IMPROVING LIFE AT WORK

IMPROVING LIFE AT WORK:

Behavioral Science Approaches to Organizational Change

Edited by

J. RICHARD HACKMAN and J. LLOYD SUTTLE

Yale University

GOODYEAR PUBLISHING COMPANY, INC.
Santa Monica, California

Library of Congress Cataloging in Publication Data
Main entry under title:

Improving life at work.

    Bibliography: p. 459
    Includes index.
    1. Personnel management—Addresses, essays, lectures.
2. Organizational change—Addresses, essays, lectures.
I. Hackman, J. Richard. II. Suttle, J. Lloyd.
HF5549.I44   658.3   76-7667
ISBN 0-87620-411-6

Y-4116-3

Current printing (last digit):
10 9 8 7 6 5

Printed in the United States of America

Interior design by Leon Bolognese
Cover design by Jaqueline Thibodeau

Contents

NATIONAL CENTER FOR PRODUCTIVITY
AND QUALITY OF WORKING LIFE
Washington, D.C. 20036

IMPROVING LIFE IN ORGANIZATIONS

How can work in American society be organized so the individual can enjoy a greater sense of participation, creativity, and dignity? How can we tap more fully the reservoir of ingenuity and intelligence of Americans, the most highly educated people in history, to improve the productivity of the economy? These are among the critical questions we must address to enhance the quality of American life.

As a people, we have made enormous social and economic progress over the past 200 years as a result of our inventiveness, organizing ability, and desire to improve the standard of living, not only for ourselves but also for the next generations. However, as economic life becomes more highly interdependent and complex, there is danger that responsibilities are becoming overspecialized; that organizational goals are being obscured; that the individual's potential for excellence is being overlooked; that we are in risk of losing our dynamism and sense of purpose.

This suggests that we must seek better understanding of how human resources can be used more effectively in large organizations and how present practices can be changed in the light of our knowledge. For our Nation's progress in this last quarter of the twentieth century may hinge as much on social research and invention as advances in earlier decades did on physical science and technology.

Nelson A. Rockefeller
Chairman, Board of Directors
National Center for Productivity
and Quality of Working Life

Acknowledgements

This book is an outgrowth of a monograph series on strategies for improving the quality of work life that was supported by the Office of the Assistant Secretary for Policy, Evaluation and Research of the U.S. Department of Labor (Contract L-73-159 to Yale University). Since contractors conducting research and development projects under government sponsorship are encouraged to express their own judgment freely, this book does not necessarily represent the official opinion or policy of the Department of Labor. The authors are solely responsible for its contents.

We are grateful to Marie Avitable for her diligence and good humor in typing the manuscript under considerable time pressure, and to Carol Truxal for her able preparation of the index. Our special appreciation goes to Richard P. Shore of the Department of Labor. Dick developed the idea for this project, and his support, encouragement, and perspective were invaluable in carrying it out. We are much in his debt.

IMPROVING LIFE AT WORK

CHAPTER 1
IMPROVING LIFE AT WORK—PROBLEMS & PROSPECTS

J. LLOYD SUTTLE
Yale University

Opportunities abound for improving the quality of work life of people in organizations. The benefits that can be gained from such improvements include healthier, more satisfied, and more produtive employees and more efficient, adaptive, and profitable organizations. Yet many of these opportunities go unrecognized, often because managers and labor leaders are unaware of the substantial gains that might be achieved from an improved quality of work life. Even in organizations where people problems have made the need for change obvious, the knowledge and abilities needed to bring about change are often lacking. The aim of this book is to provide both a greater awareness of the problems and opportunities associated with the quality of work life in contemporary organizations and a better understanding of ways to solve these problems and take advantage of these opportunities. Toward this end, the authors address questions such as these:

- How can individuals be helped to develop careers that allow them to realize the full range and extent of their capabilities and interests, while at the same time meeting both the short-term and the long-term manpower needs of the organizations that employ them?
- How can jobs be designed so that effective performance is linked with meaningful, interesting, and challenging work?
- Under what conditions do various types of rewards (such as pay, promotions, and fringe benefits) and reward systems (such as job-based

versus skill-based pay, hourly versus salary payment, and individual versus group incentive plans) prove most effective for encouraging workers to join an organization, come to work regularly, and perform effectively?

—What are the dynamics of group and intergroup relations that must be taken into account in any attempt to understand the behavior and improve the quality of work life of group members?

—What are the key supervisory strategies that produce the highest quality of work life for people in organizations? What are the structural and other constraints that influence a supervisor's behavior?

—How can the desired organizational changes, once identified, actually be brought about?

This book provides a range of perspectives for dealing with these and similar issues. It is not, of course, the first or only attempt to answer such questions. In recent years a number of strategies for improving the quality of work life have been proposed and evangelized by scholars, managers, and consultants, and numerous field experiments and surveys have been undertaken to assess the efficiency of these strategies. But the reports of these efforts are scattered through many published and unpublished documents, and their results and implications have not been organized and integrated. As a result, it is difficult to ascertain the current state of our knowledge about the nature, the causes, the consequences, or the most effective means for improving the quality of work life. Further, the knowledge that is accumulating in this area is largely unavailable to those who might learn from it or use it to design and implement change activities aimed at improving the quality of work life in their organizations.

This book is intended as a first step in remedying this lack of integration. The chapters seek (1) to bring together much of the available behavioral science knowledge about factors that affect the quality of work life, and (2) to chart some directions for future change activities intended to improve the quality of work life in contemporary organizations. It is hoped that the book will both stimulate and guide such activities.

This introductory chapter explores the nature of the quality of work life—what it is and why it is important—and examines the extent of the quality of work life problem in contemporary society. It argues not only that there is a *need* for improving the quality of work life in many organizations, but also that the investments of time, energy, and money required for such improvements are usually *justified* by the combination of economic and human gains that can accrue from them. The chapter concludes with an overview of the goals and emphases of the book as a whole and with a discussion of some of the shared values and assumptions that underlie the later chapters.

THE QUALITY OF WORK LIFE IN CONTEMPORARY ORGANIZATIONS

In recent years, increasing attention has been given to the quality of the work experience of individuals in organizations—how it affects the productivity of work organizations, how it affects the psychological well-being of workers, and how it can be changed and improved for the benefit of both. Yet there is little common understanding about what exactly quality of work life is or about whether—or why—it is important.

What Is "Quality of Work Life"?

The areas of concern and activity encompassed by the phrase *quality of work life* are broad and diverse, and many of the terms used to describe these areas (including the term *quality of work life*) imply different things to different people. To some, quality of work life refers to industrial democracy, increased worker participation in corporate decision-making, or a culmination of the goals of the human relations movement of two decades ago. To others, especially those in management, the term suggests any of a variety of efforts to improve productivity through improvements in the human rather than the capital or technological inputs of production. Unions and worker representatives often view changes in the quality of work life as leading to a more equitable sharing of the income and the resources of the work organization and to more humane and healthier working conditions. Alternatively, some union leaders suspect that management's efforts to improve quality of work life are little more than attempts to elicit higher productivity from workers without payment of higher wages. Finally, many view the quality of work life as closely related to, if not merely a broader and more up-to-date term for, such concepts as job satisfaction, humanizing work, or individualizing organizations. Thus, efforts to improve quality of work life are seen as closely akin to organizational development programs.

Perhaps the most comprehensive and widely-quoted definition of quality of work life was developed by Richard Walton (1974a), who proposed eight major conceptual categories as a framework for analyzing and assessing the phenomenon.

1. *Adequate and fair compensation*—Does pay received meet socially determined standards of sufficiency or the recipient's subjective standard? Does pay received for certain work bear an appropriate relationship to pay received for other work?
2. *Safe and healthy environment*—That employees should not be exposed to physical conditions or work arrangements that are unduly hazardous or unhealthy is widely accepted. In the future, when health will be less the

issue than comfort, more stringent standards than today's will possibly be imposed. These may include minimizing odors, noise, or visual annoyances.

3. *Development of human capacities*—To varying degrees work has become fractionated, deskilled, and tightly controlled; planning the work is often separated from implementing it. So jobs differ in how much they enable the worker to use and develop his skills and knowledge, which affects his involvement, self-esteem, and the challenge obtained from the work itself.

4. *Growth and security*—Attention needs to be given to (a) the extent to which the worker's assignments contribute to maintaining and expanding his capabilities, rather than leading to his obsolescence; (b) the degree to which expanded or newly acquired knowledge and skills can be utilized in future work assignments; and (c) the availability of opportunities to advance in organizational or career terms which peers, family members, or associates recognize.

5. *Social integration*—Whether the employee achieves personal identity and self-esteem is influenced by such attributes in the climate of his workplace as freedom from prejudice, a sense of community, interpersonal openness, the absence of stratification in the organization, and the existence of upward mobility.

6. *Constitutionalism*—What rights does the worker have and how can he (or she) protect these rights? Wide variations exist in the extent to which the organizational culture respects personal privacy, tolerates dissent, adheres to high standards of equity in distributing rewards, and provides for due process in all work-related matters.

7. *The total life space*—A person's work should have a balanced role in his life. This role encompasses schedules, career demands, and travel requirements that take a limited portion of the person's leisure and family time, as well as advancement and promotion that do not require repeated geographical moves.

8. *Social relevance*—Organizations acting in a socially irresponsible manner causes increasing numbers of their employees to depreciate the value of their work and careers. For example, does the worker perceive the organization to be socially responsible in its products, waste disposal, marketing techniques, employment practices, and participation in political campaigns?

   Walton's eight criteria are defined as characteristics of the individual's work experiences or work environment. A somewhat more direct approach to defining and measuring quality of work life, and the one adhered to in this book, is to focus on characteristics of individual workers. Specifically, quality of work life is defined here as *the degree to which members of a work organization are able to satisfy important personal needs through their experiences in the organization.* This definition implies that the quality of work life can be assessed by measures of need importance and need satisfaction, and it suggests that the two types of factors that largely determine quality of work life are (1) those that influence the importance of a particular need to an individual, and (2) those that satisfy or frustrate that need. Note, therefore, that the quality of an individual's work life is determined not by personal or situational characteristics alone, but by the interaction between these two sets of factors—by the closeness of the "individual-organizational fit." Finally, the above definition implies that the basic strategy for improving the quality of work life is first to identify and then to try to satisfy people's most important needs, presumably through their experiences in their work environments.

It is not always clear just what an individual's most important needs are, much less how well those needs have been satisfied in the past or how they might best be satisfied in the future. Several techniques and instruments are available for measuring the importance and satisfaction of different needs, but none are completely satisfactory or widely accepted as valid. It is not enough simply to ask a person what his important needs are, because people often are not consciously aware of their needs. Nor can we rely on any of the diverse and competing theoretical frameworks that identify important human needs and the means for their satisfaction (such as, Maslow's five-level need hierarchy, Walton's eight criteria, Erikson's eight stages of man), because no one of them has yet been shown to be the most valid or useful. Thus, there are crucial theoretical questions that must be answered before an adequate *operational* definition of quality of work life can be derived. It does seem clear, however, that any such definition must include both personal and external (subjective and objective) aspects of work-related rewards, work experiences, and the work environment.

The Growing Concern with Quality of Work Life

Quality of work life has become the focus of considerable and growing concern in the past few years, not only in this country but throughout Western industrialized society. Evidence for this concern is found in the expanding body of literature (in both the popular press and the management and scholarly journals) and in the growing number of national and international conferences of managers, union leaders, government officials, and behavioral scientists devoted to the analysis and improvement of life in organizations. Efforts to improve the quality of work life have been stimulated by a variety of recently established institutions, both public and private, as well as by congressional legislation.[1] Organized labor has also exhibited a growing interest not only

---

1. The National Quality of Work Center is perhaps the best known of the institutions that have been formed to generate and spread knowledge about improving the quality of work life. Other such institutions include The Center for the Quality of Working Life at UCLA, The Ohio Quality of Work Center, and The Work in America Institute.

in encouraging but also in participating in the design of organizational change activities aimed at improving the quality of work life. As further evidence of all this attention, or perhaps as a result of it, one recent reviewer has estimated that more than two thousand public and private enterprises, including business and nonprofit organizations and also state and local governments, are currently involved in some formal change activity aimed at improving the quality of work life. The number of individual plants, offices, and workplaces where such activities are underway is perhaps many times that number (Mills, 1975).

The current concern with improving the quality of work life is all the more remarkable, as noted by Mills, because of its *timing* and because it is so *deep-seated*. It has evolved in a period of both rising inflation and deepening recession, when the problems and uncertainty facing American business are all but overwhelming and the capital needed to support any new venture is especially scarce. The concern seems, furthermore, to be part of a significant change in the management philosophy in many organizations—a change that is being expressed in permanent alterations of corporate structures and policies. It appears, therefore, that the concern with quality of work life is neither a full-employment phenomenon (that is, a luxury that can be afforded by only the wealthiest and most paternalistic companies, for only the most secure and satisfied employees, or in only the best of times) nor a fad that is likely to be short-lived. On the contrary, the improvement of life at work seems to be a direct response by many organizations to problems of rising unemployment and falling productivity, and it is bringing about changes that are likely to persist long after the current popularity and novelty of the topic have subsided.

When viewed from an historical perspective, however, the concern during the mid-1970s with improving the quality of work life is not so surprising. It can be thought of as the latest—and in many ways the culmination—of a string of reform movements that have attempted during the past several decades to protect the rights and interests of the worker. These reforms began with the child labor laws, workmen's compensation laws, Fair Labor Standards Act, and other legislation passed early in this century. They continued through the unionization movement and the labor-management relations laws of the 1930s and 1940s, the human relations or power-equalization movement of the 1950s, and the concern with equal job opportunity and job enrichment in the 1960s. Thus, the quality of work life movement is not concerned with any new or additional needs of the worker, but instead tries to bring a more comprehensive and balanced perspective to the earlier diversity. It is a recognition, in many ways, that there is no one particular set of needs that is universally most important, and that the importance of any particular need varies considerably among workers and over time.

Whether the concern with improving the quality of work life is a direct response to current economic conditions and social values, the logical next step in an evolutionary series of reform movements, or merely an idea whose time has come, it is clear that concern is high and widespread. The relevant questions are *why* the phenomenon is important and whether it deserves the attention it has recently received. The following discussion considers the two basic arguments that have been used to justify organizational change activities that seek to improve the quality of work life: (1) the need to solve the quality of work life problem facing American workers, organizations, and society; and (2) the significant benefits that can accrue from such improvements for both workers and organizations.

Is There a Quality of Work Life Problem?

Perhaps the major impetus for much of the recent concern is the alarm expressed by many about what has been termed the *quality of work life problem* facing today's workers and organizations. Yet there is currently a great deal of uncertainty and disagreement about just how serious this problem is, how widespread it is, or whether it exists at all. Some argue that the problem is very real and very serious, and that it portends—and will even help to bring about—a revolution in the way productive work is done in this country. Others view it as little more than the normal and expected growing pains of American society and industry, especially as industrial organization reaches its final stages of maturity. Finally, still others view the quality of work life problem as one largely created by the media and the politicians, as little more than a passing fad or a ploy to win votes from workers.

There are few valid or conclusive data that speak directly to the existence, the seriousness, or the scope of the quality of work life problem, much less to its sources or its effects. Those who argue that the problem is important generally contend: (1) worker alienation and job dissatisfaction are increasing, primarily as a result of meaningless jobs and authoritarian managers; (2) the productivity of American workers and industry is declining while counterproductive behaviors (such as turnover, absenteeism, sabotage, theft, union militancy, and drug abuse or alcoholism at work) are increasing; and (3) the confidence of the public in large institutions in general, and big business in particular, is rapidly eroding. The poor and supposedly deteriorating quality of life in contemporary American work organizations is identified as a major cause of all these symptoms.

It often turns out, however, that the evidence cited in support of these contentions consists largely of anecdotes and personal experiences with a relatively few workers, impressions gained from a few widely-publicized cases such as the 1972 strike at the General Motors plant in Lordstown, Ohio, or social surveys that may be biased and unrepresentative. The few trustworthy data that are available often fail to support the notion that the quality of work life problem is universal. For example, Quinn, Staines, and McCullough's (1974) comprehensive review of surveys of job dissatisfaction concludes that "there has been no substantial change in overall levels of job satisfaction over the last decade" (p. 6), even among younger workers. More specifically, that review discovered a *multiplicity* of trends in job satisfaction, moving in different directions for different segments of the work force, rather than any single general trend. Even if these results were less contradictory, surveys of job satisfaction, productivity, turnover, and absenteeism can, by their nature, provide only partial assessment of the quality of work life of the workers surveyed. The reason is that while all of these attitudes or behaviors are indeed influenced by quality of work life, each is influenced by other factors as well. For example, satisfaction depends on the individual's expectations and values as well as on what happens at work; productivity is influenced by technology and skills as well as by motivation; and turnover and absenteeism may be affected more by the general state of the economy (and the unemployment level in particular) than by the quality of a person's work experiences. In short, we simply do not know, on the basis of available information, just what the quality of life is for contemporary American workers or which way it currently is changing—if, indeed, it is changing at all.

It appears, therefore, that the quality of work life problem facing today's workers may not be as serious or as widespread as the U.S. Department of Health, Education, and Welfare's report on *Work in America* would lead one to believe. It *is* clear that substantial and identifiable numbers of workers are unhappy with their jobs and are demanding more meaningful work. For example, the Quinn review cited above found that job dissatisfaction was higher than normal among blacks and other minorities, younger workers, blue-collar workers, women with small children, and workers without a college education. It also found that a growing number of workers are beginning to demand improvements in both economic *and noneconomic* outcomes from their jobs. The importance of noneconomic rewards (for example, challenging and interesting work) is increasing relative to the importance of economic ones, especially among white-collar and highly educated workers. Thus, there is need for improvement, and considerable room for improvement, in the quality of work life of many contemporary American workers.

In this context, the significance of whether there really is a quality of work life problem in contemporary society diminishes. What *is* important is that there are significant gains to be obtained—both by workers and by the organizations that employ them—through changes that lead to an improved quality of work life. The following section spells out more fully these potential benefits and lays the groundwork for the subsequent explorations of how to get there from here.

What Might Be Gained from an Improved Quality of Work Life?

The quality of an individual's work life has been shown to affect many of his responses to his job. Improvements in quality of work life might lead, for example, to more positive feelings toward one's self (greater self-esteem), toward one's job (improved job satisfaction and involvement), and toward the organization (stronger commitment to the organization's goals). They might also lead to improved physical and psychological health—fewer mental health problems and less inclination to become addicted to drugs or alcohol—and to greater growth and development of the individual as a person and as a productive member of the organization. Finally, a higher quality of work life can often lead to decreased absenteeism and turnover, fewer accidents, and higher quality and quantity of output of goods and services.

Job Satisfaction.   Perhaps the most direct and immediate gain from an improved quality of work life is higher job satisfaction. Indeed, these two phenomena are so closely related that they are often assumed (incorrectly) to be one and the same. For the purposes of this discussion, it is important that a distinction be drawn between them. As used here, the term *job satisfaction* refers to an individual's affective reactions or feelings toward his job, and the term *quality of work life* refers to the need satisfactions of the person. Job satisfaction is determined largely by how well an individual's actual rewards and experiences on his job compare with his desired or expected rewards and experiences; it is based largely on the individual's personal, subjective evaluation of the job. Often, however, subjective perceptions—desires and expectations—have little to do with reality, with how well a reward actually satisfies a particular need. For example, a worker might be perfectly satisfied with his work environment if it is clean and comfortable, even though it might be dangerous to his health, simply because he has no basis on which to judge its impact on his health. Or, a worker might not be actively dissatisfied with low pay and infrequent promotions (even if he performs his job very effectively), because he only attended school through the eighth grade and therefore does not expect to earn high wages or make foreman. Finally, workers on monotonous, demeaning jobs might not object to their work if they have never had opportunities to experience the feelings of pride and self-fulfillment that challenging jobs can provide. In short, workers might be reasonably satisfied (or at least not actively dissatisfied) with jobs that provide a low quality of work life, *because they do not have enough information, or the right information, with which to accurately evaluate how well their jobs satisfy their important needs.*

On the other hand, few workers who experience a high quality of work life experience low job satisfaction. Individuals whose important needs are being satisfied by their job-related activities invariably express positive feelings about those jobs, feelings that could lead to greater involvement and commitment as well as to more effective job performance.

Individual Productivity. For the individual worker, quality of work life and productivity are closely related, especially when productivity is defined in terms of the individual's internal work standards. It probably would be impossible for an individual to satisfy his higher-level needs for achievement or self-actualization, for example, if he felt that he was not performing effectively on the job. Further, because many organizations tie such rewards as pay raises, bonuses, tenure, and promotions to measures of job performance, productivity also has at least some influence on the individual's ability to satisfy lower-order needs for food, shelter, and security. Productivity is, therefore, meaningful and important to the worker (perhaps more so than to the organization in many ways), and high productivity is both a cause and an effect of a high quality of work life.[2]

It is important to note that the term *productivity* as used here involves much more than merely the quantity of the individual's work output. It also includes such work behaviors as turnover, absenteeism, defiance of rules and authority, grievances, strikes, union activity, sabotage, theft, accidents, and especially the quality of work output. All of these behaviors have been shown to be directly influenced by the individual's job satisfaction, involvement, or commitment; and, as noted earlier, these attitudes are directly affected by the quality of the individual's work life. Finally, quality of work life affects such personal

---

2. The impact of quality of work life on productivity (or vice versa) depends at least in part on how productivity is measured and by whom. For example, *external* measures of productivity, such as those provided by the individual's supervisor, co-workers, or the formal evaluation system, have a greater impact on extrinsic rewards such as pay, promotion, and status, and thus are related to how well particular lower-level needs are satisfied. Alternatively, *internal* measures of productivity have a greater impact on intrinsic rewards, such as pride, self-fulfillment, and growth, and therefore are related to the satisfaction of higher-order needs. If internal and external measures of productivity agree, then quality of work life and productivity are likely to be very closely related; but if the two types of measures disagree, the situation is more complicated. Thus, quality of work life improvements will probably produce the greatest increases in productivity in situations where internal and external measures are fully consistent, as is true when external measures are open to and easily verifiable (and correctable) by the individual worker.

attitudes and behaviors as creativity, the willingness to innovate or to accept change, the ability to adapt to change in one's work or environment, and the degree of internal work motivation—all of which are central to individual work productivity.

The quality of work life is not the only or perhaps even the most important determinant of individual productivity. Technological constraints, the performance of one's co-workers, personal skills and abilities, the amount of work assigned, and a variety of other factors both inside and outside the organization might also influence productivity. All of these factors must, therefore, be taken into account in any attempt to improve productivity through improvements in the quality of work life. In other words, a high quality of work life does not always or necessarily assure a high level of individual productivity, even though poor quality of work life does invariably discourage productivity to some extent.

Organizational Effectiveness.   Not surprisingly, the impact of quality of work life on the overall effectiveness or profitability of an organization is even more complex and multifaceted than is its impact on individual productivity. This impact is especially crucial because the decision to undertake organizational changes aimed at improving the quality of work life often hinges on the potential gains that these improvements will bring in the effectiveness of the organization as a whole.

Often, the interests of workers and the goals of the organization are fully congruent and mutually supportive. In such situations, improvements in the quality of work life will result in gains for both parties. For example, improvements in job design might well produce not only more intrinsically motivating and enriching tasks but also higher individual productivity. *If* these job redesigns can be implemented with relatively little cost to the organization (that is, with low capital investments and few retraining needs), *if* higher individual productivity leads directly to increased organizational productivity, and *if* the workers actually desire more challenging and intrinsically satisfying jobs, then the quality of work life improvements could be viewed as a direct means for increasing organizational effectiveness. In this situation, management's desire to improve organizational effectiveness would serve as a powerful incentive for undertaking the job redesign project.

However, there are many areas where the interests of individuals are in clear and inevitable conflict with the goals (especially the economic goals) of the organizations that employ them, or with the interests of other groups in the organization. For example, demands by workers for more pay or greater security would be in direct conflict with the profitability of most organizations; or, an increase of the power or autonomy of nonmanagement workers might be possible only if the authority of managers is reduced. In such situations, there are inherent tensions and trade-offs between the interests of workers and those of the organization as a whole, or those of other groups in the organization. These conflicts can best (and perhaps only) be resolved through bargaining. It must be recognized, however, that the practical considerations of organizational survival and economic viability impose very real constraints on the ability of the organization to improve quality of work life in areas where economic costs are involved. And the realities of power and political behavior in organizations are likely to interfere with quality of work life improvements when the interests of some groups are threatened.

Occasionally the impact of quality of work life improvements on organizational efficiency is decidedly positive or negative. Much more often, however, significant benefits can be gained from these improvements, but only at some costs to the organization. These costs and benefits must then be weighed against each other to determine if the improvements are indeed worthwhile for the organization. In gauging the overall impact of quality of work life improvements on organizational effectiveness, therefore, one of the most difficult as well as most important tasks is identification of the full range of costs and benefits that are tied to these changes. Many of these consequences are not readily apparent, and even if they were, they would not be easily measurable.

Consider, for example, the impact of quality of work life on individual productivity, discussed above. It is clear that organizational effectiveness involves considerably more than just the sum of the separate contributions of individual members. Organizational effectiveness requires, and quality of work life might well have an impact on, the ability of interdependent individuals and groups to work together toward organizational goals—to communicate effectively with each other, to coordinate their activities, to resolve their conflicts, and so forth. An improved quality of work life could make it easier for individuals and groups, both separately and collectively, to innovate, to grow, and to adapt to each other and respond to changes in their environment. Even though many of these benefits of organizational changes aimed at improving quality of work life are difficult to recognize, much less to measure or evaluate, they should all be taken into consideration when judging the value of such changes.

Finally, in identifying the impact of quality of work life improvements on organizational effectiveness, it is important to recognize that the *time frame* within which such an impact is judged has a lot to do with how the improvements are evaluated. It is necessary to distinguish between short-term and long-term consequences, because short-term costs are often unavoidable in order to achieve long-term gains. For example, any organizational change (whether associated with an attempt to improve quality of work life or not) will produce stresses and tensions in the organization as it moves through the process of change and attempts to achieve a new state of equilibrium, among its different parts and with its environment. These stresses are generally short-lived, however, and are more than offset by long-term improvements in the organization's growth and development and in its ability to adapt to internal and external change.

In summary, improvements in the quality of work life have a variety of consequences—for the individual, for the organization, and even for society. For the individual most of these consequences are positive, because quality of work life improvements are specifically designed to serve the interests of workers and to satisfy their most important needs. For the organization, however, changes in the quality of work life have more complex and contradicting consequences. In order to fully identify and evaluate these consequences, a broader, systems-level view of organizational effectiveness is needed. Such a perspective must include the personal well-being and need satisfaction of *all* members of the organization—workers, supervisors, managers, and perhaps even owners and clients—as well as the goal-achievement of the organization as a whole. In such a framework, organizational effectiveness would be defined in terms of the *congruence* between the needs of the people who belong to the organization and the goals of the organization. Quality of work life and organizational effectiveness then could be defined *interdependently,* in terms of the individuals' and organization's abilities to satisfy each other's most important needs and expectations. The impact of a change in either component on the other can be more clearly identified with such a framework, and the justification for undertaking organizational changes aimed at improving either can be more readily evaluated.

Finally, for society at large, the overall consequences of quality of work life improvements would depend on their *combined* impact on workers and organizations. When viewed from a broader societal perspective, it might occasionally turn out that quality of work life improvements that are not worthwhile in terms of their benefits to the organization or its members separately are indeed justified by their impact on people and institutions outside the organization who are affected by it—for example, the organization's customers or clients, the local economy or government, or those affected by the organization's impact on the environment. Quality of work life improvements might help to achieve such social goals as greater economic prosperity or political stability, or they might help to cure such social ills as mental health problems, unemployment, or drug and alcohol addiction among employees and their families. Last but not least, quality of work life improvements might be judged desirable on the basis of humanitarian values, especially when the other costs and benefits of such changes are rated nearly a toss-up.

STRATEGIES FOR IMPROVING THE QUALITY OF WORK LIFE: THE PLAN OF THE BOOK

The primary goal of this book is to stimulate and guide the planning, implementation, and evaluation of future research and change activities that seek to make contemporary organizations simultaneously more productive and more humane by improving the quality of the work experience of the members of these organizations. Each chapter focuses on a different point of leverage for understanding and changing quality of work life. These are: (1) the development of careers and career paths, (2) work design, (3) organizational reward systems, (4) the design and maintenance of group and intergroup relationships, (5) managerial practices, and (6) strategies for changing quality of work life where the motivation for change comes from both inside and outside the organization.

Common Goals

Although each chapter is written so that it can be useful in its own right, three common goals and emphases run through the whole book.

First, each chapter reviews and integrates current behavioral science knowledge relevant to the topic at hand. This includes scholarly knowledge generated by academics and understandings that have emerged from ongoing experiences and experiments in organizations. The material presented encompasses knowledge gained from research and experiences in European organizations as well as those in this country.[3]

Second, each chapter examines the implications of existing knowledge for the development of new conceptual frameworks. Significant advances in understanding quality of work life—and in developing the tools and techniques needed to execute planned change effectively—hinge on the adequacy of the theoretical models that organize the factors that affect the quality of work life. Thus, a high priority task for each chapter is to advance state-of-the-art conceptualizing about the processes and phenomena being considered.

---

3. The purpose is not to compare and contrast the European and American experiences, for there are significant differences between the two in their political and economic systems and their cultural norms. Instead, the purpose is simply to make use of all available knowledge, wherever it was gained, and important knowledge has been gained from research and experiences in European work organizations.

Finally, each chapter addresses issues that are specifically relevant to *changing* the quality of work life of people in contemporary organizations. Although descriptive facts and findings are an important part of each chapter, an overriding concern is to organize and present this material so that it furthers understanding of how quality of work life can be improved through planned intervention. Where possible, therefore, the book goes beyond diagnosis of quality of work life problems and their likely sources and makes specific suggestions about ways to solve these problems.

The book is addressed to anyone who is concerned or charged with bringing about, planning, directing, carrying out, or evaluating planned change in organizations. Thus, we were writing for managers, union leaders, government officials, internal and external consultants, students of organizational behavior and change, and workers who wish to increase their understanding of the uses and misuses of behavioral science knowledge in organizations. The book should be of value to anyone who seeks a general understanding of what the behavioral sciences have to offer toward the improvement of life at work.

There are areas of overlap as well as of omission in the coverage of the different chapters, though there is little redundancy. Few of the major determinants of or strategies for improving quality of work life are ignored. Some topics are touched on in two or more chapters—for example, the Scanlon Plan, leadership, change processes, and the importance of unions. Such topics are relevant for understanding different strategies for improving quality of work life and are viewed from different perspectives. There is wide diversity among the different chapters in style, content, and the degree to which each goes beyond the description and analysis of quality of work life problems and offers prescriptive guidelines for solving these problems. Such inconsistency is unavoidable, because the authors and the topics of the chapters are different and because we are at very different stages in our understanding of the different topics. In other words, there is wide variance in the amount and the quality of the research and data that are available in the different areas, and also in the sophistication and proven validity of the relevant theoretical frameworks. In some areas our understanding of ways to improve quality of work life is quite advanced—for example, in reward systems and in supervision. In other areas—such as careers and intergroup relations—there simply are few known or tried solutions to particular aspects of the quality of work life problem. Where this latter situation occurs, the authors point this out and perhaps thereby encourage more research and conceptualizing. Despite their diversity, however, there are critical links among the chapters, including common goals and shared values and assumptions (as outlined below). Taken together, therefore, the chapters form a logical and coherent whole. The book offers one comprehensive approach for understanding and improving the quality of work life.

Shared Values and Assumptions

Each of the chapters in this book represents the work and the ideas of its author. However, there are a number of shared values and assumptions about human behavior, about organizations, about change, and about the contributions of the behavioral sciences to understanding each that are common to the book as a whole. Many of these views have been stated or implied earlier but are made explicit here to help the reader integrate and interpret the arguments in the chapters that follow.

The issues discussed below represent a set of *values* shared by many of the authors regarding the relationship between individuals and organizations and the role of behavioral science theory in understanding and improving this relationship. Obviously, there is not (nor is it likely that there ever could be) complete agreement among all of the authors on all issues. Similarly, the authors' views will differ from those of the readers in some important areas. Where such conflicts exist, an effort is made to deal with them openly and fairly, rather than to suggest or require a consensus.

Other issues involve specific *concepts* used by several of the authors to analyze the causes, consequences, and ways to improve the quality of work life. However, no attempt is made to develop a single, comprehensive model of man or of organizations or to outline a general theory of organizational change. Instead, the concepts discussed below are limited to those that are most directly relevant to planning and implementing organizational changes that seek to improve quality of work life.

Quality of Work Life Versus Organizational Efficiency. It has often been suggested, either explicity or implicitly, that there is a basic incompatibility between the interests of workers (quality of work life) and the goals of the organizations that employ them (efficiency). Accordingly, any effort to advance one set of interests can only succeed at the expense of the other. As discussed earlier, however, it is our view that the quality of the interaction between individuals and organizations can be improved to the benefit of both—that quality of work life and organizational efficiency can be, and must be, improved simultaneously. It is indeed possible, and a reasonable objective for society in general and for this book in particular, to seek ways to design and manage organizations so that the goals of organizations and the interests of the people who work in them become more congruent and mutually supportive. We feel that there are tremendous but often unrecognized opportunities in many work organizations for improving quality of work life and organizational efficiency simultaneously, simply by focusing on those areas where the interests of workers and organizations coincide. A primary goal of this book is to point out such areas of common interests and to suggest ways to utilize them.

At the same time, the book recognizes that there are some areas where conflict between workers and organizations is inherent and where trade-offs between the interests of the two parties are unavoidable. In such areas, the authors seek ways to resolve the conflicts peacefully and effectively, to make constructive use of the energy that conflict creates, and to make the necessary trade-offs as fairly and painlessly as possible. The goal in these areas is to bring about effective accommodation and compromise between the two parties, rather than to strive for a pretense of harmony and cooperation.

Whether the relationship between the quality of work life and organizational efficiency in a given area is marked by compatibility or conflict, this relationship is usually so close that a change in either component is likely to affect the other. Although the focus of the book is on ways to improve quality of work life, these improvements are *not* sought at the expense of, or in disregard for their impact on, organizational efficiency. Instead, the recommended changes are primarily ones that bring about simultaneous improvements in quality of work life and organizational efficiency. Any proposed change is evaluated in terms of its impact on *both* outcomes.

The Responsibility for Improving Quality of Work Life. Because the benefits from quality of work life improvements are likely to be widespread, it is the shared responsibility not only of management and workers but also of union leaders, government officials, and behavioral scientists to work together to bring about these improvements. Each of these groups has a crucial role to play in initiating, designing, carrying out, and evaluating organizational change activities that seek to improve quality of work life. This goal can best (and perhaps only) be achieved if all of these groups work together. No one group can bring about meaningful changes on its own, but any one group might effectively block the success of efforts to improve the quality of work life, through passive nonsupport or through active resistance.

The authors devote primary attention to what the behavioral sciences have to offer toward the improvement of life in work organizations. Perhaps most important is the focus of behavioral science knowledge on specific strategies for bringing about healthy and enduring changes. The authors believe that the behavioral sciences can provide both the substantive knowledge and the catalytic influence that can help decision-makers and policy-setters in management, government, and organized labor to design and implement effective and humane change in work organizations.

It is especially important that behavioral scientists begin to work in closer cooperation with leaders of organized labor on issues of planned organizational change and improved quality of work life. In the past, such cooperation has often been notable for its absence. This has led many—especially among union leaders and members—to view the behavioral sciences as a tool used by management to gain greater control and increased output from workers. This book endeavors to help counteract this view by providing a framework and issuing a call for increased communication and cooperation between behavioral scientists and workers. The responsibility for bringing about this increased level of interaction rests, of course, with both parties. Union leaders must begin to seek out and make use of the advice and assistance of behavioral scientists, just as behavioral scientists must begin to address themselves more directly to the needs and interests of workers.

Unions and their members are viewed not only as an important part of the audience of this book, but also as a major topic to be dealt with. Throughout the book, the crucial role of unions in affecting planned organizational change and bringing about improved quality of work life is recognized. Change is shown to be a very different process, and to require different strategies, in unionized as compared to nonunionized organizations, and in organizations where the union supports the change as compared to where it resists the change.

Unions have actually played a longstanding but often unrecognized role in influencing and seeking improvements to quality of work life. Their successful efforts to win increased wages, improved job security, and due process for their members, as well as their more recent interest in such areas as occupational safety and health, career development, and job design, all have obvious and significant impacts on quality of work life. Through their negotiations with management, many unions have begun not only to demand but also to help bring about quality of work life improvements in the noneconomic areas as well. Perhaps the most notable examples of this are the recent agreements in the automobile and steel industries to form joint union-management committees that seek to improve both productivity and quality of work life. Management in these industries must also be credited with an interest in and efforts toward improving quality of work life. Such efforts are likely to be all the more successful because they are exerted in cooperation with organized labor to seek solutions to common problems.

Government leaders at all levels have shown in the past, and will no doubt continue to show in the future, a very active concern with protecting the rights and interests of workers. The federal government has intervened directly into the relationship between organizations and their employees through such legislation as the Fair Labor Standards Act, workmen's compensation laws, child labor laws, laws governing union-management relations, laws providing for minimum wages and unemployment insurance, and, most recently, the Occupational Safety and Health Act and the Equal Employment Opportunity Act. All of this legislation has helped to assure a minimum quality of work life for today's workers, at least in the areas of economic rewards and security of work. In addition, the government has provided encouragement and financial support for management and workers, as well as for scientists from inside and outside of industry, to seek ways of improving all aspects of quality of work life. This support is channeled through government-sponsored research programs in the National Science Foundation, the National Commission on Productivity and Work Quality, the Department of Commerce, the Department of Labor, the Office of Naval Research, and elsewhere. Finally, the government has sponsored broad-scale national surveys of worker satisfaction and quality of work life, and of personal, job, and organizational factors associated with satisfaction and quality of work life. Included among these are Department of Labor surveys of quality of work life and the Survey Research Center's Survey of Working Conditions in 1969–1970 and its Quality of Employment Survey in 1972–1973. The costs of such surveys generally put them beyond the means of private enterprise or individual organizations, but they have proven to be immensely valuable for evaluation and planning purposes. Given that the government has tried a number of both direct and indirect approaches to improving quality of work life in the past, what should the government's role and responsibility in these areas be in the future? Should the government attempt to legislate minimum quality of work life standards in all areas, including the content and intrinsic rewards of work? Or should it merely continue to encourage management, unions, and behavioral scientists to work toward such goals on their own initiative? There is considerable disagreement and uncertainty about what the answer to this question should be. Several possible roles or actions by the government are suggested in the later chapters (see especially Beer and Driscoll, Chapter 7).

Finally, it is clear that the owners and managers of an organization must play a central role not only in implementing but also in initiating organizational change activities that seek to improve quality of work life. Few such changes can be successful, or would even be attempted, if the leaders of the organization were not willing to commit their authority as well as the organizational resources which they control to support the changes.

In summary, the major implication of this and the previous assumption is that organizational changes aimed at improving quality of work life might be sought and supported by a number of different groups, though their reasons for such support would be quite different. The groups that share the responsibility and perform crucial roles in bringing about quality of work life improvements would benefit in different ways from such improvements. Workers and union leaders, for example, might be motivated to seek quality of work life improvements for their own obvious self-interests. To convince management of the need for changes, workers and union leaders could use the argument that these improvements often produce simultaneous improvements in individual and organizational productivity. Management's primary rationale for seeking to improve quality of work life, on the other hand, might be its desire for a preplanned strategy for improving organizational efficiency. Behavioral scientists, government officials, and others outside the organization might take the point of view of workers (that quality of work life improvements are worthwhile for their own sake), of management (that quality of work life improvements are a means for improving organizational efficiency), or even of society at large (that more efficient organizations and an improved quality of life of their members are beneficial to all those whom the organization serves or affects). Finally, quality of work life improvements might be supported by someone inside or outside the organization on purely humanitarian grounds. In that situation any productivity improvements that result would be viewed simply as fortunate by-products of the change, and any costs incurred would be seen as necessary to achieve more important ends. In short, quality of work life is a very value-laden issue. One's beliefs about whether it is important, whether it needs to be improved, how it should be improved, and how much such improvements are worth depend largely on one's perspective and set of values. The authors of these chapters feel that improvements in many areas of quality of work life are both necessary and worthwhile. They also believe that such improvements can be brought about in ways that minimize the costs and maximize the gains for both the organization and society.

The Change Process.   Changes in an organization's structure or in the way it operates, like changes in the way a person thinks or acts, take place in three separate but overlapping stages. The first involves the *unfreezing* of the existing structures or ways of functioning, thinking, or behaving. The second stage is the actual *change* to new structures and procedures, or new ways of thinking and acting. The final stage involves the *refreezing* of the newly acquired characteristics and behaviors.[4] For a change process to be successful, all three of these stages must be completed. Changes that stop halfway through the process are likely to be only temporary and superficial, and changes that start in the middle of the process are likely to be successfully resisted or diverted by the defenses of existing structures and behaviors.

The unfreezing stage of a change process is intended to overcome the natural and often unavoidable resistance of a system (a person or an organization) to any significant change in its makeup or functioning. This resistance develops because an internal change disrupts the existing state of equilibrium or internal consistency of the system and thus is likely to be seen as a threat to the system's self-image or accustomed mode of operation. The system will then defend against such a threat by resisting the change and seeking support for its old equilibrium state. In order to unfreeze this old state, it is necessary to (1) remove any of its external sources of support, (2) criticize or point out its weaknesses and ineffectiveness, and/or (3) minimize any anxiety that might be aroused by the change. In other words, the person or organization must be convinced, first that the old state is truly inadequate and undesirable, second that the change will not hurt nearly as much as might be imagined, and third that it is easier and more comfortable to change than it is to resist the change. All of these mechanisms for unfreezing the system's existing state of equilibrium are intended to create in the system the readiness and the motivation to change and the willingness to accept the risks that are inherent in any disruption of an existing equilibrium state.

Once a system's equilibrium state has been upset, it begins to seek information about the kinds of change that will help to establish a new, more effective equilibrium. It is at this point that the actual change phase of the overall change process takes place. The person or organization begins to seek out, process, and assimilate information from a variety of sources. This process results in a new definition of the situation, a new set of assumptions about reality, and a new self-image. On the basis of this new information, the system then begins to adopt new modes of thinking, behaving, or functioning, or new internal structures. In planned organizational changes that are aimed at improving the quality of work life, there is usually some person or group (a change agent) that is the primary source of information and so determines the direction of the change. There are any number of strategies for change that the change agent might use and a number of targets for

4. For a fuller discussion of the three-step change process, see Lewin (1951) or Bennis, Schein, Steele, and Berlew (1968, pp. 333–370).

change within the organization. These are all examined in detail by Beer and Driscoll (Chapter 7).

The probability that the change agent's information and influence will successfully guide the change depends on three conditions: (1) the perceived value of the change, or the extent to which the system sees the proposed change as relevant to the achievement of its goals; (2) the perceived power of the change agent to affect (enhance or block) the system's ability to achieve its goals; and (3) the prepotency of the new structures or behaviors, or the extent to which the changes are seen as clearly the best alternatives for solving felt problems. These three conditions affect not only the direction of the change (whether the change agent's proposed innovations will be adopted), but also its permanency and depth (whether it will be lasting and will influence the fundamental values of the person or the management philosophy of the organization). The stability of the change is also determined by how well it is integrated into the system's permanent makeup and functioning—how effectively it is refrozen during the final phase of the change process.

Refreezing is the third and often neglected phase of a change process. It is the phase in which the person's newly acquired attitudes, beliefs, and behaviors, or the organization's newly developed structures or modes of operation, become stabilized and continue until a later unfreezing event occurs. This reintegration phase occurs largely through the support and reinforcement the changes receive from the system's external environment. It is also necessary that the different parts of the system—the individual's attitudes, beliefs, and behaviors, or the organization's subsystems—be congruent or compatible with the change. Without such external reinforcement and internal consistency, the change often is only temporary, and the system reverts to its old equilibrium state. In organizational life, changes associated with improvements in the quality of work life must be supported by the organization's formal authority system, its formal reward system, the behavior of managers and supervisors, the expectations and norms of the work group, and the overall climate and culture of the organization. All of these sources of influence must encourage and reward the new equilibrium state if it is to be sustained.

In summary, maintaining a high quality of work life in contemporary work organizations requires almost continuous change and adaptation at the individual, organizational, and even societal levels. The three-phase model of change described above shows some of the commonalities and links among these three levels of change. This model provides useful guidelines for understanding, stimulating, and implementing a variety of planned change activities aimed at improving the quality of work life. It sheds some light on the sources of resistance to planned change, on ways of overcoming this resistance, on the conditions that are most conducive to the acceptance of innovations, on ways of directing the change to its desired ends, and on ways that can stabilize the change so that it is permanent. As suggested by the terminology used, individual and organizational changes are best understood if these processes are viewed from what is called a *systems perspective*.

A Systems Perspective.   People, organizations, and their interactions can best be viewed from a systems perspective. That is, a person or an organization can most usefully be thought of as an organism continually changing and adapting to changes in its environment. Like organisms, people and organizations are composed of many interrelated parts that interact with each other and with the larger environment of which they are parts. For the individual, these interrelated parts include his attitudes, behaviors, and cognitive thought processes (beliefs and expectations). The major components of an organization, on the other hand, include: (1) the attitudes, values, and skills of the *people* who make up the organization; (2) the *internal environment* of the organization, such as organization structure, job structure, control systems, policies, and personnel practices; (3) the *processes by which people interact,* such as communication, conflict resolution, decision-making, intergroup relations, and interpersonal relations; and (4) the *culture* of the organization, which is the perception by organizational members of what the organization stands for and thus what behaviors and attitudes are rewarded.

The struggle for survival of a person or organization is thus a struggle to maintain consistency or equilibrium among its various parts or subsystems, between itself and other systems, and between itself and the larger systems of which it is a part. Survival or health is threatened, and energy is mobilized to maintain equilibrium when various subparts of the person or organization are not in harmony with each other, or when the external environment changes enough to make past modes of adaptation ineffective.

The concept of a person or organization as an *open system,* continually exchanging resources and information with its environment and striving to maintain internal consistency and external relevance, has appeared in a number of theoretical formulations about personality and organizations.[5] This concept has important implications and applications when viewing individual-organization interactions. The im-

---

5. For a discussion of systems theory concepts as they relate to individual behavior in organizations, see Katz and Kahn (1966). For a discussion of systems theory guidelines for planned organizational change, and for a useful bibliography, see Alderfer (1976).

plications of the systems perspective for *changing* people and organizations are especially clear. External pressures are needed to create change in any one component of a person (attitudes, beliefs, or behaviors) or an organization (people, internal environment, interaction processes, or culture). These pressures will initially be resisted, because a change in any one component of a system would be a threat to its internal consistency or equilibrium. As the change in one component occurs, however, the person or organization will mobilize internal energy to maintain equilibrium. This energy will produce changes in the system's remaining components to fit the direction of the externally induced change. Change in the total system will occur, and a new state of internal consistency and external relevance will be developed.

Another crucial implication of a systems perspective is the realization that the phenomena of organizational change and individual-organization interaction are not isolated incidents but occur as part of a much larger set of interdependent events. It is not possible to look at or change only one aspect or part of a person or organization without considering the ramifications of such an action on other parts of the system. It would be foolish, for example, to introduce a new reward system or a new job design without adapting the work group structures and norms and the supervisor-subordinate relationships to these changes. These arguments might seem patently obvious, but it is remarkable how many times they are ignored in actual organizational change activities.

Finally, when viewing an organization as a system of interrelated parts, it is important to realize that the organization is actually a system of interrelated *subsystems*. In other words, an organization is composed of individuals who interact with each other and with the several groups of which they are members, and of groups that interact with each other and with the organization as a whole. In addition, the organization is a system that interacts with other organizational systems, and with the larger environmental system of which it is a part—with the economy, the society at large, or a particular industry. Between each of these systems and subsystems there are boundaries and relationships that must be maintained.

The Importance of Individual Differences.   Throughout this book the authors stress that there are no totally general or universal strategies for improving the quality of work life. Instead, the impact and usefulness of any particular strategy is shown to be contingent on characteristics of the setting in which it is used and of the people to whom it is applied. Probably the most important set of factors that determine whether a strategy will be useful for improving the quality of work life is made up of the *needs* of the people involved. People differ in the importance they assign to various needs, as well as in the types of rewards and experiences that best satisfy those needs. These differences have a major impact on the values that people assign to particular types of work-related rewards and experiences, as well as on their reactions to organizational changes that alter their rewards and experiences.

Individual differences in needs derive in part from the different types of experiences people have in different jobs, and in part from more basic differences in personality, values, life styles, social class, family and educational background, and so forth. It is important to recognize that not all workers want enriched jobs, greater autonomy and responsibility, promotions to management, or opportunities to interact with others. Some workers are more concerned with job security and financial rewards, prefer jobs that are simple and highly structured, or like to work alone. This should not, however, automatically be construed as an indication that the quality of their work lives is poor. The rewards provided by such jobs may well satisfy these workers' most important needs, and they may perform very effectively as a result. In short, it is important that quality of work life be assessed in terms of the workers' rather than the managers' or researchers' value systems. Individual differences should be taken into account in assessing quality of work life and in designing organizational changes that seek to improve quality of work life for a particular group of workers.

Finally, it must be noted that the assessment of needs and the design of ways to satisfy these needs are made even more difficult by the ever-changing nature of human needs. These changes are due in part to workers' on-the-job rewards and experiences, and in part to their nonwork experiences and their personal maturation. Further, the changes might result from a change in either the rewards they actually receive or in the subjective value that they assign to these rewards. One important implication of the fact that people's needs change over time is the realization that the minimum acceptable level of a reward—the amount of a particular reward that is required to satisfy a given need—is likely to increase over time. Once workers become accustomed to receiving a particular amount of pay, to being treated in a particular way by their supervisors, to having a particular amount of autonomy on their jobs, and so forth, they will want even further improvements in these rewards and experiences. The quality of work life tends, therefore, to be a very dynamic phenomenon and one that requires regular monitoring and almost constant readjustments if it is to be maintained at a high level.

Overview of the Individual Chapters

Chapter 2: Career Development. John Van Maanen and Edgar H. Schein take a wide-ranging and dynamic view of careers and career development in the context of (1) the life cycles of individuals, (2) the needs of organizations and organized society, and (3) the norms and values of the broader culture. The authors propose that careers emerge from a matching process that involves the individual, the organization, and the culture. The bulk of the chapter is devoted to analyzing careers in terms of three primary concepts, and to exploring the practical implications of these concepts for improving the career development process. These three concepts are: (1) the distinction and the relationship between *internal* and *external* (subjective and objective) views of careers; (2) the need to understand the person *within the total life space* and *throughout his lifetime* in order to understand his career; and (3) the need to view *career development* issues in interaction with *self-development* and *family development* issues. The authors conclude with a look toward the future, with emphasis on the emerging need for new strategies for career management, for changes in educational and organizational practices that affect careers, and for alterations of public policies relevant to occupations and careers. They suggest steps that the society, the employing organizations, and the individuals can take to improve the career development process.

Chapter 3: Work Design.   J. Richard Hackman addresses the redesign of work and work systems as a strategy for change, with special emphasis on conditions under which work redesign is and is not likely to be useful in initiating change. Hackman begins with a discussion of the meaning of the catchall term *work redesign*, and then moves to a review of the ways that job design can affect employee satisfaction, motivation, and productivity. He then examines several factors that moderate people's reactions to their work (including individual difference and interpersonal and organizational moderators) and that explain why there is no such thing as a universally good design for work. This material serves as a point of departure for a discussion of the Job Characteristics Model and of principles for designing work and enriching jobs of both individuals and groups. Several of the special problems and opportunities encountered in attempts to carry out job enrichment and other strategies for work design are noted, and a set of guidelines for installing planned changes in jobs is developed. Hackman ends with a discussion of some of the major current challenges to the future viability and effectiveness of work redesign as a strategy for planned personal and organizational change, including (1) the need to diffuse knowledge about work redesign theory and practice, (2) the need to disseminate work redesign innovations, (3) the need to pay more attention to the jobs of first-level managers, and (4) the need to pay more attention to the role of unions in work redesign efforts.

Chapter 4: Reward Systems. There is substantial literature on the design and use of reward systems to motivate employees in organizations (for example, on the effects of piece-rate incentive systems). Little is known, however, about how reward systems affect other aspects of the organization, or about how they can be used as integral parts of broadly oriented programs of organizational change. Edward E. Lawler considers both of these issues. He begins with an examination of the ways rewards and reward systems influence individual attitudes and behaviors and organizational structures and procedures. Then he identifies some of the properties that organizational reward systems must have if they are to contribute to a high quality of work life and organizational effectiveness. A number of specific rewards and reward systems—pay, promotion, dismissal/tenure, fringe benefits, status symbols, bonuses and various pay and promotion plans, performance evaluation systems, and fringe benefits packaging plans—are then evaluated in terms of whether they possess the characteristics that lead to a high quality of work life and organizational effectiveness. Turning from the *design* of reward systems to the *process* through which these systems are administered, Lawler examines such issues as the impact of communication and participation on pay system effectiveness. Finally, he examines reward system redesign as a strategy for organizational change, and the need for congruence between the way the reward system and other systems in the organization operate—and especially the need to adapt or redesign the reward system when other subsystems in the organization are changed.

Chapter 5: Group and Intergroup Relations. Clayton P. Alderfer addresses the nature and dynamics of group and intergroup relations within organizations, and the pervasiveness of their impact on seemingly unrelated aspects of organizational life. He emphasizes the importance of intergroup, as opposed to intragroup, relations, and he shows how some of the classical studies of group behavior in organizations failed to pay adequate attention to intergroup dynamics. The author then examines some of the systematic properties of intergroup relations and develops a set of basic concepts that are helpful for understanding the complex set of behaviors, emotions, attitudes, and beliefs that arise when groups have interdependent relationships. These concepts also help to explain some of the ways that group and intergroup relations influence the quality of a group member's work life. The three major classes of intergroups in organizations—(1) task-induced intergroups, which arise from the need for division of labor, (2) hierarchically-induced intergroups, which evolve from the hierarchy of authority and the inevitability of superior–subordinate relationships in organizations, and (3) historically-rooted intergroups, which are based on the personal and social characteristics that members bring into the organization—are defined and described. Alderfer concludes by presenting and discussing several behavioral science interventions that can be employed to reduce the destructive effects of intergroup conflict and enhance the possibility of improving the quality of work life for groups as well as organizations.

Chapter 6: Managerial Practices.   George Strauss deals primarily with the roles of supervision and management in implementing the practices and making the changes that affect (and presumably improve) quality of work life. He begins with an examination of the way the supervisor—management's immediate representative in the work place—influences the quality of work life and individual productive behavior both directly through his treatment of individual employees on a day-to-day basis, and indirectly through his influence on the design of jobs and reward systems and on the development of teamwork. The author emphasizes three key supervisory roles—(1) providing *consideration,* (2) serving as a *facilitator* of employees' work efforts, and (3) encouraging appropriate degrees of *participation* in important work decisions. He also examines some of the structural characteristics of organizations that have an important impact on quality of work life and productivity. Finally, Strauss considers the role of the union in improving the quality of work life of union members. He considers the quandries that quality of work life issues pose for unions and then makes some specific suggestions about how management might effectively enlist union cooperation in dealing with problems in this area.

Chapter 7: Strategies for Change.   The preceding chapters emphasize particular points of leverage for initiating changes through the design of work, managerial practices, group and system design, and so on. In this final chapter Michael Beer and James W. Driscoll focus on the change *process* and on the various strategies for bringing about the changes suggested in the other chapters. They begin with an examination of a number of choices that must be made—whether explicitly or implicitly—when organizational changes are undertaken. These include choices between power- and collaboratively-based strategies, centralized and decentralized change, fast- and slow-paced change, and individual- and structural-oriented change. The authors then turn to a detailed examination of three general strategies for approaching quality of work life changes: (1) strategies arising internally to the organization, such as organizational development approaches or a variety of management and union strategies; (2) strategies originating with political and special interest groups, such as community action approaches; and (3) societal-level strategies, such as the use of legislation as a device for putting external pressure on an organization for change. The authors conclude with a proposal for integrating organizational-based and external programs aimed at improving the quality of life in work organizations.

CHAPTER 2
CAREER DEVELOPMENT

JOHN VAN MAANEN & EDGAR H. SCHEIN
Massachusetts Institute of Technology

The quality of work life ultimately refers to the interaction between individual employees and their employing organization. The wants and needs of individual employees—for material rewards, job satisfaction, opportunities to use talents and make contributions, and chances to learn and grow—must somehow be meshed with the wants and needs of an organization—for productivity, creativity, reliability, loyalty, and high performance. A psychological contract must be worked out that permits the individual and the organization each to give and receive enough so that the important needs of both are satisfied *over a long period of time.*

Most analyses of the interaction between the individual and the organization do not take the time perspective into account. Only job factors in the immediate situation are analyzed for their potential in creating a rewarding and satisfying work environment or productive, creative, and loyal employees. Yet we know that most jobs are embedded in job histories. And we know that the job history is often thought of, both by the individual and the organization, as a *career.* It is the purpose of this chapter to spell out the importance of taking the career perspective explicitly into account in any attempt to improve the quality of work life.

What do we know about individual needs when we think in terms of a ten, twenty, or thirty year span? What factors need to be analyzed if we are looking for ways to improve the quality of working life across the entire career, not merely in a given job situation? How can individuals improve the development of their careers? How can organizations develop policies that create viable career development options? How can social institutions support the career development process so that high quality work life becomes a meaningful reality over the entire life span? These issues are the focus of this chapter.

It is important to note that concern for the issues surrounding career development is relatively new. Both the descriptive work and prescriptive work on the topic tend to be theoretical, oversimplified, and confused. Therefore, before we can begin to examine how to improve the career development process, we must understand the language used to discuss careers, and we must develop explanatory concepts that are useful for understanding career dynamics. It is to these issues that the first four sections of this chapter are addressed.

THE MEANING OF A CAREER

A career is something we all have but often fail to recognize. Although *career* is a familiar concept that is used frequently and almost automatically in our society, the commonsensical use of the term is surprisingly ambiguous. In fact, most people, when pressed, would probably find this word difficult to define.

The ancient Greeks used the term *career* to refer to a fast-paced running of a course—some sort of race. A vestige of the original use remains in the verb form—for example, *to career* a horse. But conventional use of the word is considerably more diverse. At times, the term career is used to convey *upward occupational mobility*—for example, the route taken by an individual to the executive suite, as in *business career*. At other times, it is used to imply *occupational stability*—for example, the lifetime occupation of a person who is a *career soldier*. Both uses imply *continuity* or *consistency*. Thus, whether mobile or stable, the career represents an organized path taken by an individual across time and space.

A career generally consists of a series of separate but related experiences and adventures through which a person passes during a lifetime. It can be long or short, and an individual can pursue multiple careers either in rough sequence or at the same time. In this sense, the concept is a shorthand notation for a particular set of activities with a natural, unfolding history—involvement over time in a given role or across a series of roles. In the work world, prostitutes, plumbers, doctors, factory workers, managers, housewives, bartenders, waitress-

es, lawyers, criminals, and policemen all have careers.[1] Any of these
careers can be brilliant or disappointing, a success or a failure. What is
critical about careers, however, is the degree to which they serve as
the principle around which people organize their lives. This depends
not only on the status, direction, tempo, and length of the career, but
also on the meaning the individual ascribes to it.

In earlier times, the notion of a career could be ignored or taken for
granted as an irrevocable feature of everyday life—a perfectly predictable outcome of one's position in the traditional order of things.
Whether peasant, artisan, or aristocrat, one's life work was determined
for the most part by birth. An individual experienced little separation
between his various pursuits because a person's station in life was the
fundamental reality around which family, work, and social activities
were organized—the many roles played by the person being, as it
were, fused together.

The concept of *Gemeinschaft* as used by the early sociologists
captures this sense of career nicely. In Gemeinschaft society, the individual is fully incorporated within a social network that, by and large,
defines who he is, what he is to do, and how he is to do it. The
development of individualism is minimal, and experiences in the work
sphere of a person's life are not separated from experiences in nonwork spheres. The notion of an individual choosing certain work is
essentially alien to the Gemeinschaft world. A person simply orients
his activity to the community at large—a social order based on con-
sensual folkways, mores, and religion. Thus, children can see in their
parents and grandparents fairly precise images of themselves grown
older. In that way they achieve a sure sense of the future that awaits
them. In such a society, the notion of a career spans both work and
nonwork, and the quality of a person's work life is inseparable from the
quality of his life in other areas.

It is only with the coming of relationships based on individual
exchange and calculation, rather than on mutual trust and knowledge,
that the concept of work becomes problematic to an individual. This
shift in social relationships is associated with the historical transition of
nineteenth-century Western society from its communal and medieval
character to its present competitive and industrial form. In place of the
old Gemeinschaft orientation there arose the *Gesellschaft* orientation,
in which the workman strives primarily for his own advantage. Individualism is highly developed and work, in modern society, can be

---

1. Occupational concerns do not constitute the only use of the term *career*. Certainly
one can speak of family careers, deviant careers, leisure careers, aesthetic careers, and
even moral careers. But, in the main, our interest here is with work careers that exist
within what economists glibly call the labor market.

approached in an instrumental manner, because *it is separable in theory and practice from other spheres of a person's life.*

As a result of this transformation of perspective, voluntaristic beliefs replace deterministic ones, and we now make choices that affect the course of our lives. In the world of work, for example, the ever-expanding list of job titles suggests that career possibilities are virtually limitless. Nowadays few children enter the occupations of their parents (Goode, 1964), and so a planned career is possible. The choices we make in the present can be seen to have recognizable, if only proba-blistic, consequences in the future. It is the existence of these choices that makes career development not only possible but necessary in modern society.

A career can provide order and meaning to the events and relation-ships in which a person is involved. As suggested by Hughes (1958, Preface), "a man's work is as good a clue as any to the course of his life and his social being and identity." In order to better understand both man and society, therefore, social scientists have been increas-ingly concerned with the relationship between individuals and their work. They have devoted an enormous amount of study to such issues as: the association between occupations and personality types, the connection between the division of labor and individual work at-titudes, and the process by which occupations and organizations are included within a person's self-image.

One recent by-product of this somewhat eclectic concern for the individual in the workplace has been the realization that *change* must be central to any account of the person's relationship to a job. An understanding of this relationship at any particular time must be based on knowledge of the changes that typically occur in a person's life and psychology as a result of passage through the life cycle. Career lines are not forged absolutely through the process of simply joining an organization or selecting an occupation. Rather, the nuances of mem-bership, participation, and progression are always in various stages of revision and negotiation. People change, as do organizations. Thus, a study of careers is a study of change. To improve the quality of an individual's work life through career development is essentially to guide or alter a change process that is occurring anyway.

WHY STUDY CAREERS?

The Theoretical Perspective

There are at least two major reasons why we should try to understand careers. First—and perhaps of most importance—the career concept is central to an understanding of *individual identity.* As recent work has made abundantly clear, any account of adult personality must allow for perpetual change—whether subtle or dramatic—within the individual. Experience provides the raw material from which a sense of the self grows, and experience is unceasing. To paraphrase Erikson's (1950) now classic statement, identity is never gained once and for all but is achieved continuously over a lifetime. Thus, although we cannot fail to recognize that each moment of life possesses its own inherent value, personal identity is built on the dimension of time and emphasizes both the continuity and discontinuity of experience.

Time and identity are what the career notion so nicely conveys. To develop an empathetic understanding of the individual, we must have some idea of the person's experienced past and anticipated future. More specifically, to grasp such situationally-denoted constructs as *work involvement* or *job satisfaction*, we must view people within their careers—within a context that explicitly directs attention toward the changing patterns of involvement or satisfaction. And even the most casual concern for these patterns suggests that they cannot be studied apart from personal experiences occurring within the individual's *nonwork* spheres of life—notably those that take place in the person's immediate family. To highlight this point, the interest expressed of late in what has been called the *midcareer* or *midlife* crisis suggests that a growing number of people, at particular times, critically reassess and significantly rearrange their work role, personal career, and total life situation.

The second and, for the most part, complementary theoretical interest that is served by the study of work careers revolves around research into the *nature and workings of complex organizations*. An organization cannot be understood (or changed) unless we have at least a rudimentary conception of the values, beliefs, and cognitive styles of the people located in various positions within it. And these values, beliefs, and cognitive styles are related most clearly to the training and subsequent careers of individuals. Unfortunately, a concern for the careers of people is a missing feature in all but a few organizational studies (Chinoy, 1955; Crozier, 1964; Dalton, 1959).

In one area in particular, an understanding of careers can lead to a better understanding of organizational processes. That is in the emerging trend in large, bureaucratic organizations toward a decreasing reliance on control through the fixed chain of command and an increasing reliance on more indirect kinds of control. Some prevailing indirect mechanisms are based on various incentive systems that have explicit career implications—for example, bonus plans, retirement packages, seniority rules, automatic pay increases, and so on. Even more significant is the emphasis on control through recruitment and promotion of those people whose career-related values fit organizational needs. Use of the career as an unobtrusive and indirect form of control has the advantage of seeming more legitimate than a system based on order or fiat.

Public schools, for example, encourage teachers to act as proverbial disciplinarians in the classroom, not on the basis of explicit rules and regulations but rather on the grounds that only those teachers with a reputation for running a tight ship are permitted to move into administrative positions (Lortie, 1975). Consider also the common practice of allowing ex-servicemen bonus points on police civil service examinations. Such a practice helps to insure that only those newcomers who are familiar with and presumably supportive of a strong, hierarchical chain of command are selected for police service (Harris, 1973). Such control systems are likely to excite less resistance from organizational members, and they may work more smoothly than control systems based on immediate and direct supervision. As Blau and Schonnherr (1971) suggest, "slave drivers have gone out of fashion not because they were so cruel but because they were so inefficient" (p. 71).

The criteria for selection and advancement in many organizations can be seen to define the premises and set the limits for many of the decisions made by members of the organization. Indeed, organizations are relying more and more on the judgments of those presumed to have professional expertise. This occurs because of the increased complexity of the environments in which organizations operate, and also because of the growing awareness that the efforts of people are channeled more effectively by mobilizing individuals' commitments to work itself than by coercion or bargaining. Such reliance on expert judgment opens the door for an insidious form of control over the organization itself, as well as over the participants. The form is insidious because it arises out of the background, training, and assumptions carried by the professional or expert, and because it is not easily identified or counteracted. One result of this growing dependence on professional judgment is that some decisions—for example, about laying off workers or investing corporate funds—are made on the normative criterion of technical efficiency, learned by experts during their lengthy professional, occupational, and organizational socialization processes. Many decisions, therefore, are rational only in the most local sense—serving the organization but not the society.

Even among the lower strata of organizational members, career considerations may provide a sort of membrane within which work-related decisions are limited. For example, many patrolmen working city streets tend to adopt a "lay low, avoid trouble" outlook toward their occupation lest they jeopardize their potential movement into other aspects of policing—detective work, radio communications, or up the hierarchical ranks (Van Maanen, 1973). Other occupations are marked by a sort of "backward calendar" in which workers count the days until retirement benefits can be claimed (Van Maanen, 1975b). In short, the detailed study of the career conceptions that workers in various occupations adopt can lead to a much better understanding of the assumptions underlying and guiding the day-in and day-out activities occurring in any organization.

The promise of career studies lies in learning substantially more about why both organizations and individuals act as they do. On the one hand, the career represents to the individual both an opportunity and a constraint. The ability to look ahead in terms of a career perspective may be a real source of inspiration and value for some people, but to others it may be a curse, a source of discontent and even of despair. On the other hand, organizational problems are not necessarily the same as those faced by the individual. Things are accomplished by organizations in part because people are concerned about their careers. Hence, the career must also be seen as a significant feature of the regularity imposed by the rules and culture associated with organizational life.

The Practical Perspective

When careers are considered from a practical or normative standpoint, most discussion takes place under the generic label of *career development*. Used conventionally, career development implies a lifelong process of working out a synthesis between individual interests and the opportunities (or limitations) present in the external work-related environment, so that both individual and environmental objectives are fulfilled. From the individual's perspective, career development involves "part of the merging cognitive structure of the self in relation to the world" (Tiedeman and O'Hara, 1963). And, from the environmental perspective, career development involves the many sequences and patterns by which people are linked over time to various work settings.[2] Thus, career development cannot be seen as either an individual or an environmental concern exclusively. Indeed, there are various frameworks within which to consider the topic. For the purposes of this discussion, three primary frameworks can be identified—personal, organizational, and institutional/societal.

---

2. As we emphasize in later sections of this chapter, work careers cannot be studied in isolation from family careers. And, although our main interest here is with organizational or occupational careers, to concentrate exclusively on careers defined in terms of the labor market would be equally misleading. Indeed, the so-called nonlabor market careers—those of housewives (and the growing number of househusbands), welfare recipients, criminals, volunteer workers, recreation enthusiasts, and so on—constitute distinctive ways of life organization and are therefore proper and worthy areas for career research. Some important and interesting work is going on in these areas. See for example, Bernard, 1974; Lopata, 1971; Seidenberg, 1975; Waldorf, 1973.

Personal. Human experience can be seen as a continuous stream of events in which the individual seeks to gain control over the immediate environment. Simultaneously, he is progressively being incorporated by that very environment. Thus, a dialectic process exists between the individual and the environment. Each is contained within the other, each is affected by the other, and the interaction takes place throughout the individual's lifetime. For the individual, career development is a balancing operation in which he attempts to integrate environmental demands and personal concerns. Individuals seek opportunity and stability as well as significance, meaning, and variety in the work that they do. People must also respond to career and family demands that sometimes pull in opposite directions. Events of middle and late life—such as undergoing a major job change, reaching a leveling-off point in the career, being fired or laid off, and facing one's eventual retirement—are of central importance to people. Certainly, physical and mental health are crucial personal issues closely related to work. In short, career development rests on the concerns of individuals, and it is to personal growth and satisfaction that career development programs must fundamentally be oriented.

Organizational. The issues involved in career development are of growing concern to large and small organizations in both the business sector and the government sector. The reasons for this concern are many, but two major ones stand out. First, the growth and productivity of organizations is now, more than ever, dependent on the effectiveness of human performance. Second, social values are shifting away from a view of work as the most important aspect of life and toward a view that explicitly takes into account all facets of the individual's life. Career development can no longer be considered in isolation from self-development and family development. Therefore, if organizations cannot create opportunities for career fulfillment at all employee levels, they will have an increasing number of undermotivated and ultimately unproductive workers and managers.

In other words, organizations must become more concerned about career development in order to survive economically as well as to help their human resources become more fulfilled. It is important that career development be viewed in the context of *all* of the human resources of an organization, not merely at the level of manager development where, traditionally, most of the effort has been placed. Not only do hourly workers need assistance, but various other groups within the organization—engineers, computer programmers, salespeople, and clerical personnel, for example—also need to be able to define their careers and they need opportunities to develop those careers.

It is our impression that employment patterns at all levels within organizations are becoming more stable, because of union pressures, government regulations, or cultural norms. If this trend continues, organizations will be forced to create programs that enable people to continue to grow and to remain involved in their work throughout their careers. If organizations cannot respond to this challenge, we predict that they will stagnate, become inefficient, and ultimately be displaced by other organizations that are better able to manage their human resources. Consequently, career development may well be a factor in the survival of organizations.

Institutional/societal. Career development concerns are intimately related to the goals, policies, and activities of various institutions, including educational systems, labor unions, legislative bodies, and various private and governmental regulatory agencies. Educational programs and opportunities, for example, often create and subsequently define the available career paths in the society. Governmental legislation is used frequently to help open up some career paths that historically have been closed to all but a privileged few. Manpower, welfare, and unemployment policies certainly bear directly on career-related issues. Indeed, the regulation of careers through licensing and standardization practices in various occupations and industries is today taken for granted in the world of work.

Briefly, institutional concerns revolve around three basic issues: (1) the definition of the talents and resources that will be needed by the institution/society to insure its survival and growth; (2) the development and utilization of individual abilities, skills, and talents in relation to institutional/societal needs; and (3) the guarantee that there is equality of opportunity to develop and practice the use of personal skills, abilities, and talents.

Viewed from this broadest of perspectives, career development entails an appreciation for the manner in which institutions channel and guide people through their working lives. Labor unions, to use a familiar example, provide members with continuing material and psychological benefits but they also provide members with delimited careers that can be either enriching or alienating. Adult education programs can assist people to move from obsolete or stultifying careers to others that are needed and fulfilling. Federal support programs, such as training stipends, systematically encourage people to enter some careers and discourage them from entering others. In short, the enormous impact of institutions on individuals, organizations, and careers must be recognized if we are to become responsive to the critical problems posed by work in this society.

TOWARD AN INTEGRATIVE MODEL
OF CAREER DEVELOPMENT

Matching Individual and Environment

Career development, as described, cannot be considered an individual, organizational, or institutional issue exclusively. The problems posed by inquiry into this area are many sided. Individuals, for example, cannot be expected to construct meaningful careers on their own if organizations fail to provide significant opportunities. Nor can organizations be expected to single-handedly provide adequate career opportunities without at least some institutional support available in the environment. Consequently, a notion of *joint responsibility* is central to a concern with career development.

One way to highlight this joint responsibility idea is to use a *matching model* to describe the career development problem. The match or fit between the person and the environment necessarily involves the interaction among institutional, organizational, and individual variables. Hence, we can usefully define the problem of career development in the following manner:

> How to achieve an optimum match throughout the life cycle between the needs and goals of individuals (as expressed through personal motives and values) and the requirements of work environments in society (as represented by tasks, roles, and settings).

If we also take into account the modifying role played by the different work-related norms prevalent in various societal, occupational, and organizational subcultures around the importance of work, what constitutes success, how one is to behave in the workplace, and so forth, we can illustrate this diagrammatically, as in Figure 2.1.

Society in this model represents the available (and potential) work structures in the environment. These work structures are defined by particular tasks, roles, and settings and are based on existing technology, information, and knowledge available in the society at large. They

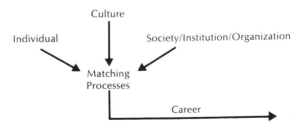

Figure 2.1 – Generic Influences upon the Career

are experienced by people in the form of organizational and occupational opportunities and demands. The *cultural* framework within
which an individual is located provides the context in which he can
make meaningful the experience associated with participation in the
work world. Thus, the individual's work-related needs, motives, and
abilities develop through interaction in the society and are contingent
on the cultural filters used by the individual to interpret such interaction.

What sets the model in action is the integration (or lack thereof)
provided by the matching processes linking individuals and work
environments throughout the life cycle. Techniques such as education,
role redesign, apprenticeship, vocational guidance, participative management, job training, and even the ubiquitous trial-and-error method
are popular matching processes—although not necessarily appropriate
in specific contexts.

The problem of career development defined in this manner becomes one of relating the key environmental, cultural, and individual
variables across time, and then discovering the differential effects
various matching processes have on the resulting integration among
these variables. We must look to organizational and institutional outcomes as well as to individual careers; to performance and productivity as well as to personal satisfaction and growth; and to occupational security and stability as well as to role innovation and task
variety. In short, a complex, interactive, and time dependent scheme is
required if we are to construct relevant career development programs
that respect both individual and environmental needs and constraints.

Given this eclectic mandate, we now examine several theoretical
approaches to the study of organizational and occupational careers. It
should be noted, however, that we are not interested in summarizing
the substantial disciplinary-based literature concerned with careers.
Such a task would take us far beyond the scope of this chapter. Rather,
we will focus on the *limitations* of the various conceptual approaches
to assist us in constructing a more useful and realistic framework for
viewing careers.

Psychological Approaches to the Study of Careers

Research into the many aspects of careers has not simply appeared
overnight. One research strand of long standing has revolved around
the effort to develop a theory of occupational *choice*. Many clinical,
vocational, and social psychologists have attempted to develop such a

theory as an aid in guidance and counseling as well as in selection and placement.

Although specific models have taken sundry forms, there are essentially two classes of occupational choice theories. One can be called the *differentialist* view (Holland, 1966; Hornaday and Kuder, 1961; Strong, 1943) because it places primary emphasis on individual differences—on the diversity of talents, abilities, and psychological endowments among people. The differentialist aim is to build a theory that will allow both jobs and people to be described with the same sorts of terms. Satisfaction and stability of occupational choice (and, by implication, the career) are judged, then, by the *congruence* between the descriptions of the job and of the person who performs it. Thus, patterns of ability, interest, style, and disposition, which are seen to be shaped early in life, are to be matched to the personal characteristics that seem to be required in a given occupation. By and large the differentialists have ignored the origins of differences and have concentrated on measuring them in early adulthood. Indeed, a whole industry has been founded on the testing and assessing of individuals prior to work and in the workplace—an industry deeply indebted to the various diagnostic devices developed by psychometricians for discovering vocational interest and ability.

On the other hand, some psychologists (Ginzberg, Ginsburg, Axelard, and Herma, 1951; Roe, 1957; Super, Starishevsky, Matlin, and Jordaan, 1963) have attempted to redress what they feel to be the static, unyielding quality of the classification and association models of the differentialists. These theorists employ what can be labeled a *developmentalist* perspective. This view implies that occupational choice is not something that occurs at a specific time, but rather that it represents an evolving sequence of individual decisions. Choice, from this standpoint, is a more or less irreversible process of limiting decisions that begin with an individual's first childish fantasies about work and end with his reflections on retirement. Occupational identity is seen to be part of the individual's wider development.

Developmentalists have attempted to identify the personality correlates of occupations and to define how early childhood experiences bias a person toward particular occupations. The sources for developmentalist theory and practice have been the writings of cognitive, educational, and child psychologists concerned with general identity formation (Erikson, 1959, 1968; Kohlberg, 1964; Kroll, Dinklage, Lee, Morley, and Wilson, 1970; Piaget, 1962, 1969). The concept of life stages—such as exploration, establishment, maintenance, and decline—is used as the starting point by many theorists interested in the developmental approach. The main aim here seems to be the construction of a theory that establishes norms for thought and behavior at various chronological ages. Because developmentalists have been less devoted to the narrow scientific approach of the differentialists, their theories have been looser, almost metaphoric, and consequently less subject to rigorous empirical test.

A third strain of psychological theorizing—*organizational*—can also be distinguished. Organizational psychologists have devoted substantial attention to the problems that stem from a person's involvement in the work milieu. For example, issues such as socialization and training, supervisor-subordinate relationships, work motivation and satisfaction, performance measurement and evaluation, and communications and decision-making patterns have been central concerns of this field (see, for example, Argyris, 1964; Hall, 1971; Leavitt, 1972; Porter, Lawler, and Hackman, 1975; Schein, 1971). However, despite considerable rhetoric about the need to view individual-organizational relationships over time, little research has been carried out longitudinally. Indeed, many empirical investigations conducted within this framework tend to reflect a static, statistically abstract, sort of name-rank-and-serial-number correlational approach that is particularly unsuited for the study of careers. In addition, all too often organizational psychologists focus on areas of study that are oriented solely toward managerial problems and priorities—such as efficiency and effectiveness. By concentrating on the official objectives of the organization, organizational psychologists tend to emphasize the point of view of people working *for* the organization rather than the point of view of people worked on *by* organizations. Career studies by their very nature must be about people who are exposed, as we all are, to actual organizational treatments and processes in their everyday lives, people who constitute the raw materials of the organization and are its customers, workers, clients, inmates, managers, beneficiaries, and sometimes victims.

Sociological Approaches to the Study of Careers

Psychologists, by focusing most of their attention on individual choice and development, have tended to neglect the considerable economic and social constraints within which people must act. Sociologists, on the other hand, have from the beginning given only slight attention to the question of occupational choice. They feel that by the time race, class, sex, religion, nationality, education, family, and area of residence have played out their respective parts, the range of individual choice has been severely restricted and so have individual expectations. Consequently, rather than concentrate on the *individual*, sociologists have focused on the *settings* in which the individual carves out a career.[3]

There are three distinct, although overlapping, sociological approaches to the study of careers. These three approaches resemble subdisciplines and can be labeled *industrial sociology,* the *sociology of occupations and professions,* and *organization theory.* Each approach typically asks different questions, employs different models and methods, and is concerned for the most part with different groups of people and settings. Industrial sociology is concerned with workers and their membership in *task* groups. Occupational sociology is concerned with all members of a particular occupation or profession. And organization theory is concerned with managers and their role in organizations. Although this academic division of labor is a source of strength and broadens our perspective on work careers, it is also a weakness. The fact is that people are concerned with all three categories at once—with task, occupation, and organization. To restrict attention to just one of the categories is unnecessarily limiting.

Sociologists have contributed in critical ways to the study of careers by emphasizing the individual's discovery of common norms and values associated with participation in a particular work role. Whereas psychologists often have a very unrealistic view of the actual requirements of particular careers, sociologists have developed rich descriptions of what it is really like to be on the inside of specific occupations or organizations. This effort to describe various occupational settings has led to a better understanding of some careers, including those of cab drivers (Davis, 1959), dance hall musicians (Becker, 1951), assembly line workers (Roy, 1960; Walker and Guest, 1952), professional thieves (Sutherland, 1937), janitors (Gold, 1964), and restaurant workers (Whyte, 1948).

Certainly sociologists have compelled us to recognize that what is claimed as the essence or critical function of a particular career is sometimes little more than rhetorical justification for occupational status and prestige, an ideology bearing little relationship to what the individual actually does within the career (Goode, 1957; Vollmer and Mills, 1966; Wilensky, 1964). For example, public pronouncements by police administrators concerning the dangerous rise in some category of crime suggest that policemen are constantly engaged in the business of crook catching. Yet, as numerous studies detail, the business of policing is far more mundane and service-oriented than professional spokesmen would have us believe (Reiss, 1971; Rubenstein, 1973; Westley, 1971). Similarly, sociological research in the area of mental

---

3. Of particular interest here are the works of Greer, 1972; Hughes, 1971; Krause, 1971; Salaman and Thompson, 1973; Stewart and Cantor, 1974; and Zald, 1971.

illness (Goffman, 1961a; Stanton and Schwartz, 1954; Scheff, 1966) demonstrates the wide gap that sometimes exists between what is officially proclaimed as an institutional mandate (heal the sick) and what is in fact practiced (classification and control).

The Need for an Eclectic Approach

Historically, the two career frames of reference—psychological and sociological—have remained remarkably independent. One comes away from reviewing the career-related literature with a sense of frustration at the dearth of cross-referencing. Although there are undoubtedly good organizational reasons for such limited theoretical accounting of careers, the situation is just short of appalling. While psychologists have been busy developing things like the Strong Vocational Interest Blank or the Kuder Occupational Preference Blank, sociologists have been busy infiltrating occupations and organizations, trying to discover general properties of the work experiences of people (Becker, Greer, Hughes, and Strauss, 1961; Dalton, 1959; Van Maanen, 1973). There exists, therefore, a curious hiatus between the two approaches. On the one hand, we have psychologists saying essentially that "people make careers" and, on the other hand, sociologists claiming that "careers make people."

What is required, of course, is a focus that shifts from an inordinate concentration on occupational roles or personal characteristics to one that emphasizes the career as an object of inquiry.[4] Researchers must begin to study both sides of the coin. Detailed study of the individual and of individual differences within an occupation must be accompanied by detailed study of the occupational setting and of the issues that participation in the setting raises for the people who are in it. The serious study of careers requires a profound respect for the dialectic quality of human experience. Man is both the creator and the created. A commitment that emphasizes either an ordered world of constraint, manipulation, and conformity or one that emphasizes man's capacity for growth, vision, and originality would be a mistake. What is needed is the recognition of the unfolding character of social life viewed from within a framework that explicitly includes the many roles a person is called on to play.[5]

---

4. It is interesting to note that several impressive attempts to do just this have appeared in the popular literature. Studs Terkel's Working (1974) and Division Street: America (1968) are perhaps the best known. But consider also Jack Olsen's Girls in the Office (1972) as well as Kenneth Larson's The Workers (1971), Philip Slater's The Pursuit of Loneliness (1970), Gail Sheehy's Hustling (1973), Martin Mayer's The Bankers (1974), Dan Lortie's Schoolteacher (1975), and E. E. LeMasters' Blue Collar Aristocrats (1975). Indeed, the quasi fiction of Joseph Heller's Something Happened (1974) is most appropriate to a concern with corporate careers. And no list of writings in the popular culture would be complete without mention of the HEW report, Work in America (1973) and Sheppard and Herrick's Where Have All the Robots Gone? (1972).

Perhaps the best direction in which to proceed is to begin con- structing a framework on which an interdisciplinary study of careers and career development can rest. Certainly we must continue to explore the processes, structures, and settings in which careers exist, and we must build learning theories that relate experience to cogni- tion. But we also must cast our conceptual net so that it captures the actual meaning people attach to situations and not simply focus on the meaning attached to situations by those of us employed to study those situations.[6] Theoretical abstraction and statistical elegance are not the goals. Rather, we seek a way to better understand the various shapes, properties, and meanings a career can have.

The remainder of this chapter represents, we think, a tentative but useful start in this direction. No claims are made, however, regarding the "one best way" to study careers, or, for that matter, the "one best way" to design and implement career development programs. Nor do we argue for the bedrock utility of using a particular set of variables to describe the contingencies on which careers depend. Rather, we have tried to portray the complexity of the situations surrounding individuals and their careers.

BASIC CONCEPTS FOR THE STUDY OF CAREERS

Three primary concepts serve to organize the following analysis. First, we suggest that there must be an explicit acknowledgement of the need to view careers from at least two basic perspectives—the *internal* perspective that refers to the individual's subjective apprehension and evaluation of his career, and the *external* perspective that delineates the more or less tangible indicators of a career—occupation, job level, mobility, opportunity, task characteristics, and the like. One is subjec- tive, the other objective, and there is little reason to assume that the two inevitably coincide on any given dimension. This distinction is

---

5. A simple example will suffice. Consider the number of studies on job satisfaction that characterize man's turning away from the world of work as an aberrant, alienated, if not destructive response. Very little positive worth has been attributed to the family or other nonwork spheres as potential wellsprings of support, self-esteem, and growth. Studies that depict the partial involvement of individuals in the workplace in disparaging terms barely conceal their managerial bias. Indeed, they represent little more than ideological pronouncements—on the sacred worth of a hard day's work—and as such fall outside the realm of scientific endeavor.

6. One useful place to begin is with the words of our subjects. Few firsthand accounts find their way into either the psychological or sociological literature. And those that do are usually concerned with deviance of some sort. Thus, for example, psychologists have their psychopathological "wolfman" and sociologists have their sociopathological "jackroller." Among the dimensions of work that we are interested in here, there are very few firsthand accounts that we can turn to for insight—although the recent works of Cottle (1974) and Fraser (1969) probably come the closest.

perhaps the most crucial for future research and applications, because in the past the two perspectives have often been confused.

Second, we suggest that work careers can be clarified analytically only by understanding the *person within the total life space* and *throughout his lifetime.* Whatever personal, occupational, and family features eventually prove to be most interesting to analyze, they must not be seen as fixed. Rather, they must always be scanned for the longitudinal evolution affecting relationships among career variables.

Third, we suggest that it is of crucial importance to develop an *interactive model*—a model that pays special attention to the interaction of *self-development, family development,* and *career development* issues. Essentially, we argue here that causal, linear models, which emphasize stimulus-and-response explanations between a limited number of variables, may be a too restricting, if not entirely inappropriate way to think about careers. The century-old strategy of varying one factor and then observing the results on another factor is suitable only when the phenomenon in question is unambiguous, controlled, and simple—something careers most assuredly are not. Patterns and relationships are what research must highlight, not deterministic equations of cause and effect. Career outcomes are the results of interaction among a fairly large set of variables existing within a complex domain. From this standpoint, rules and principles of interaction may eventually be constructed leading to what some might call a grammar of situations (Goffman, 1961b, 1967), instead of the separate and competing propositions of individual motives or external demands presently in vogue. Indeed, the metaphors and analogies that inform and frame our empirical and deductive work should be drawn from ecological, not mechanical, etiologies.

Each of the above suggestions is treated separately in the following three sections—the external and internal perspectives, careers over time, and the interactive framework. Within each section, we develop a general theoretical position, provide some examples, and denote several practical implications relevant to career development issues. It should be noted, however, that across the three sections the analytic and applied concerns become increasingly more complex. In other words, the suggestions made here are cumulative and should not be considered in isolation.

The External and Internal Careers

Basic Definitions.   The *external* career refers to the more or less objective categories used by members of society or of an occupation to describe the typical or official progression of steps through a given occupation (Bailyn and Schein, 1975; Schein, 1974; Van Maanen, 1976; Wilensky, 1961). Some careers, like that of a doctor, have clearly defined stages of education, internship, residency, licensing, hospital affiliation or private practice, and so forth. Other careers, like that of an engineer, are much more vaguely defined because occupants have many options available to them after receiving a basic education. An engineer could, for example, work in government or industry, go into private consulting, or train to become a manager during the early portion of the career. But we are still referring to external criteria, job titles, and some kind of visible progression through objectively defined stages.

The idea of stages in a progression toward culturally defined rewards is the essence of the external definition of career. Typically, we have associated this concept of career with professions like law, medicine, teaching, government service, engineering, and architecture. But the concept is just as applicable to other kinds of occupations, even occupations considered to have low prestige. For instance, although one cannot define very many career steps involved in occupations like automobile factory worker or secretary or plumber, there is nevertheless some *horizontal* progression. This may be in terms of rewards such as higher pay through the years, greater job security, cleaner and less physically demanding work, and honors for length of service or high priority work. Over the years, the individual also acquires greater knowledge of what goes on in the organization, he may become privy to some secrets shared, he may have opportunities to become a mentor to younger workers, and he may experience other rewards associated with being closer to the core of the organization (Schein, 1971). And, of course, there is always the possibility, however slight, of promotion to a better job. Many workers might regard such careers as not very challenging or desirable, but they are nevertheless careers by definition.

One of the central problems of career development is the reexamination of the options available for improving careers that are not very attractive in terms of progression toward *hierarchically* defined rewards. If an employer knows that many workers will remain with the organization for twenty to thirty years, what kind of planning can be done to create a career progression that will be more desirable for those workers?

The phrase *internal career* refers to the set of steps that make up the *individual's* concept of his progression within an occupation. This internal concept may be very vague (for example, a general ambition to get ahead) or it may be very specific (for example, a personal plan to achieve a specific rank, position, income, or skill by age thirty-five). Many people in business formulate internal careers that involve, for example, spending a few years in a large company to learn the ropes, saving some money, and then striking out to start their own enterprises. Engineers sometimes plan to stay in a technical job for five to ten years but plan then to make an explicit attempt to get into management (Bailyn and Schein, 1975). And many public defenders expect to begin their own private practice after just a year or two of experience in a government agency (Platt and Pollock, 1974).

Other workers may have less clear internal career concepts, but they do think and plan in terms of a future in which they will improve themselves by continuing their education, getting into another line of work, relocating to take advantage of an opportunity in the labor market, saving money to buy a small business, and so on (Blauner, 1964; Chinoy, 1955; Sheppard and Herrick, 1972; Shoestak, 1959).

For people within a given occupation or external career position, many internal careers are possible. For some people, increasing competence may be emphasized internally, while others may consider income most important. Although a sort of upward progression characterizes the internal careers of many, this need not always be true. Take, for example, the idea of occupational achievement. A man may, at twenty-one years of age, make $10,000 a year as an accountant. He may, at forty, make $100,000 as president of the firm. If at twenty-one his objective is to become president of the firm, his $10,000 a year job will hold an entirely different meaning for him than if he expects to remain at the same job forever. If upwardly mobile, he may see his work as good preparation or as a way to learn the discipline of work. If his future is viewed with more dismal prospects, he may interpret the same job as tedious. There are two internal careers possible for the accountant in this example—one enriching, the other deadening. Identical situations may surround people, but the meaning of these situations may vary substantially from person to person. The internal career created by an individual transforms the purely real or external career as the course of events unfolds. It reflects the goals and values held by the individual in relation to his working life and the criteria of success by which he judges himself.

Themes.   One way of capturing analytically the interplay between the internal and external careers is to consider the patterns by which people link their experienced past and anticipated future. Van Maanen (1975b) uses the term *theme* to refer to these patterns. In the workplace, a theme conveys the individual's evaluation of where he is and where he is going in his work career. A theme might be, for example, that one has an interesting, challenging job with good prospects, or, conversely, that one has a dull, routine job with no prospects. Both themes postulate a pattern that is meaningful to the individual. As such, the theme explains, provides context, and guides the person in his environment. Themes can, of course, be realistic, in the sense that they accurately depict the external career and are continuously being experienced and confirmed. Or they can be fantastic, in the sense that they fail to accurately depict the external career and are never being experienced or confirmed.

Themes place the present within a stream of work life events. The apprentice beautician assumes, for example, that if his performance is acceptable, more clients will be forthcoming, as will pay raises, job security, and the like. In this case, the theme embodies a notion of increasing responsibility and is, therefore, subject to empirical test in the everyday world. What happens when one fails to confirm a given theme as expected is disconfirmation and surprise, which lead to reappraisal and perhaps a reconstruction of the theme. A good illustration is provided by Kopelman, Dalton, and Thompson (1971). In a study of the work careers of engineers, they note that the early occupational experience of engineers is marked by highly challenging tasks, a number of pay raises, and, for many, promotion into supervisory slots. It is a time of interesting work, excitement, and high aspiration. The work situation clearly embodies an optimistic getting-ahead theme. However, the likelihood of this advancement theme being confirmed throughout the length of the career is low; as the engineer moves out in the career, plateaus are reached and promotions become less frequent. And as career lines flatten out, work themes must undergo what for some are, no doubt, painful transformations.

In many work situations, the entry level job taken by an individual represents a sort of terminal career node as well. Coal miners, garbage collectors, secretaries, janitors, and, to a somewhat lesser degree, school teachers, policemen, and social workers enter jobs at a level from which hierarchical advancement is not the norm. To a degree then, these jobs represent limited careers. Yet, there almost always exists the possibility of achieving, from the individual's standpoint, a better assignment, freedom from close supervision, higher pay with seniority, job tenure, and perhaps increasing recognition for a task well done. In such occupations, these are the work features that themes are built on.

Chinoy's (1955) auto workers or Blauner's (1964) factory hands may not see their jobs as part of a career that channels aspirations and sustains dreams, but they do construct themes based on the difficulty of their work, the nature of their supervision, and the monotony of the jobs. Work themes stressing security can be found in many occupations (Dubin, 1956; Goldthorpe, 1968; Walker and Guest, 1952); in other occupations, simply being able to retire free of occupational disease is a major theme (*Work in America*, 1973; Scott, 1974). Finally, on some jobs where people have difficulty attaching any meaning whatsoever to what they do, simply marking time is a significant work theme (Roy, 1952, 1960).[7] In this regard, Fraser's (1968) comments are perceptive: "Time is what the factory worker sells, not labor, but time, dreary time. Desolute factory time that passes so slowly compared with the fleeting seconds of the weekend" (p. 12).

A predominant theme has a number of implications. Take, for example, the careers of business executives in the United States, where the theme of upward advancement is utilized. Such careers seem to carry with them what Henry (1963) calls a "permanent sense of the unobtained." Thus, the executive who at thirty years of age considers himself successful only if he is head of the department at age forty, will, at age forty, consider himself successful only if he is head of the division at age fifty, and so on. A consumer theme revolving around the accumulation of material goods has much the same character, as does an artistic theme stressing the achievement of excellence. These themes become progressively more difficult to achieve as the individual travels through the career.

Associated with any given theme is a *timetable* (Roth, 1963). The timetable is, in essence, the test of a particular theme. Timetables refer to a range of time that surrounds the benchmarks of an internal career. Take, for example, the aspiring university professor who makes explicit his anticipated rise in the scholar's hierarchy by planning to acquire a Ph.D. before turning twenty-five, publish his first book before twenty-seven, receive university tenure before thirty, and make full professor by thirty-five. The failure to achieve any particular benchmark exactly on time is not likely to cause a revision in the overall internal career. However, there is a delicate line to be drawn here, for in some academic organizations the so-called up-or-out proviso is operative— the aspiring full professor must look elsewhere for employment if promotion does not come within five years or before he turns thirty-five. Officers in military organizations often fall under a similar external timetable fiat.

Timetables for business careers can vary a great deal from organization to organization. Thus, a failure to be promoted within a two-year stretch in one organization may lead a person to what some have called a *status panic* (a reaction to a signal that one's upward thrust in

7. Similar themes characterize life for some individuals in other settings as well— plateaued managers in some industrial firms (Warren, Ference, and Stoner, 1975), draftees in peacetime armies (Sorokin and Merton, 1937; Stouffer, 1949), students in many educational institutions (Becker et al., 1961), and railwaymen working for economically hard pressed organizations (Potratz, 1975; Salaman, 1974).

the organization has been thwarted). In another organization, such a failure is not a personal failure at all, but rather a taken-for-granted organizational policy.

A theme can be *owned* by the person or not. Ownership refers to the degree to which an individual feels he can control his career— regardless of whether this belief is imagined or real. Organizations differ in the degree to which members, through their own efforts, can control their movement through the external career steps. Civil service bureaucracies, for example, exert almost monopolistic control over the career movement of employees. Similarly, in the higher circles of managerial and professional ranks, a person's career movement may be determined largely by events not of his making. For instance, demand for a service may shift, the economy may spiral downward, or a superior may act capriciously. Any of these events could wrench temporal control from the individual's hands, reducing his sense of ownership of his career.

When ownership does not characterize the internal career, a person is quite likely to feel powerless in the workplace, perhaps confused and helpless at being the pawn of larger forces. Seeman (1959) and Blauner (1964) would regard the individual in such a situation as alienated. And this is as possible in managerial or professional occupations as it is in the so-called blue-collar occupations—whether skilled or unskilled, unionized or nonunionized, self-employed or organizationally employed, and so on—although perhaps not with the same regularity (Bailyn and Schein, 1975).

The Internal-External Concept Elaborated. Before proceeding to a discussion of how internal and external career factors can be better matched, we must note that many concepts relating to the success or failure of careers have internal and external meanings that are often blurred in the literature on this topic. Specifically, we feel that some confusion surrounds the concepts of *participation, productivity, reward,* and *success.* Each of these has internal and external meanings that need to be distinguished if we are to accurately assess the outcomes of career development programs.

Participation (participative management). This concept normally means providing employees with opportunities to become involved in decisions that go beyond the immediate boundaries of their jobs; that is, participation has an *external* meaning pertaining to *what the organization or the manager does* in the way of providing opportunities for employees to influence decisions, by expressing feelings or by actually voting (Marrow, Bowers, and Seashore, 1967). However, this same concept has a subjective, *internal* meaning pertaining to an employee's feelings of involvement, of having a sense that personal influence can be exerted over some decisions (March and Simon, 1958; Tannenbaum, 1968).[8]

Employees differ in their needs for involvement as well as in the areas where they want involvement. Therefore, whether *participative management*, used in the external sense, works will depend to a large extent on the degree to which the opportunities provided by management for participation (the external component) *match* the employees' needs to be involved or to participate (the internal component). Many programs of participation fail because they assume that employees want involvement in areas in which they do not want it. On the other hand, employees can become demoralized and angry if their internal need to participate is not matched by opportunities to do so.

Productivity.   The term *productivity* typically refers to the actual output of a person, group, or organization (an *external* criterion). This may or may not match an individual's *internal* sense of his productiveness—what he regards as a fair day's work for a fair day's pay. One of the reasons productivity programs often fail is that they only consider the organization's demands and fail to determine an employee's perception of how productive he is or can be. If there is a mismatch between external and internal perceptions of productivity, the organization must consider various options to reduce the gap; it must *not* simply assume that managerial standards are the correct ones and should automatically be accepted as valid by employees.

When one examines the subjective, internal side of productivity, one often finds that the reasons an employee does not produce more are related to factors other than fatigue. The relevant factors can include lack of meaning in the work, lack of social stimulation in the workplace, lack of a positive relationship with the supervisor, feelings of being exploited, and feelings that the work layout or the machinery or the industrial engineering standards are unrealistic. Until one finds out *why* the employee is not producing more, one cannot determine how to create a better match between external and internal productivity standards.[9]

Reward.   Much has been written about how to reward employees, but very little consideration has been given to what the employee might find rewarding (the internal, subjective side of reward). Companies constantly attempt to invent better pay systems, benefit systems, vacation systems, and promotion systems (all *externally* defined in terms of

8. The various mechanisms and outcomes of participation are discussed, from different perspectives, by Lawler (Chapter 4) as they relate to pay system redesign, by Strauss (Chapter 6) as they pertain to supervisory strategies, and by Beer and Driscoll (Chapter 7) as they affect organizational change efforts.

9. Suttle (Chapter 1) has examined how internal and external assessments of productivity, and the match between the two, influence quality of work life.

societal or organizational norms of what should be rewarding), but give relatively little effort to determining what *employees* are seeking in the way of rewards.[10] This factor is relatively less important in a well-integrated and stable society where cultural norms about rewards are fairly universal. However, in a rapidly changing society, the values of the new generations entering organizations may be quite different from traditional values. For example, according to at least one report, young people today are putting more emphasis on being given time off, on being allowed more than the customary freedom in the selection of hours of work, on having a choice about how to collect their financial rewards (salary, fringe benefits, stock options, and health insurance), on recognition for their contributions, and on challenging work (Yankelovich, 1972). Here, as in the other areas, organizations will have to try to match the externally defined rewards (incentives) with the changing internal needs of employees. If mismatches occur, both the employees and the organizations will have to reassess their values and assumptions in order to design a reward system that meets the needs of both (Adams and Rosenbaum, 1962).

Success. How often have we had the experience of talking to someone who appeared to be highly successful then discovered that he felt very unhappy and dissatisfied? Such a discrepancy in perception occurs when an observer applies external, societal criteria to the situation of an individual who is assessing his own experience according to internal, subjective criteria. Perhaps he wanted a bigger promotion than he got, perhaps he wanted more recognition for his contribution, not merely a salary increase, perhaps he wanted to help a key subordinate who failed. The professor of science at a famous university may *look* very successful, but he may *feel* completely unsuccessful unless he has made a discovery that attracts the attention of his scientific peers throughout the world. In short, we cannot assume that by meeting external criteria of success we are assured of internal feelings of success (Bailyn and Schein, 1975).

If a career development policy is to maintain high levels of motivation and involvement in employees throughout their careers, it is essential to determine what internal criteria of success those employees are using and how well those internal criteria match the external opportunity structure. If what the employees regard as success is externally unattainable (a mismatch of internal and external criteria), then new opportunities have to be created or employees have to be

---

10. Lawler (Chapter 4) also stresses the importance of taking the individual's personal, subjective expectations and evaluations of rewards into account. He shows that job satisfaction, and to some extent productivity, are influenced not so much by the actual (*externally* defined) rewards that people receive as by their personal beliefs and values (*internal* definitions) regarding these rewards. He points out as well that people vary widely in what they find rewarding about their jobs.

helped to change their criteria, or both. In some situations this will mean that employees will discover that what they want is genuinely not attainable in one organization and that they will have to change their aspirations or seek a different organization in which a different opportunity structure exists.

In summary, when we talk of careers, career development, and factors related to careers, we must always be careful to distinguish between the internal and the external needs of a given employee group, and we must examine the degree of match or mismatch across different areas of work, before we generate new career policies and programs.

Careers Over Time

Stages and Processes in the Career.   In order to better design programs of career development, we must understand the changing needs of the individual at different career stages. Both the external and the internal careers generate different issues at different times in the individual's life cycle. What are these issues and how do they fit into the *total life perspective* of the individual?

Table 2.1 shows the major stages of the career. In the lefthand column are the major stages that make up the *external* career and the individual processes that typically reflect them. In the righthand column are the major internal processes that the person is experiencing at different stages of the internal career (Ginzberg et al., 1951; Levinson, Darrow, Klein, Levinson, and McKee, 1974; Schein, 1964; 1971; Schein and Bailyn, 1974; Super, 1957; Vaillant and MacArthur, 1972). The external factors vary greatly from one occupation to another, as well as in the individual processes of different people. The ideas presented in this table are meant to identify the issues that may face organizations and people at different stages of the career. We are not suggesting however that all people go through the same processes or steps.

Table 2.1 is a drastic condensation of a very complex set of processes that occur in stages and cycles as an individual progresses through a career. To fully explore and explicate the issues involved in all phases of this model is beyond the scope of this chapter. Indeed, research into these issues is not only scanty, but somewhat shallow. It is scattered widely throughout a diverse literature and, more often than not, rests on cross-sectional, not longitudinal, evidence.[11] However, we do

---

11. What is needed is not simply longitudinal analysis but what is called *cohort analysis*. Using time as a variable is tricky and care must be taken to provide at least some control over sociohistorical variation. For an excellent methodological treatment of some prerequisites for treating time as an independent variable, see Buss, 1974, or Wohlwill, 1970.

Table 2.1–Major Stages and Processes of the Career

External Stages and Individual Processes	Internal Stages and Processes
1. *Exploration Stage*	*Exploration*

External Stages and Individual Processes

1. *Exploration Stage*
   - Occupational images from mass media, books, movies
   - Advice and example of parents, siblings, teachers, and other models
   - Actual success/failure in school, sports, hobbies, and self-tests
   - Stated constraints or opportunities based on family circumstances — economic, historical, et cetera. "We can't afford to send you to college" or "every boy of mine must try the law"
   - Actual choice of educational path — vocational school, college major, professional school
   - Counseling, letter of recommendation, and other external influences
   - Test results of manual and intellectual aptitude and achievement tests

2. *Establishment Stage (Early Career)*

   a. *Mutual Recruitment* — organization is looking for talent — individual is looking for a good job
   - Constrained by labor market and pool of available talent
   - Selection, testing, screening

   b. *Acceptance and Entry*
   - Induction and orientation
   - Assignment to further training or first job
   - Informal or formal initiation rites and conferring of organizational status (identity cards, parking sticker, uniform, company manual)

Internal Stages and Processes

Exploration
- Development of self-image of what one "might be," what sort of work would be fun
- Self-assessment of own talents and limitations — "things I could never be"
- Development of ambitions, goals, motives
- Tentative choices and commitments
- Enlarged self-image based on integration of personality, social and educational accomplishments
- Growing need for real test of ability to work and accomplish real life vocational tasks
- Anticipatory socialization based on role models, teachers, and images of the occupation

Getting Started, Finding a Job

- Reality shock
- Insecurity around new task of interviews, applying, being tested, facing being turned down
- Developing image of occupation/organization based on recruitment/selection process

- Making a *"real"* choice, take job or not, which job, first commitment
- Maximum need for self-test and fear of failure
- Exhilaration at being accepted or despair at being turned down; readjustment of self-image
- Beginning development of themes

Table 2.1—Major Stages and Processes of the Career (cont.)

External Stages and Individual Processes

c. *First Job Assignment*
-Meeting the boss and co-workers
-Learning period, indoctrination
-Period of full performance "doing the job"
-Leveling off and/or becoming obsolete
-Preparing for new assignment

d. *Leveling Off, Transfer, and/or Promotion*
-Feedback on meaning of the move or lack of move, performance review, career counseling, salary action (usually more frequent but has special meaning here)
-If transferred or promoted, repeat of the five steps under 2c

(If individual fails, "does not fit in," or has to be laid off, the process goes back to 2a)

(If individual is succeeding, he is probably developing a speciality or special areas of competence leading to a period of real contribution in that area of competence. If that area of competence is needed in the organization, the individual is given actual or de facto tenure)

Internal Stages and Processes

-Expectation of being tested for the first time under *real* conditions
-Feeling of playing for keeps
-Socialization by boss, peers, and subordinates — "learning the ropes"
-Reality shock — what the work is really like, doing "the dirty work"
-Testing the commitment to occupation/organization — developing the theme

-Feeling of success or failure
-Reassessment of self-image and how it matches perceived opportunities in occupation/organization — "Is there a career here?"
-Sorting out family/work issues and finding a comfortable level of accommodation
-Forming a career strategy, how "to make it" — working hard, finding mentors, conforming to organization, making a contribution
-Decision to leave organization if things do not look positive
-Adjusting to failure, reassessment of self, occupation and organization — effort to avoid losing self-esteem, elaboration or revision of theme
-Turning to unions or other sources of strength if feeling unfairly treated or threatened

-Growing feeling of success and competence, commitment to organization and occupation
-Period of maximum insecurity if organization has formal tenure review — "Will I make it or not?"

External Stages and Individual Processes	**Internal Stages and Processes**
e. *Granting of Tenure* (If tenure is *not* granted, individual will be moved *out* or *over* in a less central role)	−Feeling of being accepted fully by organization, "having made it" −Crisis of reassessment, trying to determine the "meaning" of not getting tenure, possible loss of work involvement, or casting about for new career options, period of high learning about self, testing of one's assumptions about self, occupation, and organization
3. *Maintenance Stage:* *(Mid career)* −Person is given more crucial, important work of the organization and expected to enter his period of maximum productivity −Occupation and organization secrets are shared −Person is expected to become more of a teacher/mentor than learner −Problem of how to deal with the plateaued person — remotivation *(Late career)* −Jobs assigned and responsibilities draw primarily on wisdom and perspective and maturity of judgment −More community and society-oriented jobs −More jobs involving teaching others, less likely to be on the "firing line" unless contacts and experience dictate	−New sense of growth and realistic assessment of one's ambition and potential (timetable revision) −Period of settling in or new ambitions based on self-assessment −More feeling of security, relaxation, but danger of leveling off and stagnating −Threat from younger, better trained, more energetic and ambitious persons −Possible thoughts of "new pastures" second careers, new challenges, et cetera, in relation to biosocial "mid-life" crisis −Working through of mid-life crisis toward greater acceptance of oneself and others −More concern with teaching others, passing on one's wisdom both at home and at work −Psychological preparation for retirement −Deceleration in momentum −Finding new sources of self-improvement off the job
4. *Decline Stage* −Formal preparation for retirement −Retirement rituals −Continued association on new basis if contribution is still possible	−Learning to accept a reduced role and less responsibility −Learning to manage a less structured life −New accommodations to family and community

know more about the early phases of a career. The section that follows contains an analysis of organizational socialization and its implications.

Pathways to Membership: Organizational Socialization in the Early Career Phases.   Most people spend much of their lives in organizations. From about the age of five on, we spend a large portion of our waking hours responding to organizational demands. According to Tausky (1970), some 90 percent of the employed population in the United States work for organizations. Socialization processes do not take place only in the intimate surroundings of family or in specialized organizations—such as schools, prisons, and mental hospitals—whose explicit mandate is to change people. Increasingly, socialization is carried out in environments where people carve out work careers— particularly in large-scale bureaucratic organizations. Whether we seek to become psychiatrists, bartenders, salesmen, or machinists, our lives are in many ways bound up in activities and organizations where learning can be expected to take place—where we enter as recruits or novices and are taught by agents or coaches (Strauss, 1959; Wheeler, 1966). The stages of this socialization process can be defined as entry, encounter, and metamorphosis.

Entry.   Most people in this society enter occupations different from those of their parents, thus shrinking the relevance of family socialization to the work career (Goode, 1964). Furthermore, advancing specialization, represented by the increase in the variety of available careers, has reduced the relevance of all but a few educational institutions to the workaday world (Lancashire, 1971). It is apparent that individual career decisions are often based on incomplete, inaccurate, and sometimes distorted information. Furthermore, sociologists argue that once such birth-determined factors as race, sex, and class are played out, an individual's range of occupational choice is indeed limited. Miller and Form (1964) suggest poignantly that within this range most people simply stumble into their occupations.

Yet, having stumbled, the individual begins to build a set of expectations and justifications that rationalize a particular choice. Vroom and Deci (1971) call this process "postdecisional dissonance reduction," a stiff but precise phrase descriptive of the *post facto* mental activities of new entrants to occupations and organizations. Several studies have shown that rather remarkable attitude changes are undergone by recruits during their first few months on the job (Berlew and Hall, 1966; Glaser, 1964; Porter, Van Maanen, and Crampton, 1972; Schein, 1961, 1964; Van Maanen, 1975a). Hence, for many if not most recruits, it is clear that they did not—or could not—know just what their work roles were about before joining organizations.

The concept of anticipatory socialization refers to the degree to which an individual is prepared, prior to entry, for an occupational or organizational position. The results of anticipatory socialization may range from an internalization of broad societal prescriptions (such as "a man must work") to specific behavioral guidelines associated with a chosen career (such as "a doctor must not become personally involved with his patients"). The amount of prior learning required of a recruit varies across organizations and occupations. For example, Wheeler (1966) suggests that most organizations require new members to be at least oriented toward the avowed purposes of the employing organization. However, some organizations—dubbed resocialization agencies by Wheeler—make no such assumptions about new members. Among these are prisons and mental hospitals.

All organizations make some effort to insure the inclusion of only the "right types." Caplow (1964) remarked: "Few organizations are exempt from that spontaneous chauvinism that makes the candidate with the conforming traits look more talented than others" (p. 177). Nepotism, psychometric tests, prerequisites, stress interviews, and background checks all are used in the organizational selection of the right types. Indeed, the ability of the individual to present the appropriate face during the selection process determines his ability to move into the organization in the first place. Thus, success depends on the degree to which the aspiring member has correctly anticipated the expectations and desires of those in the organization in charge of selection.

At times, selection procedures are so problematic and lengthy from the individual's standpoint that by the time he is chosen he has already undergone a great deal of organizationally-directed socialization. For example, the stretched-out screening process associated with police selection is a critical feature of the socialization process. Physical and mental examinations, oral interviews, psychiatric tests, character investigations (in which an applicant's friends and relatives are questioned about the most delicate matters), and polygraph tests all serve to teach the recruit a great deal about his favored occupation. Few men move through the entire sequential process—which often takes a year or more—without becoming committed to a police career (Van Maanen, 1973). Perhaps in some occupations where it is claimed that people do not undergo major changes, such changes occur during the anticipatory phases of the career.

Normally, the information exchanged by the individual and the organization is systematically biased. Each attempts to present itself in the most glamorous light, sharpening the positive and dulling the negative. And, in general, this tendency consistently produces mild to deep shock on both sides when the individual finally begins to work within the organization. It would seem, therefore, that unrealistic expectations set up the individual for a major shift upon entrance. One experimental study of West Point cadets indicates that the attitudes of those recruits who were given a fairly accurate portrait of life at the Point changed less—and, incidentaly, they performed better—than did the attitudes of those who were provided the traditional honorific and heroic image of the organization (Macedonia, 1969). Anticipatory socialization cannot fully account for the reactions of individuals to organizational settings. Yet its influence is well documented and may—depending on the role for which the individual prepares—aid or hinder his adjustment to the organization.

Encounter. When an individual enters an organization as a recruit, he is likely to experience what Hughes (1958) calls "reality shock." The extent to which the outcome of the socialization process is affected depends on the intensity of the shock. In some situations, when the shock runs deep, the person's subjective base for evaluating his organizational position will be undermined or destroyed. Anomie results.

Studies investigating withdrawal from the workplace nearly always emphasize task factors as a major cause of turnover (Porter and Steers, 1973). According to Schein (1962, 1964, 1968) one of the primary reasons for a new member's organizational disillusionment and subsequent exit is receiving, on entry, an assignment that is either too difficult or too easy. Either type of assignment constitutes a sizable reality shock, or "upending experience," and results in at least a temporary shift of the individual's situational identity. For example, some socialization agents, as almost a matter of policy, provide recruits with an extended honeymoon period in which the person is expected to do little or nothing. Thus, the person's entering image of fulfilling a responsible position within the organization must be suspended. On the other hand, some agents provide a recruit with an initial task or problem beyond his ability, destroying temporarily—and sometimes permanently—the person's sense of competence. In either situation the recruit must recast his expectations if he is not to fall into an anomic relationship with the organization.

Some tasks simply do not have the potential of supplying *any* meaning (Guest, 1960; Van Maanen, Katz, and Gregg, 1974). In fact, Roy (1960) observed that on some isolated jobs, even the "game of work" cannot be played because the task is far too dull and repetitive. In these instances the recruit must look elsewhere—to family, colleagues, and nonwork activities—for meaning. Socialization processes on such inherently anomie-generating roles must provide new members with alternative sources of meaning and control (such as pay, colleagues, and variety) if the individual is to remain in the workplace.

In general, the depth of reality shock depends on the extent to which the individual has anticipated correctly the expectations of others in the organization. If the expectations are more or less accurate, the encounter phase of socialization merely provides for a reaffirmation of the person's entering views. However, if the novice enters the organization with expectations out of line with what is actually experienced, the socialization process must first involve a destructive phase that detaches the individual from his a priori assumptions (Schein, 1973). Once unfrozen, he is ready to learn the pivotal norms that operate in the work setting through formal or informal means.

Virtually all organizational members are part of a smaller group context that constitutes perhaps the *key* source of their learning. The group to which a recruit is first assigned possesses and transmits a set of collective understandings that represent, to varying degrees, the values and norms of the group. Once the recruit is accepted into the organization, the relevant group either cushions or amplifies the impact of the reality shock. Generally, these groups are supportive and help the individual interpret the role demands dictated by the organization. Hughes (1958) notes that the colleague group assists the newcomer by providing a definition of just what constitutes a "mistake" within the group and organizational contexts. At the same time the group may also defend the recruit's right to make mistakes (Blau, 1955).

Metamorphosis.   The focus here is on the achievement of what Becker et al. (1961) called the "final perspective." This perspective consists of the solutions a recruit works out for dealing with the problems discovered during the encounter phase. In terms of this discussion, the final perspective represents the theme that is a portion of the internal career.

Kelman (1958) suggests that when the newcomer first encounters the organization, he accepts role demands because of the explicit rewards and punishments involved. A broad understanding of the role has little to do with its initial acceptance. Soon, however, the individual begins to associate with other members of the organization (whether agents or other recruits) and selectively develops positive attachments that lead to positive identification with some of these others (Kelman, 1958; Schein, 1973). Eventually the neophyte discovers that some actions are rewarding in and of themselves and are congruent with his evolving situational identity. This discovery leads to the genuine internalization of norms and values.

The end result of metamorphosis, as we use the term, refers to the point in the socialization sequence where the new member can be said to be comfortable in the environment. He has fashioned what could be called an organizational *Weltanschauung*—an outlook regarding the problems that stem from his organizational involvement. The work situation has lost its strangeness and become familiar. The role makes sense to the actor and can be put within at least a sketchy career framework. Certainly the individual's carefully constructed definitions are subject to disruption at any moment. In this sense, socialization is always open-ended and never fully completed. But, at any one moment, the individual who is to continue to participate in the organization over a long period must develop a somewhat closed perspective of just who he is in the situation and what he is to do.

Metamorphosis often involves status rituals or ceremonies that allow the person to say "I am not what I used to be." Such symbolic events may involve tests and trials followed by the granting of titles, new responsibilities and privileges, or the sharing of information that had been withheld (Van Gennep, 1960). These events celebrate individual metamorphosis. Indeed, they provide a sort of liturgical cement, holding together relationships forged during the socialization experience as well as calling to attention the common conscience arising from "going it together."

Finally, it is important to note that socialization always entails a degree of both covert and overt bargaining between agents and recruits. The final perspectives assumed by recruits do not spring unilaterally to the front. Barnard (1938) emphasized this point when discussing transitions from position to position within organizations. He remarked that, "there is no instant replacement, there is always a period of adjustment" (p. 7).

This period of adjustment involves the negotiation of a psychological contract (Schein, 1968, 1970). Whether the topic for negotiation is career timetables, role expectations, group membership, or the evaluation standards to be used externally to mark the recruit's progress in the organization, influence is potentially mutual. Of course, at entrance, the individual may possess few counters to bargain with, but he does have a physical and mental presence that is—if we are concerned with the human side of career development—worth an incalculable amount. In other words, whether it is recognized or not, a negotiation process accompanies all career transitions. Therefore, from a normative standpoint, it would seem wise for organizations and individuals alike to elevate such psychological contracting from its present *sub rosa* position to one that would allow mutual interests and constraints to be articulated openly.

Attributes of Socialization Contexts. Although we cannot go into detail in this chapter, we wish to point out that one of the least examined aspects of career development is the setting within which a career is learned and played out. As Schein (1971) has suggested, the career involves vertical (hierarchical), horizontal (changing job function), and centripetal (getting closer to the heart of the organization) movement. And as each vertical, horizontal, or inclusion boundary is passed, a new socialization sequence occurs. Socialization and resocialization are perpetual and include even preparation for retirement and ultimately for death. What attributes can be identified that would permit us to classify these many socialization settings and processes?

We would like to suggest seven such attributes as a beginning (Van Maanen, 1975a, 1975b):

1. *The degree of formality or informality of the socialization process.* Does the socialization process take place informally, on the job, or does it take place formally, in a special setting such as a school or training center? Usually, the more formal the setting the more stress there is on influencing the person's attitudes and values (Bidwell, 1962; Brim, 1966).

2. *The degree to which the process is determined or undetermined.* Does the socialization sequence operate on a fixed and known schedule, involving clear stages or steps? Educational processes are the best examples of determined processes, while promotional systems in the management hierarchies of most businesses are clear examples of undetermined processes. And in most organizations, the manner of dealing with role failures is relatively undetermined and so creates anxiety for recruits who can only guess what will happen to them if they "don't make it."

3. *The degree to which the socialization process is individually tailored or collectively administered to all recruits.* When groups are socialized collectively, as in military training, there is a much greater likelihood that a common perspective will arise based on the shared fate of all members. Such a perspective may or may not be desirable from the point of view of the organization. Thus, collective perspectives may lead to very high morale but may also provide the seeds for organized resistance. On the other hand, individually tailored socialization, such as an apprenticeship program, may promote high conformity within the organization; but such processes are expensive and time consuming.

4. *The degree to which the socialization process is sequential or nonsequential.* Some kinds of supervisory training require a set pattern of rotation through specific jobs as preparation for the managerial role; other kinds of socialization do not imply any set sequence of experiences. The more sequential the process, the more each stage builds on the previous stage, and—because of the investment he makes—the more irreversible the commitment of the person being socialized.

5. *The degree to which the persons being socialized are homogeneous or heterogeneous.* The more homogeneous the group—whether

by age, sex, prior education, geographical origin, or prior work experience—the more likely the group will develop a single perspective. Thus, organizations that wish to discourage the formation of collective perspectives often set up more heterogeneous training or socialization programs.

6. *The degree to which the socialization process is serial or disjunctive.* Does the recruit follow the footsteps of predecessors in a clearly defined and well-traveled career path, or does he follow a more or less unique career path? Police training and academic training are both examples of a highly serial process in which experienced members groom newcomers to assume similar roles. On the other hand, many industrial training programs for management trainees are highly disjunctive, in that the jobs recruits assume after training range from foreman to staff analyst to executive assistant. Institutions that follow highly serial socialization processes are much more likely to remain stable, because the value system of the older generation is always represented in the intermediate and younger generations.

7. *The degree to which the socialization process confirms and builds on the recruit's identity or destroys and rebuilds that identity.* Most open institutions, such as businesses, build up present identities. However, in the so-called total institutions—such as military organizations, religious orders, militant labor unions, and some of the lower status occupations that do the dirty work of society (Hughes, 1958)—the organization seeks to destroy parts of a recruit's entering identity while building on other parts.

We have thus far identified a number of stages and processes—both external and internal—that make up a career, and we have focused especially on the socialization activities and experiences that take place during the earliest phases of a career. We have also seen how some attributes of the organizational setting in which the socialization process takes place can have long-term effects on career development and organizational performance. A very broad and diverse set of variables has been shown to be important in any consideration of careers and career development. In the following section, we provide a degree of closure on our evolving perspective by presenting a conceptual scheme that systematically links the variables with which we have been concerned. The primary purpose of this scheme is to direct attention toward the interaction among such career variables as the settings in which careers are played out, the more stable needs/values/intentions of the individual, the temporal stages of the career, and the structure of the family. It is becoming increasingly clear that one can not fully understand the complexities of a given career without understanding such interaction.

The Career Cube: An Interactional Schema
for Studying Work, Self, and Family Issues

When we label a problem as psychological or sociological, work-oriented or nonwork-oriented, philosophical or practical, managerial or labor, we display a tenacious unwillingness to allow the problem to guide us in our study. One of the most important ways of understanding career development, however, is to perceive it in its total context within a person's lifespace. Concerns about work and career do not exist in isolation but are related to personal issues of self-development, the stages of the individual's life, his basic motives and talents, his family, the setting in which he works, his circle of acquaintances, various economic and political constraints that surround his real and imagined opportunities, and so on. As we have suggested, past research in this area has tended either to treat the problem of work as if it could be insulated from the total lifespace of the individual, or to study single variables like age, education, task properties, and social class in relation to work. The conceptual scheme presented below—to which we have thus far been building—was developed as a way of studying life/career issues in their full richness.

This schema, for pictorial reasons, is called the career cube and is presented in Figure 2.2.[12]

The career cube attempts to show the simultaneous development of the three major areas that we believe are in continual interaction throughout the life cycle—self, family, and work. Dimension A can be thought of as the *stages of life development*, especially during adulthood from age twenty to sixty-five when most of the critical interactions represented in the career cube take place. We do not analyze these stages in detail in this chapter, but seminal works by Erikson (1959), Levinson et al. (1974), Vaillant and MacArthur (1972), and Gould (1975) have begun to sketch the major stages that must be considered in a full theory of the sort we are suggesting. Dimension B represents the *stages of career development* that we outlined in Table 2.1. Dimension C can be thought of as the *stages of family development*. As time passes and critical events occur in the individual's personal life, his family, and his career, he moves into various sections of the cube. Thus, any given cell in the cube can be thought of as a particular set of forces acting on the individual; the forces derive from a particular stage of self, family, and career development. Before illustrating these interactions, we wish to comment on how cultural and

---

12. The career cube as detailed in the text was developed in collaboration with our colleague, Lotte Bailyn.

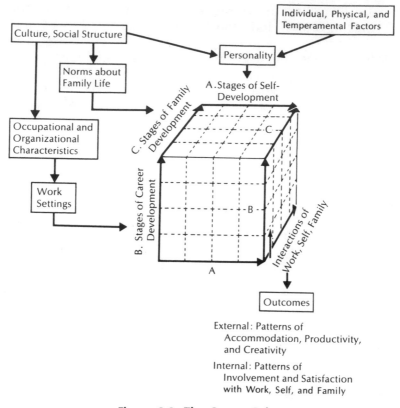

Figure 2.2–The Career Cube

biological forces influence development and what kinds of outcomes we are looking for.

The culture, or social structure, is a pervasive influence on each of the dimensions of the cube. Its influences on self-development derive from the fact that many of a person's key developmental problems and conflicts result from interaction between biological/genetic factors and the cultural and subcultural norms and roles associated with adulthood or maturity. For example, the crisis of adolescence is clearly an interaction of the physical/biological maturation process and the cultural norms about adolescence and early adulthood. How the person handles this stage and subsequent ones has to be analyzed both in terms of the individual's physical/biological growth and development and in terms of the collective social and cultural norms surrounding the person.

At the same time, cultural and social structural features determine the nature of the occupational structure, define the critical rewards and incentives for work and careers, and determine many of the critical aspects of the settings within which people work. Technological factors that create automated factories, assembly lines, and other work settings must be thought of—in this context—as sociocultural forces. Similarly, the economic/political forces that create pressures on the labor market, define what kinds of occupations are needed, and directly influence policies around unemployment have to be considered here. These institutional and societal forces are ultimately translated into laws and organizational policies that determine working hours, pay, retirement, safety, equal employment opportunity, and so on.

Finally, the culture clearly defines a family and the basic norms surrounding family life. We have seen some changes in the values around family in the past decade or so. But we must not forget that many cultural norms are very stable and are embodied in social institutions and laws—specifically those regarding marriage, divorce, and child care. Although new life styles are being explored and dual career families are forcing us to focus on new issues of child care, we are still a culture very much oriented toward a small nuclear family, fully responsible for the care and education of its children. Many of the interactive strains between work and family derive from the stability of the cultural concepts of what a family should be and how it should evolve.

Each of us is embedded in a culture and society that defines not only how adults should evolve over their total life spans but also how our careers should evolve and how our families should evolve. We are, in a sense, drawing attention by means of the career cube to typical stresses and strains that derive from the fact that our culture is not well integrated. In fact, we are increasingly experiencing conflict between what is expected of us as individuals, what is expected of us as workers, and what is expected of us as spouses and parents. These conflicts force us to accommodate in various ways. The *external* patterns of accommodation are the efforts we allocate to different sectors of our lives, thus producing long-range patterns of productivity and creativity that are externally measurable. We can devote relatively more or less effort to self-development, to family, and to career, and we can think of productivity and creativity in each of these spheres. The *internal* accommodations are the feelings we develop around the external accommodations we make. Are we satisfied with work, family, or self? Are we emotionally involved (ego-involved) with one or more of these major areas? Are we anxious and insecure about any of them? Because each of these dimensions represents development through time, we have to view the accommodation process as occurring through time and as leading to evolving patterns of accommodation that might involve shifts in allocation of energy across the three areas from one time to another.

Family States and Stages. We have referred to family issues, but we have not attempted to show how developmental issues in the family operate in the life cycle. Analysis of the family cycle is complicated because we can think both in terms of *states* (whether one is single or married) that are structural and not related to age in any necessary fashion, and in terms of *stages* (married with no children, having young children, having old children) that are age-related and developmental. Hence, for each basic type of family state that derives from marital status, the presence or absence of children, and the pattern of work followed by the spouse, one can think of a separate developmental cycle with its own stages (Bailyn, 1974; Salvo, 1969). We will not attempt to spell out a full typology based on these states and stages but will simply draw attention to some of the more important kinds of issues that derive from this method of analysis.

The impact of a person's family on his career depends, in part, on the developmental needs of children, and these are closely related to the ages and the number of children. It has been shown, for instance, that among the highly educated, the impact on parental careers of one child is dramatically different than that of three or more children, with two children representing a less distinctive, intermediate state (Bailyn, 1974). The effect of children on the career patterns of their parents derives partly from the parents' needs to develop their children. For instance, the aspirations parents have for the education of their children will affect the economic requirements of the family and thereby determine some parental career decisions. In noneconomic areas, if parents do not want to geographically dislocate their children too frequently, they will decide where they work partly on the basis of these considerations.

We also know that a person's career is very much affected by the working pattern of the spouse. Information on this pattern is therefore highly relevant for the assessment of other involvement and satisfaction outcomes. A psychologically meaningful categorization might be the following (Schein and Bailyn, 1974):

1. spouse has no paid employment;
2. spouse is supplementally employed, part-time or full-time, in a nonprofessional job defined as supplementing family income;
3. spouse is career qualified but only partially employed within the constraints of the primary career;
4. spouse is career qualified and fully engaged in pursuing own career (the dual career family).

Obviously, there is an interaction between concerns related to children and concerns related to spouse's career. Each of the stages of child development interacts with each of the possible states of employment and career qualification of the spouse; consequently, a full taxonomy of family stages and states would involve a complex grid of all the possibilities inherent in the combination.

As an example of the possible interactions, we can describe the following hypothetical evolution of a "typical" male in our society. At the point of departure from school—whether he drops out or graduates from high school, college, or professional school—the individual is usually concerned primarily with fulfilling his work-related motives and values, which can be expressed as "making money" or as "finding an exciting and challenging job." At this stage, he may or may not have a family, and it is likely that his needs for self-actualization are closely tied to his needs for developing a successful career. Consequently, there is a good deal of congruence among work, family, and self concerns in the early stages of a career.

At some point, perhaps five or ten years into the career, the balance among these three factors may shift dramatically toward family; at this stage, the individual may have young children and want to be emotionally involved with his family. Even if he is not motivated to be involved with his family, the demands of family circumstances may be such that much of his energy and attention will be drawn away from the work situation, toward the family. An important implication for an employing organization is whether or not the external career system would permit the employee at this stage to make career and work adjustments that would take into account the increasing pressures of family life. For example, moving from one city to another may be much more feasible for the individual who has preschool children and whose spouse has no employment than for the individual whose children are in school and have just begun to make an adaptation to a given school, or the individual whose spouse is also involved in a career.

At a later stage in the career, one can postulate that the individual will have learned what his level of career achievement is likely to be and will have made an adaptation to that self-knowledge. As he recognizes those factors, his concern and energy will shift not only toward the family but perhaps also toward self-actualization in a general way. That is, one can assume that the individual will begin to seek self-actualization in a broader realm than just the work career. At this stage, we must look for indicators of whether the employer permits or encourages the degree of freedom that will allow an individual to develop additional skills, hobbies, and other self-enlarging activities.

At a still later date, with the growth and departure of children, one can postulate that the individual and his spouse go through still another stage of reassessment where reinvolvement in work or heavy involvement in community or nonwork activities may result as a way of coping with the loss of the parental role. We are aware, of course, that women's careers typically have different phasing. Further, we are aware that men's career patterns are beginning to be modified by the same forces that are changing women's careers. But no matter what modifications may occur, the interrelation between career and family stages will remain, even if the particular form it takes may change. And it will be interesting indeed to watch the extent to which these modifications will lead to congruence or conflict between men's and women's roles (Schein and Bailyn, 1974).

Career Anchors: Life Cycle-Career Cycle Interaction.   Research on the types of interactions that the career cube highlights has been sparse, but some beginnings have been made in this area in the form of longitudinal studies that view the person in his total lifespace. One such study has focused on the career development of a group of alumni of the Sloan School of Management at the Massachusetts Institute of Technology (Schein, 1975a). The purpose of the study was to observe in detail how the interactions between the individual and his employing organization would shape and be shaped by his values and attitudes. A detailed interview of a group of forty-four men, when they graduated in 1961, 1962, and 1963, and again ten to twelve years later (in 1973), revealed patterns of evolution in their careers and lives which could best be captured in terms of a concept referred to as a *career anchor.*

A career anchor can be thought of as a syndrome of self-perceived talents, values, and motives that organize and give stability to career-oriented decisions and that probably provide one key element of an individual's sense of identity. The histories examined thus far suggest that career anchors emerge gradually through the individual's interaction with his family, educational, and work-related settings. Thus, one can think of the individual's basic learning process as the gradual discovery through successive choices and experiences of what he is good at and what he values or likes to do. Some of these experiences occur in school, some occur in the playground or in sports, and some occur in interpersonal or social situations. But we are postulating that people build on success experiences and avoid situations in which they have had histories of failure. If a woman is good in sports and physical activities, she may well be drawn to a career based on coordination and manual dexterity; if a man has had success in interpersonal relations, he may well seek work in which such sensitive skills are relevant, such as teaching or counseling jobs; if a person has had success in academic activities, he may be biased toward careers that are more conceptually based, such as science or engineering. Actual experiences are not the only source of career-related motives, but they are a very powerful influence. Certainly a person's needs and values influence his initial choice of an occupation, but such needs and values must also be confirmed or disconfirmed during the person's early work experiences. Individuals, when they enter the workplace, may discover some new tasks for which they are particularly well-suited but which they had not considered prior to joining the organization. Conversely, they may discover through experience that they can not do some things they once thought they were good at. Indeed, they may discover that there are particular duties they disdain and wish to avoid, although there will undoubtedly be other job duties they fully enjoy and value.

Career anchors may be latent or unconscious in the individual when he first chooses a career but become manifest both to the individual and to others as actual work experience accumulates. Career anchors are clearly inside the person, functioning as a set of driving and constraining forces. If people move into settings in which they are likely to fail or in which their values are compromised, they will be pulled back into something more congruent with their skills and beliefs—hence the metaphor of the anchor.

In the panel study of management school graduates referred to above, Schein (1975a) found that five anchors, expressed as dominant motives of what people wanted from their careers, covered all individual cases. Van Maanen subsequently applied these anchors to his study of the socialization of police recruits to determine the applicability of the concept to an entirely different kind of occupational group (see Van Maanen, 1973, 1974). These five anchors, as applied to the two different occupational pursuits, are discussed below.

Anchor #1: Managerial Competence. This syndrome implies that the person is seeking and values opportunities to manage. It is management per se that motivates the individual and that he has sought throughout his early career. The syndrome involves three further values or areas of competence: (1) interpersonal competence—the ability and desire to handle a variety of interpersonal and formal situations without excessive strain; (2) analytical competence—the ability and desire to identify, analyze, and develop solutions to problems; and (3) emotional maturity—the ability to bear high levels of responsibility and to exercise leadership, authority, and power without internal conflict.

What distinguishes the individual in this group from others in terms of his career path is the felt need to climb to a level of an organization where he believes his managerial behavior will make a real difference to the functioning of the organization. His technical skills may have brought him to a managerial level, but he is able to put aside the technical image of his personality and assume an image based on general management. The motive to become a manager has been there from an early period in his life, although we cannot fix as yet just when and how the motive first arose.

If we study the careers of policemen from this perspective, we find some young policemen who orient themselves toward their jobs in such a way that the likelihood of career advancement is increased. The life goals of patrolmen with this anchor center around promotions to responsible positions and attainment of high rank in the police service. The individual may be attending college during off-duty hours, studying conscientiously for the various civil service promotional examinations, and actively searching out ways to increase his opportunity to advance in rank. Interestingly, Walsh (1975) points out that those patrolmen most concerned with achieving managerial responsibility are the ones most likely to regard everyday patrol duties as unimportant and, therefore, to withdraw from those duties whenever possible.

Anchor #2: Technical/Functional Competence.   This syndrome implies that the individual is seeking and values opportunities to exercise various technical talents and areas of competence. What distinguishes this group most clearly from those anchored to managerial competence is that they will resist being promoted out of a technically satisfying role into one that is primarily managerial, even though they recognize that the socially desirable success syndrome is to climb as fast and as high as possible. A person will have conflict in this situation but will clearly lean toward the decision to remain in a job that permits him to exercise areas of technical/functional competence. Such areas might include engineering, systems analysis, finance, accounting, and marketing. These areas may involve some management of technically competent subordinates, but the focus is on the technical work performed; management is viewed as merely a means to its better performance.

Among alumni of the management school in this category, some were professors, some consultants, some junior and senior staff members in organizations, and some functional managers. Among policemen, one finds here the "cop's cop." Whether he be a detective or patrolman, he is seeking a role in which he can exercise his perceived police competence. Apprehending the criminal, or as the police are fond of saying, "crook catching," is the individual's *raison d'etre* in the occupation. Promotion to a higher bureaucratic level holds little fascination for people anchored here. Indeed, promotion may be viewed with disdain, for it usually takes one away from the action on the street. Administrative and service duties are likely to be seen by this group as a frivolous waste of time. This attitude can be detected in the oft-quoted motto of many officers, "We're cops, not pencil pushers or social workers."

Anchor #3: Security. This syndrome implies that the person is motivated primarily by the need to stabilize his career situation, even if that means subordinating some personal work needs or desires to those of the employing organization or the profession. That is, the person will do whatever is required to maintain job security, a decent income, and long-range stability in the form of a good retirement program. It is in this group that one will find what has come to be labeled the "organization man"—the individual who is willing to be socialized to the norms of the organization (Schein, 1968). Because these people are primarily security oriented, they will normally rise only to a certain level within the employing organization. Such moves, however, will always be determined by a need to find a more secure position, rather than more job challenge.

Although it may have been overestimated as an anchor by the nonpolice public, security is nevertheless an identifiable career anchor for some police officers. Those who fall in this category will do whatever is required to maintain their jobs and will seek out organizational locations where stability, safety, and routine characterize their day-to-day tasks—communications, jail, records, and so on. On the beat, these officers tend to adopt a public relations style with the public and with fellow officers; they will value interpersonal dealings with people and will discount the importance of interactions with training programs, supervision and the courts, for they have little interest in career advancement.

Anchor #4: Creativity. This syndrome is one of the most difficult to articulate because of the small number of cases we have. Yet it seems to be crucial for understanding some managerial careers, and in particular for understanding the entrepreneur. We found in our sample that those men who had successfully launched ventures of their own had a whole variety of values and motives that overlapped to some extent with other anchors. They wanted to be autonomous, to be managerially competent, to exercise their special talents, and to build a fortune in order to be secure, but none of these seemed to be the master motive or value. Instead, what seemed to be driving each of them was an overarching need to build or create something that was entirely his own product. It is self-extension—through the creation of a product or process that bears his name, a company that is his own, a personal fortune that is a measure of his accomplishments—that seemed to be the key to the individual in this group. We observed that such people kept getting into new ventures and trying their hands at new kinds of projects. Yet they always played a very central and visible role—hence the concept of creativity in the service of self-extension.

As is true of the managerial example, this syndrome is difficult to articulate clearly in policemen. And again this difficulty is largely due to the small number of cases we have to deal with. However, in the police world the creativity anchor is crucial for understanding the so-called rotten-apple or bent policeman. Certainly not all policemen have the situational opportunity to engage in graft, burglary, extortion, confidence games, or narcotics trade, but police do differ in regard to how far they will pursue deviance when given the opportunity. Reiss (1971) suggests accurately that there are "reactive" and "proactive" differences among the police regarding the initiation of illegal activity. For our purposes here, only the proactive would be considered to have a creative career anchor—the reactive tend to be security-minded officers who go along to avoid ostracism and possible expulsion from the department (Sherman, 1974; Smith, 1965; Stoddard, 1968). Thus, the grafter who initiates and actively builds a parallel criminal career while engaged in police work can be seen to have a creative anchor in much the same way that the entrepreneur in the managerial world has a creative anchor (Cook, 1971; Knapp, 1972).

Anchor #5: Autonomy and Independence. This syndrome implies that individuals are seeking work situations in which they will be maximally free of organizational constraints to pursue their professional or technical/functional competence. This group is different from those concerned with technical/functional competence in that their needs for autonomy appear to be higher than the needs to exercise competence. If such an individual is given the opportunity to work within an organizational context, he typically declines—even if the organization would provide better facilities or more resources for the pursuit of his work.

Most of the professors, teachers, and private consultants in the alumni sample typify this syndrome. Many of them originally pursued their work within companies but left because of the constraints, the lack of variety, the lack of freedom to set their own hours and working conditions, and so on. This syndrome does not imply an absence of interest in technical/functional competence; but it does imply that the master motive or value is the need to be autonomous and independent. Similarly, we are not implying that this group is unconcerned about creativity, but only that creativity is not the master motive. Many professors could go to work in government or private laboratories and have greater opportunities for creativity than within a university, yet will not go in order to preserve the sense of autonomy provided by a university.

In the police world we see categories of careers that offer maximal autonomy and independence—the solitary radio-car officer who refuses to work with a partner, the traffic officer who values his motorcycling adventures, or the undercover officer much romanticized by the popular press for his idiosyncratic, if not downright bizarre, approach to policing (Maas, 1973; Whittemore, 1973). Indeed, ex-policemen-turned-private-detective in the style of Sam Spade, Bulldog Drummond, and Lew Archer are prototypes of the independent police career. Again, it is not a rejection of the technical/functional competence that marks this group, but the need for autonomy that must always be pursued.[13]

Possible additional anchors. These five anchors are useful for describing the interaction of the life cycle with the career cycle of the managers and policemen examined in the two studies. However, it is far from clear whether these five anchors cover most of the careers one would find across a wide range of occupations. For example, an anchor that might be found in a very low prestige occupation would be the *need for identity*—the need for occupational activities and trappings that help define who and what the person is. A person with such an anchor would seek an occupation that would clearly define his *external* role through title, uniform, or other visible means (even though such accoutrements have little to do with the job performed). Thus, some slaughterhouse employees, when asked their line of work, respond by saying that they work for Swift (Becker, 1972). Another illustration might be the custodian who proudly remarks that he works for Harvard University. The regalia associated with full military dress may help provide identity for some people.

The urge to express *affiliative needs and interpersonal talents* might be an anchor. Here the person would seek an occupational role in which the opportunity to work with and through people is available. Such individuals would see the opportunity as an end in itself, in contrast to some individuals who tend to work with people as a means to an end. The search for *power, influence, and control* might be a separate anchor, or it might be one facet of the managerial competence anchor. Finally, there is some evidence to suggest that for some people *variety* is a very important intrinsic occupational value. This group includes people whose talents are spread evenly across many ac-

---

13. It is noteworthy that the police have also developed a typology to order their perceptions of their work and their relations with colleagues. For example, policemen who are oriented toward the managerial competence anchor often describe the security-minded policeman as a "cabbage," devoid of drive or ambition. The technically oriented policeman is seen by others as a "hunter" with "arrest fever" or as having a "big badge." The upwardly mobile (managerial competence anchor) is frequently scorned by colleagues as a "brown noser" or a "kiss ass." The autonomous officer is called a "solo." When the creative policeman is discussed, it is usually under the label of a "shopper" or a "bagman." To see this typology in action, the novels of Wambaugh (1970, 1972) are good, as are the more serious firsthand accounts of policing presented by Radano (1969, 1974) and Walsh (1975).

tivities. They seek expression of all of their talents rather than an opportunity to exercise a single talent in depth over long periods of time. Some professors, journeymen, tradesmen, consultants, and troubleshooters say that what really attracts them about those careers is the constant variety of problems they encounter; similar points are made by some general managers who get bored if their jobs become too routinized, even though such jobs usually involve a great deal of responsibility.

In summary a career anchor is a syndrome of talents, motives, values, and attitudes that provide direction and coherence to a person's career. Each anchor reflects a distinguishable career style—that is, it reflects the way a person approaches his job, interacts with others on the scene, and emphasizes some tasks in preference to others. Although we have not emphasized it in the research so far, one could analyze the predominant family patterns associated with each career anchor and thus explore even more fully the implications of the career cube. For example, it is clear that the degree of work involvement is much higher in the managerial competence and creativity group and that this leads to subordination of family involvement; conversely, the security-oriented group is more concerned with family life and stability. Without careful longitudinal studies, we will not be able to determine the causal sequences involved. But this is clearly an area that will require intensive exploration if we are to understand fully what quality of working life means to people in different life-family-career situations.[14]

The Effects of Occupation and Work Setting on Career Outcomes. The interaction of individual development, the career, and the family cycle occurs for different people in vastly different occupational settings. Thus, one might begin to study these interactions by initially locating people in occupations that differ markedly in the kinds of demands they make, in the kinds of roles they generate, and in the kinds of work settings they provide. One could then analyze the interaction of individual or family needs with occupational requirements at different career stages. For example, a woman with a strong need to prove her ability to perform in real life settings (early career), and who finds herself in an engineering occupation that involves challenging work, might have a very high work involvement, high productivity, and low accommodation to family.

That same person in a different occupation that does not permit the

---

14. We are aware that we are talking only about the nuclear family in industrialized societies—and then only of the higher economic strata in such societies. A full exposition would have to include the role of other familial institutions, including families of origin, procreation, and habitat.

display or testing of those analytical abilities (such as production work or drafting) may have low productivity, low work involvement, low job satisfaction, and high accommodation to the family (seeking more of her satisfactions within the family or nonwork-related activities). How that same person would react at a later career stage would be a function of her early career experiences. If the occupational opportunities and internal needs continue to be mismatched, she might change her internal needs, adjust to the external setting, and become productive and satisfied. If the internal needs are stable and strong, the individual might seek a different occupation or become permanently alienated from the one she is in, learning to seek outlets in hobbies or other nonwork settings.

One can also look at the effects of given *roles* within an occupation, and at the settings within which those roles are performed. Our engineer could be, for example, an isolated performer, a member of a team, a team leader, or a consultant. She could work in a large organization as part of a well-defined structure, she could work in various marginal roles such as an internal consultant, she could make frequent job shifts, or she could work in an independent setting as an outside consultant or inventor. Within the organization, she could also find herself in different settings—part of a well-defined research laboratory or engineering group, a single engineer attached to a product or marketing group, part of a team working out in the factory, or in various isolated settings such as exploring for oil or as a perpetual traveler to fix problems in outlying regions.

Each of these settings brings different role demands. High work involvement, satisfaction, and productivity will be possible only for particular kinds of individuals whose career anchors, family stages, and career/life stages match the external requirements of the setting. Some of the settings will require great physical energy and stamina, emotional stability, and low involvement with family (the marginal role or isolated setting). Older men with children who require parental guidance would be in perpetual conflict in such roles and settings. Some settings require great interpersonal skills and affiliative needs because the jobs demand constant personal interaction and patience with others (for example, the internal or external consultant). Individuals with strong analytical needs who lack the interpersonal needs or skills would become unproductive and unsatisfied in these roles, unless they were at a stage where some of their ambition in the analytical area had been satisfied and they were ready to develop new needs and talents as a way of continuing to grow and challenge themselves.

We conclude this section by reiterating our concern that careers be studied in the total life context and over time. If individual needs are to be matched with occupational and organizational requirements for purposes of achieving both higher productivity and individual growth and satisfaction, we will need to develop theories and models that do full justice to the complexity of this matching process.

IMPROVING THE CAREER DEVELOPMENT PROCESS: ELEMENTS OF A SYSTEMATIC APPROACH

The previous parts of this chapter have dealt with what we consider to be necessary theoretical issues for understanding the dynamics and complexities of career development. Given these complexities, how can we begin now to improve our efforts in career development for all employee levels and across all sectors of the economy? How can we insure a better match of institutional/organizational requirements and individual needs throughout the life cycle? Clearly, there are some things that can only be done at the various *governmental levels*—for example, education, employment, training, and subsidy programs. At the same time, there are a number of specific things that can be done by all types of *employing organizations,* just as there are some things that can be done only by *individuals* for themselves. The following sections speak directly to these three areas through recommendations and examples. We are not attempting to be exhaustive here, but rather to identify the critical issues and to illustrate the direction in which we can and must move at the governmental, organizational, and individual levels if we are to improve the career development opportunities for all employees.

Basic Assumptions for Career Development Systems of the Future

Joint Responsibility for Career Development. We have argued throughout that the key to productive career development programs is a matching of internal career needs and external career development opportunities. For this matching to occur, both the employee and the employer must know what the needs and opportunities actually are in any given setting. If either party knows more than the other, he is in a position to exploit the relationship, leading ultimately to a less than satisfactory matching. Typically, those in authority within the organization know more than most individual employees at lower levels. They know, for example, what careers have been followed in the past, what opportunities will exist in the future, and what rewards are likely to be available. Furthermore, decision-makers in an organization typically guess at or assume the needs, motives, and anchors of their employees and simply move them about at will (Alfred, 1967). This occurs not only because it has been standard operating procedure but also because employees are often unsure of their needs and desires. We are arguing here, therefore, that one of the first and most important changes to be made in organizations is to alter this unilateral decision-making about employees' careers. Organizations must share more information about external career paths, and individual employees must learn more about their internal career needs.

One must further assume that society may also come to play a key role in this matching process, because some mismatches will not be resolvable within a given organization. For example, if an organization has to terminate an employee because he has the wrong mix of talents, needs, and motives, or if an employee finds that a given organization cannot provide the opportunities he seeks, he may well need help from other institutions in making a career shift. If the person stays in the same occupation but merely moves to another organization, there may be little problem. But if the career shift involves moving into another occupation, additional education and training, and possibly even a period of extensive search for new opportunities, we must create new societal mechanisms to aid this process. This form of help may be particularly important during mid-career and late-career periods, because so many organizations are biased against investing in older employees. We will elaborate on these points below.

Interaction of Work/Career Issues with Family and Life Stage Issues. The bulk of this chapter has argued that work/career issues should not be treated as isolated in the total lifespace of the individual. The kinds of suggestions listed below as elements of an effective career development system start with the assumption that any such system must examine how the work, the work setting, the reward system, and other factors interact with personal and family issues at different stages of the life cycle.

Changing Needs Throughout the Life Cycle. Any career development system must start with the assumption that employee needs will change throughout the life cycle. Such a system must create opportunity structures and career paths compatible with those changing needs. In many situations this will require, at the outset of the career development process, that much more information be gathered about employee needs than most organizations usually collect—they guess at needs instead of studying what they actually are. By developing more complete theories of adult life stages, we can help to identify some of these changing needs and thus make it easier for those in organizations to take these needs into account in the future. For example, in some occupations it is becoming clear that retirement is a traumatic event that must be preceded by preretirement planning and counseling.

Changing Social Values Regarding Work, Life, and Leisure[15]

Breakdown of the distinctions between professional and nonprofessional work. More and more people are ignoring the traditional conception that professional work is more valuable or worthwhile than nonprofessional work. As a result they are treating work more instrumentally—as a source of enjoyment and economic security. Many people are taking jobs for which they are overeducated (for example, college graduates are going into carpentry or various decorative crafts). And many people are avoiding professions such as engineering and science that are seen as potentially dangerous to society (that is, because they create knowledge from which more sophisticated weapons can be built or create technologies that will further destroy the environment). In other words, many young people are choosing work on the basis of criteria other than the traditional ones, and with as yet unknown consequences for the future mix in the labor force (DePasquale and Lange, 1971; Ewing, 1971; Gooding, 1971; Graen and Davis, 1971; Gulland, 1969; Tarnowieski, 1973; Yankelovich, 1972).

Breakdown of the distinction between management and nonmanagement. Increasingly employees are putting a positive value on staff, technical, and craft careers that involve increasing responsibility and influence through the practice of occupational competences but that explicitly do *not* involve *managing* others. The idea of rising in an organization is no longer limited to the idea of "getting into management" but is increasingly associated with having more influence through one's technical expertise. The acceptance of *dual ladders,* the increase in *participative management,* and the rise of interest in industrial democracy are all correlated with the trend toward a wider base of influence in organizations.

Breakdown of division of labor between the sexes. One of the major results of the women's movement that is finding increasing legal support—in equal employment statutes, nondiscrimination contracts, and perhaps eventual passage of the Equal Rights Amendment—is the challenge to traditional distinctions between male careers and female careers. Increasingly, jobs and careers are being examined in terms of the work involved, and new questions are being asked about the traditional conceptions that some careers can only be done by men or women because of factors like strength, endurance, and motivation. Women are entering traditionally male careers in greater numbers, and

---

15. The four points listed in the text are based on a summary prepared by our colleague, Lotte Bailyn.

men are beginning to enter such traditionally female careers as secretary, nurse, and flight attendant. More families are examining the possibility of having the wife work while the husband stays home to tend the children, or are making accommodations that involve both partners in all facets of work and family activities (Bailyn, 1970, 1973, 1974).

Opening up of career paths within organizations. Partly because of the breakdown of male-female barriers around careers, and partly because of efforts to insure that minority group members have equal access to career opportunities, organizations have had to be much more explicit and open about career paths and have had to make such paths available to a much broader range of employees. Equality of opportunity has always been a social value. But it is only in the past few decades that we have seen in the United States serious efforts to insure that such equality exists and to support claims of employees who feel they have been discriminated against on the basis of sex, race, religion, or age. These trends have necessitated more explicit thinking about career paths, more formalization of career planning, and more individualizing of careers.

Breakdown of Barriers Between Work, Self-Development, and Leisure. More and more people are viewing life as something that can and should be integrated rather than compartmentalized. The total development of the individual is seen as something that can occur at work, at home, in hobbies, or in all of these activities. Thus, many people have come to expect more opportunities to use their talents in their work (a *challenging* job, not merely a job), or else have settled for work that is merely instrumental—a means of making a living. They put less effort and creativity into such jobs, sometimes to the detriment of the employer. We see more and more people putting minimum effort into their jobs and maximum effort into their hobbies, sports, social life, or other leisure time activities, where they feel they can fully develop themselves.[16] If technological trends continue to make work more and more meaningless, perhaps employers will have to invent other challenges for their employees. These might include temporary assignments, or actually encouraging employees to seek self-actualization away from the job by making working hours and other conditions more flexible.

---

16. This is not to say that all compensatory activities are necessarily channeled into self-development pursuits. Certainly, self-destructive pursuits are sometimes undertaken in response to deadening or demeaning work (or no work at all). And if we are to take some of the available statistics at face value, alcoholism, drug addiction, and suicide are all increasing. Although the causes are complex, work-in-America has come to be assigned at least part of the blame.

We can summarize these basic assumptions about career development systems of the future by noting that the concept of work has historically undergone a considerable transition, from something sacred and unquestioned in prefeudal society to a set of activities whose meaning has become a major issue in modern society (Berger, 1964; Gutman, 1973). Today people can choose from a wide range of occupations and careers, and society has many values surrounding the roles of different kinds of work. In a society in which there are so many possibilities, it becomes important to spell out more explicitly what society, its employing institutions, and its individual citizens can do to make the process of choosing and developing a career a more effective one. Many of the specific career development ideas and programs mentioned below reflect the social trends discussed above and support a more general concern, which we see throughout society, for improving the career choice and development process.

What Society Can Do

Improve Procedures for Forecasting Manpower Needs and Create Structures for Identifying and Training the Talent Pools Needed. As political, economic, social, and technological conditions change, the needs for different kinds of talent within a given society also change. For example, with the advent of Sputnik and the space age, the demand for scientists and engineers increased dramatically, leading to the creation of scholarship programs and other incentives for young people to enter these fields. However, it is not clear whether the forecasts were accurate or the incentive systems were appropriate. An oversupply was created and for a time there has been the painful problem of having people trained for jobs that do not exist.

Societies differ in the degree to which they centralize economic planning, and in the degree to which their educational and training systems are coordinated with whatever central planning exists (Horvath, 1975). But the questions of what talents are needed, how they are to be identified and developed, and how the labor market is to be stimulated or controlled to insure careers for those trained constitute a major problem that no society can ignore (Myers, 1974). These large-scale planning issues are beyond the scope of this chapter, but the issues are there and need to be addressed if any viable career development system is to be created for the society as a whole.

Improve Mechanisms for the Dissemination of Career Information in Order to Improve the Early Process of Career Choice. There is considerable evidence that young people develop unrealistic images of occupations from the mass media and that these images are not adequately corrected by whatever counseling occurs in our educational institutions. Society could create mechanisms through which the major employing organizations, professional associations, and other representatives of occupational groups could present, in more realistic ways, the career options open to young people. Such mechanisms might include better printed literature, movies or television shows, visits to schools by members of the occupation, subsidies for special short-run visits to employing organizations, internships, and other temporary work assignments where young people could observe the world of work and participate in it on a trial basis.

Improve Mechanisms for People to Discover Their Talents, Needs, and Motives by Improving Career Counseling. What is now primarily a private activity—aptitude testing and vocational counseling—should be offered on a much broader scale through the educational system or other public institutions. Most people do not know very much about their talents and needs when they make early decisions. As a result, many make false starts or find themselves trapped in careers for which they are not suited. If people could become familiar with their career potentials earlier, society—as well as individuals—would benefit.

The counseling function should be reexamined and improved. Many vocational counseling activities, particularly in high schools, are based on outmoded conceptions of occupations, on invalid or culturally biased tests, and on incorrect assumptions about the role of counseling. Counselor training has been biased toward the differentialist or classification approach of studying careers, an approach that gives relatively less attention to the sociological approaches to career research. If we are to help people to enter satisfying lifelong careers, we have to go beyond testing for talents and interests. We must try to provide valid information about work *settings*, about the kinds of values and motives that can be fulfilled in those settings, about how those settings will interact with family issues, and so on. Counseling should be based more on the model of "process consultation" (Schein, 1969b), where the counselor's role is to help the individual to locate information about jobs and about his own talents instead of dispersing expert advice on what the individual should do based on tests. The counseling function should help people to become more responsible for their own career decisions.

Improve Mechanisms for Career Switching. No matter how carefully people choose their careers, there will inevitably be mismatches. It is perhaps too much to expect that the employer and the employee can, by themselves, solve the matching problem. We believe that new mechanisms should be made available that will help people to reassess their career anchors and obtain additional education or training if necessary, and that will provide assistance in the search for new career paths. Such mechanisms might include assessment and counseling centers subsidized by national, state, or local governments, scholarship or loan programs to support those who decide to return to school, and employment information clearing houses to help people relocate. Various forms of assistance will have to be provided—particularly for people who have families to support. Government assistance could also go directly to employers to support training or reeducation activities, as we have seen in government aid for Equal Employment Opportunity programs.

Stimulate More Varied Adult Education Activities.   There is growing evidence that *adults* at various stages will need assistance in career development, career switching, or both. The society, through its educational institutions, can facilitate this process by providing enough opportunities for adult education at all levels. At present, graduate schools seem to be strongly biased against people who have been out of college for ten or more years, even if those people have the intellectual aptitude to complete demanding degree programs. Adult education is available for less professional kinds of careers, but probably will have to become a more open system as society's needs for professionals in various categories grow and as individual needs to change and upgrade careers also grow.

What Employing Organizations Can Do

Improve Manpower Planning and Forecasting Systems.   An effective manpower planning system must consist of the following elements: (1) a general forecast of what kinds of products and services, and in what quantities, will be needed over some future period of time; (2) a careful working out of manpower needs to meet the forecast—manpower at all levels of management and labor in terms of numbers of people; (3) an assessment of the skills and personal characteristics that are likely to be needed in the various categories of employees; (4) an assessment of the present ages, skill levels, and other personal characteristics that may be relevant to the needs of the future; (5) an assessment of the career anchors of the present pool of employees and the likelihood of their being motivated and talented enough to progress into the needed categories; (6) an assessment of the gap between the needs as defined in steps 2 and 3 and the manpower supply as assessed in steps 4 and 5; (7) identification of the development needs of present employees and the need for recruitment of new employees based on the results of steps 5 and 6; (8) development planning for employees at all levels, and the generating of development programs consonant with the plans generated; (9) monitoring systems that insure that the steps outlined above actually take place initially and continue to be implemented over a period of years; and (10) evaluative procedures to update the plan and improve the forecasting, assessment, planning, and development activities on a continuing basis.

These ten steps constitute a fairly elaborate and expensive set of procedures. They would cost money, and more important, they would cost a great deal of managerial time. Only a few organizations with which we are familiar have so far been successful in getting their key people to take the time to make the forecasts and plans outlined above. But it is becoming clearer and clearer to organizations that in a rapidly changing economic, political, social and technological environment, it is essential that manpower planning be done with the same energy and commitment as any other planning process. If effective manpower forecasting and planning are carried out, these lead automatically to the next step—the sharing of these plans with employees through better performance reviews, feedback, and career counseling.

Improve Dissemination of Career Option Information. The manpower planning process will inevitably identify for the organization some of the characteristics of the career paths that past employees have followed and that future employees will follow. As such information becomes available, even if only in very generalized form, it will become increasingly important to share that information with employees. Many organizations find that they can put such information into printed literature in the form of "Career Options at Organization X." If the information is not clearcut, it can be shared in career counseling sessions.

Initiate Career Counseling in Connection with Performance Appraisal. Much has been written about how to make performance appraisal a more effective process, but this is not the place to review that literature. It is important, however, to identify one crucial element of that process that should occur at least once a year. Every manager or supervisor should sit down with each of his subordinates, review the entire year's performance, and initiate a dialogue that would contain the following elements: (1) the employee's goals, aspirations, and expectations with regard to his own career for the next five years or longer; (2) the manager's view of the opportunities available and the degree to which the employee's aspirations are realistic and match up with the opportunities available; (3) identification of what the employee would have to do in the way of further self-development to qualify for new opportunities; and (4) identification of actual next steps in the form of plans for new development activities or new job assignments that would prepare the employee for further career growth. If the employee has unrealistic aspirations, he should be given a frank appraisal of where and how he falls short, and should have an opportunity to explore ways to rethink his internal career aspirations. This whole process may lead to the identification of a need for further assessment and counseling, which should then be made available by the organization, either inside or outside. Such activities also require that managers, particularly first line supervisors, receive more training on how to do performance appraisal and career counseling; indeed, it is perhaps more important that the supervisors receive adequate reviews and counseling regarding their own careers.

Development of Effective Internal or External Assessment Centers. One of the most dramatic developments in United States' companies in the area of career development is the supplementing or displacing of psychological testing by more comprehensive assessment centers (Bray and Grant, 1966; Cambell, Otis, Liske, and Prien, 1962; Kraut, 1972; McConnell and Parker, 1972). The essence of the concept is to replace the test with a situation in which the person being assessed has to behave in a simulated real life setting that resembles the type of setting in which he will be expected to perform in the future. Assessment centers also replace or supplement clinical psychologists with trained observers, who may be employees of the organization trained in how to observe and assess. In the past psychologists have tried to infer future performance from personality traits as revealed on projective or other tests. The assessment center makes the assumption that one can improve such inferences by putting candidates into situations that simulate the actual jobs they will have to perform. Included among the evaluators are people whose familiarity with these jobs was acquired by experience.

Candidates spend one to three days going through various exercises and simulations and are observed throughout this time by trained assessors. Following this period, there is typically a group meeting among the assessors to bring together all of the information about a candidate. The next step is a summary and feedback session with the candidate. Feedback is typically presented by someone who is trained in how to handle such a situation. He emphasizes *observations* that have actually been made and attempts to get the candidate to perceive himself more accurately by pointing out relationships between the assessors' conclusions and observed behavior that the candidate can remember. When handled properly, the whole process is more open and less threatening to the person being assessed than is a program of intensive psychological testing.

When assessment centers are being used effectively, they become not only tools for identifying and assessing employee talents but also developmental tools for the assessors. Individuals who are assigned for periods of time to the assessment center learn how to observe human behavior carefully, how to make inferences from observations, and how to give feedback to the person being assessed. Each of these skills makes the assessors more effective, especially in their future performance appraisal activities. It also makes them more aware of what is involved in the process of development, and this awareness gives them insight into their own career development.

Some assessment centers have operated entirely outside the context of employing organizations. Essentially they are extensions of consulting companies that used to rely on psychological testing and interviewing but have added simulation situations to their assessment procedures. In terms of career development, such organizations can play a key role in giving the individual employee insight into his own talents and limitations. They are less effective as developmental tools for the organization as a whole, because they do not involve organizational employees in the roles of observers and assessors.

The assessment center concept can be used by any organization on whatever scale is desirable. The various companies we are familiar with that use assessment centers (for example, AT&T, Steinbergs, Ltd., and Syntax) each use different models evolved to meet their specific needs.

Support of Educational Training Activities for All Levels of Employees. As employees become familiar with both available external career options and their internal career needs, they are likely to identify areas of education and training that are prerequisites for further career growth. It is then important that the organization have an explicit set of policies about time off and financial support for such activities. We are not arguing that every organization should finance all such activities, unless employee development is clearly seen as necessary in terms of the long-range manpower plan. We are arguing that every organization should think through these issues and have explicit policies in these areas. Then, when employees desire additional education and training, there will be an organizational framework through which they can obtain it, even if they must subsidize it themselves or get help from the organization to get outside support (via scholarships, loans, government support, and so on). It is our impression that support of educational activities is a growing trend and is becoming an important part of the reward system of many organizations.

Job Posting. Many companies have begun to experiment with making available to all employees information about openings that exist within the organization. (The more typical process has been for the supervisor to negotiate privately with the personnel department or other supervisors to locate a suitable replacement.) If all employees know what openings are available, they can apply for those openings and learn firsthand what qualifications they need and what qualifications they seem to have. If the job posting system works correctly, it has the advantage of stimulating *employees'* initiative to develop their careers by actively seeking new assignments instead of waiting to be told about them (Alfred, 1967). It also has the advantage of stimulating the *organization* to do more honest performance appraisal; employees who do not qualify for a job must be told precisely why they do not and what they would have to do to qualify. Job posting and internal assessment centers are congruent with each other. The employee can use the assessment center to find out whether he is qualified for some of the jobs that are available before going through the whole application procedure.

Companies like Polaroid and Minneapolis-Honeywell, who have used job posting for some time, have learned that the system only works when managers at all levels support the concept and put in the time and effort to interview applicants and give good feedback to those who are rejected. If the process is not handled with energy and dedication, it can become an empty ritual or a demotivator.

Special Assignments and Job Rotation. The model of career development we have been advocating puts great emphasis on an individual learning what his career anchors are. Organizations, too, need to know more about the talents, motives, and values of their employees. One way to determine these is through assessment centers, but such centers are still only simulations of reality. To provide real tests under real conditions, and to provide a new range of experience for employees, the organization must systematically rotate people through new kinds of jobs or special assignments. Job rotation can be a fairly formal process in which an individual spends one or two years in each of the major departments of an organization. Or it can be an informal process of spending a few weeks or months in a department to learn what the work of that department is all about, how the employee would like it, and how good he would be at it.

Special assignments can be in the form of committee or task force assignments, in which employees are organized into new groups around new tasks. Or they can be more formal project assignments where employees work for a time under other supervisors on specific projects, with the understanding that they will eventually return to their original departments. Such temporary assignments are usually justified by organizations because the particular skills of an employee are a scarce resource within the organization. We are arguing that such assignments should also be considered when no unique skills are involved but the employee needs the experience and self-test of working in a different setting as part of a career development plan. If such activities are to be successful, the process must contain a mechanism that provides the employee with good feedback and counseling after the temporary assignment. Then he will have an opportunity to digest and consolidate the learning that may have taken place during the assignment.

Career Development Workshops.   Some organizations are beginning to experiment with training and development activities designed specifically to explore career issues. Such programs or workshops were initially focused on improving the process of bringing high talent employees into the organization, and on easing the transition from school to work (Kotter, 1973; Schein, 1964). They focused on the initial expectations that the new employee and the organization had of each other. These *joining up* workshops provided opportunities for groups of new employees and their supervisors to meet as separate groups and explore what each expected to give and receive. They then focused on a sharing of these expectations, which revealed areas of mismatched expectations. And finally, the workshops set up work groups, consisting of both employees and supervisors, to work out procedures for reducing the mismatches by changing employee expectations or organizational procedures or both.

   These workshops revealed that different managers in the organization had very different views of what their organization expected to get from new employees and what they expected to give in return. For many managers, in particular, these workshops opened up issues related to their own careers and to the organization's reward system—issues that had not been raised before but that were crucial for any kind of career planning.

   Mid-career workshops are a logical extension of the *joining up* workshops and have been tried in a number of organizations, (for example, at Procter and Gamble and at Steinbergs, Ltd.). The participants are typically a group of professional employees or junior and middle managers and their supervisors (although they could, in principle, be from any level of the organization). A central assumption of the workshop is the joint responsibility of the individual and the organization for career development. Thus, the activities reflect self-diagnostic activities, diagnosis of the organization, and a bringing together of these diagnoses toward the identification of potential mismatches. Training people how to make life plans, how to think about the role of their work career within those plans, and how to develop concrete action steps toward implementing the plans may involve one to three days of focused individual work and group discussion. Discovering one's career anchors and how one's career fits into one's total life plan also become important elements of this process (Bass, 1966).

Once the individual has gained some insight into his needs, and once his boss has gone through the same exercise, they are better qualified to begin a dialogue with each other. The concrete planning of future career steps may occur as part of the workshop or may be planned for some future time. The workshop builds the commitment to work on career issues explicitly.

Central to the workshop is the discovery by both the employee and the organization of the internal career needs of the employee. The importance to both of determining their needs, rather than operating on the basis of assumptions, is illustrated by the following case (Schein, 1975b, pp. 5–6):

A group of executives in a large financial organization attended a career development workshop which involved some self-diagnosis by these managers as to their own aspirations and ambitions. These were all high potential managers in the forty-five to fifty-year-old range. The company had a corporate headquarters organization involving a president, executive vice-president, several group vice-presidents, and several staff vice-presidents overseeing the technical and financial functions in the organization. Below that level were geographical regions in which the various branches of the organization were operating. The executives at the workshop were all general managers at the regional level, and the question that arose was "what they really wanted out of their next several promotions?" Initially it was difficult for the group to answer this question because they did not quite trust each other enough to be entirely candid. However, after several days together they did share their real hopes and expectations.

Since most management development systems make the assumption that managers want increasing responsibility, and further assume that increasing responsibility is defined by increasing rank in the organization, the surprising result of the workshop was the wide *diversity* of managerial hopes and expectations. One or two men clearly wanted to get into corporate headquarters and ultimately to become the executive vice-president or president; most of the men wanted to move to a bigger *regional* job where they felt they would have more responsibility, but they specifically did *not* want to get into corporate headquarters because they saw that as a loss of autonomy and freedom, and a political jungle that they did not want to cope with; several people wanted to get out of "line" jobs altogether and have senior technical positions in various financial areas crucial in the business, even though they had been successful "line executives."

In other words, in a group of fairly homogeneous high potential executives, there were at least three completely distinct concepts of the ideal career, yet they and their own bosses assumed that they all wanted the same thing. It was only when they felt they could "open up" to each other that it was discovered that there was a diversity of internal careers. The conclusion is clear—if that company wants to do a good job of career development, it will have to find a way to take into account the different needs of these managers rather than simply promoting them in terms of external career criteria.

Out of the workshop should come more insight into (1) how the organizational promotion system actually does work (the characteristics of the external career), (2) what people at different levels want (the characteristics of the internal career), (3) where the areas of mismatch are, and (4) what can be done about them. Solutions may emphasize the need for the employee to alter his career aspirations, or for decision-makers in the organization to alter their career development policies, or both, in the form of new integrations or compromises.

Group sessions dealing with organizational diagnosis often lead to the discovery that there are obstacles to career development in the formal or informal policies or practices of the organization. In such situations the workshop activity should shift to a discussion of how to deal with those obstacles (accept them, plan to change them, work around them, and so on). For example, a given individual's career planning may well reveal the need for a series of rotational assignments in various divisions of the organization, but the organization's traditions may strongly dictate against any lateral cross-division transfer. The workshop participants may then have to work on whether to attempt to change the traditions, find alternate mechanisms for rotation, or give up rotation as a career development goal.

It is our impression that most career development programs fail to get off the ground because they short-circuit areas 1 and 2 above. That is, management makes assumptions about its incentive and reward structures and about what employees need and desire, and then goes directly into decisions *based on these assumptions* (Alfred, 1967). Without adequate information about the external and internal career factors, and without mechanisms for identifying mismatches, it is unlikely that adequate career development programs will ever be established.

Workshops dealing with retirement issues, leveling-off, disengaging, and making the transition to new roles outside the organization are not yet as well worked out. But the issues of the late career are pressing, and organizations should begin to plan to deal with such issues.

Sabbaticals, Flexible Working Hours, and Other Off-Work Activities. Some organizations are beginning to experiment with the idea of giving employees longer periods of time off to pursue personal goals (Finley, 1972; Myers, 1974). The reasons may be several. At the senior executive levels, the pressures of day-to-day work accumulate to the point where a few weeks vacation is not enough time for revitalization and certainly is not enough time to learn anything new that may relate to careers. For middle managers and professional staff employees in midcareer, there may be a problem of *plateauing*—a loss of motivation accompanying the recognition that not many more promotions can be expected. A period of time away from the organization may permit such individuals to develop new interests outside the work context, to readjust their thinking to their career leveling-off, and to put their work into a life perspective. The organization is likely to continue to need the contributions of such people and therefore must find vehicles that permit them to remotivate themselves. An extended period of time off can often serve that function. Indeed, employees at all levels need extended periods of time free from work pressures. And, at the lower levels of the organization, the concept of sabbaticals ties in closely with continuing education and training to permit people to learn new skills that will make career development to higher levels more feasible.

An issue related to the sabbatical concept has to do with the interaction of work, family, and self concerns. Even though the career per se might not require or benefit from a period of time off, the needs of the person to do something crucial in his family life or in relation to self-development might require such time off. For example, in a dual career family there might be occasions when the spouse has to travel and the employee is needed, either at home for a period of child-rearing or to accompany the spouse. When a baby is born, and during other family events, it may be important for both parents to be at home. Many professional employees want time off to work in the community. Time off may be one of the most important benefits a company can give to employees. It should become an explicit part of personnel policy, in the same way that sick leave is usually covered by explicit policies.

Closely related to the idea of sabbaticals are the ideas of a shorter work week and flexible working hours. Many experiments are going on in Europe and the United States that involve these concepts, especially at the hourly employee level. We cannot review these programs in detail here, but we can note that such experiments, along with flexible rewards discussed in the next section, will increasingly become a critical part of any truly viable career development system (Myers, 1974).

Flexible Reward and Promotional Systems.   This topic is a very large one that can be addressed only briefly here. It is clear from the study of employee needs and internal career concepts that organizations are too limited in their thinking about rewards and success criteria (Schein, 1975b). In the financial area, for example, there is a growing trend toward giving employees a choice among several forms of financial reward. The employee can take an increase in pay in the form of a salary increase, a bonus, increased medical or other benefits, stock options, paid leave, or whatever else makes sense to both employee and employer. Lawler (Chapter 4) describes such flexible or cafeteria-style reward systems in some detail. What is important here is that the employee is given a choice, which increases the likelihood of matching employee needs with organizational needs.

It is clear that organizations will have to develop multiple promotional ladders to reflect the fact that not all employees want to be supervisors or general managers. Some organizations have developed dual ladders in an effort to reward the highly technical contributor—the creative scientist or engineer. But as yet little attention has been given to upgrading other roles—such as the financial analyst, the computer programmer, the marketing expert, the secretary, the purchasing agent, or the skilled or unskilled worker on the factory floor. And many functional managers (sales managers, financial managers, and so on) do not want to be general managers but want career growth within their function. This may require the invention of new titles and appropriate rewards to go with such titles. More provisions will have to be made for people to leave managerial roles and go back into senior staff roles without feeling that they are being demoted. Ultimately, the cultures and norms of organizations will have to shift to recognize that, in an increasingly complex environment, the organization is highly dependent on a wide range of human resources and career development involves many paths besides the path upward.

In summary the above ten areas all interact with each other and all reflect the more general conception that has been argued throughout this chapter—that career development ultimately is the responsibility of the employee, the organization, and the supporting institutional structures of society. One of the major problems in launching career development systems is that the organization tries activities in a piecemeal fashion, failing to see that the various activities interact, depend on each other, and ultimately demand important changes in the culture of the organization.

What the Individual Can Do[17]

We would like to close this chapter with a few thoughts on the role of the individual. As society becomes more complex and as organizations become more monolithic, it is easier and easier for the individual to feel powerless in the face of unknown or unchangeable forces. What, after all, can individuals do about their own careers when so many options are controlled by the labor market (the opportunities available) and by the various organizational activities over which individuals have little control? The answer is that individuals cannot do everything. They *cannot* get control over *all* of the outside forces that determine their careers. *But they probably can do more than most of them are now doing.*

Specifically, people can do much more to increase their understanding of themselves—their needs and anchors—and they can do a much better job of negotiating with employers if their self-insight is greater. It is a shocking experience to run a career development workshop and to be told by the participants that the workshop represents the first time they have ever attempted to analyze their own needs, although they recognize the ways in which their careers do or do not fulfill those needs. It is shocking to do research interviews on career histories and to have people being interviewed say, at the end of their interviews, that this was the first time they had ever spent an hour or so thinking about their careers. Perhaps we have overcompensated. Perhaps because we feel relatively little control over our careers, we have abdicated all control. And because we have abdicated all control we have encouraged organizations to continue to control careers for us, except around specific issues such as those that arise in labor-management negotiations.

Probably the best remedy is for those interested in launching career development programs in their own organizations to start by analyzing their own careers. They cannot help others or launch effective programs if they have no understanding of the interaction of personal needs, family issues, and work issues in their own lives (Miller, 1975). Once individuals understand themselves better they can start helping others—immediate subordinates, peers, and even superiors—understand their careers better. Only when the level of such under-

---

17. In recent years, what has been called *pop psychology* has become big business. Numerous books on "How to be a successful, assertive, serene, happy, sexy, or whatever person" have become best sellers. They tell us *how to become our own best friends* and *how to live with another person* in the *prime times* of our lives all because we were *born to win.* The genre is self-help and within it people try to "cope," discover their "true selves" and establish "meaningful relationships." Much of this literature promises much more than it can deliver and is shot throughout with a sort of hardcore banality. Yet the fact that it is a growth industry in more ways than one should alert us to the importance of career development at this period in our history.

standing is fairly high among a critical mass of people in an organization or society is that organization or society ready to launch a career development program on a sufficiently wide scale.

How can this be done? There are now available many programs for career and life planning, some in the form of self-administering packages (for example, see Ford and Lippitt, 1972; General Electric Company, 1972; Shepard and Hawley, 1974; Storey, 1973; Vicino and Miller, 1971). Individuals can use these centers or self-study activities to think through their own lives and how their careers fit into them. If enough high-level managers in organizations begin to do this, organizationally sound career development programs will follow.

CHAPTER 3
WORK DESIGN*

J. RICHARD HACKMAN
Yale University

Every five years or so, a new behavioral science "solution" to organizational problems emerges. Typically such a solution is first tried out—with great success—in a few forward-looking organizations. Then it is picked up by the management journals and the popular press and spreads across the country. And finally, after a few years, it fades away as disillusioned managers, union leaders, and employees come to agree that the solution really does not solve much of anything.

It looks as if the redesign of work is to be the solution of the mid-1970s. The seeds of this strategy for change were planted more than two decades ago, with the pioneering research of Charles Walker and Robert Guest (1952), Frederick Herzberg and his associates (Herzberg, Mausner, and Snyderman, 1959; Herzberg, 1966), Louis Davis (1957, 1966), and a few others. Successful tests of work redesign were conducted in a few organizations and were widely reported. Now, change programs involving work redesign are flooding the nation, stories on "how we profited from job enrichment" are appearing in management journals, and the labor community is struggling to determine how it should respond to the tidal wave that seems to be forming (Gooding, 1972).

The question of the moment is whether the redesign of work

*Portions of this chapter are adapted from Hackman (1975b), Hackman and Oldham (1975; in press), and Hackman, Oldham, Janson, and Purdy (1975). Bibliographic assistance was provided by Kenneth Brousseau, Daniel Feldman, Linda Frank, Andrea Miller, and Irmtraud Streker.

will evolve into a robust and powerful strategy for organizational change—or whether, like so many of its behavioral science predecessors, it will fade into disuse as practitioners experience failure and disillusionment in its applications. The answer is by no means clear.

Present evidence regarding the merits of work redesign can be viewed as optimistic or pessimistic, depending on the biases of the reader. On the one hand, numerous published case studies of successful work redesign projects show that work redesign can be an effective tool for improving both the quality of the work experience of employees and their on-the-job productivity. Yet it also is true that numerous failures in implementing work redesign have been experienced by organizations around the country—and the rate of failure shows no sign of diminishing. Reif and Luthans (1972), for example, summarize a survey, conducted in the mid-1960s, in which only four of forty-one firms implementing job enrichment described their experiences with the technique as "very successful." Increasingly, other commentators are expressing serious doubts about whether job enrichment is really as effective as it has been cracked up to be (Fein, 1974a; Gomberg, 1973; Hulin and Blood, 1968).

Unfortunately, existing research findings and case reports are not very helpful in assessing the validity of the claims made by either the advocates or the skeptics of work redesign. In particular, an examination of the literature cited in Hackman (1975a) leads to the following conclusions:[1]

1. Reports of work redesign successes tend to be more evangelical than thoughtful; for example, little conceptualizing is done that would be useful either as a guide to implementation of work redesign in other settings or as a theoretical basis for research on its effects.
2. The methodologies used in evaluating the effects of changes in work design often are weak or incomplete. Therefore, findings reported may be ambiguous and open to alternative explanations.
3. Although informal sources and surveys suggest that the failure rate for work redesign projects is moderate to high, few documented analyses are available of projects that failed. This is particularly unfortunate because careful analyses of failures often are among the most effective tools for exploring the applicability and the consequences of this or any other organizational change strategy.
4. Most published reports focus almost exclusively on assessing the positive and negative effects of specific changes in work content. Conclusions are then drawn about the general worth of work redesign as a change strategy. Yet there is an *interaction* between the content of the changes and the

---

1. Similar conclusions are reached by Katzell and Yankelovich (1975), after a very thorough review and analysis of selected prototype studies of the effects of work redesign.

organizational context in which they are installed; identical job changes may have quite different effects in different organizational settings (or when installed using different processes). Existing literature has little to say about the nature or dynamics of such interactions.

5. Rarely are economic data (that is, direct and indirect dollar costs and benefits) analyzed and discussed when conclusions are drawn about the effects of work redesign projects, even though many such projects are undertaken in direct anticipation of economic gains.

In sum, it appears that despite the abundance of writing on the topic, there is little definite information about why work redesign is effective when it is, what goes wrong when it is not, and how the strategy can be altered to improve its general usefulness as an approach to personal and organizational change.

This chapter attempts to advance current understanding about such questions. It reviews what is known about how the redesign of work can help improve life in organizations and attempts to identify the circumstances under which the approach is most likely to succeed. It reviews current practice for planning and installing work redesign and emphasizes both the pitfalls that may be encountered and the change strategies that have been shown to be especially effective. And, at the most general level, it asks whether this approach to organizational change is indeed worth saving, or whether it should be allowed to die.

WHAT IS WORK REDESIGN?

Whenever a job is changed—whether because of a new technology, an internal reorganization, or a whim of a manager—it can be said that work redesign has taken place. The present use of the term is somewhat more specialized. Throughout this chapter, work redesign is used to refer to any activities that involve the alteration of specific jobs (or interdependent systems of jobs) with the intent of increasing both the quality of the employees' work experience and their on-the-job productivity. This definition of the term is deliberately broad, to include the great diversity of changes that can be tried to achieve these goals. It subsumes such terms as *job rotation, job enrichment,* and *sociotechnical systems design,* each of which refers to a specific approach to or technique for redesigning work.[2]

There are no simple or generally accepted criteria for a well-designed job, nor is there any single strategy that is acknowledged as

---

2. Because the aim of the present chapter is a *general* examination of what kinds of changes in jobs lead to what kinds of outcomes under what circumstances, there is no need to join in the occasional haggles that develop over the specific meaning of the various terms used to refer to such changes. Readers who wish to sort out the specific connotations of the various terms used in the literature are referred to expositions by Rush (1971, pp. 12–17) and by Strauss (1974a, pp. 38–43).

the proper way to go about improving a job. Instead, what will be an effective design for one specific job in a particular organization may be quite different from the way the job should be designed or changed in another setting. There are, nonetheless, some commonalities in most work redesign experiments that have been carried out to date. Typically changes are made that provide employees with additional responsibilities for planning, setting up, and checking their own work; for making decisions about methods and procedures; for establishing their own work pace within broad limits; and sometimes for relating directly with the client who receives the results of the work. Often the net effect is that jobs which previously had been simplified and segmented into many small parts (in the interest of efficiency from an engineering perspective) are put back together again and made the responsibility of individual workers (Herzberg, 1974).

An early case of work redesign (reported by Kilbridge, 1960) is illustrative. The basic job involved the assembly of small centrifugal pumps used in washing machines. Prior to redesign, the pumps were assembled by six operators on a conveyor line, with each operator performing a particular part of the assembly. The job was changed so that each worker assembled an entire pump, inspected it, and placed his own identifying mark on it. In addition, the assembly operations were converted to a batch system in which workers had more freedom to control their work pace than they had had under the conveyor system. Kilbridge reports that after the job had been enlarged, total assembly time decreased, quality improved, and important cost savings were realized.

In another case, the responsibilities of clerks who assembled information for telephone directories at Indiana Bell Telephone Company were significantly expanded (Ford, 1973). Prior to the change, a production line model was used to assemble directory information. Information was passed from clerk to clerk as it was processed, and each clerk performed only a very small part of the entire job. There were a total of twenty-one different steps in the workflow. Jobs were changed so that each qualified clerk was given responsibility for all the clerical operations required to assemble an entire directory—including receiving, processing, and verifying all information. (For large directories, clerks were given responsibility for a specific alphabetical section of the book.) Not only did the new work arrangement improve the quality of the work experience of the employees, but the efficiency of the operation increased as well—in part because clerks made fewer errors, and so it was no longer necessary to have employees who merely checked and verified the work of others.

In recent years, work redesign increasingly has been used as part of a larger change package aimed at improving the overall quality of life and productivity of people at work. A good example is the new General Foods pet food manufacturing plant in Topeka, Kansas (Walton, 1972, 1975b). When plans were developed for the facility in the late 1960s, corporate management decided to design and manage the plant in full accord with state-of-the-art behavioral science knowledge. Nontraditional features were built into the plant from the beginning— including the physical design of the facilities, the management style, information and feedback systems, compensation arrangements (see Chapter 4), and career paths for individual employees. A key part of the plan was the organization of the work force into teams. Each team (consisting of from seven to fourteen members) was given nearly autonomous responsibility for a significant organizational task. In addition to actually carrying out the work required to complete that task, team members performed many activities that traditionally had been reserved for management. These included coping with manufacturing problems, distributing individual tasks among team members, screening and selecting new team members, and participating in organizational decision-making (Walton, 1972). The basic jobs performed by team members were designed to be as challenging as possible, and employees were encouraged to further broaden their skills in order to be able to handle even more challenging work. Although not without problems, the Topeka plant appears to be prospering, and many employees experience life in the organization as a pleasant and nearly revolutionary change from their traditional ideas about what happens at work.

The Uniqueness of Work Redesign as a Strategy for Change

The redesign of work differs from most other behavioral science approaches to changing life in organizations in at least four ways (Hackman, 1975b). Together, these four points of uniqueness make a rather compelling case for work redesign as a strategy for initiating organizational change.

1. Work redesign alters the basic relationship between a person and what he or she does on the job. When all the outer layers are stripped away, many organizational problems come to rest at the interface between *people* and the *tasks* they do. Frederick Taylor realized this when he set out to design and manage organizations "scientifically" at the beginning of this century (Taylor, 1911). The design of work was central to the scientific management approach, and special pains were taken to ensure that the tasks done by workers did not exceed their performance capabilities. As the approach gained credence in the management community, new and more sophisticated procedures for analyzing work methods emerged, and industrial engineers forged numerous principles of work design. In general, these principles were intended to maximize overall production efficiency by minimizing human error on the job (often accomplished by partitioning the work into small, simple segments), and by minimizing time and motion wasted in doing work tasks.

It turned out, however, that many workers did not like jobs designed according to the dictates of scientific management. In effect, the person-job relationship had been arranged so that achieving the goals of the organization (high productivity) often meant sacrificing important personal goals (the opportunity for interesting, personally rewarding work). Taylor and his associates attempted to deal with this difficulty by installing financial incentive programs intended to make workers *want* to work hard toward organizational goals, and by placing such an elaborate set of supervisory controls on workers that they scarcely could behave otherwise. But the basic incongruence between the person and the work remained, and people-problems (such as high absenteeism and turnover, poor quality work, and high worker dissatisfaction) became increasingly evident in work organizations.

In the past several decades, industrial psychologists have carried out a large number of studies intended to overcome some of the problems that accompanied the spread of scientific management. Sophisticated strategies for identifying those individuals most qualified to perform specific jobs have been developed and validated. New training and attitude change programs have been tried. And numerous motivational techniques have been proposed to increase the energy and commitment with which workers do their tasks. These include development of human relations programs, alteration of supervisory styles, and installation of complex piece-rate and profit-sharing incentive plans. None of these strategies have proven successful. Indeed, some observers report that the quality of the work experience of employees today is more problematic than it was in the heyday of scientific management (cf., *Work in America,* 1973).

Why have behavioral scientists not been more successful in their attempts to remedy motivational problems in organizations and improve the quality of work life of employees? One reason is that psychologists (like managers and labor leaders) have traditionally assumed that *the work itself was inviolate*—that the role of psychologists is simply to help select, train, and motivate people within the confines of jobs as they have been designed by others. Clearly, it is time to reject this assumption and to seek ways to change both people and jobs in order to improve the fit between them.

The redesign of work as a change strategy offers the opportunity to break out of the "givens" that have limited previous attempts to improve life at work. It is based on the assumption that the work itself may be a very powerful influence on employee motivation, satisfaction, and productivity. It acknowledges (and attempts to build on) the inability of people to set aside their social and emotional needs while at work. And it provides a strategy for moving away from extrinsic props to worker motivation and to move instead toward *internal* work motivation that causes the individual to do the work because it interests him, challenges him, and rewards him for a job well done.

2. Work redesign directly changes behavior—and it tends to stay changed. People do the tasks they are given. How well they do them depends on many factors, including how the tasks are designed. But no matter how the tasks are designed, people do them.

On the other hand, people do *not* always behave in ways that are consistent with their attitudes, their levels of satisfaction, or what they cognitively know they should do. Indeed, it is now well established that one's attitudes often are *determined* by the behaviors one engages in—rather than vice versa, as traditionally has been thought (Bem, 1970; Kiesler, Collins, and Miller, 1969). This is especially true when individuals perceive that they have substantial personal freedom or autonomy in choosing how they will behave (Steiner, 1970).

Enriching jobs, then, may have twin virtues. First, behavior is changed; and second, because enriched jobs usually bring about increased feelings of autonomy and personal discretion, the individual is likely to develop attitudes that are supportive of his new on-the-job behaviors (cf. Taylor, 1971). Work redesign does not, therefore, rely on changing attitudes first (for example, inducing the worker to care more about the work outcomes, as in zero defects programs) and hoping that the attitude change will generalize to work behavior. Instead, the strategy is to change the *behavior,* and to change it in a way that gradually leads to a more positive set of attitudes about the work, the organization, and the self.

Moreover, after jobs are changed, it usually is difficult for workers to slip back into old ways. The old ways simply are inappropriate for the new tasks, and the structure of those tasks reinforces the changes that have taken place. Thus, one need not worry much about the kind of backsliding that occurs so often after training or attitude modification activities, especially those that occur off-site. The task-based stimuli that influence the worker's behavior are very much on-site, every hour of every day. And once those stimuli are changed, behavior is likely to stay changed—at least until the job is again redesigned.

3. Work redesign offers—and sometimes forces into one's hands— numerous opportunities for initiating other organizational changes.

When work is redesigned in an organization so that many people are doing things differently than they used to, new problems inevitably surface and demand attention. These can be construed solely as *problems,* or they can be treated as *opportunities* for further organizational change activities. For example, technical problems are likely to develop when jobs are changed—offering opportunities to smooth and refine the work system as a system. Interpersonal issues also are likely to arise, almost inevitably between supervisors and subordinates and sometimes between peers who now have to relate to one another in new ways. These issues offer opportunities for developmental work aimed at improving the social and supervisory aspects of the work system.

Because such problems are literally forced to the surface by the job changes, all parties may feel a need to do something about them. Responses can range from using the existence of a problem to justify that "job enrichment doesn't work," to simply trying to solve the problem quickly so the work redesign project can proceed, to using the problem as a point of entry for attacking other organizational issues. If the last stance is taken, behavioral science professionals may find themselves pleasantly removed from the old difficulty of selling their wares to skeptical managers and employees who are not really sure there is anything wrong. Eventually a program of organizational change and development may evolve that addresses organizational systems and practices that, superficially at least, seem unrelated to how the work itself is designed (Beer and Huse, 1972).

4. Work redesign, in the long term, can result in organizations that rehumanize rather than dehumanize the people who work in them. Despite the popular inflation of the work ethic issue in recent years (cf. Chapter 1), there is convincing evidence that organizations can and do sometimes stamp out part of the humanness of their members—especially people's motivations toward growth and personal development (cf. Kornhauser, 1965).

Work redesign can help individuals regain the chance to experience the kick that comes from doing a job well, and it can encourage them to once again *care* about their work and about developing the competence to do it even better. These payoffs from work redesign go well beyond simple job satisfaction. Cows grazing in the field may be satisfied, and employees in organizations can be made just as satisfied by paying them well, by keeping bosses off their backs, by putting them in pleasant work rooms with pleasant people, and by arranging things so that the days pass without undue stress or strain.

The kind of satisfaction at issue here is different. It is a satisfaction that develops only when individuals are stretching and growing as human beings, increasing their sense of competence and self-worth.

Whether the creation of opportunities for personal growth is a legitimate goal for work redesign activities is a value question deserving long discussion; the case for the value of work redesign strictly in terms of *organizational* health easily can rest on the first three points discussed above. But personal growth is without question a central component of the overall quality of work life in organizations, and the impact of work redesign on the people who do the work, as human beings, should be neither overlooked nor underemphasized.

As described above, the potential of work redesign as a strategy for change may sound glowing. Yet, for reasons discussed later in this chapter, that potential is realized infrequently in actual change projects in contemporary organizations. To reconcile the promise with the product—and thereby to lay the groundwork for more effective implementation of work redesign—requires understanding of why and how jobs affect people, what factors in the situation moderate the success of work redesign, and how changes in jobs most effectively can be installed and followed up. It is to these issues that we now turn.

WAYS WORK REDESIGN CAN IMPROVE SATISFACTION, MOTIVATION, AND PRODUCTIVITY

In this section, we examine several conceptual frameworks that are available for understanding how jobs affect people and for guiding the implementation and evaluation of work redesign projects. Because work redesign potentially can contribute to the improvement of work life and productivity in a number of different ways, the particular type of theory that will be most useful in a given instance will depend both on the type of problem addressed and on the kind of change contemplated. Therefore, the present review is organized in terms of three different avenues for achieving personal and organizational change through the redesign of work.

The first avenue focuses on how work redesign can minimize the negative consequences of work that is highly routine and repetitive. The second examines ways that work can be changed to provide new or increased opportunities for positive and self-sustaining work motivation and productivity. And the third avenue deals with ways that the social and technical aspects of the workplace can be changed in concert, to simultaneously enrich both the content and the context of the work. Thus, the first avenue attempts to eliminate actively negative outcomes of work; the second attempts to create new and positive outcomes; and the third takes a step back from the individual job and focuses on the development of healthier work *systems*.

Minimizing the Dysfunctional Effects of Repetitive Work

Among the earliest documented instances of human problems resulting from work design are accounts of the dysfunctional consequences of routine, repetitive tasks (Vernon, 1924; Walker and Guest, 1952; Worthy, 1950). Highly repetitive jobs have been found to diminish worker alertness, to decrease sensitivity to sensory input, and in some situations to impair muscular coordination. Because employees dislike working on such jobs, they often engage in behaviors aimed at countering their feelings of boredom. These behaviors include daydreaming, chatting with other workers, making frequent readjustments of posture and position, and finding excuses to take unnecessary breaks from work. Many of these behaviors impair the employee's work effectiveness, yet provide only temporary relief from the boredom of the job.

Psychologists have amassed a great deal of research evidence about the causes and consequences of high and low levels of psychological and physiological activation (Berlyne, 1967). Moreover, as Scott (1966) has shown, it may be possible to use activation theory both to understand the often negative effects of repetitive jobs, and to plan changes in the stimulus characteristics of jobs so that people experience nearly optimal levels of activation in their work.[3]

Yet despite the clear relevance of activation theory to job design, three thorny problems must be overcome before the theory can be applied to real jobs. The first problem has to do with differences among individuals in how activated they are by their jobs and in the amount of activation they prefer. The research literature clearly shows that different people have different optimal levels of activation—that is, levels at which they are most alert, neither bored nor overstimulated. Moreover, there is increasing evidence that personality affects how an individual will act when over- or understimulated (Bakan, Belton, and Toth, 1963; Scott, 1969). Such differences among people are obviously important in applying activation theory to job redesign. But at present the theory provides little explicit guidance about how these differences should be dealt with in designing jobs and tasks.

A second problem with applying activation theory is that means

---

3. Activation theorists have given relatively little attention to jobs that may be *over-stimulating*, perhaps because few such jobs exist for rank-and-file workers in contemporary organizations. Research on role-overload (for example, Kahn, Wolfe, Quinn, Snoek, and Rosenthal, 1964; Sales, 1970) would seem to be of considerable relevance to understanding the dynamics and consequences of excessively high levels of activation in work settings. But conceptual links between studies of role-based stress and conditions of overactivation on the job are only beginning to be drawn (for example, McGrath, 1976).

must be developed for *measuring* current levels of activation of individuals in work settings. Although some progress on this issue has been made (Scott and Rowland, 1970; Thayer, 1967, 1970), it remains very difficult to measure reliably how near an individual is to his optimal level of activation. And until better measurement techniques are developed, it will remain impractical to use the theory as a basis for the redesign of jobs except in a very gross fashion—for example, in instances where it is clear that most employees are enormously over- or understimulated by their work.

Finally, some practical difficulties in applying the theory are encountered because of the processes by which individuals adapt to changes in the level of stimulation they experience. A person's level of activation decreases markedly as a function of familiarity with a given stimulus situation. But after a period of rest, re-presentation of the same stimulus situation will again raise the level of activation (Scott, 1966). More complete understanding of the waxing and waning of activation in various circumstances could have many implications for such job design practices as job rotation. Those who advocate job rotation claim that worker motivation can be kept reasonably high by rotating individuals through several different jobs, even though each of the jobs would become monotonous and boring if an individual were to remain on it for a long period of time. If future research can identify ways to maintain activation at nearly optimal levels through planned stimulus change, then the theory can increase substantially the usefulness of job rotation as a motivational technique. If, however, it turns out that there are general and inevitable decreases in activation over time regardless of how different tasks and rest periods are cycled, then the long-term usefulness of the technique would seem to be limited.

Creating Conditions for Positive Work Motivation and Personal Growth

Even if the problems with activation theory identified above could be solved, the theory still would appear most useful for alleviating negative outcomes that result from jobs that under- or overstimulate employees. The theory offers little guidance, in other words, toward the design of jobs that elicit positive and self-reinforcing work motivation. Two other conceptual approaches to work redesign that do attempt to specify the conditions under which positive work motivation can be generated and maintained—motivation-hygiene theory and job characteristics theory—are reviewed below.

Motivation-Hygiene Theory. By far the most influential theory of work redesign to date has been the Herzberg two-factor theory of satisfaction and motivation (Herzberg, Mausner, and Snyderman, 1959; Herzberg, 1966). In essence, the theory proposes that the primary determinants of employee *satisfaction* are factors *intrinsic* to the work that is done—recognition, achievement, responsibility, advancement, and personal growth in competence. These factors are called *motivators* because employees are motivated to obtain more of them —for example, through good job performance. *Dissatisfaction,* on the other hand, is seen as being caused by *hygiene factors* that are extrinsic to the work. Examples include company policies, supervisory practices, pay plans, and working conditions. The Herzberg theory specifies that a job will enhance work motivation only to the degree that motivators are designed into the work. Changes that deal solely with hygiene factors should not generate increases in employee motivation.

It is much to the credit of Herzberg's theory that it has prompted a great deal of research and inspired a number of successful change projects involving job redesign (Paul, Robertson, and Herzberg, 1969). Especially noteworthy is the series of job enrichment studies done at AT&T (Ford, 1969). These studies demonstrate, for a diversity of jobs, that job enrichment can lead to beneficial outcomes both for the individuals involved and for the employing organization. Moreover, a set of step-by-step procedures for implementing job enrichment was generated as part of the AT&T program, and these procedures continue to guide many job redesign activities throughout the country.

The Herzberg theory (specifically, the distinction between motivators and hygiene factors) provides a clear and straightforward way of thinking about employee motivation, and of predicting the likely impact of various planned changes on motivation. The phrases "Yes, but that's really only a hygiene factor" and "But would it change the *work itself?*" have undoubtedly been used thousands of times as managers consider various strategies for attempting to improve employee work motivation and satisfaction.

More often than not, applying the Herzberg theory has helped keep change focused on issues that are central rather than peripheral to employee motivation and satisfaction. Consider, for example, such recently popular interventions as the four-day work week and flexible scheduling of working hours (Best, 1973; Fiss, 1974). Both of these changes legitimately can be viewed as devices for improving the quality of the work experience of employees in organizations. They provide workers with increased flexibility in planning leisure activities, in coordinating work and family responsibilities, and generally in achieving a higher level of personal control over their lives. As is true of most significant organizational innovations, early reports of the effects of these intervention strategies have been optimistic (*Journal for Humanistic Management*, 1973).

Yet the Herzberg theory would suggest that such alterations of work schedules are *not* likely to lead to long-term improvements in worker satisfaction, motivation, or productivity, because the nature of the work itself is not changed by such innovations. If the work is more frustrating than fulfilling, then about all that reasonably could be expected from flexible scheduling of work hours and the four-day week would be a decrease in some dissatisfactions that derive from conflicts between personal plans and work schedules. Indeed, problems arising from dissatisfying aspects of the work might actually be exacerbated rather than relieved under a four-day arrangement, because more hours would be spent on the job on any given work day. And, after the novelty of the four-day work week had worn off, the net result might be merely a change from "TGIF" to "Thank God it's *Thursday*" (Walters, 1971).

In sum, what the Herzberg theory does, and does well, is point attention directly to the enormous significance of the *work itself* as a factor in the ultimate motivation and satisfaction of employees. And because the message of the theory is simple, persuasive, and directly relevant to the design and evaluation of actual organizational changes, the theory continues to be widely known and generally used by managers of organizations in this country.

Despite its considerable merit, however, there are a number of difficulties with motivation-hygiene theory that compromise its usefulness. For one thing, a number of researchers have been unable to provide empirical support for the major tenets of the two-factor theory. (See, for example, Dunnette, Campbell, and Hakel, 1967; Graen, 1968; Hinton, 1968; House and Wigdor, 1967; and King, 1970. For analyses of the evidence that are favorable to the theory, see Herzberg, 1966; Whitsett and Winslow, 1967.) In particular, it appears that the original dichotomization of aspects of the workplace into motivators and hygiene factors may have been partly due to methodological artifact. Moreover, some aspects of the workplace can serve at times as motivators and at other times as hygiene factors. Nonspecific praise from a supervisor or an end-of-year raise in pay, for example, would not be classified as motivators by the theory. Yet to the extent that praise or pay raises are provided by the organization (and experienced by the employee) as recognition for achievement, such items would help motivate the employee—because recognition is included in the theory as a motivator (cf. Oldham, in press, b). Thus, the motivating factors are not operationally defined in and of themselves; instead, the status of various factors depends in large part on the dynamics of the particular organizational situation.

This difficulty severely compromises the degree to which the presence or absence of the motivating factors can be *measured* for existing jobs. At the least, the measurement problem makes empirical testing of the theory in organizations very difficult. It also raises severe practical difficulties in using the theory to plan and implement actual job changes, because there is no way to diagnose systematically the status of jobs prior to change, or to measure the effects of job enrichment activities on the jobs after the change has been carried out.

Finally, the theory does not provide for differences in how responsive people are likely to be to enriched jobs. In the AT&T studies based on the theory (Ford, 1969), for example, it was assumed that the motivating factors potentially could increase the work motivation of *all* employees, although the implementation procedures devised for these studies specified that enriching tasks should be added to a job only when the employee showed readiness for the new responsibilities. But the theory has not yet been elaborated to specify how such determinations of readiness should be made. Because evidence is now abundant that some individuals are more likely to respond positively to an enriched, complex job than are others (Hulin, 1971), it would seem imperative that the theory be elaborated to specify in concrete terms how individual differences should be dealt with—both conceptually and in the design and implementation of actual changes.

Job Characteristics Theory. An approach to work redesign that focuses on the objective characteristics of jobs is rooted in the work of Turner and Lawrence (1965). These researchers developed objective measures of a number of job characteristics that were predicted to relate positively to employee satisfaction and attendance. The job characteristics were summarized in a single measure (called the RTA Index) that reflects the overall complexity and challenge of the work.

Turner and Lawrence found the expected positive relationships between the RTA Index and employee satisfaction and attendance only for workers from factories located in small towns. For employees in urban work settings, satisfaction was *inversely* related to the scores of jobs on the RTA Index, and absenteeism was unrelated to the index. The investigators concluded that reactions to "good" (high RTA Index) jobs were moderated by differences in the subcultural backgrounds of employees. Subsequent research by Blood and Hulin (Blood and Hulin, 1967; Hulin and Blood, 1968) provided support for the notion that subcultural factors moderate workers responses to the design of their jobs.

A study by Hackman and Lawler (1971) provided further evidence that job characteristics can directly affect employee attitudes and behavior at work; and it suggested that such effects could be conceptualized in terms of the expectancy theory of work motivation (Vroom, 1964). Specifically, Hackman and Lawler predicted that if specific core job characteristics are present, employees will experience a positive, self-generated affective response *when they perform well*—and that this internal kick will provide an incentive for continued efforts toward good performance. The specific job dimensions proposed as necessary to create conditions for such self-motivation to develop and be maintained are: (1) variety, (b) task identity (that is, doing a whole piece of work), (c) autonomy, and (d) feedback.

In addition, Hackman and Lawler suggested that the differences they found in the way various subcultural groups of employees reacted to complex jobs might be most simply explained by how strongly group members desired personal growth and development. It was predicted that the stronger an employee's need for growth, the more the person would value the feeling of personal accomplishment obtained from doing the job well—and therefore the more likely he would be to respond positively to a job high on the four core dimensions.

Results reported by Hackman and Lawler (from telephone company employees) generally supported the prediction that employees who work on jobs high on the core dimensions exhibit high work motivation, satisfaction, performance, and attendance.[4] In addition, these researchers found that a number of dependent measures were moderated as predicted by growth need strength; that is, employees with high need for growth responded more positively to "good" jobs than did employees low in growth need strength.

A model of work design that attempts to extend, refine, and systematize the findings described above has been proposed by Hackman and Oldham (in press) and is described in detail later in this chapter. In essence, the model proposes that five core job characteristics—skill variety, task identity, task significance, autonomy, and feedback—foster work experiences for employees that, in turn, affect their work motivation and satisfaction. Job redesign activities based on the model involve increasing the standing of a job on the core job characteristics, especially for employees who have strong growth needs.

The job characteristics model (like the Herzberg approach) deals only with aspects of jobs that can be altered to create *positive* motivational incentives for the job incumbent. The model does not directly address the dysfunctional aspects of repetitive work (as does activation theory), although presumably a job designed in accord with the dictates of the model would not turn out to be excessively routine or repetitive.

---

4. These findings subsequently have been replicated by Brief and Aldag (1975), Oldham (in press, a), and Zierden (1975).

In addition, both the motivation-hygiene model and the job characteristics model focus exclusively on the relationship between an individual and his work. These theories do not explicitly address managerial, social, technical, or situational moderators of how people react to their work, even though attention to such factors would be critical to the successful installation of work redesign programs in ongoing organizations. As Friedlander and Brown (1974) note, the core of such models can perhaps better be viewed as theories of motivation than as theories of change.

Finally, both the Herzberg and the job characteristics models are framed in such a way as to apply exclusively to jobs that are done independently by individuals. They offer no guidelines for the effective design of work for interacting teams—that is, work that involves interdependent contributions from a number of employees and is more appropriately conceived of as a group task than as an individual task. An alternative conceptual approach that does emphasize the use of interacting groups in accomplishing the work, and that explicitly addresses social and technical moderators of work design, is discussed below.

Creating Integrated Work Systems

The sociotechnical systems approach to work design provides guidance for the creation of *systems* of work, in which both the social and the technical aspects of the workplace are integrated and mutually supportive of one another (Emery and Trist, 1969; Trist, Higgin, Murray, and Pollock, 1963). The two essential premises of sociotechnical theory have been described as follows:

> The first is that in any purposive organization in which men are required to perform activities . . . the desired output is achieved through the actions of a social as well as a technical system. These systems are so interlocked that the achievement of the output becomes a function of their joint operation. The important concept is "joint," for it is here that the sociotechnical idea departs from more widely held views—those in which the social system is thought to be completely dependent on the technical. "Joint optimization" is also crucial to this theory: it is impossible to optimize for overall performance without seeking to optimize jointly the correlative but independent social and technological systems.
>
> The second premise is that every sociotechnical system is embedded in an environment that is influenced by a culture, its values, and a set of generally acceptable practices. This environment permits certain roles for organizations, groups, and the individuals in them. To understand a work

system or an organization, one must understand the environmental forces that are operating on it. This emphasis suggests, correctly, that sociotechnical theory falls within the larger body of "open system" theories. Stated simply, this means that there is a constant interchange between what goes on in a work system or an organization and what goes on in the environment. (Davis and Trist, 1974, p. 247).

Thus, sociotechnical systems theory contrasts with the traditional engineering approach to work design. The latter often ignores the personal needs of the people who carry out the work, especially social needs that can be fulfilled by group memberships. The theory also differs from psychological approaches to work redesign, which often ignore or underemphasize the importance of technological and environmental factors in affecting what happens in the workplace. Changes that are undertaken from a sociotechnical systems perspective attempt simultaneously to modify *both* the technical and the social aspects of the organization to create work systems that lead both to greater task productivity and to higher personal fulfillment for organization members.

Of special importance is the contribution of sociotechnical theory to development of the idea of the *autonomous work group*. In such a group the members of a work team share among themselves much of the decision-making about the planning and execution of the work (Gulowsen, 1972; Herbst, 1962). Typically, an autonomous work group is a relatively small group (less than twenty members) that is encouraged to develop close intermember ties and a joint commitment to the task of the group. The task of such a group is designed so that it is a whole piece of work on which members can perform a variety of different roles. The group as a whole obtains feedback about its performance on the task. When autonomous work groups are formed, other aspects of the workplace (for example, the technology, the nature of first-level management, and compensation plans) typically are changed as well, so that the group, its task, and the surrounding organization are maximally congruent with one another (as in the Topeka plant of General Foods, described earlier). Strategies for designing work for autonomous (or semiautonomous) teams are discussed in detail later in this chapter.

The theory on which the sociotechnical systems approach to change is based has evolved gradually over the past two decades. It is based on findings from numerous planned changes of work systems, originally primarily in overseas organizations, but increasingly in the United States as well. Many of these change projects have provided vivid illustration of the interactions between the social and technical aspects of work, and also have proven successful as action projects (Davis, 1966; Davis and Trist, 1974; Rice, 1958; Trist et al., 1963). As revealed through reports of such experiments, sociotechnical systems theory appears to be at the same time very general and very specific. It is general in the sense that the principles of the theory are framed and discussed at a rather molar or general level of analysis, and few explicit conceptual links are forged between the tenets of the theory and the particular actions taken or outcomes observed in various applications. It is specific in the sense that the characteristics of the organizations where the experiments are conducted (and the specifics of what happens during the course of the project) usually are described in rich and complete detail.

The generality of the theory is one of the elegant features of the sociotechnical approach, and at the same time is one of its major difficulties. On the positive side, the theory can be adapted with ease to almost any organizational situation and can be used to understand and explain (albeit in systems language) almost anything that happens there. Thus, the theory remains open to continual improvement and revision on the basis of increased experience with it in actual change situations. (This is often not true of behavioral science theories that are fully articulated and highly specific.) Moreover, the theory seems quite unlikely to fall into the trap of a "new Taylorism"—that is, mechanistically overspecifying the details of tasks and relationships that are expected to contribute to an improved quality of life in organizations (Davis, 1975).

However, the generality of the theory creates a number of problems for scholars and interventionists, problems that are not remedied by the simple provision of full detail about experiments in which the theory is applied. There is no explicit specification in the theory, for example, of exactly how (and under what circumstances) the work, the social surroundings, and the outside environment affect one another. Also, the terms and concepts used in the theory lack operational specificity. Together, these ambiguities make it very difficult to conduct controlled experiments to assess the validity of the theory, or to gather quantitative data about the characteristics of the social and technical aspects of a workplace as part of a prechange diagnosis (or a post-change evaluation) of a sociotechnical intervention.

Especially troublesome is the lack of theory-specified criteria for well-designed jobs or well-constructed work groups, and the absence of a theory-based change strategy for attempting to create such jobs and groups. Some criteria and change principles have been proposed (Davis, 1966; Davis and Trist, 1974; Engelstad, 1972; Trist et al., 1963). But the various sets of prescriptions differ in numerous specifics and all appear to be based more on experiences in given research or action projects than on any tenets of sociotechnical systems theory.

Two major emphases characterize most applications of the

sociotechnical approach to change. The first is a strong tendency to form workers into groups. Indeed, almost every organizational change based on the theory involves the formation of some sort of group, to such an extent that sometimes individual people and individual jobs are overlooked. Second, research and change activities are virtually never carried out in a piecemeal fashion, as would be done if one focused solely on such topics as man-machine interaction, motivation, enriched tasks, and shared power. Instead (and this may represent one important reason why specific operationalizations of concepts and explicit guidelines for change remain mostly unspecified in the theory), applications of sociotechnical systems almost always involve simultaneous pulling of numerous levers for change in the organizational setting.

The twin emphasis on groups and on changes with many focuses is reinforced in a recent paper by Louis Davis (1975). Although Davis originated the term *job design* some years ago, he now argues that the concept *job* may be an inappropriate point of departure for planning improvements in the quality of work life. Instead, he suggests that the design of jobs is best viewed as a *consequence* of prior choices that must be made about a work system—rather than as the point of initial intervention into the system. Davis proposes that the term *job design* be replaced by *work system design*, and that the *roles* of organization members (rather than their jobs) become the basis for planning organizational changes.

This perspective highlights the differences between sociotechnical systems theory as it currently is evolving and the more individually-oriented theories of work design reviewed earlier. The individually-oriented theories start with the person and the job and then address the social and technical environment as potential moderators of the person-job relationship. The sociotechnical approach takes the opposite view; that is, it starts with the work system *qua* system, and addresses the job and the individual as derivative parts of that system.

In sum, the sociotechnical perspective on the redesign of work has been shown to be of considerable value as a way of thinking about work and its redesign, and as a framework for planning changes in work systems. Yet sociotechnical systems theory in its present form is difficult to test empirically, and the theory provides little explicit and concrete guidance about what organizational changes should be made under what circumstances. For these reasons, a more job-focused orientation will be taken in the sections of the chapter to follow— albeit a focus that attempts to acknowledge and deal with the considerable impact that the social and technical surroundings have on how people react to their work.

WHY THERE IS NO UNIVERSALLY GOOD DESIGN FOR WORK: CONDITIONING FACTORS

As implied by the above review of conceptual approaches to work design, a "good" job is a function of both the characteristics of the work itself and the circumstances under which the job is to be performed. In this section, four conditioning factors are reviewed, each of which can affect substantially the impact of a job on employee satisfaction and productivity. The conditioning factors are: (1) individual differences among the employees who do the work; (2) the social and interpersonal context of the job; (3) the climate and managerial style of the organization as a whole; and (4) the technology of which the work is a part.

Individual Differences

Obviously not all jobs are suited to all people. Some individuals prosper in simple, routinized work, while others prefer highly complex and challenging tasks; some are happier and more productive when working by themselves, while others become frustrated and unhappy at work unless other people are around; and so on. One aim of work redesign, therefore, is to increase the congruence between the workers and the work.

As indicated in Figure 3.1, achieving such congruence is very much a two-way street in which the person and the job each have specific demands that must be met and specific resources to contribute to the

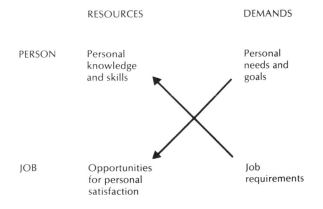

Figure 3.1–Achieving Congruence Between Person and Job

person-job interaction.[5] The knowledge and skill of the person (a resource) can be applied to completing the job requirements (a demand); and, at the same time, the job provides various opportunities for personal satisfaction (a resource) that can be used by the person in attempting to meet his own needs and goals (a demand). In a highly congruent work situation, the demands of the job and the person would be simultaneously fulfilled. And it can be argued that optimally designed work would facilitate (or at least not impair) the achievement of such a mutually beneficial situation (cf. Porter, Lawler, and Hackman, 1975). In the paragraphs that follow, we examine how differences among people in their resources and demands moderate how they react to their jobs.

Knowledge and Skills.   Probably the most important moderator of how a person reacts to a job is the level of knowledge and skill he has to perform it. When people are assigned to jobs for which they are not fully qualified, serious problems develop both for the person and for the employing organization. From the perspective of the organization, underqualified employees generate numerous direct and indirect costs—because of poor quality work, extra supervisory time, and so on. And for the individual, being underqualified can cause considerable personal unhappiness and embarrassment.

A great deal of research has gone into the development of procedures and devices for ensuring that the knowledge and skills of employees are sufficient to fulfill the requirements of their jobs. Job analysis methodologies, for example, provide a means for identifying precisely the abilities required for successful performance of almost any job, whether it is enriched or simple (Fine, 1955, McCormick, Jeanneret, and Mecham, 1972). Once job requirements are identified, numerous tests and models for selection and placement are available for matching people to jobs, so that all employees have the capability to perform adequately (Dunnette, 1966).

Such selection devices and procedures typically are quite sophisticated, and they usually achieve their intended goal quite well. But as actually applied in ongoing organizations, they sometimes encourage practices that are inconsistent with the attainment of high congruence between people and jobs. For example, the mere availability of selection devices that provide ordinal discrimination among candidates for a position can lead those responsible for selection decisions routinely to select those candidates who score highest on the tests. Although this provides excellent insurance that jobs will not be filled by people who

---

5. The dynamics of person-organization relationships are explored more generally by Suttle (Chapter 1).

are not capable of performing them, a frequent side effect is that substantial numbers of people turn out to be *overqualified* for the work they are assigned to do. Overqualification can represent just as much of a mismatch between person and job as underqualification. Overqualified individuals, for example, are likely to find themselves unchallenged by the work and bored by it. In such circumstances they may psychologically withdraw from work or attempt to find ways of injecting something of interest into the work day—and that something may have little to do with getting the job done. Neither alternative bodes particularly well for organizational productivity or for the long-term health and well-being of the individual.

A second problem with traditional selection procedures is that the analyze-test-select approach to achieving congruence between people and jobs encourages everyone to consider the a priori design of the job itself as given, and to focus solely on identifying people who are able to do the job as designed. If the job is *poorly* designed (for example, if it is excessively simplified and routinized, or excessively complex and stressful), it may be nearly impossible to find individuals who are really well suited to it (that is, who are simple enough for it, if the job is excessively simplified, or who are competent enough for it, if it is excessively complex). Although the most effective way of proceeding in such circumstances might be to redesign the job, that alternative is unlikely to be considered if the job has been carefully described and analyzed, and if tests are conveniently at hand to use in selecting people who are sure to have the minimum capability required.

There are traps for the unwary in the use of sophisticated techniques for analyzing jobs and assigning people to them. However, it should be reemphasized that both the quality of life at work and work productivity are powerfully affected by the degree of fit between the skills of the person and the demands of the job. Job analysis and selection devices, when used appropriately, can contribute in important ways to assuring that people have jobs that are neither beyond nor seriously beneath their capabilities.

Needs and Goals. A well-designed job allows employees to satisfy important personal needs (or progress toward fulfilling personally important goals) while working productively on the job. Many jobs, however, are arranged so that employees find it virtually impossible to do what the job demands and at the same time satisfy their personal needs. Admittedly, however, it is difficult to design a job that will be satisfying over a long period of time to everyone who works on it, largely because of the diversity and the changing nature of the needs that are important to different individuals (Neff, 1968; Strauss, 1974b). Indeed, even single individuals usually are simultaneously seeking satisfaction of a number of different needs, all of which can influence how the person behaves on the job (Katzell and Yankelovich, 1975).

Two general classes of needs that have clear relevance to how jobs are designed are examined below: (1) needs for personal growth and development; and (2) needs for meaningful social relationships.

Growth Needs.   When jobs are enriched, opportunities are created for increased self-direction, learning, and personal accomplishment at work. However, not all individuals respond positively to such opportunities. The question, then, is how to determine ahead of time who will and who will not prosper on a complex, challenging job. The findings of Turner and Lawrence (1965) and of Blood and Hulin (1967) suggest that the critical factor may be subcultural. For example, workers from rural settings may more strongly endorse middle-class work norms than people from urban settings, and therefore may respond more positively to challenging work. On the other hand, results reported by Hackman and Lawler (1971) suggest that it is the level of desire for higher order (growth) need satisfaction that moderates reactions to complex jobs. Specifically, they found that when jobs provide increased opportunities for personal discretion and learning, people with high needs for growth respond more positively to the work than do people with weak growth needs.

Other investigators recently have obtained results similar to those reported by Hackman and Lawler, and it now appears that measures of human needs may provide the most valid and direct way of tapping differences among people that affect their reactions to enriched work.[6] Previously reported differences in how urban and rural workers respond to complex jobs, for example, may have been obtained primarily because rural workers tend to have stronger needs for growth than do workers from urban environments.

Social Needs.   The impact of social needs is analogous to the impact of growth needs. As jobs provide increased opportunities for significant social relationships, individuals with strong social needs should re-

---

6. Findings similar to those of Hackman and Lawler are reported by a number of investigators, all of whom used a measure of growth need strength (Brief and Aldag, 1975; Hackman and Oldham, in press; Oldham, in press, a; Sims and Szilagyi, 1974; Zierden, 1975). In addition, Robey (1974) obtained similar moderating effects using extrinsic versus intrinsic work values as the individual difference measure. Failures to obtain a moderating effect have been reported by Shepard (1970), by Susman (1973), who used urban versus rural differences, and by Stone (in press), who used a measure of employee endorsement of the Protestant work ethic. Wanous (1974) directly compared the usefulness of (1) higher order need strength, (2) endorsement of the Protestant work ethic, and (3) urban versus rural subcultural background as moderators of job effects. Although all three variables were found to be of some value as moderators, the need strength measure was most powerful and the urban-rural measure was weakest.

spond more positively to the work than individuals who have weak social needs.

Many work redesign projects (especially those designed on the basis of sociotechnical systems theory) are explicitly intended to increase the extent or intensity of employees' social relationships on the job. The results of such experiments suggest that for the most part employees do respond positively when opportunities for satisfying social needs at work are expanded. What is not yet known is whether differences in measured social need strength can be shown to *moderate* how different individuals respond to jobs that provide different opportunities for social interaction. Also presently unknown is the degree to which work productivity is high when individuals with strong social needs perform jobs that provide significant social opportunities. It may turn out, for example, that in some circumstances trade-offs between satisfaction and work productivity will be encountered when job changes deal solely with the social aspects of work.

Conclusion: Individual Difference Moderators. Some researchers and managers, especially those sympathetic to a "scientific" approach to management, continue to argue that differences among people are an anathema to efficient and effective organizations. In somewhat extreme form, the argument is that work should be designed so that the idiosyncrasies of individual employees will have little or no opportunity to disrupt ongoing organizational activities. Numerous devices, ranging from extra close supervision to mechanical pacing of jobs, are used to suppress tendencies for individual differences to be expressed at work.

This point of view can now be held only if one ignores a substantial body of evidence to the contrary. Observations of individuals working on highly standardized jobs, for example, reveal that differences among people almost inevitably show themselves—and not always in the most pleasant of ways—even when management is making every attempt to encourage or enforce regularity among workers. From a more positive point of view, evidence summarized earlier in this chapter suggests that differences among people can be deliberately capitalized on in designing jobs—to the benefit of the employees as well as to the organizations where they work. Indeed, these differences *must* be taken into account if optimum congruence between people and jobs is to be achieved.

A number of significant questions about individual difference moderators remain unanswered, however, and many of these questions must be dealt with in one way or another by those who design work in organizations. For example:

1. What percentage of the work force actually desire higher order need satisfactions at work and so are likely to respond positively to enriched jobs? Some observers estimate that only about 15 percent of rank-and-file employees are so motivated (Fein, 1972, 1974b). Others are more optimistic (Herrick, 1972; *Work in America*, 1973). Although the answer to this question has obvious implications for organizational work design practices, perhaps a more critical question is the following.

2. What is the *direction* of the relationship between job complexity and beneficial outcomes for people with strong higher order needs as contrasted with people who have weak higher order needs? In particular, are people with weak needs for growth actively threatened and upset by jobs that are high in challenge and complexity? Recent evidence suggests that employees with low measured growth need strength are *not* repelled by enriched jobs; instead, they simply do not respond to such jobs as positively or enthusiastically as do individuals with strong needs for growth (Hackman and Oldham, in press; Stone, in press; Zierden, 1975; for a contrary view, see Hulin and Blood, 1968). If further research confirms that growth need strength determines only the strength (and not the direction) of the relationship between job complexity and work outcomes, then concerns about discouraging workers by enriching their jobs could and should vanish.

3. How reliably and validly can intangible individual differences (such as need strength) be measured? How can such measures be used in actual selection, placement, and job design practices? State-of-the-art methodologies for measuring and using individual differences in needs and goals in organizational decision-making are relatively primitive when compared, for example, to the sophisticated methodologies available for assessing individual differences in knowledge and skill. Managers frequently underestimate the needs of their subordinates for growth and for increased work responsibility. And so it is important that procedures be developed to provide organizational decision-makers with trustworthy data about the actual need states of their employees.

4. Finally, how are individual differences themselves affected by what happens at work? There is increasing evidence that the quality of work experiences can strongly affect both job-related skills and personal needs and goals (Argyris, 1960; Breer and Locke, 1965; Kornhauser, 1965; Porter, Lawler, and Hackman, 1975). The extent and dynamics of these effects are still far from fully understood. But they bear importantly on how individual differences are construed and managed in organizations—and in particular on the degree to which existing characteristics of people are assumed to be fixed or malleable as plans are made about how jobs will be designed.

Interpersonal Relationships

Interpersonal issues can affect the reactions of people to their jobs, and to changes in those jobs, in a number of important ways. It was proposed above, for example, that social need strength will affect how people react to job changes that alter the social makeup of their work. Moreover, there is increasing evidence to suggest that *any* job change (even if oriented exclusively to individual jobs, and not explicitly intended to affect interpersonal behavior) has some impact on the extent and quality of social relationships at work (see Alderfer, Chapter 5). As shown in Figure 3.2, such changes in social relationships can affect the productivity, motivation, and satisfaction of the people whose jobs are redesigned. Thus, job changes can have a double-barreled effect on outcomes: the direct impact of the newly-designed job, and the indirect or unintended (and often unexpected) effects on social relationships.[7]

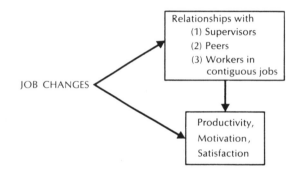

Figure 3.2—The Moderating Effects of Interpersonal Relationships on the Effects of Job Changes

Sometimes altered relationships reinforce and consolidate the direct effects of job changes; other times social relationship issues tend to counteract the direct effects of the job changes. In one project, for example, supervisor-subordinate relationships were unintentionally strained when employee jobs were enriched. This created considerable social tension in the organizational unit and, apparently, washed out any increases in motivation and satisfaction that might have resulted from the improvements made in the job (Lawler, Hackman, and Kaufman, 1973).

---

7. Research has shown that changes in jobs often affect the relationships of job incumbents with members of three other groups: (1) supervisors (for example, Alderfer, 1969b; Lawler, Hackman, and Kaufman, 1973); (2) peers whose jobs also are affected by the change (for example, Conant and Kilbridge, 1965; Rice, 1958); and even (3) workers whose jobs are not affected by the change but who can observe it (for example, Bishop and Hill, 1971; Strauss, 1955).

Based on reports and observations of similar phenomena, Reif and Luthans (1972) conclude that job enrichment often forces workers to "trade in" opportunities for social interaction to obtain in return a more interesting job. They suggest that many workers will find this trade unacceptable and therefore will resist job enrichment programs. To the extent that workers' social need strengths are stronger than their needs for personal growth and development, such a conclusion would seem warranted.

Yet we should not be too quick to assume that there is a necessary trade-off between how enriched a job is and the amount of opportunity the job provides for meaningful social contact and interaction. The reports of Trist et al. (1963) on job changes among British coal miners are instructive on this point. Initially coal miners worked together in small groups in which there was high interdependency and high cohesiveness among members, both on and off the job. A technological innovation required that jobs be changed, and as part of the change existing groups were recomposed into larger work units of forty to fifty men. Members of these new groups were under a single supervisor, but they often were widely separated from one another while working, and individuals were now identified primarily in terms of their particular work functions. As a result of the change, workers reported increased feelings of indifference to and alienation from their work, and productivity declined sharply. The changes in jobs apparently disrupted social relationships and led to unfortunate consequences for both the organization and the people.

But the story does not end there. The researchers identified some groups where the technological innovation was being used, but without apparent disruption of the groups. The jobs of these miners had been changed, but they had been redefined in terms of a total group task (that is, getting the coal out of the mine) rather than in terms of functional specialties. Moreover, members of these work groups became competent to perform a number of different functions necessary for the overall mining task, and the groups took responsibility for deploying men to different tasks and shifts. Finally, group members were paid on the basis of group (rather than individual) work performance (Trist et al., 1963). Both work productivity and employee satisfaction for these groups were more than adequate. Thus, although the technological innovation (and accompanying job changes) were initially disruptive to the existing satisfying relationships for all workers, in some groups ways were found to develop, within the constraints of that innovation, a new social structure that preserved the interpersonal ties that were of great importance to these employees.

The conclusion, then, is that job changes do sometimes disrupt on-the-job relationships in ways that are dysfunctional for both the organization and the worker, but that it may be possible to reconstruct relationship patterns so that important social ties among workers are preserved or strengthened. In practice, it sometimes may be advisable to plan and install changes in group and interpersonal relationships simultaneously with (or perhaps even prior to) changes in the work. Other times it will be better to start with changes in the work, and then undertake modification of group structures later when the need to do so has become fully apparent. But whatever the strategy for managing them, it is clear that social and interpersonal issues *do* affect the outcomes of job changes. And it is also clear that careful attention to the social consequences of changes in jobs is warranted for all work redesign programs, even those that are intended only to affect the jobs of individuals.

Organizational Climate and Style

The overall climate and style characteristic of an organization can best be summarized by using the distinction drawn by Burns and Stalker (1961) between *mechanistic* and *organic* systems. Mechanistic systems are relatively "tall" and operate in accord with the principles of classical Weberian bureaucracy. Power and authority are centralized at the top of the hierarchy, with rules and procedures clearly defined and enforced. Organic systems tend to be relatively "flat," and managers are encouraged to operate their units in any way that serves the overall goals of the organization. Thus, the particular tasks and people present in an organizational unit may dictate a way of operating that is not consistent with the operation of other organizational units.

Some types of jobs may be more tenable in a mechanistic system; others may be more appropriate for an organic system. Consider, for example, enriched jobs that provide employees with considerable discretion and autonomy in their work. Such jobs might be very difficult to install and maintain in mechanistic organizations, because decision-making and planning are clearly the prerogatives of management in such systems and consistency and regularity of employee behavior is highly valued. In organic systems, job enrichment might be expected to flourish. Such organizations should have the capability to design jobs in a variety of ways throughout the system without introducing organizational chaos. Moreover, they should be better able than mechanistic organizations to adjust job designs to individual needs and abilities on a temporary or permanent basis.

The above predictions about the interdependencies between job design and organizational climate and style are inherently plausible. But they do not tell the whole story because they ignore the role of

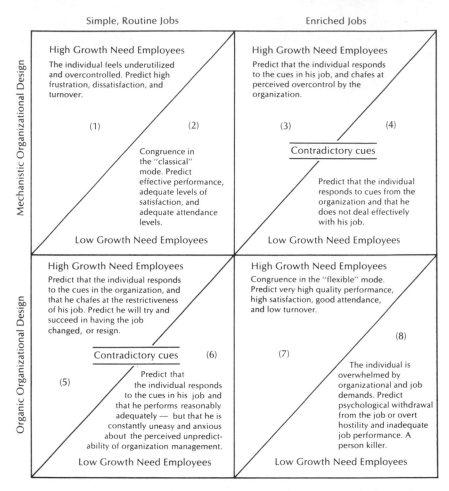

Figure 3.3 – Predicted Relationships among Organizational Climate, Job Design, and Employee Needs

employee need states (particularly growth need strength) in determining when there will be a good fit between the person and the work. A summary table showing how all three classes of variables interact in determining employee productivity and satisfaction has been proposed by Porter, Lawler, and Hackman (1975) and is reproduced in Figure 3.3. The figure specifies the personal and work outcomes that are expected from all possible combinations of (1) organizational climate and style (organic versus mechanistic systems), (2) job design (enriched versus simple work), and (3) employees' growth need strength (high versus low). Two of the cells in the figure reflect general congruence between the person and the work: Cell 2 (mechanistic system, simple, and routine jobs, low growth need employees) and Cell 7 (organic system, enriched jobs, and high growth need employees). For these two cells, generally adequate performance and satisfaction are predicted, although expectations are higher for Cell 7 than for Cell 2. Cells 1 and 8 are opposites: in Cell 1 individuals with high growth needs are faced with an entirely constraining situation in both the job and the organization; in Cell 8 individuals with low growth needs are faced with a wide-open set of opportunities that they would, in all probability, have no idea how to deal with. Thus, it is predicted that individuals in Cell 1 will feel underutilized, frustrated, and dissatisfied and probably will leave the organization; individuals in Cell 8 would be likely to feel overwhelmed by organizational and job demands and might have substantial difficulty adapting to the work situation.

Cells 3 through 6 are characterized by contradictory messages: the job provides one set of cues to the employee, and the organization provides another. While Porter, Lawler, and Hackman propose (see Figure 3.3) that for these cells individuals will tend to respond positively to the cues that are consistent with their own need states (and to ignore cues that are inconsistent with their needs), a recent study by Zierden (1975) casts doubt on that hypothesis and raises an alternative possibility.

Zierden examined the three-way interactions specified in Figure 3.3 as they affected the satisfaction of workers in two organizations. Measures of the degree to which jobs were enriched, and of the growth need strength of employees, were taken from the Job Diagnostic Survey (Hackman and Oldham, 1975, described in more detail later in this chapter). A measure of management style (adapted from Likert, 1967) was used as a surrogate for the degree to which the work environment of employees tended toward the organic model. Zierden confirmed the predictions of Porter, Lawler, and Hackman for all cells involving employees with strong growth needs (Cells 1, 3, 5, and 7). Specifically, satisfaction was high, as predicted, in Cell 7 (high growth need, organic style, enriched job); and satisfaction was relatively low, in Cells 1, 3, and 5 (where the job, the organization, or both were incongruent with the person's needs).

The prediction for Cell 2 (low growth needs, mechanistic style, simple job) received some support. Although employees in that cell were not particularly happy with the work, neither were they strikingly dissatisfied with it. Zierden interprets the moderate to low level of satisfaction observed as indicating that people in this cell were "resigned to their lot."

Of special interest are Zierden's findings for Cells 4, 6, and 8, where low growth need employees are faced with an enriched job, an organic organizational environment, or both. Porter, Lawler, and

Hackman predicted basically *negative* outcomes for these cells, but Zierden found that the satisfaction of employees in these cells ranged from moderate to very high. He explains the results by hypothesizing that the measure of growth need strength taps not only desire for growth opportunities in one's work, but also (and confounded with desire) the level of *expectation* people have about what can be obtained from their work. Thus, in Zierden's conception, low growth need employees have generally low expectations about the amount of satisfaction they will be able to obtain from their work. In Cells 4, 6, and 8, then, the employee's expectations are disconfirmed in a positive direction (in Cell 4 by a better job than expected, in Cell 6 by a more positive style than expected, and in Cell 8 by both). This happy disconfirmation of expectations, Zierden suggests, leads to high levels of measured job satisfaction.[8]

In sum, the findings reported by Zierden offer considerable support for the notion that the climate and style of the organization moderate the impact of enriched versus simple job designs. Moreover, his findings reinforce the proposition that individual need strength also must be considered for full understanding and accurate predictions of how people react to their work.

Technology

Following Blauner (1964, p. 6), technology can be defined as "the complex of physical objects and technical operations (both manual and machine) regularly employed in turning out the goods and services" of an organization. Technology can have at least two important, though indirect, effects on the person-work relationship.

First, the technology of an organization affects the type of organizational structure that evolves (Woodward, 1958). To the extent that organizational structure in turn affects patterns of interpersonal relationships and the overall climate of the organization, technology can be viewed as indirectly determining what types of jobs will and will not be appropriate and viable for various organizational contexts.

Second, technology can have a considerable impact on what types of job designs are *possible* for an organization. Sometimes the technology is such that any change in work design large enough to be meaningful is simply not feasible. For example, organizations that have huge investments in stationary equipment for which there is little

---

8. Among high growth need individuals—that is, those in Cells 1, 3, and 5—employees' *high* expectations are disconfirmed, by a less good job (Cell 5), a less organic style (Cell 3), or both (Cell 1). In these cases, disconfirmation is an unpleasant discovery and leads to low job satisfaction—which happens for those cells to parallel the predictions made by Porter, Lawler, and Hackman (1975).

operational flexibility may find it impossible to meaningfully change the jobs of machine operators. (That work design considerations might have been brought into the picture when the technology was designed is an issue of considerable significance but, unfortunately, not one that much can be done about after the equipment is in place.)

In other situations technology will provide little or no constraint on the options available to an organization about how the work can be designed. Service organizations (both public and profit-making), for example, often have substantial freedom of choice about how jobs are designed and how groups of jobs are related. Not surprisingly, it turns out that a large proportion of the successful job enrichment projects described in the research literature were conducted in service organizations.

In still other types of organizations the options for work design are neither wide open (as in the service organization example) nor completely predetermined (as in the stationary equipment example). Instead, the technology serves to render some types of work design relatively feasible and easy to install and other types very difficult to install. Anderson (1970), for example, reviewed job enrichment studies conducted for four types of technologies (service, heavy assembly, electronics, and processing) and found that what job changes were made—and how they were carried out—was dependent in important ways on which technology was involved. Friedlander and Brown (1974) reach a similar conclusion. For illustration, they point out that in a continuous process technology it may be nearly impossible to design jobs with high task identity. Increases in autonomy and feedback, on the other hand, may be more readily introduced into such jobs than would be the case for a technology involving heavy assembly work (see also Alderfer, 1969b).

As will be discussed later in the chapter, one of the most important decisions that must be made in any work redesign project is the choice between designing the work for individual employees and designing it for interacting groups. Aside from any difference in the intrinsic merits of work designed for individuals and work designed for teams, sometimes the technology is such that the *only* realistic way to enrich the work of employees is to develop teams of workers and provide the teams with substantial responsibility for a relatively large portion of the work. In some processing and heavy assembly operations, for example, technological constraints (coupled with the physical limitations of humans) make it impossible to pull together enough segments of the work to generate a genuinely meaningful job for an individual working alone.

Predicting the impact of jobs on the people who do them is not an altogether straightforward matter. Those who would argue that enriched jobs are better (or worse) for people and for productivity than are traditionally-designed jobs will be correct only sometimes. It depends on the characteristics of the people involved, on their patterns of social relationships, on the overall climate and managerial style of the organization, and on the technology of which the jobs are a part.

It also should be emphasized, however, that the matter is *not* so complex as to make situation-appropriate redesign of work impossible. Although the conditioning factors reviewed above can be powerful determinants of the outcomes of job redesign activities, no complex fourfold chart of these effects is required to sensitively plan for work redesign. Instead, simply asking the question "How would this fit with the people, with their interpersonal relationships, and with the climate and technology of the organization as a whole?" often will suffice to raise a warning flag in a given instance. When incongruencies do seem likely, then those responsible for installing the changes will be able to decide ahead of time whether developmental work is required to prepare the people and the organization for the planned job changes, or whether the job changes should be revised to increase their congruence with the existing organizational system.

Moreover, some diagnostic techniques and some principles for enriching jobs are now available that can help ensure that plans for work redesign are consistent with existing theory and experience about the characteristics of well-designed work. In the pages to follow, we examine some of these devices. First a model for guiding the redesign of work for individuals is proposed; then approaches to work redesign for interacting teams are discussed; and finally some common problems and opportunities that arise in the actual process of installing work design changes are reviewed.

DESIGNING WORK FOR INDIVIDUALS

A model specifying how job characteristics and individual differences interact to affect the satisfaction, motivation, and productivity of individuals at work has been proposed by Hackman and Oldham (in press). The model is specifically intended for use in planning and carrying out changes in the design of jobs. It is described below and then is used as a guide for discussion of diagnostic procedures and change principles that can be used in redesigning the jobs of individuals.

The Job Characteristics Model

The basic job characteristics model is shown in Figure 3.4. As illustrated in the figure, five core job dimensions are seen as creating

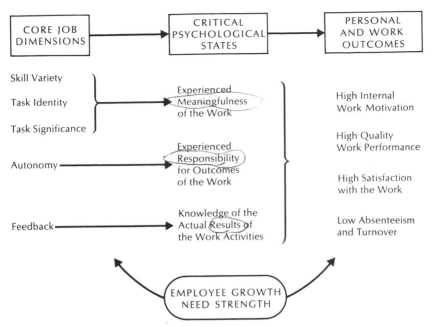

Figure 3.4–The Job Characteristics Model of Work Motivation

three critical psychological states that, in turn, lead to a number of beneficial personal and work outcomes. The links among the job dimensions, the psychological states, and the outcomes are shown to be moderated by individual growth need strength. The major classes of variables in the model are reviewed briefly below.

Psychological States. The three following psychological states are postulated as critical in affecting a person's motivation and satisfaction on the job:

1. Experienced meaningfulness: The person must experience the work as generally important, valuable, and worthwhile.
2. Experienced responsibility: The individual must feel personally responsible and accountable for the results of the work he performs.
3. Knowledge of results: The individual must have an understanding, on a fairly regular basis, of how effectively he is performing the job.

The more these three conditions are present, the more people will feel good about themselves when they perform well. Or, following Hackman and Lawler (1971), the model postulates that internal rewards are obtained by an individual when he *learns* (knowledge of results) that he *personally* (experienced responsibility) has performed well on a task that he *cares about* (experienced meaningfulness). These internal rewards are reinforcing to the individual and serve as incentives for continued efforts to perform well in the future. When the person does not perform well, he does not experience reinforcement, and he may elect to try harder in the future so as to regain the rewards that good performance brings. The net result is a self-perpetuating cycle of positive work motivation powered by self-generated rewards. This cycle is predicted to continue until one or more of the three psychological states is no longer present, or until the individual no longer values the internal rewards that derive from good performance.

Job Dimensions. Of the five job characteristics shown in Figure 3.4 as fostering the emergence of the psychological states, three contribute to the experienced meaningfulness of the work, and one each contributes to experienced responsibility and to knowledge of results.

The three job dimensions that contribute to a job's *meaningfulness* are skill variety, task identity, and task significance.

> Skill variety—the degree to which a job requires a variety of different activities that involve the use of a number of different skills and talents.

When a task requires a person to engage in activities that challenge or stretch his skills and abilities, that task almost invariably is experienced as meaningful by the individual. Many parlor games, puzzles, and recreational activities, for example, achieve much of their fascination because they tap and test intellectual or motor skills. When a job draws on several skills of an employee, that individual may find the job to be of very high personal meaning even if, in any absolute sense, it is not of great significance or importance.

> Task identity—the degree to which the job requires completion of a whole and identifiable piece of work—that is, doing a job from beginning to end with a visible outcome.

If an employee assembles a complete product or provides a complete unit of service, he should find the work more meaningful than if he were responsible for only a small part of the whole job, other things (such as skill variety) being equal.

> Task significance—the degree to which the job has a substantial impact on the lives or work of other people, whether in the immediate organization or in the external environment.

When an individual understands that the results of his work may have a significant effect on the well-being of other people, the experienced meaningfulness of the work usually is enhanced. Employees who tighten nuts on aircraft brake assemblies, for example, are much more likely to perceive their work as meaningful than are workers who fill small boxes with paper clips—even though the skill levels involved may be comparable.

The job characteristic predicted to prompt employee feelings of personal *responsibility* for the work outcomes is autonomy, which is defined as follows: PROMOTES RESPONSIBILITY

> Autonomy—the degree to which the job provides substantial freedom, independence, and discretion to the individual in scheduling the work and in determining the procedures to be used in carrying it out.

To the extent that autonomy is high, work outcomes will be viewed by workers as depending substantially on their *own* efforts, initiatives, and decisions, rather than on the adequacy of instructions from the boss or on a manual of job procedures. In such circumstances, individuals should feel strong personal responsibility for the successes and failures that occur on the job.

The job characteristic that fosters *knowledge of results* is feedback, which is defined as follows: REDUCES ABSENTEEISM + T.O.

> Feedback—the degree to which carrying out the work activities required by the job results in the individual obtaining direct and clear information about the effectiveness of his performance.

It often is useful to combine the scores of a job on the five dimensions described above into a single index reflecting the overall potential of the job to prompt self-generated work motivation in job incumbents. Following the model diagrammed in Figure 3.4, a job high in motivating potential must be high on at least one (and hopefully more) of the three dimensions that lead to experienced meaningfulness, *and* high on autonomy and feedback as well. The presence of these dimensions creates conditions for all three of the critical psychological states to be present. Arithmetically, scores of jobs on the five dimensions are combined as follows to meet this criterion:

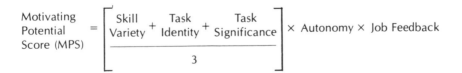

$$\text{Motivating Potential Score (MPS)} = \left[\frac{\text{Skill Variety} + \text{Task Identity} + \text{Task Significance}}{3} \right] \times \text{Autonomy} \times \text{Job Feedback}$$

As can be seen from the formula, a near-zero score of a job on either autonomy or feedback will reduce the overall MPS to near-zero; a near-zero score on one of the three job dimensions that contribute to experienced meaningfulness cannot, by itself, do so.

Individual Growth Need Strength. Growth need strength is postulated to moderate how people react to complex, challenging work at two points in the model shown in Figure 3.4: first at the link between the objective job dimensions and the psychological states, and again between the psychological states and the outcome variables. The first link means that high growth need individuals are more likely (or better able) to *experience* the psychological states when their objective job is enriched than are their low growth need counterparts. The second link means that individuals with high growth need strength will respond more positively to the psychological states, when they are present, than will low growth need individuals.

Outcome Variables. Also shown in Figure 3.4 are several outcomes that are affected by the level of self-generated motivation experienced by people at work. Of special interest as an outcome variable is internal work motivation (Lawler and Hall, 1970; Hackman and Lawler, 1971). This variable taps directly the contingency between effective performance and self-administered affective rewards. Typical questionnaire items measuring internal work motivation include: (1) "I feel a great sense of personal satisfaction when I do this job well"; (2) "I feel bad and unhappy when I discover that I have performed poorly on this job"; and (3) "My own feelings are *not* affected much one way or the other by how well I do on this job" (reversed scoring).

Other outcomes listed in Figure 3.4 are the quality of work performance, job satisfaction (especially satisfaction with opportunities for personal growth and development on the job), absenteeism, and turnover. All of these outcomes are predicted to be affected positively by a job high in motivating potential.

Validity of the Job Characteristics Model

Empirical test of the job characteristics model of work motivation is reported in detail elsewhere (Hackman and Oldham, in press). In general, results are supportive, as suggested by the following overview:

1. People who work on jobs high on the core job characteristics are more motivated, satisfied, and productive than are people who work on jobs that score low on these characteristics. The same is true for absenteeism, although less strongly so.

2. Responses to jobs high in objective motivating potential are more positive for people who have strong needs for growth than for people with weak growth needs. The moderating effect of individual growth need strength occurs both at the link between the job dimensions and the psychological states and at the link between the psychological states and the outcome measures, as shown in Figure 3.4. (This moderating effect is not, however, obtained for absenteeism.)

3. The job characteristics operate *through* the psychological states in influencing the outcome variables, as predicted by the model, rather than influencing the outcomes directly. Two anomalies have been identified, however: (a) results involving the feedback dimension are in some situations less strong than results obtained for the other dimensions (perhaps in part because individuals receive feedback at work from many sources—not just the job), and (b) the linkage between autonomy and experienced responsibility does not operate exactly as specified by the model in affecting the outcome variables (Hackman and Oldham, in press).

Diagnostic Use of the Model

The job characteristics model was designed so that each major class of variables (objective job characteristics, mediating psychological states, individual growth need strength, work motivation, and satisfaction) can be directly measured in actual work situations. Such measurements are obtained using the Job Diagnostic Survey (JDS), which is described in detail in Hackman and Oldham (1975). The major intended uses of the JDS are (1) to diagnose existing jobs prior to planned work redesign, and (2) to evaluate the effects of work redesign activities—for example, to determine which job dimensions did and did not change, to assess the impact of the changes on the motivation and satisfaction of employees, and to test for any possible postchange alterations in the growth need strength of people whose jobs were redesigned.

In the paragraphs that follow, several steps are presented that might be followed by a change agent in carrying out a diagnosis using the JDS.

Step 1. Are motivation and satisfaction really problematic?   Sometimes organizations undertake job enrichment or work redesign to improve the work motivation and satisfaction of employees when the real problem with work performance lies elsewhere—for example, in the equipment or technology of the job. It is important, therefore, to examine the scores of employees on the motivation and satisfaction portions of the JDS at an early stage in a job diagnosis. If motivation and satisfaction are problematic, and are accompanied by documented problems in work performance, absenteeism, or turnover as revealed by independent organizational indices, the change agent would continue to Step 2. If not, he presumably would look to other aspects of the work situation (for example, the technology, or the workflow) to identify and understand the reasons for the problem that provoked diagnostic activity.

Step 2. Is the job low in motivating potential? To answer this question, the change agent would examine the Motivating Potential Score of the target job, and compare it to the MPS scores of other jobs to determine whether the *job* is a probable cause of the motivational problems documented in Step 1. If the job turns out to be low on MPS, he would continue to Step 3; if it scores high, he would look for other reasons for the motivational difficulties (for example, the pay plan, or the nature of supervision).

Step 3. What specific aspects of the job are causing the difficulty? This step involves examination of the job on each of the five core job dimensions, to pinpoint the specific strengths and weaknesses of the job as it currently exists. It is useful at this stage to construct a profile of the target job, to make visually apparent where improvements need to be made. An illustrative profile for two jobs (one "good" job and one job that needs improvement) is shown in Figure 3.5.

Job A is an engineering maintenance job and is high on all of the core dimensions; the MPS of this job is a very high 260.[9] Job enrichment would not be recommended for this job; if employees working on the job are unproductive and unhappy, the reasons probably have little to do with the design of the work.

Job B, on the other hand, has many problems. This job involves the routine and repetitive processing of checks in a bank. The MPS is 30, which is quite low, and would be even lower if not for the moderately high task significance of the job. (Task significance is moderately high because workers are handling large amounts of other people's money, and therefore their efforts potentially have important consequences for the unseen clients.) The job provides the individuals with very little direct feedback about how effectively they are performing; the employees have little autonomy in how they go about doing the job; and the job is moderately low in both skill variety and task identity.

Job B, then, certainly could be improved, and there are many avenues to consider in planning job changes. For other jobs, the avenues for change may turn out to be considerably more specific. For example, feedback and autonomy may be reasonably high, but one or more of the core dimensions that contribute to the experienced meaningfulness of the work (skill variety, task identity, and task significance) may be low. In such a situation, attention would turn to ways to increase the standing of the job on these latter three dimensions.

Step 4. How ready are the employees for change? Once it has been documented that there is need for improvement in a particular job, and

---

9. MPS scores can range from 1 to 343, and average about 125.

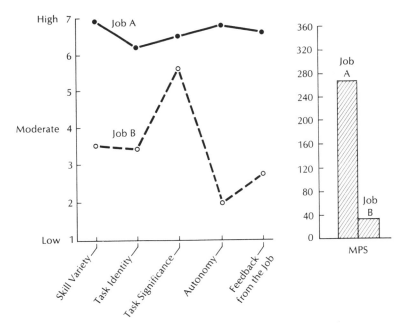

Figure 3.5–JDS Profile of a "Good" and a "Bad" Job

the especially troublesome aspects of the job have been identified, it is appropriate to begin planning the specific action steps that will be taken to enrich the job. An important factor in such planning is determining the growth need strength of the employees. Employees high on growth need strength should respond more readily to job enrichment than employees with weak needs for growth. The measure of employee growth need strength provided by the JDS can be helpful in identifying which employees should be among the first to have their jobs changed (those with high growth need strength), and how such changes should be introduced (perhaps with more caution for individuals with weak needs for growth).

Step 5. What special problems and opportunities are present in the existing work system?
Before undertaking actual job changes, it always is advisable to search for any special roadblocks that may exist in the organizational unit as it currently exists, and for special opportunities that may be built on in the change program.

Frequently of special importance is the level of *satisfaction* employees currently experience with various aspects of their organizational life. For example, the JDS provides measures of satisfaction with pay, job security, co-workers, and supervision. If the diagnosis reveals high dissatisfaction in one or more of these areas, then it may be very difficult to initiate and maintain a successful job redesign project

(Oldham, in press, a; Oldham, Hackman, and Pearce, 1975). On the other hand, if satisfaction with supervision is especially high, then it might be wise to build an especially central role for supervisors in the initiation and management of the change process.

Other examples could be given as well. The point is simply that such supplementary measures (especially those having to do with aspects of employee satisfaction) may be helpful in highlighting special problems and opportunities that deserve explicit recognition and attention as part of the diagnosis of an existing work system.

Principles for Enriching Jobs

The core job dimensions specified in the job characteristics model are tied directly to a set of action principles for redesigning jobs (Hackman, Oldham, Janson, and Purdy, 1975; Walters and Associates, 1975). As shown in Figure 3.6, these principles specify what types of changes in jobs are most likely to lead to improvements in each of the five core job dimensions, and thus to an increase in the motivating potential of the job as a whole.

Principle #1: Forming natural work units. A critical step in the design of any job is the decision about how the work is to be distributed among the people who do it. Numerous considerations affect that decision, such as technological constraints, level of worker training and experience, efficiency from an industrial or systems engineering perspective, and equity of individual work loads. Work designed on the basis of these factors usually is distributed among employees rationally and logically. The problem is that the logic used often does not include the needs of employees for personally meaningful work.

Consider, for example, a typing pool consisting of one supervisor and ten typists who do all the typing for one division of an organiza-

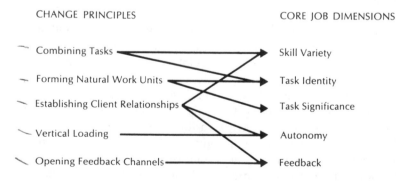

Figure 3.6—Principles for Changing Jobs

tion. Jobs are delivered in rough draft or dictated form to the supervisor, who distributes them as evenly as possible among the typists. In such circumstances the individual letters, reports, and other tasks performed by a given typist in one day or week are randomly assigned. There is no basis for identifying with the work or with the person or department for whom it is performed, or for placing any personal value on it.

By contrast, creating natural units of work increases employee "ownership" of the work and improves the chances that employees will view their work as meaningful and important rather than as irrelevant and boring. In creating natural units of work, one must first identify the basic work items. In the typing pool example, that might be "pages to be typed." Then these items are grouped into natural and meaningful categories. For example, each typist might be assigned continuing responsibility for all work requested by a single department or by several smaller departments. Instead of typing one section of a large report, the individual will type the entire piece of work, with knowledge of exactly what the total outcome of the work is. Furthermore, over time the typist will develop a growing sense of how the work affects co-workers or customers who receive the completed product. Thus, as shown in Figure 3.6, forming natural units of work increases two of the core dimensions that contribute to experienced meaningfulness—task identity and task significance.

Because it is still important that work be distributed so that the system as a whole operates efficiently, work loads must be arranged so that they are divided equitably. The principle of natural work units simply requires that these traditional criteria be supplemented so that, as far as possible, the tasks that arrive at an employee's work station form an identifiable and meaningful whole.

Principle #2: Combining tasks. The very existence of a pool made up entirely of persons whose sole function is typing reflects a fractionalization of jobs that sometimes can lead to such hidden costs as high absenteeism and turnover and extra supervisory time. The principle of combining tasks is based on the assumption that such costs often can be reduced by taking existing and fractionalized tasks and putting them back together again to form a new and larger module of work. At the Medfield, Massachusetts plant of Corning Glass Works, for example, the job of assembling laboratory hot plates was redesigned by combining a number of tasks that had been separate. After the change, each hot plate was assembled from start to finish by one operator, instead of going through several separate operations performed by different people.

Combining tasks (like forming natural work units) contributes in two ways to the experienced meaningfulness of the work. First, task identity is increased. The hot plate assembler, for example, can see and identify with a finished product ready for shipment, rather than with a nearly invisible junction of solder. Moreover, as more tasks are combined into a single worker's job, the individual must use a greater variety of skills in performing the job, further increasing the meaningfulness of the work.

Principle #3: Establishing client relationships.   Jobs designed according to traditional criteria often provide workers with little or no contact with the ultimate user of their product or service. As a consequence, workers may have difficulty generating high commitment and motivation to do the job well.

By establishing direct relationships between workers and their clients, jobs often can be improved in three ways. First, feedback increases because additional opportunities are created for the employees to receive direct praise or criticism of their work outputs. Second, skill variety may increase, because of the need to develop and exercise one's interpersonal skills in managing and maintaining the relationship with the client. Finally, autonomy will increase to the degree that individuals are given real personal responsibility for deciding how to manage their relationships with the people who receive the outputs of their work.

Creating client relationships can be viewed as a three-step process: (1) identifying who the client actually is; (2) establishing the most direct contact possible between the worker and the client; and (3) establishing criteria and procedures so that the client can judge the quality of the product or service received and relay his judgments directly to the worker. Especially important (and, in many cases, difficult to achieve) is identification of the specific criteria by which the work output is assessed by the client, and ensuring that both the worker and the client understand these criteria and agree with them.

Principle #4: Vertical loading.   In vertical loading, the intent is to partially close the gap between the "doing" and the "controlling" aspects of the job. Thus, when a job is vertically loaded, responsibilities and controls that formerly were reserved for management are given to the employee as part of the job. Among ways this might be achieved are the following:

— giving job incumbents responsibility for deciding on work methods and for advising or helping to train less experienced workers;
— providing increased freedom in time management, including decisions about when to start and stop work, when to take breaks, and how to assign work priorities;

— encouraging workers to do their own troubleshooting and to manage work crises, rather than calling immediately for a supervisor;

— providing workers with increased knowledge of the financial aspects of the job and the organization, and increased control over budgetary matters that affect their work.

Vertically loading a job inevitably increases autonomy. And, as shown in Figure 3.4, this should lead to increased feelings of personal responsibility and accountability for the work outcomes.

Principle #5: Opening feedback channels.   In virtually all jobs there are ways to open channels of feedback to individuals, to help them learn not only how well they are performing their jobs but also whether their performance is improving, deteriorating, or remaining at a constant level. Although there are various sources from which information about performance can come, it usually is advantageous for a worker to learn about his performance *directly as he does the job* — rather than from management on an occasional basis.

Job-provided feedback is more immediate and private than supervisor-supplied feedback, and it increases workers' feelings of personal control over their work. Moreover, it avoids many of the potentially disruptive interpersonal problems that can develop when a worker can find out how he is doing only from direct messages or subtle cues from the boss.

Exactly what should be done to open channels for job-provided feedback varies from job to job and from organization to organization. Often the changes involve simply removing existing blocks that isolate the individual from naturally occurring data about performance, rather than generating entirely new feedback mechanisms. For example:

—Establishing direct client relationships (discussed above) often removes blocks between the worker and natural external sources of data about the work.

—Quality control efforts often eliminate a natural source of feedback, because all quality checks are done by people other than the individuals responsible for the work. In such situations, any feedback that workers do receive may be belated and diluted. Placing most quality control functions in the hands of workers will dramatically increase the quantity and quality of data available to them about their performances.

—Tradition and established procedure in many organizations dictate that records about performance be kept by a supervisor and transmitted up (not down) the organizational hierarchy. Sometimes supervisors even check the work and correct any errors themselves. The worker who made the error never knows it occurred and is therefore denied the very information that could enhance both internal work motivation and the technical adequacy of his performance. In many cases, it is possible to provide standard summaries of performance records directly to the workers. This would give the employees personally and regularly the data they need to improve their effectiveness.

—Computers and other automated machines sometimes can be used to provide individuals with data now blocked from them. Many clerical operations, for example, are now performed on computer consoles. These consoles often can be programmed to provide the clerk with immediate feedback in the form of a CRT display or a printout indicating that an error has been made. Some systems even have been programmed to provide the operator with a positive feedback message when a period of error-free performance has been sustained.

The principles for redesigning jobs reviewed above, although illustrative of the kinds of changes that can be made to improve the jobs of individuals in organizations, obviously are not exhaustive. They were selected for attention here because of the links (Figure 3.6) between the principles and the core job dimensions in the motivational model presented earlier. Other principles for enriching jobs (which, although often similar to those presented here, derive from alternative conceptual frameworks) are presented by Ford (1969), Glaser (1975), Herzberg (1974), and Katzell and Yankelovich (1975).

DESIGNING WORK FOR TEAMS

Often it is easier or more appropriate—given the nature of the work and the organizational circumstances under which it is to be done—to design work for interacting teams rather than for individuals working alone. In such situations, the ultimate aim generally is similar to that sought when individual job enrichment is carried out. That is, the goal is to increase the quality of the work experience of the people involved, and simultaneously to increase the quality and quantity of the work produced. The difference is that the work is defined and implemented as a *group* task, rather than as an interconnected set of individual tasks. Because of this, a larger chunk of work can be included within the boundaries of the task, thereby increasing the intrinsic meaningfulness of the work. Moreover, the possibility is increased for the development of close, socially satisfying work relationships among team members. Such relationships are highly valued by many people, but difficult or impossible to achieve via redesign of individual jobs in some work settings. An example is the assembly line, where individual work stations are fixed and may be so widely separated that meaningful social interaction with others is, for all practical purposes, precluded.

Until relatively recently, most work design for teams has been carried out from the perspective of sociotechnical systems theory, and has involved the creation of autonomous or semiautonomous work groups. Specific arrangements—for example, how the group task is designed, the size and composition of the work group, and the nature of the reward system—have varied from project to project, but the following attributes are characteristic of most autonomous work groups:[10]

1. The group is assigned a whole task, in which the mission of the group is sufficiently identifiable and significant that members find the work of the group meaningful.
2. Workers in the group each have a number of the skills required for completion of the group task, and so the flexibility of the group in carrying out the task is increased. When individuals do not have a robust repertoire of skills initially, procedures are developed to encourage cross-training among members.
3. The group is given autonomy to make decisions about the methods by which the work is carried out, the scheduling of various activities, the assignment of different individuals to different tasks, and (sometimes) the selection of new group members.
4. Compensation is based on the performance of the group as a whole, rather than on the contributions of individual group members.

It should be emphasized that these four statements are simply summaries of the kinds of changes that often are made when work is redesigned for interacting teams. They do not represent the only way to design work for groups, nor are these ingredients necessarily the most appropriate ones for any given instance. Therefore, it may be useful to step back from specific change principles and attempt to identify the major *general* criteria for the design of work for teams— and then to explore alternative strategies for attempting to achieve those criteria.

Design Criteria for Interacting Work Groups

The two criteria listed below appear to be the minimum requirements for the design of interacting work teams if high team productivity and member satisfaction are to be achieved simultaneously.

1. The team should be a cohesive group, in which members feel committed to the goals of the group, and in which they can experience significant personal satisfaction through their interactions with teammates.

---

10. See, for example, Bucklow (1966), Davis (1966, p. 44), Davis and Trist (1974), Gulowsen (1972, pp. 375–378), and Trist et al. (1963, Ch. 9).

As Sayles (1958) has pointed out, there are many types of work groups within organizations—and by no means are the members of all of them able to work together in concerted fashion to achieve mutual goals. Moreover, just because an individual is in a work group does not imply that he will find the experience socially or personally satisfying; groups can be a source of anxiety and stress as readily as they can serve as a comfortable social home for members.

In a highly cohesive group, members greatly value the rewards (usually interpersonal) that fellow members can provide. This means that the quality of the social experience of members in cohesive groups is likely to be high rather than low. It also means that cohesive groups usually have considerable leverage in enforcing member compliance with group norms. That is, because members of cohesive groups strongly value the rewards controlled by their peers, they are especially likely to engage in behavior that is congruent with group norms. Failure of a group member to do so can result in those rewards being made unavailable (that is, in his being "frozen out") or can lead other group members to negatively sanction his actions (Hackman, 1976).

The problem is that, although cohesive groups have been shown to generate high uniformity of member behavior vis-à-vis group norms, the *direction* of those norms is unrelated to the level of cohesiveness of the group (Berkowitz, 1954; Schachter et al., 1951; Seashore, 1954). Sometimes highly cohesive groups enforce a norm of low performance; other times they encourage and support member efforts toward high performance. Relatively little is known about what factors determine whether group norms will encourage high or low performance (Lawler and Cammann, 1972; Vroom, 1969). It is necessary, therefore, to propose the following additional criterion for the design of work teams in organizations.

2. The environment of the work group, including its task, must be such that the group norms that emerge and are enforced are consistent with the twin aims of high productivity and satisfying interpersonal relationships.

Approaches to Work Design for Interacting Groups

Meeting the two design criteria identified above requires, at a minimum, attention to (1) the composition and dynamics of the group, (2) reward contingencies in the organizational environment, and (3) the structure of the group task.

Design and Maintenance of the Group Qua Group. Numerous issues related to the design of effective groups in organizations are addressed by Alderfer (Chapter 5), and therefore are not treated in detail here. There are, however, two issues that merit special attention in regard to the design of work for groups.

First, it is important that members of an interacting work team be able to experience themselves as part of a group that is *psychologically meaningful* to them. Usually this requires that the group be moderately small (usually fewer than fifteen members, although apparently successful autonomous work groups of larger size have been reported), and that members occupy a single workplace, or at least contiguous workplaces with easy access to one another. Calling a set of people a group for reasons other than the nature of their relationships with each other (for example, a set of flight attendants who have the same supervisor but who literally fly all over the country and rarely see one another) does not meet the conditions for creation of an effective work team.

Second, although reasonably close and meaningful interpersonal relationships can be important to the success of interacting work teams, group process interventions (for example, team-building) that focus *exclusively* on relationships among group members or on the social climate of the group as a whole should be used with caution. Direct interpersonal interventions can be quite powerful in altering social behavior in a group. For this reason, process interventions may be useful in increasing the capability and willingness of members to share with one another special skills that are needed for work on the group task. Yet research evidence also shows that when such interventions are used alone, the group's task effectiveness rarely is enhanced (and often suffers) as a result (cf. Deep, Bass, and Vaughan, 1967; Hall and Williams, 1966; Hackman and Morris, 1975; Hellebrandt and Stinson, 1971; Kaplan, 1973; Wagner, 1964). Thus, although process interventions can be of great use as part of a broader intervention package aimed at creating effective work teams, total reliance on such interventions appears inappropriate if the goal is to work toward simultaneous improvement of the social experience of the members *and* their collective task productivity.

Design of Environmental Contingencies. The way the organizational environment of the group is arranged can affect whether it is in the best interest of group members to work together effectively and, indeed, whether it is *possible* for them to do so. Especially important are the compensation system and the role of the first-line supervisor. (See Lawler, Chapter 4, and Strauss, Chapter 6, for more extended treatments of compensation and supervision.)

In almost every case in which autonomous work groups have been successfully created in organizations, pay systems have been arranged so that the pay of group members was contingent on the performance of the group as a whole, rather than on the performance of individual employees. Use of a group-based compensation system increases the chances that internal cooperation and cohesiveness will increase as members work together to obtain the group-level rewards. Moreover, dysfunctional group interaction that grows from the fear (or the fact) of pay inequities among members should diminish when compensation is tied directly to the output of the group as a whole. It should be noted, however, that simply moving to a group-level compensation system does *not* eliminate the possibility of suboptimal productivity norms. When group members mistrust management, for example, norms enforcing low productivity may emerge to protect the group against possible changes of performance standards by management. Thus, although group-level compensation plans play an important part in the design of work for interacting teams, they in no way guarantee high group productivity.

Also critical to the design of work for teams is the new role that first-line supervisors play under such arrangements. In many applications, the supervisor moves from having day-to-day (even minute-to-minute) responsibility for the work behavior and productivity of individual employees to a role that primarily involves managing the *boundaries* of the group—not what goes on within those boundaries (Taylor, 1971). Thus, the supervisor assists the group in liaison with other groups and may serve as the advocate of the group in discussions with higher management, but he leaves to the group routine decision-making about the work and about management of work crises. Under such conditions, group members should experience substantially more ownership of their work activities and output, thereby creating the conditions required for members to experience collective responsibility for and commitment to their shared task.

Design of the Group Task.   Perhaps most important in determining whether a group develops a norm of high or low productivity is the quality of the experience group members have as they work together on the group task. For example, if members find the task activities frustrating and unpleasant, they are likely over time to notice similar adverse reactions in others—and perhaps to begin sharing these reactions verbally. Gradually, group members may come to an implicit or explicit agreement that the best way to minimize the unpleasantness they experience in task work is to minimize the energy they invest in doing the task. If, on the other hand, members find work on the task exciting, fulfilling, or otherwise rewarding, these experiences are likely to be shared and a norm of high effort may be the result.

The implication, then, is that redesigning the group task may be a more powerful strategy for improving member motivation and group productivity than attacking directly group norms about productivity. To do the latter, often, would be to address the symptoms rather than the problem.

What task characteristics are most likely to generate high group commitment to effective performance? As a start, the five core dimensions used in the job characteristics model of individual work motivation would seem useful (that is, skill variety, task identity, task significance, autonomy, and feedback). Such dimensions could be applied to analysis of group tasks as readily as they are to individual tasks. Moreover, because a group can undertake a much larger piece of work than an individual, the intrinsic meaningfulness of many group tasks can exceed substantially the best possible design for individuals doing the same work. There is no way, for example, that an individual can manufacture an automobile; a group can, and with considerable positive effect on the skill variety and task identity of the jobs of group members (cf. Walton, 1975b).

If group tasks were designed to be high on the five core job dimensions, then an increase in task-relevant motivation of group members would be expected. And, over time, group norms about productivity should become consistent with the increased motivation of individual group members. Yet such positive outcomes should come about only if (1) the individual group members identify with and feel commitment to the group as a whole (it is, after all, a *group* task), and (2) the internal process of the group facilitates and reinforces (rather than impairs) concerted action toward shared group goals. The core job dimensions have little to offer toward the creation of these two conditions. How, for example, could a group task be designed so that all members see it as providing high autonomy—and therefore experience substantial *personal* responsibility—for the outcomes of the *group*? Moreover, given that it is now well documented that how group tasks are designed affects not only the motivation of group members but also the patterns of social interaction that develop among them (Hackman and Morris, 1975), how can group tasks be structured so that they prompt task-effective rather than dysfunctional member interaction?

Such questions have no simple answers. And although task design per se potentially can contribute to their solution, the issues raised are affected as well by the environmental contingencies that are operative, and by the design and composition of the group. Thus, once again it must be concluded that no single approach can create an effective design for work to be done by interacting teams. Instead, such a goal requires simultaneous use of a number of different handles for change. Some of these have to do with the group, some with the task, and some with the broader organizational context.

Group Versus Individual Task Design: Which When?

Choices about designing work for individuals or for groups are complex, and often depend on factors idiosyncratic to a given situation. In general, however, a group-based design seems indicated when one or more of the following conditions is present:

1. The product, service, or technology is such that meaningful individual work is not realistically possible (for example, when a large piece of heavy equipment is being produced). In such situations it often is possible for a group to take autonomous responsibility for an entire product or service, while the only possible job design for individuals would involve small segments of the work.

2. The technology or physical work setting is such that high interdependence among workers is required (cf., the concept "technically required cooperation" proposed by Meissner, 1969). Susman (1970) has suggested that one effect of increased automation (especially in continuous process production) is to increase interdependence among workers. The creation of autonomous work groups under such circumstances would seem to be a rather natural extension of the imperatives of the technology. When, on the other hand, there are no required interdependencies (for example, telephone installers who operate their own trucks, coordinating only with a foreman or dispatcher), then there would seem to be no real basis on which meaningful work teams could be formed, and enrichment of individual jobs might be a better alternative.

3. Individuals have high social need strength, and there is a significant probability that the enrichment of individual jobs would break up existing groups of workers that provide social satisfactions to their members. In such situations, designing work for teams would capitalize on the needs of employees, whereas individual-oriented job enrichment might require that individuals give up important social satisfactions to obtain a better job (Reif and Luthans, 1972).

4. The overall motivating potential of employees' jobs would be expected to be *considerably* higher if the work were arranged as a group task rather than as a set of individual tasks. Probably in most situations the standing of a job on the core dimensions would increase if the job were designed as a group task, simply because a larger piece of work can be done by a group than by an individual. This should not, however, automatically tilt the decision toward group work design, because of the numerous interpersonal factors that must be attended to in effectively designing work for interacting groups. Sometimes the risk or design-effort required to deal with such factors may make it more appropriate to opt for individual task design, even

though a group task might be expected to be somewhat better *as a task* than would be any of the individual tasks.

Cautions in Designing Work for Groups

In concluding this section, three caveats about the design of work for groups are suggested:

1. Existing evidence suggests that the work must provide group members with *substantial* autonomy if group members are to experience high responsibility for it. Just as pseudoparticipation in organizations may be worse than no participation at all, so it is that autonomous work groups should not be formed unless there is reasonable assurance that the result will not be a potentially frustrating state of pseudoautonomy. This, of course, requires careful attention to issues of management and supervision, to ensure that managers are both willing and able to provide the group with sufficient real autonomy to carry out the proposed group task (cf. Gulowsen, 1972). (The same, of course, is true for the design of autonomous individual tasks.)

2. The need states of employees who will make up the groups must be carefully attended to, because work in interacting teams on a complex task will not be satisfying or motivating to all people. Optimally, group members should be rather high on *both* social and growth need strength. If the social needs of group members are high but their growth needs are low, then there is risk that the group members will use the group solely as a source of social satisfaction. Even if the task is very high in objective motivating potential, members might find the group so much more involving than the task that productivity would suffer. When, on the other hand, members are high in growth need strength but low in social needs, then it might be better to consider designing the work for individuals, technology permitting. If employees are low on *both* social and growth need strength, then prospects for creating teams in which members work together effectively and productively on a challenging task would appear very dim.

3. Finally, it should be noted that virtually all of the above discussion has focused on characteristics of groups and of tasks that are likely to generate high *motivation* to perform the task effectively. For some group tasks, the level of motivation (or effort) of group members is not critical to the success of the group; instead, performance effectiveness varies with the level of knowledge and skill of the members or with the task performance strategies utilized by the group. In such circumstances, the attributes of the group, the task, and the environment that would be required for high group performance would be quite different than those proposed here (cf. Hackman and Morris, 1975).

GUIDELINES FOR INSTALLING
PLANNED CHANGES IN JOBS

We move now to exploration of issues that arise in the actual installation of changes in the design of work. The material presented below is based on observations and interviews conducted by the author and his associates over the past three years in numerous organizations where work redesign activities were being planned, implemented, or evaluated.

In general, we have found job enrichment to be failing at least as often as it is succeeding. And the reasons for the failures, in many cases, appear to have more to do with the way planned changes are *implemented* in organizations than with the intrinsic merit of the changes. Again and again we have seen good ideas about the redesign of work die because the advocates of change were unable to gain acceptance for their ideas or because unexpected roadblocks led to early termination of the change project.[11]

Our findings are summarized below as six prescriptive guides for implementing changes in jobs. Each guide includes a discussion of pitfalls that frequently are encountered in work redesign projects, as well as ingredients that were common to many of the more successful projects we observed.[12]

Guide 1: Diagnose the Work System Prior to Change

It now is clear that work redesign is not effective in all organizational circumstances. Yet rarely is a systematic diagnosis carried out beforehand to determine whether meaningful change is feasible, given the jobs being considered, the people who will be involved, and the social, organizational, or cultural environment in which the work is performed. As a result, faulty initial assumptions often go uncorrected, and the change project may be doomed before it is begun.

The choice of the job to be changed, for example, often seems to be almost random. Perhaps a manager will decide that a given job seems right for enrichment. Or he will settle on a job because it is peripheral to the major work done in the organization—thereby

---

11. In interpreting the observations reported here it is important to understand that we have *not* researched the "superstar" change projects, such as the Topeka plant of General Foods or the Kalmar plant of Volvo. Instead, we have focused on regular organizations, struggling as best they could with the resources they had to reap the purported benefits of job enrichment. For a more detailed analysis of what goes wrong in attempts to install work redesign in such organizations, see Hackman (1975b).

12. Other commentaries on the process of installing changes in jobs, which have much in common with the observations summarized here, include Chapter 7 of this book, Beer (1976), Ford (1971), Glaser (1975), Katzell and Yankelovich (1975, Ch. 6), and Sirota and Wolfson (1972a, 1972b).

minimizing the risk of severe disruption if something should go wrong. Or a job will be selected because *everything* seems wrong with it—the work is not getting done on time or correctly, employees are angry about everything from their pay to the cleanliness of the restrooms, grievances are excessive, and so on. The hope, apparently, is that somehow redesigning the job will fix everything all at once.

Yet it must be recognized that some jobs, given existing technological constraints, are about as good as they ever can be. Work redesign in such situations is at best a waste of time. Other jobs have so much wrong with them that is irrelevant to how enriched they are that job enrichment could not conceivably bring about a noticeable improvement—and instead might add even more complexity to an already chaotic situation. When such matters are overlooked in planning for work redesign, the result often is a change effort that fails simply because it is aimed at an inappropriate target.[13]

Similarly, differences in employee readiness to handle contemplated changes in jobs only infrequently are assessed before a project is installed. Line managers often express doubts that employees can handle proposed new responsibilities or skepticism that employees will enjoy working on an enriched job. Sometimes, as planning for work redesign proceeds, managers become convinced of the contrary. But only rarely are change projects designed with full cognizance that employees are likely to *differ* in their psychological readiness for enriched work.

Even less frequently is explicit assessment made of the readiness of managers to deal with the kinds of problems that inevitably arise when a major organizational change is made. In one case, the management team responsible for a job enrichment project nearly collapsed when the first serious change-related problem emerged. Time and energy that were needed for the project were spent instead working on intrateam issues that had been flushed out by the problem. And another "job enrichment failure" occurred while the managers talked and talked. An adequate diagnosis of the readiness of the management team for change-management would have increased the likelihood that the problematic intrateam issues would have been dealt with *before* the work redesign activities were initiated.

The commitment of middle and top management to job enrichment also rarely received diagnostic attention in the organizations we observed. Whether organizational change activities must begin at the top—or whether work redesign is a strategy for change that can spread from the bottom up—remains an important and unresolved question

---

13. A set of diagnostic clues for identifying jobs that may be particularly good candidates for enrichment is provided by Whitsett (1975).

(Beer and Huse, 1972). It is almost always true, however, that middle and top management can terminate a project they find unsatisfactory, whether for good reasons or on a whim. In one case, a high-level executive agreed to serve as sponsor for a project without really understanding what the changes would involve. When difficulties in implementation developed, the executive concluded that he had been misled—and the project found itself out from under its protective umbrella and in serious organizational jeopardy. In another case, a single vice-president was counted on to protect a fledgling project from meddling by others who favored alternative approaches to organizational change. When the vice-president departed the organization to attend a several-month executive development program, his temporary replacement terminated job enrichment activities and substituted a training program more to his own liking. In both cases, an early assessment of the attitudes of key top managers would have revealed the need to develop a broader and better informed base of high-level support for the projects.

A number of organizations we studied did conduct diagnoses of the work system before changes were installed. Almost invariably these studies identified problems or issues that required attention prior to the beginning of the job changes. Such diagnoses are not easy to make. They involve the raising of anxieties at a time when most participants in a project are instead seeking comfort and assurance that everything will turn out all right. Moreover, the tools and methodologies required for undertaking such diagnoses only now are beginning to become available (cf. Hackman and Oldham, 1975; Jenkins, Nadler, Lawler, and Cammann, 1975; Sirota and Wolfson, 1972b). Our observations suggest, however, that the diagnostic task may be one of the most crucial in a work redesign project.

Guide 2: Keep the Focus on the Work Itself

Redesigning a job often appears seductively simple. In practice, it is a rather challenging undertaking. It requires a good deal *more* energy than most other organizational development activities, such as attitude improvement programs, training courses, and objective-setting practices (Ford, 1971).

There are many reasons why it is so hard to alter jobs. At the purely bureaucratic level, the entire personnel-and-job-description apparatus often must be engaged to get the changes approved, documented, and implemented. If the organization is unionized, the planned changes often must be negotiated beforehand—sometimes a formidable task. Simple inertia often tempts managers to add lots of window dressing to make things appear different, rather than actually to change what people do on their jobs. Finally, when even one job in an organization is changed, many of the interfaces between that job and related ones must be dealt with as well. In even moderately complex work systems, this is no small matter.

Because of these and other forces against change, work redesign projects frequently are carried out that have very little impact on the work itself. A project carried out in the stock transfer department of a large bank is illustrative (Frank and Hackman, in press). At the end of the project the informal word among managers was, "We tried job enrichment and it failed." But our research data (which measured the objective characteristics of jobs before and after the change) showed that, although all manner of things did change as part of the job enrichment project, the work itself was not among them. Our correlational analyses of data collected in that organization showed that there were very positive relationships between the amount of skill variety, autonomy, and feedback in various jobs and the satisfaction, motivation, performance, and attendance of the job incumbents. These across-job relationships were present prior to the change project, and they were there afterwards. But it was also true that those people who held the "good" jobs before the change also held them afterward, and those people whose jobs originally were routine, repetitive, and virtually without feedback had essentially identical jobs after the work was "redesigned." Workers had been formed into small groups, supervision had been changed, names of jobs and work units had been altered, and a general stirring about had taken place. But the *jobs* were not changed much, and the effect (after about six months) was a slight deterioration in worker satisfaction and motivation. This deterioration, apparently, was due more to the failure of the project to live up to expectations than to the changes that had actually taken place.

It is easy, apparently, for those responsible for work redesign activities to delude themselves about what is actually being altered in such projects, and thereby to avoid the rather difficult task of actually changing the structure of the work people do. One way of ensuring that a project stays focused on the work is to base change activities firmly on a theory of work design. Several such theories were reviewed earlier in this chapter (activation theory, motivation-hygiene theory, job characteristics theory, sociotechnical systems theory), and others are discussed by Glaser (1975).

No doubt some theories are better than others. Our observations suggest, however, that the specific details of various theories may not be as important as the fact that *some* theory is used to guide the implementation of change. In addition to keeping the changes focused on the original objective of restructuring the work, a good theory can help identify the kinds of data needed to plan and evaluate the changes and can alert implementors to special problems and opportunities that may develop as the project unfolds.

The theory must, however, be *appropriate* for the changes that are contemplated. Therein lies one of the major difficulties of the stock transfer project described above. The project originally was designed on the basis of motivation-hygiene theory, which deals exclusively with the enrichment of jobs performed by individuals. The changes that actually were made, however, involved the creation of enriched *group* tasks. Because the theory did not address the special problems of designing work for groups (how to create conditions that encourage members to share with one another their special task-relevant skills), those responsible for implementation found the theory of limited use as a guide for planning and installing the changes. Gradually the theory dropped from their attention. Without the benefit of theory-specified guidelines for change, the project became increasingly diffuse and eventually addressed many issues that had little or nothing to do with the work. All this is not to imply that these other issues were unrelated to the change or were improper. However, they cannot be made as substitutes for changes in the work itself.

Guide 3: Prepare Ahead of Time for Unexpected Problems

When substantial changes are made in jobs, shock waves may be created that reverberate throughout adjacent parts of the organization. If insufficient attention is given to such spin-off effects of job changes, they may backfire and create problems that negate (or even reverse) expected positive outcomes.

The site of the backfire varies from case to case. In one company, employees who prepared customer accounts for computer processing were given increased autonomy in scheduling their work and in determining their own work pace. This resulted in a less predictable schedule of data input to the computer system. Because the data processing department had not been involved in the project until the changes were already made, serious computer delays were encountered while data processing managers struggled to figure out how to respond to the new and irregular flow of work. The net result was an increase in antagonism between computer operations and the employees whose jobs had been enriched—and a decrease in the promptness of customer service.

In another company work was redesigned to give rank-and-file employees a number of responsibilities that previously had been handled by their supervisors. The employees (who dealt with customers of the company by telephone) were given greater opportunities for personal initiative and discretion in dealing with customers, and initially seemed to be prospering in their new responsibilities. But later observations revealed a deterioration in morale, especially in the area of supervisor-subordinate relationships. Apparently the supervisors had found themselves with little work to do after the change (because the employees were handling much of what the supervisors had done before). When supervisors turned to higher management for instructions, they were told to "develop your people—that's what a manager's job is." The supervisors had little idea what "developing your people" involved, and many of them implemented that instruction by looking over the employees' shoulders and correcting each error they could find. Resentment between the supervisor and the employee groups soon developed, and more than overcame any positive benefits that had accrued from the changes in the job (Lawler, Hackman, and Kaufman, 1973).

Problems such as those described above often can be avoided by developing contingency plans ahead of time to deal with the inevitable spin-off problems that crop up whenever jobs are changed. Such plans can be advantageous in at least two ways. First, employees, managers, and consultants all will share an awareness that problems are likely to emerge elsewhere in the work system as the change project develops. This simple understanding may help keep surprise and dismay at manageable levels when the problems do appear, and so may decrease the opportunity for people to conclude prematurely that "the project failed."

Second, preplanning for possible problems can lead to an objective increase in the readiness of all parties to deal with those problems that do emerge. Having a few contingency plans filed away can increase the chances that change-related problems will be dealt with before they get out of hand—and before they create a significant drain on the energy and morale needed to keep the change project afloat.

Not all contingency plans can be worked out in detail beforehand. Indeed, they probably should not be. Until a project is underway one cannot know for sure what the specific nature of the most pressing needs and problems will be. But one can be *ready* to deal with common problems that may appear. For example, the training department can be alerted that some training may be required if managers find themselves in difficulty supervising the employees after the work is redesigned. And those responsible for the reward system can be asked to engage in some contingency planning on the chance that the new work system may require nontraditional compensation arrangements. One does not *begin* with these matters. But one is well advised to anticipate that some of them will arise, and to be prepared to deal with them when and if they do.

Guide 4: Evaluate Continuously

When managers or consultants are asked whether a work redesign project has been evaluated, the answer nearly always is affirmative. But when one asks to see the evaluation, the response frequently is something like "Well, let me tell you . . . only one week after we did the actual job changes this guy who had been on the lathe for fifteen years came up to me, and he said . . ." Such anecdotes are interesting, but they provide little help to managers and union officials as they consider whether work redesign is something that should be experimented with further and possibly diffused throughout the organization. Nor is it the stuff of which generalizable behavioral science knowledge is made.

Sometimes hard data are pointed to, such as financial savings resulting from reductions in personnel in the unit where the work redesign took place. Such data can validly document an improvement in worker productivity, but they are of little value in understanding the full richness of what has happened, or why. And, of great importance in unionized organizations, they are hardly the kind of data that will engage the enthusiasm of the bargaining unit for broader application of work redesign.

There are many good reasons why adequate evaluations of work redesign projects are not done—not having the capability to translate human gains into dollars and cents, not being able to separate out the influence of the job changes on measured productivity and unit profitability from the many other factors that influence these outcomes, having an organization-wide accounting system that cannot provide data on the costs of absenteeism, turnover, training, and extra supervisory time, not really trusting measures of job satisfaction, and so on.

These reasons can be convincing, at least until one asks what was done to try to *overcome* the problems and gets as a response "Well, we really didn't think we could get the accountants to help out, so . . ." And one is left with several unhappy hypotheses: (1) nobody knows *how* to do a decent evaluation—nor how to get help in doing one; or (2) management does not consider systematic evaluation an essential part of the change activity; or (3) the desire of the people responsible for the program to have it appear successful is so strong that they cannot afford the risk of an explicit evaluation.

In a retailing organization, for example, job enrichment was sold to top management by a single individual. And soon the program came to be known throughout the organization as "Joe's program." Joe, understandably, developed a considerable personal interest in managing the image of the program within the organization. When offered the chance for a systematic evaluation of the project to be conducted at no cost to the organization, Joe showed considerable initial hesitation, and finally declined the offer. Later discussions revealed that although he recognized the potential usefulness of the information he would gain from an outside evaluation, that benefit was more than countered by the risk of losing his *personal* control over the image of the project that eventually would emerge.

Because of the pressure on lower-level managers and consultants to make job enrichment programs at least *appear* successful, it often is necessary for top management or union leaders to insist that serious and systematic evaluations of such programs take place. For such evaluations to be valid and useful, management must attempt to create an organizational climate in which the evaluation is viewed as an occasion for *learning*—rather than as an event useful mainly for assessing the performance and competence of those who actually installed the changes.

Such a stance permits interim disappointments and problems to be used as times for reconsideration and revision of the change project, rather than as a cause for disillusionment and abandonment. And it encourages those responsible for managing the change to learn as they go how most effectively to design, install, and manage enriched jobs. This is a matter of considerable importance, because there is no neat package for redesigning work in organizations and there probably never will be.

Taking a learning orientation to work redesign is, however, a costly proposition. It is expensive to collect trustworthy data for use in monitoring a project throughout its life, and to experiment actively with different ways of changing jobs. It is painful to learn from failure, and to try again. Yet such costs may actually be among the better investments an organization contemplating work redesign can make. Paying such costs may be the only realistic way for the organization to develop the considerable knowledge and expertise it will need to reap the full benefits of work redesign as a strategy for change.

Guide 5: Confront the Difficult Problems Early

Individuals responsible for work redesign projects often find it tempting to get the project sold to management and union leadership, and only then to begin negotiations on the difficult problems that must be solved before the project can actually be carried out. This seems entirely reasonable. If such problems are raised *before* the project is agreed to, the chances are increased that it will never get off the ground. It appears, nevertheless, that in the long run it may be wiser to risk not doing a project for which the tough issues cannot be resolved beforehand than to do one under circumstances that require compromise after compromise to keep the project alive after it has begun.

Vigilance by those responsible for the change is required to ensure that the tough issues are not swept under the rug when the project is being considered. Among such issues (that too often are reserved for later discussion) are:

— The nature and extent of the commitment of management and union leaders, including the circumstances under which a decision may be made to terminate the project. It is especially important to make sure that both management and union leadership realize that problems will emerge in the early stages of a project, and that a good deal of energy may be required to protect and nurture the project during such down phases.
— The criteria against which the project ultimately will be evaluated and the means by which the evaluation will be done, including measures that will be used. Given that there are serious measurement difficulties in assessing any work redesign project, it is important to make sure that all parties, including management and union sponsors, are aware of these difficulties and are committed at the outset to the evaluation methodology.
— The way that learnings gained in the project (whether they are "successful tactics we discovered" or "roadblocks we unexpectedly encountered") will be made available to people who can use them as guides for future action, in the same or in other organizations.

Guide 6: Design Change Processes That Fit with Change Objectives

Most work redesign projects provide employees with increased opportunities for autonomy and self-direction in carrying out the work of the organization. Employees are allowed to do their work with a minimum of interference, and they are assumed to have the competence and sense of responsibility to seek appropriate assistance when they need it. The problem is that far too often the process of *implementing* job enrichment is strikingly incongruent with that intended end state.

It appears unrealistic to expect that a more flexible, bottom-loaded work system can be created using implementation procedures that are relatively rigid and bureaucratic, and that operate strictly from the top down. Yet again and again we observed standard, traditional, organizational practices being used to install work redesign. More often than not employees were the last to know what was happening, and only rarely were they given any real opportunity to actively participate in and influence the changes. In many situations they were *never* told the reasons why the changes were being made.

What happens during the planning stages of a work redesign project is illustrative of such incongruence between means and ends. Typically, initial planning for work redesign (including decision-making about what jobs will be changed) is done privately by managers and consultants. Diagnostic work, if performed at all, is done using a plausible cover story—such as telling employees that they are being interviewed "as part of our regular program of surveying employee attitudes." (The rationale is that employee expectations about change should not be raised prematurely; the effect often is that suspicions are raised instead.) Eventually managers appear with a fully determined set of changes that are installed in traditional top-down fashion. If employees resist and mistrust the changes, managers are surprised and disappointed. As one said: "I don't understand why they did not respond more enthusiastically. Don't they realize how we are going to make their work a lot more involving and interesting?" Apparently he did not see the lack of congruence between the goals being aspired to and the means being used, between "what we want to achieve" and "how we're going to achieve it."

As an alternative approach, managers might choose to be public and participative in translating from theory through diagnosis to the actual steps taken to modify jobs. Such an approach could be advantageous for a number of reasons.

First, when diagnostic data are collected and discussed openly, everyone who will be affected by the changes has the chance to become involved in the redesign activities and knowledgeable about them, and so everyone is less threatened. In one organization, managers initially were very skeptical about employee participation in planning for job changes. After employees had become involved in the project, however, a number of managers commented favorably on the amount of energy employees contributed to the planning activities and on the constructive attitudes they exhibited.

Second, the quality of the diagnostic data may be improved. If employees know that changes in their own work will be made partly on the basis of their responses to the diagnostic instruments, they may try especially hard to provide valid and complete data.

Third, chances are increased that learnings will emerge from the project that can be used to develop better action principles of work redesign for future applications. The involvement of people from a diversity of organizational roles in diagnostic and change-planning activities should facilitate attempts to piece together a complete picture of the change project—including the reasons that various changes were tried, what went wrong (and what went right), and what might be done differently next time.

Fourth, expectations about change will be increased when employees are involved in diagnostic and change-planning processes. Rather than being something to be avoided, therefore, heightened employee expectations can serve as a positive force for change. For example, such expectations might counter the conservatism that inevitably creeps into changes planned and implemented downwards through several hierarchical levels in an organization.

Despite these potential advantages, it is not easy to carry off a fully participative work redesign project. Nor do openness and employee participation guarantee success. Indeed, some experienced commentators have argued explicitly *against* employee participation in planning job changes, because (1) participation may contaminate the change process with "human relations hygiene" (Herzberg, 1968), (2) employees are not viewed as competent to redesign their own jobs, or (3) job design is viewed solely as a management function (Ford, 1969).

Our observations of work redesign projects turned up few projects in which employee participation was actively used in the change process. And the ideas for change that employees proposed in these cases did focus mainly on the removal of roadblocks from the work and on the improvement of hygiene items. This is consistent with the predictions of Ford (1969) that employee suggestions usually deal more with the context of work than with its motivational core.

The circumstances under which employees participated in work redesign activities in these organizations, however, were far from optimal. Often employees simply were asked "What would you suggest?" and given little time to consider their responses. In no case were employees provided with education in the theory and strategy of job redesign before being asked for suggestions. And in all cases we studied, employees had no real part in the final decision-making about what changes actually would be made. They were contributors to the change process, but not partners in it.

To develop and utilize the *full* potential of employees as resources for change would be an exciting undertaking, and a major one. It could require teaching employees the basics of motivation theory, discussing with them state-of-the-art knowledge about the strategy and tactics of work redesign, and providing them with training and experience in planning and installing organizational innovations. Such an approach would be costly, perhaps too much so to be practical. But it would have the advantage of encouraging employees to become full collaborators in the redesign of their own work, thereby creating a *process* for improving jobs that is consistent with the ultimate *objectives* of the change. Moreover, and of special importance to the quality of work life in organizations, the approach would provide employees with greatly increased opportunities for furthering their own personal growth and development—and at the same time would significantly increase their value as human resources to the organization.

CONCLUSION: CHALLENGES FOR THE PRESENT

Work redesign is in its adolescence. If it is to survive and develop into a robust and widely used strategy for personal and organizational change, it must mature quickly. For this to happen, progress on the following issues seems imperative.

1. *Education about the theory and practice of work redesign must be taken more seriously than it is at present and must be made more widely available—particularly to members of organized labor.*

Work redesign is not a prepackaged innovation that can be simply plugged into an organization and forgotten about. Instead, it involves some rather basic alterations of traditional thought and practice about how to structure and manage work. Considerable skill and sophistication are required to successfully design, install, and maintain work redesign programs.

Unfortunately, personnel responsible for implementing work redesign often receive only minimal educational preparation before a project is begun in an organization. Such preparation often includes only a one- or two-day workshop offered by a consulting firm or a university, or a series of visits to other organizations where redesign projects already have been carried out. The result is that job changes often are planned and installed by people who are operating very near the limits of their own understanding and expertise. The quality and impact of the changes that are made often suffer as a consequence.

Moreover, the reservoir of talent available nationally for carrying out work redesign activities is, at the moment, insufficient to meet the opportunities for change that exist. Unless the pool of available talent is expanded soon (through more extensive and broadly available education in the theory and strategy of work redesign), numerous opportunities to initiate change will be lost, some forever, simply because the human resources needed to carry them out were not available when the time was right.

A particularly pressing educational task is to redress the imbalance in knowledge about work redesign (and other approaches to changing the quality of work life) held by managers and by union officials. Virtually all available resources for learning about the redesign of work (for example, courses in business schools, books and articles in management periodicals, advanced management seminars and conferences, and services offered by academic and private consultants) are more readily available to management and tend to deal with the goals and techniques of change from a managerial perspective. As a result, any misperceptions or stereotypes union leaders hold about work redesign (for example, that it is "a stopwatch in sheep's clothing") may persist uncorrected. When a work redesign project is undertaken in a unionized organization, such disparities in knowledge and in attitudes about the change strategy and its objectives may make real collaboration between union and management extraordinarily difficult (see Chapters 6 and 7).

2. *Better ways must be found to diffuse work redesign innovations throughout organizations.*

Usually work redesign projects are first tried at a single location in an organization. Then, if the trial is successful, programs are developed to spread the innovation throughout the organization, drawing on the learnings gained and expertise developed in the first project (Beer and Huse, 1972; Walters and Associates, 1975).

Unfortunately, only rarely does substantial diffusion take place, even when the trial project is markedly successful. Walton (1975a) studied eight organizations in which highly successful work design projects had been conducted, and found that significant diffusion occurred in only one of the eight. The factors identified by Walton as hindering the spread of a successful innovation within an organization are numerous and powerful. Clearly, devising new strategies for facilitating the diffusion of work design innovations is an undertaking as challenging as it is important.

Perhaps especially critical (and problematic) in the diffusion process is the role of the internal behavioral science consultant. In many organizations internal consultants have major responsibility both for shepherding an initial work redesign trial and, if it is successful, for spreading the learnings gained throughout the organization. Yet internal consultants often are not well-respected as professionals in their organizations (sometimes with justification, sometimes not). And often they are asked to take responsibility for the diffusion of innovation without having either the expertise or the resources they need to do so. Significant rethinking of the role of internal behavioral science consultants is required if conditions are to be created that enable people who hold that role to become more effective in helping organizations design and spread new work structures.

3. *Increased attention must be given to improving the jobs of first- and second-level managers.*

Relatively little research and few change programs have focused on the design of lower-level management jobs in organizations. These jobs deserve careful attention for at least two reasons. First, in many organizations the jobs of first- and second-level managers are as poorly designed as are those of the employees they supervise. Especially troublesome are built-in restrictions on the autonomy these managers have to carry out their work, and the limited amount of feedback they receive from their jobs. Yet in the rush to attend to jobs held by supposedly alienated rank-and-file workers, very real problems in the design of managerial jobs often are overlooked.

Second, the jobs of managers invariably are affected when their subordinates' jobs are improved. As noted earlier in this chapter, improvements in employee jobs sometimes are made directly at the expense of the managerial job. Decision-making responsibilities and special tasks that traditionally were reserved for management are given to the worker, and the job of the manager may be denuded to about the same extent that the jobs of the subordinates are improved.

If work redesign is to have a chance of diffusing throughout an organization, the jobs of lower-level managers must be improved simultaneously with (or shortly after) the enrichment of subordinate jobs. Otherwise, managers may become justifiably angry at the effects of work redesign on the quality of their own work experiences, with predictable effects on their willingness to participate in further work design activities. Moreover, if managers are to develop a style of supervising that supports rather than erodes the new responsibilities of subordinates whose work has been enriched, they will have to experiment a good deal with their own behavior at work. The constraints that traditionally are built into lower-level managerial jobs often diminish both the manager's motivation to undertake such experimentation and the degree to which it is objectively possible for him to do so.

4. *The role of labor unions in initiating and executing work redesign projects must be expanded and elaborated.*

The stance of organized labor toward work redesign presently is very unclear. Some reports characterize labor leaders as basically supportive of alterations in work that are aimed at improving both the quality of employee work experiences and organizational productivity; others describe union leaders as rather vehemently opposed to job enrichment and most other work design innovations (cf. Calame, 1973; Katzell and Yankelovich, 1975). Perhaps the most that can be said with confidence at present is that there are many labor leaders who have yet to make up their minds about the value of work redesign as a strategy for organizational change, and about how well work redesign fits with union objectives and with the needs of union members.

Also unclear is the role the local union should play when work redesign activities are undertaken in an organization. The most negative role, of course, is to resist the changes and to block them whenever possible; locals occasionally have taken this position in some organizations. But when unions *do* participate in work redesign projects, what should they do?

There are a number of options. For one, unions can take the initiative in suggesting that work redesign activities be carried out, rather than waiting for management to make the suggestion. By and large, unions have not exercised this option in this country—although it is not uncommon in some European countries. Another possibility is for unions and management jointly to "own" a work redesign project, sharing both formal sponsorship of the project and responsibility for seeing it through. This approach is being followed with apparent success in the quality of work experiments now being carried out under the sponsorship of the National Quality of Work Program (see Chapter 7). Finally, it is possible for the union, as an organization, to participate actively in work redesign projects even when the projects primarily are owned by management. Local unions, for example, could take responsibility for collecting diagnostic data prior to change and could share with management the tasks of interpreting the data and designing changes in jobs based on the diagnostic findings. Or the union could undertake to systematically evaluate the effects of changes in jobs on union members. At present, however, little is known about how best to structure union participation in such activities, or what the implications of participation might be either for union-management relations or for union-member relations.

Clearly, research on union involvement in work redesign is needed, and needed soon. The problem is that the people most appropriate to conduct such research are behavioral scientists who are knowledgeable about organizations and change processes. And thus far behavioral scientists, as a group, have been so dominantly oriented to the needs and objectives of management that gaining acceptance by organized labor—even for research on ways to enhance the effectiveness of union involvement in quality of work programs—may turn out to be problematic.

In sum, the challenge facing unions, management, and behavioral scientists in articulating and elaborating the role of unions in work redesign activities is a substantial one. But it also is a challenge that is worthy of considerable effort on the part of those who care about improving the quality of life in organizations. For without the active involvement of organized labor, it is doubtful that work redesign ever can evolve into a strategy for change that actively *develops*—not just utilizes—human resources in organizations.

CHAPTER 4
REWARD SYSTEMS

EDWARD E. LAWLER III
The University of Michigan

Organizations distribute a large number of rewards to their members every day. Pay, promotions, fringe benefits, and status symbols are perhaps the most apparent but certainly not all of the important rewards. Because these rewards are important, the ways they are distributed have profound effects on the quality of work life that employees experience as well as on the effectiveness of organizations.

Despite the importance of rewards in organizations, most of the writings concerned with quality of work life have tended to ignore or play down their impact. This is a serious oversight and one that needs to be corrected if organizations are to be designed in ways that provide a high quality of work life. One reason for this oversight may be the often-made assumption that there is a very simple and direct relationship between the amount of reward received and the quality of work life. If this view is accepted, then improving the quality of work life is simply a matter of giving everyone more rewards. The research that has been done, however, shows that this is too simple a view. Some rewards have been found to contribute more to a high quality of work life than others and problems of equity cannot be solved simply by giving more rewards. These findings will be reviewed later in this chapter when we focus on the characteristics of different rewards and on some of the approaches to reward system design that promise to increase both the quality of work life and organizational effectiveness.

But before specific rewards and reward practices are considered, it is necessary to review briefly what is known about the determinants of people's affective reactions to rewards, and about the impact of reward systems on organizational effectiveness.

REWARD SYSTEMS AND INDIVIDUAL SATISFACTION

A great deal of research has been done on what determines whether individuals will be satisfied with the rewards they receive from a situation. This research has shown that satisfaction is a complex reaction to a situation and is influenced by a number of factors. The research can be summarized in five conclusions:

1. *Satisfaction with a reward is a function of both how much is received and how much the individual feels should be received.* Most theories of satisfaction stress that people's feelings of satisfaction are determined by a comparison between what they receive and what they feel they *should* receive or *would like* to receive (Locke, 1969). When individuals receive less than they believe they should, they are dissatisfied; when they receive more than they believe they should, they tend to feel guilty and uncomfortable (Adams, 1965). Feelings of overreward seem to be easily reduced by individuals and therefore are very infrequent (surveys often show about 5 percent of an employee group feel overpaid). Feelings of overreward are usually reduced by individuals changing their perceptions of the situation. For example, they increase their perceptions of their worth, or their perceptions of the amount of pay deserved. Feelings of underreward are less easily reduced and often can be reduced only by an actual change in the objective situation—by higher pay or a new job.

2. *People's feelings of satisfaction are influenced by comparisons with what happens to others.* A great deal of research has shown that people's feelings are very much influenced by what happens to others like themselves (Patchen, 1961). People seem to compare what others do and what others receive with their own situations. These comparisons are made both inside and outside the organizations they work in, but are usually made with similar people. As a result of these comparisons, people reach conclusions about what rewards they should receive. When the overall comparison between their situations and those of others is favorable, people are satisfied. When the comparison is unfavorable, they are dissatisfied.

People consider such inputs as their education, training, seniority, job performance, and the nature of their jobs when they think about what their rewards should be. There are often substantial differences among people in which inputs they think should be most important in determining their rewards. Typically people believe that the inputs that they excel in should be weighed most heavily (Lawler, 1966). This, of course, means that it is very difficult to have everyone satisfied with their rewards, because people tend to make their comparisons based on what is most favorable to them. Individuals also tend to rate their inputs higher than do others. It has often been noted, for example, that average employees rate their job performances at the 80th percentile (Meyer, 1975). Given this and the fact that the average person cannot be rewarded at the 80th percentile, it is not surprising that many individuals often are dissatisfied with their rewards. Still, it is possible to influence how satisfied employees are by altering the total amount of rewards that are given and by altering how those rewards are distributed. Some distribution patterns clearly are seen as more equitable and satisfying, because they are more closely related to the inputs of individuals and therefore to what people feel they should receive.

It is because individuals make comparisons that people who receive less of a given reward often are more satisfied with the amount of the reward they receive than are those who receive more (Lawler, 1971). For example, people who are highly paid in comparison to others doing the same job often are more satisfied than are individuals who receive more (for a different job) but are poorly paid in comparison to others doing the same kind of job.

3. *Overall job satisfaction is influenced by how satisfied employees are with both the intrinsic and extrinsic rewards they receive from their jobs.* A number of writers have debated the issue of whether extrinsic rewards are more important than intrinsic rewards in determining job satisfaction. No study has yet been done that definitely establishes one as more important than the other. Most studies show that both are very important and have a substantial impact on overall satisfaction (Vroom, 1964). It seems quite clear, also, that extrinsic and intrinsic rewards are not directly substitutable for each other, because they satisfy different needs. To have all their needs satisfied, most individuals must receive both the intrinsic and the extrinsic rewards they desire and feel they deserve. This means, for example, that money will not make up for a boring, repetitive job, just as an interesting job will not make up for low pay.

4. *People differ widely in the rewards they desire and in how important the different rewards are to them.* Probably the most frequently and hotly debated topic related to the quality of work life concerns how important different rewards are to employees. One group of writers says money is the most important, while another group says interesting work is (*Work in America*, 1971). Both groups, of

course, are able to find examples to support their points of view, because for some people money is most important and for others job content is most important. People differ substantially and in meaningful ways in what is important to them. Some groups, because of their backgrounds and present situations, value extrinsic rewards more than do others. For example, one review gave the following description of a person who is likely to value pay highly: "The employee is a male, young (probably in his twenties); he has low self-assurance and high neuroticism; he comes from a small town or farm background; he belongs to few clubs and social groups, he owns his own home or aspires to own it and probably is a Republican and a Protestant" (Lawler, 1971). People with different personal and background characteristics, on the other hand, value an interesting job more highly.

The research on the importance of different rewards also quite clearly shows that the amount of reward a person has strongly influences the importance attached to it (Alderfer, 1969a). In the case of extrinsic rewards, for example, those individuals who have a small amount of a reward typically value it the most. It also appears that the importance individuals attach to rewards shifts as they acquire and lose quantities of different rewards. Some evidence suggests that minimal amounts of the rewards that are required to maintain a person's physical well-being and security are needed before other rewards become very important (cf. Cofer and Appley, 1964).

Overall, reward systems seem to have a greater influence on individuals' *satisfaction* with rewards than on the *importance* attached to those rewards (Lawler, 1971). Both satisfaction and importance can be influenced by the amount of rewards that organizations provide. But satisfaction seems to be much more susceptible to influence, because it is directly affected by reward levels. The importance of rewards, on the other hand, is influenced by things that are beyond the control of organizations (such as family background and the economic climate), as well as by satisfaction.

5. *Many extrinsic rewards are important and satisfying only because they lead to other rewards.* There is nothing inherently valuable about many of the things that people seek in organizations. They are important only because they lead to other things or because of their symbolic value. A particular kind of desk or office, for example, often is seen as a reward because it is indicative of power and status. Money is important only because it leads to other things that are attractive, such as food, job security, and status. If money were to stop leading to some or all of these things, it would decrease in importance (Vroom, 1964). Because extrinsic rewards typically lead to other rewards, they can satisfy *many* needs and thus remain important even when conditions change.

Necessary Reward System Properties

On the basis of what has been said so far about rewards and satisfaction, we can identify four important properties that any organizational reward system must have if it is to produce a high quality of
work life. First, the system must make enough rewards available so that
individuals' basic needs are satisfied. If these needs are not met,
employees will not be satisfied even if external comparisons are favorable. Fortunately in most work situations the employees' basic needs
are satisfied, often because of the requirements of federal legislation
and union contracts. It is often pointed out, however, that sometimes
these needs are not met, particularly the need for security. When the
need is not met, action to increase job security must be taken before a
high quality of work life will be present. Just meeting basic needs is not
enough.

Second, the reward levels in the organization must compare favorably with those in other organizations. Unless the reward levels compare favorably with what other organizations provide, individuals will
not be satisfied with their rewards because they will inevitably note
that they are not as well off as others.

Third, the rewards that are available must be distributed in a way
that is seen as equitable by the people in the organization. People
compare their own situations with those of others inside the organization. And they are likely to be dissatisfied if in their organization
people they perceive as less deserving receive more rewards, even
though they themselves are in a favorable position with respect to the
outside market. People have a sense of equity, which involves considerations of how much they receive in comparison to what others
around them receive, regardless of the absolute amount they receive or
their position in the outside market. To construct a reward system that
is high on internal (within organization) equity, it is necessary to base
that system on the perceptions of the people in the organization. As
will be emphasized later, the most direct way to take these perceptions
into account is to have people in the organization make the decisions
about how much different individuals will be rewarded.

Finally, the reward system must deal with organization members as
individuals. This means recognizing their individuality by giving them
the kinds of rewards they desire. This point is crucial because of the
large differences among people in what rewards they want. Unless
these differences are explicitly recognized, it is unlikely that a reward
system will be broad enough and flexible enough to encompass the
full range of individual differences.

In summary, because of the nature of people's reactions to reward
systems, a reward system must be built in a way that allows it to

provide four things: (1) enough rewards to fulfill basic needs, (2) equity with the external market, (3) equity within the organization, and (4) treatment of each member of the organization in terms of his or her individual needs.

REWARD SYSTEMS AND ORGANIZATIONAL EFFECTIVENESS

In looking at the role of rewards in organizations it is not enough to look only at their impact on the quality of work life. Consideration must also be given to the impact of rewards on organizational effectiveness. Indeed, the adoption of any reward system hinges partially on the impact it is expected to have on organizational effectiveness. A reward system that substantially reduces organizational effectiveness is not likely to be voluntarily adopted, no matter how much it contributes to a high quality of work life. Further, quality of work life and organizational effectiveness are closely tied together, because without some level of organizational effectiveness, there is no organization and no work life at all. Thus, the challenge is to find reward systems that contribute to *both* organizational effectiveness and a high quality of work life.

Organizations typically rely on reward systems to do four things that contribute to organizational effectiveness: (1) motivate employees to join the organization, (2) motivate employees to come to work, (3) motivate employees to perform effectively, and (4) reinforce the organizational structure by indicating the position of different individuals in the organization. The considerable amount of research that has been concerned with each of these functions of reward systems is summarized in the following four sections.

Reward Systems and Organizational Membership

There is a great deal of evidence which shows that the rewards an organization offers directly influence the decisions people make about whether to join an organization, as well as their decisions about when and if to quit (see Lawler, 1971, and Yoder, 1956, for reviews). All other things being equal, individuals tend to gravitate toward and remain in those organizations that give the most desirable rewards. This behavior seems to be explainable because high reward levels lead to high satisfaction. Many studies have found that turnover is strongly related to job satisfaction and somewhat less strongly related to satisfaction with the extrinsic rewards a person receives (Porter and Steers, 1973). Apparently this is true because individuals who are presently satisfied with their jobs expect to continue to be satisfied and as a result want to stay with the same organization.

The relationship between turnover and organizational effectiveness is not so simple. It is often assumed that the lower the turnover rate the more effective the organization is likely to be. This probably is a valid generalization, because turnover is expensive. Studies that have actually costed it out have found that it often costs an organization five or more times an employee's monthly salary to replace him (Macy and Mirvis, 1974). However, not all turnover is harmful to organizational effectiveness. Clearly organizations can afford to lose some individuals, and indeed may profit from losing them. Thus, turnover is a matter of both rate *and* who turns over.

The objective should be to design a reward system that is very effective at retaining the most valuable employees. To do this a reward system must distribute rewards in a way that will lead the better performers to feel satisfied when they compare their rewards with those received by individuals performing similar jobs in other organizations. The emphasis here is on *external* comparisons, because turnover means leaving an organization for a better situation elsewhere. One way to accomplish this, of course, is to reward everyone at a level that is above the reward levels in other organizations. However, this strategy has two drawbacks. In the case of some rewards (for example, money), it is very costly. And it can cause feelings of intraorganizational inequity, because the better performers are likely to feel inequitably treated when they are rewarded at the same level as poor performers in the same organization, even though they are fairly treated in terms of external comparisons. Faced with this situation the better performers may not quit, but they are likely to be dissatisfied, complain, look for internal transfers, and mistrust the organization.

What, then, is the best solution? It would seem to be to have competitive reward levels and to base rewards on performance. This should encourage the better performers to be satisfied and to stay with the organization. It is important to note, however, that not only must the better performers receive more rewards than the poor performers, but they also must receive *significantly* more rewards because they feel they deserve more (Porter and Lawler, 1968). Just rewarding them slightly more may do no more than make the better and poorer performers *equally* satisfied.

In summary, managing turnover means managing satisfaction. This depends on effectively relating rewards to performances, a task that is often difficult. When it cannot be done, about all an organization can do is to try to reward individuals at an above-average level. In situations where turnover is costly, this should be a cost effective strategy even if it involves giving out expensive rewards.

Organizational Effectiveness and Absenteeism

Absenteeism, like turnover, is expensive. Like its twin, tardiness, it leads to overstaffing. Another result is that untrained and inexperienced individuals do the jobs of those who are absent. Thus, it makes sense for organizations to adopt reward policies that minimize absenteeism. What kind of reward policies will do this? A great deal of research has shown that absenteeism and satisfaction are related. When the workplace is pleasant and satisfying, individuals come regularly; when it isn't, they don't. Basically, therefore, reward policies that make work a satisfying place to be and that tie rewards to attendance will reduce absenteeism.

Several studies (discussed later in detail) have shown that absenteeism can be reduced by tying pay bonuses and other rewards to attendance. This approach is costly, but sometimes it is less costly than absenteeism. It seems to be a particularly useful strategy in situations where both the work content and the working conditions are poor and do not lend themselves to meaningful improvements (see, for example, Hackman, Chapter 3). In situations where work content or conditions can be improved, such improvements are often the most effective and cost efficient way to deal with absenteeism. Thus, reward system policies are only one of several ways to influence absenteeism, but they are potentially effective if an organization is willing to tie important rewards to coming to work. In many ways this is easier to do than tying rewards to performance, because attendance is more measurable and visible.

Reward Systems and Motivation

When certain specifiable conditions exist, reward systems have been demonstrated to motivate performance (Lawler, 1971; Vroom, 1964; Whyte, 1955). What are those conditions? Important rewards must be perceived to be tied in a timely fashion to effective performance. Stated another way, research shows that organizations get the kind of behavior that is seen to lead to rewards employees value. In many ways this is a deceptively simple statement of the conditions that must exist if rewards are to motivate performance. It is deceptive in the sense that it suggests all an organization has to do is to actually relate pay and other frequently valued rewards to performance. Not only is this not the only thing an organization has to do, but it is very difficult to accomplish (Tosi, House, and Dunnette, 1972; Whyte, 1955). Tying rewards to performance requires a good measure of performance, the ability to identify which rewards are important to particular individuals, and the ability to control the amount of these rewards that an individual receives. None of these things are easy to accomplish in most organizational settings, a fact that has led some to conclude that it is not worth trying to relate rewards to performance (Meyer, 1975).

Organizations must not only tie important rewards to performance, but they must do so in a manner that will lead to employees' perceiving the relationship. This means that the connection between performance and rewards must be visible, and that a climate of trust and credibility must exist in the organization. The reason why visibility is necessary should be obvious; the importance of trust may be less so. The belief that performance will lead to rewards is essentially a prediction about the future. For individuals to make this kind of prediction they have to trust the system that is promising them the rewards. Unfortunately, it is not entirely clear how a climate of trust can be established. However, some research, discussed later, suggests that a high level of openness and the use of participation can contribute to trust.

Reward Systems and Organizational Structure

In all complex organizations there is division of labor. Organizations differ, however, in the degree to which members have unique, highly specialized jobs, and in the degree of hierarchical differentiation that exists (Galbraith, 1973; Lawrence and Lorsch, 1967; Lorsch and Morse, 1974; Perrow, 1967). Some organizations, for example, are characterized by relatively flat structures and only a few levels of management; others have many levels—often as many as twenty in very large organizations. Some organizations are broken up into many departments, each of which has a function; others as a matter of policy try to discourage a high level of functional specialization.

In any organization, reward systems can be used to reinforce the existing or desired structure, and to help it operate effectively. The military is perhaps the clearest example of an organization that uses the reward system very effectively to differentiate between people in different positions. Each rank in the military has different privileges; there are even separate officer clubs and housing areas on bases. The argument in favor of such differentiation is that it helps make the organization more effective, because it clearly establishes who has authority and makes it easier for subordinates to take orders because they come from the position rather than from the person. Thus, the whole use of rewards in military organizations is designed to be congruent with the reliance on steep, strict hierarchies with decision-making centered at the top.

At the other extreme are organizations that consciously try to give everyone the same fringe benefits, parking spaces, and offices, to diminish the distance between different organizational levels. The argument here is that the lack of differentiation among people in terms of rewards and symbols of office, when combined with a relatively flat organization structure, produces an organization that is highly participative, equalitarian, and flexible. The further argument is that large differences among people in a more participative organization are incongruent with this style of management and organization structure and would be counterproductive. This is an interesting argument but one lacking substantial research support. Nevertheless, as various reward system practices are considered, it is important to think about whether they lead to differential or similar treatment of organization members who are at different management levels.

REWARD SYSTEM REQUIREMENTS

Table 4.1 summarizes what has been said so far about what a reward system must do if it is to contribute to organizational effectiveness and the quality of work life. Although there is not perfect agreement between the reward system characteristics that lead to a high quality of work life and those that lead to organizational effectiveness, there is a high degree of overlap. Rewards that are seen to be fair in terms of both internal and external comparisons are functional for both, because they lead to high satisfaction, low absenteeism, and low turn-

Table 4.1–Overview of Reward System Requirements

Quality of Work Life

a. Reward Level	A reward level high enough to satisfy the basic needs of individuals
b. External Equity	Rewards equal to or greater than those in other organizations
c. Internal Equity	A distribution of rewards that is seen as fair by members
d. Individuality	Provision of rewards that fit the needs of individuals

Organizational Effectiveness

a. Membership	High overall satisfaction, external equity, and higher reward level for better performers
b. Absenteeism	Important rewards related to actually coming to work (high job satisfaction)
c. Performance Motivation	Important rewards perceived to be related to performance
d. Organization Structure	Reward distribution pattern that fits the management style and organization structure

over. Tailoring the rewards to the needs of the individual can also contribute to both a high quality of work life and organizational effectiveness. This approach leads to high satisfaction and can help make a performance motivation system more effective by assuring that valued or important rewards are tied to effective job performance.

Tying rewards to performance contributes to motivation. It can also contribute to satisfaction because people only feel equitably treated when rewards are based on their contributions, one of the most important of which is job performance. Satisfaction of basic needs and provision of high overall reward levels contribute primarily to a high quality of work life; congruence with organization structure seems to contribute primarily to organizational effectiveness. In order for reward systems to operate in the manner that we have identified as optimally effective there are five identifiable characteristics that the rewards themselves should have. These include (1) importance, (2) flexibility, (3) frequency with respect to administration, (4) visibility, and (5) low cost.

A reward must be *important* to some individual or group of individuals if it is to influence organizational effectiveness and employee satisfaction. Thus, the first question that needs to be asked about any reward is whether it is valued by the particular individuals involved. Although it is possible to identify some rewards as more important than others *on the average*, there are large individual differences in how important rewards are.

A reward system that relies solely on generally important rewards inevitably is going to miss some employees, because even rewards that are important to most employees are not important to everyone. This creates the need for individualizing rewards (Lawler, 1974) so that employees will receive the rewards each specifically desires. In some situations, individualization can be accomplished—and the quality of work life improved—by giving people the choice of which extrinsic rewards they will receive. For example, one company allows workers who have finished their daily production quota the choice of going home or receiving extra pay. If rewards are to be tailored to individuals, those rewards must be flexible with respect to both the amount given and whether it is given to everyone in the organization. It is impossible to create individualized reward packages without flexibility. Further, unless there is flexibility in who receives rewards, it is impossible to vary rewards according to the performance of individuals; thus, equity is difficult to achieve. Overall then, *flexibility* is a desirable characteristic for a reward to have.

Related to the issue of flexibility is the issue of *frequency*. Giving rewards frequently is often helpful for sustaining extrinsic motivation and satisfaction. Thus, the best rewards are those that can be given frequently without losing their importance.

The *visibility* of rewards is important because it influences the ability of the reward to satisfy esteem and recognition needs. Low visibility rewards cannot satisfy these needs and therefore often are less valued by employees. Visibility is also important in clarifying the relationship between rewards and performance.

Finally, the *cost* of the reward is relevant because it is a constraint that the organization must consider. A high cost reward simply cannot be given as often, and when used reduces organizational effectiveness as a result of its cost.

Table 4.2 presents an evaluation of the common rewards that are used by organizations in terms of their average importance, flexibility, visibility, frequency, and cost. As can be seen from the table, none of the rewards rate high on all of the criteria. Interestingly, pay seems to possess all the characteristics that are necessary to make it the perfect extrinsic reward except one—low cost. It is particularly expensive to use as an extrinsic reward, because individuals need to receive frequent pay increases or bonuses in order for sustained extrinsic motivation and satisfaction to be present.

Promotion, dismissal, and tenure are all low in flexibility. They cannot be easily varied in amount according to the situation. They also cannot be given very regularly. This makes it difficult to tie them closely to performance over a long period of time. Job tenure or a guarantee of permanent employment, for example, is a one-shot reward, and once it is given it loses all ability to motivate. These rewards also tend to be expensive. Their high cost is not as visible and obvious as is the cost of pay, but it is real. Special awards, certificates, and medals are examples of rewards with quite a different set of characteristics. They are high in flexibility and visibility. However, they can only be given a few times before they lose their value. And because

Table 4.2–Evaluation of Extrinsic Rewards

	Average Importance	Flexibility in Amount	Visibility	Frequency	Dollar Cost
Pay	High	High	Potentially High	High	High
Promotion	High	Low	High	Low	High
Dismissal	High	Low	High	Low	High
Job Tenure	Moderate	Low	High	Low	High
Status Symbols	Moderate	High	High	Low	Moderate
Special Awards, Certificates, and Medals	Low	High	High	Low	Low
Fringe Benefits	High	Moderate	Moderate	Low	High

many people do not value them at all, their average importance is relatively low.

In summary, there is no one reward or class of rewards that meets all the criteria for being a good extrinsic reward. Furthermore, organizations have little control over how important different outcomes are to individuals. However, organizations do control which outcomes they use. It is important that each organization carefully diagnose its situation and use the one or ones that are right for its particular situation. Failure to do this assures that the reward system will fail to contribute to a high quality of work life and organizational effectiveness.

Table 4.2 points out that promotion, fringe benefits, and pay are the extrinsic rewards that can have the greatest impact on the quality of work life as well as on organizational effectiveness, because they are important to most individuals. Each of these rewards also has other characteristics that make it potentially effective. Thus, as we turn to an examination of how specific reward system practices, structures, policies, and procedures contribute to those reward system characteristics that enhance organizational effectiveness and the quality of work life, the discussion will focus on these rewards. The discussion will then turn to a number of new approaches to reward system design that have been suggested as ways to improve the quality of work life.

PROMOTION

Promotions, and indeed virtually all movements of employees from one job to another in an organization, are handled in a similar manner by most organizations (Campbell, Dunnette, Lawler, and Weick, 1970). Decisions about who will be moved where and when are made by managers who are at least one organization level above both the position that is to be filled and the individuals who are being considered to fill it. Promotion and job change decisions are typically regarded as so important that only individuals higher up in the organization can be trusted to make them. It is usually reasoned that individuals at the same or lower levels do not have the knowledge to make good decisions, and that they cannot be counted on to put organizational effectiveness first in the decision process because their self-interest is so directly involved.

The whole promotion process is kept secret in most organizations. Often, even the people who are being considered for a position are not aware of this fact. Sometimes they are not even aware that a position is open or about to be open, and that a decision is pending. Even when it is known that a position is open, it often is not known who will make the decision about filling it. Further, individuals often do not know what kinds of career plans the organization has in mind for them, even though in many organizations considerable effort is put into planning the careers of individuals. All planning is done by top management, usually with the aid of the personnel department, and the individuals are not asked their preferences or even informed of the results of the planning process. It is not uncommon, for example, to find that organizations have secret manning charts that show the backup people for all positions in the organization.

Are there alternatives to the secretive top-down approach to making promotion decisions—alternatives that will lead to greater organizational effectiveness and a higher quality of work life? Let us consider first the issue of secrecy and then the decision process.

Secrecy

A number of organizations have established the practice of openly posting the availability of jobs and inviting individuals to nominate themselves. This is an established practice in many government organizations, in unionized companies such as Xerox, and in such nonunion companies as Texas Instruments and Graphic Controls. An interesting variant of the open posting approach has been tried in some of the new Procter and Gamble plants. In these plants individuals are asked to draw up two-year development plans. These include new jobs that they would like to hold and new skills that they would like to acquire. These plans are then presented by the individuals to their work group, and a decision is made by that group as to whether the plan is acceptable or not. Other organizations have instituted similar planning processes at the management level, except that managers plan their careers with someone in the personnel function or in higher management.

Open posting does entail some extra administrative work. A number of announcements have to be made, a time delay is necessary so that applicants can respond, a large number of applicants usually have to be processed, and those applicants who fail have to be told why they did not get the job. These activities all take time and are costly, and can thus hurt organizational effectiveness. On the other hand, they may very well lead to better promotion decisions as well as to a more efficient decision process in some situations. For one thing, open posting helps assure that all qualified applicants who want a job will be considered and that those who are not interested will not be considered. Often when jobs are being filled, the individuals who are charged with the decision simply are not aware of who is available or who can do the job. This is particularly true in large operations. Thus, the decision-makers fail to consider every individual who can do the job. Further, and perhaps more important, they often do not know who is interested in having the job. As a result they consider and even offer the job to people who do not want it.

Open posting potentially can also lead to increased employee motivation. If promotion decisions are based on performance, an open system can make this clear. It can also help communicate to individuals in the organization that they can be considered for any position that comes along. This should help to improve motivation because it can help make individuals aware that a valued reward—promotion—is open to anyone who performs well. Of course, openness will not help motivation, and may even harm it, if promotion decisions are poorly made and not based on performance. This is a real concern, because performance and potential to do a higher level job are often not the same, and it is sometimes desirable to promote individuals who are high on potential but not necessarily high on past performance.

When no one individual or set of individuals is publicly identifiable as responsible for a decision, there may be a tendency for whoever makes the decision to put a little less energy into it, and perhaps to do some things that would not be done if a public defense of the decision were necessary. Public accountability can be a powerful motivation, and sometimes can even prevent individuals from making decisions based on questionable criteria (such as hunches, friendship, or sex). Public accountability, of course, does not always lead to better decisions, but it seems to contribute to good decisions.

In addition to contributing to organizational effectiveness, open job posting and career planning systems can be positive factors in quality of work life. Unfortunately, there is little research to show just how much these practices increase satisfaction, but they should have a positive effect. This conclusion is based on the assumption that open job posting and career planning systems should help individuals to end up in jobs that fit their needs. Individuals are often better able than others to decide which jobs are best for themselves. Thus, if they are given adequate information about the jobs that are open, having employees nominate themselves for jobs should increase the number of individuals who are placed in jobs that satisfy them.

It is important to note that not all aspects of an open job posting system necessarily contribute to a higher quality of work life. For one thing, this system forces the individual to publicly declare interest in a position. In most situations there are many more applicants than openings, and consequently a number of people have to be rejected. Rejection is not an easy thing to accept, particularly when the individual has made a public declaration of interest. Under a more secret system the individual does not have to make a statement of interest and thus may not feel the rejection quite so strongly, even though it is equally real. The fear of rejection may also discourage some individuals who would do a job quite well and find it very satisfying from even nominating themselves.

Finally, public declaration of interest in a position may make the promotion decision somewhat less satisfying and rewarding for those individuals who are selected for the job. Some individuals may value rewards more when they are received without being requested. Overall, though, it seems safe to conclude that open, self-nominating promotion systems probably increase the quality of work life, because they facilitate the process of placing individuals in jobs they find satisfying.

Decision-Making

As was mentioned earlier, in most organizations promotion decisions are made by individuals at organization levels that are above the position to be filled and the individuals who are being considered. There is an obvious, albeit controversial, alternative to having only higher level employees involved in decision-making about promotions. It is to have the present peers and subordinates of the person being considered, as well as the future peers and subordinates from the situation where the job opening exists, participate in the decision-making. This is now being done in some situations. In universities, students and lower level faculty members often sit in on selection and promotion committees for higher level academic and administrative positions. In some organizations work groups are given the opportunity to interview and select future members and future supervisors (for example, the Topeka plant of General Foods; see Walton, 1972). There are reasons and a little data to suggest that this can lead to greater organizational effectiveness and an improved quality of work life. Let us first consider the issue of having present peers and subordinates involved in promotion decisions.

A great deal of evidence exists to show that peers typically see an individual's performance pretty much as it is seen by the superior, although sometimes peers are a little more accurate in their assessments (Campbell, Dunnette, Lawler, and Weick, 1970). This is hardly surprising, because peers often have more contact with their co-workers and get a less guarded and staged picture of behavior. There are also some aspects of behavior that co-workers are in the best position to assess, such as cooperation with fellow workers. Although evidence is strong that peers can do a good job of assessing performance, there is little evidence to establish that subordinates can do a good job. It cannot be denied, however, that subordinates are in a uniquely advantageous position to assess such qualities as leadership style.

Unfortunately, much of the research on peer evaluation has only tried to determine if peers can evaluate performance accurately for research. The results of peer involvement in decision-making have not been studied extensively. Thus, although it is possible to argue that peers should be involved because they have relevant information, it is not possible to definitely state that if involved they will be motivated to make decisions that will contribute to organizational effectiveness.

As was noted earlier, perceived equitable distribution of rewards is an important attribute of a high quality of work life. One way to increase the likelihood that rewards are distributed in a way that is perceived to be equitable is to allow all the relevant parties to be involved in the allocation of the rewards. Having just one group of individuals (superiors) make the allocation decisions virtually assures that the decisions will be seen as inequitable by others. Not surprisingly, individuals sometimes feel that the basis for a promotion decision is not equitable even though the decision-maker believes it is. This, incidentally, is particularly likely to be true if the reasons for the decisions are kept secret. With secrecy, individuals often do not have the information they need to understand why the rewards were allocated the way they were.

A few studies have looked at the impact of having work groups select their own members and supervisors. The results, although very limited, are basically favorable. One study (Van Zelst, 1952) has shown that such selection procedures can lead to increased productivity. In addition, logic and some data suggest that these procedures have a positive impact on the quality of work life. Participation by future peers and subordinates should help satisfy the often stated desire of individuals to have some say in choosing their co-workers and supervisors. It should also help assure a good fit between the new individual and the members of the existing group, for two reasons. First, group members are likely to select someone who will fit in well, and second, because it is their decision, they will be committed to seeing that it works. This point is supported by some data G. D. Jenkins and I have recently collected at the Topeka General Foods plant. It shows very high group cohesiveness scores, as well as high organizational effectiveness, in groups that select their own members and supervisors. A note of caution is in order here, however, with respect to selecting individuals from outside the organization. Some aspects of the procedures (such as assessing abilities, evaluating past experiences, and affirmative action) may best be done as prescreening by the personnel department.

Overall, it seems that widening participation in promotion decisions has the potential to improve both organizational effectiveness and the quality of work life. It is important to note, however, that there is little research to support these conclusions. Further, it should be noted that increasing the number of participants in decisions has added some costs in the areas of time and administrative procedures.

FRINGE BENEFITS

The typical fringe benefit program provides equal amounts of such benefits as life insurance and health insurance to all organization members who are at similar levels in the organization. Typically, there is one fringe benefit package for hourly employees, one for salaried employees, and a third for the top levels of management. This approach emphasizes the differences between levels of the organization but fails to emphasize the significant differences among people who are at the same level. Yet research quite clearly shows that a benefit that is valued by one employee sometimes is not valued by another (Nealey, 1963). When researchers ask employees to allocate a hypothetical raise among a number of benefits, such things as age, marital status, and number of children influence which benefits a person prefers. For example, young unmarried men want more time off the job and young married men want less vacation; older employees want greater retirement benefits and younger employees want more cash.

These findings are hardly surprising; people in different life situations have different needs. The fact that many people do not get the fringe benefits they want, however, has some interesting implications for the degree to which fringe benefit programs contribute to the quality of work life and to organizational effectiveness. Essentially, it means that most fringe benefit programs fail to optimally contribute to either. These programs end up costing an organization money for benefits that are not valued by the employees and therefore do not contribute fully either to their satisfaction or to their desire to work effectively.

One way to improve employee satisfaction with fringe benefits is simply to increase everyone's coverage in all benefits so that everyone has an ample amount of each benefit. This, of course, would contribute to improving the quality of work life but would be very costly. A less costly alternative is a cafeteria-style fringe benefit compensation plan. This kind of plan involves telling employees just how much the organization is willing to spend on their total pay package and giving them the opportunity to spend this money as they wish. They can choose to take it all in cash, or they can choose to take some cash and use the rest to buy the fringe benefits they want. This plan makes clear to employees just how much the organization is spending to compensate them, and it assures that the money will be spent only on the fringe benefits the employees want. Such a program can increase an employee's perception of the value of the pay package, and this in turn can increase pay satisfaction. Thus, from the point of view of quality of work life, the cafeteria-style plan clearly seems superior to the traditional pay and benefit approach.

A cafeteria-style plan also can contribute to organizational effectiveness. It involves no additional direct costs and yet it has the potential to decrease absenteeism and turnover and allow the organization to attract a more competent work force. These benefits come about because working for the organization is more attractive, since individuals receive the benefits they want rather than the benefits someone else thinks they should want.

There are some practical problems with the cafeteria approach, but they are far from insurmountable. One obvious difficulty is that the plan complicates the bookkeeping aspects of wage and salary administration. With computer assistance, however, this difficulty can be readily overcome. Some managers feel that if employees are given the chance to choose their own pay and benefit package they will be irresponsible and choose only cash; then if illness or other problems occur, the employees will not be protected. This concern can be dealt with on three levels. First, the research evidence indicates that most people will behave responsibly, given the choice (Lawler and Levin, 1968; Nealey, 1963). Second, there is real doubt that employers should intervene if people take all cash. Controlling the kind of fringe benefit package an employee selects is a form of parental control and places the employee in a dependent and passive position. Such control is also in direct opposition to providing a work life that allows freedom of choice. Finally, if an organization wants to be sure everyone has certain minimum amounts of coverage, it can simply give everyone a minimum benefit package and then allow employees to supplement it according to their needs.

Probably the most serious practical problem with the cafeteria approach stems from the fact that the costs and availability of many fringe benefits (such as insurance plans) are based on the number of people who subscribe to them. Thus, it is difficult to price a benefit plan and to determine its availability in advance, so that an employee can make an intelligent decision about participating in it. In large companies this is not likely to be a serious problem, because a minimum number of participants probably can be guaranteed. Smaller companies may have to try to negotiate special agreements with insurance companies and others who underwrite aspects of the benefit package, or they may simply have to take some risks when the plan first goes into effect. After some experience with the plan, however, an organization should be able to judge in advance the number of employees who will select different benefits, and thus be able to price them accordingly.

Despite the practical problems with cafeteria-style plans, two organizations—the Systems Group of TRW Corporation and the Educational Testing Service—have put them into effect. The largest and first plan is the one at TRW. It started with a series of surveys designed to estimate how many people would choose different benefit options. The plan, as it was finally put into place in the fall of 1974, is far from a full cafeteria plan. It allows for a limited number of choices and requires everyone to take minimum levels of the important benefits (the ETS plan allows for more choice). The TRW plan does, however, put all twelve thousand employees in the organization on the plan. It allows for new choices each year, and it gives employees choices among significantly different benefit plans (over 80 percent of the employees took advantage of this opportunity and changed their benefit packages when the plan first went into effect). At the present time, for example, the employees can choose among four hospital plans. It should be noted that the plan is supported by an extensive computer software program, and that its introduction was preceded by several years of developmental work.

The TRW project represents an important initial effort to make cafeteria compensation plans a reality. At present, more organizations are needed that are willing to try this approach. Unions could provide the impetus to get many organizations to experiment in this area. So far, no union has tried to bargain for a cafeteria-style plan, but there are reasons why they might begin to do so. First, these plans promise to make union members more satisfied, and second, unions often are in the position of having to bargain for benefits many of their members are not interested in. Cafeteria plans could eliminate this problem.

Hopefully, more organizations will soon have full cafeteria plans operational. Only if this is done will we be able to fully assess the degree to which they can contribute to organizational effectiveness and to the quality of work life.

PAY: ADMINISTRATIVE APPROACHES

A few approaches to pay administration have appeared in the last twenty years that have the potential to contribute to both a high quality of work life and organizational effectiveness. Overall, however, this area has not been characterized by a great deal of innovation. Rather, it has been characterized by efforts to refine existing approaches. In this section we will concentrate on what is new, and review such approaches as skill-based job evaluation plans, all-salary pay plans, and lump sum salary increase plans. In addition, we will look at the old issue of how pay can be related to performance, and at an old approach—the Scanlon Plan—that seems to be enjoying new popularity.

Job Evaluation and Skill Evaluation

The pay systems of most organizations are built on job evaluation programs that first describe the job and then assess the characteristics of it. Once a job has been evaluated, it is compared to what other organizations pay for jobs with similar characteristics and pay is set at a level that is in line with the outside market. As noted earlier, this step is crucial. Salaries must be in line with the outside market if they are to contribute to organizational effectiveness and a high quality of work life. In most plans, the next step is to set a pay range for each job; the salaries of individuals are then based on an assessment that usually considers some combination of the individual's job performance, seniority, and a host of other factors. An almost infinite variety of systems are used to evaluate jobs (see, for example, Belcher, 1974). However, it is not clear that any one of them consistently produces pay decisions that are perceived as equitable by employees.

The job evaluation approach to setting salaries does meet some of the requirements for good reward system practice, but it fails to meet others. For example, it is particularly strong in producing internal and external equity. However, critics of this approach have noted that it fails to reward individuals for all the skills they have, and it fails to encourage individuals to learn new job-related skills. This comes about because the job evaluation approach treats employees not as individuals but as job holders.

In an attempt to improve traditional job evaluation plans, some organizations, both in the United States and abroad, have introduced skill evaluation pay plans. In these plans people are paid according to what they can do rather than what they actually do—that is, in terms of their abilities rather than their performances. Most of these plans pay individuals according to the number of jobs in the organization they can perform and do not take into account the job the person is actually performing at a given time. This has the effect of focusing on the individual rather than the job and encourages individuals to learn new skills.

Like most new approaches to management, it is not clear when or where skill evaluation pay plans were first used. They first came into prominence in Norway through the work of Einar Thorsrud (Jenkins, 1973). As part of a program of industrial democracy, several Norwegian companies adopted such plans in plants that were structured around autonomous work groups and job rotation (see Hackman, Chapter 3). This approach seemed to fit well there because of its emphasis on job rotation and on the need to acquire new skills. At present, the skill evaluation approach has enjoyed limited acceptance in the United States. Procter and Gamble has used it in four of its new plants, and General Foods has used it in the Topeka, Kansas plant.

The plan at Topeka provides a good example of how a skill evaluation pay plan works. It is based on a starting rate that is given to new
employees when they first enter the plant. After five different jobs are
mastered, the next higher pay rate is obtained. After all the jobs in the
plant are mastered, the top or plant rate is obtained. Employees are
given encouragement and support to learn new jobs, but it usually
takes a minimum of two years for an employee to learn all the jobs.
The members of an individual's work team decide when a job has
been mastered. After individuals have learned all the jobs, they continue to rotate among the same jobs, and the only opportunity for
additional pay lies in acquiring a specialty rate, which is given to an
individual who has gained expertise in a skilled trade (such as plumb-
ing).

One study of the Topeka plant reports that the pay plan seems to be
successfully contributing to both organizational effectiveness and a
high quality of work life (Walton, 1972). Organizational effectiveness
seems to have been improved because of the flexibility of the work
force and the broader perspective of the work force on how the plant
operates. A high quality of work life seems to have been achieved
because the plan reinforces a spirit of personal growth and development and produces wage rates that are perceived to be equitable. The
latter point is supported by the data collected by Jenkins and myself.
We compared the attitudes toward pay of the Topeka employees with
those of employees in other similar plants that did not have skill-based
pay plans, and we found rather dramatic differences. The Topeka plant
had much higher levels of pay satisfaction, and the employees generally felt their pay was well and fairly administered. The plant also
showed very low absenteeism and turnover rates. Thus, at least in this
one case, a skill-based pay plan does seem to have contributed to both
organizational effectiveness and a high quality of work life.

Despite their high degree of promise, skill-based pay plans are not
without their problems. Even under such plans, for example, individuals run up against the top end of a pay range because they have
learned all the jobs there are to learn. Depending on the complexity of
the plant or work situation, this may take from a few months upward.
When it happens, it may decrease an individual's motivation to perform well. There is nowhere to go financially unless some type of
bonus or other pay-for-performance system is used. This "topping out"
effect may be a substantial problem as a plant matures and many
people reach the top pay rate. And it may become a more serious
problem if a highly trained work force is developed whose skills
cannot be used fully by the organization. So far this does not seem to
be a problem at Topeka. But it may be in a few years if the plant does
not expand and make available new opportunities for learning and

skill utilization. Because of these problems, it is not clear that skill-based plans are as functional in older plants as they are in new ones, where the emphasis needs to be on skill acquisition.

These plans also require a tremendous investment in training. This investment can take many costly forms, ranging from formal classroom education to having inexperienced individuals doing jobs. One other problem that has arisen with skill-based pay plans has to do with setting pay rates. Most pay plans set pay rates in terms of the rates paid on similar jobs in the same community. This is difficult with skill-based plans, however, because the emphasis is on individuals, not on jobs. Further, because each organization has its own unique configuration of jobs that individuals learn, it is unlikely that individuals with similar skills can be found elsewhere. The situation is further complicated by the fact that an organization that has a skill-based plan is likely to be the only one in a community with such a plan. My interviews at the Topeka plant indicated that the employees had no clearly developed idea of whose pay their pay should be compared with. They did feel that their pay should be higher than that of people who did only one of the jobs they did, but beyond that they had no clear position.

It is interesting to note that most of the plants where skill-based plans have been used successfully are essentially process production plants (for example, chemicals or bulk food). This seems to be a production technology that is particularly advantageous for the use of skill evaluation plans. With process production, there is a definite advantage in having employees know a number of jobs and understand the total plant as a system. The latter is particularly important in process plants, because jobs are so highly interrelated.

The type of production technology may also moderate the desire of employees to have a skill-based plan. As part of an experiment in worker participation in pay system design that I am doing with G. D. Jenkins, we asked workers in a plant to vote on whether they wanted a skill-based plan. They voted it down, giving as one reason that they are skilled machinists who want to learn their own jobs better. There might have been some advantages to the company if the machinists had learned the other jobs—it would have created a more flexible work force. But the advantages would have been limited because of the nature of the workflow. The company manufactures products in a way that creates fairly independent jobs. The employees finally decided in favor of a system that pays individuals more as they become more skilled at operating a single machine.

Overall, skill-based plans appear to be a promising approach to administering rewards in a way that will provide a high quality of work life and contribute to organizational effectiveness. They seem to be particularly appropriate in process production plants, in situations where skill acquisition and personal growth should be emphasized, and in situations where they can be combined with a pay incentive plan so that the pay of individuals will not hit an artificial ceiling. Little is known about the usefulness of skill-based plans in nonprocess production situations. Thus, some experimentation with them in service and mass-production situations would seem worthwhile.

The All-Salaried Work Force

Most organizations distinguish between their management and non-management employees in terms of both the fringe benefits provided and whether employees are paid on an hourly or salaried basis. As a rule, hourly employees punch time clocks, lose pay when they are late, and have less generous sick leave and absenteeism privileges. The idea of putting all employees on salary, however, seems to be slowly growing in popularity. The presumed advantages of this approach include increases in both organizational effectiveness and the quality of work life (Hulme and Bevan, 1975). The all-salaried work force is supposed to increase organizational effectiveness by reducing administrative costs and producing more committed and loyal employees. It is supposed to increase the quality of work life of employees because it gives them more flexibility and treats them as mature and responsible adults.

There is some evidence that workers prefer to be on salary. Typical of these data are the results of a survey I recently did with G. D. Jenkins in a New England factory. Such a plan was favored by 55 percent of the work force. On the other hand, a company president (Sheridan, 1975) has pointed out one reason why employees do not always like salary pay plans: "We took the right not to work away from our people by putting them on salary. When they chose to go hunting or fishing or drinking instead of coming to work, it didn't make sense to them to be paid for not working. They felt a little guilty, so they didn't enjoy the day off. The couldn't understand how the company could stay in business that way—which is a helluva good perception."

Although an all-salary plan does not allow for individual treatment, it does give the individual more freedom, because it allows for later arrivals and departures and more free time. Overall, most employees probably prefer a salary plan to an hourly plan, because it accords them more mature treatment and because it eliminates an inequity that is experienced when some but not all employees are on salary. Thus, it probably does represent an improvement in the quality of work life for most people.

The UAW has raised the issue of all-salary plans in negotiations with the big three auto manufacturers, and indeed such a plan has been implemented in one UAW contract (Kinetic Dispersion). Still, there has been little widespread union support for these plans. Some unions see them as a strategy to prevent unionization (for example, at Boston Edison), and indeed they have been tried mostly in nonunion companies. IBM, for example, went to all-salary plans in the 1950s, as did Gillette. Still, because most workers seem to prefer salary plans, there is good reason for unions to make them a negotiating issue.

There is no solid evidence to indicate that an all-salary pay plan contributes to organizational effectiveness. However, to the extent that it makes working for a particular organization more attractive, it should help to reduce turnover, and this can contribute to organizational effectiveness. Although it is frequently argued that such a plan produces increased commitment to the organization, there is nothing but secondary evidence to support this claim. Typical of the kind of statements that are made is the following one (Sheridan, 1975, p. 32) by Frank Pluta of Kinetic Dispersion Corporation: "I don't think the men work any harder as a result, but there are some benefits to the company. There is a sense of loyalty. And the men come up with ideas to help keep things going a little better. There is an easy kind of relationship between the workers and supervisors. I can't say there has been a measurable gain in productivity, but the employees will help you to innovate, especially in a time of shortages."

This statement probably represents a valid assessment of how employees react to salary plans. Still, it would be useful to have some solid data showing that, in fact, important benefits do come about when employees are placed on salary plans.

Critics of the all-salary idea argue that there is a real danger that it will lead to increased absenteeism and tardiness. They argue that when time clocks disappear and the threat of lost pay decreases, employees may think they have been granted a license to cheat the company. The counter to this argument is that workers will be less motivated to cheat because the company has trusted them (besides, who says you cannot cheat on a time clock?). Further, just because a time clock is not present does not mean that management cannot be concerned when people do not come to work or show up late. Management has not given up its ability to notice and even dismiss individuals who do not show up on time or are frequently absent. Finally, white-collar workers show up even though they are not on time clocks, and there is little reason to believe they are more responsible than hourly employees.

Unfortunately, there is little firm evidence as to whether all-salary plans lead to higher absenteeism and tardiness rates. A number of companies have been quoted as saying that when they moved to an all-salary plan, absenteeism either went down or stayed the same (for example, Gillette and Dow Chemical; see also Hulme and Bevan,

1975). Others report that such plans led to a slight increase in absenteeism. There simply is not adequate evidence, however, to indicate what the most common effect is. A good guess is that, on the average, an all-salary plan leads to a small increase in absenteeism, but that under some conditions, it might lead to a reduction.

Absenteeism might be reduced, for example, in situations where an all-salary plan is combined with a more participative approach to management and with more attention to absenteeism by supervisors. If it is to result in a decrease, supervisors cannot simply forget about tardiness and absenteeism completely. Rules must be made and enforced, and the few that abuse the privilege must be disciplined. If the all-salary pay plan is the only thing management does to communicate to the workers that they are expected to be responsible, it probably will not decrease absenteeism and tardiness. Although such a plan gives the workers a message that they are trusted, it has to compete with a lot of messages that say just the opposite. This message is often a difficult one to get across and cannot stand a lot of competition, particularly when the desired behavior (coming to work) has to compete with other attractive alternatives (such as sleeping). If, however, an all-salary plan is combined with more challenging jobs, greater decision-making latitude, and other changes in the reward system, it can be a useful base on which to build a better relationship between the organization and the individual.

In summary, the all-salary pay system appears to be a promising approach, one that can accomplish the twin objectives of increasing both the quality of work life and organizational effectiveness. However, it is not likely to be accepted by all. And it is likely to be effective only if it is part of an overall management strategy and organization design that emphasizes employee participation, meaningful work, and mature treatment of employees.

Lump Sum Salary Increases

Most organizations provide no flexibility with respect to when pay raises are distributed to employees. Although many organizations speak in terms of annual salary increases, in fact all but a few organizations give raises by adjusting the regular pay checks of employees. For example, if employees are paid weekly, then their weekly pay check is increased to reflect the amount of the annual salary increase. Similar changes are made for employees paid on a biweekly or monthly basis. This approach allows the employees absolutely no flexibility with respect to when they receive their raises. To get the full amount of their annual increase, they have to wait a full year. This approach also often has the effect of perceptually burying a raise so that it is hardly visible to the recipient. Once the annual raise is divided up among the regular pay checks and the tax deductions are made, very little change usually occurs in take-home pay.

Recognizing these problems, some organizations have started a lump sum increase program that is aimed at making salary increases more flexible and visible, and at the same time communicating to their employees that they are willing to do innovative things in the area of pay administration. Under a lump sum increase program, employees are given the opportunity to decide when they will receive their annual increase. Just about any option is available, including receiving it *all* in one lump sum at the beginning of the year. The employee can also choose to have the increases folded into regular salary checks, as has been done in the past. The following quote from a publication of an insurance company that has installed such a plan illustrates the philosophy behind it:

> The Lump Sum Increase Program (LSIP) is a payment option offering you the flexibility to tailor part of your total compensation to your specific needs. Under this program you can elect to receive all or part of any salary increase—whether merit, promotional, or a special adjustment—in the form of one lump sum payment (less a small discount for payment in advance). By making the full amount of your increase available as soon as it is effective, LSIP allows you to plan realistically for large expenditures without using retail credit plans having high interest rates.

Each year the employees can make a new choice. They are not bound by any of their past choices, and each year they have the opportunity to allocate not only the current year's raise but the raises from all the years since the program began. Obviously this can give individuals a considerable amount of flexibility in when they receive their pay increases.

The money that is advanced to employees is treated as a loan. This means that if an employee quits before the end of the year, the proportion of the increase which has not yet been earned has to be paid back. Also, because the money is advanced to individuals before they earn it, they are charged interest at a low rate to offset the cash flow problem such payments cause.

Unfortunately, there is no research evidence on how effective the lump sum program is. All that can be reported so far is that the employees who are subject to it seem to be enthusiastic about it. Most people see it as contributing to a high quality of work life. It costs individuals very little, but they gain the opportunity to shape their income to fit their unique needs and desires. In short, a lump sum program represents one way in which employees are treated more as individuals by the organizations that employ them, and as such it can improve the quality of work life.

There are some reasons to believe lump sum increases can also contribute to organizational effectiveness. For one thing, the costs involved to an organization are minimal. The administration of a lump sum increase plan does involve some extra costs, because, like a cafeteria fringe benefit program, it requires extra bookkeeping and record keeping. There also will undoubtedly be some situations where money will be lost because employees quit and do not pay back the advances they receive. Organizations need not lose interest income on the cash they advance, since they can charge interest on it. The organizations that have tried the plan so far have charged relatively low interest rates (for example, 6 percent). These organizations realize that they might be able to invest their cash more profitably, but they feel nevertheless that the lump sum program is worthwhile.

What are the advantages to an organization of a lump sum increase plan? The major positive outcome from such a plan should be that it makes working for a particular organization more attractive. All other things being equal, organizations that give employees choices about when they will receive their pay increases should have a competitive advantage in attracting and retaining employees. Like other practices that make organizations more attractive, the lump sum plan can pay off in a number of ways—better selection ratios, lower turnover, and lower absenteeism. These, in turn, result in lower personnel costs and a more talented group of employees.

Giving lump sum increases also increases the visibility of the amount of a salary increase. A large raise tends to come across clearly as a large amount of money and a small raise comes across as just what it is—a small increase. Increasing the saliency of the amount of a raise may or may not be functional for an organization, depending on how well pay is administered by the organization. If pay is administered in an arbitrary and nonperformance-based manner, then it is hardly functional to highlight the size of an increase. On the other hand, if an organization does a good job of administering pay, then increasing the saliency of raises can be functional. For example, if the increases are based on performance, then the lump sum approach has the potential of making pay a more effective motivator, because pay will be more clearly tied to performance. If pay increases are equitably distributed, lump sum increases can make this clear, thereby increasing pay satisfaction and reducing the tendency of individuals to look for other jobs. On the other hand, if pay increases are inequitably distributed, lump sum increases can highlight these problems.

In summary then, the lump sum increase approach can magnify both the positive and the negative aspects of a pay plan. It can help an organization if pay increases are well administered, and it can hurt if pay increases are poorly administered. It is, therefore, a tool to be used only when an organization has a reasonable, well-functioning salary increase plan.

Relating Pay to Performance

Given our discussion of what determines human behavior, it is difficult to argue with the view that relating pay to performance can contribute to organizational effectiveness. When pay is tied to performance, it can motivate performance as well as contribute to satisfaction among the higher performers. As a result of their being satisfied, high performers are less likely to turnover when pay is related to performance.

Pay that is related to performance can also make an important contribution to a high quality of work life under some conditions. Specifically, when employees feel that pay should be based on performance, feelings of intraorganizational reward equity cannot exist unless people are paid in relation to their perceived contributions to the organization. A number of studies have looked at whether employees generally feel they should be paid on the basis of their performance. Almost without exception these studies have shown that employees feel pay should be based on performance. For example, one study measured managers' attitudes about how their pay should be determined. The results showed that managers prefer to have their pay based on performance and that they believe performance should be the most important determinant of their pay (Lawler, 1966). The study also found a consistent tendency for a large gap to exist between how important managers felt performance actually was in determining pay and how important they felt it *should* be. This gap reflects the inability of the organizations to develop pay plans that fit the needs of employees. It also indicates that pay can make a much stronger contribution to a high quality of work life in these organizations.

Studies done among blue-collar workers to determine their preferences with respect to pay plans do not show as strong an acceptance of performance-based pay plans as has been found among managers. The studies are a little difficult to interpret, however, because many of them asked for reactions to specific pay plans, such as piece rate plans, rather than to the general idea of performance-based pay. Workers often object to piece rate plans but still favor other kinds of performance-based pay systems. Thus, it is hard to tell if the workers studied objected to the principle of having pay based on performance, or to the specific plans being considered.

Illustrative of the studies on this topic is one by *Factory* (1947), which reports that 59 percent of the workers sampled who were not paid on an incentive basis said "they would like to work under such a system if it were fairly run." The results of another study by the

Table 4.3–"On a job which could be paid by either piece rate or hourly rate, which would you rather work on?"

	No. of Mfg. Manual Workers	Percentage Who Prefer		
		Piece Rate	Hourly Rate	Do Not Know
Total	919	36	61	3
Paid by:				
Hourly Rate	658	24	73	3
Incentive Plan	131	57	39	4
Piece Rate	130	75	22	3
Union status:				
No Union	220	43	53	4
Have Union	699	34	63	3
Members	597	33	65	2
Nonmembers	102	35	54	11

Opinion Research Corporation are presented in Table 4.3. This table shows replies to the question: "On a job which could be paid by either piece rate or hourly rate, which would you rather work on?" (*Opinion Research Corporation*, 1946). The results show a pattern that is typical of many similar studies—workers on incentive plans prefer such plans, and workers on hourly rates prefer hourly rates. The data show, however, that overall only 36 percent of the workers studied prefer piece rate plans. It is possible that a far larger proportion would be in favor of performance-based pay in principle, but would not prefer the piece rate plan to an hourly pay rate.

Several studies have analyzed what determines whether an employee will prefer performance-based pay. The data suggest that individual preferences are influenced both by the individual's needs and by the situation (Lawler, 1966). Employees high in achievement needs seem to prefer performance systems; those with strong security needs do not. The more competent employees are, the better their past experience with the system; and the better their relationship with the boss, the more they prefer performance-based pay.

Some writers stress that reward systems which base extrinsic rewards on performance place the employee in an uncomfortable dependency situation, because they specify what must be done to receive valued rewards (Argyris, 1957). Admittedly, this represents a dependency situation and there is evidence that severe dependency situations lead to lower satisfaction, alienation, hostility, regression, and a lack of growth. However, it is interesting to compare this situation with one where rewards are given on an arbitrary or random basis, so that the employee has no influence over the reception of rewards. This situation would seem in many ways to place the individual in an even more uncomfortable and dependent position. When rewards are based on performance, the individual has control as is illustrated by the cartoon that shows two rats in a Skinner box. One rat is saying to the other: "Boy, have I got this guy trained. Every time I press the bar he gives me a pellet." This cartoon highlights the point that when rewards are dependent on performance, a two-way dependence situation exists—the receiver is dependent on the reward giver, but in many ways the giver is dependent on and obligated to the receiver. This point is elaborated in Figure 4.1. It shows that dependency feelings are a function of both the basis for giving rewards and the degree to which individuals are treated differently by the system. Dependency is shown to be greatest when rewards are given in different amounts to individuals on an undefined basis, and lowest when individuals are paid on the basis of the jobs they hold so that all individuals are treated the same.

	Rewards on Group or Organization Basis	Rewards on Individual Basis
Agreed to Measures of Performance	Low Dependency	Moderate Dependency
Agreed to Measures of Job Characteristics	Very Low Dependency	Low Dependency
Not Defined or Agreed to	High Dependency	Very High Dependency

BASIS FOR REWARDS

Figure 4.1–Relationship of Dependency to Reward Distribution Policies

In summary, the evidence suggests that workers are not necessarily opposed to performance-based pay systems, but that the situations in which they work and their work histories may lead them to oppose such systems. Presumably opposition to incentive pay often comes about because the employees feel they cannot trust the company to administer incentive plans properly.

Methods of Relating Pay to Performance. There are nearly as many methods of relating pay to performance as there are organizations, and at times it seems that every organization is in the process of changing its approach. One study found, for example, that one out of every three companies had "recently" changed its method of paying salesmen (Research Institute of America, 1965). However, some types of plans clearly are more capable than others of relating pay to performance,

Table 4.4—Classification of Pay Incentive Plans

	Performance Measure	Reward Offered	
		Salary Increase	Cash Bonus
Individual Plans	Productivity		Sales commission Piece rate
	Cost Effectiveness Superiors' ratings	Merit rating plan	
Group Plans	Productivity Cost Effectiveness Superiors' ratings		Group incentive
Organization-Wide Plans	Productivity	Productivity Bargaining	
	Cost Effectiveness Profit		Kaiser, Scanlon Profit Sharing

and thereby of contributing to organizational effectiveness and a high quality of work life.

The mechanics of various types of pay plans can be grouped according to their characteristics on three dimensions: (1) the organization unit where performance is measured for reward purposes (individual, group, or organization-wide basis); (2) the way performance is measured (measures typically vary from admittedly subjective, such as superiors' judgments or ratings, to somewhat objective, such as costs, sales, or profits); and (3) what rewards are offered for successful performance (salary increases or cash bonuses). Table 4.4 presents a breakdown of various pay plans on these three dimensions. This classification system yields eighteen different types of incentive plans.

Table 4.5 provides an effectiveness rating for each plan on four criteria. These ratings attempt to summarize what has typically happened when each kind of plan has been used. First, each plan is evaluated in terms of how effective it is in creating the perception that pay is tied to performance. In general, this indicates the degree to which the approach ties pay closely to performance, chronologically, and the degree to which employees believe that higher pay will follow good performance. Second, each plan is evaluated in terms of whether it results in the negative side effects that often are produced by pay-for-performance plans. These include social ostracism of good performers, defensive behavior, and the giving of false data about performance. Third, each plan is evaluated in terms of the degree to which it contributes to teamwork and cooperation. Finally, each plan is evaluated in terms of the degree to which it usually is acceptable to employees. The ratings range from 1 to 5; a 5 indicates that the plan is generally high on the factor and a 1 indicates it is low.

Table 4.5–Ratings of Various Pay Incentive Plans

		Tie Pay to Performance	Produce Negative Side Effects	Encourage Coopera-tion	Employee Accept-ance
Salary Reward					
Individual plan	Productivity	4	1	1	4
	Cost effectiveness	3	1	1	4
	Superiors' rating	3	1	1	3
Group	Productivity	3	1	2	4
	Cost effectiveness	3	1	2	4
	Superiors' rating	2	1	2	3
Organization-wide	Productivity	2	1	3	4
	Cost effectiveness	2	1	2	4
Bonus					
Individual plan	Productivity	5	3	1	2
	Cost effectiveness	4	2	1	2
	Superiors' rating	4	2	1	2
Group	Productivity	4	1	3	3
	Cost effectiveness	3	1	3	3
	Superiors' rating	3	1	3	3
Organization-wide	Productivity	3	1	3	4
	Cost effectiveness	3	1	3	4
	Profit	2	1	3	3

A number of trends appear in the ratings. Looking only at the criterion of tying pay to performance, we see that individual plans tend to be rated highest, group plans are rated next, and organization-wide plans are rated lowest. This is because in group plans to some extent, and in organization-wide plans to a great extent, individuals' pay is not directly a function of their behavior. The pay of individuals in these situations is influenced by the behavior of others and also by external market conditions with some types of performance measures (for example, profits).

Bonus plans are generally rated higher than pay raise and salary increase plans. Under bonus plans, a person's pay may vary sharply from year to year in accordance with recent performance. This does not usually happen with salary increase programs, because organizations seldom cut anyone's salary. As a result, pay under the salary increase plan reflects not only recent performance but also performance over a number of years. Consequently, pay is not seen to be closely related to present behavior.

Finally, note that approaches that use objective measures of performance are rated higher than those that use subjective measures. In general, objective measures enjoy higher credibility; that is, employees will often accept the validity of an objective measure, such as sales or units produced, when they will not accept a superior's ratings. Thus, when pay is tied to objective measures, it is usually clearer to employees that pay is determined by performance. Objective measures, such as sales volume and units produced, are also often publicly measurable. When pay is tied to them, the relationship between performance and pay is often much more visible than when it is tied to a subjective, nonverifiable measure, such as a superior's ratings. Overall, then, the suggestion is that individually-based bonus plans that rely on objective measures produce the strongest perceived connection between pay and performance.

The ratings of the degree to which plans contribute to negative side effects reveal that most plans have little tendency to produce such effects. The notable exceptions here are individual bonus and incentive plans at the nonmanagement level. These plans often lead to situations in which social rejection and ostracism are tied to good performance, and in which employees present false productivity data and restrict their production. These side effects are particularly likely to appear where trust is low and where the kinds of quotas and performance measurements that are frequently part of piece rate systems are used.

In terms of the third criterion—encouraging cooperation—the ratings are generally higher for group and organization-wide plans than for individual plans. Under group and organization-wide plans, it is generally to everyone's advantage for an individual to work effectively, because all share in the financial fruits of his higher performance. This is not true under an individual plan. Thus, good performance is much more likely to be supported and encouraged by others when group and organization-wide plans are used. In short, if people feel they can benefit from another's good performance, they are much more likely to encourage and help other workers to perform well than if they will not benefit and might even be harmed.

The final criterion—employee acceptance—shows that, as noted earlier, most performance pay plans have only moderate acceptance. The least acceptable seems to be individual bonus plans. Their low acceptance, particularly among nonmanagement employees, seems to stem from their tendency to encourage competitive relationships between employees, and from the difficulty in administering such plans fairly. The low acceptance of individual bonus plans is shown by the negative attitudes of most unions toward them. However, some unions favor group and, particularly, organization-wide plans. They correctly recognize that these plans potentially allow employees to share in any gains in organizational effectiveness that they produce, and thus solve many equity problems before such problems arise. They also recognize that these plans can unify a work force instead of dividing it as many piece rate plans do.

The ratings in Table 4.5 show a general tendency for employees to prefer salary increases to bonuses. The reason for this is obvious—a salary increase tends to become a permanent part of a person's pay, but a bonus does not. Unless the bonus potential is much larger than the raise potential, employees naturally prefer raises. Finally, the ratings show a slight tendency for plans based on objective measures to be preferred to those based on superiors' ratings. This stems from the preference for valid measures that individuals trust because they can control and influence them.

It should be clear from this short review that no one performance pay plan represents a panacea. Unfortunately, no one type is strong in all areas. Thus, it is unlikely that any organization will ever be completely satisfied with its approach. Further, some of the plans that make the greatest contributions to organizational effectiveness do not make the greatest contributions to quality of work life, and vice versa. Still, the situation is not completely hopeless. Clearly, some approaches contribute more than others to both a high quality of work life and organizational effectiveness. When all factors are taken into account, group and company-wide bonus plans that are based on objective data, and individual level salary increase plans, rate highest. We also know that many of the approaches not mentioned in the table, such as stock option plans, across the board raises, and seniority increases, have no real effect on the performance motivation of most employees because they do not relate pay to performance. It is interesting that many of the quality of work life projects in Scandinavia also seem to have concluded that group plans are desirable. Many of the experiments there have involved switching to group bonus plans as part of larger work redesign programs (see Linestad and Norstedt, 1972).

Perhaps the most important conclusion arising from the research on different performance pay plans is that the effectiveness of all pay plans varies according to a number of situational conditions. A plan that works well for one organization often is unsatisfactory for another, for a whole series of reasons. Thus, although it is tempting to say that a particular approach to pay administration is always best, it is wiser to consider the factors that determine which kind of plan is likely to be best in a given situation.

Factors Influencing the Effectiveness of Performance Pay Plans. One factor that must be considered when a pay plan is evaluated for a particular organization is the degree of cooperation that is needed among the individuals who are paid by the plan. When the jobs involved are basically independent of one another, it is reasonable to use an individual plan. Independent jobs are quite common; examples include outside sales jobs and some kinds of production jobs. In these, employees contribute relatively independently to the effectiveness of the total group or organization. Thus, it is appropriate to implement an incentive plan that motivates these employees to perform at their maximum and to pay little attention to cooperative activities.

Many jobs, however, demand that work be done either successively (work that passes from one person to another) or coordinately (work that is a function of the joint effort of all employees). With successive jobs and especially with coordinate jobs, individual incentive plans are usually inappropriate. For one thing, on these jobs it is often difficult to measure the contribution of any one individual, and therefore it is difficult to reward individuals differentially. Another problem with individual plans is that they typically do not reward cooperation, because cooperation is difficult to measure and to visibly relate to pay. Cooperation is essential on successive and coordinate jobs, however, and it is vital that the pay plan reward it. Thus, the strong suggestion is that group and organization-wide plans may be best in situations where jobs are coordinate or successive.

A related issue has to do with the degree to which inclusive objective performance measures or criteria can be created for individuals. For many jobs, it is quite difficult to establish criteria that are both quantitatively measurable and inclusive of all the important job behaviors. The solution to this problem often is to establish a group or organization-wide incentive plan. Inclusive criteria sometimes can be stated at the group and organizational levels even when they are not possible at the individual level. It is quite easy to think of jobs for which a criterion like productivity might not be inclusive enough when individuals are looked at, but might be inclusive enough when a number of jobs or employees are grouped together. In choosing an incentive plan, an organization must consider whether the performance measures that are related to pay include the important job activities. Plans that have backfired in this area are legion and diverse (for example, salespersons who have only sold and have harmed long-term customer relations, profit margins, and trade-in prices; and city maintenance crews that have filled potholes without regard to whether they will stay filled).

There are many situations where objective measures do not exist for individual or even group performance. One way of dealing with such situations is to measure performance on the basis of larger and larger groups until some objective measures can be found. Another way is to use subjective measures of performance at the individual or

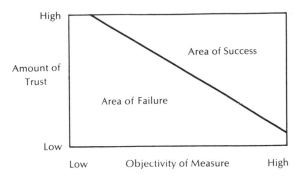

Figure 4.2—Relationship of Trust and the Objectivity of Performance Criteria to Success of the Program

small group level. This is possible in some situations but not in others. The key factor is the degree of superior-subordinate trust—the more subjective the measure, the higher the degree of trust needed. Without high trust there is little chance that the subordinate will believe that pay is fairly based on performance. Figure 4.2 illustrates the relationship between trust and the objectivity of the performance criteria (Lawler, 1971). It indicates that, even with the most objective system, some trust is still required if the individual is to believe in the system. It also suggests that unless a high degree of trust exists, pay plans based on subjective criteria have little chance of success.

One further issue concerned with performance measurement that must be considered is whether the individuals under the plan will actually be able to influence the criteria on which they will be evaluated. All too often the criteria used in pay plans are unrelated to the individual worker's efforts. This creates low motivation and a poor quality of work life. Certainly this is true of most profit-sharing plans. The individual workers usually are not in a position to influence the profits of most companies, yet this is a criterion on which part of their pay is based.

Although it has not been explicitly stated, it should be clear from the discussion so far that there are situations in which pay should *not* be related to job performance, because such a relationship will not contribute to both organizational effectiveness and a high quality of work life. These situations would include organizations where the following conditions exist: (1) the trust level is low; (2) performance must be measured subjectively; (3) inclusive measures of performance cannot be developed; (4) the organization is large, and performance cannot be measured at the individual or group level.

Reward Schedules.   The approach that has been taken to performance motivation so far in this chapter has stressed the importance of relating pay closely to performance. Expectancy theory argues for a one-to-one relationship (Lawler, 1973a; Vroom, 1964) between performance and rewards. It is important to note that not all psychologists agree with this point of view. For example, a number of psychologists recently have stated that the work of B. F. Skinner suggests that rewards sometimes are more effective when they are related to performance on a *variable ratio schedule* (Jablonsky and Devries, 1972; Nord, 1969; Yukl, Wexley, and Seymour, 1972). A variable ratio schedule is one in which the reward is given only after some number of the correct or desired responses, and in a variable or nonregular way. For example, a reward might be administered after the first desired behavior, then after three more, then after one more, and so on. Typically, a determination is made in advance about what percentage of the desired responses will be rewarded.

Although it is often stated that Skinner's work (1938, 1969) shows that variable ratio schedules are more effective in motivating performance than are *fixed ratio schedules*, which reinforce or reward individuals every time they exhibit a certain behavior a specific number of times, this is a controversial and grossly simplified interpretation of Skinner's work (see Bandura, 1969). It simply is not clear that better performance results when people are rewarded on variable ratio schedules. Although Skinner's work does suggest that variable ratio schedules slow the extinction of a behavior after rewards are no longer given, it shows just the opposite with respect to the acquisition of particular behaviors. Further, there is reason to believe that a variable ratio reward schedule has a negative impact on the quality of work life, because this kind of schedule places people in a high dependency situation.

It is hardly surprising that the practical implications of Skinner's work have intrigued some researchers and managers. Consider what a help it would be to organizational effectiveness if performance could be increased by decreasing the frequency with which people are paid for good performance. This would pay off for the organization in both lower costs and higher performance. Three recent studies have tried to determine if, in fact, variable reinforcement schedules can be of value. These studies are worth reviewing briefly because they reveal something important about the impact of these schedules on organizational effectiveness and quality of work life.

In an interesting study, Pedalino and Gamboa (1974) introduced a poker incentive plan to reward attendance. The plan worked as follows: "Each day an employee *comes* to work and is *on time*, he is allowed to choose a card from a deck of playing cards. At the end of the five day week, he will have five cards or a normal poker hand. The highest hand wins $20. There will be eight winners, one for approximately every department." The plan seemed to have the desired effect of reducing absenteeism (18.7 percent). Unfortunately, the study did not compare the effectiveness of this plan with a nonlottery bonus system for rewarding attendance, so we do not know whether the system was better than other bonus systems might have been (for example, 100 percent reinforcement systems). However, it clearly is better than no reward system at all. The researchers reported no data on the reactions of the employees to the plan. We do not know, for example, if their satisfaction increased as a result of the plan being installed or if they would have preferred to receive the extra money that was involved in the lottery as part of their regular salary. Thus, we do not know what the impact on quality of work life was.

Two other studies have compared the impact of different approaches to reinforcement schedules. The first (Yukl, Wexley, and Seymour, 1972) was a laboratory study of a small number (n = 15) of subjects. The results tended to support the view that variable ratio reinforcement schedules are more effective. In the study, the same amount of money seemed to buy higher levels of performance when it was given on a variable ratio schedule. In addition, the same level of performance was obtained by giving twenty-five cents reward for every correct response as was obtained by giving twenty-five cents for 50 percent of the correct responses. This, of course, is a rather effective way to reduce costs. The variable ratio reward schedule did not, however, seem to lead to an improved quality of work life. The subjects on the variable ratio reward schedules were significantly less satisfied with their pay, which is hardly surprising because they received less.

In a later study (Latham, Yukl, and Scott, 1974; Yukl and Latham, 1975) an effort was made to replicate the results of the earlier study in an actual job situation (tree planting). Three work crews were studied.

> Each crew was approached individually. The first crew was told that in addition to their normal hourly pay, they would receive two dollars contingent upon planting a bag of trees. The second crew was told that in addition to their normal hourly pay, they would receive four dollars contingent upon planting a bag of trees *and* correctly guessing the outcome of one coin toss. The third crew was told that in addition to their normal hourly pay, they would receive eight dollars contingent upon planting a bag of trees *and* correctly guessing the outcome of two tosses. Thus, the amount of money paid by the company to each individual was to be approximately the same over the long run— two dollars 100 percent of the time, four dollars 50 percent of the time, or eight dollars 25 percent of the time. A fourth crew, geographically isolated from the other three, was selected as a control group. That is, individuals in this crew did not receive a monetary bonus for planting a bag of trees. Thus, the performance of this group enabled us to determine what changes in performance could be

attributed to seasonal fluctuations or simple recording of the data (Hawthorne Effect).

Each reinforcement was administered in the form of a token immediately after a bag of trees was planted. Since the data were collected
for approximately twelve weeks, twelve days were randomly selected in
which the planters could cash in their tokens until they were present on a
subsequent exchange day or until the study ended (Latham, Yukl, and
Scott, 1974, pp. 3–4).

The results were rather dramatic. The continuous reinforcement
group showed the biggest performance increase (33 percent). The
second group, which received four dollars on a 50 percent schedule,
actually decreased their performance, and the third group showed an
increase (18 percent). The only plan that was cost effective from the
organization's point of view was the first plan.

The authors report that one reason the two variable ratio schedules
did not work well was that some employees opposed them. These
employees felt that the schedules were a form of gambling and therefore were morally wrong. Open discussion seemed to reduce this
problem. But the fact that the reaction did occur suggests that variable
ratio schedules may not be seen as contributing to higher quality of
work life, even when they pay the same as continuous schedules.

In summary then, it is not clear that variable ratio reinforcement
schedules meet either of our criteria—that they contribute to either
organizational effectiveness or a high quality of work life. It does seem
clear, however, that they should never be used as a way of spending
less money. This will only contribute to employee dissatisfaction. It
may be, as has been suggested, that as long as a variable ratio
schedule does not cost them any money, some individuals might prefer
the gambling nature of the system. However, it remains unclear
whether this preference will hold up over time if the alternative is to
receive the *same* amount of money without going through coin flips
and lotteries. If employees still prefer the gambling, there is no reason
why they cannot be given the option of being paid on a variable ratio
schedule.

As far as performance is concerned, it still remains to be shown
that the same amount of money can produce greater productivity
under a variable ratio schedule. In some situations it may, because
some individuals do enjoy gambling and they may work harder for the
opportunity to gamble. However, it is doubtful that this is a general
phenomenon, and it is probably counterbalanced in many situations
by individuals who find gambling unattractive. Perhaps the answer is
to give those individuals who prefer to gamble the opportunity to work
on variable ratio schedules, while leaving the others at 100 percent
reinforcement schedules. This would give everyone the kind of plan

they want and might increase organizational effectiveness at the same time.

The Scanlon Plan.[1]   The Scanlon Plan is undoubtedly the best known company-wide incentive plan. It was developed by Joe Scanlon, a union leader, in the middle 1930s. As was noted in Table 4.3, in this plan bonuses based on a measure of company performance are given to all employees. Proponents of the plan argue it should not be regarded as just another incentive plan.

> Scanlon deeply believed that the typical company organization did not elicit the full potential from employees, either as individuals or as a group. He did not feel that the commonly held concept that "the boss is the boss and a worker works" was a proper basis for stimulating the interest of employees in company problems; rather, he felt such a concept reinforced employees' beliefs that there was an "enemy" somewhere above them in the hierarchy and that a cautious suspicion should be maintained at all times. He felt that employee interest and contribution could best be stimulated by providing the employee with a maximum amount of information and data concerning company problems and successes, and by soliciting his contribution as to how he felt the problem might best be solved and the job best done. Thus, the Scanlon Plan is a common sharing between management and employees of problems, goals, and ideas (Lesieur and Puckett, 1969, p. 112).

Scanlon realized that if his management philosophy was to be implemented, some structural changes were needed in organizations. He pointed out that most wage systems fail to reward individuals for cooperative behavior, and they also fail to produce a convergence between the goals of employees and the goals of the organization. His solution to this problem was a company-wide bonus plan. Scanlon also believed that in most organizations the opinions and ideas of people lower down in the organization are ignored, even though they are of value. To correct this situation, he suggested that organizations use a suggestion system that involves an elaborate committee structure. The Scanlon Plan, then, is a philosophy of management that is basically participatory and that involves using a pay incentive system and a suggestion system.

The genius of the Scanlon Plan and of the man, Joe Scanlon, is the recognition that a commitment to participation and joint problem-solving is not enough. Effective use of participatory management requires a congruence between the structure of an organization and the style of management. This point will be discussed in greater detail in

---

1. The Scanlon Plan is also discussed in Chapters 5 (Alderfer) and 6 (Strauss) from different perspectives, and as it relates to different aspects of improving life at work.

the next section. It is mentioned here to stress that it is an integral part of the Scanlon Plan and because Joe Scanlon was one of the first to articulate the important influence that the fit between the pay system and the management philosophy can have on an organization.

Companies following the Scanlon Plan use widely varying methods of calculating the amount of bonuses employees receive (all members of the organization receive bonuses, usually the same percentage of their salaries). Some plans, particularly the early ones, used a straight profit-sharing approach. In recent years, the most common approach has been to base the bonus on a ratio measure that compares total sales volume to total payroll expenses. This is, in effect, a measure of labor cost efficiency (if wages and sale prices are corrected for inflation). A base rate is established at the beginning of the plan, and money savings resulting from improvements over the base are shared (usually equally by the company and the employees). The ratio is used instead of profits in order to have a measure that is more responsive to the behavior of the employees.

In concept, then, the pay system is an important part of the overall Scanlon approach to management, because it ties the goals of individuals to the goals of the organization. When it is operating properly, the better the organization functions, the better off the employees are. It is to the advantage of employees to produce more, to work faster and more effectively, to cooperate with other employees, to adopt new technologies, and to make suggestions that improve organizational effectiveness. Clearly, then, as McGregor (1960) and many others have pointed out, when it operates properly the Scanlon Plan can contribute to both organizational effectiveness and a high quality of work life.

The Scanlon Plan has been around long enough (since the mid-1930s) to allow some conclusions to be drawn about its effectiveness. The conclusions must be tentative, however, because little actual research has been done on the plan, and most of what has been done is of low quality. Estimates vary on how many firms have tried the plan, but the figure is generally thought to be less than five hundred (Howell, 1967). One recent review of the literature found studies covering fifty-three situations where the plan was tried (Moore and Goodman, 1973). This is a rather large number of cases, but unfortunately the data on most cases are poor, and it is therefore difficult to determine just what impact the plan has had in most situations.

It is possible to code forty-four of the cases in terms of whether the plan was successful in contributing to organizational effectiveness (see Moore and Goodman, 1973). The apparent successes outnumber the failures by thirty to fourteen. This is an impressive success rate, but it may be inflated, because it seems probable that organizations that are successful in introducing the plan are more likely to write about their experiences than are those who fail. Similarly, researchers are more likely to report positive results than negative ones. However, even if we discount the two-to-one success to failure ratio because of selection bias, the success ratio is still impressive and probably indicates that a Scanlon Plan is successful at least half the time. The following are outcomes which Moore and Goodman suggest often occur when the plan is successful:

1. The plan enhances coordination, teamwork, and sharing knowledge at lower levels (Lesieur, 1958; McKersie, 1963; Scanlon, 1949).
2. Social needs are recognized via participation and mutually reinforcing group behavior (Frost, Wakley, and Ruh, 1974; Whyte, 1955).
3. Attention is focused on cost savings—not just quantity of production (McKersie, 1963).
4. Acceptance of change due to technology, market, and new methods is greater because higher efficiency leads to bonuses (McKersie, 1963; Shultz, 1958b).
5. Attitudinal change occurs among workers and they demand more efficient management and better planning (Lesieur, 1958).
6. Workers try to reduce overtime; to work smarter, not harder or faster (Lesieur, 1958; Scanlon, 1949).
7. Workers produce ideas as well as effort (Shultz, 1958b; Whyte, 1955).
8. More flexible administration of union-management relations occurs (Helfgott, 1962).
9. The union is strengthened because it is responsible for a better work situation and higher pay.

It is interesting to note that higher employee satisfaction and a better quality of life are not among the outcomes listed. There is a reason for this. Few studies have looked at the impact of the Scanlon Plan on quality of work life. There is some evidence, however, that it does have a positive impact. First of all, it leads to higher pay because of the bonus and, as was noted earlier, this increases satisfaction. Further, the kinds of outcomes listed above often do contribute to employee satisfaction. Finally, several studies, including one by the author at Donnelly Mirrors, have found high satisfaction and commitment levels in Scanlon companies (Frost et al., 1974; Moore and Goodman, 1973).

There are a number of reasons why Scanlon Plans fail. Some of these can best be regarded as simply poor implementation of a potentially good plan. Others reflect more basic flaws in the approach that limit its effectiveness in a number of situations. The following are areas where poor implementation often leads to plan failures.

1. *Formula construction.* The formula needs to accurately measure what is going on in the organization and must be adjustable to changing conditions. Often, rigid formulas that do not reflect employee behavior are developed and lead to failure.
2. *Payout level.* It is important that some bonuses be paid, particularly at the beginning. Sometimes this does not happen because the performance level that must be achieved before a bonus is paid is set too high.
3. *Management attitudes.* Unless managers are favorable to the idea of participation, the plan will not fit the management style of the organization. In some organizations, the plan has been tried simply as a pay incentive plan without regard to the management style, and it has failed because of a poor fit.
4. *Plan focus.* Most plans focus only on labor savings. This presents problems in organizations where other costs are great and are under the control of the employees. It can lead to the other costs being ignored or even increased in order to reduce labor costs.
5. *Communication.* For the plan to work, employees must understand and trust it enough to believe that their pay will increase if they perform better. For this belief to occur, a great deal of open communication and education is needed. Often this is ignored and, as a result, plans fail.
6. *Union cooperation.* For the Scanlon Plan to succeed, the local union must be supportive. In most of the places where it has been tried the local union has supported it. However, some failures have occurred in situations where unions have not supported it sufficiently.
7. *Threat to supervisor.* The plan changes the roles of supervisors. They are forced to deal with many suggestions, and their competence is tested and questioned in new ways. Unless supervisors are prepared for and accept these changes, the plan can fail. This point goes along with the general point that management must be prepared to manage in a different way.

The following are attributes of the Scanlon Plan that limit its applicability and cause it to fail in some situations.

1. *Organization size.* The plan is based on employees seeing a relationship between what they do and their pay. As organizations get larger, this is harder to accomplish. Most successful Scanlon Plan companies have less than five hundred employees. One solution to this problem is to have several plans in one company (Dana Corporation has done this).
2. *Performance measurement.* In some organizations, good performance measures and a reasonable performance history simply do not exist and cannot be established. This is often true in organizations where rapid technological and market changes occur. When this is true, the Scanlon Plan is not appropriate.
3. *Measurement complexity.* Often performance can be measured only in very complex ways. The truer this is, the more difficult it is to make the plan work, because there is no clear, easily understood connection between an individual's behavior and rewards.
4. *Administrative costs.* It costs money to administer a Scanlon Plan. Substantial bookkeeping and clerical costs are involved, as well as meeting

and administrative time. In some organizations, these can be so large as to discourage use of the plan.

5. *Worker characteristics.* The plan depends on workers wanting to participate and wanting to earn more money. Admittedly, most workers have these goals, but certainly not all do. Unless a substantial majority of the employees want the benefits the plan offers, there is no way it can succeed.

In summary, there is evidence that the introduction of a Scanlon Plan can lead to a higher quality of work life, greater organizational effectiveness, and stronger unions. However, the evidence clearly shows that these benefits have not always been obtained when Scanlon Plans have been introduced. The following conditions seem to favor the successful implementation of the Scanlon Plan:

1. management commitment—from top to bottom—to participative management;
2. union support and the feeling that the Scanlon Plan will strengthen the union;
3. small organization size;
4. an organization whose performance can be measured by a simple formula;
5. a good communication program about the plan;
6. a high level of trust in the organization;
7. employees who value money and who want to participate and offer suggestions;
8. competent, confident supervisors;
9. an organization history of stable, measurable performance that can be used as a baseline for the payout;
10. an organization where cooperation among employees is important to the success of the organization;
11. base salaries that are perceived to be equitable.

PAY: PROCESS ISSUES

The emphasis so far has been on the strengths and weaknesses of different pay systems. It is very clear that no pay plan is perfect. It also seems that little progress is being made toward developing better pay plans. During the last ten years only three new approaches to pay administration have been suggested and tried—cafeteria-style fringe benefit programs, lump sum pay increases, and skill-based evaluation plans. This suggests that the time has come to direct some attention away from the mechanics of pay systems (for example, how the point system of job evaluation and profit-sharing formulas can be improved) toward other issues.

A growing body of research and theory suggests that more effort can profitably be directed toward two areas—the *process* side of pay administration, and how pay plans *fit* the rest of the management systems in organizations. In considering process, attention needs to be focused on who should be involved in decisions concerning the design and administration of pay plans, and on what kind of communication structure should exist with respect to pay policies and rates. In considering fit, attention needs to be directed to whether the type of pay plan that is used and the way decisions are made about that plan are congruent with such things as how jobs are designed and how decisions in other areas are made. We will return to the fit issue later; first we will focus on the process issues of decision-making and communication.

The reason for focusing on process can be found in the notion that people respond to the world as they perceive it, not as it exists. How pay is *actually* administered certainly is an important determinant of people's perceptions concerning pay. But the technical details of the plans and the amount of money distributed cannot explain all the variations in perceptions, because people often misperceive situations where pay is involved. This point is made by studies on the effects of communication practices, as well as by a group of studies that have looked at how decisions about pay are made. The communication studies will be considered first, and then we will look at the decision-making studies.

Communication and Pay

Secrecy about management pay rates seems to be an accepted practice in most business organizations, whether they use individual or group plans, bonus or salary increases, objective or subjective performance measures. Secrecy policies, however, are not limited to the area of management compensation, as the following newsnote from the February 18, 1975 issue of the *Wall Street Journal* illustrates:

> *Money Talks:* Jeannette Corporation illegally prohibited employees from discussing wage rates among themselves, an NLRB judge rules. He orders reinstatement of a secretary who was fired for talking about her pay, and tells the company to permit such conversations among employees.

The actions of the Jeannette Corporation also illustrate just how serious some organizations are about pay secrecy. Exactly why some organizations are so concerned about keeping pay rates secret, however, is not easy to determine. There certainly is no evidence that secrecy leads to greater organizational effectiveness or to a higher quality of work life. Still, most managers seem to assume that people should not know what their co-workers are earning. The following letter from the president of one company shows how he justifies secrecy in his organization.

MEMORANDUM TO: LOIS JONES

Certain selected employees of this company have been chosen for a salary increase effective February 1, 1975. I am pleased to advise you that a salary increase in the amount of $600 has been approved for you beginning February 1, 1975.

This salary increase should not be discussed with other employees simply because some of our employees have received no salary increase at all.

Most managers, when asked why they favor secrecy, argue that everyone is more satisfied (the people who do and do not receive pay raises) when the pay is secret. They also point out that most individuals prefer secret pay. What they do not point out, however, is that secrecy also gives pay administrators more freedom in administering pay, because they do not have to explain their actions.

It certainly is true that in most organizations that have secrecy, there is no great demand by employees that pay rates be made public. However, it is also worth noting that unions frequently do make such demands, and that pay is public at nonmanagement levels in most unionized organizations. It is interesting to note what happened at one university when the faculty unionized, because it shows that the desire of management to keep pay secret is not necessarily shared by either the union or the employees, despite the claims of management. The following is part of a memorandum from the administration:

In the present interim-bargaining situation, the University has been advised by legal counsel that it is required by law to comply with the request of a certified bargaining agent for certain individual salary and fringe benefit information on bargaining union members. We therefore intend to comply with the AAUP's request, and we expect to release this information to your bargaining agent shortly.

The AAUP Executive Committee has assured us that they are cognizant of the sensitivity of faculty to this matter, and they recognize the need for confidentiality.

A later memorandum noted:

In my May 5 memorandum to the faculty I ascribed to the AAUP Executive Committee an attitude towards the release of heretofore confidential salary information. I said, you may recall, that

"The AAUP Executive Committee has assured us that they are cognizant of the sensitivity of faculty to this matter, and they recognize the need for confidentiality."

I have now learned that I misunderstood their attitude on this matter. In a letter dated May 8, 1975, the president of the bargaining agent notified me as follows:

"Your memorandum of May 5, 1975, contains an error. The AAUP Executive Committee does not know that the faculty is sensitive about the matter of salary confidentiality."

There is some evidence which shows that making pay public can lead to both a higher quality of work life and greater organizational effectiveness. This is true because openness can help to clear up the kinds of misperceptions that occur when secrecy exists, and because openness generates pressure for a credible, trustworthy, and equitable pay system.

The earlier discussion of pay satisfaction stressed that it is strongly influenced by social comparisons. Obviously, secrecy has a strong impact on the kinds of comparisons that individuals can make. There is no evidence that secrecy eliminates pay comparisons, but there is evidence that when pay secrecy exists, people base their comparisons on inaccurate information, innuendo, and hearsay. If pay secrecy leads employees to estimate the pay of others correctly, then pay satisfaction should be roughly the same with secrecy or without. But if secrecy causes people to overestimate the pay of others, pay satisfaction should be lower with secrecy. The question of whether secrecy leads to high, low, or accurate comparisons has been researched extensively at the management level (see Lawler, 1972; Milkovich and Anderson, 1972). The results show that secrecy tends to lead people to overestimate the pay of individuals at the same levels in the organization (the most important comparison group); further, it shows that the greater the overestimation, the greater the dissatisfaction. The research evidence also shows that individuals tend to overestimate the pay of people below them and to underestimate the pay of individuals above them. These findings suggest that pay secrecy may do more to cause pay dissatisfaction than to reduce it, because it encourages misperceptions that contribute to dissatisfaction.

There is reason to believe that secrecy also can reduce motivation. As was stressed earlier, motivation with respect to pay depends on the rather delicate perception that performance will lead to a pay increase. This perception requires a belief in the organization and a trust in its future behavior. Secrecy does not contribute to trust. Openness does, because it allows people to test the validity of an organization's statements, and it communicates to employees that the organization has nothing to hide (Steele, 1975). In fact, with openness it is quite possible that more individuals would favor the idea of merit pay. One study (Beer and Gery, 1968) found that employees who had accurate information about the pay rates in their company were more favorable to the idea of merit pay than were those who had little information. This finding is hardly surprising. It seems logical that employees will be more willing to accept the risk of a merit system if they have clear evidence that the company can be trusted to distribute pay fairly. With pay secrecy, it is difficult to see how this trust can be established.

Making pay information public does not automatically establish the belief that pay is based on performance or ensure that people will get accurate performance feedback. All public pay information can do is clarify those situations where pay actually is based on merit, where this fact might not otherwise be obvious because relative salaries are not accurately known. This was true in one organization that had a merit-based plan and pay secrecy. At the beginning of a study, data showed that the employees saw only a moderate relationship between pay and performance. Data collected after the company became more open about pay showed a significant increase in the employees' perceptions of the degree to which pay and performance were related (Lawler, 1971). The crucial factor in making this change to openness was that pay was actually tied to performance. Making pay rates public where pay is not tied to performance will only serve to emphasize this more dramatically and thereby further reduce the power of pay to motivate effective performance.

The general tendency of managers to overestimate the pay of managers around them probably explains why managers may not see a relationship between pay and performance even when a relationship exists. For example, in one organization the average raise given was 6 percent, but most managers believed that it was 8 percent; further, the larger a manager's raise was, the larger the manager believed other people's raises were (Lawler, 1972). These misperceptions had the effect of wiping out much of the motivational force of the differential reward system that was actually operating. No matter how well managers were performing, they believed that they were getting less than the average raise. This problem was particularly severe among the high performers, because they believed that they were doing well and yet receiving average rewards. This was ironic, because their pay did reflect their performances. Thus, even though pay was actually tied to performance, these managers were not motivated because they could not see the connection.

There is another way in which pay secrecy may affect motivation. Several studies have shown that accurate feedback about performance is a strong stimulus to good performance (Vroom, 1964). People work better when they know how well they are doing in relation to some meaningful standard. For a manager, pay is one of the most meaningful pieces of feedback information—high pay means good performance, and low pay is a signal of poor performance. The research discussed already shows that when managers do not really know what other managers earn, they cannot correctly evaluate their pay and the feedback implications of it. Because they tend to overestimate the pay of subordinates and peers as well as the raises others get, the majority of managers consider their pay low; in effect, they receive negative feedback. Moreover, although this feedback suggests that they should change their work behavior, it does not tell them what types of changes to make. When managers are not doing their jobs well, negative feedback is undoubtedly what they need. But it is doubtful that it is what is needed by managers who are performing effectively.

In addition to clarifying the relationship between pay and performance, openness has another important effect. It forces decision-makers to defend their salary practices. Secrecy makes it difficult for people to obtain the kind of factual information they need to question their salary, to understand the raise they have received, and to determine the validity of what supervisors say about the relative size of the raise. With secrecy, all most individuals can say is that they feel they deserve more money. Without secrecy, the individuals who want to confront their boss and ask for a raise can say specifically that "X makes Y amount of money. Why don't I?" Potentially this is desirable for both organizational effectiveness and quality of work life. It gives individuals the opportunity to find out how they are being dealt with by the organization, and it can motivate the superior and the organization to do a better job of administering pay. There is danger here, however, that openness may lead superiors to decide to pay everyone the same amount, so that they will not have to explain or justify pay differences.

There is one final question that arises whenever greater openness about pay is discussed: How much information about pay should be made public? In other words, should everyone's salary be made public, or only pay ranges and distributions? The answer depends on the situation. If the organization has always had strict pay secrecy, then it would be foolish to try to move to complete pay openness overnight. As a beginning, an organization might release some information on pay ranges and median salaries for various jobs. Most individuals do want at least this much information to be public. Next, organizations might give out information about the size of raises and about who is getting them. Finally, the organization could move to complete openness. This should be done only when the whole organization has become more democratic and is characterized by a high level of trust among supervisors, subordinates, and peers. The pay system must fit the climate of the organization. Authoritarian and democratic organizations require different pay systems. The latter can easily tolerate openness about pay and the basing of pay on performance. It is much less clear that openness can be easily tolerated in an authoritarian organization.

Participation and Pay System Effectiveness

A number of decisions need to be made about pay. The most important are those concerned with pay system design and those concerned with how much particular individuals are paid. Although these decisions are typically made by top management, there is evidence to suggest that they might best be made by the individuals who are affected by the decisions. Two recent studies provide clear evidence that participation by lower level employees in pay system design can make a difference in the impact of the plan. In the first study, two work groups were studied; in one, productivity was very high and had continued to go up for more than ten years (Cammann and Lawler, 1973; Lawler and Cammann, 1972). In the other group, productivity was low and had remained relatively stable for years. Both groups did the same kinds of jobs, and they had similar pay incentive plans. In the second study, identical incentive plans designed to motivate attendance were installed in a number of work groups (Lawler and Hackman, 1969; Scheflen, Lawler, and Hackman, 1971). In some groups the plan was highly successful in reducing absenteeism, but in others it was only moderately successful.

We can explain why the same pay plans worked well in some of these situations but not in others by looking at who was involved in designing the pay plans. In the attendance bonus study, the one characteristic that distinguished the groups where the plan worked from those where it did not was decision-making. The plan was designed and developed by the employee groups where it worked, but it was imposed on those groups where it was less effective. In the other study, the group where the plan worked had a long history of participating in decision-making, and they had actually voted on the plan when it was put into effect years earlier. In the other group, no history of participation existed, and the plan had simply been designed by management and imposed on the employees.

Thus, we have some evidence that participation in the design of a pay incentive system can influence its effectiveness. This raises the question of why participation makes a difference. In some situations it may lead to the design of a better plan, because it involves a high level of information exchange. However, in the studies cited above this cannot account for the differences, because similar plans produced different results. Other research shows that participation contributes to the amount of information employees have about what is occurring, and also to their feelings of control over and commitment to what is decided (Vroom, 1964).

As has been stressed, for incentive pay plans to work, employees must see a relationship between pay and performance. One possibility is that when employees participate in the design and administration of a system, they are more likely to trust that a pay-performance relationship exists for three reasons: (1) they have more information about the plan, (2) they are committed to it, and (3) they have control over what

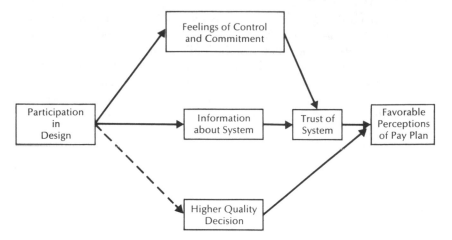

Figure 4.3–The Effects of Participation on Perceptions of Pay

happens. This reasoning is summarized in Figure 4.3. This figure also shows that under some conditions participation leads to higher quality decisions, and that this in turn leads to favorable pay perceptions.

In the two studies mentioned above, the factors shown in Figure 4.3 probably did contribute to the success of the plans in the groups that participated in their design. In the attendance bonus study, for example, the employees in the groups that developed the plan did seem to feel a sense of commitment that was not present in the other groups. In the production bonus study, the group that increased in production clearly seemed to have more commitment to the plan, to have a clearer perception of how it operated, and to feel more control over it.

So far the emphasis has been on the effect of participation on pay incentive systems. The same kind of thinking would seem to be applicable to systems that are designed to set salary levels and to influence pay satisfaction, absenteeism, and turnover. To test this out, G. D. Jenkins and I have been conducting a study in a small manufacturing plant. As a part of this study, the employees were asked to design a pay system for their plant. This was handled by a committee of workers and managers who did considerable research on different kinds of job evaluation plans and gathered salary survey data. They ended up developing a plan that gave control of salaries to the employee work groups. This plan was put into effect, and the employees set each other's salaries.

The results of the new pay program were an 8 percent increase in the organization's salary costs and a significant realignment of employees' salaries. A survey of the company six months after the new system went into effect also showed significant improvements in turnover, job satisfaction, and satisfaction with pay and its administration. Why did this occur? The workers seemed to feel better about their pay because the additional information they received gave them a clearer, more accurate picture of how it compared with others' pay. Further, participation led to feelings of ownership of the plan, and produced a plan where the actual pay decisions were made by peers. These factors led to a belief that the plan was fair and trustworthy. It also seemed that the new pay rates were more in line with the workers' perceptions of what was fair, so that pay satisfaction would have increased somewhat even if the employees had not developed commitment to the plan. This is not surprising. What constitutes fair pay exists only in the mind of the person who perceives the situation, and in this particular organization the plan allowed the people with the relevant feelings to control the pay rates. Thus, employee participation led to more understanding and commitment and to better decisions.

Similar findings have come from the data collected by Jenkins and myself at the General Foods Topeka plant. There pay rates are based on the skills of the employees, and other employees openly decide when the skill has been acquired. In this situation, pay satisfaction is high and turnover is practically nonexistent. It is interesting to contrast the situation in this plant, and in the plant previously discussed, with the way pay is handled for managers in most organizations and for most employees in nonunion companies. The process is almost completely reversed. That is, in most organizations pay rates are set by supervisors or higher management, and the individual has little influence on these rates. Further, pay rates of all employees are kept secret, as are the results of salary surveys, so that the individual has little information about what others are paid. Given such a system, it is hardly surprising that employees often do not have any commitment to the pay plan and do not trust company statements that say they are fairly paid.

At first glance it may seem surprising that, when given the chance, employees gave themselves only an 8 percent raise (in the Lawler and Jenkins study). This did not come about because they were highly paid already; rather it came about because they decided to behave responsibly and set their wages at the 50th percentile of their labor market. There is other evidence of workers behaving responsibly when they are asked to set wages. Lawler and Hackman (1969), for example, noted that the employees asked for a very small bonus in that study. Gillespie (1948) has reported on a study where workers were allowed to participate in setting rates:

> When a new job was to be quoted, the job description was sent to the shop and the men got together and worked out methods, times, and prices; the result went back via the foreman to the sales department in order that a

quotation could be sent. I was surprised and horrified at this unplanned, nonspecialized and dishonesty-provoking procedure and set out to improve organization and method. As I went deeper into the study of department economics I found:

    a. The group's estimates were intelligent,

    b. The estimates were honest and enabled the men, working consistently at good speed, to earn a figure LESS THAN THAT COMMON TO SIMILAR SHOPS ON ORGANIZED PIECEWORK,

    c. The overhead costs were lower than they would have been if the shop was run on modern lines.

Perhaps the most interesting case of workers setting their own pay has occurred at the small Friedman-Jacobs Company. According to news reports ("Arthur Friedman's Outrage," 1975), Friedman decided to allow employees to set their own wages, make their own hours, and take their vacations whenever they felt like it. Apparently this rather radical approach has worked well for Mr. Friedman.

"It was about a month before anyone asked for a raise," recalls Stan Robinson, 55, the payroll clerk. "And when they did, they asked Art first. But he refused to listen and told them to just tell me what they wanted. I kept going back to him to make sure it was all right, but he wouldn't even talk about it. I finally figured out he was serious."

"It was something that I wanted to do," explains Friedman. "I always said that if you give people what they want, you get what you want. You have to be willing to lose, to stick your neck out. I finally decided that the time had come to practice what I preached."

Soon the path to Stan Robinson's desk was heavily traveled. Friedman's wife Merle was one of the first, she figured that her contribution was worth $1 an hour more. Some asked for $50 more a week, some $60. Delivery truck driver Charles Ryan was more ambitious, he demanded a $100 raise.

In most companies, Ryan would have been laughed out of the office. His work had not been particularly distinguished. His truck usually left in the morning and returned at 5 in the afternoon religiously, just in time for him to punch out. He dragged around the shop, complained constantly and was almost always late for work. Things changed.

"He had been resentful about his prior pay," explains Friedman. "The raise made him a fabulous employee. He started showing up early in the morning and would be back by 3, asking what else had to be done."

Instead of the all-out raid on the company offer that some businessmen might expect, the fifteen employees of the Friedman-Jacobs Co. displayed astonishing restraint and maturity. The wages they demanded were just slightly higher than the scale of the Retail Clerks union to which they all belong (at Friedman's insistence). Some did not even take a raise. One serviceman who was receiving considerably less than his co-workers was asked why he did not insist on equal pay. "I don't want to work that hard," was the obvious answer.*

---

*Copyright © 1975 by The Washington Post and reprinted with their permission.

Thus, it seems that when employees are given the responsibility for decisions about something important like pay, they often behave responsibly. This is, of course, in contrast to the kinds of demands employees make when they are placed in an adversary relationship, such as most union-management negotiations. Here large demands are the norm. The crucial difference seems to be that in negotiations the workers are bargaining for salaries, not setting salaries.

Of course, having employees set their own wages may not work in all situations. Small organization size, for example, probably is helpful. In small organizations there is a better chance for employees to see a relationship between their behavior and the success of the organization. They quickly realize that if they take too much pay the organization will not be able to function. Type of business also may be another important factor in determining how successful employee control of pay will be. Consumer businesses like the appliance business that Friedman is in probably are relatively amenable to this approach. All employees are usually aware that the firm operates on the margin between selling price, which is known to all, and the cost of goods, which is also known. Because most employees meet customers, they realize that higher prices mean less business, and so they are aware that sales costs (translate salaries) can only be so high or the company will go out of business. It also probably is very important that salaries be public if they are to be self-set. Public pay allows group pressure to be used against anyone whose pay is too high and who is harming the business and jeopardizing the pay of all.

A great deal more research is needed on what kind of participation in pay decisions is appropriate. A number of different kinds of participation are possible. Decisions need to be made about system design, about where individuals should fall in the system, and about what the salaries of individuals should be. In other words, decisions need to be made about how big the pie will be, what procedure will be used to divide it up, and what size piece each person will get. Further, there are, as many have pointed out, different levels of participation. These range from consultation to full participation, when the employees make the final decision (Tannenbaum and Schmidt, 1958; Vroom and Yetton, 1973). In the study by Jenkins and myself that was mentioned earlier and in the Lawler and Hackman study (1969), the employees were asked to make all the pay system design decisions, but were told that their recommendations with respect to amount of pay were subject to veto by the company president. This approach seemed to work well. The employees made recommendations that management considered realistic. It is quite possible, however, that research will show that this approach cannot be used in many situations, and that the type of participation that is appropriate depends on a number of situational factors as well as on the type of decision to be made.

In unionized situations a different approach is needed, but there are possibilities for participation in pay decisions nevertheless. Decisions concerned with the type of pay system and the relative pay of individuals could be made jointly by the union and management outside of the normal adversary relationship. At present this rarely happens. Unions do play an important role in assuring that external equity exists, because they try to get similar pay for their members in different organizations. They also act as appeal agents for individuals who feel inequitably treated. However, only a few unions participate in joint union-management job evaluation committees. This would seem to be an area where more unions could make a significant additional contribution to the quality of work life. Unions could also become more proactive with respect to system design and could start trying to influence the kinds of pay systems organizations use.

It seems likely that participation can most easily be employed in designing the basic pay system. Although individuals clearly have vested interests here, there is basic agreement in most organizations about the guiding principles that should be used (for example, that pay should be based on seniority, job level, and performance). It seems to be much more difficult to take a participative approach to deciding how much will be given out in wages or how much each individual will receive. In most situations the employees have too much self-interest in such decisions. In most organizations, therefore, management probably will, for the foreseeable future, determine just how much money will be spent.

Decisions about how individuals will be treated within an established pay structure are different from decisions about how much money will be spent. In the Topeka plant and a few other plants around the world, for example, this decision is made by peers, and this approach seems to be working reasonably well despite a few problems. Probably the most important of these problems is the difficulty peer groups have in refusing a pay raise request when there are no limits on how many individuals can get raises for good performance ratings. This is a particular problem where there are no objective standards for job performance. Some organizations have tried to handle this by giving the group a lump sum to allocate among its members. This prevents the group from deciding that everyone is doing well and deserves the maximum increase the organization can offer. But this lump sum approach does not prevent the group from deciding to give everyone the same raise. This often is not functional for the reasons noted previously, and yet it seems to be a frequent outcome because individuals have trouble talking about each other's performances. This seems to be particularly true when there are no agreed-upon standards. Most groups that have handled this issue successfully have had agreed-upon standards. They also have engaged in considerable process work and have had expert process consultation available.

In summary, data are accumulating to support the thinking represented in Figure 4.3. Participation in pay decision-making in some situations does seem to increase pay satisfaction and motivation. It has this effect because it increases trust and commitment, improves decision quality, and assures that employees will have accurate information about how pay is administered. It also seems to help assure that pay will actually be allocated in ways that fit the employees' perceptions of equity and lead to pay satisfaction.

REWARD SYSTEMS AND ORGANIZATION CHANGE

The apparent relationship between participation and trust in pay system design has some interesting implications for organization change efforts. Many organization change theorists argue that participation can increase trust and satisfaction, but few suggest that participation *start* in or even include the reward systems of the organization. A recent review of participation in management by the International Labor Organization fails to note any examples where participation has included pay system design or administration (Walker, undated). In most writings on organization change, pay administration is seen as a difficult area to work in and one that, if it is to be dealt with at all, is dealt with only after a spirit of trust and participation has been established (Likert, 1961, 1967). For example, a recent book on the Scanlon Plan suggests that if a climate of participation and trust exists, then a Scanlon Plan should be installed because it is likely to be successful (Frost et al., 1974).

The arguments presented so far do not disagree with the view that pay and reward systems can be easily changed after a spirit of trust and participation has been established. Indeed, some of the studies cited earlier supported this point, in the sense that the pay system changes were made easier because a good climate already existed (for example, Lawler and Cammann, 1972). However, I would like to suggest the possibility of starting organization development efforts with participation in pay administration, precisely because this is such an important and difficult issue to deal with. An alternative approach is to begin with some other rewards (for example, promotion), although there are reasons for favoring pay. As has already been noted, pay is important to most employees, and there are a number of interesting and significant changes that can be made in pay systems that have the potential of improving both the quality of work life and organizational effectiveness.

The idea of starting an organization development program with changes in pay system decision-making is consistent with the literature that suggests that participation is likely to be meaningful only when it involves decisions that are important to employees, that they have information about, and that they want to participate in (Vroom, 1964). Such an approach also seems likely to lead to organization-wide changes, because of the importance of the pay issue and because pay changes affect all levels in an organization. This is in notable contrast to some other approaches (for example, job redesign), which start with small groups and often have trouble spreading to the rest of the organization. Success in the area of pay system decision-making can strongly reinforce a more participative style of management and thus can lead to experimentation with other issues. Pay system changes are also highly visible and immediate, and so can produce rapid change. What better indication of the seriousness of an organizational development effort and of the trustworthiness of management than for management to turn over pay administration to employees? Such an action can provide dramatic proof to employees that management is serious when it talks about a new approach. Finally, in order to design an adequate pay system (particularly an incentive system), employees must have a good idea of how their organization operates from an economic point of view. This requires some education, but it often pays dividends. This knowledge can help employees do their jobs better and can lead to valuable suggestions from employees.

Some evidence in support of beginning an organizational development effort with pay changes is provided by the results Jenkins and I are obtaining in the manufacturing plant where the employees were asked to design their own pay system. Prior to this, the plant was run in a very traditional way. Trust of management and satisfaction were low, and turnover was high. After the experience with redesigning the pay system, trust, job involvement, and job satisfaction all went up in a manner that indicates the experience affected other areas of the relationship between the employees and the company. The experience of many Scanlon Plan companies also suggests that organization change efforts can begin with pay system changes. Lesieur (1958) argues quite convincingly that a Scanlon Plan often leads to a high level of worker involvement in decision-making, and that when this happens it is very effective.

Even if an organization does not want to begin by using participation in the pay area, pay system changes can be helpful in establishing the significance of an organization change project. Putting everyone on salary, for example, can communicate that things are different. Doing an attitude survey and then adjusting the pay system according to the results can communicate to employees that the organization is concerned about their preferences. Starting a job redesign change effort by giving everyone a pay increase so that they are paid for their new job before they start doing it can be a way of indicating that individuals will be doing more important jobs and that the change is real.

Finally, a strong case can be made for the argument that the reward system implications of an organization change project should always be considered *before* the project is begun. Often organizations begin projects without thinking about pay, or by simply saying that pay system problems will be worked out later. For example, a number of organizations that have gone into job enrichment projects have said that a gains-sharing system will be worked out later if gains materialize. The advisability of this approach is doubtful. A good guess, and it is only a guess at this time, is that it is easier to work out a gains-sharing plan before there is anything to share than after there is a fixed amount available. It would seem that waiting until the gains have materialized is more likely to create a dysfunctional bargaining situation. Organizations also have been known to give pay increases to employees in job enrichment experiments without considering the effect of such raises on other employees. Even though the other employees are not adversely affected, they still often feel inequitably treated. In some situations this has led to employee demands that they be allowed to participate in the project or that it be cancelled. This kind of pressure can be functional, because it can encourage dissemination of the job enrichment experiment. But it can also be dysfunctional if dissemination is difficult or premature.

SYSTEM CONGRUENCE

It is frequently pointed out in the literature on organization structure that organizations have multiple systems; it is less often pointed out, but equally valid, that in an effective organization all systems are congruous (Katz and Kahn, 1966; Leavitt, 1965). When incongruence exists, a role conflict situation is set up. Employees receive conflicting messages about what behavior is expected of them and how the organization regards them. Although employees are capable of some degree of compartmentalization, it is difficult and uncomfortable for them to undergo this for a long period of time in an area as important as rewards (Kahn, Wolfe, Quinn, Snoek, and Rosenthal, 1964). Thus, systems usually head toward balance. This often leads employees to reject the changes that have been introduced unless those changes are part of a total system change (Katz and Kahn, 1966; Leavitt, 1965). One implication of this is that changes that start with the reward system must spread to other areas; another is that changes that start elsewhere must, before too long, deal with the reward system so that system congruence will exist.

Unfortunately, relatively little research has been done on what constitutes system congruence or symmetry or just how it can be achieved. Thus, there is little empirical evidence about congruence. Nevertheless, a few observations can be made. It would seem that congruence must exist within and between two areas—decision-making process and system design or structure. As far as decision-making process is concerned, congruence would seem to mean that decisions about such things as rate of production, product quality, new employee selection, and purchasing must be made in the same way that decisions about rewards are made.

As far as design or structure is concerned, congruence would seem to mean that the type of job evaluation plan (for example, skill based versus point method) and incentive plan (for example, group or individual) used must be supportive, in a measurement and reward sense, of the way jobs are designed and decisions are made. Specifically, the reward system needs to measure and reward those things that are critical (for example, cooperation and skill acquisition) in making the job and the organization design work. It also needs to measure behavior at the level (individual, group, or department) that the job design emphasizes. Congruence also would seem to require that the reward system emphasize only those differences among people that are supportive of the basic structure and decision-making approach in the organization.

The importance of congruence has often been overlooked by people who take job enrichment and participative management approaches to organizational development. I have come across a number of cases where either a traditional job enrichment approach or an autonomous work group approach was tried, and nothing was done to change the structure of the reward system. In almost every instance problems were caused by a misfit between the structural design of the pay system and the new job designs. In several instances job enrichment and job rotation were implemented, but a traditional job evaluation plan was left in place. As a result employees demanded higher pay because they now had more responsibility. In one plant a woman who was asked to take notes at team meetings asked for a raise because she had taken on secretarial duties. Management had trouble answering this demand because the job evaluation plan was designed for situations where employees did not rotate and acquire new skills. It is interesting to note that in the Topeka plant, where both job enrichment and a skill-based evaluation plan were installed, these problems are not present because the evaluation approach is supportive of people changing jobs and acquiring new skills; in fact it rewards them for doing so.

In another case, a large airline tried an autonomous work group experiment with its maintenance employees. The experiment failed because the pay system was not changed. The employees were not on an incentive plan, but they had come over the years to expect large amounts of overtime. In effect, because harder work did not get them more money and slower work did (it got them overtime), they had decided to work overtime to earn more money. Thus the establishment of an autonomous work group failed to increase performance not because the concept was defective but because good performance was against the best economic interests of the employees.

Lindholm (1974) has reported on a Swedish case that emphasizes what can happen when a pay system does not fit the way jobs and organizations are structured. In this situation a piecework system was abandoned in favor of an hourly wage plan, and the jobs of the employees were enriched. The result was a failure—performance went down and turnover went up—apparently because both the financial incentive to perform well and the positive effect the system had on scheduling were gone. Two years later a plant-wide incentive system was added. Suddenly productivity went up 45 percent, and turnover dropped to a lower level than before the piecework plan was dropped. This pay plan seemed to fit perfectly with the new organization design. It provided motivation by tying pay to performance. And because it rewarded plant performance, it encouraged the cooperation and teamwork needed to make the new approach to job and organization design work effectively.

It was noted earlier that in many of the successful Scandinavian experiments in job and organization redesign, pay incentive plans have been used (see Jenkins, 1973; Linestad and Norstedt, 1972). The plans have never rewarded individual performance but instead have focused on group, department, or plant-wide performance. These experiments seem to point to the same conclusion as the research mentioned earlier on the Scanlon Plan—that some kinds of pay incentive plans can be very effective in an organization that uses participative management, autonomous work groups, and job enrichment. In some ways, this is an ironic conclusion, because the proponents of these approaches often argue that they are powerful motivators and make pay incentives unnecessary. It is also ironic that traditionally-run organizations usually are in a poor position to use pay as an incentive because the trust level is low—yet these are just the organizations that need to use pay as a motivator the most.

As summarized in Table 4.6, this discussion suggests some interesting conclusions about what constitutes system congruence. This table shows what types of reward system practices are most congruent with a more traditional or authoritarian approach to organization design and management (theory X in McGregor's terminology), and what

Table 4.6–Appropriate Reward System Practices

Reward System	Traditional or Theory X	Participative or Theory Y
Fringe Benefits	Vary according to organization level	Cafeteria — same for all levels
Promotion	All decisions made by top management	Open posting for all jobs; peer group involvement in decision process
Status Symbols	A great many carefully allocated on the basis of job position	Few present, low emphasis on organization level
Pay		
Type of System	Hourly and salary	All salary
Base Rate	Based on job performed; high enough to attract job applicants	Based on skills; high enough to provide security and attract applicants
Incentive Plan	Piece rate	Group and organization-wide bonus, lump sum increase
Communication Policy	Very restricted distribution of information	Individual rates, salary survey data, all other information made public
Decision-Making Locus	Top management	Close to location of person whose pay is being set

types are more congruent with a human resources or participative approach (theory Y). The term *traditional approach* implies strict specialization and standardization of function, and a tall organization structure with a strict hierarchical approach to decision-making. The term *human resource approach* implies management based on pushing decision-making down to lower levels, an emphasis on creating meaningful jobs, a flat organization, and an emphasis on openness within the organization.

The recent work on contingency theory suggests that neither of these approaches is necessarily superior to the other. According to contingency theory, what happens depends on the type of environment that is being dealt with and the type of technology being employed (Galbraith, 1973; Lawrence and Lorsch, 1967). Thus, we cannot conclude that one style of reward system administration is always or necessarily best. Rather, we must conclude that congruence is always best and that participative decision-making with respect to pay, openness about pay, group and plant-wide incentives, all-salary pay plans, openness about promotion, participation in promotion decisions, cafeteria-style fringe benefit plans, and skill-based bonus plans are congruent with new approaches to organization design that emphasize autonomous work groups and job enrichment. We also end up concluding that standard job evaluation plans, piecework incentive or no incentive at all, many status symbols, low openness about promotion and pay decisions, and the use of an hourly pay system and little participation with respect to promotion and pay decisions are congruent with the more traditional, top-down approach to management.

OVERVIEW: REWARD SYSTEMS

If there is one message that the readers of this chapter should take away with them, it is that there are reward system practices that can contribute to a high quality of work life. True, there are no ideal practices, no universal "goods," but there are better practices and worse practices. Admittedly, what is good and what is bad depends partially on organizational and environmental conditions, but these can be identified and dealt with. This chapter has provided a great deal of data to refute the two extreme positions about the relationship between extrinsic rewards and quality of work life. On the one hand it seems clear that improving the quality of work life is not simply a matter of providing more extrinsic rewards, as some would have us believe. On the other hand it also seems clear that reward systems cannot be ignored in efforts to produce a high quality of work life, as others would have us believe. Any serious effort to improve quality of work life must consider reward systems and must deal with the complexities and conflicts inherent in them.

Table 4.7 summarizes what has been said about the effect of new reward system practices and processes. Each of the practices discussed is rated on six dimensions. The first three are dimensions that contribute to a high quality of work life, and the next three are dimensions that contribute to organizational effectiveness. Because these are new practices, the question that concerns us is whether they represent improvements over traditional practice (for example, secrecy versus openness). Thus, each practice is rated on a five-point scale running from 0 to 4. A rating of 0 indicates that the practice leads to a negligible *increase* over what is usually present in organizations. A rating of 4 indicates that the practice produces a large increase over what is usually present. A note of caution is in order in interpreting these figures. They should be viewed as averages across all situations. They obviously may not be applicable to any particular situation because of the many situational factors that condition their validity.

Table 4.7—Evaluation of Reward Practices

Reward Practice	External Equity	Internal Equity	Individuality	Performance Motivation	Membership	Absenteeism
Open Promotion and Job Posting	1	3	0	2	2	1
Participation in Promotion Decisions	1	4	0	2	2	1
Cafeteria Fringe Benefits	2	0	4	0	2	1
Skill Based Evaluation Plans	0	2	3	2	2	2
All-Salary Plans	2	0	1	0	1	0
Lump Sum Salary Increase plans	0	0	3	1	2	1
Performance Pay Plans	2	2	3	3	1	1
Scanlon Plan	2	0	0	2	2	1
Variable Ratio Plans	0	0	0	0	0	0
Open Pay	1	2	0	2	0	1
Participation in Decisions	1	2	0	2	1	1

Further, they represent the opinions of the author and are supported by little research.

The ratings suggest that improvements can be obtained by changing both the process and the mechanics of reward administration. The process changes of moving to a more open and participative system are rated favorably. The one mechanical practice that seems to offer little is variable ratio reward plans. All the others seem to have something to contribute to both a high quality of work life and organizational effectiveness. Because many of these practices are new, it will be interesting to see if this optimistic conclusion will stand up under the research that needs to be done to test its validity.

CHAPTER 5
GROUP AND INTERGROUP RELATIONS*

CLAYTON P. ALDERFER

Yale University

Marian was a black, older female research assistant in a production department of a large industrial corporation. She was also an officer of the local union and an employee with more than twenty years of service to the company. I am a younger, white male professor from a local university. I met Marian because she was a member of a division task force set up by management to improve hierarchical and lateral communication. The task force was very close to being a microcosm of the 250-person division it represented. It consisted of eleven members—five female, six male; two black, nine white; eight nonmanagement, three management; and at least one from each of the major work groups in the division. Consulting with this group, I noticed that Marian's contributions were frequently ignored by other group members, even though her words seemed to me very insightful and pertinent to the work of the group. Gentle interventions to the effect that people weren't listening to each other had little impact on Marian's being ignored, so I became more directive. "Hey, how about listening to what Marian has to say!" did make it easier for Marian to be heard. There were several occasions when Marian's words saved the group from serious errors. Nevertheless, members of the group were sometimes troubled by Marian's style; some even commented on her "hangups."

---

* Bibliographic assistance for this chapter was most effectively provided by Leroy Wells, Jr.

After several months of work with the task force, I developed an alternative way of understanding Marian's relationship to the group, instead of thinking of it in terms of her personality. The tendency of the task force not to hear her directly paralleled the way the groups she embodied were treated within the division as a whole. Her work group was the smallest in the division. Shortly after the communications project began, a corporate-level decision declared that research was no longer a permissible job title, thereby robbing Marian and others of a desirable professional symbol. Although labor-management relations in the company were not severely strained, normal conflicts of interest did exist between the parties. When Marian sensed that the task force was ignoring or putting down a labor position, she was quick to champion it. Awareness of the plight of female and minority employees was never far from Marian's consciousness. She viewed herself—and her work history confirmed her self-image—as a liberated woman years before it was fashionable to be so identified. White male managers several levels above Marian recognized her as a "spokesman for her people."

Marian was identified with many groups in the division. Her role in the task force made her many group memberships salient because of her efforts to improve communications among these groups in the division. Moreover, the cumulative effect of Marian's group identifications was especially potent because so many of her groups occupied comparatively lower power positions in relation to other groups in the system. She was labor in a management run corporation; female in a male dominated system; black in a predominantly white company; research in a production oriented division; and more than fifty years old in a setting where the average age was less than forty.

To survive, Marian had to understand intergroup relations. In contrast to many older high seniority employees, she retained a delightful sense of vitality. Despite her enthusiasm and commitment, however, she was sometimes hurt by people's reactions to her, and at these times she would either become angrily insistent or quietly defiant. Marian paid a price for these reactions, because the emotions she expressed interfered with the ability of many to hear her.

Her special contribution to the task force was to be alert for areas of jurisdictional conflict among groups. Stimulated largely by Marian's concerns, the group conducted itself in a way that ultimately earned the endorsement of the union. Yet few people seemed to understand the number of intergroups Marian carried within her or the insights she produced as a consequence. Her behavior was most often explained as a function of her personality, and the painful truths she spoke were frequently overlooked or inadequately appreciated.

Marian's story powerfully illustrates the many tensions that may accumulate for a person who has many group identifications within a work organization. All organization members belong to several groups according to their hierarchical position, function, profession, ethnicity, sex, and age. Thus far organizational psychology has paid more attention to individuals than to groups in organizations. But the changing American culture—stimulated by the civil rights movement, the women's movement, and the rebellion of youth—has caused changes in all of our major social institutions. The need to cope humanely and effectively with the impact of groups in organizations grows as the number of recognized group identifications of members increases.

Marian's experience shows the many ways that intergroup relations may affect a person's quality of work life. For example, an individual's group memberships may influence his pay, probability of promotion, and job duties. The combination of groups to which people belong may determine the amount of tension they experience, the degree of respect they receive from others, and the extent to which their behavior serves their own interests, the organization's interests, or both.

At this moment there is no well-accepted view of groups and intergroups in organizations that takes account of the complexity I believe to be present. Therefore the aims of this chapter are, first, to examine the nature of group and intergroup dynamics as they occur in work organizations, and second, to relate those understandings to a series of behavioral science interventions that can be employed to reduce the destructive effects of intergroup conflict and to enhance the possibility of improving the quality of work life for groups as well as individuals. The starting point is the assertion that many approaches to understanding group behavior in organizations fail to give an adequate account of intergroup dynamics because they focus almost exclusively on intragroup processes. The next section provides a definition of the human group that gives more attention to intergroup relations than most previous concepts of group behavior. After that we will examine several classical studies of group behavior to detect how the original investigators dealt with intergroup dynamics. Then a series of propositions explaining the nature of intergroup conflict are outlined, and a series of specific intergroups within organizations are defined and described. The chapter concludes by presenting and discussing several behavioral science interventions that might be employed to improve intergroup relations in organizations.

GROUPS IN SOCIAL SYSTEMS

One well-known sociologist declared that the human group is "the most familiar thing in the world" (Homans, 1950). Without some thought, most people would probably agree with Homans. They would feel as though they know what a group is, how to understand group behavior, and perhaps even how to be an effective group member. Because groups abound everywhere and most people are members of several groups, each of us does possess the accumulated knowledge of his *personal* experiences with group life. But widespread *general* understanding of group behavior does not exist. The preceding example showed how Marian's associates tended to explain her behavior in personality terms rather than in group dynamics terms. Social scientists whose professional commitment is to advancing knowledge about group behavior do not agree among themselves about the definition of a group (Cartwright and Zander, 1968; Deutsch, 1973). Therefore, one cannot begin an analysis of groups in social systems by quoting a generally accepted definition of the human group, for there is no single legitimate authority to call on. A definition is necessary, however, and the one proposed here has several origins—the life experiences of the author, the analyses of several social scientists, and the problems to be examined in later portions of the chapter.

> A human group is a collection of individuals (1) who have significantly interdependent relations with each other, (2) who perceive themselves as a group by reliably distinguishing members from nonmembers, (3) whose group identity is recognized by nonmembers, (4) who have differentiated roles in the group as a function of expectations from themselves, other group members, and nongroup members, and (5) who, as group members acting alone or in concert, have significantly interdependent relations with other groups.

This definition of a group differs from many proposed by other writers in the relative attention it pays to external compared to internal group relations. Human groups are open systems—they regularly exchange matter, information, and energy with other groups and the wider social system of which they are a part. Other group definitions have been more inward looking and have failed to recognize fully the extent that behavior among group members is affected by the external relations of the group as a whole and of individual members.

The idea of significantly interdependent relations among members does not imply that all members must have face-to-face interaction with each other. It does mean that members share common concerns, because such concerns have been imposed from outside or initiated from within. Group members without regular face-to-face interaction can distinguish members from nonmembers because all members use symbols that are not as well known to nonmembers as to members. The members of the sales department of a large corporation, for example, may never directly interact with all the other members, but they will be familiar with a common approach to selling company products.

Thus, two members of the sales department, who are not personally known to each other, could distinguish their common group membership by reference to information and procedures known only to members of the department. In general, symbols used by group members need not be secretly guarded in order to be comparatively unfamiliar to nonmembers. Interdependence among group members simply causes them to evolve a common set of symbols and behavior patterns that would not be well known to nonmembers.

A collection of individuals known only to each other is not a group. For a group to exist, some nonmembers must know that there is a group in which they are not members. This knowledge is necessary for the group as a whole to relate to its external environment. Knowledge of a group by nonmembers is not equivalent to formal recognition, however. The black managers in a large, predominantly white corporation petitioned higher management to recognize them as a formal unit in the system. Although top management refused the request, the black managers were known both to each other and to the corporation. They were a group.

Role differentiation among group members varies widely depending on the nature of the group, the number of members, the type of individuals who belong, and the way the group relates to its environment. Role differentiation among members establishes their interdependence with one another.

The survival and vitality of a group depends on the evolution of roles to manage the internal and external problems of group life. If the internal concerns of group members are not satisfied, members will begin to drop out, and eventually the group will cease to exist. If the external demands on a group are not met, the group will be unable to obtain new resources from the environment for survival and growth. Some roles emerge to express particular internal concerns of group life. Other roles are established to deal with the group's relations with its external environment. Methods of selecting individuals for leadership and other roles in groups differ according to the relative power available to members (inside forces) and nonmembers (outside forces). Some leaders derive their legitimacy from the wider social system in which their group is embedded through appointments by higher ranking executives. Others are selected by the group. Regardless of how they are appointed, however, group leaders manage the crucial tensions between the internal and external transactions of their groups.

The present idea of a human group begins with individuals who are interdependent, moves to a sense of the group that is confirmed from inside and outside the membership, recognizes the varied roles played by members because of their internal and external relationships, and concludes by noting that the group is a significant interacting unit in the social system in which it is embedded. In the following pages this concept of group life will be an organizing principle.

SMALL GROUP BEHAVIOR
AND INTERGROUP RELATIONS

Small groups in organizations behave as they do because of relations that develop *among* groups as well as *within* groups. The earliest studies of work groups in organizations tended to emphasize *intra*group more than *inter*group dynamics. This section reviews three well-known studies of small groups in organizations to highlight the often overlooked effects of intergroup dynamics in small group behavior.

Study 1: The Bank Wiring Room. A landmark study in the field of organizational behavior was conducted by Roethlisberger and Dickson (1939) at the Hawthorne Works of the Western Electric Company between November 1931 and May 1932, in a work unit called the Bank Wiring Room. In some important ways this study marked the discovery of group dynamics in industry. Fourteen nonsupervisory male employees held primary responsibilities in the room. Thirteen of the group were twenty to twenty-six years old, and one man was forty. After extensive observation and interviewing, the researchers learned that the social organization of the Bank Wiring Room consisted of two subgroups of different status, plus a number of individuals who were not included in either subgroup. In the front of the room the higher ranking subgroup worked on connector banks. This assignment was more desirable to all the employees than working on selector banks, which were the responsibility of the lower status subgroup at the back of the room. The patterns of relations among the men within the two cliques differed significantly, however, and the cliques differed in their relations to the wider social system in which they were embedded.

Within the Bank Wiring Room there were three different jobs—nine wiremen, three soldermen, and two inspectors. Both cliques in the room were composed of men with different occupations. There were differences in occupational status among inspectors, wiremen, and soldermen. Inspectors had the highest status because they held authority to approve or reject the banks put together by the wiremen and soldermen and thereby partially controlled their income. Inspectors, although they functioned both physically and psychologically inside the Bank Wiring Room, had a different departmental reporting relationship outside the room. Their relationship to wiremen and soldermen was therefore potentially problematic on two counts—authority and external identification.

As it turned out, the relationship of the inspector to the other members of his clique was different in each clique; the core of this difference was found in how the tensions between the inspectors and others in the group were managed. In the high status subgroup, the inspector managed to be both an integrated member and an outsider with authority. As a member of the group he engaged in arguments with members and participated in various games of chance enjoyed by the operators. One of the ways he integrated his authority role with his membership was by proposing and supervising a contest among the operators to determine whose work was of highest quality. Among the other members of the high status clique there was one wireman who seemed to function as an internal leader of the group. He was the most esteemed of all the employees in the Bank Wiring Room, a high producer, and a frequent host of card parties outside of work. There were noticeable contests for dominance between the internal leader and the inspector in the high status subgroup. These contests seemed to help cement the subgroup into a smoothly functioning unit, however, rather than to disrupt it. Furthermore, the inspector of the high status subgroup did not readily accept all directives from outside authorities. He was observed to disagree with higher ranking officials who made requests of his group and to influence their behavior directly.

The production performance of the high status clique was clearly superior to the performance of the low status clique, even though tests administered by the researchers revealed no difference between the groups in IQ or manual dexterity. Because the Bank Wiring Room as a whole was on a group incentive system, the high status clique contributed more to the total income of the room than the low status members. But because the pay rates of individuals reflected their unique performance history, the members of the high status clique also earned more money individually than the members of the low status subgroup. Both inside and outside the Bank Wiring Room, therefore, the higher social-economic status of the clique at the front of the room was confirmed.

In contrast to what happened in the high status clique, the inspector for the low status clique was not at all well integrated with the other members of his subgroup. During the course of the study he was actually driven from the Bank Wiring Room by the members of his own subgroup. On the surface, it appeared as though he had to leave the group because he inadequately performed his job and thereby impeded the performance of the unit. In fact, members of his own clique sabotaged the equipment he used to test their banks. On leaving the group he reported four factors that could have been responsible for his difficulties. First, he felt like a perpetual outsider to the group; unlike the inspector for the high status group, he did not enter into the various informal activities of the clique. Second, he believed that his Armenian nationality presented a major barrier between himself and the operators, all of whom were from northern European or "American" ancestry. Third, he blamed the inspection department for not training him properly. And fourth, he felt he could not get along with the "boys" because they were just irresponsible kids. At forty, he was fourteen years older than the next oldest member of the room. Thus, the contrast between the roles that evolved for the inspectors in the two cliques could not have been more marked.

Similarly, there was also a decided difference in how internal leadership was handled in the low status subgroup. There was a member of the low status subgroup whose performance was outstanding and who aspired to the informal leadership of the clique. But his efforts to speak for the group were not accepted by the membership. His leadership attempts were openly rejected, and he personally was a target of sarcastic remarks. As a person of Polish descent, he belonged to a minority ethnic group that was the target of abuse by other members of the Bank Wiring Room. The low status subgroup seemed to be without either internal or external leadership, but there was a central member who seemed to manifest a high proportion of this subgroup's norms. Although he had the highest IQ and the third highest manual dexterity score of any member in the Bank Wiring Room, he also had the poorest performance. This behavior led him to become a target of much kidding by his peers and an object of attention from higher management. At one time he was taken from the room to receive additional training. Although he willingly accepted this training, he also assured supervisors that he would not improve his performance and kept his word. The key to his success in the room seemed to be the good-natured way he accepted criticism from both his peers and management about his poor performance.

The Bank Wiring Room study has become a famous classic because it showed the effects of the informal organization, in contrast to the organization's formal structure, on employee job behavior. Traditional organization charts had no method of identifying the informal subgroups that emerged from the work structure and from the interpersonal relations among the workers. But the original Bank Wiring Room study did not explain variations in individual and group behavior by reference to dynamics among these subgroups. Nevertheless, it is clear that behavior within the Bank Wiring Room was partially a function of relations *between* the two cliques. In addition, the leadership dynamics of the two subgroups were partly determined by how their internal and external authorities related to each other, and how they maintained or failed to maintain membership in groups outside the room.

Even though all people in the Bank Wiring Room were white males, ethnicity was also an important but overlooked factor in the original explanation. The rejected inspector noted the influence of his ethnic group in determining his difficulties. Other observations by the original researchers showed the prevalence of ethnic concerns in the minds of the employees (Roethlisberger and Dickson, 1939). A solder-man in the high status group whose background was German told a wireman in that group whose nationality was Polish that his family was moving into a neighborhood "where no Polacks are allowed." The wireman responded, "I suppose they won't allow *any* (emphasis his) white people there." The dialogue continued:

Solderman: The only trouble is that we can't take the wireman along with us. They don't allow Polacks below the Mason-Dixon line.
Wireman: No, they just allow niggers down there.

Study II: British Coal Mining. Another well-known study of industrial work groups in which the intergroup dynamics tend to be overlooked is that of Trist, Higgin, Murray, and Pollock (1963) in which the consequences of different sociotechnical systems for mining coal are compared. For generations coalmen were organized by a method called *single place working*. In this procedure the primary work group consisted of six men who shared the same location in the mine and whose pay was jointly determined. Members of such a *marrow group* chose themselves and held autonomous responsibility for all shifts in their territory. Each miner carried out a *composite work role* because he possessed the range of skills required to carry out all tasks demanded of his unit at the coal face.

A technological innovation in the method by which coal was carried out of the mines, called the *face conveyor,* caused a radical change in the single place working tradition. Many problems, both technological and social, grew out of the change to the new method of coal getting, called the *conventional longwall method.* Furthermore, the expected economic returns were not realized. Miners no longer operated in composite work roles but took on much more specialized functions. The sense of autonomous responsibility, shared by all members of a marrow group and extending across a full day's work, disappeared. And the specialized duties performed on separate shifts provoked destructive individual and intergroup competition among members of different shifts, among various role encumbents, and between labor and management. Overall, the technological innovation had disrupted an effectively functioning social system, which in turn had undermined the potential of the new technology.

The social science researchers discovered that not all work groups were organized according to the conventional longwall methods. In some settings they found groups that had evolved a *composite longwall method* that seemed to combine the technological advantages of using the face conveyor with the social system benefits of single place working. Key to the functioning of the composite method was *task continuity*. Rather than basing a group's work identifications on particular functions (for example, cutting, filling, and stoning) and building barriers between roles, the newer method focused on the total task of taking coal out of the mines. It thereby served to unify the group around the task as a whole rather than around its subparts. The focus on the task as a whole was further supported to the degree that (1) miners as individuals were competent to carry out several roles, (2) the work groups contained the requisite variety of skills among the men, and (3) the members were paid on the basis of their group's performance rather than their individual roles.

Trist et al. (1963) observed additional features of the composite method. For one thing, internal leadership functions tended to be shared and rotated among the members of the composite work groups. When work situations became especially stressful, however, the relatively egalitarian method of allocating leadership roles changed, and those most competent to do certain tasks undertook them. Such flexible group processes were undoubtedly aided by the fact that the work teams were permitted to select their own members. The three levels of management above the work teams tended to work primarily on external affairs that influenced the groups. The composite work team approach also minimized occupational status differences among team members. And a group payment method avoided differentiations based on job titles and encouraged people to recognize their interdependencies with each other.

A comparative study between the two modes of work organization (conventional versus composite longwall mining) was undertaken. The results showed that the composite organization surpassed the conventional system in a number of key features.

1. Members working by the composite method showed a tendency to anticipate the effects their work would have for others, while conventional miners were concerned only about their own narrowly defined assignment. As a result, the conventional workers made more extra work for each other than did the composite miners.
2. Individuals in the composite system had greater variety in the tasks they undertook and in the groups with whom they worked than did people in the conventional system.
3. Absence was more than twice as frequent in the conventional system as in the composite system.
4. The conventional system fell behind in its work cycle on 69 percent of the

shifts, while the composite organization lagged in only 5 percent of the shifts. In overall productivity, the conventional system ran at 78 percent of potential while the composite method operated at 95 percent efficiency.

5. Demands for coordination and settlement of jurisdictional disputes by management were far greater under the conventional than under the composite method. Destructive intergroup conflicts that had been set off by the conventional longwall method were substantially reduced by the composite method for organizing groups—probably because the whole task around which each group was organized served as a superordinate goal for the members, and the work teams were not dependent on each other.

In sum, on all measures reported, the composite system was superior to the conventional mode of organization (Trist et al., 1963).

Study III: Hierarchical Relations among Occupational Groups. Although many approaches to group behavior do not make differentiations among types of groups, other observers recognize that some groups consistently react quite differently from others. One dimension on which nonmanagement work groups vary considerably is their level of protest activities, or their tendency to petition for improved working conditions. Between 1951 and 1955, Leonard Sayles (1958) studied three hundred work groups from a hundred plants in a variety of industries. The purpose of his study was to determine what factors seemed to influence the nature and frequency of protest actions taken by work groups. In reviewing the data from his sample of groups, he determined that there were four basic styles in which work groups reacted to authority—apathetic, erratic, strategic, and conservative.

Apathetic groups were least likely to develop grievances or engage in concerted action to pressure management or the union. These groups were not inclined to challenge management decisions or to seek something extra for themselves. They did not distinguish themselves in productivity and were frequently noted for having petty jealousies and interpersonal problems among members. Their members also tended to be low participators in union activities.

Erratic groups showed more frequent protest activity than apathetic groups. But their overall behavioral pattern was termed *erratic* because the seriousness of the issues about which they objected frequently had little relation to the intensity of their reactions. Problems considered minor by union and management might erupt, in other words, into a major confrontation. Simultaneously, longstanding serious difficulties might remain beneath the surface without any attention being given to them. Members of erratic groups were often quite participative in the organizational phase of union activity but moved to less central positions after the union became more established.

Strategic groups were consistently in the center of grievances involving major economic considerations. In contrast to the erratic groups, they were not characterized by sudden flashes of activity. Rather, they were shrewdly calculating pressure groups that demanded constant attention to their problems and could reinforce their demands by group action. Often these groups contained many union regulars who succeeded in getting one of their members elected to a top union office, even when they comprised only a small proportion of the membership.

Conservative groups were the most stable of all those observed. On the surface there was little evidence of turmoil, trouble, or concerted activity. The niche they had carved for themselves in terms of compensation and working conditions was very satisfactory. Their rare grievances against management were pursued inside and outside of formal channels, and it was characteristic of management to respond positively. In fact, there was a tendency for management to be more likely to have grievances against these groups, rather than vice versa. When members of conservative groups participated in union activities— which was less often than strategic groups did—they were noted for selfish pursuit of their own interests.

Sayles (1958) identified both intergroup and intragroup dynamics that seemed to explain the variations in group protest activity. He argues convincingly that a work group's relative ranking among other groups in the system (in terms of the rewards it receives from the organization) was an important factor in predicting its reaction to system authorities. Apathetic and erratic groups, for example, tended to be among the lowest ranking groups in most organizations. It was difficult for groups at this level to develop cohesion among their members because membership in these groups was so unattractive to organization members. Some people in these positions were new to the system and expected to move upward shortly as a result of their own efforts; they did not particularly need group support to improve their standing. Other members of lower ranking groups were senior employees who, for various reasons, had no hope of significantly improving the rewards they obtained from the organization.

Strategic forms of protest, on the other hand, were most likely to come from middle-level groups that were almost at the top of the prestige ladder among groups. Such groups had the self-confidence that emerges from having real value to the organization. Their middle position in the hierarchy of organizational privileges told them that there was hope for improving their relative deprivation. Because membership in these groups was valued by both members and nonmembers, they were able to develop enough cohesion to mount sustained protest activities.

Conservative groups tended to be those who were at the top of the privilege system for nonmanagement employees. Because they had already obtained the best pay, job conditions, and work design, they had fewer reasons to engage in strategic and sustained efforts to improve their relative standing. They were, however, interested in preserving their privileges and acted to be sure that they did not lose what they had gained.

Intergroup Effects Shown in the Three Studies. The three studies just reviewed were selected for discussion because they illustrate different ways that intergroup dynamics might influence small group behavior. In the Bank Wiring Room, external group membership, ethnicity, and age were prominent variables that were ignored in the original analyses. Yet these variables appear to have been an important source of the tensions between the two subgroups. These tensions were related to the behavior of individual members of the groups, and resulted in difficulties in the relations among group members and in poorer group performance than the potential of the individuals who composed the group. Problems facing the lower ranking subgroup from outside group memberships probably increased the frustrations that members of this subgroup faced inside the work room.

In the coal mining studies it was possible to observe the intergroup consequences of the breakdown of small work group boundaries. When the marrow groups were destroyed as a result of the change in work technology, severe intergroup tensions broke out. Left to their own devices without supportive work groups, the miners drifted toward new groups to protect their turf and their other prerogatives. Members with common roles banded together to contest members with other roles, and one shift competed with another for evasion of responsibility and placement of blame. The consequences of this intergroup warfare were harmful for both the miners personally and for their work performance. The breakdown of external work group boundaries set off a process by which new groups formed around the special anxieties of the individual members. These new groups served more to express these anxieties covertly than to solve the personal difficulties facing the miners or to execute the task facing the workers.

Sayles' (1958) study illustrating the various stances toward managerial and union authority taken by work groups points out how small group behavior may be influenced by the intergroup dynamics of the broader social system in which small groups are a part. Occupational rank among work groups was a powerful variable in determining the extent to which specific groups withdrew from, rebelled against, bargained with, or resisted the initiative of higher authorities—regardless of whether the power was localized in union leadership, management, or both. Apathy or rebellion were most frequently observed in the lowest ranking groups that might have conceived of their options in the most polarized fashion. Either they had nothing to gain from investing their energy in task performance or negotiation, or they held out a glimmer of hope for constructive change through revolution. The emotional stance of these groups has much in common with the flight-fight basic assumption identified by Bion (1961). Within a group this emotional condition is most likely to arise when individual members are disenchanted with the degree of gratification they have received from figures of authority (Slater, 1966). Strategic investment in work and negotiation was most frequently observed from middle ranking occupational groups. Their history included past rewards for similar performances, and their future suggested hope for improvement by working within the system.

Most resistance to changes initiated by labor or management came from the oldest, most senior, most established occupational groups. According to most measures of success in the blue-collar culture, these groups had made it, and they were not very interested in rocking the boat in ways that might endanger the positions of relative security and satisfaction they had achieved. In sum, hierarchical standing among work groups within a broader social system seemed to affect the emotional dynamics within the groups so that lower, middle, and upper class showed substantially different group climates.[1]

Events growing out of intergroup relations, therefore, play a significant part in determining the behavior of small groups in organizations. Relations with other groups in its environment may determine how a group forms, the nature of its emotional climate, how roles are structured for individuals who represent group interests, the distribution of resources for group members, the reaction of the group to system authorities, and the effectiveness of the group in achieving its objectives. Thus, to understand group behavior in organizations, knowledge of intergroup dynamics is essential.

DYNAMICS OF INTERGROUP RELATIONS

Aware of the limitations of analyses based only on the dynamics of individual personalities or on the internal relationships of small groups, we now examine explicitly the systematic properties of intergroup relations. A number of basic concepts are helpful for understanding the complex set of behaviors, emotions, attitudes, and beliefs

---

1. My thinking in reviewing Sayles' analysis was also influenced by Smith's (1974) work on hierarchical intergroups.

that arise when groups have interdependent relationships with one another. This section provides a discussion of those concepts as they have been developed from social science research.

Development of Intergroup Relations. The analysis of intergroup relations is in part the study of *power relations* among groups. An important variable influencing the dynamics of groups who are interdependent is their relative power. In some situations power differences between related groups in an organization are relatively small, as in the case of sales and production departments in many manufacturing organizations (see Walton, Dutton, and Fitch, 1966). On the other hand, there are many situations where gross power differences exist among related groups (see Van Den Berghe, 1972).

Significant power differences among groups usually arise from their developmental histories. For example, low power groups often arise initially to express their identities and to protest against frustrations inflicted on them by high power groups. Thus, the earliest developmental phase of an unequal power intergroup relationship occurs when *individuals* who share a common condition induced by actions of a high power group begin the process of forming a group in order to improve their common fate. On the other hand, related groups that have relatively equal power from the outset are not burdened with a history that includes a time when the high power group(s) so dominated the low power group(s) that the very existence of the low power group(s) was not recognized by the high power group(s).

The study of intergroup relations is also closely related to the analysis of *conflict.* Among groups of relatively equal power, the emergent relationship may vary in how conflictful (that is, competitive versus cooperative) it turns out to be. Among groups of unequal power, the degree of conflict is likely to be significantly higher, in part because the relationship began with at least one group's fight to be recognized as a legitimate group in order to express grievances against some other group(s). Conflictful intergroup relations, regardless of how they became that way, are characterized by a systematic pattern of emotional relations among the related groups.

Internal and External Effects. William Graham Sumner (1906) first used the term *ethnocentrism* to characterize the pattern of reactions found among groups in conflict. From the point of view of a given individual, one's own group was the ingroup and the other groups were outgroups. More recently, Levine and Campbell (1972) reorganized Sumner's original formulation and differentiated the properties of groups according to whether they apply to ingroup or outgroup. Table 5.1 summarizes these properties.

Table 5.1-Properties of Ethnocentric Intergroup Relations

Ingroups	Outgroups
Ingroup members see themselves as virtuous, superior, universally human, and strong.	Ingroup members see outgroup members as contemptible, inferior, immoral, and weak.
Ingroup members are prohibited from stealing from or killing ingroup members.	Outgroup members are either encouraged to or not discouraged from stealing from and killing outgroup members.
Ingroup members are encouraged to obey ingroup authorities and cooperate with ingroup members.	There is a general absence of cooperation between ingroup and outgroup members and of obedience to outgroup authorities by ingroup members.
Among ingroup members there is a willingness to remain a member and to fight and die for the ingroup.	Ingroup members are unwilling to join the outgroup, or fight and die for the outgroup. Ingroup members are rewarded for killing outgroup members in warfare.
Ingroup members fear, distrust, and blame outgroup members for ingroup difficulties.	

Cutting across all of these properties is the polarization of feelings between ingroup and outgroup. Rather than holding mixed feelings about both ingroup and outgroup, ingroup members tend to associate positive affect with the ingroup and negative affect with the outgroup. This process relieves members from some of the pain of internal dissent and self-criticism by psychologically locating bad traits more outside than inside their own boundaries (Coser, 1956).

Among some scholars there has been a tendency to assume that interdependent relations among groups virtually assure intergroup conflict and ethnocentrism (Levine and Campbell, 1972). This point of view rests in part on the assumption that the cohesion necessary to bind individual members into a group can exist only if negative affect is not directly exchanged among members. Thus, an *external enemy* is functional for any group, because it provides a target toward which internally generated negative feelings can be aimed. An alternative view implied by Coser (1956) and stated explicitly by Alderfer (1976) is that group cohesion can be built on the capacity of a group to tolerate and work through negative affect among its members. Cohesive groups that permit conflict among members have less need for external enemies on whom to project negative feelings unacceptable within the group. They are, therefore, less likely to form ethnocentric relations with other groups with whom they are interdependent.

On the other hand, there is extensive research evidence supporting the proposition that external threat induces internal cohesion. Sherif and Sherif's (1969) studies of intergroup conflict and competition documented the rise of ingroup cohesion as external conflict increased. Members were more likely to have friends from within their own group and less likely to select associates from the other group. Blake, Shepard, and Mouton (1964) observed that less dissent was permitted in groups in conflict as pressures mounted for members to develop a common front against their enemies. Further, studies of time-bounded conflicts with definite winners and losers showed that being declared victorious or vanquished had different effects on groups (Blake, Shepard, and Mouton, 1964). Winning groups retained their internal sense of positive feelings and cohesion, even to the point of becoming "fat and happy." In contrast, losing groups were much more self-critical and internally conflictful after the outcome had been determined.

Cognitive Distortions   Because of the pattern of emotions just identified, intergroup conflict usually is marked by various forms of irrationality. It is common for groups in conflict to sense this irrationality in others, but it is uncommon for them to see it in themselves.

During an intergroup conflict simulation conducted by this author based on the work of Sherif and Sherif (1969) and of Blake, Shepard, and Mouton (1964), nine groups in competition were asked to give percentage estimates of how much evaluations of their own and the other groups' products were influenced by group loyalty. Eight of the nine groups estimated *other* groups would be more influenced by loyal pressures than their own group. The average percentage given to *own group* loyalty was 23 across all nine groups, while the average percentage of *other group* loyalty was 36. By the end of the exercise two-thirds of the groups thought their own product was best, despite the announcement of independent judges who had selected one product as the winner.

Blake, Shepard, and Mouton (1964) also found that factual distortions occurred as groups judged each other's products during intergroup competition. The researchers allowed competing groups to examine the items produced by each other and then assessed the validity of the information absorbed by the groups. They found that groups showed more accurate understanding of their own than of other groups' products. Also, characteristics common to several products were frequently not identified as such but instead were attributed *only* to the participants' own product.

Sherif and Sherif (1969) found that groups competing in a tug-of-war estimated the length of the contest quite differently depending on whether they were nearly winning or nearly losing. Estimates of the near winner ranged from twenty to forty-eight *minutes* while estimates of the near losers varied from one to three and one-half *hours*. The two groups produced nonoverlapping distributions in their answers— neither of which contained the correct duration of the contest, fifty-five minutes, and both of which reflected their emotional experiences with the intergroup conflict.

Leadership Behavior.   The relationship between internal group cohesion and external conflict also relates to the role of group leaders (Deutsch, 1973). In situations where external threat provokes internal cohesion, observations indicate that some traits are commonly found among individuals who move to occupy leadership roles. Blake, Shepard, and Mouton (1964) found that leaders were distinguished from nonleaders by their tendency to dominate group effort, to express themselves clearly and concisely, and to push the group to stay on the work agenda. Sherif and Sherif (1969) report that the rise of intergroup conflict changed the status of a young man—who had been considered a bully—to that of hero. Another group deposed a leader who, in the minds of his followers, did not take a sufficiently belligerent stance in relation to other groups. In sum, intergroup conflict tends to set in motion forces that bring more authoritarian leaders to prominence. Likewise, it has been suggested that leaders with authoritarian styles tend to provoke external conflict as a means of justifying suppression of dissent among their followers (Frank, 1967). A leader who felt he was losing power within his group might argue that members should put aside their differences with him so that *together* they might fight against a common external threat. A leader with imperialistic desires might justify his actions by providing opportunities for followers to increase their scope of influence.

It is, therefore, reasonable to suggest that the association between internal cohesion and external conflict may be based on causal processes that operate in both directions (Deutsch, 1973). In other words, groups of people do band together more tightly when they face a common threat. And threats may be provoked by leaders who wish to enhance their power by increasing the cohesion of their followers.

The role of leader in a network of intergroup relations is hazardous. We have already noted how the intensification of intergroup conflict may lead some individuals to rise in influence while others decline. For someone outside the pressures generated by such conflict, it may appear as though a leader acting as negotiator for his group is free to respond to "the facts" as they are presented to him. But this view is often erroneously simple. Experiments on intergroup conflict show that leaders whose groups lose in competition face substantial reduction of their influence within the group (Blake, Shepard, and Mouton, 1964). Even during the conflict, negotiators face strong pressures to concede little to their opponents; followers reward them for being tough and for making nonnegotiable demands. Signs that they are open to views from the other side evoke doubt, mistrust, and other forms of punishment from their associates. In this way authoritarian leadership behavior is provoked by followers as well as by the leader's own needs. In addition to pressures from the leader's own groups, their adversaries question their motives and are quick to highlight personality flaws that become noticeable under the pressures of negotiation. Thus, the group leader-negotiator in intergroup relations is a person in the middle whose behavioral alternatives are often severely constrained. After a series of negotiating attempts, leaders learn to anticipate possible responses from their adversaries. Their future behavior is further constrained to those options that they believe (however validly) will lead to desirable responses from their adversaries (Dubin, 1962).

Implications of the Theory. This concludes the discussion of concepts essential for understanding intergroup dynamics. To perceive fully the impact of intergroup relations, one must recognize their effects on single individuals, such as Marian, and on the internal dynamics of small groups, such as in the three small group studies reviewed. When one accepts the validity of an intergroup perspective, it influences how one understands individuals and the internal dynamics of small groups. But the source of intergroup dynamics ultimately rests with *interacting* groups. The previous section presented concepts explicitly addressed to the dynamics of intergroup relations—the conditions that promote the start-up of intergroup relations; the pattern of emotions that occurs during intergroup conflict; the impact of intergroup conflict on intellectual processes; and the mutual influence of leadership and intergroup processes.

Each stage in this analysis has implications for improving the quality of an individual's work life. For example, the identity of an individual cannot be separated from his multiple group memberships. Problems encountered by groups in organizations influence the personal lives of their members. Challenges and opportunities presented to groups may be incorporated into the experience of individual members, thereby enhancing the self-worth and meaningful personal identity of each member. The nature of intergroup life in an organization may also determine whether a person has a group in which he feels fully included, whether he develops harmonious or antagonistic relations with other people in his immediate environment, whether he accurately or inaccurately perceives relevant information, and whether he rises or falls from positions of leadership in the system.

In subsequent sections of this chapter we examine specifically the major classes of intergroups in organizations. Task and hierarchically induced intergroups arise from the principles of division of labor and hierarchy of authority and thereby are rooted in the internal dynamics of pyramidal organizations. Generational, sexual, and ethnic intergroups arise from historical forces external to the traditional objectives of work organizations. But the dynamics of these latter intergroups are not independent of the former ones. Indeed, as we shall see, people's roles, positions, and experiences with the internally determined intergroups are likely to be intimately related to their membership in the externally rooted groups.

TASK INDUCED INTERGROUPS

Classical writers in the field of management viewed division of labor as the reason for and essence of organization (Sofer, 1972). For example, Fayol (cited by Sofer, 1972, p. 130) wrote: "Division of work permits a reduction in the number of objects to which attention and effort must be directed and has been recognized as the best means of making use of individuals and of groups of people." Division of labor affords a means whereby complementary activities may be allocated to related individuals and groups and so allows organizations to produce outputs that would otherwise be impossible. But the process of dividing work contains the seeds of conflict, in part because, as Fayol notes, it encourages the narrowing of attention to one's own area of responsibility. Individuals and groups so oriented can lose sight of broader objectives of the organization and pursue their own goals at the expense of other groups and of the organization. Because division of labor is not limited to any given hierarchical level, intergroup conflicts induced by differences in tasks may occur at all levels of a hierarchy.

A French Bureaucracy. In studying a French industrial monopoly, Crozier (1964) identified a three-way intergroup conflict among operators, machinists, and supervisors at the bottom of the organization hierarchy.

The Operator-Supervisor Intergroup. One of Crozier's major findings was the unusual pattern of relations between machine operators and supervisors. Workers had quite low personal involvement with their supervisors. They were tolerant and cordial but showed no essential respect for the supervisory role. If supervisors made efforts to alter this pattern, they faced strong resistance from operators, and the tolerance formerly experienced was withheld. Further, the position taken by the operators was strongly reinforced by their group norms. Supervisors, on the other hand, had somewhat complementary attitudes toward the operators. They had a low regard for the production workers and thought of them as neglectful, irresponsible, and careless. Among the supervisors, however, there was no consensus about how to treat the operators. Some thought being strict was best. This subgroup admitted that they had discipline problems, and they tended to be younger, better trained, and hostile to the seniority principles employed in the system. Other supervisors took a more laissez-faire position with regard to discipline or said that they decided what to do on the basis of specific issues in question. In short, operators and supervisors had evolved a relationship with each other that minimized personal involvement, kept latent conflicts suppressed, and preserved stability.

The Maintenance Worker-Operator Intergroup. Maintenance workers were a source of considerable tension in relation both to operators and to supervisors. There was a strong dependency relationship between the operators and the maintenance workers (not unlike the kind of relationship one might have expected between real supervisors and subordinates) although the operators and maintenance staff reported to two different hierarchical lines of authority. A sizable minority of the operators felt that the maintenance workers did not do all they could to aid the production process. There was a strong sense of jealousy and resentment about what was perceived as the privileged position occupied by the maintenance group. Crozier concludes that: "Production workers, mostly women, behave as if they were dependent on the maintenance men and resentful of it. The sex difference, of course, is probably an important element of the situation. But this influence should not be exaggerated. No comments were ever made about it" (p. 97).

The maintenance workers showed a reluctant awareness of the operators' problems and some tolerance. Like the supervisors, they thought the workers did harm by not working at a regular pace, and they viewed the workers as having little understanding of technical problems or anything beyond the narrow requirements of their own jobs. Maintenance men frequently intervened in the working behavior of "their" production workers, whom they viewed as rather careless subordinates. They often gave advice to the workers, although they also reported that this advice was usually ignored. Many maintenance workers said they got along well in their relations with production workers but thought their colleagues did not. Such a response pattern suggests covert tension that was easier for the maintenance workers to attribute to others than to admit to themselves.

The Supervisor-Maintenance Worker Intergroup.   The relationship between the supervisors and maintenance workers was the most overtly conflictful of the three separate paired relations in the three-way intergroup. Maintenance workers and supervisors were on more or less equal footing hierarchically. Both groups showed a willingness to express their feelings openly. For example, 46 percent of the maintenance workers expressed doubts about the foremen, and 33 percent of the foremen directly attacked the maintenance group. Although each group expressed displeasure with the other, the costs of this antagonism seemed to be higher for the foremen than for the maintenance staff. Thus, despite the tension in their work, the maintenance crew managed to retain high morale, but the foremen did not. Maintenance people did not think the foremen were very important—an opinion similar to that held by the production workers. But a large proportion of the maintenance workers held this view and with greater underlying hostility than felt by the production workers. Seventeen percent of the foremen reported that the maintenance workers jeopardized their authority over production people, and 33 percent refused to discuss that issue.

Sources of Intergroup Conflict.   As it turned out, the three-way intergroup among maintenance, production, and first line supervisors was influenced by more than task differences among the groups. The lowest ranking group, the operators, turned out to be almost exclusively women. Their mode of defending themselves from supervision and maintenance was to band together to resist initiatives that would alter their group norms. Foremen were caught in the middle. They were responsible for the machine operators but did not have enough power to significantly influence the operators. Although hierarchically similar to the foremen, the maintenance staff acted with more influence and less personal duress than their counterparts. It is possible that they were able to do this because they had an independent power base outside the chain of authority that linked operators and foremen. The greater power of staff over line in this setting at the bottom of the chain of command contrasts, however, with the more common finding that individuals in staff positions feel less influential than line managers.

Purchasing Agents.   The significance of outside reference groups in intergroup struggles is further emphasized by George Strauss' (1962, 1964) study of purchasing agents (PAs). Although the operator-supervisor-maintenance conflict described by Crozier occurs at the bottom of the organizational hierarchy, PAs find themselves slightly higher in the system. They are charged with securing raw materials for

an organization at the lowest cost consistent with quality requirements; yet PAs are often viewed as little more than order-takers. At
worst they are seen as freeloaders who enlarge their private coffers
with favors from vendors with whom they place orders. Among themselves, PAs fear that their positions are dead-end jobs, because few PAs
ever get promoted into higher management. They envy other professionals in the organization, such as accountants, lawyers, and engineers, whose words are generally taken without question. Further,
PAs are harshly critical of members of their own profession who "act
like two bit shysters" and thereby prevent fuller acceptance by management.

In the flow of work, PAs stand between salesmen for outside vendors and multiple departments within their own organization. With
salesmen, PAs are relatively powerful as they attempt to place orders
on the best possible terms and see that those orders are delivered on
time. But internally the PAs' relationships are much more problematic.
Their internal role improves, however, as more departments grant them
discretion in determining what the company will buy, as more departments consult with the PAs on the components of items to be pur-
chased, and as more departments permit the PAs to influence allied
functions such as receiving, inventory control, and production control.
But frequently PAs find themselves at the end of a process in which
engineering and scheduling determine all facets of the order, except price and supplier, without consulting with the PAs. This situation
heightens the likelihood that the PAs will become embroiled in conflicts with engineering and scheduling.

The PA-Engineer Intergroup.   PAs strongly prefer that engineers avoid
telling them what brands to purchase. Instead, they want functional
specifications of the needed product, which will enhance their discretion in dealing with vendors. However, this request from the PA generally calls for additional work from the engineer. He must then provide
greater detail in his order than a product plus brand name, and he also
must test alternatives to see whether they do meet specifications. It is
not surprising, therefore, that interactions between PAs and engineers
often have the flavor of status battles. Engineers may perceive PAs as
intruding into areas where they feel uniquely qualified. In response
they may shut PAs out of the deliberations that they feel are crucial to
performance of their work. The frequent educational discrepancy between PAs and engineers adds to the hazards of that relationship.
Engineers may feel that it is beneath their dignity to accept influence
from people with less education than they have, and the PAs may react
with resentment of what they perceive as arrogance from the engineers.

The PA-Production Scheduler Intergroup. Production schedulers determine order size and delivery date. Problems between PAs and production schedulers tend to be less severe than those between engineers and PAs. Educational differences between schedulers and PAs are less likely than between PAs and engineers, and so PA and production scheduling disputes more often have the quality of bargaining between equals. The major conflict between PAs and production schedulers concerns lead time, because PAs feel that they are often given inadequate time to place orders. When purchasing is left out of early deliberations and their input is solicited only at the end of the line, accumulated delays must be made up at their expense. Usually they must pay some price for this additional burden they place on salesmen. They may be charged more for the products, or they may have to promise salesmen future orders in order to obtain the kind of prompt response deemed necessary.

The PA-Management Intergroup. PAs often feel that they do not obtain adequate recognition and support from top management. One reason is that there is no standard as to whom the PAs should report. Some PAs feel they should report directly to the company president. More often, however, they actually report to someone whose higher priority concerns do not include purchasing. As a result, PAs lack frequent contact with their boss and resent being ignored. And their ability to conduct successful negotiations with other departments within the plant—especially those with more power—suffers from lack of administrative support in their own chain of command.

The PAs' External Identification. In response to their tenuous and conflictful roles, PAs often seek support outside their organization. One place that they turn is to salesmen and vendors. PAs from Strauss' study (1964, p. 141) reported comments such as:

> The vendor helps me; management doesn't.
> They are our allies in dealing with engineering.
> All I know, I've learned from salesmen, they are PAs' biggest support.

They also turn to each other in an effort to develop professionalism. The National Association of Purchasing Agents, professional education programs, certification, and the development of a code of ethics help in this quest. The professional association, in particular, meets a number of real needs for members. It provides them with a sense of cosmopolitan identity (Gouldner, 1957). For some, friendships in the association become more important than ties in the employing organization. The professional association also aids mobility by providing contacts that make it easier to find jobs outside the PAs' current organization. The association provides ways for the PAs to improve their education through programs it sponsors. Informal conversations at association meetings with colleagues who share similar problems provide PAs with an opportunity to let off steam about their organizational stresses. The cafe environment also gives them an opportunity to try out ideas that might be rejected by nonprofessionals at their workplaces. Finally, the professional association promotes the occupational and economic interests of its members, much the way a union does.

Adrift without real group support within their organization, PAs band together in professional meetings outside to obtain the group support and power lacking within. Intergroup conflicts involving PAs with engineers, scheduling, and upper management are inevitably influenced by membership in the external professional group. The individual PA also increases the loyalty conflict he feels between the employing and professional organization as he attempts to improve his power and status by moving outside the organization for a significant portion of his life.

Staff-Line Struggles.   Dalton (1959) reported another pattern of staff-line relations that cut across several hierarchical levels in plants employing complex chemical technology. Although staff outnumbered line in these organizations, the line had undisputed control over the system, and staff members were expected to serve the interests of line managers.

In one example of what Dalton (1959) euphemistically called a *monitoring function*, staff members were asked to help line executives learn about irregularities at the production level. Passing hidden information helped line executives to correct the tendency for problems to be hidden as communication moved upward in normal hierarchical channels. Staff members who provided this kind of information to line executives earned their favor, but they also provoked the enmity of lower ranking supervisors who felt that the staff members were "ratting." The stakes of higher and lower ranking staff members in this practice were different, however. Higher ranking staff members could ingratiate themselves with top level line executives by reporting what their subordinates had learned about the practices on the production floor. But the lower ranking staff members, by pleasing their own supervisors, risked their standing with the line managers whom they most wanted to influence.

Ideas and initiatives taken by staff to improve productivity were frequently resisted by line managers, even when they realized the potential value of these contributions. One example reported by Dalton (pp. 75–76) concerned a new method for handling shop tools. Devised by an industrial engineer, the new method would reduce costs by prolonging the life of tools. But despite the acknowledged merits of the new idea, it was resisted by line management. One man explained,

> Jefferson's idea was pretty good. But his damned overbearing manner queered him with me. He came out here and tried to ram the scheme down our throats. He made me so damn mad I couldn't see. The thing about him and the *whole white-collar bunch* [italics mine] that burns me up is the way they expect you to jump when they come around. Jesus Christ! I been in this plant twenty-two years. . . . I've worked with all kinds of schemes and all kinds of people. . . . I've been around, and I don't need a punk like Jefferson telling me where to head in. I wouldn't take that kind of stuff from my own kid—and he's an engineer too. . . . Him and the whole white collar bunch . . . can go to hell. We've got too damn many bosses already.

It is clear from these comments that the line manager was reacting to a lot more about Jefferson's proposal than the merits of the concept. He objected to the staff man's interpersonal style, to his group membership ("the white-collar bunch"), to his age, to his profession, and to his potential authority. Further, members of Jefferson's own staff group objected to what he had done because it seemed as though he was trying to get individual credit for the idea when it might have been presented as a contribution from the whole department rather than just from him.

Other instances of line resistance to staff proposals were related to the monitoring functions sometimes performed by staff members. Dalton reported that foremen were likely to regard most staff projects as manipulative devices. Under such circumstances they "cooperated" with production workers and general foremen to defeat staff initiatives.

As suggested by the quotation on the Jefferson project, there was more to the staff-line conflicts in the Dalton study than just differences in tasks. Systematic examination of the social backgrounds of the two groups revealed differences on several other dimensions. Staff members tended to be younger, better educated, more professionally conscious, and more concerned about their appearance and manners than line managers. Despite these apparent advantages, however, staff members were frustrated in their mobility aspirations within the firms studied, and their turnover rate was nearly three times that of line managers.

Common Properties of Task Induced Intergroups.   This section has reviewed three major studies of conflicts among groups in organizations where the primary basis of the group differences was task assignments. These particular studies were selected because together they permit comparison among intergroup conflicts as they occur at the bottom, lower middle, and upper middle sectors of work organizations. A major finding cutting across all of the studies was evidence of *correlated intergroup* conflicts. Just as Marian as an individual embodied several groups, various task groups within organizations may contain other groups within their membership.

The Crozier study suggested that sex differences among operators, supervisors, and maintenance men may have influenced the relations among these parties. It is probably no accident that the lowest level job in that setting was held by women. Staff-line struggles as revealed in the Dalton study were also a partial function of other underlying group differences. Particularly important in this setting were age and educational differences. Underlying the staff-line struggle was a generational conflict where less powerful, younger, and more educated men contested with more powerful, older, and less educated men for authority in the production system.

Also common to each of the internal intergroup conflicts was at least one party with a significant external reference group. The maintenance group in the Crozier study, the purchasing agents in the Strauss study, and the engineers in the Dalton study each identified with a cosmopolitan group whose influence was more broadly based than the employing organization. Although the cosmopolitan groups were not always the most powerful in the local setting, their external reference group provided them with mobility potential not available to groups without a professional base. Thus, the external reference group provided a means for a deprived group to compensate for internal difficulties or to enhance its local status.

HIERARCHICALLY INDUCED INTERGROUPS

Hierarchy of authority is a second essential property (along with division of labor) of modern organizations. Individuals who hold higher ranking management roles have legitimate power and expect their work orders to be accepted by those in lower positions. But the power of some to command is limited by the willingness of others to obey, despite whatever normal expectations follow from a person's position in a table of organization. This willingness to obey arises from the individual's history, because each human being has a long period of dependency during normal development. Assumption of adult roles in organizations frequently reproduces some aspects of the parent-child relationship, in the sense that nearly everyone is subject to the organization and has some one person to whom he is accountable. It is normal, however, for adults to resist being dependent, and to seek ways to minimize their dependence and increase their own power. Thus, hierarchical relationships often lead to the creation of subgroups and the development of intergroup conflict, as those lower down in the hierarchy seek to increase their power and counteract the dependency relationships produced by the hierarchy. One of the most common types of hierarchically induced subgroups is between unions and management.

Origins of the Labor-Management Intergroup. Individuals at the bottom of an organization's hierarchy not only are dependent on those above them, they also tend to fare poorly on most measures of human welfare (Argyris, 1964). To protest and change the extremely poor conditions faced by individuals at the bottom ranks of many organizations, labor unions have arisen. Initially unions attempted to organize nonmanagement employees in order to improve their wages, hours, and working conditions. More recently, first-line supervisors and professionals in some settings have also begun to organize. Labor-management relations define the major hierarchical intergroup in most organizations. It is clearly a relationship between parties of unequal power.

The basic conflict in labor-management relations involves how cooperative the parties should attempt to be with each other. In the early phases of union organizing, there is little doubt about this issue, for if the choice were left to management, there would never be a union. Thus, in establishing a union in a previously management-dominated system there can be no compromise. Labor must win the right to organize, and they cannot do this without overcoming very fundamental management resistance to the reality of having an alternative source of power and allegiance for employees.

During the earliest phases of labor-management relations, existence is at stake for the union. Management fights union organizing activities forcefully, because they experience their power as threatened. The organizing period generally draws a specific sort of person to prominent leadership positions in the union. The labor leader of this period is likely to be an aggressive and militant individual willing to press almost any issue if there are signs that it will increase the vulnerability of management. There also tend to be common structural attributes of labor leaders chosen during the earliest phase of labor-management relations. When the primary union task is to establish its existence, labor leaders are more likely to emerge from the lower ranking, more deprived occupational groups. These characteristics follow from the general properties of intergroup development and leadership behavior identified in the earlier section on the theory of intergroup dynamics.

Intergroup Conflicts Within the Labor Movement. Struggles about how the interests of lower ranking members are best served do not take place only between labor and management. There are also contests between rival unions or factions within unions to determine who shall represent employees in particular organizations. The dynamics of these relationships are very similar to those between labor and management when a system is first being organized. At this point in the intergroup development, the fundamental issue turns on whether a new power group will come into existence.

Sayles and Strauss (1953) described a situation where an independent union was replaced by the CIO. The struggle lasted eight years before the international replaced the local in the loyalty of the workers in a large manufacturing plant. During the conflict the CIO lost three elections, then finally won the fourth. Charges and countercharges were exchanged between the two union groups while the contest was underway. Local leaders warned, for example, that acceptance of the international would "cause trouble" from outside influences who might be dominated by "Communists." The CIO charged, on the other hand, that the Independent was not sufficiently aggressive in seeking pay raises and promotions for members.

The CIO organizers saw the basic contest as between higher and lower paid workers. In their view the older men in the top level (nonmanagement) jobs were not interested in getting anything else. Younger men just starting out had futures to protect and were the best people to contact. After the CIO had won the right to represent the workers, the center of union power in the plant moved sharply downward on the pay scale. The last president of the Independent had come from one of the highest paid occupational groups, but the first one elected under CIO auspices came from one of the lowest paid groups. Moreover, 85 percent of the officers elected under the first round of CIO elections had *not* held office under the Independent. Many of the Independent officers had occupied top level nonmanagement positions as lead-men or inspectors. Members had become fearful that they had grown too close to management.

Within eighteen months after reorganization by the CIO there were definite signs of reversion back to the older pattern of officer selection. The first president of the CIO was replaced by the former president of the Independent. In six of eight officer elections where there were serious contests, higher paid workers replaced lower paid ones. In the first CIO election, candidates from the two highest paid occupational groups got less than 20 percent of the vote, but in the second they received more than 30 percent.

Sayles and Strauss note that as union-management relations move away from points of transition or severe economic stress, a more stable, less overtly conflictful pattern tends to emerge. Industrial peace becomes more common. Yet within the union executive board, differences on how to relate to management remain. The split is sometimes formulated as between the *radicals* and *conservatives*. These labels do not refer to external political affiliations but to internal views about how to relate to management.

Radicals often feel as though they have been elected to union office with a mandate to clean house. They are very critical of union officials who make informal agreements with management that threaten to sell out the contract. The radical position is one of consistent resistance to management. Radicals are anxious to harass and annoy company officials whenever possible, and they are inclined to believe that every grievance should be pushed as far as possible. Radicals do not particularly differ with conservatives on the merits of specific grievances, but they do differ on how hard grievances should be pushed.

By and large conservatives are the older, higher paid men who are not adverse to direct union action when careful analysis shows it to be necessary. Nevertheless, their preference is to reach their goals by businesslike bargaining. Proud of the individual relationships they have developed with management, they are anxious to keep the respect of both company and community. Noisy, antagonistic confrontations over what they consider minor issues threaten those relationships. Conservatives view informal agreements as essential to maintaining a flexible working relationship with management.

It is clear that the two stances toward company authority have different costs and benefits. The orientation that best serves member needs is more likely to be a function of the circumstances than of any overriding principle. Radicals serve best during the time when recognition and survival are uppermost problems for unions, and when conservative labor leaders have lost touch with the fundamental needs of rank-and-file members. Escalation of conflict, open confrontation, and attention-seeking strategies are often essential to begin the process of correcting longstanding grievances that influence large numbers of severely deprived people. But once legitimation for union activities has been achieved and as long as member needs are being served, provocative actions tend to be counterproductive to union and company interests.

Sayles and Strauss found evidence that when the labor-management relationship is serving the interests of both parties, leaders from both parties may collude to stifle the behavior of a radical officer whose activities threaten the working relationship. Management representatives told one man, for example, that even if he would not settle on terms they found agreeable, they would get other union officers to agree with those terms. Union officials said, "There is no use fooling yourself. If the company doesn't like you, you can't bargain with them at all." The radical protestor was unable to muster enough political support to press his concerns under these circumstances.

Other Nonmanagement Subgroups.   Within the union there are often contesting interest groups whose benefits are influenced by whether the officers take a radical or conservative stance toward management. But these groups also have autonomous concerns that turn as much on how they stand in relation to other groups in the union as they do on the relationship to management. For example, wage differentials that do not correspond to the significance of the jobs as employees view them can be a source of protest directed to both union officers and management.

Variations in the *methods* of payment can be especially provocative of intergroup conflict among related occupational work groups. Suppose workers on an assembly line are being paid by an incentive system based on the number of units they produce. If their equipment is serviced by craftsmen who are paid on a daily rate, a natural conflict may arise. The production workers may want their equipment repaired as rapidly as possible so their incentive earnings are not damaged. The maintenance staff, in contrast, may be in no hurry to complete their work because their wages are not directly linked to output. If the day work group prevails, the incentive group may feel as though they are being deprived of an opportunity to earn money. A satisfactory accommodation is not always easy to reach under these circumstances.

Other internal disputes among union members turn on the demographic characteristics of seniority, sex, and ethnicity. Seniority has become an increasingly crucial determinant of a worker's economic security. Depending on the situation, seniority may influence layoffs, demotions, promotions, and shift assignments. But the operation of seniority principles is often complex and forces labor leaders to make difficult choices with or without management consultations. When the work load is uneven and people are frequently laid off, the determination of who goes is usually made on the basis of seniority and the rank order of jobs. Individuals with high seniority may bump others downward in the job progression. This situation not only plays senior employees off against their juniors, but it also sets occupational groups into competition with each other. Men in each occupational group wish to maximize the number of groups below them in order to increase their own likelihood of keeping jobs when cutbacks are made.

Women's Roles in Unions.   Even though their study was done in the early 1950s before the recent civil rights and women's movements, Sayles and Strauss were alert to the special problems faced by women and minority ethnic groups in unions. Male-dominated unions looked upon women as a major problem. A field representative interviewed by Sayles and Strauss commented, "Organizing and servicing those (predominantly female) locals is a pain in the neck. I know a lot of men who won't touch it with a ten foot pole." Women were rarely elected to union office. One local that was 80 percent female had only five women among the twenty-seven members of its executive board. A survey of steward selection showed that departments with fewer than 50 percent women elected no female stewards; departments with 50 to 79 percent women elected more male than female stewards; and units with 80 percent or more females selected only female stewards.

Sayles and Strauss note that the role of women in unions may arise from a feeling shared by both men and women that union activity is a man's job. "Many rank-and-file male unionists show signs of resenting female 'intrusion,' while women seem to agree that their place is in the home rather than in the union hall." A union president interviewed by the researchers summarized the situation: "Women in a local are a lot of trouble. They are either trying to use their charms to get you to do something for them or people are accusing you of using your office to make time."

Sayles and Strauss suggest that the observed pattern of male-female relations may be partially class determined. Most of the really active women in a white-collar local came from middle income families. They note a tendency for lower and lower middle classes to segregate membership in associations by sex. The woman's role in the home was seen by both male and female union leaders as a major factor in limiting female union activity. A middle-aged female organizer commented, "But I suppose if I was in love enough with a man, even I would be less interested (in union business)."

Temporal and geographical factors also influenced the ease with which women could participate in union activities. Meetings lasting until late evening held in halls located in deserted, run-down sections of town cause women to pay a heavy psychological price for participating in union activities. Some unions found that after changing the location of their meetings to more desirable settings the proportion of female members who attend substantially increased. Others increased the social and educational content of their programs to make them more responsive to the interests of female members. Sayles and Strauss conclude their discussion of women in unions by saying, "Those unions which have interested themselves in the special problems involved in obtaining female participation have found a new source of energy for union activity." Their data suggest that the experience of women in labor unions differs little from what females face in other kinds of organizational settings.

Ethnic Differences in Unions.   Ethnic divisions were also observed in the unions studied by Sayles and Strauss, although they had no direct experience in locals with any sizable number of black members. The ethnic groups they encountered were primarily based on religious and European nationality differences—Irish versus Italian, Jewish versus Italian, and so forth. Sometimes the ethnic struggle was overt and out in the open. Other times it was more covert. Regardless of how the conflict was expressed, however, Sayles and Strauss observed that, "In most situations ethnic differences are significant." Thus, despite union ideology favoring equalitarianism, union leaders showed the same degree of prejudice and discrimination as average members of their communities. Quotations from union leaders reported by Sayles and Strauss include:

> You know why the Jews are so important in CIO headquarters? They got in early, when unionism was very unpopular. They don't care how people think. All they want is the buck.
> It's the damn Wops that are always pushing themselves and trying to take over the local. The minute a "white man" gets out, they're ready to jump in.

Although Sayles and Strauss' study had little material on the special situation confronting black Americans, Dalton's (1959) work did describe in detail some aspects of the situation confronting blacks in the industrial world dominated by white management and labor leaders. The Attica plant in Dalton's study was located in a community with a substantial and organized black population. Reynolds, Attica's head of Industrial Relations, was in charge of all employment in the factory and also held a public political office in the community. His desire to attrack black votes at election time caused him to become involved in the racial struggles at the plant in some unusual ways. Because of his political ties, black community leaders were able to prevail upon him to aid in the hiring of more blacks than might otherwise have been possible.

Although blacks in the plant were most frequently employed in the lowest skilled jobs, there were exceptions to this general pattern. One sector of the black community had made special arrangements to prepare their members to qualify for the higher level positions when they became available. Eventually a substantial number of black employees were in fact hired for the more skilled positions. Whites responded with open abuse of the higher status, higher paid blacks, and violence nearly erupted. Throughout the struggle the union was unwavering in supporting black members. The grievance committee consisted of one black and two white members, and despite the protests of white workers and the unofficial orders of white management, the committee remained vigilant to any discriminating practices.

Reynolds was in a difficult position. His own management ordered him to hold down the percentage of blacks in the "class jobs," and the union was looking over his shoulder to be sure that he adhered to the contract. He compromised by promising to hire, subject to testing, blacks who were qualified for the higher level positions. Although the test was based on a work sample, Reynolds instructed the foreman who administered it to "flunk them, regardless of how good they are" (Dalton, 1959, p. 135). The black rejectees approached the black member of the grievance committee; protests were filed by the union, but they were unable to prove that the tester discriminated. Then the black community organization entered the struggle. Reynolds met with them and apparently was able to diffuse their complaints. (Dalton's account is not entirely clear on this point.) But Reynolds nevertheless changed his methods of employment discrimination and his contest with the union was later renewed.

It is clear from these examples that sometimes unions collude with prejudice and discrimination against women and ethnic minorities and other times they provide potent forces to counteract these destructive patterns. Singerman (1975) has recently provided a useful review that attempts to define more carefully the conditions that promote cooperation or conflict between black and white workers in labor unions.

Union as Microcosm. In summary, unions arise to counteract the inhumane consequences of hierarchical structures. Collective bargaining over the years has counteracted the unilateral power of management to determine wages, hours, and working conditions. But unions also are hierarchical systems. The leadership group may lose touch with the membership. Occupational, sex, and ethnic intergroups may form within unions from deprivations experienced by individuals as a function of their various subgroup memberships. As unions work at one level to improve the quality of work life for members, they may spawn other problems that are directly analogous to the conditions they seek to ameliorate. Quality of work life interventions may, therefore, be directed toward union organizations as appropriately as toward other kinds of human systems.[2]

HISTORICALLY ROOTED INTERGROUPS

The preceding sections have described intergroup conflicts that arise in organizations as a result of division of labor and hierarchy of authority. The origins of these divisions are within work organizations. Now we shall turn to another class of intergroup conflicts, those that arise in social systems but do not originate in the organizations. Instead, they

---

2. See the chapters by Strauss (Chapter 6) and by Beer and Driscoll (Chapter 7) in this book for further discussion of the role of unions in influencing and improving the quality of work life.

are brought into the organization by members who carry various personal and social histories with them as they become system members. Because they are open systems, work organizations often mirror the surrounding cultures in which they are embedded. In the preceding section we noted the phenomena of *correlated intergroups*—variables of age, sex, and ethnic group affiliation were often associated with individuals' positions in the division of labor and hierarchy of authority. Recognition that additional intergroup conflicts often exist beneath those induced by the nature of formal organization is not the same as examining the unique dynamics of those struggles. That is the purpose of this section.

Conflicts arising from age, sex, and ethnic group differences are heavily influenced by history. The feelings, attitudes, beliefs, perceptions, and behaviors that people bring to interactions influenced by these variables reflect the cumulative results of unique personal experience, socialization and education, and the collective history of the ethnic groups with which they identify. Age, sex, and ethnic group identification vary, however, in the amount of history affecting the perspectives of members who differ on these variables. For example, age-based intergroups occur within the lifetimes of the individuals involved. In fact, during a lifetime a person may participate in both sides of this intergroup conflict (Bengston, Furlong, and Laufer, 1974). Sex differences cross generations. Peter Filene (1974), an American historian, found that to explain sex roles in modern America he had to review phenomena dating from 1890 to the present. Finally, ethnic group differences often reflect the effects of centuries of inequitable treatment. Lerone Bennett, Jr.'s (1962) *History of the Negro in America* traces the most oppressed of the United States' minority groups over more than three centuries to explain the revolt of the 1960s. We now turn to a consideration of the unique characteristics of intergroups based on age, sex, and ethnicity, discussed in order of increasing historical complexity.

Differences Between Generations

Campus unrest from the mid-1960s to the early 1970s called the nation's attention to conflicts between generations in unmistakable ways (Bengston, Furlong, and Laufer, 1974). During the height of the disorders, when fears were aroused and anxieties were increased, it was natural for observers and participants to shorten their time perspectives and react as if the events through which they were passing were unique. In fact they were not. Feurer's (1969) historical review of student movements in different nations at various points in history found that generational conflicts had some common properties, regardless of the particular situation in which they arose.

Basic Dynamics of the Generational Intergroup. Feurer wrote in terms of student movements, but his own data reveal that the conflict may be more broadly defined as between younger and older generations. The root of a younger generation's cohesion is rebellion against the older generation. There is disillusionment with the older group, who are viewed as having failed in their mission. Rejecting the (often materialistic) values of their elders, younger people see themselves as having a special historical mission to fulfill. They possess a reserve of emotional energy that impels individuals toward a revolutionary experience. Although the generational conflict often shares common concerns and methods with other movements (for example, with social class conflict), it also has its own unique dynamics. Drawing on the similarities of generational conflict with those of class conflict in order to portray the differences, Feurer (p. 32) developed a "Generational Manifesto," part of which is as follows:

> The history of all hitherto existing society is the history of generational struggles. Old and young, fathers and sons, aged masters and young apprentices, aged employers and young laborers, old professors and young students have since the primal parricide contended with each other for the mastery of society. Every revolutionary movement has been heralded by an uprising of the young. . . . The fight continues uninterrupted, now hidden, now open; thus far it has never ended with a clear triumph of the young, for by the time they have won, they have become middle aged. Only in recent times, with the rise of great student communities brought about by the new affluence, has it become genuinely possible for the student movement as the vanguard of the young to take decisive power.[3]

An ethical charge fuels the younger generation's rebellion. Typically they have ideals toward which they are striving and against which they measure the older generation's performance. Turned outward these ideals may serve to reactivate society's conscience and to establish new standards of ethical behavior. Turned inward the ideals have the potential of destroying both older and younger generations. During the political struggles it was not unusual for the young to attempt to assassinate the old. Whether or not such an act succeeded, it frequently brought countermeasures—inflicted by the young on themselves or by their adversaries. Sometimes assassins committed suicide; other times they were killed by police or military action.

---

3. From *The Conflict of Generations: The Character and Significance of Student Movements*, by Lewis S. Feurer, © 1969 by Lewis S. Feurer, Basic Books, Inc., Publishers, New York.

Youth in rebellion usually share a common intellectual elitism. Generational conflict may not be confined to colleges and universities, but it frequently starts there. Young people from middle class origins have the opportunity to escape from the immediate problems of providing for their own and others' economic well-being. They are able to think, reaffirm (or change) their developing ideals, and prepare themselves for the time when they shall take power from their elders —whether by revolution or evolution. This period of higher education tends to unite the youth of each era, for to some degree they read the same books, hear the same intellectual disputes, and reflect on the same national and international conflicts.

The less developed the culture of a social system is, the more separated an intellectually elite youth movement is inclined to be. When the elders of a system are also poorly educated, it provides the youth with another factor on which to base their deauthorization of the old. The old must be displaced because they shame the young. They might also be blamed for the backwardness of the people as a whole.

The more power is held exclusively by the elders in a social setting, the higher the likelihood of generational conflict. To the degree that power is concentrated in the hands of an exclusively older group, youthful leaders must contest their elders on a *group* basis in order to increase their own influence. Thus, the battle may be polarized between the young with ideas (and ideals) and the old with power.

Among the young rebels, the relations between men and women are often closer than they might be when the youth are not united against their elders. Feurer (1969, p. 12) cites David Kamen, a Berkeley, California, student writer who, in 1966, made the sexuality explicit when he commented,

> "The radical political fraternity has taken a hint from the old saying that a family thay prays together stays together, and believes that a movement that screws together glues together. Or to be specific, that Socialists who sleep together creep together."[4]

Feurer further relates generational rebellion to "a secret society of sons and daughters banded against the father." The secret organization may become a new primary group, replacing the biological family, in which members to a limited degree can choose their own brothers and sisters. Secrecy about the youthful organization may stem a lot less from real danger than from the felt need to distinguish this group from its elders.

There is usually a strained ambivalence between the elite youthful rebels and other disenfranchised groups when generational conflict is

---

4. Feurer, *The Conflict of Generations: The Character and Significance of Student Movements.* Used by permission of Basic Books, Inc.

present. As Feurer notes, youth movements frequently have a "back to the people" flavor to them. But rather than building an alliance with "the people" on the common pursuit of concrete objectives, such as better wages, hours, and working conditions, the youthful elite try to forge a coalition out of common ideals. Only a fragile cooperation can emerge because "the people" recognize that the youthful intellectuals already have privileges which have been denied them. So, however much the young elite wish to tie their movement to other causes, the nonelite remain suspicious. Class divisions separate students and workers of the same age. The workers recognize that the students always have the option of walking away from the deprivations involved in their daily existence. And the students do just that, thereby confirming the validity of the workers' suspicions.

Generational intergroups do not always appear. Like other group dynamic events, the nature of group formation is problematic. As a result, research in this area has had to struggle with the definition of a generation (Feurer, 1969; Bengston, Furlong, Laufer, 1974). Feurer (p. 25) suggests the following:

> A generation . . . consists of persons in a common age group who in their formative years have known the same historical experiences, shared the same hopes and disappointments, and experienced a common disillusionment with respect to elder age groups, toward whom their . . . opposition is defined.[5]

He goes on to recognize that a generation's consciousness is heightened and its cohesion enhanced by what he terms "a generational event." Generational events are of many kinds but the most binding are those that create a sense of martyrdom among age mates. The experience that one's own fellow students were assaulted, imprisoned, or killed by actions carried out or sanctioned by the elders helps to pull the youth of an era together in an unmistakable way. The Vietnam War had such an effect in the United States from the mid-1960s to the early 1970s. Analogous events may be found for other groups in other time periods (Feurer, 1969, pp. 25–27).

Generational Conflict in Management Development. The characteristics of generational conflicts just reported were abstracted, with some minor interpretative modifications, from Feurer's more extensive historical treatment. He noted, and subsequent investigators have repeated, that generational analysis has not taken a firm place in American behavioral science theories. Feurer's work for the most part relied

---

5. Feurer, *The Conflict of Generations: The Character and Significance of Student Movements.* Used by permission of Basic Books, Inc.

on historical accounts of sociopolitical struggles. He was mainly concerned with student movements whose organizational base was inside universities and whose targets for change were national governments. The infrequent use of generational conflict theories to explain social processes in general is further related to their almost total absence in explaining organizational behavior. However, there was an organizational study of intergroup conflict by the present author (Alderfer, 1971) that might, in retrospect, more fully be explained by reference to a generational conflict model. The study analyzed the intergroup relationships that had developed between members of a management development program and other sectors of the bank in which it was located. The review of this study that follows includes data taken from the original report, and additional information available to the author but not included in the original paper because its theoretical relevance had not been identified when the article was prepared.

The management development program was begun in the late 1950s by senior officers in the bank who wished to improve the quality of managerial talent that became available to fill higher ranking positions in the institution. In part the decision to start the program was inspired by a study done by Chris Argyris (1954), in which he identified the bank's tendency to attract employees with high desires to be secure and to avoid aggressive behavior in themselves and others. The new management program was explicitly oriented toward selecting and developing a corps of highly intelligent and aggressive young managers who would be more dynamic and outgoing than their predecessors.

The very existence of this program, although it was initiated at the very highest levels of the bank, was an implicit recognition that the elder generation of the bank had failed to provide the kind of developmental leadership that was necessary for the institution to survive and grow during the dynamic 1960s. Members of the training program (that is, younger managers) experienced this partial sense of failure by many (though not all) top executives. They were aware of the Argyris study, and they knew that, on the bank's standard personality inventory, their profiles differed markedly from many officers who had come up through the ranks. Particularly, the more successful members of the training program thought of themselves as the wave of the future in the bank's management.

Recognizing their own lack of experience in many technical areas of banking, the younger group was nevertheless critical of their elders on key dimensions of general management. They faulted the older men for the conservatism of their management decisions, and they objected to their elders' tendency to withdraw from difficult matters in handling personnel. The younger group viewed themselves as the carriers of new ideals for the bank. A conservative, secure, and soft managerial style was to be replaced by a tough, performance-based, risk-taking approach to governing the system. The struggle between the older and younger elite generation in this bank was not over a political revolution in the nation but over a managerial revolution in the bank.

Although no one talked of physical violence of the sort associated with political assassinations and suicides, an important battleground for the war between the generations was in the area of career development. Some divisions of the bank were managed by pairs of older and younger men. In some cases the older man viewed himself as preparing the way for the younger man's ascension and acted as a mentor. In other cases the pairing was characterized by a high degree of mutual distrust and fear. The results of the latter pattern sometimes led to the "career death" of one or both parties; the senior man might take early retirement or the junior person might find a better position in another bank.

The two generations had grown up in different eras, and their value systems reflected those variations in life experience. Senior men had started their careers when the country was in the midst of the Great Depression. They knew the fears associated with threatened layoffs and the collapse of banks. They were deeply loyal to their employing institution, partly because the bank had survived the depression without eliminating any employees from the work force. Several of the senior managers had come from elite families in the community and had attained degrees from Ivy League institutions. Others had achieved top managerial positions without the benefit of a completed college education.

Although the family backgrounds of the new corps of managers varied, their personal experience was primarily rooted in an era of abundance and affluence. All were college graduates and a high proportion held degrees from Ivy League institutions. As a whole the management development program was symbolized by the bank as a place open only to Ivy League graduates, although some members of the program had other than Ivy League degrees. The intellectually elite nature of the program was well established within the organization.

There was no evidence of a "back to the people" ethic in the management development program. In fact, the most negative attitudes about the program were held by male employees who had not yet entered management ranks. They believed that the accelerated mobility prospects of the new trainees were direct barriers to their own career aspirations.

For some demographic groups in the bank, the management development program had earmarks of a closed, secret society. People tended to see members of the program as having closer relationships with each other than with other members of the bank. This feeling was especially strong among the other males in the bank (both management and nonmanagement). The trainees denied that they operated as a closed group. Slightly less than half of the female members of the bank saw the program as more open than the trainees themselves did, suggesting a kind of alliance of "sons and daughters" similar to that identified by Feurer for political movements.

Program members talked about happenings that could be conceptualized as generational events. By the time of my study, the first member of the program had left the bank to take a position with another institution. For the trainees this event was symbolized as one of their number being killed off by a system that did not provide upward mobility opportunities rapidly enough to utilize the young man's talents. Older members of the institution viewed the loss, however, as an indication of the disloyalty of the younger generation.

In summary, except for lacking a "back to the people" ethic, the management training program showed almost all the traits of generational conflicts proposed by Feurer. The student movements described by Feurer were rooted in universities and advocated leftist-liberal political philosophies. Politically the bank could hardly have been more different. But in terms of intergroup dynamics, the other parallels could not have been more striking. Historically speaking it was probably no accident that the generational struggle within the bank between the younger and older managers was occurring at approximately the same time (the mid and late 1960s) that the nation's campuses and communities were erupting with generational struggles tied to political issues—racism, the Indochina war, and governance and curricula at colleges and universities.

Differences Between Men and Women

The kinds of experiences that women have in organizations mirror their positions in the larger society. More specifically, in comparison to men, women are more deprived of the rewards available to full members of work organizations. But we are at a point in history when women are not passively accepting male domination of major institutions. Male-female intergroup conflicts exist in many organizations because women are organizing to obtain their rights. This section identifies organizational conditions that provoke conflict between men and women, points out the intellectual biases that have arisen from male accounts of females, and describes the pattern of sex-role stereotyping that has arisen in many social systems.

Origins of Male-Female Intergroup Conflict in Organizations. The history of women in relation to men in organizations is one of relative deprivation and oppression. One recent report showed that the median annual earnings of white women was $4,279 as compared to $7,396 for white men. The analogous statistic for black women was $3,194 as compared to $4,777 for black men (Loring and Wells, 1972). Slightly more than 1 percent of the women in the work force received over $15,000 per year, while more than 13 percent of the men did.

One reason for the lower pay of women compared to men is that females have been systematically excluded from higher paying managerial jobs. A 1970 study by the Bureau of National Affairs showed that 39 percent of the companies surveyed had no female managers at all, and in 93 percent of the companies less than 10 percent of the management positions were filled by women (Loring and Wells, 1972). Moreover, the highest job level held by men in the survey was top management, although less than 20 percent of the companies surveyed had women in top management. Controlling for educational differences between men and women did not alter the income differences. In 1970, the average income for female college graduates was $8,156, while for male college graduates it was $13,264. The female college graduate group even had a lower average annual income than men with one to three years of high school education.

A study published by the U.S. Department of Health, Education, and Welfare in 1970 found that more women than men reported signs of poor mental health—symptoms such as nervousness, insomnia, trembling hands, nightmares, fainting, and headaches (Chesler, 1972). These results were consistent with an earlier survey by the Joint Commission on Mental Health and Illness, which showed that for nonhospitalized American adults greater distress and symptoms were reported by women than men in all adjustment areas (Gurin, Veroff, and Feld, 1960).

Like other people who have found themselves at a relative disadvantage in social systems, women have drawn together to form groups to combat the inequities they encountered. In the United States, women have a long history of struggling with the male establishment to achieve equal treatment in the political process, the workplace, and the family. Firestone (1972) has provided a history of American feminism, which shows that the women's movement has demonstrated dynamics similar to those we have observed in other groups who have attempted to change their relatively deprived conditions. Specifically, there has always been a tension between radical and conservative feminists that is analogous to the split observed earlier between radical and conservative labor leaders. Radicals have consistently been alert to the plethora of factors that prevent women from having full power

in all sectors of their lives. They have been more assertive and confronting—willing to harass and embarrass the male establishment
wherever it seemed as though there was an opportunity to gain more
power. Conservatives, on the other hand, have selected broader issues
of a more unifying nature, such as suffrage, and have attempted to
work within the system for change. Radicals such as Firestone view the
conservative position as collusive with the male establishment as long
as full equality for women has not been won.

Cognitive Biases in Analyses of Women.   The presence of a variety of
women's organizations leaves little doubt as to whether male-female
differences have taken the form of intergroup conflict. The general
proposition from intergroup theory, which states that each group tends
to distort factual information to make it consistent with the group's
perspective in the contest, applies to the conflict between men and
women. Firestone notes how male historical accounts have consistently omitted discussing the most vibrant radical feminists, preferring
to devote their attention to more acceptable, less threatening female
leaders. Discussions of women's "freedom" in the workplace have
shown a similar pattern.

As recently as 1966, Ginzberg (p. 48), a male writing about "the life
styles of educated women" said,

> Young boys and girls think differently about work . . . . Every young man
> knows that he must become concerned about his occupational choice
> . . . The parallel social expectation for a young woman is that she . . . will
> marry and raise a family. She may expect to work regularly or intermittently,
> full or part time, but she is not required to make her plans accordingly . . .
> Men have no option except to plan their lives around work. On the other
> hand women are *free* of this requirement. *Their options are much broader*
> (emphasis mine).

Contrast this with Simone de Beauvoir (1952, p. 755), writing about
"the independent woman."

> A woman supported by a man . . . is not emancipated from the male
> because she has a ballot in her hand; if custom imposes less constraint
> upon her than formerly . . . It is through gainful employment that woman
> has traversed most of the distance that separated her from the male; and
> nothing else can guarantee her liberty in practice.

For the male Ginzberg, perhaps feeling the pressures of his own
occupational predicament, a woman has more options (is freer) because she is not forced to make an occupational choice. For the female
de Beauvoir, a woman is not free until society has permitted and she
has accepted the dilemmas of remunerative occupational choice.

But the intergroup relationship between men and women does not begin in the political arena or the workplace. It starts in the family between brothers and sisters, mothers and sons, daughters and fathers. Probably the most influential view of personality development and family relations has been psychoanalytic theory—the creation of a male genius who himself was raised in the paternalistic culture of Victorian Europe. According to Freud (1933, pp. 172-173), a significant determinant of female inferiority feelings arises from the anatomical differences between men and women.

> The discovery of her castration is a turning point in the life of the girl . . . She is wounded in her self-love by the unfavorable comparison with the boy who is so much better equipped . . . No doubt this turning away from her mother does not come to pass at one blow, for at first the girl looks on her castration as a personal misfortune, and only gradually exends it to other females.

But as Horney (1967), a female psychoanalyst, was to point out, there is more than one significant anatomical difference between men and women. Men and women have quite different roles to play in the reproductive function. Women have, in the capacity for motherhood, quite an indisputable physiological advantage. Men are never able to bear a new life within themselves or experience the pleasure of suckling a young child. These facts are a source of envy among men as Horney (pp. 60–61) reports from her psychoanalytic work:

> This is most clearly reflected in the unconscious of the male psyche in the boy's intense envy of motherhood . . . When one begins, as I did, to analyze men only after a fairly long experience of analyzing women, one receives a most surprising impression of the intensity of this envy of pregnancy, childbirth, and motherhood, as well as of the breasts and of the act of suckling.

Thus, it is not just women whose views of themselves and of the male-female relationship are influenced by major biological differences with the opposite sex. Men, too, experience psychic pain as a result of limitations in their natural endowments. In a male-dominated society, however, men have the power to rationalize their feelings into theories that emphasize female rather than male limitations and to create roles that more often than not perpetuate male dominance. Horney's critique was not confined to the analysis of fantasy— whether in men or women—but also pointed out that female inferiority feelings were based on social reality. She was significantly affected by Simmel's analysis of male-female roles as analogous to masters and slaves. In terms of human defenses, Simmel recognized that a privilege (and perhaps a necessity) of a master (male) is to forget that he is in charge while the slave (female) can never afford that privilege.

Emergent Sex Roles in Organizations. Work roles for men and women have evolved into stereotyped patterns that have been accepted with only minor modification by both sexes. A *woman's place* has been defined both by the types of organizations that are most likely to employ females and by the types of assignments that are open to women in organizations. In one study, men and women sex-ranked classes of organizations from feminine to masculine as follows: education; retailing; media; government; finance; consumer manufacturing and service trades; industrial manufacturing; defense; transportation and public utilities; and construction (cited by Loring and Wells, 1972, p. 12). Women are more likely to be admitted to the more feminine organizations, and they are more likely to advance within them. It violates few expectations, therefore, for a woman to be director of a social welfare agency or a top manager in an advertising agency.

But it is generally more difficult for women to advance in management in male-oriented enterprises. In part this must be because being a manager is more consistent with the male than with the female sex-role stereotype. A sample of male managers from the life insurance industry reported *no* relationship between their concept of "Women in General" and their concept of "Managers" but a high relationship between their concept of "Men in General" and "Managers" (Schein, 1975b). The male managers also reported no relationship between "Men in General" and "Women in General." A sample of female managers from the same industry reported a positive relationship between "Women in General" and "Managers" and between "Men in General" and "Managers." The women managers, however, showed a higher relationship between "Men in General" and "Managers" than between "Women in General" and "Managers." They also showed a positive relationship between "Women in General" and "Men in General." Thus, in this study, the women showed that they shared some of the male stereotypes about the qualities necessary to be a manager; but on the whole the women did not stereotype men, women, or managers as much as men did. For the female managers, being emotionally stable, steady, analytical, logical, well-informed, and consistent were characteristics unrelated to being a manager. For the male managers these same traits were what made managers more similar to men than to women.

Similar results were obtained in a study of men entering the nursing profession—an occupation that has been predominantly feminine in sex-role stereotype. Lynn, Vaden, and Vaden (1975) surveyed the attitudes of 1,000 nurses in Kansas to obtain their views of male and female roles in nursing. They found marked differences between men and women on a wide variety of items. Male nurses and nursing administrators tended to feel that men were more effective in supervision, that most women would prefer working for a male rather than a female supervisor, and that men would prefer working for a male rather than a female supervisor. Female nurses and nursing administrators disagreed with these views. However, male and female nursing administrators basically agreed that more men entering the nursing field would upgrade the profession, that career advancement for men was more rapid than for women, and that the increase in the number of men in nursing would enhance the attractiveness of the profession for both men and women. Male and female nurses significantly disagreed on these items; the male nurses' opinions were more like the administrators' opinions (regardless of the sex of the administrators) than like the female nurses' opinions. Thus, even in a predominantly female occupation such as nursing where men are just beginning to enter in significant numbers, nonmanagement males agree more with some management attitudes than do nonmanagement females.

The emerging picture of women in relation to management in both predominantly male and female work roles is that men have sharper sex-role stereotypes than women. The average man believes that management is more clearly a male than a female function. Women share this view to a degree—no doubt because of their socialization in a predominantly male culture. But women also have a more complex, less polarized view of themselves and of management than men do.

Although many discussions do not address the issue directly, sexual feelings between men and women often influence their working relationships in organizations. Bradford, Sargent, and Sprague (1975, p. 45) quote a male manager as follows: "I don't know whether it's right for me to act this way, or whether it makes me a Male Chauvinist Pig, but the first time I meet a woman, I respond to her as a sexual object and only later as a person." Not all people respond to heterosexual encounters as this man reported, but the possibility of strong positive feelings between men and women may make relationships as difficult as any of the negative feelings evoked by the unequal treatment of women. In fact, Horney (1967, p. 112) has even proposed a connection between the two kinds of male reactions. She noted that sexually attractive women are often feared by men and kept in bondage to control such emotions.

Loring and Wells (1972, p. 113) reported the fantasied reactions of married male managers to the sentence, "If I had a woman boss, my wife would feel . . ." One said his wife would be jealous. Another said it would be "OK if the woman boss were unattractive." As women become members of management, they join areas of work activity that until recently have been almost exclusively the territory of men. A woman's responsibilities may require her to travel with men or to participate in work-social meetings that do not take place during normal business hours. Events such as these are likely to evoke sexual fantasies and may even lead to sexual behavior between men and women. Some organizations may be tempted to assume a parental role in such affairs, when marriages that do not allow for talking through the issues that arise from male-female relations at work are threatened.

At the workplace, sexual feelings between men and women may also lead to stereotyped role behavior. Kanter (1974) and Bradford, Sargent, and Sprague (1975) have identified "the Macho and the Seductress" as a set of interlocking roles. Although actual seduction may or may not occur, the predominant theme in this kind of male-female relationship is sexual, emphasizing flirting and game-playing. The man wants to be seen as a potent male who can affirm the sexual attractiveness of the female. And the women behaves as a sexually desirable object who is potentially available. Bradford, Sargent, and Sprague (1975, p. 57) also report that it is sometimes possible for men and women to discuss their feelings of sexual attraction directly and thereby reduce either Macho-Seductress game-playing or the maintenance of unnecessary distance and formality. But often such a discussion is too uncomfortable for the people involved. I know of no easy or simple way to handle sexual feelings—largely because these emotions are so intense and conflictful. But there can be little doubt that sexuality is a part of organizational life; to believe otherwise is to deny a very significant part of reality.

In summary, the male-female intergroup relationship in organizations is one of extensive inequality reflecting the status of women in American society at large. A woman's situation is often viewed differently when seen through male eyes. Not all societies, and therefore not all relations within and among organizations, have been based on the pattern of male dominance characteristic of the United States today. One finding that has emerged from the data on the male-female intergroup—and that will be seen again in the discussion of ethnic differences—is that the subordinate group has a tendency to share partially the superior group's view of itself. Facts become incorporated into the ideology (sometimes called history or analysis) of the dominant group. Female personality and career development were explained differently depending on whether the scholar reporting was male or female. The emotional forces operative in intergroups of unequal power are further complicated in men and women by the possibility of feelings of sexual attraction between the conflicting parties.

Ethnic Differences

Until the most recent decade there has been little explicit attention paid to the relations among ethnic groups in organizations. But the reawakening of concern for the civil rights of oppressed minorities—especially black Americans—has stimulated many groups publicly to identify their cultural heritages. This revitalization of ethnic consciousness represents a major change in the American (white Anglo-Saxon Protestant) ethos in relation to ethnicity. Reflecting the larger culture of which organizational life is a part, studies of organizational life have also been slow to recognize that ethnic differences may have a strong effect on the quality of life of individuals in organizations. Notable exceptions to this pattern may be found in the work of Sayles and Strauss (1953); Zaleznik, Christenson, Roethlisberger, and Homans (1958); and Whyte (1961).

The very term *ethnic* is one that writers may use uncomfortably. Novack (1975, p. 4) reports a series of dictionary definitions for the word which show its underlying negative connotations.

> Ethnic, adj. 1 pertaining to or characteristic of a people, esp. to a speech or cultural group . . . pertaining to non-Christians . . . belonging to or deriving from the cultural, racial, religious, or linguistic traditions of a people or a country, esp. a primitive one.

In part ethnic is contrasted with belonging to the "right" (that is, Christian) religion and being part of an "advanced" (that is, nonprimitive) cultural tradition. Often Americans have treated ethnicity as a dirty secret, in the hope that it might go away. They have attempted to reject ethnic analysis in at least three ways, according to Novack (pp. 1–3). Some people try all their lives to *get over* their ethnic origin and join the influential mainstream. Others who have joined the "superculture" *lose touch* with other individuals who must work very hard for the barest economic return or may be unable to find employment at all. A third type of rejection comes from people who are largely *unconscious* of their own ethnicity, either because they are white Anglo-Saxons in homogeneous ethnic settings or because their family histories include many ethnic groups without specific attention to the differences. For a long time the concept of the United States as a melting pot for diverse cultural traditions was not questioned. The psychic damage to individuals, the threat to families, and the danger to cultural traditions that this view of our country justified was not admitted by the dominant white Anglo-Saxon groups.

Black Americans in Relation to Organizations.   There is little doubt that black Americans have been the most oppressed of the various ethnic groups that have entered the United States and attempted to obtain membership in its organizations. No other group has the history of slavery or the degree of exclusion from the most basic rights of citizenship (that is, voting, housing, and education) encountered by black Americans. A focus on the black experience in American organizations provides some indications of the extreme conditions that may confront a minority ethnic group and affect the quality of work life of its members.

Blacks first arrived in what today is the United States in 1619. By 1775 there were approximately five hundred thousand blacks held as slaves or indentured servants in the United States. When the colonies declared their independence from England, about one-sixth of all people living in this country were slaves (Kerner, 1968). This beginning established a pattern for black Americans that has been only slightly altered to this day, even though slavery as a legal condition in the United States has been abolished for more than one hundred years.

In ratios greatly disproportionate to their numbers in the population as a whole, blacks who are able to find employment have been forced into unskilled and service jobs where wages are poor, job tenure is insecure, and status is low. U.S. Bureau of Labor statistics for 1966 showed that 20 percent of nonwhite male workers were nonfarm laborers where the median income for 1965 was $2,410, while only 6 percent of the white male population held similar positions. Sixteen percent of nonwhite males were service workers with a median annual income of $3,436 by 1965, but again only 6 percent of white men were employed in such jobs. The contrast with employment in professional, technical, and managerial jobs, where the median income in 1965 was $7,603, could hardly be more marked. In 1966, 27 percent of white males held these positions, whereas only 9 percent of black males were so employed.

Stirred by the civil rights movement and pressed by federal legislation and executive orders, industry began by the mid-1960s to remove some of the barriers to black employment and upward mobility. Between 1966 and 1968 there were increases in black employment in the automobile, aerospace, steel, rubber, tire, petroleum, chemical, and electrical industries (Purcell and Cavanagh, 1972). But in every industry except one (petroleum) the employment increases were greater in blue-collar than in white-collar occupations. Moreover, the two-year increases were not large. The rate of change varied from .2 percent for the tire and petroleum industries to 1.6 percent for the electrical industry.

Purcell and Cavanagh made a special study of the electrical industry. They assumed an objective of having blacks employed in the electrical industry at 10 percent of the working population at all levels. This was a conservative figure, because blacks are actually about 12 percent of the total population, and their unemployment rate is usually at least twice that of whites. Then they estimated the excess (+) or deficit (−) in black employment for 1969 in each of the nine occupational categories in the electrical industry. As a crude way to estimate how long it would take for black employment in each occupational category to achieve parity with the population as a whole, they divided the change rates for each job category (estimated over the 1966-1969 period) into the employment deficits for the six job categories where deficits existed, and obtained the results in Table 5.2. Uncertain as these estimates are, they provide a potent signal about how long it may take to reverse a pattern of discrimination that has been more than three hundred years in the making. Moreover, the estimates are based on the culmination of the most prosperous decade in American history—a period when unemployment was generally declining. A recession is therefore likely to increase estimates of the time required to achieve employment parity for black Americans.

Efforts to Increase Black Employment in Industrial Settings. Although an account of the barriers to black employment and upward mobility must start with a statistical analysis of employment figures to provide a sense of the magnitude of the problem, it cannot end there. The intergroup warfare between blacks and whites has been severe. Riots and other political demonstrations have been reported in the press. Less well known are the processes and outcomes that have been experienced by individuals in work organizations.

Purcell and Cavanagh report several episodes that detail the effects of some earlier efforts to provide employment opportunities for blacks in predominantly white industrial settings. In the summer of 1917, while World War I was being fought, General Electric hired one black among more than twenty-five students to whom it offered summer employment. The young man went to work at the company's huge plant in Schenectady, New York. On hearing about his presence, the International Association of Machinists called an eight-day strike in

Table 5.2—Employment Rates for Blacks in the Electrical Industry

	1969 Employment Excess or Deficit	Years to Employment Parity based on 1966–1969 rates
Service Workers	+91.6	none
Laborers	+27.5	none
Operatives	+15.2	none
Craftsmen	−58.0	14
Office and Clerical	−61.0	9
Sales Workers	−93.5	70
Technicians	−68.5	22
Professionals	−89.6	87
Officials and Managers	−90.8	55

Source: Purcell and Cavanagh (1972).

which their sole demand was that the young man be fired. The company refused, but promised the machinists that, "It is not the intention of the company to introduce colored labor into the shops or displace any white labor with colored labor, not is it the intention of the management to bring numbers of colored people to Schenectady to work in the shops" (p. 15).[6] In 1965, prodded by stronger federal legislation, the Westinghouse plant in Vicksburg, Mississippi began a campaign to hire "qualified Negro women for jobs as clerks, stenographers, and secretaries." Shortly after the announcement appeared, three fire bombs were thrown into the garage of the industrial relations manager. His two cars and the garage itself were damaged. Westinghouse management reacted quickly. The corporate level security director explained that the company could not throw away 20 percent of its business from government contracts because of one plant. He implied that if such incidents continued the corporation would move its plant from Vicksburg because it intended to comply fully with government laws requiring equal employment opportunity. In a letter to all employees the local plant manager said, "Westinghouse and local management will not tolerate any actions that jeopardize the personal safety of employees" (Purcell and Cavanagh, 1972, p. 35).[7] The incident reported here was the fourth within a year in the Vicksburg area. There were no more after Westinghouse refused to be intimidated.

Katie Fuller was the first black employee in the Fairbanks International plant in Memphis, Tennessee. She was hired by the firm in 1961, after the company decided to change its employment policies lest it risk losing government contracts. Cavanagh and Purcell were able to interview her and her work associates about the events accompanying her entry into the plant. Fuller was very carefully chosen by the plant management because they anticipated a hostile reaction from whites in the plant—in part because the racial climate in Memphis during the early 1960s was quite tense. A bright high school graduate, Fuller had held three jobs successfully before coming to the Fairbanks organization. To keep a careful watch on what happened to Fuller, plant management scheduled her to work on the first shift, as management did, rather than on the second or third shift where new employees usually started. She was given a regular assignment that required regular interaction with only one other person — another young woman who was hired about the same time she was.

The senior woman assigned to train Fuller accepted the task on two

6. From *Blacks in the Industrial World*, by T. V. Purcell and G. F. Cavanagh. Copyright © 1972 by Macmillan Publishing Co., Inc.

7. Purcell and Cavanagh. *Blacks in the Industrial World*. Used by permission of Macmillan Publishing Co., Inc.

conditions, according to Cavanagh and Purcell (p. 181): "I will train her just like I would train a white girl. I'm not going to give her any whip because she's a Nigger. . . . I am not her buddy either. I do not go on break with her."[8]

Fuller was not told that she was the only black person hired at that time; she had imagined that other blacks would be hired, too. It was reassuring to her that management seemed genuinely concerned with how she was doing, but that concern did little to reduce the harassment she experienced from her workmates. "Nigger Datie and Katie, you're from the Congo" were examples of the insults written on washroom doors. She found a doll with a hangman's noose around its neck in her locker, and she received anonymous telephone calls threatening to bomb her house if she did not quit the job. Her first foreman encouraged racist reactions to her and told her to leave the plant if she did not like what was happening. But the second man for whom she worked put a stop to some of it after Fuller went to him in desperation. Katie Fuller's reaction to her experience:

> Nobody but me and the good lord know what I went through. But I just pray. I asked God to help me. I said: Help me, Jesus, I got to work somewhere. . . . And they come through here hollering 'Nigger,' and talking all kind of ugly talk. . . . And I'd look at 'em and I would laugh. . . . It took a whole lot out of me, you know. . . . I don't know how to describe it. Devil action![9]

Despite the harassment she stayed. Within several months another black employee was hired, and the pattern was set. Black and white employees were to work together in the Memphis plant of Fairbanks International. By 1970, 27 percent of the employees in the plant were black. Katie Fuller had been a successful pioneer.

Black Professionals in Predominantly White Institutions. Whites sometimes believe that experiences like Katie Fuller's are restricted to black members of the lower socioeconomic classes. They often erroneously assume that well-educated, economically secure, and professionally competent blacks do not encounter similar prejudice. Jonathan Bramwell (1972) has written about the "Black Professional Today" and has discussed the experience of the small proportion of blacks who have been able to reach the top of this country's socioeconomic ladder.

Bramwell's background, education, and achievements can be

---

8. Purcell and Cavanagh. *Blacks in the Industrial World.* Used by permission of Macmillan Publishing Co., Inc.

9. Purcell and Cavanagh. *Blacks in the Industrial World,* p. 181. Used by permission of Macmillan Publishing Co., Inc.

matched by few individuals — black or white. A Ph.D. in biophysics, he is a staff member of *International Science and Technology*. His father is a chemical engineer, and his mother is a leading innovator in education who has been praised by the *New York Times, Who's Who of American Women*, and the *New York Post*. Other family members have been physicians, dentists, and scientists. Bramwell was a Yale National Scholar at sixteen. When he wrote *Courage in Crisis* he was also occupied writing articles about the management of science, translating Russian scientific works, directing an environmental institute, and heading a small prepschool science department. Despite considerable white resistance, he was living in a "definitely upper class section of New York." In spite of his background, schooling, ability, and achievements, Bramwell is limited by the pigmentation of his skin as, he reports, are thousands of other black professionals with similar credentials.

Here is a summary of Bramwell's (1972, pp. 8–9) findings about the black professional:

1. Extraordinarily gifted individuals, they are usually *overqualified* for the positions they hold.
2. Many feel that their positions, while equipped with impressive titles and salaries, are more than token but less than truly influential.
3. Many feel that corporations and other institutions of power have little, if any, place for talented blacks.
4. There is a marked difference between the life styles of black and white professionals—the whites being more attuned to a Madison Avenue style of life.
5. According to many, the surest path to financial success is to practice a profession in the ghetto—an impression suggesting that little has changed in fifty years.
6. A large number feel that America as a whole needed a more human atmosphere, and the black professional is in a unique position to provide the needed communication.
7. There is a growing gap in communications between black and white professionals on matters of race.
8. Almost all are involved in some efforts to improve the plight of blacks, but few saw equality around the corner.
9. Among a sample of about one thousand professionals, *all* had been directly and strongly affected by an overt act of white racism.
10. Many felt that overt racism is minor in comparison to the more subtle forms of racism they encountered on their jobs.[10]

Bramwell's data complements the earlier information about black experiences in obtaining lower level jobs in organizations. There is

---

10. From *Courage in Crisis*, copyright © 1972 by Jonathan Bramwell, reprinted by permission of the publisher, The Bobbs-Merrill Company, Inc.

little indication that black professionals escape the consequences of institutional racism, despite their possession of solid middle and upper middle class credentials. The effect of being the one black person in a predominantly white system or subsystem can be enormously stressful.

Effect of Support Groups for Minorities. As their numbers grow, blacks are sometimes able to develop support groups that provide needed counterpressures to the forces of white racism. Sometimes these groups can form within existing organizations; often they must be found outside. In 1968, black workers at Fairbanks International established a formal black caucus, called the Unity Security Association, within their local of the Electrical Workers of America (Purcell and Cavanagh, 1972). Although the local had not overtly resisted bringing blacks into the plant, the leadership found more indirect ways to be unresponsive to black employees. One of the first black employees had to go to an international representative to obtain a union card because his steward refused to provide one. White union leaders had diverted union funds to support white segregationist causes. The locals failed to support the striking sanitation workers of Memphis in the struggle that ultimately was associated with the assassination of Martin Luther King, Jr. But by 1968 blacks represented 20 percent of the hourly workforce. The Unity Security Association was formed to help black employees participate more effectively in union activities. Blacks especially felt that their grievances were not receiving adequate attention by union and company officials. In June of 1969, a black man was elected vice-president of the local, and a year later he became the union president.

When Bramwell entered Yale in September, 1957, he was one of five blacks at the institution. Being chosen as a Yale National Scholar meant he was evaluated as one of the top fifty entering students in his class. He determined that the average dropout rate at Ivy League colleges (for whites) was about 1 percent, in part because the schools financially supported any student who was performing. He also learned—after he joined the university—that the analogous statistic for highly qualified black students was about forty times as great. As one of five black students at Yale at the time, he was not likely to be able to form a support group there to help him to cope with the extensive nonacademic pressures he confronted. Instead he turned to the New Haven community, where he established black friends outside of Yale, and to a summer vacation area in Sag Harbor, New York, where the families of many middle and upper class blacks gathered. There he was able to share, with contemporaries facing similar struggles and with adults who had met the same problems before him, information about how to survive in elite predominantly white institutions. A milieu that contained so many black people of talent and achievement communicated a very different message to the young man than did the institution where he was almost the only black member.

The effects of ethnicity in organizations are rarely discussed and even less frequently changed. The case of black Americans in predominantly white institutions is an extreme one by most measures of deprivation one obtains. Other ethnic groups have faced and will continue to encounter discrimination and prejudice. Awareness of the problems has rarely been sufficient motivation to effect lasting change. Testifying before a presidential commission, Kenneth B. Clark, a distinguished psychologist, noted the repetitive pattern of knowledge and resistance to change across decades of black-white tension: "I must again in candor say to you members of this Commission—it is a kind of Alice in Wonderland—with the same moving picture reshown over and over again, the same analysis, the same recommendations, and the same inaction" (Kerner et al., 1968, p. 29). The costs of ethnic intergroup conflicts are easily denied or rationalized by dominant groups. Consequences deeply felt by the victims are often ignored by individuals who have never faced or eventually escaped such effects. Ethnic intergroup conflicts are probably the hardest to change because the cumulative effects of history are so difficult to reverse.

BEHAVIORAL SCIENCE INTERVENTIONS TO IMPROVE INTERGROUP RELATIONS

The range and complexity of intergroup dynamics in social systems should now be clear. Some group conflicts are set off by the way pyramidal systems are designed. Various task groups are pushed toward narrow understanding of their own assignments. Some groups occupy higher ranking positions in the social structure and can dominate others. Age, sex, and ethnic differences among groups are the products of ongoing life events that are brought into organizations by members. These various sources of intergroup conflict have existed since humans first formed social organizations. Methods for resolving or containing such conflicts also have existed throughout the course of history. Among the various approaches to reducing destructive intergroup conflict, applied behavioral science methods are relative newcomers.

As we have seen, the roots of many intergroup conflicts arise from real conflicts of interest among the parties. Open warfare is perhaps the oldest method for settling disputes among collectivities (Frank, 1967). Legal systems, on the other hand, provide rules and procedures for settling conflicts without war but within the framework of distributive bargaining (Walton and McKersie, 1965). Within organizations, the budget-making process also becomes a method for resolving inter-departmental conflicts (Pondy, 1973).

Behavioral science methods may complement some of the older methods of conflict management, or, in some situations, may supplant them. These methods often contain the potential for enriching the lives of the individuals and groups who become part of this type of conflict management process. Individuals may derive self-insight and improved personal functioning from such methods, and groups may grow in the esteem of both their own members and other groups. Social systems may find new energy, which prior to intervention was devoted to unproductive attacks and defense, and higher morale, which formerly was damaged by the consequences of organizational politics. A more cooperative atmosphere may evolve throughout the organization. In-terventions with intergroups also have implications for the unique individuals and groups that define the intergroup relationship.

Effective behavioral science intervention in intergroup dynamics depends both on the *level of analysis* (individual, small group, or large system) and on the *type of conflict* (task, hierarchical, generational, sexual, and ethnic). Nielson (1972) has also discussed conditions when an intervention designed to change the quality of interaction among warring groups might better be replaced by physically separating the groups. This final section describes a series of social science ap-proaches to intergroup conflict management and specifies the condi-tions when they might most fruitfully be employed. As a note of cau-tion, the reader should be aware that these methods should not be attempted by people who have not had the appropriate supervised training in applied behavioral science.

Interpersonal Peacemaking. Intergroup conflict is observable in many forms. Perhaps the most frequent occurrence is between indi-viduals who happen to represent different groups. Often the individu-als in conflict are leaders (either formal or informal) of their groups. Indeed, one view of the leader's role in a group is that he is a boundary person charged with managing the relationship between internal and external affairs (Rice, 1965).

Walton (1969) has systematized the process of interpersonal peacemaking as a social intervention. The basic paradigm is for two individuals in conflict to meet in the presence of a trusted and impar-tial third party who helps them confront their differences openly and seek a more satisfactory resolution than had been possible previously. Walton's presentation speaks primarily in interpersonal terms, but each of three cases he describes involves individuals whose difficulties with each other arose in connection with their roles as group leaders.

Intervention with the group leaders in an intergroup conflict can thus be a powerful means of changing the relationship between the groups, because a leader's power—both formal and informal—permits him to influence the behavior of his followers. At the same time one must keep in mind that leaders are also influenced by their followers, and in some instances may be captives of their groups. Interpersonal peacemaking interventions with group leaders to influence intergroup dynamics thus may not be possible or may be unsuccessful depending on the nature of the relationship of both leaders to their groups. For example, a leader whose standing with his own group is tenuous may not be free to cooperate with the leader of another group without extensive checking with his followership. This is not possible in the usual third-party peacemaking setting, because only the leaders are present. A leader may even attempt to enhance his power with his own group by escalating conflict with an outgroup. A person with this strategy could misuse a third-party peacemaking intervention to exacerbate rather than reduce intergroup conflicts.

At the outset of interpersonal peacemaking, the third party must establish a trusting relationship with each conflicting party, ensure that both understand the process they are beginning, and be sure that each actively and voluntarily chooses to participate. Unless he is already intimate with the situation, the third party must then collect information about how each person sees the conflict—both on the substantive issues at stake and on the feelings evoked. This is usually done by intensive one-on-one interviewing of each person by the consultant.

Having informed himself about the conflict, the third party then tries to arrange a meeting among the clients and himself to clarify and work through the ideas and feelings separating them. The physical setting for such a meeting is important. It is best to find neutral territory that is comfortable and relaxing to all parties—including the consultant. Meeting in one of the party's offices is usually a bad idea. Joining the consultant at his office might be all right if that does not present severe travel problems for anyone.

When the parties actually meet, the third party has a number of important functions to perform. He needs to synchronize the pace at which the participants proceed with their discussion. A common human tendency is to avoid direct discussion of the issues dividing the parties, even though the purpose of the meeting was clearly set in advance and both parties voluntarily agreed to be present. The third party attempts to pace the airing of differences between the parties so that each is able to express his point of view without unproductive escalation or denial. But the *differentiation phase,* as Walton calls it, requires more than joint catharsis to be effective. Each party must develop a sense that his side of things has been understood by the other side. The third party can facilitate this by checking to be sure that words are heard as intended and that disclosures by one side are not used as ammunition by the other. An *integration phase* in which the parties find bases for accommodation may follow differentiation, if clarifying the issues shows that there are reasons for cooperation that had not been utilized previously. Resolution of some conflicts involves several cycles of differentiation and integration, as initial solutions prove to be unstable or more elaborate understanding of the issues is achieved.

Interpersonal peacemaking, of course, can be employed when conflict between the parties is largely interpersonal or when the individuals in dispute are not acting as group representatives. But when this approach is employed for conflict containment or resolution between group leaders, then provision must be made for informing group members about the outcome. There are a variety of ways this might be done, and even if it is not, group members will undoubtedly detect changed feelings on the part of their leader. The conclusion of interpersonal peacemaking might be reserved for both leaders to derive a plan for how they can best communicate the results of their work to their respective groups.

Intergroup Problem-Solving. The limitations of interpersonal peacemaking for resolving intergroup conflicts can sometimes be overcome by working with entire groups. The next approach to be described is a method for identifying and working through differences with whole groups. It was originally developed by Blake, Shepard, and Mouton (1964) and later was elaborated by Burke (1972).

The process begins with the consultant establishing his role and his relationship to the parties before actually bringing the groups together. Before deciding that an intergroup intervention is called for, in fact, the consultant must do some preliminary diagnostic work. His efforts at this phase are similar to what the third-party peacemaker does initially, except that in preparing for intergroup problem-solving the consultant does preliminary diagnosis and establishes a contract with related groups as well as with individuals. Once it is clear that an intergroup problem-solving session might be helpful and the parties agree to participate, an off-site location is selected for the activity. A comfortable central setting away from the pressures and distractions of day-to-day operations allows the participants to devote their full energies to working on their conflict. Even informal time between meetings can be used productively if clients so choose.

The first formal activity of the off-site workshop is for the groups to prepare and exchange *images* of each other. Each group is asked to prepare answers to three questions about the intergroup relationship as it currently exists:

1. How do we see ourselves?
2. How do we see the other group?
3. How do we think they see us?

Answers to these questions may be one-word adjectives, phrases, or sentences. This phase of intergroup problem-solving is analogous to the differentiation portion of interpersonal peacemaking and relates directly to the properties of ethnocentrism detailed earlier in this chapter. Burke (1972, p. 259) provided the following examples of characteristics from an intergroup problem-solving session between engineering and manufacturing groups:

Engineering		**Manufacturing**
	We See Ourselves:	
stable		competent
cooperative		error prone
creative		hard working
•		•
•		•
•		•
	We See Them:	
unstable		error prone
not creative		no sense of urgency
industrious		unified as group
•		•
•		•
•		•
	They See Us:	
in ivory towers		constantly changing
error prone		error prone
intrusive		inflexible
•		•
•		•

Groups work privately to articulate images of each other and then present them publicly. The time of presentation is a period of heightened involvement and emotionality. Because there is some danger of escalating the conflict at this point, the consultant permits only *questions of clarification* as images are exchanged.

After all three lists are reported to the total group and questions of clarification are answered, the workshop moves to a *problem identification* phase. First as individuals and then as groups, the parties are asked to identify the problems that exist between them. When each group has consolidated the problem lists of its individual members, the group lists are exchanged in a public session. Again, only questions of clarification are permitted and participants are encouraged not to propose solutions.

The lists from the separate groups generally have some overlap, redundancy, and inconsistency. Two members from each group are selected to combine the separate lists into a single list containing all the problems between the groups that have been identified. This *grand list,* which may contain a large number of problems, must then be arranged in order of priority, because it is unlikely that all problems can be addressed in a single workshop. Individuals report their personal priorities, which are combined to establish a rank order of problems to be addressed in the workshop.

Individuals are then asked to form groups to solve the most important problems that have been identified. People volunteer for the problem group they wish to join, with the additional provision that half of each task force derives from each of the warring groups. When the problem-solving groups have completed their work, the results are shared with the entire workshop. Plans for implementation in the work setting are developed, and arrangements for a future meeting to assess the effects of the solutions are made.

Burke's presentation included an example of intergroup problem-solving between an engineering department and manufacturing—an intergroup based on task differences between the parties. His results indicated that the intervention had decidedly constructive effects. Blake, Mouton, and Sloma (1964, pp. 155–195) employed a similar approach in a labor-management conflict and obtained a more problematic outcome. After three years of behavioral science-based interventions with management alone, the consultants suggested that intergroup problem-solving could be employed to ameliorate longstanding labor-management difficulties. Neither party was very optimistic about the possibility of change but both agreed to try. The union in particular was suspicious, and early in the workshop attempted to exclude a consultant from their deliberations. Despite the consultants' efforts to remain impartial, it is likely that several years of successful association between the consultants and management biased the former's views of the situation. The consultants (Blake, Mouton, and Sloma, 1964, pp. 161 ff.) wrote the following about the start of the workshop:

> Union members had great difficulty understanding the task. . . . At the beginning, then, the union members did not have the concept of examining the *process* of behavior. . . . Their thinking pattern was so deeply ingrained on the *content* side that they were not able to think about the dynamics of the relationship. . . . Management launched into this first task with a feeling of confidence. They were sure they could quickly put their finger on the real problems. . . . In contrast to the union, *management had the process orientation* (emphasis theirs).

The groups were able to proceed with the workshop, however. Although they did not solve the problems that were dividing them, they were able to achieve greater understanding of major factors underlying their difficulties. Lack of trust, ideological differences, inadequate knowledge, and attitudinal differences were pervasive in the relationship.

A System-Wide Intervention into Labor-Management Relations.

There are probably several basic reasons why intergroup problem-solving was not more effective in the labor-management context. The case presented by Blake, Mouton, and Sloma derived from a long history of conflictful relations between labor and management in that setting. How realistic was it to expect several days of intense interaction between the parties to reverse grievances built up over years of unresolved disputes? Throughout the intergroup problem-solving design, implicit assumptions are made about the essential equality of the parties—in terms of numbers, control of resources, and structural arrangements. Although these are often reasonable assumptions when the intergroup dispute occurs between different task groups within management, they are less likely to hold for hierarchical intergroups whose power bases rest on the control of quite different kinds of resources. We do not suggest that intergroup problem-solving cannot work between labor and management—only that by itself it is not adequate to deal with the kinds of forces set in motion by years of mistrustful relations between parties of vastly different and unequal power bases. It is also crucial that the consultants who enter the situation have not been closely identified with management (Lewicki and Alderfer, 1973). Long-term interventions that recognize the structural differences between the parties offer more hope, in other words, than short-term methods that assume equality.

The Scanlon Plan was the social invention of Joseph Scanlon, a labor leader who late in his career became an academician at MIT (Lesieur, 1958). The plan consists of two basic parts—(1) a structural system for cooperative intergroup problem-solving between labor and management to effect labor cost savings in the production process, and (2) a formula for sharing the labor cost savings on a plant-wide basis. A complex committee system touching all departments and groups in a plant provides a structure for obtaining information about how to produce more effectively. Distribution of the economic fruits of this system to the entire plant gives everyone—management and labor alike—a stake in the outcome. The plan is not a short-term intervention, although a crisis may be the precipitating event that leads a plant to introduce it. It is part of the normal, everyday operations. Advocates of the plan suggest that cost savings (or lack thereof) should be distributed monthly so that people regularly realize how the plan is working.

Intergroup cooperation throughout a plant under the Scanlon Plan is based on a structure consisting of two types of committees—

production committees in each major department, and a screening committee for the plant as a whole. Several small departments may be grouped together for a single production committee. Membership on the production committee is from both labor and management—usually in unequal numbers. Typically a single management person who is a key decision-maker in the area meets with several employees elected from the ranks to form a production committee. Meeting at least once a month (and more often if desirable), the committee discusses methods to eliminate waste, to improve methods of doing work, and to schedule the workflow. The employee side of the committee reports suggestions they have obtained from their colleagues and attempts to convince management to try them—often by bringing the person who thought of the idea to the meeting. Records are kept of all suggestions and people are informed about the consequences of their ideas, regardless of whether the ideas are used. When labor and management agree about the merits of an idea (whether it is positive or negative), disposition of the suggestion is handled by a production committee. When the two parties disagree, or when implementation of the idea involves additional departments, the suggestion is passed upward to the plant-wide screening committee.

The plant-wide screening committee is usually made up of an equal number of management and union members and typically consists of eight to twelve people. Labor and management members should include the top people from both organizations. Also meeting at least once a month, the members of the screening committee have three major tasks—(1) to determine the bonus for the month, (2) to hear reports from management about any factors that might influence future operations of the plan, and (3) to act on any material that has come to them from the various production committees. Management reserves the right to accept or reject suggestions, but observers report that the acceptance rate under this system is very high (Lesieur, p. 49).

The system for determining labor cost savings and for sharing those benefits is system-wide and affects everyone from the president (or plant manager) to the lowest ranking member of the organization. Thus, the Scanlon Plan is not an individual or group incentive, but is based on the performance of the whole system. A critical element in the labor cost savings is selecting the base point from which comparisons are to be made. The most common ratio is sales volume of production in relation to payroll for the entire unit. Usually the best base point is the preceding year's results—providing that was not a period of losses for the company. Seventy-five percent of the bonus is normally paid to the participants, while 25 percent is retained by the company. Additional adjustments are made to both company and employee shares to establish a reserve to cover months when there are no labor cost savings (Puckett, 1958).

Adjustments for technological changes, price variations, and product mix can all be made within this basic framework. Difficulties arise, however, when the employees do not trust the accounting figures presented by management. As long as confidence in the data exists, employees readily see the direct relationship between the company's ability to stay in business and their own job security.[11]

Efforts to evaluate the Scanlon Plan have been conducted by a number of scholars (Shultz, 1958a; Strauss and Sayles, 1957). From these studies we obtain suggestions about problematic features of the plan and about the conditions necessary for its effective utilization. Shultz, for example, was able to rule out a number of environmental factors that might have been viewed as critical for the plan's success. Plant size, economic condition of the organization, and proportion of labor cost did not seem to be major determinants of the plan's success. Most difficulties with the plan could be traced to existing problems between labor and management, to factions within the union, or to poor communication among levels of management. Strauss and Sayles (1957) make the point that a successful Scanlon Plan requires tremendously increased interaction among all levels of union and management. Such interaction, they note, should be balanced and should include all segments of the plant community. They document how problems might arise if top management imposes the plan on lower management, if union leaders lose touch with the rank and file and become coopted by management, if production committee members do not regularly consult with their constituencies, if the union uses the plan as a means to harass management rather than to problem-solve, if foremen are resistive or unresponsive in production committee meetings, and if the group cohesion of individual work units is either excessive or nonexistent. In sum, the plan feeds on itself. It is a complex means for improving intergroup relations, and its impact is directly related to the already existing maturity of relations within and between labor and management.

Throughout this discussion I have written as if the existence of the union in a Scanlon Plan was assumed. In fact, most of the plans reviewed by Shultz (1958a) were ones with intact unions whose survival was not at stake. But not all plants with Scanlon Plans were unionized, despite the origin of the plan in the mind of a labor leader. Nonunionized plants could develop a nonmanagement structure for the plan that was analogous to what exists within the union when one is present. However, the plan functions at a time when survival for the union is not a problematic issue—either because the union is well

---

11. The Scanlon Plan is discussed by Lawler (in Chapter 4) in terms of its merits as a group incentive plan, and by Strauss (in Chapter 6) in terms of its usefulness as a method for increasing employee participation in decision making in the plant.

established (the most common case) or because it is nonexistent (the unusual case).

Sexual and Racial Consciousness Raising. Interpersonal peacemaking, intergroup problem-solving, and the Scanlon Plan are methods for intervening in intergroup conflicts that arise from division of labor and hierarchy of authority—issues whose origins are primarily inside organizations. Group dynamics methods have also been applied to historically rooted intergroups based on sex and race.[12] These approaches are in a more formative stage than the techniques just reviewed, and the literature pertaining to them is not as extensive. Nevertheless, related theoretical and technical principles apply.[13]

All-Female and Male-Female Encounter Groups. Meador, Solomon, and Bowen (1972) have written about "Encounter Groups for Women Only." This social invention is a derivative from encounter groups in general (Solomon and Berzon 1972) and from the women's liberation movement. Although the women participating in these activities are sometimes uncomfortable about this, the women's liberation movement tends to be restricted to white middle and upper middle class females. Black and other minority women tend to be oppressed more by the culture at large than by men in families, and therefore identify less strongly with women's liberation. Participants in the Meador et al. groups showed the expected demographic backgrounds.

The basic issues addressed in these groups were independence, conflicting role expectations, and self-identity. A first step toward establishing one's own identity for participants was the struggle to dispel the notion that the woman was primarily someone's wife or lover. Many women did not begin the process with the idea that they had equal rights to self-fulfillment. But as they considered their own personal development, a sense of the traps they had gotten themselves into became clearer. For example, an easy life with someone to take care of one's needs is a dependence trap. Full liberation means that a woman must feel as though she can make it on her own. Women also

---

12. Except for the work of Brown (1975) and the consultation reported at the end of Alderfer (1971), I know of no interventions that have been explicitly applied to generational conflicts. I suggest that many of the points appropriate to the other historically rooted intergroups apply to these conflicts as well.

13. Conflicts based on sex and race share with labor-management struggles the property of being heavily tied to political processes. The labor movement, the civil rights movement, and the women's movement each have influenced the legitimacy with which the respective groups can pursue their interests inside as well as outside of organizations. Political activities and applied behavioral science intervention may either complement or conflict with each other. The question of which approach serves better the interests of various groups, when the two methods are in conflict, is itself part of an intergroup conflict arising from task and hierarchical differences between professional behavioral scientists, lawyers, and politicians.

discovered that they had strength and aggression to express, but that brought another set of conflicts. For women to be strong violated some sex-role stereotypes. Women who could express these facets of themselves, however, found support from others in the group. In an all-women's group the participants did not feel as though they might lose male affection by demonstrating parts of themselves that normal role expectations prohibited. An all-female group also provides women with an opportunity to explore their more private feelings about sexuality, motherhood, and child-rearing. They could discuss the pressures they felt to be sexy in front of men and also the barriers they felt when they wished to be sexually aggressive. Body image and the sense of one's own sexual adequacy were explored openly in the all-female groups. Overall, the single sex groups provided women with an opportunity to face more squarely their confusions and fears in a setting where they discovered others with similar concerns. When she could face her own dilemmas, a woman could begin to see a variety of alternatives to her own particular child-care and motherhood problems. Women also found that they enjoyed being with other women as a result of being in the groups. Some confessed that they had secretly preferred male to female company until the group experience enabled them to develop genuinely close friendships with other women.

There is some apparent disagreement among female scholars about the merits of *sensitivity training* as a means for effecting change in male-female relations. Kanter (1974) argues that the values promoted by experiential group methods can aid males to free their emotional lives. But using the same approach for women may simply reinforce female sex-role stereotypes. According to Kanter, women do not need to become more open, caring, concerned, and supportive (at least in relation to men) but rather more assertive, aggressive, logical, and active.

The issue may not be as simple as it seems, however. Herald and Dann (1975), a woman and man, describe an experiential group conference in which male-female issues were explored together by men and women in the context of their work relationships. But the *structure* of this conference did not show the usual pattern of male domination. Staff included both men and women, and the highest status roles— external consultant and dean—were filled by a woman and a man, respectively. Each group was staffed by a male and female trainer, and the number of female participants in each small group was slightly less than half the total. Under these structural conditions, which do *not* reproduce the pattern of society at large, it was possible for men and women to learn together about their respective contributions to sex-role stereotyping without falling blindly into the more common behavioral patterns. Comparing the descriptions of the Meador et al. (1972)

groups with the Herald and Dann groups gives one the sense that the all-female groups reached somewhat deeper emotional exploration than the mixed sex groups. The mixed sex groups, however, did examine both male and female behavior and feelings, so that transfer from the conference to the real world seemed more likely from this design than from the all-female groups. The target for change in the all-female groups was more likely to be the *individual* woman while in the male-female design it was the male-female *relationship*.

Ethnotherapy.   After working with black and white psychotherapy patients and observing the increasing ease with which both races examined their racial feelings after the civil rights movement became prominent in the 1960s, Cobbs (1972) developed a new method for dealing with the emotional dynamics of racism. He called the innovation *ethnotherapy*. Because the origins of racism were in group dynamics, a group approach was selected as the model for intervention. Ethnotherapy groups consist of twelve to fourteen participants, approximately half male and half female, a black *and* a white staff member, and at least six black members. Like the mixed-sex design for changing male-female relationships, the structural arrangements for ethnotherapy do *not* reproduce the pattern for society at large. Blacks are represented in the highest status positions as staff members and in sufficient participant numbers so that if they were in the minority, it was a sizable minority. In ethnotherapy, black participants are not forced into roles which predetermine that they will be subordinate to whites. In no small measure this is due to the fact that the inventor of ethnotherapy is a black male psychiatrist who used his power to reverse in microcosm the destructive patterns he had observed in the wider culture.

All members of ethnotherapy groups are volunteers. Many whites consider themselves educated and tolerant on racial matters. They do not come to examine their racial prejudices as much as to place blacks "under the microscope of interracial understanding." Blacks also come to the groups for their own special reasons—mainly to vent their rage at each other and at whites. Group leaders try to create a climate that enables blacks who are normally ignored by whites to be heard. Individuals are invited to discuss what it means to them to be black or white in American society. Early in the group a black may launch an attack on a white and two factors become clear at once. The black is very angry, and the white is very hurt. From this point there is an escalation of feelings as whites deny the contempt blacks sense from them. Blacks then dominate the group discussion as they probe their life experiences against a backdrop of current social issues. Eventually whites begin to speak up again and explore the nature of white guilt. Individuals tend to develop different perceptions of the black and white leaders. The black leader is frequently symbolized as more feeling-oriented and less intelligent, and the white leader is viewed as weak and more technically competent. As these differential perceptions are examined in the group, they provide a potent means to understand the dynamics of racism in American society.

Appropriate use of experiential group methods can create greater awareness of male-female sex-role stereotypes and the dynamics of racism. When competently led and properly structured, these approaches allow the ingroup-outgroup patterns for both types of historically rooted intergroups to merge in the here-and-now of the interacting group. Participants can obtain rich personal learning if they are able to tolerate the stress and anxiety provoked by the intense discussion and self-study. These specially focused intergroup dynamics techniques differ from the more traditional experiential methods in terms of the demographic characteristics of the staff and membership. To prevent the interventions from merely repeating society's oppressive patterns, women and minorities must be represented in staff roles and in significant numbers among participants. Again, as in the case of labor-management relations in the Scanlon Plan, reversing destructive intergroup conflicts depends on whether designs can be established that do not reproduce the problems they attempt to solve.

Long-Term Improvement in Intergroup Communication. The preceding intergroup interventions each focused on a specific type of intergroup problem (task, hierarchical, sex, and race). But as we have seen, the several organizational intergroups are not independent; the various splits tend to be interrelated with one another. The final intervention to be described is a method for dealing with several intergroups simultaneously on a long-term basis (Alderfer, 1975).

A group of twelve people, consisting of members from all significant groups, is formed to reflect the concerns found in the larger system. In one application of this technique, the members represented four major interdependent work groups (sales, production, engineering, and research); management and labor (on a one to two ratio); women and men; and the ethnic differences present in the work force. The group was charged with helping to improve communication in the larger system by discovering what issues people wished to know about and providing the relevant information.

The group was structured to have a quasi-stable membership in which members were elected to staggered eighteen-month terms. All meetings of the group were open to members of the larger system who wished to attend as observers or participants. Specific interventions were directed toward improving communications among members of the group and between the group and the larger system. Conflicts between activities of the group and the union and between some

requests for information and perceived middle management prerogatives served to clarify the group's mission and improve its effectiveness. Ultimately the union endorsed the validity of the group, after it
was clearly determined that they would not deal with issues related to
the company-union contract. Middle managers in the system stopped
resisting group activities when the origins of their feelings were identified and the consequences of their acts were clarified.

Three major areas of concern received sustained attention by the
group—socialization of new employees, group meetings for work
groups, and promotion-rotation policies for employees. The group
found that inadequate attention was being paid to explaining to new
employees what their job duties were and what work groups they had
to know. Within the larger system there was no common practice of
group meetings between supervisors and subordinates. Some work
teams had regular meetings and others rarely met. Those who had
regular meetings found them very beneficial, and those who did not
wanted to establish the practice. Concerns about mobility in the system were intense and pervasive, because employees felt largely in the
dark about how such important decisions were made. There was
widespread belief that performance had relatively little to do with the
probability of promotion. People were unsure about how and when
affirmative action considerations influenced the mobility of individuals. After much struggle, the group sponsored a dialogue between an
employee who asked the tough questions and a manager who
answered them. This discussion was transcribed, typed, and circulated
to the entire system. Overall, the scope of issues addressed by the
group covered the full range of a person's life cycle in the
organization—from entry into the system through day-to-day work
problems to exit by job rotation or promotion. The group was also a
forum where more mundane issues of system-wide concern, such as
parking policies and fire drills, could be brought for review.

A system-wide survey of employee attitudes was taken with the
help of the group. Members helped in the construction of questions,
the administration of the questionnaire to all employees, and the
feedback of data to the whole division. Items in the questionnaire also
provided a means for the group to examine the consequences of its
activities and to alter its activities where appropriate. Key managers in
the system were also prompted to initiate changes in areas under their
responsibility as a result of the feedback.

By attempting to be responsive to such a wide range of intergroup
issues in a social system, the group found itself under constant stress.
Members found that they were sometimes blamed for events beyond
their control. Managers found themselves confronting many issues that
are normally suppressed by pressures of hierarchical systems. The net

effect, however, was that people in this system developed greater access to information pertaining to their organizational lives than is normally expected. The microcosm group improved communications in a wide range of areas of concern to members in the system.

CONCLUSION

The first challenge in any effort to improve destructive intergroup relations is understanding. Intergroup dynamics in organizations are pervasive in their effects and all too often are misperceived by the conflicting parties. It is usually much easier to see how an adversary's acts provoke one's self than to understand how one's own behavior affects someone else. The most easily understood intergroups are those where the parties have approximately equal power. The consequences of intergroups based on unequal power are usually more accurately perceived by the subordinate than by the dominant group.

The development of this chapter was designed to reflect the unfolding nature of intergroup dynamics as they might be observed by an increasingly perceptive student of human behavior. Intergroup dynamics influence individual behavior—the easiest level to observe. I began with an account of an individual whose impact in a task force was heavily influenced by her multiple group memberships. But the problem with understanding the behavior of individuals is that observers frequently explain what they see by reference to the person's personality rather than to externally generated pressures that impinge upon him. We saw that was true of the group's response to Marian.

Early attempts to go beyond the individual in explaining organizational behavior led researchers to the investigation of small group behavior in organizations. Fascinated by this new way of understanding human behavior, investigators made a subsequent error in confining their attention only to what happened inside the group. I reviewed a number of classical studies of group behavior in organizations to show how the original researchers ignored or underplayed the impact of intergroup dynamics on the groups they observed.

An explicit discussion of intergroups in organizations started with an analysis of the relationship between groups consciously created to meet organizational objectives—those arising from division of labor and hierarchy of authority. Intergroup dynamics arising from these structural decisions are most directly under the control of organization members who design systems that may increase or decrease intergroup conflict. A distinction was made between organizationally induced and historically rooted intergroups. Organization members bring their historically rooted group memberships with them when they join. In this way, the intergroup dynamics within an organization are further complicated by the intergroup dynamics of groups formed outside the system. I further observed that organizationally induced and historically rooted intergroups tend to be interdependent. Youth, women, and minority ethnic groups tend to occupy lower ranking organizational positions, so the relative deprivation they experience outside the system was correlated with similar experiences inside. The phenomena of *correlated intergroup relations* adds to the complexity of real life conflict and makes the task of effective intervention more difficult. Arising from forces set in motion by the developmental processes in individuals, the relations among family members, and the acts of whole nations, historically rooted intergroup conflicts are the most potent, painful, and hidden of the group dynamic conflicts in organizations.

Within the social technology of applied behavioral sciences are a range of treatments for the destructive effects of intergroup conflict. We observed that some techniques are more fruitful for some kinds of difficulties than for others and should be employed under some circumstances but not others. It is also possible to use the approaches in combination (for example, ethnotherapy within a Scanlon Plan organization, interpersonal peacemaking prior to intergroup problem solving). Implementation of the various technologies is likely to be more effective if the professionals involved base their interventions on a sound knowledge of intergroup theory and research findings. The social technologies can more easily be modified to fit the special circumstances where they are to be applied if the basic knowledge is related to a thorough diagnosis of the situation where intervention is to be undertaken.

Perhaps the most difficult problem in reversing destructive intergroup dynamics is to avoid reproducing the very patterns one is attempting to alter. The more effective social technologies are structured by participant selection and staff assignment to counteract this tendency. As might be expected from the foregoing analysis, the various social technologies are more likely to be accepted by those who need them least and rejected by those who could benefit most by their effective implementation. Ultimately, improvement in the *intergroup quality of work life* requires greater mutual respect and acceptance from and for all the *groups* in organizations than exists today. When that happens (if it does) *individuals* whose self-identity is partially determined by their multiple group identifications will also experience more humane work lives.

CHAPTER 6
MANAGERIAL PRACTICES

GEORGE STRAUSS
University of California, Berkeley

Previous chapters have dealt with specific aspects of the quality of work life question. In this and the following chapter, we will consider how *management* can pull these various strings together so as to improve the nature and quality of the work experience. It is management that is responsible for developing career ladders, designing jobs and reward systems, and creating the conditions under which effective teamwork can develop—all issues discussed in previous chapters. Beyond this, management influences quality of work life directly through its daily interactions with individual employees. There are few surer ways of guaranteeing employee dissatisfaction than to have a tyrannical or incompetent boss.

My discussion begins with the supervisor, who is management's direct representative at the workplace. Supervisors can affect quality of work life in a variety of ways, of which I shall emphasize three: (1) they provide *consideration*, understanding, fair and humane treatment, and the kind of psychological support that makes the tensions of the job endurable; (2) they serve as *facilitators*, providing direction, supplies, and information, so that work effort is not wasted; and (3) they can organize the work force as a team and encourage appropriate (a key word here) degrees of *participation* in making important work force decisions. All three functions directly relate to productivity and job satisfaction.

Supervisors are rarely free, however, to perform these three key functions as they wish. They are subject to a variety of constraints from the rest of the organization and are often buffeted by conflicting pressures from their subordinates and their bosses. For supervisors to be effective, therefore, they need solid support from higher management. They need substantial freedom and encouragement to engage in efforts that develop and motivate subordinates. Several of the functions that supervisors perform in addition to keeping watch over their subordinates are examined in this chapter, as are the organizational constraints that affect how well supervisors are able to perform these functions.

Important as the direct supervisor may be, there are numerous other ways the organization can influence the quality of work life. I will examine, for example, the types of organizational structures that are needed to permit workers to feel that they are making contributions as members of an overall work team. More than this, employees seek to influence decisions significant to them. There are a variety of ways to accomplish this in nonunion companies; nevertheless, the union permits employee interests to be represented directly at the highest management levels. The final section is a discussion of some of the problems faced by both unions and management in devising joint efforts to improve the quality of work life. (The union's important role in quality of work life improvements is discussed at greater length in Chapter 7.) Here I will look at the union-management relationship primarily from management's point of view and will discuss briefly the various strategies that management might adopt to facilitate a better meshing of the efforts of union and management in the process of enhancing the quality of work life. Both parties are critical, of course, to successful quality of work life efforts.

In this chapter I am concerned primarily with such subjects as supervision, participation, and union activity. These are terribly important. However, management also affects quality of work life more directly by its personnel policies, especially its concerns for workers' security, work amenities, the pace and hours of work, and safe and healthy working conditions. Although I do not stress these points here, they are of crucial significance.

One final introductory point. I am concerned—as are the other authors of this book—with the impact of managerial practices on both production and satisfaction, and I recognize that some situations require trade-offs between the two.

THE ROLE OF THE SUPERVISOR

The supervisor is critical to the quality of work life of employees. A University of Michigan study (University of Michigan, 1971), which sought to relate a large number of characteristics of workers' jobs to overall satisfaction, illustrates the wide variety of ways in which supervisory behavior influences subordinate satisfaction. The eight factors most closely related to satisfaction are listed below, in order of the strength of this relationship:

1. A "nurturant" supervisor
2. Adequate help, assistance, guidance
3. Few "labor standards problems," such as safety hazards, poor hours, or poor transportation
4. Fair promotional policies
5. Supervisor not supervising too closely
6. A technically competent supervisor
7. Autonomy in matters affecting work
8. A job with "enriching" demands

Of the eight factors, three refer directly to supervisors (1, 5, and 6), three are often primarily their responsibility (2, 7, and 8), and even the remaining two (3 and 4) are substantially subject to the influence of supervisors.

As illustrated by the above list, supervisors influence the quality of work life both directly and indirectly. They affect subordinates *directly* through their daily interactions with them. They can be supportive ("nurturant") or not understanding, friendly or distant, available to provide help or always busy, they can supervise closely or permit autonomy, they can make technically competent or incompetent decisions, and so forth. Whatever they do inevitably influences satisfaction and productivity. However, as we shall see, the relative importance of supervisory attitudes and behavior may vary considerably from situation to situation.

Equally important, in most instances, is the supervisor's *indirect* impact as a participant in the design and management of various environmental and work systems, including those discussed in previous chapters. Supervisors influence the design of jobs (Chapter 3), they play a key role in the administration of career and reward systems (Chapters 2 and 4), and they are in a position to foster the development of social systems, especially the various forms of social interaction discussed in Chapter 5. In none of these areas can supervisors act alone; they are subject to a variety of constraints placed on them by higher management. Nevertheless, the alert supervisor can take a systems view that will help integrate all these factors—and a number of others—in ways that enhance the quality of work life of their subordinates as well as help to achieve organizational objectives of efficiency and adaptability.

Research in this area may stress either the supervisor's day-to-day interactions or his long-term role as a systems designer and manager. Regardless of which view one takes, however, the manager is concerned with maintaining *both* a satisfactory work environment and high levels of employee motivation. The discussion that follows will take all these factors into account. But first it may be helpful to say a few words about the research context of the material.

The Research Context

A great deal of energy has gone into research on supervision, but unfortunately the findings are not as clear in this area as they perhaps are in some of the areas discussed in previous chapters.[1] Over the years the research on supervision has become increasingly sophisticated. Yet it is fair to say that the more rigorous the research the less useful it has been to management. This may be another way of saying that as research techniques have become more sophisticated they have exploded the glib generalizations that management had originally accepted so eagerly.

Early research concentrated on isolating the specific *personality* traits of the ideal leader. By the early 1950s, this quest was largely abandoned as it became increasingly clear that leadership was a behavioral rather than a personality trait. Much research in the 1950s and 1960s was devoted to finding a style of supervision that would optimize both performance and satisfaction in all managerial situations—from managing an automobile assembly line, for example, to leading a symphony orchestra. For a while it was believed that the secret of successful supervision was emphasis on people rather than on production; later it was hypothesized that the best supervisor was the one who gave equal stress to both people *and* production.

In recent years, there has been progressive disenchantment with simplistic conclusions of this sort. Although it is possible to say that the effective supervisor shows high concern for production and people, such a statement merely defines the problem and does not provide a specific answer. How is concern for people to be shown? The answer obviously differs from situation to situation. About the only conclusions the research can offer with any confidence at the moment, therefore, are the fairly negative ones discussed below.

1. It has proven difficult to isolate any single set of dimensions that are uniquely suited for describing the many-faceted nature of supervisory behavior. With the exception of *consideration* (a factor to be described later on), no single measure or set of measures of supervi-

---

1. There is a whole stream of review work on supervision by sociologists. This includes studies dealing with legitimacy and authority, with the forms of leadership required for different forms of worker commitment and organizational goals (such as Etzioni, 1961), with transaction and exchange theory and its relationship to leadership (such as, Homans, 1961; Blau, 1964), and with the impact of technology on supervision (such as, Perrow, 1967).

sory behavior predicts either satisfaction or productivity in a consistent manner.

2. Supervisory behaviors that maximize productivity may not maximize satisfaction, and vice versa. Usually some trade-off is required, at least in the short run.

3. There is no one best style of supervision. What is best in a given situation depends on such factors as task, technology, organizational climate, and the expectations and personalities of the employees. Further, the "best" supervisors may be the ones who vary their style of supervision according to the conditions they face.

4. It is difficult, if not meaningless, to try to study supervision apart from the organizational and cultural environment in which it occurs.

Three Key Supervisory Roles

Although the research is confusing and offers few clear guides to management, one thing is certain—the supervisor performs a number of functions that are critical to a high quality of work life. For the purposes of exposition, I will lump these functions under *consideration, facilitation,* and *participation.*

Consideration. This function relates to the supervisor's activities in providing a satisfactory work environment—the way he treats employees on a day-to-day basis, his personal relations with them, his approach to the disciplinary process, and the like. In terms of the University of Michigan survey just discussed, the considerate supervisor is "nurturant," a factor that heads the list of those most closely linked to overall job satisfaction.

A considerate supervisor makes even a boring job more tolerable. However, consideration may be particularly important for the *instrumentally*[2] oriented worker who does not seek satisfaction from the work itself. In most situations consideration affects satisfaction more than it does productivity; however, it can also influence productivity in some rather interesting ways. For example, consideration is a necessary, though not sufficient, condition for participation. And without consideration, job redesign experiments are almost sure to fail.

A parenthetical note. The term *consideration* is somewhat condescending and almost negative in tone. I would have preferred to call

---

2. Workers who are *instrumentally* oriented view work as a means (instrument) to another end; *expressively* oriented workers find work a valued end in itself (a means of expression). The main goals of instrumentally oriented workers are to earn more money, to obtain greater job security, and to enjoy more leisure; for such workers commitment to work is secondary to commitment to family, home, and community life (Dubin, 1959). Expressively oriented workers generally have the same objectives as those who are instrumentally oriented; in addition, they seek challenge and meaning from their work. For them pay and security are important—but not enough.

this factor *psychological support*. However, because the term *consideration* is better established in the literature, and because there is a widely used consideration measure developed by psychologists at Ohio State University (Fleishman, 1957), I have chosen to use it in this chapter. Furthermore, this measure has been the subject of a great deal of research, even though much of it is inconclusive (for an early review, see Korman, 1966).

Facilitation.   Items number 2 and 6 in the University of Michigan survey relate respectively to "receiving adequate help, assistance, and so on" and to "having a technically competent supervisor." Clearly, in the absence of these factors the job will be frustrating and dissatisfying and productivity will almost certainly be low. Both factors are included in the function I call *facilitation*.[3] Facilitation generally includes those things the supervisor can do to make it easier for workers to do their jobs. Without facilitation, work effort is wasted—there will be little likelihood that work effort will be converted into performance or lead to rewards. If consideration can be viewed as social support, facilitation provides technical support, although (as we shall see) the concept involves more than purely technical support, because important elements of direction, guidance, and training are included.

In Herzberg's (1966) terms (see Hackman, Chapter 3) facilitation is a hygiene factor, yet its presence makes positive motivation possible. It is important for instrumentally-oriented workers, but is perhaps more important for expressive workers who are especially likely to become upset if their work efforts are frustrated by supervisory incompetence or lack of support.

Participation.   Participation involves allowing subordinates greater opportunities to make work decisions. As such it is closely related to items number 5, 7, and 8—"supervisor not supervising too closely," "autonomy in matters affecting work," and "a job with 'enriching' demands"—in the University of Michigan study.

The relationship between participation and facilitation is a bit tricky. When there is a high degree of participation, subordinates either individually or as a group perform much of the facilitation function on their own. Supervisory facilitation is in one sense the opposite of participation. That is, when participation is low facilitation may be provided by the boss, but when participation is high it may be provided by the group. In either situation, for the organization to be effective, facilitation has to be performed by *someone*.

---

3. For the technically inclined let me note that my concept of facilitation is closely related to Bowers and Seashore's (1966) measure of "work facilitation," but it also includes elements of their "goal emphasis."

Participation is also akin to work redesign. Most forms of job redesign involve increased participation in some types of work decisions. Indeed, the amount of discretion permitted on a job is an important element in its design. Give subordinates more freedom to make job decisions, in other words, and their jobs *are* different.

Participation is of particular importance to the expressive worker. However, the opportunity for participation may increase the involvement of instrumental workers in their jobs and so may make them more expressive in their orientation. Participation is primarily what Herzberg (1966) would call a motivator, but lack of participation may be felt as lack of consideration and therefore a hygiene factor.

With this somewhat lengthy introduction, let me discuss these three concepts in greater detail.

CONSIDERATION

One of the presumed lessons of the early human relations movement was that supervisors should be considerate, treat their subordinates as human beings, look out for subordinates' welfare, be fair, show interest in subordinates as individuals, and so on. Today we are less convinced than we were twenty-five years ago that this is all that is required to make a successful supervisor, but clearly consideration is an important element in determining quality of work life. Regardless of what else it might do, consideration reduces the sense of oppression that workers feel when they are confronted by the pressures, rigidities, and sterilities of their jobs. By providing fair treatment, consideration helps meet management's end of the psychological contract (see Chapter 2), and in return for this workers are more likely to do their "fair day's work." A valuable by-product of consideration is that it tends to strengthen employees' beliefs that work effort will lead to satisfying rewards.

"Treating people as human beings," "being fair," "showing interest in them as individuals"—all these sound like parental virtues. They are not that simple, however. Being a nice guy or gal is not enough. Supervisors must adjust to the special needs and expectations of their group, as well as to those of each individual in it. Whether supervisory behavior in a given situation is viewed as considerate and whether it actually contributes to productivity and satisfaction depends, therefore, on at least three factors: (1) the subordinates' *expectations,* (2) the boss's actual *behavior*, and (3) the subordinates' *perception* of this behavior. Or, to put this in sociological terms, consideration is related to legitimacy—the considerate leader is one who behaves in a way that his subordinates feel is appropriate for a supervisor.

Four of the most critical elements of consideration are: (1) creating a feeling of approval, (2) developing personal relations, (3) providing fair treatment, and (4) enforcing rules equitably.

Creating a Feeling of Approval

The personal, one-to-one relationships between supervisors and their subordinates have a lot to do with the way subordinates view their jobs. Because employees are dependent on their boss, it is important for them to feel that he approves of their work and of them as individuals, and that he is concerned with their personal development (Likert, 1961).

Supervisors can communicate their feelings of approval of subordinates in many ways—by taking an active interest in their home lives, listening to their problems, giving praise when justified, showing tolerance when mistakes are made, and so forth. However, the subordinate's psychological perception, the *feeling* of approval, is what is significant.[4] The overall supervisory pattern may be more important, therefore, than any one specific act. In fact, the existence of such a general feeling helps determine how individual acts are interpreted. If a feeling of approval exists, employees may tend to excuse their boss's mistakes; if it does not, they may exaggerate his mistakes out of proportion. Feelings of approval also provide the atmosphere of trust that Lawler (Chapter 4) argues is essential if pay systems based on evaluation are to be successful. In the absence of a feeling of approval, supervisors' attempts to show interest in their employees may be seen as meddling. Patchen (1962, p. 290) wrote:

> When the supervisor is interested in the welfare of his subordinates and is accepted by them as a member of their "team," then his close attention to what his subordinates are doing is welcomed by them. When the supervisor is around and showing interest in what they are doing, subordinates may be eager to please him and win his approval. On the other hand, when the supervisor is held by subordinates as indifferent to their welfare, or even as a hostile outsider, then his close supervision will probably meet with apathy and resentment.

In short, the existence of a feeling of approval permits the establishment of an "exchange relationship" (Blau, 1964) or psychological contract. The existence of such a feeling may be interpreted as meaning that the supervisor has demonstrated a personal loyalty to his subordinates. Until he has done so, he cannot expect loyalty to flow the other way.

---

4. The subordinate's feeling that he is approved may depend as much (or more) on his own ego strength or sense of self-esteem as it does on anything the supervisor might do.

Note, though, that approval means different things to different people. I once interviewed two lacquer-mixers who worked pretty much by themselves at opposite ends of a long factory floor. They did the same job and were under the same foreman (who said both did a good job). The first mixer said, "I've got a good boss. He knows I know the job, so he leaves me alone. He never bothers me." The second mixer said, "My foreman doesn't care whether I am dead or alive. He's a bum foreman who doesn't show any interest in his men or how they are doing." What one mixer perceived as a vote of confidence, the other perceived as neglect. Support is highly idiosyncratic, in other words, and is hard to capture in a few hard-and-fast rules.

Developing Personal Relations

A feeling of approval is more likely to result if the boss shows personal interest in his subordinates. After all, an organization is impersonal and only individual members of management, particularly the immediate boss, can make it personal.

The key importance of good interpersonal relations has been a major theme of human relations literature through the years (Argyris, 1973b). However, most of the earlier discussions stressed nonjob-related matters. The general assumption was that good informal relations on matters not directly related to the job set the stage for better communications between manager and subordinate on problems related to work. After all, it was argued, employees rarely feel completely free and easy when talking to their boss about their work, for they are quite aware that the boss is the one who hands out rewards and punishments. But when they talk about the employee's fishing trip, the employee is the expert for the moment, even if there is no true equality between them. Some of the air of permissiveness and informality created by discussing baseball or the weather might carry over to on-the-job affairs. Once the manager and the subordinate know each other as individuals, both will feel freer to bring up mutual problems. Further, by acting as a careful listener the supervisor may be able to defuse family and other off-the-job problems that might be bothering the employee and disrupting the work.

So went the conventional wisdom of early human relations literature. However, there is another body of literature that warns against reducing the social distance between supervisors and workers too much. In most situations a boss is expected to "be friendly" (and this is particularly true where the American tradition of equality prevails), but the meaning of friendliness varies greatly from one situation to another. Usually there are well-defined expectations about how close the relationship should be. Military officers should be aloof from their men, for example, while deans should invite all new faculty to dinner (but not visit their classes), plant managers are expected to make "howdy rounds" in the plant and to be good fellows at the company picnic (but perhaps only there), and supervisors should show interest in their subordinates' vacation stories and in some plants (but not others) go out drinking with their men on payday.

A wide variety of factors affect the *expected* closeness of supervisor-subordinate relationships. For example, life insurance agents feel under great pressure from their job and their boss. As a consequence (according to Wispe and Lloyd, 1955; see also Blau and Scott, 1962), agents feel that if the boss gets too close, he will discover their inadequacies. At sea, there is a traditional social gap between officers and men—although this is rapidly breaking down under the impact of automation, and on smaller ships this traditional formality tends to dissolve. Further, there is more of it in the navy than in the merchant marine, and on European ships (where officers and men come from different social classes) than on American ships (Richardson, 1956).

The question of expected social relationships is closely tied in with technology. In situations where instant obedience is expected (as in the navy), social distance (and frequent rotation of subordinates) reinforces legitimacy and shields the supervisors from subordinates' questions about their abilities and uncertainties (Thompson, 1961). Cultural differences are also especially relevant. Behavior acceptable in small towns is considered "hick" in the big cities. Appropriate social distance varies even more between countries (Rapoport, 1964). To mention only one of the many available examples—Australians insist on greater affability than do the stiffly correct, status-conscious British, while Americans may fall in between.

Finally, the youth rebellion of the last decade and a half has changed expectations about social distance considerably. Respect for authority has declined, and supervisors are expected to be less aloof than they once were. This process will be accelerated by job redesign and by other changes that give workers greater freedom or require that supervisors and subordinates interact with each other more frequently. Social distance facilitates obedience, but it inhibits communication— and the pendulum has swung toward closer boss-subordinate relations.

The best publicized job restructuring experiments have been accompanied by symbolic reductions in status differentials. These changes have begun to reduce what UAW Vice-President Bluestone (1974) calls "the double standard that exists between workers and management. . . . Workers challenge the symbols of elitism traditionally taken for granted, such as salary payment versus hourly payment; time clocks for blue-collar workers; well-decorated dining rooms for white-collar workers versus plain, Spartan-like cafeterias for blue-collar workers; providing parking for the elite, but catch-as-you-can parking for workers" (p. 47).

At General Foods' Topeka dog food plant, for instance, there are no reserved parking lots, no time clocks, and no differentiation in decor between management offices and worker lounges. Most important, perhaps, workers in at least one department are free to make phone calls on company time (Schrank, 1974). Such reductions in status differentials not only tend to reduce dissatisfaction, they also help create an atmosphere of trust and confidence between workers and management, and, to some extent, they lead to a covert renegotiation of the psychological contract. Indeed, some might argue that these hygiene factors have a more significant impact on job attitudes than any changes in the design of the jobs.

Providing Fair Treatment

Because subordinates are directly dependent on their bosses, they are understandably anxious to receive fair treatment in the distribution of rewards and punishments. "The highest praise a worker can give his foreman is to say 'he's fair' " (Dubin, 1965, p. 65). Again, however, what is considered fair may vary widely from one local culture to another.

In general, "being fair" involves the following elements: (1) letting subordinates know clearly and in advance exactly what is required of them, thus reducing frustration caused by uncertainty; (2) making decisions on clearly explained grounds that can be defended as legitimate; and (3) dispersing rewards in a manner that seems to make them proportional to contributions and that meets the requirements of "distributive justice" (Homans, 1961). In terms of expectancy theory, fairness of this sort increases the subordinate's perceptions that effort on his part will lead to his receiving valued rewards.

"Being fair" from the employees' standpoint may also mean that their bosses respect local work customs—that is, secretaries have twenty-minute coffee breaks; no one gets a rush job Christmas Eve; deans should not drop into the classes of senior faculty; an employee may take home small items without being considered a thief (Gouldner, 1954). Many of these work customs have status or symbolic meaning. It should be kept in mind, therefore, that even innocent decisions about parking lots or the arrangements of tables may upset delicate social relations, lead to turmoil and antagonism, and be viewed as viciously unfair.

Employees also feel it unfair for a superior to ask them to perform duties other than those customarily associated with their jobs (especially when this threatens their status), unless there is some clearly justified, special reason. Further, in most socially cohesive work groups there are well understood expectations ("bogies") governing the amount of work each employee may be legitimately required to do ("a fair day's work"). Finally, employees accept those rules that seem to have a legitimate relationship to the purpose for which they were hired (or that protect individual safety, such as rules against smoking in explosive plants)—and resist and view as unfair those rules that seem to be imposed for no justifiable reason. Particularly, they resent being made to "look busy" after their "fair day's work" is done.

Rules are also more likely to be accepted if the workers who are affected have some chance to participate in development of the rules. The following story illustrates this point and also suggests an approach to labor-management relations.

The superintendent of machine operations was convinced by his Safety Department that long-sleeved shirts were a hazard even when rolled up. So he posted a notice that beginning next Monday morning wearing long sleeves on the job would be prohibited.

Monday morning four men showed up with long sleeves. Given the choice of working without shirts or cutting their sleeves off, they refused to do either and were sent home. The union filed a sharp grievance, asking for back pay for time lost.

Then the Personnel Department stepped in. The rule was suspended for a week and a special meeting was called with the union grievance committee. The safety director explained that if a worker got his sleeve caught in the machine his whole arm might be ripped off. The union agreed to the rule provided that it was extended to management (who originally had been exempt on the grounds they didn't get close enough to the machines).

Next Monday the rule was reinstated. A few men, forgetfully, arrived in long sleeves. The other men handed them a pair of scissors and insisted that the offending sleeves be eliminated on the spot. Later in the afternoon a union vice-president and a company time-study man were treated in the same way. The rule was in full effect!

Enforcing Rules Equitably

The early human relations literature stressed the importance of the supervisor avoiding unfair, punitive discipline (Katz, Macoby, and Morse, 1950; Argyle, Gardner, and Coffi, 1958), a natural reaction to the activities of Neanderthal foremen in the dark days before the advent of unions. In unionized plants an elaborate code of "industrial jurisprudence" has evolved that provides "due process" in cases of discipline. Important elements of this code have been extended to nonunion organizations. Thus, "fairness" is often viewed as requiring at the minimum that (1) punishment should be inflicted only for violations of known rules and that the degree of punishment should not exceed expectations, (2) first offenses, unless serious, should receive only a warning, and (3) opportunities should be provided for appeals. The union grievance procedure provides an elaborate review mechanism that reduces the possibility that discipline will be applied arbitrarily or inconsistently. Many nonunion plants provide similar appeal channels (Scott, 1965).

Personnel texts stress that considerate supervisors avoid nagging or repeated criticism for trivial inadequacies, that they wait to hear the employee's side of the story before criticizing or imposing discipline, and that "the criticism should be focused on the job operation and should, as much as possible, avoid laying of personal blame" (Whyte, 1956, p. 12). Learning theory is in basic agreement with these points, in that it suggests that praise is a more effective motivator than punishment. For example, performance evaluation is less likely to lead to improved performance if it is accompanied by criticism.

Employees often expect the boss to show *leniency* and ignore minor or technical violations of rules as long as the job is getting done (Gouldner, 1954). They also expect that when unexpected conditions occur (when employees are having family problems, for example), the supervisor will relax his performance standards and even, if possible, give them some time off. This expectation is an element in the psychological contract, in that in exchange for this "good turn" the employee may feel some obligation to work extra hard in genuine emergencies.

Early Human Relations was criticized for being "soft" and "namby pamby," in part because of its stress on such factors as *nonpunitive behavior* and *leniency*. True, a major objective of the pioneers in this field was to defang the arbitrary foreman. Thus, some of the literature seemed to suggest that the supervisor should abandon all efforts to evaluate employee performance or to punish even persistent failures to meet performance standards. In recent years, however, social scientists have taken a much tougher position. It is now argued that supervisors should indeed evaluate performance, but they should do so fairly and, if possible, with subordinate participation. Further, rewards should be distributed on the basis of performance alone, and firmly withheld when there is nonperformance; and formal discipline should be used sparingly but most certainly should be used when necessary. "Unconditional 'consideration' on the part of the supervisor," concludes Vroom (1964, p. 217), "may be less effective in motivating subordinates than 'consideration' which is dependent on the effectiveness of the subordinate." And the discerning reader will note the approach to rewards in Chapter 4 is far from namby pamby.

While rules and procedures for discipline have become reasonably well codified, especially in industrial plants, there have been some experiments with new approaches to rule enforcement that are worth mentioning here.

1. Traditional, "progressive" discipline provides for increasingly severe penalties each time an employee is disciplined, with the sequence typically running as follows: (a) oral warning, (b) written warning, (c) layoff, and (d) discharge. Some companies have experimented with eliminating the layoff step altogether, on the grounds that a stern warning will accomplish just as much—and can be less humiliating or resentment-arousing for the worker involved (Huberman, 1964). Most companies still feel, however, that the layoff step is essential to convince workers that management intends to take rule violations seriously.

2. Traditionally, when a worker is discharged he is expected to leave the plant immediately, even if he has an appeal in process. Several unions have proposed that, except for the most serious and obvious rule violations, the individual be allowed to continue to work until his case is finally resolved. This is the practice in a number of government agencies as well as in portions of Swedish industry. It is also the position of the American Association of University Professors with regard to discipline of faculty members.

3. In some situations workers have won the right to discipline their fellow workers. This is the case at the Topeka dog food plant of General Foods. Workers' self-discipline also occurs under union auspices in some parts of the clothing industry. Even the militant National Union of Mineworkers in England has participated on occasion in peer disciplinary programs. One such occasion occurred in a mine that was threatened with closedown because of poor productivity, part of which was caused by high miner absenteeism. The union interviewed over three hundred of its members and recommended that forty be dismissed for bad attendance. This and other measures contributed to a doubling of productivity and saved the mine (Horner, 1974, p. 64).

Peer discipline, of course, is a well-established *principle* (even if an indifferently achieved practice) in many professions. The standard union position, however, is that discipline is management's function and that the union's role, if any, is to protect the worker involved.

4. The growing recognition that alcoholism is a disease has led many companies to reevaluate their use of discipline to handle cases of drunkenness. Referrals to counseling or to such organizations as Alcoholics Anonymous have been employed increasingly as substitutes for traditional discipline.

Although each of these innovative approaches to rule enforcement suffers from serious disadvantages that may limit its applicability, as a group they represent attempts to provide workers with greater dignity on the job—and thus to enhance the quality of work life.

The discussion above has dealt with four factors in supervisory consideration. There is at least one other relevant factor—the willingness of the boss to go to bat for his men with higher management. I will discuss this factor in another context below.

Impact of Consideration on Satisfaction and Productivity

What is the impact of consideration on the quality of work life? Common sense suggests that workers who are treated considerately are likely to feel more satisfied. But what forms of consideration have any impact on productivity? Research in these areas has proven difficult, but let me suggest some possible relationships.[5]

Impact on Satisfaction. Despite the lack of firm evidence, common sense suggests that consideration does lead to higher satisfaction. "Except for a few masochists, it is probably safe to assume that subordinates will desire a high level of considerate behavior by their leaders" (Yukl, 1971, p. 420). However, there are some important differences among workers in what consideration means and the kinds of needs it satisfies.

1. For the dependent worker or the worker brought up in an authoritarian culture, the considerate supervisor may provide a father image or a role model and may be viewed as someone whom the subordinate may lean on in time of trouble.

2. Where the work load is uneven or the supervisors have some discretion in handing out rewards, their reputations for fairness may be especially important.

3. For workers with high social needs who are assigned to routine jobs, the activities of the supervisor may facilitate or hinder the development of a friendly cohesive work group. For example, supervisors can cooperate with or disrupt such activities as pay-check-number pools, birthday parties, after-work parties, and the like. Good social relations are especially important, also, when the job is anxiety-arousing or intensive teamwork is required.[6]

---

5. The following section is fairly technical—and some readers may prefer to skip over it. Nevertheless, it is useful to be fairly precise in sketching the mechanisms involved.
6. "Where tasks are interdependent, varied, and ambiguous, consideration will result in social support, friendliness among group members, increased cohesiveness, and team effort. The social outcomes will be positively valent to the members and thus increase the net sum of the positive valences associated with interdependent jobs requiring cooperation and team spirit" (House, 1971, p. 325).

4. Where the job is either substantially more or substantially less challenging than employees want, supervisors can at least make themselves available to listen to gripes. Where the job is less challenging, they can also seek to divert workers' attention to social activities (see above); where it is too challenging, they can provide encouragement and support.

5. Where the job requires that supervisors interact frequently with their subordinates, it is important that the supervisors be supportive and not socially distant, so as to counteract the oppressive features of the constant interaction.[7] Consideration, in other words, makes the exercise of power more palatable.

Consideration and Productivity.   Even common sense makes the relationship between consideration and productivity somewhat uncertain. In general, consideration involves the *context* in which work occurs. Therefore, according to Herzberg, consideration should not operate as a motivator or be related to productivity.[8] On the other hand, although there may be no *simple* relationship between consideration and productivity, some relationships probably do exist. As illustrated below, these have been formulated or explained in a number of different ways (some of which merely represent alternative ways of saying the same thing, and some of which involve expectancy theory—see Vroom, 1964; Porter and Lawler, 1968).

1. Happy workers work harder. Implicit in the philosophy of paternalism rampant during the 1920s (Strauss and Sayles, 1972) was the assumption that there was a direct relationship between morale and productivity. Decently treated workers would be happier and *therefore* would work harder, possibly out of sheer gratitude. Although such a simplistic view of the relationship is no longer in vogue, it is still the unspoken basis of some management rhetoric.

2. Consideration reduces frustrations and therefore reduces barriers to production. This hypothesis comes in two versions.

First, according to human relations theory of the 1950s (such as Maier, 1955), too little consideration (autocratic, unfeeling, high-handed supervision) leads to frustration, and this in turn leads to either aggression or withdrawal, both of which reduce productivity. Although the frustration-aggression hypothesis is also out of style, there is some evidence that when workers are denied consideration, turnover and absenteeism go up (Fleishman and Harris, 1962) and resistance to

---

7. Note the Fleishman and Harris (1962) finding that closer supervision (in their terms, "higher initiating structure") increases turnover and grievances when consideration is low, but not when it is high.

8. Support for the Herzberg hypothesis comes from Korman's (1966) review of studies that used the Ohio State Consideration scale but found no consistent relationship between this measure and productivity.

change increases (Schacter, Willerman, Festinger, and Human, 1961). This may be particularly true when the boss supervises closely.

Second, a more contemporary statement of the frustration-productivity relationship has been provided by House, who stresses the frustration introduced by the *task* (rather than by lack of consideration). For unsatisfying tasks, consideration may serve as a "stress reducer," counteracting the oppressive nature of the job. "Where the path [to higher productivity] is not viewed as satisfying, that is, for lower level jobs, it can be hypothesized that consideration serves as a source of extrinsic social satisfaction and support to the employee, thus making the path easier to travel" (House, 1971, p. 326). Among other things, for example, consideration reduces intergroup tension (Oaklander and Fleishman, 1964).

3. Consideration is a reward for productivity. This reward may involve just a simple exchange, or it may serve as one of the issues in an "implicit bargain" or psychological contract.

Yukl, for example, suggests a very simple exchange relationship between consideration and productivity: "A leader can improve subordinate performance by being highly considerate to subordinates who perform well, while withholding consideration from subordinates who show little task motivation" (1971, p. 423). There is a danger here, however, in that such a differential reward system may be viewed as blatant favoritism unless supervisors make clear the grounds for their decisions.

Alternatively, group standards can be taken into account if we look upon consideration as one of the elements in an implicit bargain. If a supervisor behaves in a manner that subordinates feel is fair, if he overlooks minor violations of rules, if he looks out for his subordinates, and so forth, then in return for this, the subordinates implicitly agree to turn out a "fair day's work" (Gouldner, 1954; Turner, 1957; Whyte, 1948). If we adopt this view, consideration may be seen to contribute to workers doing this fair day's work, but increased consideration will not result in increased productivity above this "fair" amount unless a new bargain is struck.

4. Consideration may reduce productivity because workers are no longer as afraid of being punished. This hypothesis, at first glance, is merely another version of the pre-human relations philosophy that supervisors have got to be tough if they are to get the work out. In sharp contrast to the hypotheses described above, it suggests that highly considerate, easygoing, nonpunitive supervisors may actually inhibit production because subordinates may conclude that such a supervisor is too nice a person, too much of a good friend, to punish them for goofing off (Yukl, 1971). Yukl suggests that such behavior is particularly likely on jobs that lack intrinsic satisfaction, especially

where the boss provides little direction. Under these circumstances, where positive rewards for higher productivity (either intrinsic or extrinsic) will be lacking, negative sanctions may play an especially important role. Supervisors who renounce their disciplinary role under these conditions may reduce productivity.

5. Consideration may change subordinate values. More specifically, the supervisor may be able to induce individuals or groups to place higher values on performance as a goal.

Consideration may make the subordinate "more favorable" toward the supervisor (Yukl, 1971), thus increasing the supervisor's influence and "referent power" (French and Raven, 1959). If the supervisor then communicates a concern for productivity, this will be translated into motivation. In simpler language, if you like your boss, you are more anxious to do things that will win his approval, such as working harder.

Somewhat the same relationship applies to group participation. Unless the supervisor wins respect from the group and is able to persuade it to accept organizational goals, participation may lead the group to resort to output restriction rather than increased productivity. Practicing consideration is one way for the supervisor to win respect—which in turn may contribute to the group's acceptance of organizational objectives.

6. Consideration may strengthen the effort-performance relationship. This means that consideration may make it easier for workers to get the job done. For example, considerate bosses are more approachable, and so subordinates will be more likely to ask them questions about how to do the job (Indik, Georgopoulos, and Seashore, 1961). A considerate boss will create a friendly atmosphere where teamwork will be easier to develop.

7. Consideration may make the performance-reward relationship seem more equitable. A boss who is seen as fair will also be seen as handing out rewards in terms of contribution (that is, in terms of Homan's [1961] "distributive justice"). This will strengthen the employee's belief that increased effort will be rewarded.

A Final Word on Consideration

The above discussion should make it clear that it is difficult to make sweeping statements about either the nature or the impact of consideration. What is viewed as appropriate or considerate depends upon a variety of circumstances—cultural, technical, and organizational—and a contingency approach is required. For example, among the difficulties faced by Americans operating overseas is that what is viewed as consideration in the U.S. context may not be viewed as consideration by people in other countries.

It is clear that supervisory consideration does contribute to making a satisfactory work environment and therefore to worker satisfaction. But this is more important for some workers and in some situations than it is for others. Further, despite the absence of a demonstrated direct relationship between consideration and productivity, consideration may reduce worker frustration and make other motivational approaches more effective. Even where the presence of consideration does little to increase productivity, its absence is likely to reduce productivity.

Having looked at supervisors' contributions to work environment, let us now consider various steps they might take to increase employee effectiveness directly.

FACILITATION

Most of what has been written about supervisory behavior has stressed the supervisor's role in establishing the work environment and in providing rewards. Here I would like to highlight another role, that of increasing the efficiency by which employee energy (effort) is converted into performance. It is commonly said that "the supervisor has two jobs: he must be concerned with his subordinates and he must get the work out." Accurate as the first part of this statement may be, the second is too simple. Supervisors do not get the work out by themselves. Instead, they structure the work situation so that *others* can do the job more effectively. Earlier I called this function *facilitation*—the ability to organize work and direct subordinates. Facilitation may seem a rather humdrum virtue, compared with concern for people or ability to foster participation or enthusiasm for organizational goals. Nevertheless, supervisors who waste their employees' efforts are likely to suffer not only from a poor productivity record, but also from working with a group of frustrated, dissatisfied employees whose quality of work life is low.

The facilitation function may be approached in a number of ways. Here I propose to stress its impact on the quality of work life, through the use of the expectancy theory of work motivation (Vroom, 1964). In terms of this theory, I will discuss a variety of activities that are designed to increase employees' expectancies that their efforts on the job will pay off in terms of satisfaction of needs that are important to them.

Given the breadth of the topic (and the fact that it overlaps several others that are discussed elsewhere), let me begin with a check list of potentially facilitating activities. Having indicated the broad gamut of possibilities, I will then discuss four of these—indicated in the following list by an asterisk—at greater length. Most of the other possibilities are more conveniently discussed elsewhere.

Strengthening the Expectancy Relationship: A Check List

How can supervisors strengthen the expectancy relationship so that employees perceive that increased efforts are rewarded in a manner that provides valued satisfactions? Among the things they can do are the following.

1. Supervisors can increase the likelihood that increased effort will lead to higher performance in the following ways:
— by providing clear goals, that is, by indicating the nature of the performance desired;*
— by providing guidance, for example, by teaching their subordinates *how* to work for desired goals;*
— by providing the tools and supplies required to do the job;*
— by encouraging the development of cohesive work teams (see Chapter 5);
— by obtaining efficiency-improving suggestions from subordinates through the process of participation (see discussion below).

2. Supervisors can increase the perceived likelihood that greater performance will lead to rewards through the following actions:
— by working with higher management to recast the reward and promotion (career) systems so that rewards and promotions more closely reflect performance (see Chapters 2 and 4);
— by providing rewards of their own (that is, praise) for higher productivity;
— by redesigning jobs so that completing a unit of work becomes a reward in itself (see Chapter 3);
— by encouraging participation in work decisions (see discussion below).

3. Supervisors can increase the feeling that the relationship between performance and rewards is equitable, by monitoring the rewards to insure the following:
— rewards are commensurate with performance;
— rewards are distributed fairly;
— employees have adequate opportunities to participate in deciding how rewards will be distributed;
— employees have their grievances heard when apparent inequities occur.

4. Supervisors can increase the value of rewards in terms of satisfaction.*

5. Supervisors can develop (or influence higher management to develop) adequate methods of feedback so that employees can more accurately perceive the effort-reward relationship. As Chapter 4 argues, one way of doing this is to eliminate salary secrecy.

The purpose of the above list has been to sketch the range of supervisor activities that strengthen the expectancy relationship. Below I will enlarge on the four activities marked with asterisks.

Establishing Performance Standards

Employees' efforts are often misused unless they have a clear understanding of the goals toward which these efforts should be directed. The establishment of goals or performance standards seems to be a necessary (but not sufficient) condition for productivity. Concrete goals direct effort, reduce uncertainty, and serve as an instrument of communication. Under most circumstances, clear standards also contribute to higher satisfaction; ambiguity and uncertainty lead to wasted effort and frustration.

Performance standards may be set in a variety of ways. They may be qualitative (in terms of *what sorts* of things to do) or quantitative (in terms of *how much* to do); they may be set arbitrarily by the boss, through group discussion, or as a result of either explicit or implicit bargaining; new standards may be set every few minutes or on a long-term basis.[9] Regardless of how standards are set, however, it is important that subordinates know what they are expected to accomplish.

Some jobs are so routine, of course, that no one has any problem knowing what he is expected to do. Under such circumstances, supervisors who emphasize the obvious sound as if they are nagging. Nevertheless, there are times when assignments are clear to the boss who makes them but totally unclear to the subordinates who receive them. All this may of course seem so self-evident as not to be worth mentioning, and yet, hard nosed as managers are supposed to be, many find it difficult to operationalize their goals, or to be really specific about what they want their subordinates or the work group as a whole to accomplish. Quite frequently employees say, "I'm not really sure what the boss wants me to do," or "when I was hired nobody told me what my exact responsibilities were."

Too often supervisors, imbued with the human relations point of

9. A variety of factors may determine the optimum time span of goal setting, and this time span may relate to what Jaques (1961) called the time span of discretion.

view, avoid the seeming unpleasantness of being explicit about their expectations (although they may later crack down without warning on the unsuspecting subordinate when these unspoken expectations are not met). These supervisors recognize that setting and insisting on high standards sometimes leads to hostility.[10] As Douglas McGregor argued (1944), such hostility is almost inevitable because of the supervisor's role as a father figure, and so the competent supervisor must learn to accept and deal with that hostility. An executive put the same thought in somewhat cruder (and perhaps exaggerated language): "Every organization has to have a bastard to get things done, and I'm the one picked to do it."

Standards, of course, do not have to be set unilaterally by the boss. Many of the experiments aimed at improving the quality of work life (such as Monsanto and PPG, as reported by Jenkins, 1973) have involved group-set production goals, usually within broad limits set by higher management. Among the organizations that have utilized this approach to goal setting is the R. G. Barry Company. "We got the operators involved in setting goals," its production manager reported, "because we wanted to have individual and company goals the same" (Jenkins, 1973, p. 192). Indeed, a number of instances have been reported in which production levels under group-set standards were considerably higher than the standards set by management. Participation of this sort may not be universally appropriate, however, and later on I will suggest some of the conditions under which it may not work.

Management by Objectives (MBO) is an example of participatory goal setting on a managerial level. MBO involves (1) the setting of concrete goals for each manager (2) on a participatory basis, usually through discussion between the manager and his boss. Among the advantages of MBO (when it works as it should) are that it requires that management define exactly what it wants to accomplish and specify all important objectives, especially those commonly ignored (such as employee development). Further, MBO forces the development of a plan that tells each manager exactly what he is expected to accomplish during the next evaluation period. MBO includes a strong element of participation, yet the evidence suggests that it is the setting of concrete goals, not the participation, that makes the critical difference in productivity and morale (Carroll and Tosi, 1970; French, Kay, and Meyer, 1966). There is no essential reason why MBO might not be applied at the worker level, at least on a modified basis. (For a discussion of some of the problems and limitations of MBO, see Strauss, 1972).

Standards can be set by the boss, on an autonomous basis by the

---

10. Oldham (1974, p. 93) reports on a firm in which there was a negative correlation between satisfaction with supervisor and goal emphasis.

work group, or jointly by boss and subordinates (as in MBO). The important thing is that they *be* set, and that people know what they are expected to do.

Three final points about setting standards and their use should be noted:

1. *High* standards contribute to both productivity and satisfaction.[11] Reaching a tough goal—as long as it is fair and reasonable—provides more of a sense of achievement than does reaching an easy goal. History, our everyday observations, and research (Likert, 1967) all tell us that the inspiring, respected leader is the one who urges his men to the very limits of their capabilities. This was Vince Lombardi's secret.

2. Short-run standards are generally more motivating than long-run standards (provided the period is not *too* short). Finishing a chapter in an hour is usually a more compelling goal than reading a long book over a weekend. When work is broken down into units or batches, employees achieve a feeling of completion every time they finish a batch. The desire to finish a unit has strong pulling power and also enhances the worker's efficiency (Baldamus, 1961).

3. Standards are generally more motivating if frequent feedback is provided. All of us like to know how we are doing; lack of such knowledge can be very frustrating. Indeed, feedback can be motivating, as Hackman (Chapter 3) argues, and as the following story illustrates. In a plant that manufactures a large number of small items at high speed, management installed counters on each of the production lines, just for supervisory purposes. Soon the employees were spending so much time sneaking a look that additional counters were installed at each workplace. Informal competition developed both between lines and between shifts at each workplace. Then the foreman brought in a blackboard and the men began posting their records, thus increasing the spirit of competition.

Guiding Employee Efforts

The employee wants to know not only *what* to accomplish but also *how* to accomplish it.[12] If the employee does not have appropriate training or instruction, his efforts are wasted and both productivity and satisfaction suffer. Supervisors can provide guidance to their subordinates in a variety of ways:

---

11. The importance of high standards is emphasized by Bowers and Seashore (1966), who call them "goal emphasis," and also by Likert (1967). Concern with productivity is one of Blake's two dimensions (Blake and Mouton, 1964). Several items in Ohio State's Initiation Structure scale refer to high performance standards (for example, "he emphasizes the quality of work," "he sees to it that people under him are working up to their limits").

12. The factors we are discussing now are closely related to Ohio State's Initiating Structure. These factors, plus those listed under "providing technical support" together constitute what Bowers and Seashore (1966) call "work facilitation."

— by supervising them closely on a minute-by-minute basis, telling them exactly what to do;
— by providing detailed advance instructions (rules) covering most contingencies;
— by making themselves available to answer questions, but otherwise letting subordinates work things out by themselves;
— by providing broad forms of training that impart appropriate skills.

Typically, supervisors will use a combination of these techniques. However, the particular mixture used in any given situation has considerable implications for the quality of work life. The supervisor who supervises on a minute-by-minute basis, for example, is normally felt to be supervising more closely than the one who emphasizes training or is merely available to provide help when needed.

How close should guidance be? The answer depends on the nature of the job, on the subordinates' previous training and skills, and to some extent on subordinates' personalities and orientations toward work. Insufficient guidance can be frustrating and can lead to wasted work efforts, reducing both satisfaction and productivity. However, forcing people to solve problems by themselves often provides a useful learning experience. Guidance that is too close can be felt as being restrictive—and as indicating lack of consideration—and sometimes leads to reduced productivity and to heightened resistance to change.

On routine work it is relatively easy to supervise too closely (Lowin, Hrapchak, and Kavanagh, 1969). It is chiefly on routine work that evidence has been collected associating close supervision with low productivity and dissatisfaction. On nonroutine work, however, rather close supervision may be viewed as helpful. As House (1971, p. 235) puts it: "The more ambiguous the task, the more positive the relationship between leader initiating structure and subordinate satisfaction and performance. Structure serves to reduce role ambiguity and to clarify path-goal relationships for ambiguous tasks but is viewed as unnecessary and redundant for nonambiguous tasks."

Oversupervision can be particularly frustrating for employees who have high growth needs and who are "expressively oriented" toward their jobs. Such workers want a fair amount of freedom to develop their own approaches to work problems, and perceived close control may be particularly threatening to their egos. On the other hand, "instrumentally oriented" workers and those with low growth needs may be somewhat more tolerant of bosses who supervise closely, provided they adhere to the civilities of consideration. In fact, for some highly dependent employees, close supervision may provide security and a sign that their boss is interested in them as individuals.

Some forms of work require close coordination. Such coordination may be provided either by the work group members (as in a string quartet), or by the boss (as in a symphony orchestra) acting as a close supervisor. Failure to achieve such coordination lowers both satisfaction and quality of product.

Many of the quality of work life experiments have involved the development of autonomous work groups or self-managing work teams that provide most of their own guidance (see Chapter 3). At the Topeka dog food plant, each work group is responsible for assigning duties to its members and for training newcomers.

In order for supervisors to provide effective guidance, they must be viewed as technically competent. As indicated earlier, "having a technically competent supervisor" ranked high among factors correlated with overall job satisfaction. Competence is especially important, of course, where the work is technical or the nature of the job is rapidly changing. Technical skill is even more critical where close coordination is required between members of the work team—in flying a plane, conducting an orchestra, or operating on a patient. In such situations, "unpleasant personal characteristics are often overlooked if competence is high enough. The irascible surgeon who is, nevertheless, highly respected for his skill is almost a legend. Colleagues and nurses judge doctors according to the mastery they exhibit" (Burling, Lentz, and Wilson, 1956, p. 266).

Technically competent supervisors are able to provide more effective guidance to their subordinates. In addition, their competence increases their subordinates' respect for them and provides them legitimacy as supervisors. Indeed, subordinates often subject new supervisors to a period of testing and initiation to determine whether they measure up to standards. This feeling that the boss should show technical skills is particularly strong among employees who take pride in their work and closely identify with their occupation (building tradesmen or pilots, for example).

Providing Technical Support

Even the most motivated workers find it hard to get their work done without adequate tools or supplies, or when they have insufficient information to do the job. Therefore, it is critical that a supervisor provide his subordinates with the information and materials they need to accomplish their jobs. The importance of this function is underscored by the previously mentioned Michigan survey. In that study, "I receive enough help and equipment to get the job done" was ranked "very important" by more employees (69 percent) than any other item on a long list.

Technical support often depends heavily on the supervisor's ability to build good working relations with his superiors, with staff groups, and with other departments. Organizing effective liaison relations of this sort requires time. It also requires substantial top management support. A supervisor's ability to develop effective relations *outside* his department may be as critical for employee satisfaction and productivity as anything he does *within* the department.

There have been numerous quality of work life experiments in which work groups have undertaken to provide their own support. In some groups one individual has been made responsible for dealing with the supply department, another for relations with maintenance, and so on. Increasingly groups are handling functions formerly within the province of staff departments. For example, members do simple maintenance themselves, or they keep track of their supplies.

Increasing Satisfaction Gained from Productivity

For most workers completing the job well provides *some* sense of satisfaction. However, the value of this reward (as some say, its "valence") may be increased if the job is seen as significant. Work that seems purposeless is bound to lead to frustration. One of the most unpleasant forms of punishment used by the military, for example, is to have men dig holes and fill them in again. Two British researchers (Wyatt and Langdon, 1933), in a study of a candy factory, found that the greatest dissatisfaction centered in a small work group whose job consisted of unwrapping defective chocolates as part of a salvage operation. On the other hand, telephone supervisors report that production and morale are always higher during an emergency. As one said, "It's amazing. An operator may be a low producer and a disciplinary problem, often tardy and absent, but come a blizzard when highways are closed, she will walk long distances to come to work."

Thus, anything the supervisor can do to increase the satisfaction gained from completing the job will also strengthen the expectancy relationship. One way to enhance a worker's sense of achievement is to stress the social value of the product being made—for example, in relieving suffering, advancing knowledge, or accomplishing organizational objectives. This approach to motivation is used in China and Cuba, and by almost every country in time of war. It works best when the individual (or group) already strongly identifies with the organizational objectives, as is common in some hospitals or educational institutions. Nevertheless a certain amount of pride and organizational identification is possible in almost any organization, provided subordinates feel they are being treated fairly and provided—especially for expressively oriented individuals with high growth needs—there are some meaningful opportunities to do challenging work.

The discussion above has highlighted the supervisor's old-fashioned function as manager and organizer. This function is vital not only to organizational success but also to the quality of work life. In theoretical terms, facilitation strengthens the expectancy relationship so as to increase the probability that effort will lead to performance and performance will lead to meaningful rewards. In practical terms, facilitation means that the supervisor, by properly structuring the job and providing support, ensures that effort is not wasted but is instead directed toward ends that are meaningful to the organization and to the individual. Misdirected efforts are wasteful, frustrating, and degrading to quality of work life.

Facilitation must be provided somehow. But facilitation need not be provided by the supervisor alone. Many of the supervisor's facilitating functions can be shared with subordinates through participation. However, facilitation without participation is preferable to participation without facilitation. That is, a participating but aimless group is almost always more frustrated than a group which is nonparticipatory but well directed. Facilitation, direction, good organization—whatever you want to call it—is basic. Participation is a nice added plus.

PARTICIPATION

Participation has been widely recommended as a means of improving the quality of work life and of raising productivity. In theory, participation releases creative energies and provides workers with a sense of accomplishment. Thus, it strengthens the expectancy relationship, enhances the work environment, and harnesses the energies of the informal group to work toward management's objectives. Furthermore, it is consistent with the American ideas of equality, democracy, and individual dignity. As such it offers a morally attractive solution to many of the problems of industrial life—a solution that becomes increasingly attractive as society becomes increasingly equalitarian and abandons authoritarian leadership styles.

The two examples below illustrate how participation can increase both the quality of work life and productivity by providing facilitation. The first example was developed under the Scanlon Plan (see Chapter 4); the second was initiated by employees on their own behalf.

> The first case involved a situation in which "the Planning Department had an idea for the rearrangement of the machines and the use of a conveyor to facilitate certain transport problems. ... A blueprint was made and posted on the bulletin board, but the employees stated that they could not read the blueprint and that, therefore, they could make very few, if any, suggestions about the proposed plan. Consequently, a small-scale model or

templet of what the layout would look like under the new plan was placed
at a central location in the department.[13] . . . [After this was done] a great
many comments were made both by the foreman and by the employees.
These comments were gathered together and a [joint union-management]
production committee meeting held, attended by the Industrial Engineer
responsible for the proposal. At this meeting the employees and the foreman joined together in strenuous criticism of the conveyor part of the plan.
After about two and one-half hours' discussion, the committee agreed that
the rearrangement of the machines would be beneficial but wanted the
engineer to reconsider several aspects of the conveyor system.

"About a week later . . . the committee agreed to a modified version of
the conveyor system, with the understanding that it would be installed in
such a manner that they could make changes fairly easily. Subsequently,
the committee did make several important changes, especially in the manning of the new system. The drastic revision in the department layout and
the revised conveyor system are now accepted as an improvement by the
workers and the foreman concerned and the productivity of the department has been increased by about 20 percent" (Shultz, 1951, pp. 206–
207).[14]

A second example of facilitative participation, entered into without
the fuss of calling it an experiment, comes from the author's own
experience at the Institute of Industrial Relations at Berkeley.

The Institute consists of faculty and professional staff, who spend their time
in teaching, research, and various forms of community service—and
hardworking clerical staff who keep the place going. The director and
associate directors have primary responsibilities in teaching departments
and, in effect, have largely abdicated their roles as facilitators. As a consequence work was often poorly coordinated and important meetings were
scheduled at the same time, resulting in substantial work overloads. Although personnel practices were good by most standards, relatively little
attention was given to career development.

A number of the staff met together fairly spontaneously to discuss these
problems. Committees were established to deal with such issues as building maintenance, work scheduling, and supplies. As a result of staff initiative, a program of performance appraisal was introduced and an instructor
invited to teach a course on how this worked. The supply committee
investigated alternative forms of duplicating equipment and introduced
new equipment which substantially saved on staff time at no great increase
in cost. Measures were taken to insure better scheduling of events and to

---

13. Prior to the situation described, management had tried to introduce a different conveyor belt system without consulting with the workers involved. The other system was
installed while many of the workers were gone over Christmas vacation. This quick-
and-dirty approach turned out to be disastrous. Production dropped to as much as 20
percent below the previous average, due to the inflexibility of the new system and negative attitudes toward it, and management eventually eliminated it (Shultz, 1951).

14. G. P. Shultz, "Worker Participation on Production Problems." *Personnel Journal*, 28
(1951), pp. 206–207. Copyright © 1951 by Personnel Journal. Reprinted with permission.

provide for work sharing during peak periods. The maintenance committee pressured the University Building Department to replace a leaking roof and to wash down the interior walls. A semimonthly paper was started, with a rotating editorship.

The facilitative activities (scheduling, planning, dealing with maintenance, and so on) described in these two stories would normally have been initiated by management; in both cases the work groups handled the problems themselves.

Participation typically takes less dramatic forms than the ones indicated above. Just as Moliere's hero had been talking prose all his life, so many managers have been practicing a lot more participation than they realize. On a day-to-day basis, participation may occur in locker rooms, at coffee breaks, and when a few workers and the foreman gather for beer after work. It may occur when two workers discuss how to do a job, or one man gives another some tips on how to deal with quality control. It also occurs through de facto delegation when a foreman neglects to pay attention to an able worker, who then corrects a serious problem on his own. And finally, it may occur when the union steward and foreman discuss grievances or the workers unilaterally set production "bogies." (There is no guarantee that participation will be of benefit to management, either immediately or in the long run.)

Management through its acts (and omissions) can do much to determine the form and shape of participation. The supervisor's "open door" or his practice of sharing coffee with subordinates—as well as the *genuine* receptivity to new ideas which his behavior reflects—may do more to encourage real participation than any regular series of formally scheduled meetings, although these do have a purpose.

But just what is "real" participation? There are some serious definitional problems that we will need to examine in order to clarify the context within which this term is used. Then I will briefly evaluate participation in the now familiar terms of expectancy theory. Finally, I will consider the general conditions that affect the success of participation.

Defining Participation

Participation is an overworked and somewhat imprecise term. It appears in a variety of forms and contexts. In the European context, the term often refers to workers' participation in management, usually through formal mechanisms that permit workers' representatives to influence and even control decisions affecting the organization as a whole. In the United States, participation is usually thought of as a management style that permits subordinates to make or at least influence decisions about matters of importance to them—especially decisions about how they do their work.[15]

Even within the United States context, participation can take a variety of forms, each of which is effective under different conditions and for different reasons. Precise analysis requires that the various forms be carefully distinguished (Whyte and Hamilton, 1964, p. 207). This is especially so because the evidence suggests that the shotgun approach to participation does not work. It is not enough, in other words, to try any old kind of participation to help solve any old type of problem. Researchers and practitioners alike should use the small bore rifle (with telescopic sights) rather than the blunderbuss.

There are two main schools of thought. The first looks on participation as a *resultant,* the extent to which subordinates are able to *influence* decisions (or more frequently the extent to which they *perceive* themselves as influencing decisions). The second views participation as a *decision process* and is interested in how decisions are made—for instance, whether decisions are made by the boss, by subordinates, or jointly. Let us examine these two perspectives briefly.

Influence.   A widely cited definition of participation is that of French, Israel, and As (1960). They call it "a *process* in which two or more persons *influence* each other in making certain plans, policies, and decisions [which] have future effects on all those making the decisions and on those represented by them" (p. 3, emphasis provided). French, Israel, and As make it clear that processes, such as joint decision-making, merely provide *opportunity* for influence—and that influence is the essence of participation.

How is that influence to be measured? Tannenbaum (1968) has developed an ingenious technique based on asking respondents to estimate the amount of influence exercised by various hierarchical levels within the organization. Among his findings are the following:

1. The *distribution* of influence (that is, how influence is divided among hierarchical levels) is less closely related to organizational effectiveness and member satisfaction than is *total* influence—the sense

15. To be more specific, among the differences between the two forms of participation are the following: (a) European style tends to be more formal and to be based on legal or contractual charters; (b) European style tends to be "indirect" (Lammers, 1967, pp. 201–216), through representatives of the workers who may deal with a number of different levels in the management hierarchy; United States style participation is "direct" and is concerned almost exclusively with relations between subordinates and their direct bosses; (c) European style participation is concerned with plant-wide and company-wide problems; what we call participation in this country involves chiefly workplace problems (broader problems are handled by collective bargaining, which is a separate form of participation not discussed here); (d) in this country we are concerned with participation by managers at least as much as we are with participation by workers; in Europe participation is *workers'* participation and largely ignores issues within management.

Table 6.1 – Form of Decision Process

Decision made by	Decision involving	
	An individual	A group
Superior	(1a) Individual direction	(1b) Group direction
Jointly	(2a) Consultation	(2b) Joint discussion
Subordinate	(3a) Delegation	(3b) Group decision making

that *everybody* has some influence within the organization. Effective organizations are those in which subordinates feel that both they and their boss have a considerable amount of influence. Ineffective organizations are those in which no one has influence. Thus the goal to work for is "power enhancement," rather than "power equalization."

2. Employees would like the organization to become more equalitarian but would accomplish this by increasing their own influence, not by reducing that of higher management. In most situations, subordinates are willing to have less influence than that of higher management.

On the basis of these findings, Tannenbaum argues that effective participation need not mean power equalization and that it is indeed possible to have situations where everyone gains in power. But note that what Tannenbaum measures is *felt,* not actual influence. "Counterfeit" (imagined) participation is always possible. Furthermore, we cannot be sure of cause and effect. It is entirely possible that subordinates report that they have more influence *because* the organization is more effective—that is, felt influence is the result, not the cause, of effectiveness. The influence approach tells us something about the end result desired, therefore, but not how to get there. For that we have to be concerned with participation as a process.

Process.   Obviously decisions can be divided among (1) those made by the superior (direction), (2) those made in some sense jointly by the superior and subordinate (consultation), and (3) those that the superior lets subordinates make on their own (delegation). Similarly, decisions can be made on (a) an individual or (b) a group basis.[16] Combining the two dimensions we get the matrix in Table 6.1 (with some fairly arbitrarily selected terms).

More than semantics is involved here. I submit that the manager who leaves his subordinates alone to work out problems by themselves is very different from the manager who promotes endless committee

---

16. As Heller (1971, p. 25) suggests, many writers imply that the only form of participation is group participation. My own view is that individual participation (2a and 3a) is more important and more common than group participation (2b and 3b), although the latter may be more novel and therefore more interesting.

meetings and different again from the manager who is receptive to suggestions but makes the final decisions.

If we define participation very broadly as a process in which subordinates have a say regarding decisions affecting them—as, in a sense, the opposite of being told what to do—then participation includes all of categories 2a, 2b, 3a, and 3b. *Autonomy* might be defined as including 3a and 3b, and delegation as 3a. So-called autonomous work groups (see Chapter 3) fall into category 3b.

Which is more important, influence or process? Both are important, and they reinforce each other. As indicated by the matrix in Table 6.2, which brings the two concepts together, it is the subordinates' influence and the boss's concern for subordinates that often transform mock participation into the real thing. Bosses who do not hold formal meetings with their subordinates may actually permit them more influence than bosses who hold frequent meetings in which they mastermind subordinates until the group comes up with the decisions the boss wants.

The increased communication generated by the participation *process* leads to the expression of better ideas, and this contributes to the quality of organizational decisions. But it is the feeling of *influence* that facilitates commitment to the decisions that are finally reached.

How Participation Works

The discussion above has highlighted the limitations of an oversimplified approach to participation. We know that participation—in

Table 6.2–Combining Process and Influence Approaches

Process	Subordinate influence	
	Low	High
Direction	Boss makes decisions ignoring subordinates' preferences completely	Boss makes the kinds of decisions he thinks subordinates would want him to make (he follows the Gallup Polls)
Consultation	Boss meets with subordinates, asks for their agreement on a course of action, but makes it clear by his tone of voice that he will accept no disagreement	Boss acts as chairman of the meeting, but gives no indication of his preference
Delegation	Subordinate is formally free to make any decision he wants, but from prior experience he knows that he will be punished if he deviates from the boss's preference	Subordinate is completely free to make decision on his own without guidance

some circumstances—has a positive effect on the quality of work life. The question is *how* and *when* this positive effect occurs. In other words, it is not enough to think of participation as a little black box into which participation is fed at one end and out of which higher production and satisfaction come at the other end. What happens within this box? What are the essential steps and the major variables within the participation process, and how important is each?

Expectancy theory suggests that participation might lead to higher productivity if it contributes to workers perceiving that (1) increased effort will lead to increased performance (productivity); (2) increased performance will lead to the satisfaction of important needs, especially achievement and group acceptance; and (3) the satisfaction obtained from this effort is sufficient to make the effort worthwhile (the equity factor) and thus affect the psychological bargain between the organization and its employees. Let us look at each of these influences in turn.

Participation makes it easier to convert effort into performance. Participation may, on the one hand, result in the development of better and easier ways of doing the job, so that a given degree of effort will result in higher performance. This may occur because the participative atmosphere permits subordinates to suggest and implement valuable new ideas that will make the organization more efficient. The participative atmosphere may also permit subordinates to question their boss's idea or provide him with additional information that he can use in making decisions. Where participation occurs in a group, members may exchange ideas on how to improve performance. And practice in participation may lead subordinates to develop valuable new skills.

Whether participation of this sort can occur depends on a number of questions, such as the following:

— How much relevant information can the subordinate contribute?
— Is the technology one that workers, individually or as a group, are in a position to change? Meaningful suggestions are less likely to be forthcoming, for example, if the production process depends on costly machines that would be expensive to change.
— Is there still "slack" in the sense that group discussion is likely to unearth significantly improved ways of doing things, or has the process been around for so long that most bugs have already been worked out?

Participation may also help subordinates define their objectives and so direct their efforts more effectively. As discussed earlier, much organizational inefficiency and employee dissatisfaction occur when individuals are not really sure what they are supposed to be doing.

People are more likely to understand and accept goals that they set for themselves.

Finally, participation can lead to greater team work. For example, work moved more smoothly at Corning when the women involved scheduled their own work (Glaser, 1975).

Participation makes it more likely that performance will be viewed as leading to valued rewards.   Participation may lead workers to believe that by working harder they will obtain (1) a sense of achievement or (2) a sense of social approval from their peers.

Achievement.   Following Patchen (1962, 1970), I suggest that a person is more likely to develop a sense of achievement in performing his job when the following conditions prevail:

— the individual has a generalized need for achievement (McClelland, Atkinson, Clark, and Lowell, 1953);
— he feels that he has specific skills (for example, he is a good carpenter or is good at deciding how carpentry work should be done);
— these skills are valued by him (they are an important part of his self-concept);
— he feels that doing the job (carrying out the decisions he has participated in making) is in some ways a test of whether he has these skills;
— there is some kind of feedback that tells him whether he has passed the test.

The above analysis should help us to understand why people might feel greater achievement in carrying out a decision they made than one that they did not make. For example, if they decide to make twenty units a day, they may work harder just to prove that this is a realistic goal. If they decide to do a job in a particular way, they may work hard just to prove that they picked the best way. Further, meeting a goal that they themselves have set may be viewed as a valid test of their skills as workers.

This analysis also suggests conditions under which participation would not lead to higher motivation. For example, participation may not work if the individuals involved do not value the skills tested. Thus, one might predict that participation would work less well with transient day laborers than with skilled tradesmen who are proud of their craft, or less well with a salesman whose main interest is in becoming a musician than with a salesman who looks on sales as his career. Participation would also be less likely to be successful if decisions reached through participation are viewed as trivial or as not involving a valid test of abilities.

Finally, individual forms of participation may provide stronger motivation for *achievement* than forms of participation involving groups, especially when the individuals perceive their participative contribution as lost in the larger setting. Indeed, group participation may rely less on autonomy and achievement (growth needs) than on the satisfaction of social needs.

Group Pressures.   When participation takes place in a group setting, a new element is added—group pressure to conform to decisions adopted. A three-step process may be involved.

> **Step 1.** Participation in a group discussion or decision may increase the individual's identification with or attraction to the group, particularly if he values the group or if he has a high need for social approval. The mere fact of participation may make the individual feel that his status within the group has increased and thus lead to his valuing the group more highly (because it now plays a more important part in his self-concept). In a sense the individual says, "If the group wants my opinions, it must be a pretty good group; at least, since I like having my opinions considered, I better pay more attention to it."

> **Step 2.** Once the individual values the group, he becomes more sensitive to group norms, because he wants to be a good group member. Among the group norms is carrying out the decisions that the group has made. (Normally one would expect that participation would have little impact on an assembly of individuals who have no feeling of being a group and therefore no group norms.)

> **Step 3.** To the extent that groups (or, more exactly, individuals within groups) participate in the decisions of the larger organization, group norms may develop that support those of the larger organization (that is, there may be greater commitment to the larger organization). If participation leads the group as a whole to feel that it has higher status within the organization, then the group may value the organization more highly and become more receptive to its norms—and enforce them. On the other hand, if the norms of the group are not congruent with those of the larger organization, then participation in group decisions may actually render the individual less receptive to the values of the larger organization (Seashore, 1954). For example, if the group promotes bogies or ceilings restricting output, then participation may result in lower production.

All this would suggest that the group participation should be very powerful. However, for the process to work, each individual must feel that he, by himself, has made a significant contribution to the group, and the group must feel that it has significantly influenced the decisions of the organization as a whole. These conditions are often difficult to meet.

Also, participation does create some dangers. As group members become more involved in group processes and as cohesion increases, the group may learn to expect to be consulted about every problem that arises. Because in a large organization it may not be possible to consult everyone about every problem, expectations will often be frustrated, and it might be better not to get the members so involved.

Bargaining and consideration as forms of participation. Bargaining—implicit or explicit—is a form of participation. Participation may set up an exchange relationship in which workers feel that they should work harder in return for concessions in other areas. For example, in exchange for management's agreement to let everyone go home an hour early before a big weekend, the employees may decide (with or without any explicit agreement) that they should work especially hard that day.

Participation is often a form of consideration, and as such it may reduce resistance to change. As illustrated in the Scanlon Plan case discussed above, participation may make change easier, in part because it reduces resentment that may stem from the fact that orders go only one way—downward—and from the fact that workers never feel they have any say about their jobs. Similarly, participation is a form of consideration in that it permits catharsis (letting off steam) and a reduction of general antagonism against management or the job. Participative decisions are considered more equitable just because the workers have been involved in making them. (Thus, promotions and job assignments will be more easily accepted if these are made on the basis of peer group preference.) In American society, participation has become almost a form of "industrial courtesy." In many organizations there are strong expectations that the supervisor will at least go through the motions of eliciting participation, certainly about such relatively trivial matters as how desks are to be arranged. Those who refuse to accept this convention are viewed as autocratic and inconsiderate.[17] The presence of limited, mock participation may not increase motivation or productivity; however, its absence will reduce satisfaction. In Herzberg's terms (1966), therefore, such participation is a hygiene factor.

Requirements for Effective Participation

The trouble with much previous writing about participation (including perhaps the previous pages) is that it deals with participation in the

---

17. In terms of the Ohio State scheme, "He gets the approval of his men on important matters before moving ahead" is an item measuring Consideration, not Initiating Structure. Lowin, Hrapchak, and Kavanagh (1969) conclude that the "concept of participative decision-making bridges those of consideration and initiating structure" (p. 252).

abstract rather than in terms of specific situations. And where specific situations are discussed, these tend to be highly dramatic examples of radical new innovations that involve substantial departures from typical patterns of managerial behavior. Too frequently participation has been sold as a cure-all, and as a consequence the concept has acquired ideological overtones. All of this serves to persuade managers that opting for participation requires an all-or-none decision. Consequently, conservative managers play it safe and let others experiment with this gimmick.

However, opting for participation does not require an all-or-none decision. Rather, it is useful to think of participation as something which comes in various shades of grey. Vroom (1973) suggests that we think in terms of "feasible sets." By this he means that for every managerial problem there is a feasible set of alternative decision-making approaches that are generally appropriate and another set that are inappropriate. Among these forms of decision-making are various forms of participation. There are some problems for which a specific form of participation is almost absolutely required (for example, under law, management is required to participate with its certified union representatives in setting wages). There are other situations where participation is clearly contraindicated (for example, in many emergencies). And there is a broad set of decision situations in which the degree and form of participation are largely a matter of individual managerial preference.

Thus, rather than seeking to determine the one *best* method of handling any given situation, a manager should be encouraged to think in terms of eliminating those approaches that will not work and then to adopt from the remaining feasible set the approach that is most comfortable for him and most consistent with his philosophy of management. The first step, therefore, is to determine the conditions under which participation is or is not likely to succeed—the limits of the feasible set. Some of the considerations that the manager might take into account are outlined below.

Supervisory Trust.   Participation will not work—at least for long[18]—if the supervisor does not have faith in it. As Lufton (1959) points out, "pseudo-democratic" methods, such as nondirective listening, are quite common in such professions as social work, but are frequently used in a manipulative manner that reduces individual autonomy and leads to subordinate resentment. For participation to be successful, supervisors should believe that the process will lead to positive results

---

18. "You can fool all of the people some of the time. . . ." (P. T. Barnum, c. 1860).

and they must be willing to accept, or at least give careful consideration to, their subordinates' suggestions.

Supervisory trust is critical here. According to studies by Ritchie
and Miles (1970), supervisors' attitudes toward their subordinates have
a greater impact on subordinate job satisfaction than does the sheer
amount of participatory consultation. Where supervisors have confidence in their subordinates' abilities, satisfaction tends to be high.
Where such confidence is lacking (for example, where the supervisor
views participation merely as a morale builder), the parties go through
the motions of what then becomes "counterfeit participation" (Heller,
1971). Employees eventually see through the deception; consequently,
the desired payoff in terms of morale does not result, and productivity
is even less likely to improve than without such fake participation.
Unless supervisors trust their subordinates, the subordinates are unlikely to trust their supervisors or to have any faith that the participatory process affords them any influence. Only when trust is present are
subordinates likely to express their views with honesty (Maier and
Hoffman, 1965).

As Dutch research suggests (Lammers, 1967), unsatisfactory consul-
tative meetings may have a more harmful impact on employee morale
than no meetings at all. Ritchie (1974) criticizes what he calls the
"quantity theory of participation"—the more meetings the better. He
distinguishes between supervisory *attitudes* (which he feels are reasonably constant) and supervisory *strategies* (or behaviors), which he feels
should change according to the situation. The fact that a supervisor has
a participative attitude or philosophy does not mean that he is required
to hold endless meetings, to consult at length prior to taking action
during emergencies, or to discuss endless trivia. Indeed, subordinates
will generally mistrust participatory gestures if they are inconsistent
with the supervisor's overall leadership style and may well perceive
such gestures as manipulation rather than genuine power-sharing.

Personality and Culture.   Individual personality factors are certainly
relevant. Vroom's (1960) research suggests that those with authoritarian
personalities and low need for independence are likely to react relatively unfavorably to participation. Similarly, it would seem likely that
high need for achievement (McClelland, 1961) would have to be present for participation to provide a sense of achievement; and high need
for affiliation would have to be present for participation to operate
through group pressures.

Cultural and occupational factors are also important. There may be
substantial differences between cultures in terms of the value given to
participation or the willingness of subordinates to accept the responsi-

bility for making suggestions, particularly in the presence of the boss—especially if the boss is viewed as representing another culture. For example, Ganguli (1964) reports that Indian workers feel that decision-making is the job of top management, not of workers. There are also differences among occupational groups. Professionals tend to value participation more than nonprofessionals (Patchen, 1970), and in collegial organizations, such as many universities, nonparticipative approaches fall outside the feasible set.

Organizational Commitment. As Douglas McGregor put it, "Theory Y assumes that people will exercise self-direction and self-control in the achievement of organizational objectives *to the degree that they are committed to these objectives*" (1960, p. 56, emphasis added). Such commitment is more likely to occur in "normative" (Etzioni, 1961), nonprofit, public service organizations (such as schools, hospitals, and political parties) than in most profit-making companies. It is also more likely to occur in professionally-oriented organizations, during wartime, and in communist countries (to the extent that workers in such countries accept national goals either voluntarily or as a result of indoctrination).

On the other hand, participation is often a means of generating commitment. (For example, among the best ways to raise money for a charity is to have rich donors participate on the fund-raising committee.) And successful participation may generate some commitment to the goals of profit-making organizations, at least where these goals are viewed as fair and legitimate.

Subordinates are at least unconsciously aware that the price they pay for participation is commitment, and for some this price is too high; in other words, to the extent that people resist commitment they will also reject participation. Apparently there are large subcultures of employees with strong instrumental (as opposed to expressive) orientations who view participation as reducing their freedom. Blau's (1955, p. 173) study of civil servants suggests that "the group's insistence that the supervisor discharge his duty issuing directives—that's what he gets paid for—serves to emphasize that their obedience to him does not constitute submission to his will but adherence, on his part as well as theirs, to abstract principles which they have socially accepted." And among these principles is limited commitment to organizational objectives.[19]

---

19. French, Israel, and As (1960) were discussing roughly the same phenomenon when they suggested that participation had only limited success in a Norwegian context because the particular form of participation practiced (group decision as to work changes) was viewed as not legitimate.

Organizational Factors. The success of participation in a given situation depends heavily on the climate in the organization as a whole. Participation will be less likely to be successful where there has been a history of labor-management strife or if management has been autocratic in the past. If the organization is generally authoritarian, then attempts to bootleg (without official approval) participation into a single department or work group are likely to face difficulties unless the rest of the organization is involved and appropriate adjustments are made (Bavelas and Strauss, 1955).

Organizational structure may also discourage participation. If supervisors have little discretion, they have little opportunity to implement subordinate suggestions. The more centralized and more rule bound an organization, the less opportunity there is for subordinates to develop new ways of doing things.[20] And in large organizations participation in organization-wide problems is very difficult to arrange—direct, mass-meeting participation tends to become either counterfeit (manipulated) or ineffective, and indirect participation through representatives often leads to inadequate communications and alienation.

Cohesive Groups. Group forms of participation are less likely to be effective when the group is divided, especially when members of the groups differ greatly in their values and expertise. To some extent the supervisor can help build cohesion. Or, organizational development techniques (see Chapters 5 and 7) can be used to foster increased group effectiveness.

Nature of the Decision-Making Task. There are some subjects that are appropriate for only fairly restricted forms of participation. Given company legal obligations, for example, the question of *whether* to desegregate a department is not appropriate for participation; the question of how to do it may be. Fruitful participation is also not likely to occur over the question of whether a company should make layoffs during a recession; nevertheless, the company should be prepared to consider suggestions for alternative means to save money and should allow fairly full participation in determining *how* to implement such layoffs (unless this question has already been determined through union negotiations).

The supervisor, of course, is interested in getting not only a sound decision but also one that is accepted by the group. An *adequate* decision that is enthusiastically implemented may well be better than a

---

20. Two recent trends—the growing use of computers and the increasing impact of government regulation—have induced tendencies to make the organization more centralized and so made effective participation more difficult to obtain.

perfect solution that meets with stubborn antagonism. Thus, the participative process is particularly appropriate where the supervisor is concerned more with getting acceptance of a decision than with its quality.

Actually, there are many such areas in which management does not care (within broad limits) what decision is made, as long as there is not excessive dissension. For example, management is largely unconcerned with how employees divide up the dirty work as long as the work is done—or how rest periods are scheduled, so long as the time allotted is not exceeded. And, because no vacation schedule can satisfy everyone, managers who can pass the scheduling responsibility to the group save themselves a major headache. (Note, however, that supervisors still must preside over the process by which the decision is made. If they say merely "you decide" without helping to establish a procedure, there may be endless bickering and confusion. It is the supervisor's responsibility, therefore, to help the group resolve its internal difficulties.)

In other areas the supervisor's objectives coincide with those of the group—in matters of accident prevention or avoiding jam-ups in the parking lot, for example. Possibly management should reserve a veto power over decisions in such matters, although it is unlikely that the group will make decisions that are, from the supervisor's point of view, far wrong.

There are still other areas that are probably not appropriate for participation. A crisis that demands immediate decisions does not permit a formal meeting. On the other hand, such a meeting may be useful, if held before the crisis, to develop contingencies and procedures in anticipation of future need. Furthermore, a participative atmosphere and experience in working together to develop plans will often result in greater teamwork when a crisis actually occurs, and when decisions are made with little or no participation.

Inappropriate subjects for participation may also include those about which subordinates have little information, few requisite skills, or little concern for the final results. Even so, the assignment of such problems to a work group may widen its members' horizons, develop their personal skills, and generate fresh new thoughts unsullied by conventional wisdom.

Limits to Freedom. Ideally the supervisor provides broad areas of freedom in which subordinates can regulate their own behavior (this is simply teamwork). However, there are bound to be areas of basic conflict between superiors and subordinates—at one time or another, every boss must face the inevitability of making and announcing distasteful decisions. And so we come to the question of how a supervisor can keep a meeting from encroaching on areas of decision-making that are not its proper concern.

One way of dealing with such issues is to set clear *limits* to the group's area of freedom. For example, instead of asking his subordinates "How much vacation time should you get?" the supervisor might ask "How many people can we spare at any one time during vacation and still meet customer needs?" or "Who should go when?" And supervisors should make it clear in advance that they reserve the right to reject proposed group decisions if they feel that (from their point of view) the quality of those decisions falls below an acceptable minimum. Then the most the supervisor can do is explain why he has rejected a particular decision and ask for questions.[21] In any case, it is the boss's responsibility to ensure that participation does not degenerate into a "laissez-faire" situation in which nobody accepts responsibility and nothing gets done.

Rewards for Participation. As much of the foregoing discussion suggests, if participation is to be more than counterfeit and if employees are to be enthusiastic, participation must provide significant payoffs (valued rewards) to all those involved. One payoff, as Tannenbaum insists, is increased influence for everyone. But workers may feel that intangible rewards, such as the sheer pleasure of additional responsibility, are not reward enough; they may also want higher pay. One of the strengths of the Scanlon Plan, as discussed in Chapter 4, is that the higher production resulting from participation is rewarded in solid cash.

Questions of equity enter here. When workers work harder or more efficiently, they see the company making more money, and they want more pay for themselves. Thus, when workers take on managerial tasks, it should not be surprising if they seek some (tangible) compensation for themselves.

There are a variety of possible organizational outcomes from participation. Much of the discussion, here and elsewhere, has emphasized the impact of participation on productivity. Yet this may be among the hardest of outcomes to obtain, among other reasons because productivity is a function of many things besides supervisory behavior and subordinate motivation. Among the other and more likely outcomes from participation are greater group cohesion, reduced resistance to change, better communication, reduced alienation, and improved job satisfaction (especially when subordinates have

---

21. Alternatively, top management may make the formal decision, but levels below may identify the problem and propose solutions (Blankenship and Miles, 1968).

strong needs for achievement or affiliation and when the concept of participation is accepted as legitimate in the local culture).

One especially important outcome, commonly ignored, is the better organization of work. Indeed, participation is often thought of as a motivator (and has been so treated here). In practice it may play an even more important role as a form of consideration and work facilitation. Another significant payoff is increased managerial power in the sense that participation *increases* rather than decreases the boss's influence. Bosses gain a better feel for what their subordinates are thinking, they obtain the benefit of employees' suggestions, and, above all, they have some commitment from the subordinates to implement agreed upon plans. Thus, the organization, management, and employees can all benefit from valued, relevant forms and degrees of participation.

SUPERVISION: A SUMMING UP

Supervisors have a great impact on quality of work life through both their everyday contacts and their influence on motivational systems. I have stressed consideration as a contributor to satisfactory work environment, and facilitation and participation as alternative means of strengthening the expectancy linkage between effort and satisfaction. But supervisors affect the quality of work life in many other ways—for example, through their actions in establishing high performance standards. Further, consideration, facilitation, and participation interact with each other and all contribute to satisfaction and productivity. It is misleading to examine them separately.

One thing emerges from all the research—there is no one best way to supervise. Consider a few examples. Foremen on the automobile assembly line can allow their subordinates only the most limited opportunities for participation; here the good foreman is the person who shows concern for the inevitable frustrations induced by the work process (consideration) and is able to obtain adequate supplies and support for the workers (facilitation). By contrast, university deans must allow broad opportunities for participation; if they fail to do this, their personal efforts to be considerate will be wasted or resented and largely irrelevant. Finally, the symphony conductor must be a close supervisor; there is little opportunity for independent decision-making in a symphony orchestra (as opposed to a jazz combo). Technical competence and an ability to coordinate activities is what counts here. Concern with subordinates' feelings is a desirable plus, but is essentially secondary—some of the best conductors have been unfeeling autocrats.

Supervisors play an important role, but it would not be wise to exaggerate their significance. Supervisors' freedom to vary their styles of supervision is heavily constrained by such factors as technology, company policies, and union contracts. About the only reward directly under their control is praise; and praise, unaccompanied by other rewards, soon loses its value. Consideration is the only element supervisors are reasonably free to vary.

Often the impact of staff departments, such as production scheduling and industrial engineering, on the individual worker is greater than the impact of the direct supervisor. Higher management usually makes the policies with regard to reward systems, career ladders, and job design. We now turn to broader issues such as these.

THE SUPERVISOR AND
THE LARGER ORGANIZATION

As I have stressed above, supervisors are subject to numerous constraints from the various managerial levels above them. Let us examine the nature of this relationship, especially those elements related to the quality of work life.

Supervisors have other responsibilities besides watching over their subordinates. Among other things, they are concerned with coordination between their work groups and other departments, and especially with obtaining appropriate supplies and services. Indeed, there is evidence that effective supervisors (as measured by a number of standards, including subordinate satisfaction) are likely to spend less time with their immediate subordinates, and more time with their superiors and with staff people, than are ineffective supervisors. By and large, the time spent in this fashion is devoted to obtaining resources for their departments, fighting for the interests of their departments (and the workers in them), and long-range planning.[22]

Representing Subordinates

Not surprisingly, there is considerable evidence suggesting that the effectiveness of a supervisor is in part a function of his ability to go to bat for his subordinates (Downes, 1958; Walker, Guest, and Turner, 1956). He serves as their spokesman and protector, particularly with higher management. After all, most supervisors have relatively few

---

22. Of course, there is something of a cause and effect relationship here. One reason effective supervisors can spend so much time away from their departments is that the departments are already running smoothly. Supervisors of difficult work groups may be spending so much time handling immediate emergencies (fire-fighting) that they lack the time to develop effective external relations.

rewards they can hand out on their own. And so, if they wish to reward their subordinates, they must obtain rewards from higher up. Similarly, the subordinates are relatively unprotected from higher management's pressures (particularly if there is no union). Thus, effective supervisors act as shock absorbers, shielding their men from outside influences that jeopardize their welfare and productivity.

However, being a spokesman for their subordinates is not enough. Supervisors must be successful in getting results. Twenty-five years ago, Katz, Macoby, and Morse (1950) found that supervisors of the less productive departments in an insurance company were likely to recommend promotions; but supervisors of the more productive departments were successful in obtaining them. The successful supervisor must have "influence" (Pelz, 1951). In fact, general supervision without influence may lead to poorer results than close supervision with influence (Morse, 1953). Subordinates become highly frustrated when they go through the motions of making democratic decisions that their supervisor cannot get implemented.

To the extent that supervisors are able to deliver the goods, they can reward subordinates for effective performance and they can live up to their end of the implicit bargain. However, most supervisors suffer from a classic case of role conflict, because they are also expected to stand up for the interests of the organization as a whole. Their subordinates pressure them to be considerate, and their bosses want them to be task oriented. Likert (1967) argues that the manager can resolve this conflict by acting as a "linking pin," a go-between who represents the interests of each group to the other. The concept is an attractive one in principle; however, I suspect that the number of circumstances in which a supervisor can successfully serve two masters may be limited. Considerable—and frequently painful—role conflict is common, and the linking pin can easily shear.

What can higher management do to reduce these tensions? Certainly sympathetic recognition of the supervisor's plight can help. More important, the supervisor should be permitted to participate in managerial decisions and should be entrusted with as much freedom to handle his own departments as the technology and their own skills permit. Under these circumstances, his status and ability to deliver what his subordinates need will be enhanced. He will be in a better position to obtain resources for his department and implement his subordinates' requests.

Transmittal of Supervisory Styles

How can higher management persuade supervisors to adopt the kinds of supervisory styles that enhance the quality of work life? Strengthening supervisors' positions with their subordinates is one approach. Training and organizational development (discussed in Chapter 7) and executive selection techniques are others. Management may also change the nature of the organization's reward system, because this system often determines supervisory style (as discussed in Chapter 4).

Equally important is supervisory influence. It is perfectly natural for a manager to reflect the supervisory style of his boss. The evidence suggests that those who receive general (or vice versa, close) supervision are likely to practice the same general (or close) supervision. Managers' actions are looked at for clues to the behavior they expect from their subordinates. For example, if a manager is subjected to pressure by his boss, he will have a strong tendency to transmit that pressure to those below—perhaps even increasing it a bit in the process as a way of relieving frustration and soothing a wounded ego. On the other hand, if the boss invites a manager to participate in relevant decisions, that manager will probably involve his subordinates in decision-making.

Furthermore, no manager can permit his subordinates to exercise freedom in areas in which he does not have freedom. If top management, for example, issues strict rules that describe in detail what it wants subordinates at all levels to do in almost every conceivable situation, the supervisor obviously has little discretion to delegate and little freedom to allow subordinates to engage in participation.[23]

The most promising solution under such circumstances is for management at each level to delegate sufficient authority to lower level managers so that they in turn can practice participation where appropriate. As we shall see below, delegation may also require reward systems that emphasize long-range human development rather than productivity or contributions to short-run profit.

Changing Reward and Control Systems

Most organizations make use of statistical control as a means of guiding and monitoring subordinates' behavior. Cost accounting develops standard costs for all items produced and all services rendered. If the standard cost of an item is eighty-seven cents and the foreman can make it for eighty-five cents, he makes a "profit" (part of which may accrue to him, personally, as a bonus). If he spends eighty-nine cents to make it, he incurs a "loss." Such *variance accounts* provide a measure of departmental efficiency.

Statistical controls of this sort serve a number of purposes that I will mention only briefly here. For example, they reduce the need for

---

23. On rare occasions the subordinate manager may "bootleg" participation (that is, permit it to occur without his boss's knowledge), especially on the night shift.

close, detailed supervision; they set objectives and thus act as a means of downward communication; and they serve as a springboard for personnel evaluation and reward. However, when improperly used, they have the following deleterious effects:

1. Human nature being what it is, greater weight is normally given to those factors that are seemingly easier to measure than to those that are more difficult. Productivity and costs can be measured with seeming exactness; the state of employee morale or the quality of human relations cannot.

2. Measurements can be made monthly, weekly, or (with the help of computers) even daily. Because the data are available so quickly, the temptation is to look at the data frequently and watch short-run trends. Realizing that their bosses do this, lower level managers become inhibited about making changes that will not result in immediate, short-run payoffs.

3. Statistical controls typically report the performance of each department, but not its impact on others. Thus, the way to look good is to suboptimize—to concentrate on the selfish interests of one's own group.

4. The availability of numerical, deceptively "hard" measures of supervisory performance makes it attractive for management to develop a seemingly fair reward system based largely on these figures.

Unfortunately, all of these consequences of the use of statistical controls encourage supervisors to push their workers to obtain short-run productivity at the expense of developing long-range human assets, sound interdepartmental cooperation, or good relations with customers. Supervisors are thus motivated to keep short reins on their subordinates, and the subordinates' opportunities to experiment are reduced. Individual needs get ignored, pressures build up, and the quality of work life is harmed.

The problems that can develop when statistical control systems are used can to some degree be ameliorated if supervisors participate in the development of data measuring devices they feel are fair and appropriate. Management by Objectives (MBO) is one such participative technique. It involves setting specific objectives (or control measures) that are appropriate for each manager and against which his (or his workers') performance can be measured. Acceptance by managers and workers of such control systems reduces the need for close supervision and reduces uncertainty about what an individual needs to do to win valued rewards (such as praise and promotion).

Another approach to control is the concept of Human Resource Accounting (Flamholtz, 1972, 1974; Rhode, Lawler, and Sundam, 1976). This technique is designed to take into financial account items other than (tangible) profit and loss. By placing monetary values on human systems, it seeks to account for people as an organizational resource that changes over time, as people improve their skills and move up within the organization. Human value is extremely difficult to measure in dollar amounts, and it is unlikely that Human Resource Accounting will receive early endorsement from the accounting profession. But this technique for obtaining information about human resources, as opposed to the more tangible resources, has excellent potential as a *supplement* to standard accounting reports. Within the framework of this approach, rewards and promotions can be based on supervisors' contributions to sound human relations and the development of subordinates' skills, as well as on productivity.

Every statistical control system has its limitations. Higher management frequently gives too much weight to statistical evidence (just because it is tangible) and so is tempted to correct short-run trends and solve immediate problems by intervening too soon. Thus, in order to avoid premature intervention and allow time for the important but less tangible, long-run measures to enter the picture, it might be better for top management to receive statistical reports at much less frequent intervals than lower level supervisors. The latter need more constant data feedback to keep the organization running smoothly on a day-to-day basis. Finally, feedback data should include not just statistical measures of costs and productivity but also information on labor turnover and employee morale (the latter based on attitude surveys and on other valid sources of information).

In summary supervisors cannot effectively perform the key roles discussed earlier (facilitation, consideration, and participation) unless they have top management's support. They must be encouraged to represent the interests of their subordinates. They must be afforded opportunities to experiment with new forms of work organization on their own and to participate in critical decisions made by higher management. The evaluation and rewards of supervisors should take into account their contributions to the development of a high quality of work life for their subordinates.

STRUCTURAL ALTERNATIVES

Organizational structure influences quality of work life in a variety of ways. It affects the nature of jobs people do, the kinds of interpersonal contacts they have while on the job, and the character of the supervision they receive. Examples of each of these impacts are provided below.

Of the large number of important structural issues, I will discuss two that seem especially relevant to quality of work life. These are span of control and the product versus functional organization question. Each has a significant influence on employee satisfaction, directly and through its influence on supervision.

Span of Control

This concept relates to the number of subordinates who report to one boss. There is no *simple* relationship between span of control and either subordinate satisfaction or efficiency (Porter and Lawler, 1965). However, a relationship does exist because span of control directly affects the nature of the supervisor-subordinate relationship and also organizational communication patterns.[24] According to classical management theory, effective management requires rather narrow spans (not more than seven to one). However, a widely publicized study done at Sears Roebuck in 1950 suggested that "flat" organizations with spans of control as broad as thirty-five to one were more effective than "tall" organizations with narrower spans (Worthy, 1950). Today it is generally recognized that the appropriate span depends on (and partly determines) the style of supervision practiced. This in turn depends on a variety of factors, especially the nature of the job, the character of the work force, and the extent to which managerial responsibilities are delegated to subordinates.

If the span is narrow, supervisors have only a few subordinates, and, other things being equal, they can spend more time with each subordinate. However, too often management imposes a narrow span of control on work operations that would be more receptive to delegation. Not only is this a waste of supervisory manpower, but it provides an almost irresistible temptation for supervisors to make use of their free time by supervising more closely than necessary. Thus, an inappropriately narrow span of control can have a deleterious effect on the quality of work life.

On the other hand, a broad span almost forces supervisors to delegate, because they have too many subordinates to supervise each closely. Thus, a broad span of control normally gives employees greater freedom, but it does so at the cost of reducing their opportunity to consult with their bosses. One of the presumed advantages of a broad span of control is that it implies that there are relatively few levels between the worker and top management, thereby permitting more rapid communication with the top. This seeming advantage becomes

---

24. There are a number of methodological problems involved in studying span of control. For example, allowance must be made for whether the supervisor has an assistant, and also for the percentage of his total day he spends in supervising as opposed to other activities. Having an assistant increases the number of people a supervisor can supervise; spending only part time on supervision reduces this number.

meaningless, however, if managers at each level have so many direct subordinates that they can devote little time to receiving communication from any given subordinate.

In determining the appropriate span of control, a manager needs to take stock of his work group. By and large, a narrow span is appropriate where the following conditions exist:

1. A great deal of coordination and facilitation is required—and the members of the work group are not able to provide these by themselves.
2. The members of the group have a strong need to consult with the boss, either as individuals or in groups, and it is not feasible to transfer this consultation function to the group as a whole.
3. A great deal of coordination with other departments (such as maintenance, supply, or a department adjacent to the workflow) is required, and members of the work group are unable to perform this external relations function themselves.
4. Many of the employees require on-the-job training, which other members of the group are unable to provide.
5. High standards of performance are required, but subordinates can neither be trusted to meet these without being checked on nor can appropriate indirect methods of inspection be developed.
6. The supervisor spends only part of his time supervising and the rest of his time performing a work function, so that he is really a working supervisor or *straw boss.*

Thus, as managerial functions (such as coordination, training, or inspection) are transferred to subordinates, the need for a narrow span of control declines. This should be a natural concomitant of job redesign or increased participation.

> At the Philips TV plant in the Netherlands "the group responsible for assembling the black-and-white sets, for example, not only performs the entire assembly task, but it also deals directly with staff groups such as procurement, quality, and stores, with no foreman or supervisor to act as intermediary or expediter. If something is needed from another department or something goes wrong that requires the services of another department, it's the group's responsibility to deal with the department" (Dowling, 1973, p. 54).

A broadening of the span may lead, in and of itself, to an increase in the assumption of managerial tasks by the group. At Philips, the foreman level was eliminated *before* autonomous groups of the type described above were introduced. Indeed, failure to broaden the span may jeopardize the success of quality of work life experiments.

Theoretically, the development of autonomous work groups frees the foreman to engage in long-range planning or to take over other functions now performed by higher management. There is a limit to the amount of long-run planning that can be done at the foreman level, however. If supervisors take over some of their bosses' functions, what will their bosses do? Somewhere there will be some supervisory redundancy. If the number of supervisors is not reduced, the temptation will be strong for them to resume close supervision. And there are reports of several quality of work life experiments that floundered precisely because underemployed supervisors found this temptation too great.

It could be argued that a narrow span is not inconsistent with greater autonomy and participation, provided supervisors function in a chairman's role, facilitating consensus, smoothing over human relations differences, and in general providing the various kinds of support activities discussed under the heading of consideration. Possibly, if their supervisory style involves much consultation and many group meetings, subordinates might view supervisory behavior as supportive rather than restrictive. But, particularly in routine operations, high levels of consultation and endless meetings can be counterproductive. Even consideration can be felt as smothering when provided in excess.

Some Final Caveats. Broad spans of control are appropriate only where high degrees of delegation or participation are feasible, and, as we have seen earlier, this occurs far from universally. Furthermore, a broad span of control does not imply creation of completely leaderless groups. It requires development of strong informal leadership to take over various managerial functions as formal leadership withdraws. (For a discussion of when this is possible, see Chapter 5.)

Product versus Functional Organization

Another structural issue that is relevant here is related to the question of whether activities should be grouped by product or by function. As we shall see, this issue has significant implications for promotional opportunities, sense of achievement derived from the job, and ease of work-related communications—all factors that contribute to a high quality of work life.

The example in Figure 6.1 depicts a functionally organized manufacturing group with three functions—maintenance, production, and inspection (all other functions are ignored for the moment). Each function reports to its own boss, and (as is typical) each function works in its own separate section of the plant.

By contrast, Figure 6.2 shows the same manufacturing plant organized on a product basis. This consists of three relatively independent miniplants, each with its own maintenance, production, and inspection groups.

Product organizations group people according to their common

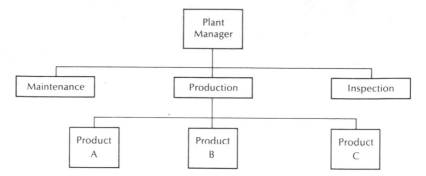

Figure 6.1–Functional Organization

objectives (workflow, product, client, and so forth). Functional organizations group people by their organizational specialties. Other examples of this product-function distinction are indicated in Table 6.3.

This product-function issue has numerous implications for organizational effectiveness and responsiveness to outside pressures. Here I will deal only with quality of work life issues felt by the individual worker.

Product organization has the advantage of short communications lines. Manufacturing workers can easily communicate with assembly workers, and they can coordinate their efforts quickly without going through a long chain of command. Typists and bosses see each other more often and, hopefully, in the process, much misunderstanding is eliminated.

With product organization, workers obtain a clearer picture of the production process. Thus, they can identify more closely with the work group and are more likely to feel pride in the product they make. Typists, for example, will be more likely to identify with their boss's work when they are assigned to work directly with him; statistics professors may become more concerned with the ability of their students

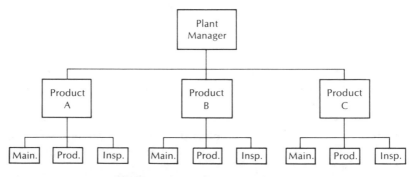

Figure 6.2–Product Organization

Table 6.3–Examples of Functional and Product Organization

Functional Organization	Product Organization
A typing pool	Each typist attached to his own boss
A central purchasing department	Each division has its own purchasing unit
A central city health department	The school district and prison each have their own health unit
A university statistics department teaching statistics for entire university	Each department hires statisticians to teach its own students

to apply what they learn if each department has its own statisticians. Product organizations may also increase the sense of satisfaction obtained from the final product (whether it be a complete manuscript or a student well trained in statistics).

The fact that in a product organization each department is technologically self-contained means the department manager can be given broad autonomy. This permits greater flexibility and quicker responsiveness to work group problems. Following our earlier analysis, because supervisors in a product organization have more autonomy delegated to them than their counterparts in a functional organization, the chances of their delegating to subordinates or engaging in participative management are increased.

Finally, product organization makes it much easier for workers to exchange or even merge jobs. Indeed, many of the recent quality of work life experiments have involved the creation of what are, in effect, product organizations. For example, Monsanto broke down one of its organic chemical plants into "product teams, each of which sets its own goals in line with those of the plant as a whole and measures its own results. Instead of being supervised closely, operators now do most of their own process control (foremen have been eliminated entirely on two shifts)" (Jenkins, 1973, p. 206). At R. G. Barry, workers do their own inspection (result—"quality levels improved tremendously") and much of their own maintenance (Jenkins, 1973).

Other groups have taken over the supply and expediting functions formerly handled by staff departments. For example, the material controls department at Corning Glass was divided into four functionally separate sections—purchasing, inventory control, scheduling, and expediting. (Communications problems between these sections were immense and the plant was plagued by parts shortages.) After the manager reorganized the department on a product basis, with each product team taking complete responsibility for material controls for a single product, the parts shortage list was reduced from fourteen IBM pages to less than one page (Glaser, 1975).

All the previously mentioned advantages of product organization should foster greater teamwork and satisfaction. The case is not entirely one-sided, however. Functional organization has its strong points as well, particularly when the workers involved are technicians or professionals. Functional organization permits workers to associate with others who have the same training and interests. Craft or professional pride is enhanced here—as opposed to pride in product. Communications about functional activities are simpler. Thus mechanics can more easily exchange tips about how to handle new equipment, and statisticians will be more likely to discuss new developments in their profession. This means that with functional organization workers will keep more up-to-date with their fields and may well be more creative. In addition, with functional organization, lines of promotion will be clearer. For example, a single purchasing agent attached to a manufacturing organization has nowhere to go. If he were part of a central purchasing department, however, his promotion opportunities would be much less ambiguous. Finally, functional organization may permit people to be transferred more easily. Maintenance men can be switched around as needed, rather than tied down to a single assignment.

The advantages of the two kinds of organization are summarized in Table 6.4.

In short, ignoring its many technological disadvantages (chiefly loss of economies of scale), product organization would seem to provide more quality of work life advantages for unskilled and semi-skilled workers. For craft and professional workers, however, the net advantages are less clear.

Finally, note should be taken of some of the problems that can

Table 6.4—Advantages of Product and Functional Organization

Product	Functional
Easier work-flow communications	Easier communications about function or craft
Identification with product and product excellence	Identification with function or craft and function or craft excellence
Department has greater autonomy from larger organization	Workers can do their own thing, but at the cost of considerable tensions with other groups
Easier coordination	Clearer promotional channels
Opportunities to exchange or merge jobs	Easier transfer between assignments

accompany a shift from functional to product organization. One of the advantages of functional organization is that the various departments can check on each other. (Certainly an independent inspection department, or to a lesser extent, independent maintenance and health departments discussed in previous examples, serve this function.) By contrast, product organization requires that higher management learn to trust each product department to develop its own inspection controls and adhere to organizational standards. Thus, managers in a product organization must learn how to supervise a much broader range of activities, some of which may be completely new to them. Fortunately, this burden may be eased somewhat by the fact that their external relations role in dealing with other departments will become easier.

BRINGING IN THE UNION

In unionized organizations, management's policies must take the union into account. Indeed, chances of improving the quality of work life through unilateral management action, without union cooperation, are slim. Most reforms aimed at improving the quality of work life require workers' participation; in many, participation is the essence. Such participation is unlikely if the union disapproves. And union cooperation is especially critical if quality of work life changes involve practices previously subject to collective bargaining. Changes in career ladders, for example, may require modifications in seniority systems, and job redesign alters job descriptions. These matters traditionally have been determined through negotiation and rendered unalterable by contract.

Beyond this, the state of union-management relations directly affects the quality of work life. Neither productivity nor morale is likely to be high in an atmosphere of constant bickering and suspicion, even if strikes are few. Thus, good union-management relations are essential to successful quality of work life reforms, and are a determinant of a high quality life on the job. Finally, the union represents an important means of providing a better quality of work life, both as a channel for upward communications and as a vehicle for participation. For all these reasons, management must give careful consideration to the union's role when making changes that seek to improve the quality of work life.

The discussion that follows examines the quandries that quality of work life issues pose for unions, and then makes some specific suggestions on how management might effectively enlist union cooperation in dealing with problems in this area. (Note: Some of these issues are also discussed in Chapter 7. Here we are concerned with the union's role when management is the party that seeks to take the initiative in making changes. Chapter 7 deals with the union as initiator and with the relations between the union and outside consultants. Thus, although there may be some apparent overlaps between the two discussions, the perspectives are very different.)

What Management Needs to Know about Union Quandaries

Quality of work life issues present problems for unions, and many union leaders are uncertain about the best ways to deal with these problems (in this they are no different than members of management). Unions are involved as equal participants in three projects being monitored by the National Quality of Work Center. And a union played an important supporting role in what was perhaps the most elaborate (and best reported) company reorganization according to behavioral science principles to date, at the Weldon Company (Marrow, Bowers, and Seashore, 1967). Unions have been involved in numerous quality of work life changes under the auspices of the Scanlon Plan. And, without using the concept of quality of work life specifically, unions at the shop level have initiated and supported countless job changes that have had the effect (and frequently the purpose) of increasing teamwork and individual discretion. Finally, Scandinavian unions have been leaders in seeking quality of work life reforms in their countries.

Despite these experiences, quality of work life issues still present some serious quandaries for unions. Union leaders are generally suspicious about the quality of work life movement and uncertain about how they should react to it. In part their uncertainty arises from lack of knowledge and even interest in these areas, because unemployment and inflation generally have higher priority than quality of work life. In part their suspicion has been caused by the way quality of work life reforms have been packaged. Many union leaders doubt the sincerity of management's sudden interest in workers' welfare, and they wonder whether management may have in mind such other objectives as introducing a speedup or weakening the union. And even union leaders who are sympathetic to the goal of improving the quality of work life recognize that implementing these changes may require painful adjustments, by unions as well as management, to traditional values and collective bargaining procedures.

Let us look at some of these union concerns, for only with an understanding of these concerns can management develop realistic plans for dealing with them.

Suspicion of the motives of quality of work life advocates.   Much of the writing on quality of work life totally ignores the union. Almost all of the early experiments in this area took place in nonunion plants. At least one prominent consultant has publicly argued that job enrichment is an effective way of keeping unions out. And a number of social critics have charged that the labor movement, because it is so single-mindedly concerned with workers' economic and possibly social needs, has been insufficiently responsive to their growth needs. Management, these critics conclude, has been more up-to-date and as a consequence unions have become somewhat outmoded.

Unions naturally react to such charges with anger. They hotly claim that they have contributed more to improving the quality of work life than management ever will. And any fair observer will agree that this union response contains a large element of truth. For example, workers in union plants earn higher wages than those in nonunion plants. Unions also have fought hard and generally successfully for safer working conditions, more humane supervision, and more equitable application of management rules. Above all, they provide the single most significant means whereby workers can meaningfully and effectively participate in resolving matters of importance to them.

Given this impressive record of protecting workers' interests, unionists feel considerable annoyance with the self-congratulatory tone of some social scientists and management spokesmen who have suddenly discovered, after all these years, that quality of work life problems do exist—and who then propose to solve them on management's terms and without recognition of the union's role. Furthermore, many union officers are apprehensive of behavioral science consultants and of academicians in general. Early consultants were frequently time-and-motion study speedup experts. As an article in the official AFL-CIO journal put it, "Substituting the sociologist's questionnaire for the stopwatch is likely to be no gain for the workers" (Brooks, 1972, p. 1). The recent interest in quality of work life questions by those in "radical-chic academic and intellectual circles" (Brooks, 1972, p. 4) is viewed as somewhat patronizing, especially when this interest is accompanied by suggestions that union officers no longer know what their members want.

In sum, there is considerable (and perhaps justifiable) suspicion among workers and union leaders of management's motives, as well as of the motives of the behavioral scientists who are associated with the quality of work life movement. However, the extent of this suspicion doubtlessly varies from work site to work site—and depends heavily on the past history of the labor-management relationship in question. Where the relationship has developed amicably and an atmosphere of trust has been created, management's interest in quality of work life proposals is likely to be accepted in good faith.

The Adversary Relationship. Unions often find it a bit difficult to deal with quality of work life problems because, as Nat Goldfinger of the AFL-CIO put it, "A union demand is a negotiable demand which, if not satisfied, can be met by a strike. How do you talk about these [quality of work life] questions in terms of a negotiable demand and a possible strike?" (Jenkins, 1973, p. 317). In general, unions have resisted making management decisions, particularly when this requires making invidious choices among members or when it might lead to membership resentment (as in the case of union participation in peer discipline). As an official of one union commented, "We want management to make the decisions so we can be free to start a grievance about it. Otherwise we could be accused of helping make bad decisions. So we have always left decisions up to management."

These comments may exaggerate the problem, however. In the first place, unions frequently participate in making hard decisions that favor one group of members over another. They do this whenever they negotiate a new seniority system or agree to a contract that provides greater benefits for one group (for example, skilled tradesmen) than for others. These may not always be quality of work life decisions, but they do require the union to make potentially unpopular choices. Further, experienced negotiators are able to live in "mixed motive" situations (to use Walton and McKersie's, 1965, terminology) in which "distributive" bargaining (where one party can gain only at the cost of the other) exists side by side with "integrative" bargaining (where the solution can provide gains for both parties). Quality of work life is an integrative issue par excellence.

Fortunately, unions have a long history of dealing with such integrative problems—from plant picnics to job evaluation—through the establishment of joint union-management committees that function separately from mainstream, distributive bargaining (Sayles and Strauss, 1953). Quality of work life improvements may well be more easily accepted and more effective when such committees are used.

Downgrading Traditional Economic Objectives. Implicit in *some* of the writings relating to quality of work life is the assumption that workers' economic needs have already been reasonably well satisfied and that personal growth needs should now be given top priority. Unionists reject this assumption and object strongly to any effort to downgrade the primacy of economic needs. They are in no way prepared to trade off concrete gains, such as wage increases, for anything as nebulous as greater freedom to make work decisions. As the evi-

Table 6.5-Attitudes of Union Officers Toward Selected Issues

	Issue "very important"[a] (percent)	Issue integrative[b] (percent)	Issue appropriate for joint program[c] (percent)
Earnings	92	26	6
Fringe benefits	79	48	4
Safety	75	68	41
Job security	68	44	12
Control of work	47	34	54
Adequate resources	46	46	61
Interesting work	41	39	68
Productivity	30	30	51
Work load	22	29	44

[a]Percent rating issue "very important."
[b]Percent reporting that with regard to given issue "my union and company want to accomplish completely the same thing" or "my company and union want to accomplish somewhat the same thing."
[c]Percent feeling that the "best way" to deal with issue is to "set up a joint program with management outside collective bargaining."

dence below suggests, unions have been willing to experiment cautiously with quality of work life changes, but only if these are the sideshow. They will strongly resist any effort to move economic questions off center stage.

Table 6.5, adopted from a survey of union activists in upstate New York (Kochan, Lipsky, and Dyer, 1974), provides some indication of union attitudes. Several interesting conclusions emerge from this study. As expected, basic economic issues are ranked most important. Yet substantial numbers of unionists also rate as "very important" such quality of work life issues as safety, control of work (described as "having more to say about how the work is done"), adequate resources (described as "improving conditions that interfere with getting the job done"), and interesting work.[25] Both productivity and work load receive reasonably low votes. In sum, the results suggest that improving the quality of work life is a secondary but still important issue for these activists.

The second column in Table 6.5 contains some surprises. With the exception of safety, a majority of the activists do *not* believe that their company and union wish to accomplish the same thing in these areas. Even "adequate resources" (an issue closely equivalent to facilitation) was viewed as a distributive issue. Presumably (we can't be sure) this majority felt that the company was not interested in "improving condi-

25. The standard deviations for the quality of work life items are considerably higher than for the economic items—suggesting more disagreement among union leaders about the importance of quality of work life questions.

tions that got in the way of getting the job done." The final column suggests considerable union support for joint programs in these areas. (Other data, not reported here, indicate that the collective bargaining route was not felt to be effective for these issues.)

The study reported above is consistent with the trend of discussion in a two-day Workers' Assembly sponsored by the Institute of Industrial Relations, University of California, Berkeley, and attended by about fifty active unionists. The announced subject of this conference was "The Changing World of Work." Nevertheless, most of the comments in various small groups during the first day emphasized the need for higher wages and job security during a period of combined inflation and recession. By the end of the day, the discussion in most groups had moved to conditions on the job, with the stress at first on such grievances as tyrannical supervision, oppressive management policies, job hazards, and excessive work loads. During the second day some individuals began distinguishing between various kinds of jobs, especially between those that are closely supervised and those that allow a man to be his own boss. By the end of this second day, there was general (but not unanimous) agreement that unions should move in the direction of increasing freedom on the job and that perhaps there should be experiments with foremanless work groups.

The conference discussions reinforce the following conclusions of the attitude survey: (1) union leaders are concerned about quality of work life conditions, although the degree of their concern probably varies from one situation to another; (2) they are somewhat uncertain about how to handle these issues within a collective bargaining context; and (3) economic issues still are of primary concern. From this I draw one further generalization: If properly approached, unions will be supportive of the kinds of quality of work life reforms discussed in this book; but, like management, they will have to feel their way into this terra incognito.

Fear of Speedup.   For management, higher productivity is an unquestioned good. Union leaders are less sure. There is general recognition that companies must be profitable if they are to pay decent wages, but the term *productivity* is often associated with the speedup and loss of jobs. Note that, of the union sample discussed above, 70 percent viewed productivity as an issue about which the union's interests were likely to diverge from those of management. Thus, union leaders are hardly likely to be enthusiastic about quality of work life changes sold in the name of increasing productivity. (Two important exceptions—these leaders' attitudes may well change if (1) higher productivity is clearly needed to save jobs, or (2) higher productivity will be compensated by higher wages.)

Fortunately, there are numerous other issues, besides productivity, on which quality of work life changes can be focused.

Traditional Work Rules.   Regardless of how they are introduced, quality of work life programs will have an impact on a number of collectively bargained policies. The thrust of collective bargaining in many industries has been to rigidify and codify managerial practices—that is, to define job classifications ever more strictly and to insist that no one work outside his job classification. Job enrichment requires movement in the opposite direction—that is, combining some jobs, blurring the boundaries between others, and even the blending of worker and supervisory functions. Also, new career patterns disturb established promotional ladders, and reforms of reward systems involve the heart of bargaining agreements.

Some unions may adopt the policy of "no backward step" and refuse to make concessions of any kind, even when these concessions might bring about a higher quality of work life. But this attitude is unlikely to be the norm. Once unions' suspicions are allayed, exceptions and changes may be permitted, subject to carefully negotiated safeguards. After all, difficult problems like those mentioned are constantly being resolved through bargaining; for example, in many plants work rules are the subject of constant renegotiation. Once union leaders discern a clear mandate for an improved quality of work life from their members, job redesign problems may well be solvable within this work-rule context.

In short, once their initial (and well-founded) suspicions have been laid to rest, unions may well cooperate in introducing quality of work life changes. Until this happens, however, both parties may have to develop some innovative new mechanisms that will overcome the problems I have been discussing.

Mechanisms for Cooperation

As suggested above, quality of work life issues pose new questions both for unions and for the collective bargaining relationship. How should management approach the union in these matters? The ideas discussed below may be useful in determining the most effective approach.

Separate Quality of Work Life Committees.   Experience with negotiations on such subjects as job evaluation and safety indicates that it might be better to establish separate union-management committees (and in large organizations, separate committees for each major department or area) to deal with quality of work life issues, rather than to subject issues in this area to the regular bargaining process. Although many of the same personnel may participate, a separate institutional framework may help divorce quality of work life from the adversary atmosphere that usually surrounds collective bargaining. Nevertheless, it will never be possible or desirable to make decisions in this area without considering their impact on the broader union-management relationship.

Joint Diagnosis of the Problem. It would be a mistake for management to decide in advance about the kinds of quality of work life changes it wishes to make—new compensation systems, for instance, or job redesign—and then to "propose" these to the union (regardless of how tentatively). This smacks too much of traditional bargaining procedures. The union may well react to such proposals by demanding offsetting concessions, and soon the parties are back to bargaining as usual.

Hopefully, proposals for change can be developed jointly by the parties, as a result of mutual agreement about the nature of the problems to be solved. One approach is for the joint quality of work life committee to begin its task with an assessment of the present state of quality of work life, although there is a danger that assessment may degenerate into blame placing. For the most part this assessment can be based on the committee members' own experiences. However, outside consultants, *jointly selected,* may be useful in polling workers' attitudes or in suggesting other ways of making the assessment activity more successful.[26]

Once the parties have diagnosed their problems and reached an agreement about what problems to deal with, the next step—not always an easy one—is to move to suggested solutions.

Proceeding Experimentally. It may be helpful to consider each step in the procedure as tentative. The fact that a suggestion is made by one party should not bind that party to it. Similarly, each change should be tried on an experimental basis at first. Wherever possible, final agreements about changes should be deferred until all parties have agreed as to their desirability.

---

26. Standard attitude analyses may not be of much value to such committees, possibly because workers are accustomed to thinking in qualitative rather than quantitative terms. An attitude survey was taken at the beginning of a quality of work life experiment at the Bolivar plant of Harman International. However, the Bolivar workforce did not show much interest in the results of the survey; only a handful of the workers ever saw or wanted to see the results of the questionnaire.

Stressing Areas Other than Productivity. Given workers' fears that quality of work life improvements may involve speedups and perhaps job losses, the productivity issue should be deemphasized, particularly at the beginning. Safety, housekeeping, equipment maintenance, and supplies are all issues that involve less radical changes in thinking than job redesign or new reward systems. The quality of work life committee may wish to defer moving into these latter areas until its members gain confidence from working together on more traditional types of reforms. On the other hand, in some situations it might be a great mistake for the committee to get itself bogged down in trivia. Possibly the important issues should be tackled first. In Chapter 4, Lawler suggests that under some conditions, quality of work life changes may begin on issues related to pay.

When the time comes to deal with job redesign, it should be approached with the goal of making jobs more intrinsically rewarding and satisfying, and not just with the goal of raising productivity. If the experiment is a success, production will increase in due course. Similarly, new reward systems should be viewed as a means of increasing workers' incomes and job security.

Economic Guarantees and Payoffs. Workers need to be reassured that quality of work life programs will not hurt them economically. If feasible, guarantees should be made that layoffs will not result from reforms. There should also be recognition that redesigned, enlarged jobs involve greater responsibility. Once workers assume some of management's functions, they may legitimately demand some of management's pay as well. Psychological rewards may not be enough; increased earnings may also be required. The Scanlon Plan (see Chapter 4) provides one mechanism for rewarding productivity gains achieved through participation.

Maintaining Union Involvement. As quality of work life experiments evolve, some decision-making authority is transferred to workers on the shop floor and the functions of the joint committee may be downgraded. Nevertheless management should continuously acknowledge the role of union leadership in helping to initiate the project. Perhaps the best way to keep the involvement of union leadership high is to bring a continuous stream of new problems to a quality of work life committee for consideration.

Consultants. Outside consultants can be useful, both in suggesting new approaches to quality of work life problems and in helping the parties work through human relations problems that may develop at either the shop-floor or the plant union-management levels. Unfortunately, not every consultant will be equally successful in this regard. Some consultants have developed life styles, value systems, modes of grooming, or specialized language that tends to turn off the average worker. Experience with management groups through organizational development (OD) efforts does not automatically qualify one to deal with union-management relations. Fortunately, there are some able consultants in this area, and it is reasonable to expect that others will develop—possibly out of the union movement, as the late Joe Scanlon did.

The Rushton Project.   This project, jointly sponsored by the United Mine Workers and the Rushton Mining Company, illustrates some of the principles described above. The following is taken from a report on the project to the Ford Foundation (University of Michigan, Institute for Social Research, 1975, Appendix A).

> The first action step at the workplace site is the establishment of a labor management committee, sometimes called a work improvement committee, or a quality of work committee. The project does not begin unless this committee has total project control and a lifetime sanction from the highest levels of the International Union and of the company. . . . At Rushton . . . it took the participants in the committee a while to fully understand that the quality of work committee was to improve work and work performance at the mine and not to focus on the usual contractual and/or grievance matters discussed in meetings between the two parties. At first, particularly among the union members, there was hesitance to speak out. This passed quickly. They found themselves beginning to examine all work-related aspects of the mine and how to improve them. The result was the preparation of what they still call "the document" (which described the experiment).
>
>   The document was ratified by a vote of the full membership of the union as an experiment. . . . A joint labor-management committee . . . supervises and monitors the experiment. . . . The original and larger group of management and union officers who drew up the "proposal" still remain. . . . This group (now called the steering committee) deals with broader policy issues while the joint labor-management committee deals with day-to-day operations.

In addition, the project has an outside consultant and an independent evaluator. One final point—in keeping with the experimental nature of the project, participation is purely voluntary and any worker may withdraw from the experimental groups at any time (and some workers have done so).

Given the tremendous diversity within the union movement and the wide variety of collective bargaining relationships that have developed throughout the country, it is very difficult to generalize with any confidence about how unions are likely to react to quality of work life

issues, except that the nature of the reactions will probably be a function of the previous bargaining history. Where the parties have developed trust and the ability to resolve differences amicably, this trust will
probably carry over to quality of work life issues. Without this kind of
relationship, however, the discussions regarding quality of work life
may well be marked by suspicion and resistance.

For participation to be effective, it must be recognized that the
union can provide an extremely important vehicle for the expression of
workers' views. If management expects to make workers so happy with
participation in quality of work life experiments that they will cast off
their union, mistrust will be inevitable. In fact, the tensions and uncertainties that almost inevitably arise during the period when quality of
work life reforms are being introduced may well bring workers closer
to their unions. Careful coordination between union and management
will be required during this transition period; certainly the human
relations skills on both sides will be sorely tested. But if the parties
work together successfully in introducing changes, relations overall are
likely to improve. Indeed, good union-management relations with regard to quality of work life experiments may reinforce participation on
other matters, including collective bargaining issues. Thus, quality of
work life issues can provide an opportunity to improve labor relations
generally.

CONCLUSION

This chapter has been concerned with the key role management plays
in influencing the quality of work life through (1) the day-to-day contacts of individual managers with members of the work force, (2) establishing policies and promoting an atmosphere that either inhibits or
facilitates a high quality of work life, and (3) redesign of jobs, administration of career and reward systems, and promotion of cohesive work
groups (the subjects of previous chapters). The first-line supervisor has
a more direct impact on quality of work life than any other member of
management, although his role should not be exaggerated.

The effective manager needs to be more than just a good guy.
Although its exact nature varies from situation to situation, consideration (emphasized during the human relations movement) is still
viewed as a necessary although no longer sufficient condition for
maintenance of a high quality of work life. Facilitation is another important function. In this chapter, facilitation has been discussed in
terms of expectancy theory, as a means whereby individual energy can
be more efficiently channeled toward organizational objectives in a
manner that leads to greater job satisfaction.

Participation is also important in achieving a high quality of work life and may not be as radical as some argue. Here I have viewed it as involving the transference of supervisory responsibilities (especially with regards to facilitation) to individuals and groups. But participation is not a panacea, despite some of the "success stories" described. Workers are still interested in higher incomes, greater job security, the elimination of health hazards from the job, early retirement, and other economic concerns. Thus, participation can be viewed by workers as a manipulative technique unless management gives them appropriate rewards, including a bigger share of the economic action, for their ideas on improving the quality of work life.

In discussing how managers can become effective in improving quality of work life, I have recognized that they must work within constraints imposed by the necessity to operate within the larger organizational system. The supervisor must have top management encouragement, support, and rewards in attempting quality of work life experiments. Top management should also recognize that organizational structure, especially span of control and the product-function issue, has an important impact on work-group effectiveness and employee satisfaction.

Some Final Words

In closing, let me confess that this chapter may well have presented a rather incomplete or distorted picture of the relationship between management and the quality of work life. In emphasizing the supervisor's personal relations with his subordinates and some aspects of participation, I have purposely slighted other considerations that may be more important to the typical worker. Quality of work life, for most workers, is heavily dependent on receiving adequate wages, having secure jobs, and working in safe, healthy environments. Whether these are present depends in part on top management's policies and in part on the general health of the economy. High quality of work life is not likely to be achieved as long as millions of workers are oppressed by fear of unemployment, industrial illness, and inability to make ends meet. Even as we pass the two hundred year mark in this nation's history, a large part of our population is still relegated to second-class economic citizenship. In the light of these problems, the issues discussed here may appear relatively trivial.

True, the approaches to improving quality of work life suggested in this chapter may have only limited utility in dealing with basic economic and social issues. Nevertheless, they can contribute both to the quality of human life and to productivity. Consideration, for example, can reduce the frustration induced by job pressures, and facilitation can reduce the frustrations that occur when work efforts are poorly directed. Participation can increase the workers' real control (not just their *sense* of control) over how they do their jobs (and for most workers, how they do their jobs is not an item of trivia). And for unionized workers participation in deciding how the job is done supplements the form of participation represented by collective bargaining. The reduction of frustrations on the job represents a worthy objective.

CHAPTER 7
STRATEGIES
FOR CHANGE*

MICHAEL BEER
Harvard University

JAMES W. DRISCOLL
Massachusetts Institute of Technology

The preceding chapters have suggested a variety of approaches to improving the quality of work life in organizations. Redesigning jobs, changing reward and pay systems, giving individuals greater influence over their careers, and more fully involving employees in decision-making are just a few of the solutions proposed. But why should managers and workers in organizations want to create these kinds of changes? If they do not want to change, can any changes in the quality of work life take place? How, for example, can the need for change be stimulated by events either internal or external to the organization? What might these events be and what social forces are required to activate them? If change is desired by people within some organizations, how can it be effected in a successful manner? Finally, what will cause these changes to be adopted by other organizations?

These are just a few of the questions to be considered when thinking about large scale changes in the quality of work life. They raise the prospect that change may be difficult to achieve. From long experience we know that perfectly good solutions often go unused because

*We would like to acknowledge the help and support of Vivian Dexter, Katherine Whitehead, and Della Burger in typing and reproducing this manuscript. Vivian Dexter was also responsible for the administration of the authors' contract and Katherine Whitehead provided editorial assistance. Their dedication and commitment have contributed substantially to the successful completion of this project.

of resistance to change by individuals, groups, and social institutions. It is likely that the innovations and improvements in the quality of work life proposed in this book will meet similar resistance. This is because improvements in the quality of work life mean changes in organizational practices, which in turn require workers and managers to modify long held attitudes, behaviors, and values.

Fortunately, there is a growing body of knowledge about the process by which change occurs. Most of the knowledge we have about organizational change stems from our observations of actual attempts, both successful and unsuccessful, to create change within organizations. We have learned, for example, that successful change follows a specific pattern of events, and we are acquiring a body of knowledge and social technology that make it possible to plan and direct those events. The field of organization development (Bennis, 1966, 1969), which will be described briefly later in this chapter, is perhaps the most notable example of our expanding knowledge and social technology of change.

If the quality of work life is to change within society as a whole, our perspective of the change process must broaden considerably to incorporate not only the necessary conditions for change required *within* an organization but also the conditions that must be developed *outside* the organization. In this chapter, we will consider not only strategies for change applicable within an organization but also strategies that originate in the community and the society at large.

Writers about and advocates of change typically take a relatively narrow view of how change can and should be brought about. Some advocate structural change in organizations and society. Others advocate knowledge or attitudinal change as the means for bringing about broader organizational or societal changes. Some hold that the development of trust and collaboration is an important precondition for change, while still others suggest that change can be created only through the development and use of power. It is not our purpose, however, to prescribe a particular strategy for changing the quality of work life, because we do not believe that any one best strategy exists. Instead, the desirability of a given strategy will depend on the perspective and values of the individual or interest group that makes the choice to change, the locus in society of the organization or the person making the choice, the situation in which the change is to occur, the stage in the overall change process at which the choice is made, and many other complex factors. In other words, the question of how to create change cannot be answered simply through a better understanding of the change process. It depends equally on our values and on the position we occupy in relation to the issues or the institution in question.

In this chapter we present a broad conceptual framework for understanding the change process, and a broad range of options for creating change in the quality of work life. The important point we wish to make throughout is that there are many different strategies, that choices must be made, and that not one but several change strategies can be effective in improving the quality of work life.

PATTERNS OF SUCCESSFUL AND UNSUCCESSFUL CHANGE

To increase the probability that change in the quality of work life will occur within organizations, we must know more about how successful changes unfold. With such knowledge the change agent or agency (consultant, manager, government, union, or community interest group) can more effectively plan actions and programs that will result in desired permanent changes. Too often lack of such knowledge has caused substantial waste in time, money, and resources. What appears to be a good means to create change may (1) trigger no change at all, (2) create change that is only temporary, or (3) trigger change that has many unplanned and often undesirable consequences.

Conditions Required for Successful Change.   The study of change has led to an understanding that successful organizational change usually occurs because some key conditions exist (Buchanan, 1967; Greiner, 1967). Below is a list of conditions that have to exist for quality of work life changes to get started and to become permanent.

1. People in the organization must feel *pressure* in order to be ready to change. High rates of turnover or absenteeism, high grievance rates, sabotage, complaints and hostility, and labor problems can create *internal* pressures for improving the quality of work life. *External* pressures include poor productivity that makes the firm less competitive, pressures for change from community interest groups, or pressures for change from government regulations enforceable by sanctions. These pressures often result in changes of leaders or leadership behavior, which in turn cause reexamination of past practices and current problems and prepare the way for organizational change. Many of the community and societal level strategies we discuss in later sections serve to create pressures on the organization and thereby force reexamination and change. On the other hand, the organization development strategy, also discussed later, stresses the need for *continual* reexamination so that external pressures and changes in leadership hopefully will not be necessary to get change moving. Reexamination is expected to create readiness to change.

2. Participation and involvement of people in reexamining prob-

lems and practices are needed to build commitment to change, and to assure that behaviors and attitudes once changed remain changed without surveillance and control. As discussed by Strauss (Chapter 6), a collaborative change process also assures higher quality solutions to problems, because people in the organization often know more about the problem than so-called experts from outside the organization or leaders at the top. Furthermore, participative practices help management learn about the needs of people and allow these needs to be reflected in the final solution. This suggests that employees who might be affected by changes should be involved in restructuring work and management practices. This is not to say that change cannot or should not occur through unilateral directive. Sometimes this is the only feasible alternative. However, this approach does not result in the same level of commitment and therefore requires tighter control to assure continuation of the change. Even when external directives are the means by which leaders are stimulated to create change in their organization, these leaders must still involve those who must change their behavior in order to gain commitment.

3. Some new ideas, models, or concepts must be brought in from the outside to help people in the organization find new approaches to management and to work that will improve the quality of work life. Thus, organizations must have access to new alternatives of the kind discussed in the other chapters in this book. As we shall see in later sections, this means that a change strategy at the organizational or societal level calls for research and perhaps even the development of experimental organizations to demonstrate the feasibility of improvements.

4. To ensure early success and prevent massive failures that can slow the momentum of change, early innovations leading to improvements should be *limited in scope*. Not until the change has been demonstrated to be feasible and learning has occurred from small-scale experimentation should changes be spread widely throughout an organization. As we shall see in later sections, this is not only true for changes within an organization, but also for changes conceived on a societal level. Government must encourage and subsidize leading-edge applications before broad-scale societal changes are undertaken.

5. A skilled leader or consultant is often needed to bring in new ideas, catalyze the process of reexamination, and support individuals in the process of improving the quality of work life. The leader serves as sponsor of the change, and can help people learn and move through the change. Even when change is triggered by external pressures, a leader or consultant is often needed within the organization to translate these pressures into change. As we shall see in later sections, an organizational or national strategy to change the quality of work life

must be concerned with making these types of change resources available. The field of organization development provides professionals capable of helping organizations improve the quality of work life.

The Three Phases of a Change Process.   Research on the patterns of successful changes suggests that they unfold in a three-phase process. These phases were first postulated by Kurt Lewin (Schein, 1961) to describe how people change. Organizations are composed of people, and so it is not surprising that this same three-phase pattern seems to be descriptive of organizational change as well (Greiner, 1967). The three phases are as follows (see Chapter 1 for a fuller discussion of the change process):

1. **Unfreezing.** A decrease in the strength of old attitudes, values, and behaviors. This results from new information or experiences that disconfirm the individual's perception of self, others, and events.
2. **Change.** The development of new attitudes, values, or behaviors through imitation of a model or through successful experimentation with new behaviors and attitudes.
3. **Refreezing.** The stabilization of change through supportive group norms, culture, or structures such as organizational policy, reward systems, and so forth.

The reader will recognize the similarity between Lewin's three-phase change model and the conditions for successful change listed above. For example, external and internal pressures are needed to unfreeze people in an organization. Participation is an important means for achieving attitude and value changes, as is experimentation with new ideas and concepts that are later found to be successful. Throughout this chapter the reader will want to evaluate the potential effectiveness of any given change strategy or combination of strategies by the extent to which they encompass all three phases in Lewin's model.

The Issue of Power.   We have already pointed out that participation in change by those affected is important if the change is to be successful. But participation also means sharing of power by those in positions of power. A major factor in unsuccessful change efforts has been found to be the use of unilateral power by those at the top of the organization, as opposed to shared decision-making between those in positions of power and those who have to change their behavior (Greiner and Barnes, 1970). Failure also results when top management totally delegates the responsibility for change to lower levels and remains uninvolved in the planning, execution, and evaluation of change.

It is our view that changes in the quality of work life require a *shared* power approach. This means redistribution of power, with lower levels gaining considerable influence in managing the change —and in many cases increasing their influence in the management of the organization as well. For example, uninteresting and un-challenging jobs are usually due in part to the fact that decision-making and control have been placed at too high a level (see Hackman, Chapter 3). To deal with this problem, management must be willing to have its power to determine the nature of jobs challenged. Management must further be willing to sit down with workers and discuss the situation, so that new solutions can be developed that draw on workers' experience. The problem cannot be solved unilaterally, because much of the knowledge about how jobs might be restructured effectively resides at lower levels. Finally, management must be willing to make permanent changes in the amounts of responsibility, decision-making, and control at lower levels in the organization. It must be willing to give up some controls now present in higher level jobs and move this control downward.

Why must the power and influence of people at lower levels be increased (relative to those at higher levels) for improvement in the quality of work life to occur? Unless those in positions of power are willing to accept influence from lower levels, (1) they will not hear those at lower levels and so will not learn about their values and needs or about the conditions in the organization that require change, (2) they will not obtain feedback about how their own behaviors or policies are contributing to problems because those at lower levels will see such feedback as futile, (3) relevant information from the bottom will not get into the decision process to increase the quality of the final solutions developed, and (4) people at the bottom will not develop independence, responsibility, and self-directed behavior. In short, power differentials in organizations prevent either effective sensing of what is going on or adaptive behavior to cope with what is sensed. This is particularly true when management must sense and respond to concerns about the quality of work life. These issues are often a reflec-tion of the way power and influence are distributed, and their elimina-tion requires that the influence of those at lower levels increase.

It is doubtful that the top management of any organization can be counted on to voluntarily increase the influence and power of those at lower levels except when the performance of the organization is so poor that its very survival is threatened. In other words, pressures beyond those generated by the natural forces of the marketplace will probably be needed. We will discuss numerous change strategies that originate outside the organization and involve community interest groups, unions, and government. Many of these strategies create direct pressures on organizations to improve the quality of work life and thus force redistribution of influence in dealing with these issues. Many of these external strategies also directly increase the psychological or legal power of those at lower levels, enhancing their ability to raise issues, provide feedback to the top, or influence quality of work life decisions.

The important point we wish to make here is that any broadly conceived effort to improve the quality of work life, whether within an organization or on a national level, must find ways to increase the influence of those at lower levels over factors that affect the quality of work life. The dynamics of successful change require this. Interestingly, such changes in power distribution can result in more power for everyone (Tannenbaum, 1962) and more control for the whole organization (Buchanan, 1967). Thus, many of the fears that more power for lower levels will result in an out-of-control organization do not seem well founded.

STRATEGIC CONSIDERATIONS IN MANAGING CHANGE

In order to move change along, the change agent (manager, union leader, employee, consultant, government official, or outside agitator) must decide on a strategy. What will be the target of his change effort? What divisions of the organization should he attack first? What should be the pace of change? Should the change effort start at the top, the middle, or the bottom? These and many other questions face the change agent in planning and evaluating a change effort. The answers to some of these questions will be determined by the situation. Others may be within the control of the change agent.

In this section we will present a series of dilemmas that must be considered by the change agent in creating and managing change. In most cases we discuss the dilemma as if the change agent must choose between extremes. Obviously, a strategy need not adhere to extremes, for a middle course is possible in most situations and is often desirable. But the change agent must be clear about how the change program measures up with respect to each of the dilemmas, and he must be aware of the impact or consequences implied or predicted. The reader will want to use these strategic considerations in evaluating the various change strategies reviewed in this and the other chapters. For the change agent, such a review can be useful at various stages in a change effort because it can lead to modifications in strategy to achieve desired results.

Appropriate versus Inappropriate Definition of Change-Target Boundaries. An effort to improve the quality of work life must define appropriate boundaries for the change. Is the objective to change an individual, a group, a plant, a corporation, or society as a whole?

Clarity about the boundaries of the change target is important for a number of reasons.

First, institutions are self-stabilizing systems that can absorb extremely large amounts of energy without changing very much. Thus, any successful change effort must concentrate change resources to achieve a critical mass—a self-sustaining momentum of change energized by people in the organization, rather than forces outside it.

For this reason, the size of the change target must be proportional to the change resources available. By change resources we mean the people, money, and time needed to unfreeze, change, and refreeze the system.[1] It is better to concentrate change resources successfully on a limited target than to waste inadequate resources on a larger target. Many change efforts go astray because they target a whole corporation, a whole community, or a society in general. If the target is a large system, then developing a critical mass in a subunit such as a plant or division may be a more effective first step. Change resources can then be freed to concentrate on the next larger subunit. Furthermore, the momentum in the first subunit can be used to move change along in other subunits, by utilizing experiences and resources from the first unit and by leveraging success. The federal government's Equal Employment Opportunity Commission (EEOC) enforcement strategy reflects this approach. It targeted American Telephone and Telegraph Corporation (AT&T) as its first major test case rather than attempting across-the-board enforcement.

A second reason change-target boundaries must be clearly defined is that failure can result when key people in the organization are against the change. Thus, the change target and its boundaries must be defined with the orientation of the key power figures in mind. It is important that the change effort be aimed at a system where the power figures are (at a minimum) neutral to the change, and preferably positive, supportive, and even involved in it.

Finally, an effective change program must be able to affect enough of the critical organizational dimensions (such as leadership, job structure, communication, and rewards) and components (people or subunits) so that the total system can change. Thus, the change target should be reasonably autonomous. If an organization is highly interdependent with other parts of a larger system, sufficient progress cannot be made without also including the subsystems with which it is interdependent.

The decision about the appropriate boundaries for a change program is never clearcut. A series of trade-offs must be considered. The less encompassing the change target (small department versus whole

---

1. By system we mean a social system like an organization, community or society. For a more complete definition of systems, see Suttle (Chapter 1).

corporation), the less autonomous it is likely to be (it is usually affected by structures and policies of the larger system) but the more practical it is to concentrate enough change resources. A corporation is more autonomous than a plant, for example, but it is rarely practical to think about attacking such a system as a whole. Furthermore, the appropriate boundary will depend on one's perspective. From the perspective of a government, the corporate unit may be an appropriate target. From the perspective of the community, various plants of larger corporations may be the appropriate targets. From the perspective of a change agent inside the corporation, a division or other reasonably autonomous but receptive unit may be the appropriate target.

The need to define change-target boundaries is particularly critical for quality of work life changes initiated by the government. It seems unlikely that a whole society is a meaningful target, even though broad social change might be the ultimate objective. A critical mass could probably not be achieved. Government's role might be to create a context that will unfreeze large systems within the society, and then to encourage the appropriate application of resources within the system to facilitate change.

Changing People versus Changing Social Structure.   There are two schools of thought about the best way to create change in social institutions. The first has focused on changing *individuals* through a variety of training and educational experiences. At an organizational level this school of thought has led to the widespread use of management training programs and sensitivity training programs. At a societal level this approach is reflected in the development of an extensive educational system.

The second school of thought is more concerned with changing the *structures* of organizations and society than it is with modifying the knowledge or attitudes of individuals. This school maintains that changes in people are best accomplished indirectly, by creating changes in those social structures that shape behavior. At the organizational level this approach would lead to changing organizational structure (see Chapter 6), compensation and reward systems (see Chapter 4), technology, administrative controls, and job structure (see Chapter 3). At a societal level, this approach to changing the quality of work life might lead to legislation that sets standards in this area, or to policies regarding the use of technology in the manufacturing of goods or the delivery of services.

An effective change program must come to grips with the choice presented by these two strategies. Are the primary resources to be put into educating managers in how to improve their managerial approaches? Or is the main thrust to be change in the structures of the organization or society? The evidence indicates that both of these approaches are needed in an effective change program. This is because individuals whose attitudes and knowledge change through educational programs are often unable to maintain the change in the face of organizational constraints (Fleishman, Harris, and Burtt, 1955), and changes in organizational and social structures often unfreeze people but do not provide sufficient guidance in how attitudes and behaviors are to change.

It is our contention that a program leading to change in the quality of work life needs to employ and balance both of these strategies (Beer and Huse, 1972; Seashore and Bowers, 1963). The questions which need continual examination are: (1) How much of each of these strategies is appropriate? and (b) What is the best sequence for employing these two strategies (that is, should they be employed simultaneously or should one usually precede the other)?

The sequencing of structural changes and attitude or knowledge changes should depend on the outcomes the change agent finds acceptable and the situation surrounding change. More specifically, structural changes will create behavioral changes very rapidly, but will also create uncertainty and insecurity in people (Tushman, 1974). Thus, frustration and anger directed at the change agent or the change effort are likely to arise. On the other hand, a change effort aimed at involving people and creating attitude change first, while slower, will result in a building of commitment; however, it may also result in frustration as individuals attempt to employ new behaviors and find them blocked by structural constraints. In this situation, anger and hostility are likely to be focused at the organization rather than at the change agent or effort. The change agent's motivation and values will determine which of these two sets of consequences is most desirable. Fortunately, however, a choice between consequences is not always necessary. For example, structural changes can be accompanied by efforts to help people adjust and adapt.

In what situation is one strategy more likely to be effective than another? It would seem to us that when those empowered to make structural changes have a good diagnosis of the situation, structural changes can be made first. On the other hand, when it is not clear what structural changes are required, educational interventions aimed at knowledge and attitude change must come first, so that the people who will be most affected by the structural changes can be involved in determining what form those changes will take. It is likely that the latter condition will exist in organizations and situations with highly complex and changing tasks. In routine situations, changes can start with structure, because problems are probably known to those who must make the structural changes.

Power Strategies versus Collaborative Strategies.[2]   A major choice facing an agent of social change is between the use of power tactics and the use of collaboration. In the first approach, the focus is on building a power base and using that power to create change through pressure and coercion. In the second approach, the focus is on developing a relationship of trust and mutual influence leading to voluntary change.

Power to create change may be built by gaining control over valued resources and making the target of change dependent on the agent of change. For example, if the government were to legislate quality of work life standards and threaten court action for the violation of such standards, this would constitute a power strategy. The legislation would provide the power. However, other groups who do not have such power could attempt to develop it by pressuring an organization in which change is desired. For example, groups with common grievances about the quality of work life could band together within one organization, within one community, or on a national scale to demand and advocate change. Threats of unfavorable publicity, work stoppages, unionization, strikes, or even violence would build a power base that could compel change.

To create change through collaboration, the change agent increases the level of trust and attraction between himself and the change target. For example, if the government were interested in using such a strategy to create change in the quality of work life, it might create an agency concerned with helping organizations to collect information about quality of work life and to move toward its improvement. A corporation might create an organization development group to accomplish the same purpose. An organizationally or community-based advocacy group might act to minimize the perceived differences between itself and those in power. To do so, it would advocate cooperation and problem-solving as the means for creating change. It would probably attempt to act reasonably and with restraint.

Creating change often means combining the power and collaborative strategies. Depending on the situation, the strategies may be mixed simultaneously or sequenced to achieve maximum impact. The most obvious way to mix these strategies is for different groups to apply different strategies. However, simultaneous use of power and collaborative strategies by different groups probably requires that the groups be independent of each other. This is because an individual or group associated with a power strategy would have difficulty developing the trust needed to implement a collaborative strategy. For example, a community group or union might use power strategies, while an

---

2. This discussion is based in part on an article by Richard Walton (1965).

internal organization development group or outside agency uses the collaborative model to facilitate change in the quality of work life. In this situation, pressure from the union or community group would hopefully create the conditions that would lead to utilization of the organization development (OD) group within the organization.

In other situations, a single group, such as a union or advocacy group, might apply a power strategy to equalize power and then use collaboration to problem-solve toward change. In these situations, it is unlikely that the power and collaborative strategy will be acted out in the same forum. For example, cooperative efforts between union and management on such issues as safety usually occur in committees that are commissioned by the collective bargaining process but operate outside the arena of contract negotiations. A single group might also choose to use collaboration first, in the hope of minimizing the need for the power strategy; the power strategy would be considered only as a backup.

Each of these alternatives has different costs and benefits that must be weighed in light of the change objectives, the time frame of the change, the readiness and willingness to change on the part of the change target, and the importance of sustaining change in the future. Power strategies are probably needed where (1) the change target is not ready for change, (2) the change agent is not recognized as legitimate by the change target, (3) time is critical, and (4) the change target knows what must be done to bring about change. Collaborative strategies are more likely to be useful (1) where power is more or less equal, (2) when an organization is unfrozen, (3) where there is plenty of time, and (4) where the target of change needs help in changing. All other things being equal, collaborative strategies have the advantage of creating changes to which people are committed. Power strategies require surveillance to assure continuation of new practices and therefore can only be applied when desired changes are clearly observable or measurable.

The change agent should consider using either of the two strategies, recognize that they represent alternatives, make a choice between them, or perhaps use them in concert.

Research and Development versus Process Facilitation. Is the best way to create change in the quality of work life through the development of new knowledge and social technology, or is it through helping people and organizations to identify human problems and develop their own solutions to these problems? The first strategy, *the research and development (R&D) model,* has been used successfully in the physical sciences. This model requires sizable expenditures in social science research leading to new knowledge and solutions to human problems in organizations. The second strategy, the *process facilitation model,* emphasizes the need for people to become aware of specific quality of work life problems in their own organizations, and to develop their own solutions to these problems. Awareness, new solutions, and action are *not* brought in from the outside but are developed by those affected, with the help of process consultants (Schein, 1969b) who catalyze a process of inquiry, invention, and action. Such an approach calls for substantial expenditures in developing process consulting resources.

Underlying each of these approaches are specific assumptions about change. The R&D strategy assumes that when new knowledge is developed it will be utilized. An inadequate amount of new knowledge and innovation prevents change. The facilitation model assumes that change is prevented by a conflict between new solutions and existing attitudes and values. New organizational and work solutions must be developed by the organizational members who are to be affected, not brought in by experts—although experts can be a significant resource (Argyris, 1973a; Schein, 1969a).

Changes in the quality of work life will require that both of these strategies be used in some situations. The key questions have to do with the mixing and phasing of the two. In the domain of human affairs, we have historically placed too much emphasis on the traditional research models. In many instances a significant lag exists between the development of knowledge and its utilization. In the field of education, for example, innovations that have been available for a quarter of a century are still not used in many schools and colleges (Stiles and Robinson, 1973). This would suggest that more emphasis should have been placed on developing systems and processes for delivering innovations. Perhaps even more important—needed changes in education should have been defined by those who have had to adopt them; these same people could even have begun to develop solutions themselves. R&D could then have become an outcome of early attempts at innovation in practice rather than a *guide* for such changes.

Because creating quality of work life changes in organizations requires significant changes in the values, attitudes, and traditions of workers, unions, and management, the process facilitation strategy must be a key. This is not to say that research on attitudes and values could not help shape a more effective process facilitation strategy. Research that points toward major problems, toward means of change, and toward alternative organizational and work models can indeed complement a process facilitation strategy. Efficiency would probably dictate, however, that the development of resources to facilitate change should precede any substantial investment in R&D. If this were done, greater readiness to utilize R&D would exist.

In summary, careful balancing of the R&D and process facilitation strategies is required for successful change to occur. For the change agent this represents a constant dilemma that must be managed. At both the societal and the organizational levels, difficult decisions must be made about the amount of money to be spent on process facilitation resources and on applied research.

Market Strategies versus Collective or Revolutionary Strategies. In the planning of change, a choice exists between a strategy that relies on market forces and a strategy that relies on collective action (Coleman, 1973). In a market strategy, the change agent attempts to develop a few individuals and organizations who, because of their superior capability, clearly perform better than individuals and organizations that have not undergone similar development. Change in an organization or in society as a whole is achieved gradually, as the virtues of the changed way of doing things are recognized and the changes are adopted by others. In effect, market forces move change along. Thus, changes in society as a whole are an aggregate of many changes in individuals and organizations.

Collective or revolutionary strategies approach change from a different direction. Their emphasis is on changing societal or organizational constraints that shape the behavior of many individuals and organizational units. To achieve these changes a number of different approaches are possible, depending on the situation. Where the change agent is in a powerful position, he can impose structures, policies, and rules to assure uniform adoption of new practices or behaviors. Where the change agent is *not* in a powerful position to change system-wide constraints, he can organize individuals and organizations into political interest groups aimed at removing any constraints that might block the adoption of new behaviors. This approach also has the secondary effect of changing the participants themselves. Involvement in the collective movement causes participants to undergo changes in attitudes and values which, in turn, fuel further change. The Community Action Program, part of the War on Poverty, is an excellent example of this strategy. It changed individuals' capacities for initiative and self-direction as much if not more than it changed communities (Marris and Rein, 1973). The development of a network of organizations with similar problems and lobbying intentions would be an example of collective action by organizations. When collective action does not create sufficient change to reduce the level of frustration created by system constraints, revolution or societal upheaval can result.

Within an organization, a market strategy would call for the development of model plants or organizations that hopefully stimulate others to try similar changes. A collective strategy would organize individuals with common grievances and aspirations to seek change, or, if the change agent is in a position of power, would result in top-down directives aimed at achieving uniform change by everyone.

At a societal level, a market strategy would provide funds to organizations seeking to experiment with improving the quality of work life. Effective performance of these organizations would, over time, cause others to adopt similar changes. Similarly, a market strategy would dictate removing barriers that prevent individuals from moving from one organization to another. Presumably differences in the quality of work life between organizations would result in a flow of labor that would influence organizations to change. A collective strategy at a societal level might include the development of organizational associations or associations of individuals dedicated to improvement in the quality of work life. Models for this are the OD Network and the Scanlon Associates of the Midwest. The former is a collection of individuals dedicated to changing organizations through organization development. The latter is a collection of corporations dedicated to principles of the Scanlon Plan (Frost, Wakeley, and Ruh, 1974). Other forms of collective action at the societal level might be more militant. An example is the formation of a political interest group whose aim would be to pressure organizations to improve the quality of work life through changes in policy and practices.

The government can create conditions for a collective strategy at the societal level by providing resources to groups, of individuals or organizations, that encourage collective action, and by legislation that protects such groups against arbitrary action by those in powerful positions. For example, the National Labor Relations Act provides such protection to unions. Also, the government would be implementing a collective strategy by passing legislation that enforces uniform adoption of specific management and work practices.

Market and collective strategies have their advantages and disadvantages. An effective change strategy will probably mix these approaches, depending on a variety of situational considerations and desired outcomes. Market strategies are inherently slower; collective strategies are faster but potentially more threatening to those in power and to those opposed to change. Thus, polarization, extreme conflict, and even violence are more likely with collective strategies. Market strategies allow individualized applications of innovation in the quality of work life; collective strategies are likely to standardize and reduce differences.

Perhaps the most important determinant of the effectiveness of the two strategies is the extent to which an organization or society is centralized, hierarchical, controlling, or authoritarian (Coleman, 1973). Market strategies are more likely to work in a pluralistic society, in decentralized organizations, and in open and loose systems. For example, Marris and Rein (1973) describe an experimental or market approach employed by the Ford Foundation in the fight against poverty and juvenile delinquency. No across-the-board national programs could be started because President Eisenhower was a conservative. On the other hand, collective strategies, whether they are top-down or bottom-up, are more likely to develop and be applicable in a hierarchical system where controls are too tight to allow a market strategy to evolve. Such strategies will apply to highly centralized companies and authoritarian societies.

Centrally Planned Change versus Decentralized Change. The choice between market and collective strategies discussed in the previous section overlaps somewhat with the choice of whether change should be centrally planned from the top or allowed to unfold decentrally from the middle or bottom. In many instances, the extent to which a choice between centralized and decentralized change exists is determined by the circumstances. One cannot speak of top-down or centrally planned change unless the society or organization is hierarchically run and those in power are willing to initiate change. Indeed, centrally controlled and planned change is not likely to be possible in a pluralistic and democratic society or a highly decentralized organization. It is only when an opportunity exists to move change by utilizing the power invested in those at the top that the change agent is faced with this choice.

When opportunities for top-down change are present, should they be taken? Such a decision should be based on the advantages and disadvantages of top-down change, not on the availability of sympathetic power to push change through. There are several important considerations in resolving the dilemma between top-down and bottom-up change (Morris, 1964; Rogers, 1973).

1. Do all the members of the organization or society have common goals and values? To the extent that an organization or society is homogeneous on these dimensions, top-down change is possible without creating major resistance and incurring hostility caused by lack of involvement.

2. To what extent do people in the system desire personal involvement and participation? To the extent that they do, a decentralized or bottom-up strategy is more desirable.

3. To what extent are the costs of inaction greater than the costs of action? If inaction is more costly, top-down change—which is more rapid—is desirable, even though negative consequences accrue because of lack of ownership and commitment to change.

4. To what extent are various subsystems (organizations in a soci-

ety or departments and divisions in an organization) similar in their tasks, people, and problems? To the extent that they are dissimilar, a decentralized strategy is more appropriate because unique solutions are required.

5. To what extent are the changes likely to threaten the power elite's basic values and power? To the extent that changes are threatening, they are likely to be squashed by those in power. Thus, when changes of this type are planned they should begin at the top.

6. To what extent are the change agent and the system willing and able to tolerate conflict? Bottom-up change involves more conflict as change affects successively higher levels of authority that are resistant. The change agent and system must be able to tolerate this conflict to allow the change process to run its course.

The dilemma between centrally planned change and decentralized change probably cannot be solved by a choice of one or the other. Some aspects of planned change, such as changes in system-wide policies or structure, may be better handled centrally; other aspects, such as changes in local practices, should be handled in a decentralized manner. Furthermore, an organization or a society is not purely authoritarian or pluralistic. In making choices about a strategy, the nature of authority in the system, the objective of the change, and considerations described above need to be taken into account.

The reader will also recognize that top-down change will probably induce new behaviors because people fear sanctions; bottom-up change will be more voluntary and self-directed. To the extent that the objective is change in the basic values and personal competence of individuals, bottom-up change will be the desired choice. Improving the quality of work life in organizations sometimes requires changes in personal values. When it does, top-down change can be considered only at a cost to this outcome.

Rapid versus Slow Change. In a planned change effort, the pace of change is governed by strategic decisions about the *means* of change. Once determined, the pace has specific consequences that must be clearly understood in planning the change. The contrast between a rapid pace and a slow pace is clearly demonstrated in the following descriptions of two different change efforts (Rose, 1965).

The first excerpt summarizes the impressions that observers had of a community development effort in Eastern Quebec.

> The [change agents] of Eastern Quebec are clearly in a great hurry. Their constituents must be motivated quickly; their plans must be accepted quickly by the provincial government. The times are urgent. Justice must be done. The alternatives are serious—social disaster? revolution? If their recommendations are not accepted and implemented quickly, the [change

agents] themselves may be forced to seek political power. They hold that the term "Welfare State" is in contrast to the concept of "true planning." Welfare services are apparently equated with attempts by "The Establishment" to adjust people to the social and economic structure rather than adjust the structure to the needs of the people. Planning, on the other hand, requires the development of a new structure based upon new discoveries in the applied social sciences and social administration as practiced in the underdeveloped nations of Africa and Asia.

The second description is a report on a community development effort sponsored by UNICEF in the Ivory Coast. It conveys an entirely different impression of the pace of change.

On the Ivory Coast a team of two [change agents] (one male, one female) travel to a village and take up residence. They must wait several months, perhaps six, before their assistance is requested in such tasks as securing a new water supply by digging a well in an appropriate location, or building some form of community structure, or assisting in the cultivation of a crop through a new technique. Their stance is one of patient reticence until asked for help, and then they proffer advice with the most careful attention to social and culture roles of the villagers.

In the first case the pace of change was rapid, even feverish. The air is one of excitement and a commitment to political change, by radical means if necessary. In the second case, the pace is slow, deliberate, and patient. It is as if there is all the time in the world to introduce a higher material standard of living.

The difference in pace is a function of the strategies chosen. A fast pace is created by the use of power strategies rather than the more collaborative strategy in the second example; by a collective strategy rather than a market strategy; and by structural changes in policy and planning rather than gradual educational strategies aimed at changing people. Rapid change is further fueled by a deliberate attempt to raise expectations and to develop a constituency for the goals of the change program. On the other hand, slower paced change takes people where they are and gears the pace of change to people's growth in needs and expectations. Structural changes, collective action, and power strategies can be used to raise expectations or to create discontent.

Perhaps the best example of the effects of rapid change comes from the Community Action Programs that were part of the Office of Economic Opportunity's (OEO) War on Poverty of the late 1960s. The involvement of the poor in planning and organizing programs (collective strategy) through a new community action organization separate from existing community agencies (power strategy) often resulted in polarization, conflict, and the alienation of people in established community agencies and in the political structure. The rapid pace at which community action organizations were set up and expectations were created developed a constituency for change and developed people's sense of responsibility for their own destinies. But it also resulted in failures, such as the Job Corps. These failures occurred in part because solutions were hastily developed and support for the changes was not developed. They were ultimately used by the opposition as reasons for withdrawing political and economic support (Marris and Rein, 1973). In other words, the forces that were set in motion by a rapid pace of change ultimately killed the program.

How fast should a change effort progress? This is a continuing dilemma that must be managed by the change agent. He must find the appropriate balance between a slow pace that does not create the conflict needed to change things and a rapid pace that creates so much conflict that polarization develops and those opposed to change move to stop it.

Solving Problems versus Changing Individual Dispositions and Organizational Culture. Is the objective of a change effort to solve a particular problem, or is it to create healthy personal dispositions and organizations immune to a reappearance of the same problems? A variety of symptoms might trigger the need for improving the quality of work life—high levels of dissatisfaction, a large number of grievances, turnover, absenteeism, low cooperation between labor and management, destructive behavior by employees, or outside pressure by community groups. A program to improve the quality of work life could concentrate primarily on alleviating these problems. The emphasis would be on diagnosing problems and developing solutions to them. On the other hand, a change program with longer-range objectives might also be developed. Such a program would not only contend with immediate problems, but would, through the process of solving immediate problems, attempt to create permanent changes in the psychological disposition of individuals and in the culture of the organization. These changes would be aimed at creating an organization in which such problems would not occur, or at the very least an organization capable of dealing with these problems without help or intervention from outside.

Solving organizational problems does, obviously, contribute to the individual's and organization's capacity to deal with similar problems in the future. To the extent that this is true, there is no distinction between short-range change programs aimed at solving problems and long-range change programs aimed at creating changes in people and culture. It is our contention, however, that the character of a change program would be substantially different if an explicit objective of changing organizational culture and personal dispositions were held by the change agent.

In a change program aimed at long-range individual and organizational development, the change agent would go well beyond the immediate solution. Considerable effort would be expended in helping people in the target organization learn about how their personal dispositions have contributed to the problems experienced, and how group and organizational norms shape behavior. Significant efforts would be undertaken to help people examine themselves and develop skills, attitudes, and values that increase the range of behaviors available to them, and thereby increase their adaptive, coping capabilities. Similarly, time and energy would be invested in redesigning group and organizational culture to reinforce more adaptive behavior. In other words, people and groups would be helped to learn how to learn.

A long-range program aimed at personal and cultural changes would require a longer time frame. The change agent would continue a relationship with the organization well beyond the initial change introduced to solve a problem. Furthermore, participation and involvement of organizational members would be high, to provide opportunities for personal learning and cultural change. Significant efforts would be undertaken to help people grow and develop through educational and training experiences.

What is the relevance of this issue to the improvement of the quality of work life in organizations? The change agent must be clear about the extent to which a particular change introduced to improve the quality of work life can stand alone, or the extent to which more fundamental changes in values or personality are required for quality of work life to be maintained or improved. For example, if control systems are modified to provide more freedom for the individual, do supervisors and workers need to learn new attitudes and behaviors required to operate within this new structure? It is doubtful that a highly controlling supervisor or a highly dependent worker could function in a work structure that increased worker responsibility and freedom.

Mainly because individual needs and expectations will continue to change in the future, organizations that want to improve and maintain a high quality of work life will require adaptive workers, managers, and structures. To achieve this, organizational members will have to become more independent, less authoritarian, more capable of trusting and collaborative relationships, more capable of making choices, more open and capable of listening, less power-oriented and more achievement-oriented, less quick to attribute motives, and more supportive. To support these changes in personal orientations, the cultural norms of organizations also will have to change. It is hard to conceive that organizational members will be able to negotiate better congruity between personal needs and organizational requirements unless management and workers alike take on at least some of the dispositions cited. This is particularly true with respect to power and authority orientations.

Short-range problem-solving goals will probably be accomplished by an expert or R&D strategy, a power strategy, within a short time horizon, or by structural changes. But fundamental changes in people and culture will probably best be accomplished through a process facilitation strategy, a collaborative approach, within a longer time horizon, and through a people-change strategy. We do not want to suggest an irreconcilable dichotomy, for it is primarily a matter of emphasis. The change agent must be clear about his change goals and choose his strategies and time horizons accordingly.

The extent to which a change effort accomplishes the long-range and more fundamental goals of personal and cultural change will depend on the extent to which the change target feels ownership of the change. We now turn to this issue.

Are the Source, Target, and Vehicle of Change the Same?   The extent of commitment to change, permanency of change, and depth of change is directly related to whether the person or organization that is to undergo change (the target) is both the initiator of change (the source) and the mover of change (the vehicle). To the extent that the source, target, and vehicle are one and the same, fewer potential problems arise from the change process, more ownership and commitment to change are developed, solutions are more appropriate and of higher quality, and change is self-sustaining.

Unfortunately, change cannot always be self-generated. Organizations that may need to examine the quality of work life may not experience sufficient dissatisfaction to energize them to start down a road to change. In such situations the source of energy for change may have to come from pressures created by employee groups, community groups, or government. When such pressures are required to trigger change, careful attention must be given to transferring the energy and motivation for change to the target organization. Unless this is done, the organization will cease to change once the pressure is removed. Current efforts by EEOC to increase minority hiring and advancement represent a situation where energy and motivation have not yet been transferred to target organizations. The threat of legal action is still the primary stimulus for these types of change in most organizations.

Ownership and self-sustained change may be possible even when the source and target of change are not one and the same. One way to do this is to ensure that the target organization becomes the vehicle for change. It plans and implements the changes, rather than having them imposed by the source of change. Thus, where outside pressure is required to initiate change in the quality of work life, it is important that specific solutions not be imposed. Rather, the pressure should be directed at stimulating a process of change that involves people in developing their own solutions.

This probably means that a national strategy for improving the quality of work life should start with organizations that want to change. These organizations have the best probability of changing, and changes in them can develop a momentum that will carry others along. We are not suggesting that less willing organizations should not be targeted. This should only be done, however, with a clear understanding of the approaches needed to overcome lack of motivation and ownership. For example, the external pressure group (community or government) that arouses the need to change (source) should concern itself with whether the organization has the consulting resources (vehicle) to lead it through a collaborative change process. Unless this occurs, the organization will be unable to change, and the external group will have to become more and more specific in the solution it would like. Ownership of change will be lost and only surface change is likely.

Phasing of Change.   The process of change is usually not smooth, and dysfunctional changes often occur. Individuals and organizations are comparable to biological organisms in that they are equilibrium-seeking and are composed of interdependent components or subsystems (see Chapter 1). Thus, planned change in one part of an organization will have an impact on other parts. This impact may have negative consequences that can slow the change process and even cause regression, unless they are properly anticipated and dealt with.

Two particular unintended outcomes are likely in many change efforts, and knowledge of them may be useful in dealing with them (Kelman and Warwick, 1973). *Psychological and organizational strain* is one potential outcome of change. Changing the quality of work life in organizations can cause considerable anxiety for those affected. Managers' traditional roles and power may be threatened; traditional functions, such as industrial engineering and industrial relations, may have to change their ways; the union's roles may change. Second, changes in organizational structure and practice will result in *changes in expectations and aspirations.* Employees who have tasted autonomy and increased self-control will want more. Their desires can easily outstrip the organization's or society's ability to deliver. It may be said that in almost any change the capacity of the organization or society to satisfy people's aspirations tends to rise at a slower rate than the aspirations.

Knowing that these consequences are likely, the change agent must attempt to plan a sequence of changes that are facilitative and reinforcing of each other. For example, changes in structures and policies must be followed by efforts to help people live within these new structures. Attempts to unfreeze an organization through pressure must be accompanied by an effort to help people in the organization solve problems and find new attitudes and behaviors. A continuous balance must be sought between phases in the change process that raise expectations and phases that are aimed at removing organizational constraints that prevent satisfaction of new expectations. Unless change sequences are carefully phased, the change process may be severely impaired and human cost may be high. It is, of course, often difficult to anticipate all the spin-off effects of a change effort. Therefore, the change agent must always be ready to deal with the unplanned consequences of a planned change effort.

Growth versus Decrement Strategies.   A change effort may be distinguished by the kinds of pressures that trigger it. Most changes occur because severe problems are affecting the organization or society. A feeling of pain and dissatisfaction with the existing state of affairs will generate the energy necessary for change to occur. A planned change launched from this platform we call a *decrement program.* An example of a decrement program in the quality of work life area would be a change effort triggered by dissatisfied employees. Such change efforts typically develop a lot of thrust because a constituency for change is already energized and the motivation to change is high.

Planned change efforts can also begin when someone feels that things could be better—that improvement and growth are possible. We call such change efforts *growth programs.* People feel dissatisfied because the organization is not coming close enough to an ideal state. Change efforts based on the desire to improve and grow do not typically develop the same thrust as decrement efforts. This is because frustrations with being less than ideal are typically not as strong or as broadly based. Thus, a large and highly energized constituency does not usually exist under these circumstances.

The change agent must be clear about the motivations for change, so that the change effort can be properly managed. In a decrement strategy the key problem is managing the building of momentum in such a way that productive and functional changes result. The changes that occur are usually rapid and system-wide. In a growth strategy, the main problem is generating a constituency for change. Typically, only a few people feel dissatisfied with the state of affairs and have the vision to see alternatives. The growth strategy is aimed at capitalizing on this limited constituency. A small and limited change effort is planned with those who want to grow and improve in an attempt to heighten the differences between the change target and others. The purpose is to create dissatisfaction in those less interested in change through demonstration of successful applications and superior performance in a model organization. Such dissatisfaction is then used to start new change efforts.

In a growth effort, conflict is likely to arise when the constituency for change grows and begins to advocate changes in the larger system (organization, community, or society). This is particularly true if the advocacy is aggressive and high profile. It is at this point that factions unsympathetic to the advocated changes will attempt to block the new constituency from achieving the changes they desire. Attempts are made to dismantle or weaken the constituent organization. Again, the Community Action Programs of the late 1960s are a good example. Such efforts harnessed some existing dissatisfaction among the poor, but to a larger extent those efforts were an attempt to build a constituency for change that was not well organized and focused. Such a constituency was indeed built, but the rapid speed with which this progressed resulted in the mobilization of strong anticommunity action forces at the local and national levels, and these forces ultimately killed the effort (Marris and Rein, 1973). This suggests that a low profile and deliberate speed are called for when the strategy involves building a constituency for change. This is because the lack of an early constituency makes the effort vulnerable to more powerful groups who may be opposed to the change in the early stages.

One can ask to what extent a real constituency for change exists in the quality of work life area, and whether a decrement or a growth strategy is likely to evolve. We cannot answer this with any degree of certainty, but the extensive debate about whether employees generally are dissatisfied with the quality of their work lives suggests that strong concerns about the quality of work life may not exist. Therefore, a strong constituency for change may not be present on a national level. If this is so, a strategy for change would have to be aimed first at building a constituency. This suggests a growth strategy. The main purpose of the strategy would be to create pressures for change by applying new approaches aimed at improving the quality of work life in a limited number of receptive organizations. These would hopefully stir others to adopt similar approaches. Managers and employees who have experienced improvements in the quality of work life could then become a growing constituency, capable of advocating changes for the society at large. It is at this point that legislation to heighten the pace of change would have the best chance of being enacted and accepted. Similarly, this would be the time when community-based strategies aimed at creating external pressure for change would have the best chance of success.

We have described the problems of initiating change and moving it along under two different situations. In one a powerful constituency exists; in the other it must be built. In improving the quality of work life, it must be determined if a constituency exists and its extent. The strategies for change (power versus collaboration, rapid versus slow, market versus collective, and so forth) must be chosen accordingly.

Summary of Strategic Considerations.   In this section we have attempted to present some major strategic choices that the change agent faces. Whether the change agent is a dissatisfied employee or manager, an organized community group, a professional behavioral scientist inside the firm, or an agency or department of the federal government, an attempt to change the quality of work life at any level of society will mean facing these strategic choices. Furthermore, the choices are not made once and forgotten. The change agent continues to face the same strategic choices as the change effort unfolds and moves through various phases. The choices will depend on the orientation and values of the change agent, the change agency's time perspective, the resources available, the readiness of the change target to change, and a variety of other situational factors.

Perhaps one of the key dilemmas in choosing a change strategy has to do with the need for consistency between means and ends. It is difficult to envision a strategy that attempts to utilize power tactics when the purpose is to increase trust and collaboration. Similarly, it would be difficult to foresee a strategy that used a collaborative approach to create change in an authoritarian institution. In choosing a strategy for changing the quality of work life, the agent of change must be clear about what improved quality of work life means. If it means increasing trust, collaboration, self-control, and flexibility in meeting people's needs, then strategies that use power as the means of change may be contradictory and may undermine this ultimate objective.

INTERNAL ORGANIZATIONAL STRATEGIES

In the previous section we presented a general framework for thinking about the change process and for evaluating the potential effectiveness of change strategies. We now turn to an examination of specific types of strategies for changing the quality of work life in organizations. The approaches discussed in this section have in common that they are internal to the organization. That is, the source of change and the vehicle for change are within the organization, although in one case (union strategies) those involved are also members of another organization. Later sections discuss strategies for change that have their origins primarily outside the organization—in the community and in the government. In each case we first describe the nature of the approach to change, and then evaluate it within the framework of the process for change and strategic considerations discussed in earlier sections.

Organization Development

A plant manager and his staff are interested in checking the morale of their organization and in improving it. With the help of an OD consultant they form a task force of people from the hourly and salaried work force. The task force, with help from the OD specialist, designs a questionnaire which is administered to all employees. The data are collected and analyzed. Results are fed back to each department by members of the task force. The data serve as a platform for discussion about problems in supervision, communications, motivation, coordination, and so forth, and changes are planned.

A top manager and his staff experience difficulty in communicating and making decisions. They invite an OD consultant in to help. After determining that the manager and his subordinates are interested in working on these problems, the consultant interviews every member of the group. He collects information on what they see as the strengths of the group, the barriers to effectiveness, and how they see each other's behavior helping and hindering effectiveness. This information is carefully organized and fed back to the group in a two- or three-day meeting away from work. With the help of the consultant an atmosphere of trust and openness develops, problems are confronted, and action plans for change developed. This process is usually repeated several more times with the help of the consultant until the group becomes self-sufficient.

A plant manager asks for help from an OD consultant in solving turnover and absenteeism problems on the plant floor. Discussion indicates that morale is low and productivity is down. A task force of union and management people is formed and is commissioned, with the help of a behavioral scientist, to diagnose the problems and propose solutions. They interview people and administer a questionnaire. This shows that people find their work dissatisfying and unchallenging. With the involvement of several additional task forces and help from professionals, jobs are redesigned to include more variety and more information about productivity and performance. In some cases groups are formed to run certain lines on their own. As a result, the span of control for each supervisor is increased and his role is changed. To support those changes, supervisors receive training in how to manage in this new situation.

These examples of OD applications illustrate the diversity of techniques that fall under the umbrella of OD and the variety of situations in which it can be applied, but they also illustrate a similarity in process. Organization development is a long-term *process* by which people in an organization become involved in examining how they and the organization are functioning or might want to function. It is a process for developing solutions and action plans for change. The techniques used to apply this process of inquiry and action are quite different depending on the problem, the client, and the situation. Furthermore, the process can spin off many diverse programs and changes, from training programs to a new organization structure or policy. But the idea is always to surface concerns, attitudes, views, and ideas not normally talked about and to develop plans for action and change based on the information surfaced and the problems identified. The process is designed not only to solve immediate problems but also to create more openness in the organization. Through this openness, organizational members at all levels become more aware of what others' views are and what they themselves must do and how they themselves may have to change to improve the situation. The process of OD is aimed at bridging the gap in communications and influence between those who have less power and those who have more, and between people and groups who would not normally collaborate and coordinate although they have common goals.

An OD effort may begin because a manager or his people sense problems that block organizational performance or employee satisfaction. Or it may begin because people want to improve their organization and themselves. Sometimes, an OD effort begins when a new organization is formed and the opportunity to design and shape it in advance exists. Regardless of how OD begins, however, the process described above ideally encompasses the organization as a total system. This means that a variety of dimensions—such as individual performance, interpersonal relations, policies, supervision, organization and job structure, planning, communication, pay systems, and decision-making—may all be examined for change and acted on.

The OD process is ideally implemented by a manager knowledgeable and skillful in its use. Often, however, an organization may call in an OD consultant for help. He may be from inside or outside the firm, but he usually has had training in the behavioral sciences and in techniques of OD. The consultant helps the organization apply a process of collecting data, diagnosing, planning and implementing change, and evaluating results to a variety of problems or in various parts of the organization. He supplies techniques for carrying out this process, and provides the expertise needed to solve organizational problems. Throughout the process the consultant acts as a third party and catalyst—helping people see problems, proposing alternative solutions, helping people examine themselves, and stimulating change. The consultant moves change along, in other words, but does not control the change process.

Organization Development and the Quality of Work Life. It should be clear that OD is an approach to organizational change and improvement that seeks to create self-directed change to which people are committed. This approach has grown from a number of assumptions about change supported by behavioral science research. The assumptions are as follows:

1. People and organizations must be ready and motivated (unfrozen) to change in order for change to "take."
2. Changes in individuals' knowledge and attitudes must be accompanied by changes in organizational constraints that shape behavior, such as organizational structure, practices, leadership, and reward systems.
3. People learn best from their own experiences. For this reason change comes about from opportunities to experiment with new ways of doing things.
4. People become committed to changes they are involved in and help to create.
5. The quality of the solution improves when people who are part of the problem participate in shaping the final solution.
6. People can only become self-directed in creating change when they have learned to take responsibility for change.
7. Trust, collaboration, and open confrontation of conflict are needed in order for organizations to be continuously adaptive.

These assumptions about change and the process that emerges from them make OD particularly congruent with the objective of improving the quality of work life in organizations. The means of change, which emphasize self-direction, collaboration, participation, and mutual influence, are consistent with the thrust to increase responsibility, collaboration, and individual choice inherent in the quality of work life improvements discussed in previous chapters. In many organizations that have embarked on quality of work life improvements, OD processes, techniques, and professionals have been involved in creating the changes. Without a doubt, future quality of work life improvements within organizations will mean hiring OD professionals and asking them to take significant responsibility for planning and implementing a change strategy in collaboration with managers. We now turn to the questions of how OD might be implemented and how OD resources might be organized within an organization so that the desired improvements might be achieved.

Implementing OD Within an Organization   Because top-down directives to use OD would be inconsistent with the OD philosophy, how does the OD process spread through the organization? What is the strategy for penetrating the organization?

There are basically two ways for implementing OD. First, top management can involve itself in the use of OD. As the top people begin to model the OD process by applying it within their respective groups, it spreads through the organization. This is quite different from directing others to apply OD techniques without first involving yourself. It probably involves the least risk that the OD effort will run across barriers that prevent it from encompassing the whole organization. Yet in many organizations, OD does not start at the top. Someone at the bottom or middle sees a need and begins OD. Thus, the second approach is the bottom-up approach. OD begins to be used by a growing number of units because the first unit's application is successful. This success is communicated to others. Or managers from the unit applying OD are transferred to other units and bring the OD process with them. It should be obvious that both of these approaches, but particularly the second, reflect a market strategy as opposed to a collective strategy for change. People and organizations become involved because they see benefits, and benefits sell themselves.

The bottom-up strategy has some obvious risks. As long as the people at the top are not involved, they probably do not understand OD and cannot be committed to it. Thus, the top people can at any time use their power to stop OD in the organization. This is likely to happen if they see OD as a threat to their power and control, or if they are forced by economic circumstances to reduce expenses and staff groups. Thus, the bottom-up approach puts a premium on the involvement of top management in OD soon after OD has begun to spread sufficiently and becomes an important force to reckon with. However, in a bottom-up approach there is no guarantee that the hurdle of getting top management involved will be passed successfully. It is hoped that a manager who has experienced OD will be promoted to a key position, or that success at lower levels will give OD sufficient credibility so that top management will want to become involved. But involved they must become if the process is to become truly system-wide.

There are many corporate constraints, such as procedures, controls, and policies, that eventually must be examined if quality of work life improvements in various subunits are to proceed. Although many changes occur at lower levels, top-down policies on manufacturing technologies, job evaluation systems, industrial relations, and the like usually affect how far changes at lower levels can go. This is not to say that the top-down approach is not without risk. Even when the top takes pains not to force OD down, those at lower levels may begin to ask for OD help because they see it as the politically smart thing to do. Political motivation for getting started does not constitute readiness for change, and the OD effort is likely to fail. Thus, the OD specialist must be on guard *not* to start an OD effort with a manager who is politically motivated to fall in line.

Organization of the OD Resources.   In recent years a number of corporations have hired applied behavioral scientists as external or internal change agents under the banner of organization development.

Some corporations have formed OD groups staffed by professional applied behavioral scientists and located them in the personnel function. In other organizations personnel professionals have acquired skills and competence to apply OD. These and other alternatives for organizing an OD effort have worked reasonably well in some corporations, but in others they have not resulted in significant innovations in the quality of work life or in significant changes in the status quo. In still other corporations significant impact by the OD group has been followed by their demise. With this in mind we will briefly review a model for organizing OD efforts which we believe can increase their impact on the quality of work life.

When an organization first becomes involved in OD, at least some professionals should be hired and a central group created where OD specialists can offer each other professional and emotional support. Change agents are required to challenge their client organization, and this often brings hostility and rejection from people in the organization. Consultants must also be objective about their client organization and its problems, and this requires the challenge of a professional colleague not directly involved as a consultant to the organization. Finally, the OD field is growing at a rapid rate, and so an effective OD consultant needs the stimulation of new ideas from professional colleagues within his organization. This can be significantly augmented by bringing outside consultants into the organization to work with internal people, and by letting internal OD specialists do some outside consulting.

A key factor in the success of the OD unit is its capacity to maintain some independence from the power centers in the organization, which it will have to confront in the course of a change effort. Second, the OD unit must have access to all levels of the organization, and especially to some of the people in key power positions. Placement in the personnel function, where OD groups are commonly found, limits their scope. The OD unit cannot counsel an organization of which it is a part, because it is not independent of that unit from a power point of view. For example, it could not confront the personnel function with changes in personnel policies and practices needed to improve the quality of work life. For similar reasons, the OD group should be independent of other staff functions that create policies affecting the quality of work life. For example, it must be able to raise questions about the design of technology in new and old plants, or about the impact of control systems on freedom and innovation.

The optimum arrangement would be for the OD group to report directly to the top of the organization, or perhaps to a steering committee composed of key power figures and constituents. In the latter model, the committee might be composed of managers who are key users of the group, but it could also include union leaders if they are users, employees from several levels of the organization, community representatives, and even customers or suppliers who associate regularly with the organization. Union leaders and hourly employees would be particularly important members of such a committee when the OD effort is aimed at changing quality of work life on the production floor. More than one such steering committee could exist. One top level committee would be required to provide overall direction to the OD group and review its activities. Each organizational subunit involved in an OD program could then form its own steering committee to guide its particular program. Having the OD unit responsible to a group that represents various constituencies for change gives it the freedom it needs to challenge the system, catalyze change, and deal with those in power positions who, by virtue of their formal position, could block change.

To make the model proposed here work, the OD group would have to support its activities by selling its service to units within the organization. An internal charge-back system would have to be set up and guaranteed by the top management. Level of staffing would be determined by client purchase. This system would give ultimate control of the change effort to client organizations and free the OD unit from top-down control. This is as it should be if change is to be truly directed and controlled by those who must change, and if the OD unit is to have the freedom to confront those in power about needed changes. Thus, a plant manager may purchase OD services to improve the quality of work life, but so could a union. Preferably, they would join together to pay for such efforts. The charge-back system does create some problems in the early stages of an OD effort, because managers may not be willing to pay for an unproven service. To deal with that problem, the OD unit will need seed money from the larger organization to demonstrate its effectiveness.

Change cannot be brought about by OD professionals alone. To be sure, they are needed as resources early in any change effort. To speed up change in the quality of work life within an organization, however, others would have to be trained in OD techniques, in how to function as change agents, and in the main issues surrounding quality of work life problems. Thus, an effective OD effort would increasingly be supported by managers, employees and union members trained as paraprofessional change agents. An effective OD strategy would provide them with training and would link them to each other and to the OD unit for emotional and professional support.

The Experimental Plant. One of the main OD strategies for changing the quality of work life in organizations has been the experimental unit. For example, at both Corning Glass Works (Beer and Huse, 1972) and General Foods (Walton, 1972) a single plant has been identified as a target for change and OD resources have been successfully massed to create a model that might be tried and replicated in other plants.

The strategy of developing a model organization is consistent with the OD strategy and the broader strategic considerations discussed earlier. First, it limits the boundaries of the change effort, thus allowing a concentration of sufficient resources. Second, it makes it possible to start with a unit that is receptive and willing to change. Third, and most important, it allows a change effort that deals with the experimental unit as a total system. Thus, the change effort is consistent with the OD definition of being system-wide and system-oriented (Beer, in press). When the change effort is concentrated in one plant, attention can be paid to changing job design, selection procedures, policies and practices, communication, trust levels, supervisory practices, pay systems, the process for goal setting and planning, accounting systems, and many other aspects of the organization that affect both the quality of work life and productivity. The experimental unit approach allows the development of an internally consistent organization where employees get consistent cues about the nature of the organization. Further, comprehensive changes remove ambiguity inherent in piecemeal changes.

The objective in developing a model plant is to use a collaborative strategy in building a successful new approach to managing, and then to use success as a platform for spreading change to other parts of the larger organization. This is the market strategy for change discussed earlier. Thus, innovations in the experimental unit must not only be successful, but they also must be sustained and picked up by others. Walton (1974b) investigated twelve experimental plants in eleven companies. He found that in three situations innovations in work structure and management regressed to more traditional states, and in several other situations the innovation in the experimental plant was sustained but did not diffuse to other parts of the corporation. Thus, in order to understand how the experimental unit approach might be made to work more effectively, we must have some understanding of the factors that prevent a quality of work life innovation from being successfully initiated, sustained, and spread.

Conditions for an Experimental Project.   There appear to be specific conditions that are favorable for a pilot plant attempting innovation in the quality of work life. Such projects have typically had the following characteristics (Walton, 1974b):

1. The plant is located in a small town.
2. The work force in the plant is small (usually less than one hundred people).

3. The plant is new or the technology and product are new.
4. The experimental unit is geographically separate from headquarters.
5. Outside consultants are used as resources for their experience and objectivity.
6. Lead time is provided for planning the new innovations and training management.
7. There is no union, or union-management relations are good.
8. There is relatively little turnover in management personnel in the early phases of the experiment.
9. The management of the experimental unit is favorable to the change or, at a minimum, neutral.

These characteristics suggest that change is relatively easier to start in situations where historical relationships and ways of doing things are not a drag, the larger organization's influence does not interfere, there is organizational slack (that is, more people and financial resources than are needed), there is no polarization of attitudes, and reasonable trust and mutual confidence exist among workers, management, and union. These conditions indicate that the experimental plant is unfrozen and provide it with an opportunity to change. However, refreezing and continuation of the change is not assured by these conditions, nor is diffusion of the change.

Conditions for Refreezing and Sustaining the Innovation. Several conditions are important in sustaining quality of work life changes in an experimental plant (Beer and Huse, 1972; Walton, 1974b).

1. *Management support.* Management directly responsible for the experimental plant must continue to favor and support the innovations and protect the plant from interference and attack from other parts of the company.

2. *Management turnover.* As key managers are replaced, they must be selected for their compatibility with the management philosophy. They must be trained and given newly required skills.

3. *Economic stability.* There must be a favorable business climate. A business that is unprofitable or a general economic downturn early in the change program can create pressures for cost reduction and retrenchment that cause managers to regress to old practices. Once changes are institutionalized such economic downturns will not have the same effect.

4. *Corporate interfaces.* Innovations require increasing independence of the experimental unit from corporate policies and constraints. Staff groups such as industrial relations, engineering, and finance often require particular approaches to problems because standardization is valued or equity with other units is a problem. These constraints, unless lifted, will prevent continuation of innovations.

5. *Reenergizing the innovation.* Innovations regress because people lose interest and the novelty wears off. Ways have to be found to sustain interest, particularly by managers. Continued training, additional innovation, and continued rewards for maintaining the innovations are needed.

These conditions for sustaining innovations are required if the initial success is to lead to other attempts to improve the quality of work life. If the original experiment regresses and looks less successful after a period of time, an important support for new change efforts will be lost. New change can only occur from a base of strength and success. Continuation of old innovations is as important as new successes. Naturally, a balance must be struck between these. So much energy cannot be put into sustaining old innovations that there are no resources for new innovations; yet new innovations cannot be started at the cost of support for old innovations. Nevertheless, sustaining the first innovation is not enough. Diffusion of change must occur.

Conditions for Diffusion of Innovation.   Innovations in an experimental unit must find their way into other units, for otherwise a momentum for change will not develop. The experimental unit will become more and more isolated, enemies of the innovation will begin to successfully marshal their opposition, and managers of compatible managerial philosophy needed to transfer into the experimental plant and sustain change will be hard to find. In order to diffuse change, a number of steps must be planned (Walton, 1974b).

1. *Top management.* They must be helped to understand the implications of the innovation for the corporation. Their commitment to the innovation must be obtained. A statement of policy, support for the resources needed to create further change, approval for lifting traditional constraints, and a periodic review of progress are all needed. Yet, top management involvement cannot be so heavy-handed as to create surface compliance and deep resentment.

2. *Manpower flow.* The best talent in the organization must be transferred into the experimental plant or plants so that they can learn the new approaches to management. These people must then be transferred out to key positions where they can apply the innovations.

3. *Identifying new targets.* Successful diffusion requires accurate identification of ready and potentially successful change targets. If mistakes are made in identification of the next targets, valuable time and resources are wasted and the momentum for change is slowed.

4. *Communicating innovations.* The experimental unit must openly plan to communicate what is going on. Communication can be facilitated by having people from other units visit the experimental unit, and by having people in the experimental unit respond to requests for help

and travel to other units. In all of this, it is important that the nature of the innovations is communicated clearly so that people can grasp the principle. A danger exists, however, that the experimental unit will spend more time communicating to the outside world than to others in the corporation.

5. *Rewarding innovators.* The organization must reward innovators with pay, recognition, and promotions. Promotions are particularly visible and are read as clear support. Their absence is interpreted as lack of support and will reduce risk-taking and innovation.

6. *Getting unions involved.* Unions can offer substantial resistance to work restructuring if they are not involved. They can block change or slow it down if they are not committed. At the experimental unit, local union-management cooperation is needed, and the international union may also have to be involved. For diffusion to occur the international union *must* be involved. (See Chapter 6 and the later section in this chapter on unions.)

7. *Preventing religious fervor.* There is a tendency for any unit at the leading edge of change to acquire an almost religious zeal and commitment to new approaches. Innovations in the quality of work life are particularly prone to be justified on the basis of moral values and beliefs. However, religious fervor creates early polarization between believers and nonbelievers, and prevents the adoption of the change and accurate appraisal of costs and benefits.

8. *Removing bureaucratic barriers.* Changes that improve the quality of work life will require exceptions from standardized practices, procedures, and policies which usually pervade a large organization. This means that the staff groups that control these policies must be persuaded—or directed—to allow exceptions. Clearly top management involvement is critical in making this happen.

9. *Credibility of experimental unit.* The more the experimental unit is seen as effective, and the more its technology, products, and size are like those of the larger system, the more likely others will be to adopt the innovations.

A knowledge of the conditions that are needed to start, sustain, and spread innovation in the quality of work life is useful in planning a strategy of change. In an overall sense, an experimental unit strategy creates a significantly different unit that produces tensions in the larger organization. These tensions must then be resolved—the larger organization must change or the smaller unit must turn back. From the point of view of the change agent, it is hoped that the creation of tension and conflict will result in adaptation by the larger organization. This is more likely to occur, as we have pointed out, if the experimental unit is the same as the larger organization in every respect except the dimension on which change is being created. But the tensions must be resolved, and the manner in which the tensions are handled will have a lot to do with successful diffusion. The trade-offs that must be considered in planning this strategy are the unfreezing effects of a radically different experimental unit against the potential rejection of the innovation and an attempt to bring the dissident unit into line. If the innovation is not radical enough, on the other hand, the experimental unit and its innovations are not rejected, but the necessary tensions needed to create change are not developed.

Summary of OD. This section has described organization development as one strategy for improving the quality of work life in organizations. We have attempted to show how the OD process works and how an organization interested in quality of work life improvements can organize its OD resources and apply them. It is our belief that OD will become an important and effective social technology for improving the quality of work life within organizations, and that OD units, when properly created and organized, can be important agents for change in organizations. The experimental plant strategy is a specific example of OD applied to improving the quality of work life at the plant level. However, the notion of identifying a target of change and concentrating OD resources and innovation there is a general OD strategy applicable to other organizational units (such as divisions and subsidiaries) as well.

In the context of the change processes and strategies discussed earlier, OD appears to be a fairly comprehensive approach. It includes all phases of change. However, it is built on the assumption that a system must be unfrozen before change can be attempted. In this regard it is a market strategy for change. The OD resources in an organization rely on pressures from outside or inside the organization to create readiness for change. OD does use data feedback techniques to unfreeze organizations, but such data are rarely sufficient to motivate change unless there are other compelling reasons. Thus, external strategies to be discussed later in the chapter are needed to complement internal OD strategies for changing the quality of work life.

Management Strategies

In the traditional hierarchical organizations in which most of us live and work, the people at the top hold most of the power. They hold it because they control rewards and punishments for most organizational members. This power orchestrates the activities of the organization, provides direction, and maintains coordination. But it is also this power that often prevents change when that change represents a serious challenge to the beliefs, values, and interests of those in power. Changes in the quality of work life are no exception. To the extent that these changes further the objectives of management, they will be welcomed. To the extent that changes challenge their values, their power, their control, and their objectives, those changes will almost always be resisted.

·Our earlier discussion clearly pointed to the need for a shared-power approach to change. That is, change is likely to occur only to the extent that management is willing to share power in examining the current status quo, and is willing to be influenced from below or outside the organization. In a sense, change can only be brought about if management is willing to have its beliefs and values disconfirmed and acts positively to create conditions for this to occur. Otherwise management's natural power position prevents serious challenge to its beliefs. It is our contention that this is particularly true in changing the quality of work life.

For the reasons just given, we must examine what role management can play in stimulating improvement in the quality of work life. A more detailed discussion of managerial methods and approaches is found in Chapter 6. Our intention here is to discuss two possible orientations management can take to the improvement of the quality of work life. Managers can either (1) share power and allow a process of mutual influence to emerge, or (2) recognize their power and use it to create changes in the quality of work life.

Changing the Quality of Work Life Through Sharing Power. Management can use its unilateral power to change the basic power equation voluntarily. It can do so by restructuring the decision-making processes of the organization to allow for more influence by various interest groups who may have a desire to improve the quality of work life.

There are a number of examples of enlightened managers who saw that the future would bring change. They realized that they would be better off taking the initiative in changing the quality of work life than holding back until overwhelmed by pressures for change. Interestingly, examples of enlightened managers are mainly found in small companies owned and managed by one man or family. Probably the earliest attempt to improve the quality of work life by this strategy occurred at Non-Linear Systems, a small electronics firm managed by its owner. Other examples include Donnelly Mirrors in Holland, Michigan, the Raymond Corporation in Green, New York, and the Siddons Corporation in Melbourne, Australia.[3]

---

3. Descriptions of these company efforts to create change and improve quality of work life are difficult to find. Donnelly Mirrors and the Raymond Corporation are cited in Conference Board publications on organization development and behavioral science applications (*Behavioral Science: Concepts and Management Applications*, 1969). The Siddons Corporation was visited by one of the authors and is not described anywhere to our knowledge. Non-Linear Systems has been written up in a number of popular press articles, including in *Business Week*.

Apparently it takes a consolidated position of power to accept the risks associated with a fundamental change in the decision-making process. When this secure power position is combined with a management philosophy that values participation and shared power, significant changes are possible. Argyris (1973a) makes clear the risks involved for management in creating fundamental changes in the distribution of power. He lists the following questions management should ask itself prior to starting a change effort.

1. Is management aware that they are about to undertake an experiment?
2. Is top management aware of the costs of failure, and that—once started—many changes are difficult to stop?
3. Is the commitment deep enough to deflect feelings of guilt when failure has occurred and to strengthen conviction to experiment anew?
4. Is top management united enough to overcome the period of counterproductiveness and to resist reverting to the old style of leadership?
5. Is top management committed enough so that it will be able to live with and effectively overcome internal conflict, ambiguity, intergroup conflict, and other upheavals that come with change?
6. How does top management cope with the fact that it is experimenting with basic changes in societal values and behavior deeply ingrained in individuals? How will it deal with the demand for quick results?
7. Is management ready to face the aloneness and fear that come with any experiment that focuses on changing some of the most basic values in society?

These questions make clear that changes in the dynamics of power involve substantial risk, and for this reason are not frequently undertaken. Yet it is our view that management interested in improving the quality of work life could create change most quickly if it examined how it might start sharing decision-making and power. Examining what prevents it from sharing power and preparing to do so, rather than responding to pressures, has substantial advantages. If top management takes the initiative, the power of all parties is likely to increase, rather than the power of management declining, because the sharing of power will have occurred in a climate of collaboration and trust. In the end all interest groups in the organization, not just management, would be concerned with overall system effectiveness and health. Management would not be locked into a win-lose conflict with various interest groups concerned just with maximizing their own interests and enhancing their own power. Management initiative can avoid this period of polarization, which, unfortunately, often precedes more collaborative and problem-centered approaches to conflict resolution.

It is not our intent to discuss here all of the specific steps management could take to redistribute power so that quality of work life changes can begin to occur. These have been discussed in other chapters (see especially Chapter 6). However, several major action categories are listed below.

1. Management can take the initiative in starting quality of work life experiments with the collaboration of unions and other groups.

2. Management can establish an OD unit concerned with change and give it total freedom to identify constituents for change and challenge top management and the system (see earlier section on OD). The OD unit then becomes an independent force for change.

3. Management can initiate bold changes in the economic structure of the enterprise by adopting plans like the Scanlon Plan (Frost et al., 1974), which distributes company-wide bonuses to employees based on cost savings and productivity improvements. Suggestions for increasing productivity come from employee committees formed to examine operations in their own work areas (see Lawler, Chapter 4). By changing the distribution of economic rewards, the Scanlon Plan creates conditions for more integrative solutions (solutions that enhance the interest of all parties) to improving the quality of work life. Further, when trade-offs have to be made between improving the quality of work life and increasing productivity, they will be more easily negotiated.

4. Management can make major structural changes in decision-making (a) by inviting a variety of interest groups to be represented on the board of directors, (b) by voluntarily introducing participative decision-making structures like works councils or the committee structure associated with the Scanlon Plan, or (c) by developing joint union-management committees on the quality of work life.

Changing the Quality of Work Life Through Unilateral Power. Management groups that may not be willing to take the risks associated with the shared power strategy could use their power to create changes in the quality of work life more rapidly than a bottom-up strategy. Such a benevolent-autocratic approach to change can have positive effects on the quality of work life, but it does not deal adequately with the need of unions or workers to participate in planning and carrying out the change process. Change can be created, but management may be suspected of having ulterior motives. Such change is not likely to increase the sense of personal responsibility, independence, and confidence of employees. To the extent that personal growth and development are part of a high quality work life, these will not be achieved. Nevertheless, management could take some significant steps in a unilateral power approach.

1. It could establish an OD unit that is geared to improving the quality of work life where possible, but without serious challenge to the power structure. Many OD units in organizations today are of this nature.

2. It can significantly affect managerial behavior by changing the pattern of rewards to encourage management decisions that foster a high quality work life. One of the keys to this is to lengthen the time a manager is held responsible for the results of his operation and to add quality of work life measures to the criteria for rewards. Efforts to improve the quality of work life often do not occur because managers know they will be promoted out of their current jobs before the effects of their decisions are felt. Holding managers responsible for consequences long after they have been transferred and promoted can change this.

3. It can begin experiments to improve the quality of work life without involvement and participation by workers or unions.

4. Management can set up data collection and feedback systems that help managers assess the quality of work life of their organization (see later discussion of social audits). Attitude surveys are one possible system, and the emerging technology for human resource accounting is another (Brummet, Framholtz, and Pyle, 1969).

Summary of Management Strategies. In this section we have outlined the alternatives open to management interested in improving the quality of work life. Although a unilateral strategy has been offered as one alternative, we believe that a shared and participative approach is the only meaningful and effective long-term strategy. Anything else runs the same risks that paternalistic and benevolent-autocratic strategies have always run. Sooner or later those who are dependent will want independence, even when dependence has been benign. This will be even more true in the future, as educational levels increase and individuals' desire for freedom, responsibility, and growth emerge as a result of increasing economic security. If a high quality work life has to be demanded, the cost to organizational effectiveness will be very high, while, as some of the early experiments have shown (Huse and Beer, 1971; Walton, 1972), a joint process of improving the quality of work life may not cost at all—and could easily increase organizational performance.

Union Strategies

The most important question to be answered in assessing the viability of the union as a change agent is whether union leaders perceive the overall quality of work life—including not only such traditional areas of union concern as fair payment, secure employment, and fair treatment, but also less tangible issues such as increased decision-making responsibility, greater participation in work decisions, and more interesting jobs—as an important issue and are motivated to push for change. If union leaders do not see all these quality of work life issues, and especially the intangible ones, as important, no tactics that we might outline here will have any value.[4]

Historically, unions have concentrated on a few key issues on which there have been rank and file consensus (Salpukas, 1974). These have been primarily *tangible* issues. That is, American unions have bargained successfully and contributed significantly to the improvement of the quality of work life by achieving economic gains, grievance procedures, better general working conditions, and job security for their members. The overwhelming consensus of workers' views on these tangible quality of work life issues has made them ideal for a collective bargaining process that relies on support of the rank-and-file and the threat of a strike for gains. Furthermore, the cyclical nature of our economy has kept economic and security issues in the forefront. Finally, bargaining at the national level and the pattern of longer-term contracts have kept the focus on economics. This is because worker frustrations tend, by their very nature, to vary with local conditions and work force characteristics. Thus, they tend to be difficult to negotiate on a national level.

As the discussion concerning the quality of work life and the "blue-collar blues" has emerged, the reaction of union leaders has been mixed. It appears that no overwhelming interest in the *intangible* quality of work life issues currently exists among union leaders. A recent study by Kochan, Lipsky, and Dyer (1974) provides some data on the importance union leaders attach to newer quality of work life issues as compared to more traditional issues. Almost without exception, traditional bargaining issues—such as earnings, fringe benefits, and job security—were seen as more important than quality of work life issues—such as interesting work, supervisor relations, and productivity. Only two intangible quality of work life issues, "Having more to say about how the work is done," and "Improving conditions that interfere with getting the work done," ranked fairly high in importance.

It would appear that union leaders do not see intangible quality of work life issues as particularly important, which would explain why unions have not been leading the charge in this area. This does not, of course, mean that workers do not seek improvements in the quality of work life, for union leaders can be just as inaccurate as management in assessing the needs of workers. Furthermore, past successes are proba-

---

4. We do not in any way want to imply that unions have not in the past contributed to improved quality of work life, nor that their primary interest in tangible issues such as job security and fringe benefits does not constitute concern for quality of work life. We do, however, want to distinguish between their concern for these tangible issues and their relative lack of interest to date in the more intangible issues.

bly preventing change. Traditional issues have been the basis of union gains up to now, so why change the focus and increase the chances of failure? Thus, if unions are to take leadership in expanding the range of quality of work life issues on which they seek improvements, they must first deal with their own apathy and lack of knowledge concerning these issues.

Building Knowledge and Interest in Quality of Work Life Within Unions. To date, applied behavioral scientists and organization development specialists have been employed almost exclusively by management. It is not surprising, therefore, that behavioral scientists are seen by union leaders as biased toward management. If unions want to explore the potential of quality of work life as a major issue in which they take leadership, they will have to employ behavioral scientists on their staffs and as external consultants. These behavioral scientists can serve in any or all of the following capacities.

1. Behavioral scientists can help to educate union leaders in theories, ideas, findings, and techniques that have led to the current interest and concern with intangible quality of work life issues. They have done so for years with management, and this accounts for the difference in knowledge between the two groups. The education process for union leaders could be both informal and formal. Informally, the behavioral scientist can help union people understand the practical usefulness of his discipline by helping solve day-to-day union problems at the national and local levels. Formally, education of union leadership can occur through structured training programs attended by regional and local union leadership. These programs would not only inform, but would also provide union leaders with skills in the use of organization development techniques. Then, as quality of work life problems become apparent, union leaders at the local level could take the initiative in applying these techniques—they could diagnose problems using surveys, and could approach supervision with suggestions for problem-solving meetings.

2. Behavioral scientists on the staff of an international union can help local union leadership plan and propose changes in the workplace that will increase the quality of work life. To date, management has taken the initiative in this area, and the union has been in a reactive posture. However, intangible quality of work life issues can become an important means of building enthusiasm among rank-and-file members and their leaders. This will occur if members see union leadership as instrumental to valued quality of work life improvement. Samuel Gompers said "more" when asked the aims of the American labor movement. "More" does not refer only to tangible issues like salary, however. It can also refer to freedom and job challenge. This

would be particularly true in the white-collar area, where unionism is just beginning to grow.

3. Behavioral scientists can act as internal OD consultants to union organizations. Unions have many of the same problems in management, conflict resolution, communication, role differentiation, and alienation that other organizations have. In fact, some have argued that unions have not fulfilled their original intent of gaining for union members more human conditions and control over their destiny. They see unions themselves as bureaucracies in need of substantial reform (Hunnius, Garson, and Case, 1973). One of the authors has discussed these problems with a local union leader, who saw many of the OD techniques being applied in his plant as applicable to his problems as president of the union. One of the main problems discussed was that of increasing member participation. Concern for involvement, participation, and self-control at the workplace will increase among union members if they experience involvement and participation in union affairs. Such involvement will increase their sense of confidence, responsibility, and self-direction, and these dispositions will then also be applied to work.

The potency of the local union as a force for change in the quality of work life can be further increased by the application of team-building techniques to union leadership. One of the authors is aware of such an application in a local plant where the union president and his committee began to explore their own effectiveness as a team. It became clear that this local leadership had done little thinking about long-range goals, objectives, and strategies. Changes in the quality of work life will require unions to take a longer view than the time frame of the immediate contract. The OD specialist working for a union can help develop a long-range thrust at the national and local levels by helping groups become more effective through team-building methods.

In summary, unions can reverse their reactive stance and take the initiative in changing the quality of work life by hiring behavioral scientists to (a) educate union leaders, (b) help propose change programs in quality of work life to management, and (c) develop more democratic and effective managerial processes within the union. Initiative by the union can pressure management and unfreeze them. Union competence in OD techniques can help create change effectively.

Collective Bargaining Strategies.   Can the collective bargaining process be used to improve the less tangible areas of quality of work life in organizations? The previously cited study by Kochan, Lipsky, and Dyer (1974) found that most union leaders in their sample did not think so. In general, union leaders judged the process of collective bargaining to be an effective instrument in dealing with the more traditional issues, rather than with the newer quality of work life issues. These more traditional issues were the ones that union leaders saw as most important and on which there was most agreement as to importance. If the opinions of union leaders are to be used as a guide, these findings suggest that collective bargaining can only be an effective instrument when quality of work life issues become more salient and a consensus develops about them. The previous discussion about educating union leaders in the behavioral sciences and applying OD to unions is, of course, a strategy for achieving this objective.

Despite the view of union leaders that collective bargaining is not a viable instrument for improving the intangible areas of quality of work life, we would like to explore some ways in which bargaining might be effective. It must be kept in mind, however, that these strategies will first have to overcome the inherent problem that these quality of work life issues are less tangible than the more traditional economic issues.

The union's use of collective bargaining as an instrument for improving health and safety provides some understanding of how collective bargaining might be used to improve the intangible aspects of quality of work life. Substantial gains in health and safety in the workplace have been made in the past several years through collective bargaining, due primarily to the enactment of the Occupational Safety and Health Act (*OSHA and the Unions,* 1973). This law has provided unions with significant leverage in entering negotiations. The existence of the law not only gives union and management a set of standards against which they can compare the conditions in their company, but the union has a potential club in the provisions for filing complaints and requesting action by the Department of Labor against a recalcitrant management.

We see no reason why unions could not negotiate improvement in the quality of work life if they had a law similar to OSHA. What type of law this might be will be discussed in more detail later in this chapter. For now, we want to make the point that collective bargaining can be used by unions to improve the quality of work life if appropriate legislation is provided to focus attention on this issue. Such a law would be most effective if it spelled out processes for the systematic examination and correction of quality of work life problems at the local level, where they are felt and occur, as opposed to listing specific standards. This is because, as discussed in Chapter 1, quality of work life is relative and depends on the specific relationships between employees and their organizations.

Examination of negotiated agreements on health and safety provides some clues for the parameters of a quality of work life law, as well as some specific demands that might be negotiated by a union seeking to improve the quality of work life (*OSHA and the Unions,* 1973). Unions might demand or a law might require:

1. a company-financed survey of employee attitudes and concerns in the quality of work life area conducted by an independent consultant selected by the company with union approval and reviewed by a labor-management committee;
2. joint union-management committees at several levels to review quality of work life issues, plan change programs, and follow up on progress in this area;
3. the right of the union and employees to obtain feedback on major problems identified by company attitude surveys;
4. protection for the right of the union to review the content of any survey aimed at examining the quality of work life;
5. protection for the right of the union to initiate an investigation by a labor-management committee of any quality of work life problems reported by workers;
6. the right of any employee to submit a grievance or seek a transfer because of poor supervision and management of his department;
7. company payment for time spent by union representatives on quality of work life committees;
8. the right of the union to obtain in advance of implementation information on company plans to develop quality of work life programs;
9. the right by the union to initiate an investigation into any quality of work life problems;
10. the right of the union to review the impact on quality of work life of all plans for new machines and technology.

These suggestions for demands a union can make in negotiations are not comprehensive. The point we would like to make is that unions can negotiate processes for assuring that quality of work life issues are examined by management and unions jointly, and that change programs resulting from these investigations are sponsored jointly or at least with union approval. This eliminates the problem of negotiating for intangibles that differ across individuals, jobs, and organizations. The *process* can be negotiated because it is always the same. The outcome and the solutions are different, however, depending on the situation.

Collective bargaining strategies for improving the overall quality of work life could place significant pressure on management and could unfreeze them. If proper resources to help the organization create quality of work life improvements are also negotiated, real progress is possible.

Union initiative in collective bargaining on quality of work life issues is a power strategy, but this strategy need not preclude collaboration once an agreement has been reached (provided, of course, that distrust and hostility have not been raised to high levels in the negotiation process). It is our opinion that collective bargaining initiatives can be used to speed up change without incurring the problem of uncontrollable conflict found in other power strategies. This is because the collective bargaining process recognizes that both parties have equal power and mechanisms are built in for controlling conflict. Furthermore, structures—such as union-management committees—that allow a collaborative process within the context of collective bargaining are frequently used and could be applied to quality of work life improvements.

Although we have pointed to the need for a law to give unions some leverage in negotiation, it is also possible for unions to negotiate quality of work life improvements without such a law. They can attempt to achieve less tangible quality of work life improvements by reducing other demands. They might also negotiate these improvements in return for productivity gains. Experience with job enrichment, autonomous work groups, and other innovations in work structures suggest that both employer and employee can gain in most situations. If unions want to take the initiative in improving the quality of work life, such strategies need to be examined.

Union-Management Collaboration in Quality of Work Life Improvements

Up to now we have described the strategies that either a union or management could use on its own initiative to improve quality of work life. We have tried to outline the leverage that each party has and the strategies that are open to them. In this section we will briefly discuss the need and the potential for joint union-management collaboration in bringing about improvements in the quality of work life.

Most OD programs initiated by management to improve the quality of work life have concentrated on management personnel or have been implemented in nonunionized plants. Where unions exist, however, management and the union need to explore the possibilities of jointly sponsored programs. Such programs are more likely to create long-term changes consistent with quality of work life objectives. It is difficult for us to conceive how significant gains in some quality of work life areas can be made without collaboration. For example, formal rules for employee participation in decisions and freedom on the job could be obtained through threat and subsequent bargaining—a power strategy. But these means could not increase employees' psychological involvement and sense of well being. These can be achieved only when an atmosphere of trust between management and workers has been developed through collaboration.

There are a number of differences between the application of OD in an organization with and without a union (Dyer and Kochan, 1974). Where unions are involved, the change agent must be aware of the differences in goals of the unions and management. Of particular importance is the fact that the union and its leaders have an interest in survival. To the extent that changes in the quality of work life threaten their survival or reduce their credibility with their constituents, they will not cooperate. Furthermore, management does not have unilateral power to initiate and move change along, because union and management share power. Finally, the conflict between union and management is more than interpersonal—it is structural. Thus, any attempt to manage this conflict must recognize its structural roots. A collaborative change process must therefore be built on the following premises.

1. A change in the quality of work life cannot threaten the survival of the union or the political viability of its leaders. Further, union leaders must be given a clear and important role in these changes. Union members must see their leaders as highly instrumental to quality of work life improvements, for otherwise these improvements may eliminate the usefulness of the union in the eyes of workers.

2. A collaborative process can get both parties to test their perceptions and awareness of worker needs. Although there are structurally-based differences between management and unions, in many situations these differences are exaggerated and both parties make erroneous assumptions about workers (Gluskines and Kestelman, 1971). The collaborative process can get both parties closer to a valid identification of worker needs. This shared knowledge, rather than myths and stereotypical thinking, can then form the basis for agreement on new ways to manage and structure work.

3. An effective collaborative process will occur only when interpersonal conflict and distrust have been eliminated so that fundamental differences can be negotiated. Too often, hostility stemming from distrust prevents good-faith negotiations. Instead of bargaining or problem-solving, therefore, conflict over irrelevant issues prevails.

4. A collaborative process will be enhanced if both parties can develop a longer time perspective. Often differences in short-term goals get in the way of recognizing commonness in long-range objectives.

A number of collaborative approaches are being developed and used to enhance union-management cooperation in improving the quality of work life. We list them only briefly below, because a more detailed discussion can be found in Chapter 6.

1. *Union-management committees to improve the quality of work life.* The first attempt at this type of collaborative effort was established in prenegotiation discussions between the United Auto Workers and the automobile manufacturers. The committee in each company is

composed of representatives of the international union and the company. It has the responsibility for reviewing and evaluating corporate programs to improve the quality of work life and for developing experimental projects in that area. Furthermore, the National Quality of Work Center, in Washington, D.C., has been active in promoting joint union-management experiments in quality of work life with the help of government funding. A union-management committee is formed to plan and review the effort. The reader will find a more detailed discussion of this program in a later section on government programs.

2. *Union-management OD steering committees.* Another version of the joint union-management committee is the OD steering committee. These committees can exist at several levels of the corporation, but their most obvious value is at the plant level. Such a committee is formed to diagnose plant problems through surveys or other means, and to ensure joint action on problems identified. The advantage of this data-based approach is that potential conflict between the union and management can be dealt with by referring to the results of the diagnosis.

3. *The union-management intergroup laboratory.* The committee mechanisms described above cannot function effectively unless trust exists between union and management. Often, hostility and distrust work against any potential collaboration or effective negotiations and bargaining. The intergroup laboratory has been developed and used by behavioral scientists to improve the relationship between groups and has been applied successfully to union-management relations (Blake, Shepard, and Mouton, 1964; Hundert, 1974). The procedure used involves the exchange of perceptions between a union and management group, in accordance with ground rules for giving and receiving feedback enforced by a behavioral science consultant. This exchange is then followed by a listing of key problems and action planning for their solution.

In summary, union-management cooperation in improving the quality of work life in some areas is dependent on a collaborative process. Both parties need each other in this endeavor. There are a number of approaches and techniques that appear to hold promise for increasing trust and developing collaboration between union and management as they jointly attempt to improve the quality of work life.

ORGANIZING COMMUNITY AND POLITICAL INTEREST GROUPS

We will now shift our attention to strategies for improving the quality of work life that originate outside a given organization. As we indicated earlier, pressure for change from outside increases readiness for change by those inside the organization. This section presents several strategies to bring external pressure on organizations by organizing community and political interest groups to improve the quality of work life.

For each external strategy, we will first present a general description and examples of its use to achieve organizational change. Then we will discuss its adaptation to quality of work life problems, along with our assessment of its costs and benefits as a means for improving the quality of work life.

The strategies considered in this section are ways of bringing to bear on organizations pressure from various interest groups in the society for improvements in the quality of work life. In the section that follows, we will turn to a wide range of alternatives open to government as the formal representative of these interests in the society.

Community Development

By community development (CD), we mean a coalition of existing organizations within a community that attacks some problem of concern to that geographical area. Historically, communities have relied on this strategy to revitalize a sagging local economy, perhaps by attracting new businesses. Chambers of commerce and appeals by combined charities are coalitions of this type. Jamestown, New York, has received national attention for its community-based attempt to resolve economic problems. This attempt has included some effort to improve the quality of work life for workers in the community. We will examine the Jamestown program as an example of an organizational change strategy based in a community rather than in a single organization. This example provides some guidelines for a community-based quality of work life strategy and an indication of its likely effects.

Jamestown, New York. In late 1971, this western New York state manufacturing center was suffering serious economic decline (*Three Productive Years,* 1975). Two thousand manufacturing jobs had left the area in a two-year period; unemployment stood at 10 percent, almost twice the national average at that time; and the town endured a wide reputation for labor-management conflict.

At that low point, leaders of the local community, with the recently reelected mayor taking a pivotal role, hit on the idea of a community-wide labor-management committee to improve local labor relations and reverse the negative economic trend. Both management and union representatives from most local manufacturing plants agreed to serve on the community committee. This group began to utilize community resources to facilitate change in individual plants. For example, the local community college helped provide employee skill training programs. Furthermore, outside funding was obtained from the U.S. Economic Development Administration and the National Commission on Productivity, and a full-time coordinator was hired to work with individual plants.

The community labor-management committee served largely as a catalyst in the change process. Members communicated the goals and results of local changes to each other, and thus created pressure on others to consider similar changes. In addition, plant-level labor-management committees were set up, and it was in these committees that the bulk of the change activity took place. These lower level committees identified specific problems facing each plant and devised their own solutions. In some cases, such as skill training, these solutions involved several different plant committees. Several committees contracted with behavioral science consultants to undertake work re-design projects and attitude surveys with feedback of the data to the employees. Not all members of the community level committee have undertaken in-plant activity to date, however, and in several plants the change process has been sporadic because of other labor relations problems.

A reliable evaluation of the Jamestown program, beyond individual anecdotes, remains to be undertaken. A major new business has entered Jamestown, but many factors besides the labor-management committee figured in the location decision. At a minimum, this community based change strategy retains a high energy level. On the quality of work life, the committee's three-year report concludes that the total program of quality of work life and productivity is ultimately intended to become a self-sustaining process of inquiry and action within the Jamestown area.

Community Development as a Change Strategy.   This example demonstrates some general characteristics of CD as a change strategy. Many of these same characteristics might also be observed in other examples of CD change programs, such as in Muskegon, Michigan, or Newport, New Hampshire.[5] At first a community—often a small community—feels a hurt from problems located in specific employing organizations. The problem may be labor relations or economic stagnation. Next, a coordinating group activates existing organizations in the community and encourages a process of data collection and feed-

---

5. We have learned of these community-based strategies for improving quality of work life through personal communication from Jesse Christman, the consultant involved in Muskegon, and Roy Lewicki, who was involved in the Newport project as a faculty member in the Tuck School of Business Administration at Dartmouth.

back within the employing organizations. This data collection may help the organizations identify problems they had not recognized. Finally, specific change programs are tailored to each organization. Other organizations represented in the coordinating group, as well as the whole community, provide pressure for change in a given organization as well as resources to execute the proposed change. Individuals with behavioral science training provide help to the coordinating group by gathering data and executing specific changes. Also, government funding and outside resources are brought in to initiate and sustain the local changes.

In terms of our strategic considerations, CD is a slow paced attempt at long-term change in an entire community. Specific change decisions are decentralized to particular organizations, and in general there is a dependence on collaboration and on facilitation of the change process within each organization.

Community Development for Quality of Work Life. The poor quality of work life provided by local employers directly affects the whole community, because community members have families, friends, and neighbors who work for these employers. The community also suffers the costs of treating traumatized employees who experience poor health, alcoholism, drug abuse, and mental illness associated with a poor quality work life (*Work in America,* 1973). Although it is not clear how much work conditions contribute to such consequences relative to such other factors as heredity or family surroundings, it is clear that community members might consider several community-based strategies for improving the quality of work life. Several such strategies are described below.

1. Local health and welfare agencies might pool their information on the effects of poor quality of work life experienced by the community's work force. Statistics on the frequency of alcoholism, psychosomatic illness, mental illness, or family problems stemming from work practices can be gathered and provided to local employers and unions. These same agencies would then advocate a coordinating group to address specific quality of work life issues with each organization. Their role in collecting data, advocating change, and coordinating change could have a significant impact on the quality of work life.

2. Employers already concerned about the quality of work life might adopt the CD strategy and involve other community employers and unions in a coordinating group. Such a group could more easily afford a trained behavioral science consultant to conduct educational programs on the quality of work life, to conduct surveys, and to undertake change efforts in several organizations.

As a strategy for improving the quality of work life, CD can be expected to demonstrate the same costs and benefits that characterize it as an approach to other problems. CD will work best only when organizations in the community already feel the need for change. When organizations recognize the need for quality of work life action in general, they can pool their energy and resources in a community-based program to identify the specific actions each might take (for example, job redesign, supervisor training, and so forth). However, this strategy is slow paced, and requires political skills to coordinate the specific long-term and strongly-held interests of participating organizations. Also, because any single organization relies on the expert resources brought into the community by the CD coalition and on the support of the coalition, CD may delay the development of internal quality of work life resources in each organization. This reliance on outside resources makes any particular organization's quality of work life program vulnerable to disruption if the outside groups that comprise the coalition remove their support.

On the other hand, CD does encourage the development of quality of work life programs tailored to each organization. We expect such programs to persist and succeed more often than prepackaged programs developed in other settings and imposed on a particular organization. In principle, CD also encourages a collaborative approach to change in each organization. This should reduce the problems of resistance and rejection that may occur over time when a power strategy is used to demand quality of work life improvements. For those same reasons, CD as a strategy to improve the quality of work life has limited application where employers feel *no* need for such improvement. It is best applied after a need for improving the quality of work life is both felt and acknowledged.

In general, CD strategies emphasize the often neglected community aspects of the quality of work life problem. In particular, community health and welfare agencies might document the negative consequences of poor quality of work life. Identifying these problems is a beginning of a growth program to improve the quality of work life. In such a growth program, these agencies would heighten local awareness of the problem and show local employers and unions the need for action. The agencies might even become advocates for quality of work life improvement in the community. It should be recognized, however, that CD strategies involve action by existing power groups in the community in areas where their concern would be seen as legitimate. This gives them leverage in influencing members of the community, and obviates the need for interest groups in the community to organize for quality of work life improvement. When the appropriate power groups either do not exist or decide not to take action on the quality of work life problem, other community interest groups might have to be formed to deal with the problem.

Organizing Interest Groups

Putting pressure on an organization to improve the quality of work life of its employees requires some source of power. If those concerned with the quality of work life in an organization or community are currently powerless to exert pressure for change, they can organize as an interest group to press their claims. The organization of workers into labor unions has created pressure on employers to improve the quality of work life with respect to wages and working conditions. However, there are other forms of organizing that might be equally useful as strategies to effect change in the quality of work life. In this section we will present a general model of organizing, evaluate one example of its use, and examine its applicability to quality of work life issues.

A Model for Organizing.   Saul Alinsky (1972) developed a strategy for social change based on giving power to the powerless in a community by organizing them. Alinsky organizes the powerless in the following four steps: (1) entry (gaining their credibility), (2) data-collection (identifying their self-interests), (3) setting particular kinds of goals for them (specific, immediate, and realizable), and (4) organizing them (establishing at a convention a formal organization of the powerless group with officers, bylaws, and a constitution) (Peabody, 1971).

As a change strategy, Alinsky's organizing is unique in two aspects. First, it emphasizes the building of power through organization at the expense of particular change objectives. He would sacrifice a particular issue to gain power in order to facilitate change more generally. Second, Alinsky has advocated a completely pragmatic selection of influence tactics—use whatever resources the powerless have available. Threats are particularly emphasized because the opposition often overreacts to threats. This overreaction—counterthreats, police action—helps unify the powerless into a strong organization.

Organizing involves the powerless in a collective action for change. It creates the power to press for change and simultaneously raises the aspirations of the powerless for change. As we stated above, collective action also raises the confidence of the powerless and increases their personal efficacy. Alinsky and his students have applied this strategy to organize many communities. We will briefly consider one example especially relevant to quality of work life issues.

FIGHT.[6] This black community organization in Rochester, New York, was organized by Alinsky according to the model just outlined. In its early stages (1966–1967) FIGHT focused particular pressure on Eastman Kodak, the major employer in the community. On one occasion, FIGHT's president, Reverend Franklin Delano Roosevelt Florence, and fifteen of his associates went directly to Kodak's headquarters and demanded to see the "top man." FIGHT demanded that within eighteen months Kodak hire six hundred hard-core unemployed recruited by FIGHT; FIGHT threatened a "long, hot summer" if its demands were not met and staged a demonstration at Kodak's annual stockholders meeting.

The results of FIGHT's campaign were mixed. Its immediate goal of jobs for the unemployed was met. Rochester began a local program to hire the hard-core unemployed and placed almost eight hundred workers in jobs in the first eleven months of that program. Kodak's share in this program was estimated as the six hundred jobs originally demanded by FIGHT. FIGHT also gained visibility and power as an organization in the community during the campaign. It even began a $600,000 company in conjunction with Xerox, the other large local employer. On the other hand, Kodak had already been a leading equal opportunity employer and it never specifically agreed to FIGHT's demands. A more collaborative approach might have obtained even more jobs at Kodak without creating undesirable resistance. As an example of that resistance, Kodak refused to take part in a joint venture with FIGHT similar to the one undertaken with Xerox.

Organizing for a High Quality Work Life. Just as FIGHT raised the aspirations of Rochester's black community and built a solid power base to pressure Kodak and other employers, change agents can follow Alinsky's model and organize employees or members of the community to demand quality of work life improvements. Because the quality of work life covers a range of issues, from job security to a sense of work accomplishment, the likely form of an organizing campaign would vary with the particular problem encountered. Historically, where workers sought job security and economic gains, organizing to elect a formal union has proven to be an effective change strategy. More recently, minority workers fearing discrimination by employers—even where a union already exists—have organized associations to advance their interests. Many companies now have a caucus of black employees, for example. Organizing can also apply to the less tangible issues associated with the quality of work life. An

6. This account relies heavily on Sethi, 1970.

advocate of improved quality of work life might follow Alinsky's model
to organize all the members of an occupation, such as nurses or social
workers, into a local association. Those employed by several organizations could demand quality of work life improvements such as an
increase in the amount of responsibility allowed them in their jobs.
They could even adapt the tactics of demonstrating in behalf of such
demands.

Organizing along the Alinsky model is most appropriate as a
strategy to improve quality of work life in the following situations:

1. when individual members of a potential interest group lack the power to
   press for change in the quality of work life within their respective
   organizations, and are not recognized as legitimate participants in
   decision-making within these organizations;
2. when the members of a quality of work life interest group are employed by
   organizations that are unreceptive to quality of work life issues and require
   unfreezing;
3. when individuals feel strongly dissatisfied with specific quality of work life
   issues and feel the need for immediate change;
4. when individuals lack the self-confidence or resources to press quality of
   work life issues on their own;
5. when the quality of work life issues of concern are highly visible, so that
   compliance by the target organization can easily be observed and
   monitored.

Indeed, unions have traditionally organized in such situations. As better assessment techniques make quality of work life issues more
measurable and visible (a topic we discuss below), organizing can be
more widely applied to pressure unreceptive organizations to improve
the quality of work life they provide for their employees.

The FIGHT campaign allowed the black community to build confidence and put pressure on Rochester employers; however, FIGHT
seemed to be an inappropriate strategy against Kodak as a *single*
employer. Kodak was already receptive to equal employment opportunity, and thus a more collaborative approach might have produced
similar change without creating the resistance, breaks in communication, and refusal to participate in joint ventures that characterized the
FIGHT-Kodak relationship. The best use of an organizing campaign
like FIGHT is to unfreeze a target organization to the need for change.
Kodak was already unfrozen to equal employment issues.

As a change strategy, organizing has two additional disadvantages.
First, it only elicits surface compliance in response to pressure. Thus, if
the outside pressure lessens, even this surface compliance may disappear. Second, and perhaps more critical, organizing arouses counterforce by the target organization as it tries to resist the pressures being
applied to it. This counterforce could crush the newly organized qual-

ity of work life group in its infancy, if sufficient resources and power were brought to bear against it.

Pressure-Focusing Mechanisms

Mobilizing—either existing organizations in community development (CD) or groups of individuals into formal associations (the Alinsky model)—is not the only way to bring the pressure of interest groups to bear on improving the quality of work life. An alternative principle is the creation of a general mechanism to focus pressure on organizations. Organizations or individuals can then use these mechanisms whenever they experience a quality of work life problem. We will consider three such pressure-focusing mechanisms.

Whistle-Blowing.   The Clearinghouse for Professional Responsibility, one of Ralph Nader's efforts, provides access to Nader's various organizations by any employee who wishes to make public an illegal or morally objectionable practice in his organization—blowing the whistle on the practice (Nader, Petkas, and Blackwell, 1972). A whistle-blower can (1) report the practice internally to supervisors or investigative units within the organization, (2) complain externally to the media, government agencies, or the courts, or (3) resign from the organization either as a silent protest or with a strong public condemnation of the practice.

The Nader Clearinghouse receives inquiries from potential whistle-blowers and counsels them on the likely effects of these alternative actions while preserving their anonymity. Nader has helped publicize these complaints by publishing reports on a number of employees who objected to organizational practices.

These same action alternatives are available to an employee concerned about quality of work life issues. A whistle-blowing center devoted to such issues could provide employees with comparative information and current research results to establish the validity of their quality of work life complaints. This information could answer such questions as: How does the objectionable condition compare with that in other organizations or communities? and, What are the likely effects on employees of this condition? Then, the center could describe the alternative sources of pressure open to the employee— media channels interested in the quality of work life, organizations interested in quality of work life issues in the industry, locale, or profession, and legal recourse that may be available to the complainant. Besides counseling the employee on these alternatives with the protection of anonymity, the center could later publicize important quality of work life complaints in support of interested employees.

This strategy complements other approaches to quality of work life change. For example, the strategy of organizing interest groups could utilize such a center. A whistle-blowing center would also facilitate the use of government legislation and information-gathering strategies on the quality of work life (described below).

The major disadvantage of whistle-blowing is that it relies heavily on outside resources. For example, media coverage, public attention, and legislation have facilitated whistle-blowing on the issue of pollution. Thus, whistle-blowing will be an effective strategy for improving the quality of work life only to the extent that public attention focuses on quality of work life issues or legislation requires action in this area by employers. Only where such conditions exist do the benefits of whistle-blowing offset the inevitable personal costs to individuals who make public complaints.

The Ombudsman. An ombudsman is another way to bring external pressure to bear on organizations to improve the quality of work life of their employees.[7] In Sweden and Finland, an ombudsman is a politically independent, impartial investigator in the legislative branch of government (Rowat, 1968). By tradition, all political parties agree on the ombudsman's appointment. The ombudsman handles complaints against government administrative decisions directly, informally, quickly, and inexpensively. A citizen appeals an administrative decision by a letter to the ombudsman, whose main power is the right to investigate. If warranted, the ombudsman by using his prestige and reputation for personal objectivity, competence, and superior knowledge, persuades the decision-maker to change. When persuasion fails, publicity can often secure remedial action. Because of this simple, inexpensive procedure, many complaints can be and are settled.

The government in a local community or a professional association could appoint an ombudsman to receive quality of work life complaints. That person would investigate the complaint and attempt to persuade the employer to develop or accept quality of work life changes. If persuasion based on the ombudsman's personal qualifications and objectivity failed to achieve change, then the ombudsman would publicize the complaint and an assessment of the quality of work life problem. The local government or profession could also attach penalties to the employer. As an example of such penalties, the American Association of University Professors publishes a blacklist of those colleges and universities that do not meet its standards for conditions of academic employment.

---

7. An ombudsman can also be used internally to effect organizational change. This strategy rests on the same basis of power as the external strategy and has similar limitations.

Personal persuasion by the ombudsman is preferable. Such a personal method constitutes a collaborative approach to change and increases the probability that an employer will accept the need for change and will change voluntarily. However, personal persuasion will work best only if the employer accepts quality of work life as an important issue. If he does not, persuasion will fail and the ombudsman will be left with the alternatives of putting pressure on the employer through publicity or mobilization of outside groups. Furthermore, to do this successfully, these groups must have power and be previously committed to achieving a high quality work life. For these reasons, the ombudsman is most effective when he uses a collaborative strategy. When pressure groups are invoked, the ombudsman's reputation for objectivity suffers and his future effectiveness is reduced.

Social Audits. A social audit is an attempt to measure the performance of an organization in areas of social concern—such as civil rights and equal opportunity, pollution abatement, and so forth. Such an audit could include the broad area of quality of work life and could form the basis for several change strategies.

To date most social audits have been conducted within corporations (Bauer and Fenn, 1972; Dierkes and Bauer, 1973). For example, a business might assemble in one document all its social responsibility goals and its current programs to reach these goals. Some external groups have also audited organizations on social topics other than quality of work life. The Dreyfus Third Century Fund conducts investigations to identify socially responsible firms for investment purposes. The Council on Economic Priorities accumulates and disseminates information on the performance of organizations in areas of social concern. These two groups rely on the media, and ultimately on investors, to act on their findings. Gathering the information for such external audits is an obvious problem. Target organizations must cooperate and provide needed data. However, simply announcing the names of noncooperating companies to the media has, in some cases, influenced those organizations to give information.

An external audit of the quality of work life of an organization's employees requires the ability to measure quality of work life effectively, a need that affects a number of change strategies discussed in this chapter. As discussed in Chapter 1, there are two major approaches to measuring the quality of work life of employees (Lawler, 1973b). The first focuses on the subjective reactions of employees to their work, such as their job satisfaction, frustrations, tensions, and so forth. The second considers the behavioral outcomes for persons working on particular jobs—turnover, illness, absenteeism, drug abuse, and the like. Organizational psychologists have developed effective instruments for measuring employees' reports of their subjective reactions to work. However, these reports may be distorted, either positively or negatively, if the employees feel that the information they provide will form the basis for actions toward either themselves or the employer. Although such distortions provide important information about the state of employee morale, behavioral outcomes may be preferable for quality of work life audits because they are less subject to overt distortion.

A quality of work life audit could be implemented in a variety of forms, as described below.

1. College and graduate school placement offices dealing with highly talented personnel are a source of leverage on employers. Such offices desire information about potential employers to improve their service to job seekers. A quality of work life audit of potential employers would help them do this and indirectly pressure employers to improve the quality of work life they provide, in order to attract mobile and talented employees. Thus, one strategy to improve the quality of work life is to encourage placement offices to conduct such an audit, or to feed the results of quality of work life audits undertaken by other groups to placement offices.

2. Financial leverage can be used in conjunction with social audits as a strategy to improve the quality of work life. External social audits can guide investment decisions by concerned individuals and institutions (churches, employee pension funds) in favor of organizations that are taking positive steps to improve the quality of work life of their employees. Such decisions reward these firms with capital and favorable stock prices. Even a single share of stock enables a shareholder to take symbolic actions, by voting against management recommendations or by using the stockholders' meeting as a source of publicity on quality of work life performance. In the FIGHT-Kodak confrontation described above, FIGHT used both symbolic and direct financial leverage against Kodak. They demonstrated at the stockholders' meeting and encouraged holders of large amounts of stock to vote against management.

3. Media publicity based on a quality of work life audit can also be used to put pressure on employers to improve the quality of work life.

4. The federal government could facilitate this change strategy by requiring publicly-held companies, government contractors, and government agencies to publish an internal audit of behavioral outcomes associated with the quality of work life. (We recommend such an audit in our section on government strategies.)

The social audit is a long-range strategy for improving the quality of work life. It can place pressure on employers to improve the quality of work life as market forces affect the movement of human and financial resources to prominent quality of work life employers. However, the use of social audits to improve the quality of work life, like the whistle-blowing center, requires outside support from the media, investors, and job seekers. It is vulnerable to shifts in attention by these outside groups. In addition, for successful pressure, the audit assumes easy market movement for both human and financial resources over time.

Whistle-blowing, the ombudsman, and social audits rely primarily on *information* from inside an organization to focus outside pressure on employers. Interest groups outside the organization also can rely on more aggressive sources of pressure to improve the quality of work life. In the next section, we briefly consider violent and nonviolent protests to pressure organizations to make such improvements.

Protests: Violent and Nonviolent

By protests we mean the threat or use of physical action to influence another's behavior. These can take the form of violent physical force aimed at injuring the change target or nonviolent physical actions such as a sit-in.

Historically, protest has been an important approach to organizational change. It has been used perhaps most frequently in labor-management relations. For example, in 1937, a massive sit-down strike marked the climax of the campaign by labor to organize General Motors. During the forty-four days of the strike, the strikers destroyed property and used fire hoses as weapons; the police used riot guns and tear gas. The strike ended when General Motors agreed to recognize the UAW as the bargaining agent for the workers. Thus, protest—including violence—was used to obtain recognition of the union. This recognition laid the basis for the later involvement of the union in negotiations and other more collaborative approaches to change. In general, violence usually disappears from labor-management relations after recognition has been won and collective bargaining has been established (Ross, 1954).

Both violent and nonviolent protests are possible strategies to pressure organizations to improve the quality of work life. Employees, whether organized into a union or not, can strike or demonstrate to protest unacceptable quality of work life conditions. As noted above, a community organizing campaign might well call for such protests on quality of work life issues.

In order to assess the likely effects of protest as a strategy for improving the quality of work life, let us consider briefly a prominent example of the use of protests—student protests against war-related recruiting on college campuses. During the 1967–1968 academic year, students at many colleges and universities protested against recruiting on campus by the military and by companies associated with the Vietnam war. At those campuses where students protested with sit-ins and human blockades, the administration was three times more likely to restrict on-campus recruiting by war-related employers than was the administration at campuses where no protest took place (Morgan, 1972). Another effect of these demonstrations was that they contributed to the increase in formalized influence of students on college campuses during this period. However, the protests also caused problems for student demonstrators. Besides the personal risks involved, campuses with these protests were also twice as likely to adopt new regulations for future demonstrations.

These results on campus protests suggest that protest is a potentially effective strategy to pressure organizations to change. Indeed, unions have always used both the threat of a strike and actual work stoppages to pressure employers to change working conditions. Protest, therefore, deserves consideration as a general strategy to improve the quality of work life. It is most likely to be used or to be necessary when a group is not recognized as having legitimate influence on a particular issue. Once recognition is obtained, as in the labor movement, violent protest is less often required. Thus, protest may enable the use of other collaborative change strategies after recognition is obtained.

Besides the obvious personal risks involved in protests, this strategy has general disadvantages. It creates resistance in the organizations that are the objects of protest, although they might otherwise be open to influence. The adoption of campus restrictions on future protest activity illustrates this resistance. Although protest may accomplish short-term change, or the promise of change, long-term change may not follow unless the target considers future protests a possibility.

We feel that protest, particularly violent protest, requires careful consideration before it is used as a change strategy for improving the quality of work life. Unfortunately, however, protests often result from the release of built-up frustration rather than from rational analysis. Although the history of our work organizations and our universities indicates that the possibility of protests always exists, and that they can effect change, protest will remain a strategy of last resort, used only after strategies with less personal risk have failed. Moreover, protests for quality of work life improvements will probably focus on fundamental and tangible issues like job security, occupational safety, and equal employment opportunity. Indeed, violent protest may be incongruous with some quality of work life changes. Threats of injury destroy the trust and collaborative spirit that underlie quality of work life improvements such as increases in responsibility, trust, and discretion at work. Nonetheless, protest is a change strategy whose costs and benefits—like those of any other strategy—must be assessed from the perspective of the advocate desiring change.

Community and Political Pressure Strategies in Perspective

Advocates inside and outside employing organizations can utilize outside resources to initiate or focus pressure for change in the quality of work life. The external pressure may make it possible for those inside the organization who favor an improved quality work life to increase their influence, or it may create an awareness of quality of work life issues where previously none existed.

The community surrounding an employing organization is one likely source of this external pressure. The best strategy to activate community pressure will vary with the resources a change advocate possesses in a given situation, and with the costs of applying each strategy. In a community where existing employers and unions are receptive to quality of work life improvements, a CD strategy is called for to bind these organizations into a coalition. The coalition can share change resources and influence its members to adopt specific changes. Where such receptivity is lacking, however, local health and welfare agencies or other interest groups may be able to unfreeze organizations to the need for change.

Organizing along the Alinsky model is a more costly and uncertain approach. It attempts to create receptivity to quality of work life issues. Alinsky's model selects immediate, specific, realizable demands as the basis for building a community organization. It will drop particular demands and raise others to appeal to different individuals as the organizer attempts to build an organization quickly. Where tangible and deeply felt issues of job security, occupational safety, or discrimination concern either the community or some employees, Alinsky's strategy may succeed. Indeed, it may take the form of organizing a labor union. However, less visible issues, like the lack of intrinsic satisfaction from work, are less suited to Alinsky's model. Community or employee organizing for such issues generally awaits better measurement techniques to make both issues and demands more visible. However, repeated refusal by employers to consider such intangible quality of work life issues may result in community organizing and protest as a last resort.

Besides developing external pressure for quality of work life improvements, a change advocate can also establish mechanisms that allow dissatisfied individuals or groups to focus pressure for quality of work life improvement on organizations. We discussed only three possibilities—a whistle-blowing center, an ombudsman, and social auditing. The role of the change advocate, his resources, and his power are among the factors that will determine the mechanism established or utilized. For example, an advocate involved in a mental health clinic might sponsor a local whistle-blowing center to counsel and advise local quality of work life complainants. Establishing a quality of work life ombudsman, on the other hand, would require more powerful sponsorship by a local government, a union, or a professional association. Widespread social auditing for quality of work life would be expensive, and substantial financial resources or power would be required to get organizations to do self-audits.

All of these strategies for organizing community and political interest groups attempt to bring external pressure to unfreeze the target organization and make it aware of the general need to improve the quality of work life. All these pressure strategies run the risk of antagonizing the target organization in order to obtain recognition for quality of work life issues and encourage possible changes. After the target organization accepts the need for change, however, other long-term collaborative strategies are appropriate and possible. Of the strategies in this section, a CD program to coordinate local quality of work life changes and change resources offers the best potential external support for such a long-term collaborative undertaking.

The strategies we have discussed so far to improve the quality of work life have neglected the most obvious source of external pressure—government action. We now move to an examination of the government's role in improving the quality of work life.

GOVERNMENT STRATEGIES TO IMPROVE QUALITY OF WORK LIFE

Improving the quality of work life is a reasonable goal for our society. However, many individuals who recognize the value of a high quality work life would oppose government pressure on employers to improve it. Managers in the private sector might cite such government action as a misdirection of energy away from adding to the nation's economic well-being through the pursuit of profits. Others might see government action on this issue as an encroachment on the collective bargaining process. Any attempt to legislate quality of work life strategies will require trade-offs between such opposition and the advantages of government action. Our personal view is that some government action to stimulate improvement in quality of work life is both appropriate and necessary.

As noted in the previous sections, without external pressure some organizations will not undertake change to improve the quality of work life. As the formal representative of the society, government has unique capabilities to bring such pressure on organizations. Only government pressure can stimulate some organizations to undertake quality of work life changes; for other organizations, however, positive government programs would both hasten and extend the range of their voluntary activity in this area.

At present, government legislation puts substantial pressure on conditions of employment in organizations in areas such as equal opportunity, safety, and labor relations. Given the overall impact of government on employment and its specific effects on quality of work life change programs, the question of government strategies is not whether but *how* government action will affect the quality of work life.

The federal government might undertake any of a variety of possible strategies to improve the quality of work life:[8]

1. The government can modify existing laws affecting the quality of work life.
2. New legislation can set and enforce quality of work life standards of employment.
3. New legislation can reward organizations with government incentives for adopting quality of work life innovations.
4. New legislation can require all employers to begin a change process within each organization to improve the quality of work life it provides its employees.
5. Government funding can support programs to advance the state of the art in quality of work life practice and knowledge.
6. The government can serve directly as a model quality of work life employer or encourage its contractors to become such models.
7. Finally, the government can alter policies on education and the economy to improve the quality of work life.

We will evaluate each of these alternatives according to the strategic considerations for change presented above, and conclude with suggested guidelines for government policy at the national level to improve the quality of work life.

Modifying Existing Legislation

The government might modify any piece of legislation that interferes with attempts to improve the quality of work life, or that causes quality of work life problems. For example, the wage and hour laws establish different classes of employees with respect to overtime pay. If a work team composed of exempt and nonexempt personnel works overtime,

---

8. For reasons of space we will emphasize actions by the federal government. State governments might take similar actions, especially in states with strong quality of work life constituencies.

some will receive extra pay while others will not. This puts an additional constraint on attempts to restructure work groups and to integrate different levels of the organization. Some provisions of the tax code also have unintended negative effects on the quality of work life. For example, investment tax credits have encouraged capital-intensive technology, even though jobs in such technologies often provide a poor quality work life and are difficult to restructure economically.

We would encourage a reexamination of this and other legislation. However, we recognize that many of the laws seek reasonable policy objectives—increased economic activity for the tax credit, or protection of the worker by wage and hour laws. Indeed, much of the legislation restricting the actions of employers with respect to their employees seeks improvements in fundamental aspects of the employees' quality of work life—equal job opportunity, adequate payment, health, and safety. Therefore, the government must carefully assess any modification of existing employee protective legislation as a means to improve the quality of work life.

Across-the-board modification of legislation affecting employers is also a questionable governmental strategy based on our consideration of the change process. Such a collective approach would remove constraints on all organizations and give them the potential to adopt quality of work life changes. This approach would materially effect change only in those organizations currently attempting to improve the quality of work life. As we indicated earlier, a collective strategy works best when all organizations are homogeneous. At present, all organizations do not have equal interest in quality of work life change programs. An across-the-board change is thus an inappropriate strategy to encourage experimentation in a few organizations. Moreover, a collective change would jeopardize the advances in other aspects of quality of work life accomplished by the pressure of these laws.

As an alternative to collective change, legislation might allow the creation of sheltered experiments by exempting individual organizations from problematical federal employment statutes if they propose quality of work life changes. For example, an employer might want to allow all members of a team composed of exempt and nonexempt employees to determine their own form of payment (see Chapter 4). This might require exemption from required overtime payments to the nonexempt members of the team. Similarly, tax credits for investment might be increased on an individual basis if a firm were to make capital investments that also increased quality of work life. A small federal agency would coordinate such proposals with the various government enforcement personnel and ascertain that approved quality of work life proposals are actually executed. Such exemptions are a market strategy; they encourage innovation in exceptional plants and companies that no longer require the pressure of earlier legislation to maintain minimum standards of employment.

Setting Standards

The federal government might legislate minimum standards for quality of work life and pressure all employers to conform by means of fines or other penalties for noncompliance. There are three broad categories in which standards might be applied—organizational practices (that is, types of jobs, personnel policies, reward systems), subjective employee reactions to the organization (attitudes toward jobs, supervisor, company), and employees' behavioral outcomes (turnover, absenteeism, alcoholism, mental illness).[9] Although the government might tax or fine employers for reliance on practices associated with poor quality of work life such as assembly line jobs, current research indicates that for almost any organizational condition imaginable (routine work, close supervision) there are some employees who find that condition satisfying or at least acceptable. Therefore, government standards should only be considered in the categories of subjective reactions and behavioral outcomes where indications of low quality of work life reflect poor *fit* between the needs of the individual employee and organizational conditions. In order to gain some insight into the feasibility of government setting standards in these quality of work life categories, we will consider two employment areas where federal legislation has already applied standards. These are occupational safety and health, and equal employment opportunity.

Occupational Safety and Health. Prior to the passage of federal legislation in 1970, this area suffered relative neglect in state and federal legislation and in union activity. Through the provisions of the 1970 Occupational Safety and Health Act, the federal government threatened the employers of 57 million people with substantial fines if they violated nationally established standards for conditions affecting health and safety. These standards focused on hazardous organizational practices in order to prevent negative outcomes for employees. Any worker observing a hazardous condition was empowered to request a federal inspection. In practice, a small staff has usually limited inspections to cases where employees have already suffered serious outcomes, either accidents or widespread illness.

The establishment of occupational safety and health standards proved to be a problem. Initially, many inappropriate standards were

9. The discussion of government use of standards relies heavily on Lawler (1973b) and an unpublished manuscript by the same author.

incorporated into the act (Foulkes, 1973; Mallino, 1973). More generally, the introduction of new substances and technologies in industrial
processes creates a continuous demand for new standards.

Although this legislation has pressured organizations to improve
working conditions, improvement has not been equal in all organizations. Strong unions can take advantage of the legislation as a source of
outside pressure in negotiations or as a source of standards to be
referenced in the bargaining agreement (OSHA and the Unions, 1973).
Large employers often possess sufficient financial resources to correct
safety and health hazards and to maintain a staff specializing in this
area to stimulate needed action. Small companies have complained
about the difficulty of understanding safety and health standards. We
suspect they have also been less likely to initiate action in this area.

Equal Employment Opportunity. The 1964 Civil Rights Act, other
legislation, and various executive orders clearly prohibit employment
discrimination based on race, color, religion, sex, national origin, or
age. Employers, employment agencies, labor organizations, and joint
labor-management committees controlling apprenticeship programs
must follow the various nondiscrimination laws or suffer penalties.
These range from contract cancellation to awards of back pay for
groups of employees who were discriminated against. Government
contractors and subcontractors must observe executive orders on nondiscrimination as well. Most business organizations are subject to
both.

Enforcement of these standards against organizational practices of
discrimination necessarily follows a slow, organization by organization
approach. Thus, relatively few penalties are administered, and some
penalties—contract cancellations, for example—are rarely enforced.

Evaluation of Standard-Setting. Standard-setting certainly puts pressure on organizations to change. This external pressure has most effect
where some already organized group (a union, a civil rights group, or a
specialized management staff) can focus this pressure on organizational practices. The standards also provide internal pressure because
they provide some stimulus to organize employees into unions to demand better treatment. However, the strategy raises some problems. Its
greatest difficulty lies in the establishment of standards. Organizations
will gather the data required by law (accident reports or employment
summaries), but the administration of penalties requires a clear, quanti-
fiable standard. Setting standards also assumes technical capability to
measure organizational practices or their outcomes, and an inspection
staff to apply these measurements to alleged violations. The use of
penalties in conjunction with standards reduces the government's ef-

fectiveness in encouraging change. For example, employers hesitate to call the federal agencies for occupational health and safety advice for fear they will instigate an inspection and fine. Employers' fear of penalties may also tie up social scientists in organizations in justifying past practices. This may have been true in equal employment opportunity. Paradoxically, these individuals are critical to developing and applying quality of work life improvements. Finally, standard-setting creates no incentive for internally generated changes or progress beyond the minimum requirement in the standard.

Standards for Quality of Work Life. Despite the potential effectiveness of standard-setting as a means of pressuring organizations to improve the quality of work life, the technology for measuring employees' subjective reactions to their work or the behavioral outcomes they demonstrate is not yet adequate to support regulation of organizations by the government. Employee reports of their subjective reactions to work (for example, attitudes, or extent of satisfaction or tension) are too easily distorted by employees either to please or penalize their employers. These subjective reactions can provide extremely useful information for diagnosing organizational problems. Distortions do reflect employee feelings about the organization. However, such data is not sufficiently understood to justify government penalties.

Behavioral outcomes—such as turnover, absenteeism, psychosomatic illness, or mental illness—have been too inconsistently measured to provide accurate standards or norms. Further research might develop usable standards for such outcomes. An equally critical shortcoming is that the relative contribution of organizational factors, such as routine work or job tension, to undesirable outcomes has not been adequately determined. Other factors outside the organization, such as inherited tendencies or problems in the home, also affect these outcomes.

For the above reasons, both subjective employee reactions and behavioral outcomes are inappropriate to regulate organizational practices in the quality of work life area. They cannot at this time be measured with sufficient accuracy, nor is there any well-understood relationship between organizational practices and employee reactions and outcomes.

Lawler (1973b) has suggested federal legislation requiring employers to make public internal information on objective employee behavioral outcomes such as turnover, absenteeism, alcoholism, and mental illness. This would set a government standard for a quality of work life *reporting process* rather than for quality of work life practices and employee outcomes. Initially, this internal information need not be verified by auditors outside the organization, although such validation would ultimately be required. Such a strategy makes visible the consequences of organizational practices that affect the quality of work life. Visibility of these consequences can focus attention on them and can generate external pressure on the organization from stockholders, unions, and the public at large if warranted. In addition, visibility of consequences can stimulate internal pressure for quality of work life improvements.

This strategy retains one key advantage over across-the-board standard-setting. Because all organizations must undertake a similar expenditure, there is no special economic burden on any single organization. This strategy puts less government pressure on the organization than setting standards for quality of work life outcomes, and it reduces many of the negative effects of penalties. Because employers are only required to undertake a reporting process, they are free to seek government assistance without fear of penalty, as long as they report the required information. Social science resources would be free to focus on generating new information and solutions. In addition, giving visibility to these negative consequences creates an incentive for internal innovation in quality of work life.

In summary, the present level of scientific understanding and measurement of quality of work life outcomes does not allow the government to penalize organizations for providing a poor quality of work life. Even if this barrier were removed, setting quality of work life standards has enough negative effects, such as creating employer resistance, to render this strategy questionable. However, setting of standards for an internal process of monitoring and reporting quality of work life outcomes would reduce these negative effects, and could still create pressure for quality of work life improvement.

Incentives for Adopting Quality of Work Life Innovations

The government can adopt the general strategy of rewarding organizations with incentives such as tax advantages, financial bonuses, or public recognition. Such incentives to employers for meeting quality of work life standards would avoid some of the negative effects of government strategies involving penalties. Unlike penalties, incentives do not create resistance in employers. Indeed, as time passes, rewarded employers are more likely to feel a sense of ownership for the practices they adopt. However, using government incentives to meet quality of work life standards raises some of the same problems we discussed in connection with across-the-board standards. These are the problems of measuring quality of work life effects and the cost of surveillance to assure that incentives are justified.

The government might achieve the positive advantages of incentives and avoid the problems of standard-setting by rewarding employers for adopting innovative quality of work life practices. This general strategy—providing government incentives for innovation—has been used in a variety of situations. We will examine two examples of the strategy to gain some insight to its effectiveness, limits, and consequences.[10]

Examples of Incentives for Innovation. Since the 1930s, the U.S. Soil Conservation Service has made payments to farmers for adopting innovative conservation techniques. This governmental strategy has stimulated farmers to adopt conservation techniques—such as the use of lime—that conform to farmers' existing values. On the other hand, the incentives have less effectively encouraged more unusual practices, such as terracing of fields. American farmers frequently adopted conservation techniques only for the incentive provided and did not understand or internalize the conservation value of those practices. Thus, when incentive payments stopped, the farmers often abandoned the techniques.

In India, local governments in the mid-1950s began offering financial payments as incentives to encourage married couples to adopt birth control practices. Couples did increase their use of these practices, although the incentive program had its share of problems. Many individuals adopting birth control practices were outside their fertile years. They forged age certificates to obtain the financial incentive for adopting birth control. Because incentives were also paid in some areas to canvassers who successfully encouraged couples to adopt these techniques, these canvassers often relied on coercion and deception to influence couples to adopt birth control. It should also be noted that the couples adopting birth control for incentives were most often people from the lower economic classes to whom the financial payment was most attractive (Rogers, 1973).

These two examples suggest that a strategy of government incentives can be used in some cases to increase innovation. However, the strategy has at least the following probable limits and unintended consequences, which should be examined in considering it as a potential strategy for encouraging quality of work life innovations: (1) only a limited range of innovations is stimulated; (2) innovation adopters often do not understand the innovation's value—they merely seek the incentive; (3) the incentives encourage cheating and deception; and (4) indirectly the incentive causes the use of threats by parties seeking incentives, the very influence tactic this strategy might have been hoped to avoid.

---

10. The examples and evaluation of government incentives in the United States and Asia are drawn from Rogers (1973).

Incentives Applied to Quality of Work Life Innovation.   To apply this strategy to improving the quality of work life, the federal government might well reward organizations for undertaking any number of the innovative practices described in this book. The experimental plant we described in the section on OD is one example of such an innovation. To encourage the use of experimental plants, the government could legislate such incentives as permitting an employer to gain a tax advantage through the accelerated depreciation of new plants that incorporate quality of work life innovations; or, tax payments could be reduced in proportion to the costs of the quality of work life program in an existing, but newly designated experimental plant. In order to prevent deception, this strategy would have to include specific criteria for an experimental plant. A board of behavioral scientists might even have to be established to certify the existence of quality of work life innovations in the plant—such as job redesign and individualized reward systems, effective communication practices, and participation in decision-making—in order for a plant to qualify for an incentive.

The strategy of providing incentives for innovation has some limitations. For one thing, it will tend to encourage the spread of specific, previously developed innovations, because most organizations do not have their own behavioral science resources. As we discussed earlier, such innovations may not fit local conditions. Furthermore, the incentive strategy does not facilitate the development of a continuing change process internal to the adopting organization. In order to overcome this limitation, the government might specifically reward organizations that have developed their own quality of work life innovations.

Implementation of this strategy must also consider the undesirable effects of incentives suggested by the examples of soil conservation and birth control. As noted, the government must undertake some surveillance against cheating by those employers who claim the incentives. The incentive strategy does avoid the use of threats and penalties, but high level managers, like the canvassers for birth control, might frustrate this advantage by forcing lower level management to adopt quality of work life innovations. Both cheating and forced compliance are undesirable consequences that result when organizations adopt innovations solely to obtain incentives. The same motive may lead those organizations that need the financial incentive most to adopt legislatively supported innovations. These financially troubled organizations may be least ready or able to develop additional quality of work life programs beyond the specific innovations adopted. If only such organizations adopt quality of work life innovations, this strategy will not facilitate a widespread effort to improve quality of work life among employers in the society.

The advantages of incentives to encourage innovations suggest that this market strategy is a reasonable approach to improving the quality of work life, despite its potential limitations and undesirable effects. This strategy could be a slow-paced, decentralized means of building positive momentum for quality of work life improvement.

Legislating a Quality of Work Life Change Process for Organizations

The government could directly legislate specific processes internal to all employing organizations. This change strategy has been widely utilized in countries outside the United States where national governments have legislated internal organizational processes to increase employee participation in decision-making. Legislation of worker participation as a particular internal process is directly relevant to the quality of work life, because increased employee responsibility and control over work decisions are often cited as improvements in quality of work life.

We will examine the West German experience with legislated worker participation from two perspectives. We will look at it first as an example of how internal organizational process and practices can be legislated to improve the quality of work life. Second, and more important, we will look at it as an example of how internal organizational processes might be legislated to encourage quality of work life examination and change.

Worker Participation in West Germany. Legislated worker participation in West Germany takes two forms—a traditional works council at low levels in the organization, and codetermination, or participation in high level decision-making in the coal, iron, and steel industries.[11] According to legislation passed in 1951, half the board of directors of companies in these three industries must be employee representatives. A labor director, also an employee representative, sits on the executive committee and takes part in the management of the enterprise on a day-to-day basis. For other industries, a second codetermination law (passed in 1952) strengthened the low level works council that is elected by blue- and white-collar workers. This council negotiates with management over more limited decisions—such as conditions of employment, grievances, wage systems, work rules, and the administration of social welfare services.

Employees in West Germany are satisfied with this legislated process of codetermination. However, one survey showed the sources of this satisfaction to be better social services and higher wages and salaries rather than increased participation in personnel and business

---

11. Hartman (1970), Strauss and Rosenstein (1970), and Seybolt (undated) provide the basis for this discussion of German worker participation. Walker (undated) provides an excellent overview of the variety in worker participation.

policies (Hartman, 1970). In operation, codetermination does not increase the influence of *individual* employees over decisions at work. The labor director participates in policy decisions of the organization, but the workers who reach that position are not in close contact with rank-and-file employees. The director is actually prohibited by law from disseminating business secrets. Thus, few employees take part in or know about high level decision-making. The low level works council deals with issues usually taken up in collective bargaining in the United States. It does not involve individual employees in production or policy decisions of the organization.

This example demonstrates the direct legislation of an internal organizational process. The German experience also suggests that legislating this particular process—worker participation—does *not* necessarily increase the individual's control over his job. Furthermore, employees who participate in high level decision-making deal with management problems requiring technical expertise and information that they may not have. In general, as employees acquire that expertise and information they often change their relationships with other employees and thereby their representativeness (Strauss and Rosenstein, 1970). In any event, this legislated attempt at worker participation does not involve shop floor production issues where the employee may have the most knowledge to contribute to organizational effectiveness, and where participation is most likely to yield a feeling of personal satisfaction (Strauss, 1963). Improving the quality of work life will probably require some other process (such as work redesign, as described in Chapter 3, or group tasks and group decision-making, as discussed in Chapter 6) to satisfy needs for influence over important decisions about the employee's job.

In summary, participation by employees in decision-making can contribute to improving the quality of work life for some employees in some situations. In Chapter 6, Strauss outlines various ways participation may have this effect. The formally legislated use of employee representatives in plant-wide works councils can contribute to improving the quality of work life by representing employee concerns at high levels. Such representation may also increase the trust employees feel in the organization's decision-making. However, it seems unlikely to contribute to an individual employee's feelings of responsibility and control over his work.

Legislating Actions by Organizations to Improve Quality of Work Life. Although the legislation of formal worker participation in decision-making has the limits cited above, there may be ways to legislate participative processes that increase individual feelings of responsibility and control. Such legislation would encourage participation at lower levels and on day-to-day work problems. We will discuss this approach briefly before turning to a more attractive alternative—legislating a process for examining and changing the quality of work life.

Legislation might require some variation of current practice such as the Scanlon Plan. Government might even legislate practices that are not as well documented, such as an ombudsman internal to the organization to receive quality of work life complaints. The major problem with legislation to require such organizational practices is the low probability of enacting such precedent-breaking legislation in the United States. In addition, such a collective strategy attempts to force specific changes in practice on a variety of different and possibly inappropriate organizations. Instead of requiring specific organizational practices such as the Scanlon Plan or an ombudsman, therefore, legislation might require that each organization initiate participative processes for self-inquiry and change directed toward improving the quality of work life. Such legislation might require the following process:

1. Data would be collected internally on employees' satisfaction with job, salary, supervisor, participation, influence, and other important dimensions that affect the quality of work life. Data on behavioral outcomes such as grievances, turnover, absenteeism, employee sickness, and personal problems might also be collected.
2. A joint council of employee and management representatives would undertake the survey and feed the results back to all organizational members.
3. The same council would solicit comments and complaints from employees based on this feedback, formulate official recommendations to improve the quality of work life, and report the survey results to management, the public, and stockholders.
4. Where a union represents employees, a joint labor-management council would undertake this process and the results would also be reported to the union.

This process presents a number of problems. Again, it requires a departure from American legislative tradition. Also, it imposes on established collective bargaining relationships a new requirement that both parties may oppose. Finally, improvement in the quality of work life would be a relatively slow-paced and long-term process.

Despite these limitations, legislating a process for improving the quality of work life through a participative process of self-examination and change seems worth considering. Compared to West German worker participation, it increases the number of employees participating, it distributes information on these issues widely, it raises quality of work life issues relevant to employees of the organization, and it does not impose a practice that might not be relevant to a given group of employees or a particular organization. Yet it ensures examination and change.

In terms of the strategic considerations we have discussed, this strategy is dependent on data about the quality of work life, as seen by employees, to generate power for individuals and groups who feel a need for improvement of their quality of work life. This power, based on information that makes visible the consequences of particular organizational practices, is relatively nonthreatening compared to other forms of government pressure. And it would support and encourage a collaborative process of change within the organization. The energy unleashed by this process would be focused on quality of work life issues within the organization. It would not be dissipated in the same way that energy generated by external pressures is dissipated by the organization's resistance to pressures from outside groups. A legislated process of examination and change would result in the development of quality of work life improvements suited to local conditions. It would facilitate the development of a self-contained and sustained change process within the organization. Yet this legislation would put pressure on all organizations to begin a process of quality of work life improvement.

Advancing the State of the Art

The government can facilitate the improvement of quality of work life in the society without involving itself as deeply or widely in the operations of employing organizations as the previous strategies require. Simply advancing knowledge about the quality of work life and the means to improve it, and disseminating this information, is a strategy that can function in isolation or in conjunction with other government approaches.

Three general forms of this strategy deserve consideration:

1. The government can create or sponsor model quality of work life programs. Other employing organizations can then observe and imitate them.
2. The government can generate new information through research to evaluate current quality of work life change efforts, to develop understanding of the quality of work life change process, and to identify emerging quality of work life issues.
3. The government can serve as an information clearinghouse disseminating existing information.

Unlike most of our previous discussions, in this section we can report some concrete programs. At the national and state levels government has begun information-based strategies to improve the quality of work life.

Developing Models.   The National Quality of Work Center (NQWC), funded by the U.S. Department of Commerce and the Ford Foundation as an affiliate of the University of Michigan, continues a program originated under the Federal Price Commission in 1972 to establish experimental quality of work life projects. Each project lasts eighteen months and involves both labor and management of the participating company in restructuring work patterns with the help of behavioral science consultants. Over the long term, the center also seeks to evaluate the impact of these projects on both productivity and the quality of work life, to disseminate this knowledge, and ultimately to provide technical assistance to interested labor and management.

The National Quality of Work Center projects originally received support from the government; the center now seeks funding from the unions and companies involved. The fact that a company and union must both agree to the project and jointly apply for or provide funds assures that they are serious about improving the quality of work life, and that such improvements will be supported by both parties and will have some permanency. Finally, innovations in the quality of work life that require union-management cooperation are likely to be the most difficult to implement. Thus, these models are likely to be seen as relevant and credible examples of quality of work life innovation.

The approach of developing model organizations is a market strategy for change. It is hoped that model organizations will be sufficiently successful in improving the quality of work life and increasing productivity that other organizations will imitate them in adopting innovations. Many companies that are ready to innovate need models as a guide to action.

However, this strategy must be combined with other actions. In isolation it resembles the research and development approach to change in assuming that awareness of an innovation leads to its adoption. We can go back to our earlier discussion of innovations to illustrate the tenuousness of that assumption. In one example, farmers refused to adopt some conservation innovations. In the Indian example, although 75 to 80 percent of fertile couples know about contraceptive methods, only 12 to 15 percent adopt these practices (Rogers, 1973). The world is not likely to beat a path to a successful technique for improving the quality of work life. An organization that sees no need for such improvements will not adopt any changes, even if those changes have improved the quality of work life and productivity elsewhere. Some other factors must first pressure many organizations to make them want to undertake change.

If the government were interested in expanding the strategy of developing quality of work life models, it might consider improving this approach in three areas. First, the government might support additional demonstration projects with emphasis on the development of internal change resources to supplement outside consultants. This would increase the probability of continued change beyond the initial demonstration project. Second, new demonstration projects might maximize the involvement of those affected by the change program in the design of its evaluation (the NQWC projects separate responsibility for the change program from its evaluation). Although this suggestion would sacrifice some objectivity in the evaluation, it focuses evaluation on dimensions critical to local participants and may increase use of the evaluation in a continuous change process. Finally, the government might support the demonstration of non-OD quality of work life strategies, including some external to the organization such as community development or community quality of work life audits.

Generating New Information.   Innovation requires research and the development of new knowledge. The government might support gathering new information of two quite different types.

1. Fundamental research is still required on quality of work life issues. For example, we need to better understand the negative physical and psychological consequences of poorly-designed work (for example, mental illness), and the effects of particular organizational practices such as repetitive work. A high priority for new research is a coordinated evaluation of current attempts at quality of work life improvement. These attempts should not remain unrelated experiments. Coordinated evaluation of them could help build a theory of change that specifies the particular change strategy most appropriate to different organizational situations and different quality of work life improvements.

2. Continuous monitoring of the quality of work life in this society is also required to indicate the extent of the national quality of work life problem, its change over time, and the distribution of attitudes relevant to it within the different segments of the work force. The Quality of Employment Survey is an example of this strategy (Herrick and Quinn, 1971). Regular monitoring of employee reactions to work and their quality of work life outcomes can focus policy toward the most critical segments of the work force. Such surveys also provide data on the fundamental quality of work life research issues described above.

As a change strategy, gathering new information depends heavily on other groups (industries, communities) to utilize the information in efforts to improve the quality of work life. But it will both encourage reality in the claims of quality of work life advocates and guide government to focus its change efforts on industries or segments of the work force that are experiencing particularly severe problems.

Disseminating Information.   The government can play a role as an information clearinghouse. It can gather and disseminate existing information on quality of work life experiments and innovations initiated by organizations throughout the country. In order to disseminate this information, a national clearinghouse might (1) provide quality of work life information on request, (2) attract media attention to new developments, or (3) inform a quality of work life network through newsletters or regular meetings.

Congress has provided limited support for this strategy within the broader charter of the National Center on Productivity and Work Quality. This center is publishing evaluations of quality of work life innovations undertaken by employers (see, for example, *A Plant-Wide Productivity Plan in Action,* 1975). Such publications, conferences, and other activities provide information on quality of work life innovations to labor and management across the country and indeed around the world.

At least one state government has taken the third approach to disseminating information. As of this writing (1975), the Ohio Quality of Work Project serves as a source of information on quality of work life demonstration projects in the state and publishes a quality of work life newsletter. This is the least costly of these alternatives, but it also increases significantly the probability that quality of work life information will reach individuals and organizations who are ready to use it. Information dissemination is a minimal government strategy to facilitate improving quality of work life. It will help those organizations who are motivated and ready, but will do nothing to stimulate change in organizations not motivated to improve the quality of work life.

Government as a Model Employer

Government agencies at all levels employ a large and growing proportion of the American work force. Federal, state, and local governments today employ one-sixth of the nation's work force. Government operations account for 22 percent of the gross national product. Government has been the fastest growing employment sector (Spiegel, 1975). The government can substantially influence the quality of work life in the total society by direct strategies to improve the quality of work life of its own employees.

Government at all levels has not been in the vanguard of change as a model employer. For example, government employees are not covered by OSHA and were only brought under Title VII of the 1964 Civil Rights Act by a 1972 amendment. Quality of work life issues are no exception. At present, quality of work life receives only limited attention within the government sector, although some related programs are underway. For example, the American Federation of State, County, and Municipal Employees, AFL-CIO, one of the fastest growing unions in the country, has embarked on a career development program relevant to the quality of work life. Workers doing the lowest jobs in some hospitals (mopping floors, changing sheets, and emptying bedpans) have been upgraded and given some of the responsibilities of practical nurses (Salpukas, 1974).

Improving quality of work life is no easier in governmental organizations than in the private sector. But government has the unique advantage of being able to start with its own organization because it has direct control over its management. The management policy of elected and appointed officials can affect conditions of work, without new legislative action, in such massive organizations as the Department of Defense and of Health, Education and Welfare. Further, the internal strategies discussed earlier (management, union, and OD) are available to management and workers in government organizations.

Government organizations also present unique problems for organizational change to improve the quality of work life. First, civil service regulations impede some change efforts. They fix and standardize reward systems and encourage reliance on formal authority. Second, the top leadership of government agencies turns over frequently, weakening the continuity required for an effective change program. And finally, government organizations are more openly political than are private employers. Historically, many organizational change techniques (OD and some management strategies) have been developed in organizations where differences in the goals and constituencies of managers are less openly expressed and perhaps less pervasive. Political organizations may resist such change techniques or require their modification.

Government Contractors.   Employers under contract to the government represent another employment sector where government has some influence on the quality of work life. Here government action would require implementation of external change strategies. The federal government has already singled out government contractors for special pressures to improve equal employment opportunity in the society. The threat of contract cancellation attempts to enforce compliance with government standards against discrimination.

We have already indicated that the technology for measuring the quality of work life is not sufficiently developed to support governmental regulatory action on quality of work life standards. However, the government might utilize other change strategies with its contractors. For example, it might require public disclosure of quality of work life outcomes or give contractor employees official access to a quality of work life ombudsman. Through such strategies, the government can have an impact on a large number of employees directly. It can also seek to create a set of model employers among contractors for other organizations in society to imitate.

The application of standards, or any other external strategy that applies pressure to contractors, has the same advantages and disadvantages discussed earlier. The advantage of more direct government access must be balanced against the negative effects of relying on the threat of penalties, such as contract cancellation, for noncompliance. As we have already mentioned, if government uses threat of penalties to create quality of work life improvements in contractor organizations, it will be difficult for government to work collaboratively with them to help improve quality of work life. Penalties also fail to encourage the development of a self-sustaining change internal to the threatened organization. Nevertheless, with sufficient cognizance of these potential problems, government, through its influence over contractors, can influence the quality of work life in a significant proportion of the private sector.

Effects of Related National Policy on the Quality of Work Life

So far we have examined government strategies that place direct pressure on organizations to improve the quality of work life of their employees. In all of these strategies government acts as a force in the external environment of employing organizations. However, less direct factors in the organization's environment—such as the kind of people available for recruitment, alternative job opportunities for its employees, and competitive forces—affect the organization's effort to improve the quality of work life. Government policies on education, labor markets, and the economy can alter the forces impinging on organizations and thus facilitate changes in quality of work life.

Education.   Every employer relies on personnel who have received a general education in the school systems of the larger society. Although employers can select their personnel and train them after hiring, they must deal with individuals whose attitudes, expectations, skills, and values are fairly well developed by the time they enter the organization. Changing the educational system that shapes employees before they begin employment is, therefore, one strategy for initiating changes in the quality of work life within organizations. In terms of our strategic considerations, this is a people-changing approach rather than an attempt to change social structures. The current educational system in the United States has been criticized for fostering various characteristics in students—dependence on authority, competitive orientations toward peers, and, in deprived segments of the population, limited capacities for trust and motivation to achieve (for example, see *Work in America,* 1973). These individual characteristics limit not only the capacity of workers to accept some quality of work life improvements but also the capacity of managers to provide them. For example, employees must be capable of accepting increased responsibility for decision-making in programs such as job enrichment or individualized pay systems. At the same time, managers must develop better interpersonal skills and rely less on formal power and authority if the responsibility, challenge, and freedom of their subordinates is to increase.

The government might encourage open classrooms, self-paced learning, and equalized power between the teacher and students, if research were to show the effectiveness of these practices in developing individuals capable of adopting quality of work life changes. In addition to facilitating quality of work life changes demanded by others, such individuals would themselves demand from employers more improvements in the quality of their work lives. Thus, they would constitute an internal source of pressure for change.

As an alternative to these broad changes in the educational system, the government might use education to increase the exposure to quality of work life issues received by specific groups within the society (organizational supervisors, managers, and officials in the labor movement). A generation of managers has already received exposure to the social sciences during undergraduate and graduate programs, though quality of work life could be given even greater emphasis in these programs. Labor leaders, however, have received less exposure to the social sciences, despite the fact that quality of work life is an area of equal concern to labor and management. For example, labor union officials can effectively utilize survey techniques to assess directly the quality of work life concerns of their constituents. In addition, we outlined a variety of union or union-management strategies to improve the quality of work life that a labor official might profitably examine and utilize (also see Chapter 6). Government funding could support specific quality of work life educational programs for supervisors, managers, and especially for labor officials.

Of these two educational strategies, the strategy of educating specific groups able to influence quality of work life directly has more immediate payoff and potential. We do not know enough yet about the impact of educational practices on predisposition to quality of work life improvements. Furthermore, broad educational change has limits because of the heavy impact of nonschool factors on individual development. Indeed, the quality of work life problem comes full circle here. The work that parents do may well affect the values they hold for their children (Kohn, 1969). Changing the parents' jobs rather than changing classroom techniques might better foster in children values favorable to a high quality of work life.

The specific strategy of educating organizational and labor leaders is also subject to criticism. As our discussion of people-changing strategies suggested, even if education changes the disposition and knowledge of these individuals, they must return to the unchanged social structure of their organizations. Their new values and skills may disappear unless changes in the organizations support their personal changes. Nevertheless, quality of work life education programs targeted at critical groups in the society could be an important *component* of a broader government strategy.

Labor Market. A highly mobile work force puts pressure on employers to increase the quality of work life they offer in order to be able to hold and attract new employees. Government labor market strategies that increase labor mobility thus have indirect beneficial effects for quality of work life. A key to high labor mobility is full employment. Thus, in the inevitable discussions of the trade-offs between full employment and inflation, quality of work life considerations emphasize the importance of full employment.

The following are some additional government strategies that will increase labor mobility and indirectly benefit quality of work life.

1. Legislation creating completely portable pensions that would allow employees to consider alternative employment without sacrificing retirement benefits built up with their current employers.
2. Providing funding or tax incentives for the retraining of individuals who experience a midcareer crisis and who seek a change in occupation and organization (see Chapter 2).
3. Legislating mandatory open posting of job openings within organizations to increase mobility in the organization's internal labor market. Presumably people would move toward parts of the organization with a high quality of work life, thereby placing pressure on other parts to change (see Chapter 2).

The strategy of improving labor mobility is a necessary but not sufficient condition for creating pressure on employers to improve the quality of work life. Unless some organizations have not only made such improvements but also communicated them to job seekers, labor mobility will not create pressure for change.

Economy. A healthy economy is a prerequisite to a high quality of work life. Quality of work life includes the satisfaction of higher order needs at work, such as accomplishment, independence, and growth.

However, satisfaction of these needs will not be demanded unless an employee satisfies more compelling needs for physical survival and security. This means holding a well-paid job, being free from hazards to health and safety, and having some guarantee against arbitrary action by the organization. A healthy national economy helps ensure these minimal requirements. Thus, government strategies to stimulate economic activity will usually have a positive indirect effect on the nation's quality of work life. However, not all strategies to encourage economic growth necessarily improve the quality of work life. Some actions, such as an increase in production through expansion of assembly line technology, may reduce quality of work life for some people.

The existence of international competition puts some limits on the compatibility of national economic health with a high quality of work life. Some resources spent to increase the quality of work life do not add value to the goods and services produced. Rather, they benefit the employee and society in general. Because such goods and services will cost more, they cannot compete with goods produced in other societies that do not emphasize a high quality of work life or charge their quality of work life costs directly to the whole society through general taxation. In our market economy, costs of quality of work life change programs are charged directly to the producing organization.

The national government can manage this problem by recognizing the differences among quality of work life strategies and types of industries. Those strategies that immediately increase productivity, such as is often the case with job redesign, do not create this problem. Increased quality of work life raises the value of the product, and thus competitive pressures encourage quality of work life improvement. However, some strategies and some jobs—such as autonomous work groups as a substitute for assembly line production—might render an organization less competitive. These situations present trade-offs. The government might be forced to select among the following policies.

1. Increase quality of work life, but protect the jobs by tariffs restricting imports, or tax incentives to spread quality of work life costs over the society.
2. Accept a proportion of low quality of work life jobs in the society and give holders of these jobs special benefits (shorter hours, higher pay, early retirement).
3. Allow such jobs to migrate to other nations and accept the economic consequences—some economic decline or increased international interdependence as our society specializes in industries that provide a higher quality of work life to their employees.

The tension between quality of work life and economic growth can be eliminated through a long-term national program that optimizes both economic growth and quality of work life. Such a program would emphasize economic growth through the expansion of those sectors in our economy—such as research and development, professional jobs, and service jobs—that provide greater opportunity for improved quality of work life.

The natural competitive forces of the international marketplace are pushing us in that direction anyway. As our labor costs increase, more routine manufacturing operations are finding their way abroad. This trend can be viewed positively by a government concerned with improving the quality of work life in America. Naturally such a policy would require additional programs to deal with the immediate discontinuities that such a movement of jobs creates.

Framework for a Government Quality of Work Life Strategy

Change at the societal level depends on the simultaneous presence of many conditions. The absence of a single critical condition can prevent successful change (Coleman, 1973). As an area for societal change, quality of work life at present suffers from several critical deficiencies—most organizations do not feel the need for quality of work life improvement, techniques and demonstrations of such improvements are just developing, and isolated quality of work life change efforts have not yet generated a theory of change to guide advocates. In terms of our original strategic considerations, the current national posture on quality of work life will probably result in a slow-paced attempt at long-term change. It relies on gradual change in people's values, and on the marketplace appeal of a few largely uncoordinated, almost coincidental, programs of innovation. In the absence of some pressure on organizations to change, we would expect this strategy to result in the adoption of quality of work life programs by only a few organizations where internal forces—such as the interest of top management or the perceived value of a specific quality of work life program—combine to create high readiness to change.

The slow pace of this strategy for change underlines the potential advantage of government action. Government's ability to act will depend, however, on the existence or development of a broad coalition of interests that supports such a major strategy for improving the quality of work life. Government can lead, in other words, but its leadership is dependent on the consent of a sufficiently large constituency. The appeal to employees of successful quality of work life innovations or gradual change in cultural values may generate this constituency over time. Without the support of such a constituency (and no such constituency currently exists), the government will not be able to successfully undertake a strategy of pressuring employers for quality of work life improvements.

The need for government to lead and catalyze improvement in quality of work life, together with the limits on its ability to do so, suggests four possible strategies that can comprise a national policy on quality of work life.

1. Government can generate some pressures on organizations to become aware of quality of work life problems, and can begin some change programs. This might best be done by legislation requiring management and labor to jointly engage in an internal process of surveying quality of work life problems and making changes, or by legislation requiring employers to report outcomes such as turnover, absenteeism, and employee satisfaction to stockholders and the public. Such legislation would increase the pace of change somewhat, but might create less of the resistance experienced by government in the equal employment area.

2. Government can stimulate the spread of quality of work life innovations by supplementing the current market strategy with a collective strategy encouraging action by all employers. A program of tax incentives, limited exemptions from federal employment regulations, and continued direct government funding of quality of work life demonstration projects could encourage organizations, especially government contractors, to innovate in improvements in this area.

3. Government can expand efforts to advance the state of the art in quality of work life. Research is especially needed on the measurement of quality of work life and the type of change strategies that apply to various situations. Education programs for managers and labor leaders can help disseminate information obtained from experiments and research.

4. Government can undertake major efforts to innovate and improve quality of work life in its own organizations, thus becoming a model employer. Changes in quality of work life that increase productivity and efficiency would be particularly well received by a public concerned about government size and responsiveness.

These strategies are interdependent. For maximum impact they should be phased in an optimal sequence. Initially some pressure is required to increase the readiness of organizations for change. This pressure could result from government legislation requiring employers to make visible the quality of work life in their organizations. For most effective results, efforts to disseminate information, to increase knowledge through research and model programs, and to reward innovation should be increased after the need to improve quality of work life is felt. This means that these strategies should gain more prominence after legislation of the type described above creates a readiness for change. This is not to say, of course, that research and development programs or funding of experimental projects should not be continued. We are only suggesting that their effectiveness can be enhanced by a greater concern for quality of work life in organizations. The minimal government legislation of the type we suggest can create such interest and concern.

This leads us to a final role for government not mentioned earlier. As concern and interest in improving quality of work life increase as a result of the interventions described above, organizations will need behavioral science consulting resources to implement change. Government can play a role in assuring that these resources are available by supporting financially (directly or indirectly) the education of individuals who seek to develop competence and expertise in the applied behavioral sciences.

Our discussion of phasing implies a speedup in the pace of change by introducing some governmental pressure, minimal as it may be. However, economic conditions in our society and other governmental demands on employers need to be taken into consideration in decisions about the phasing of different change strategies. Government pressure to improve quality of work life is unlikely to be received well by employers when there is an economic recession, when there are high rates of unemployment, and when government is already pressuring employers on other issues, such as equal employment. Additional pressure during these times is likely to generate high and lasting resistance to quality of work life improvement. For this reason a delay in government pressure on quality of work life is called for until these conditions change. We are not saying, however, that economic recession and the other conditions mentioned should stop all government activity in the quality of work life area. Several of the strategies mentioned should be continued until conditions warrant more government initiative through legislation. However, we should not expect widespread change until pressure is applied to employing organizations.

The quality of government legislation to improve the quality of work life could be substantially enhanced if government took an experimental approach to its interventions. Where possible, we would encourage limited experiments with various governmental programs and legislative strategies outlined above. Another possibility is the evaluation of legislation on quality of work life passed by state and local governments. Where this occurs, an experiment with limited risk is possible. Evaluation of experimental programs and legislation can lead to more effective legislation at the national level. This recommendation parallels our earlier discussion about the change process. Successful changes usually start with limited experiments that allow improvements in the quality of the solution and increases in commitment to the change. Government intervention in quality of work life is no exception.

At the appropriate time, the importance of quality of work life as a national priority must be tested by an attempt to pass legislation requiring quality of work life reporting or by some other form of pressure on organizations. By that time, measurement of quality of work life may have improved sufficiently to warrant outside auditing of organizations' quality of work life reports or the development of industrial and geographical norms for quality of work life effects on employees. Regardless of this future improvement in quality of work life measurement, substantial improvement in this area and the success of other change strategies probably requires governmental pressure on organizations to improve quality of work life. If the national government cannot legislate such pressure, improvement in quality of work life will remain a relatively slow and uncertain process.

SUMMARY

We have presented in this chapter an array of strategies for changing the quality of work life, ranging from internal strategies available to individuals and groups inside the organization to means for organizing political and interest groups outside the organization. Also presented were a variety of strategies available to government. In doing this, we have tried to be all encompassing. Our intent has been to describe all the levers available for changing quality of work life, so that someone *planning change* in quality of work life on a national level might be able to identify some of the strategies that are being used, some which are not, and some which might be needed to create further change. We have assumed that such a change agent or agency has a systems perspective of society and is interested in determining which mix of strategies might best be applied to move change along. Obviously, the U.S. Department of Labor, with its interest in workers and work organizations, might be one such party.

Change in the quality of work life will result from and probably requires several change strategies working in parallel or sequenced and phased in some optimum manner. But what rationale might be applied in making decisions about the mix of strategies needed and their phasing? To help answer this question, we propose that all of the strategies discussed fall into one of two categories—a strategy either *creates pressures* on people and organizations to change, or it *helps* people and organizations to change. The first set of approaches to change we call *pressure strategies*. These strategies may come from management or union inside the organization or they may come from outside the organization, from the community, or government. They are characterized by the agent of change using power against the target of change, a fast pace of change, and the advance of change through collective action or structural changes designed to affect behaviors. The second set of approaches to change we call *facilitation strategies*. These strategies may be applied by OD groups within the firm, by joint union-management committees, by community groups working in cooperation to develop an improved quality of work life, or by government providing funding for research and development or disseminating information about quality of work life. These strategies are characterized by collaboration between change agent and change target, by a relatively slower pace, by the advance of change through market forces, and by attempts to change attitudes and knowledge of people before creating major structural changes. Table 7.1 presents a breakdown of the strategies discussed in this chapter into pressure strategies and facilitation strategies.

Table 7.1–Pressure and Facilitation Strategies

	Pressure	Facilitation
Internal to Organization	Unilateral management strategies Union strategies	Organization Development Management strategies that equalize power Union-management collaboration
External to Organization	Organizing interest groups Whistle-blowing Social audits Violent and nonviolent protest	Community development (CD) Ombudsman
Government	Standards for QWL Incentives for QWL Legislating worker participation Legislating a QWL change process within the organization Legislating a QWL report by organization	Modifying existing legislation Funding demonstration projects Disseminating information on QWL Funding research and development Government as a model employer National policies on education, labor mobility, and economy Funding the education and development of behavioral science consulting resources

Pressure strategies and facilitation strategies complement each other. Pressure strategies are needed to unfreeze an organization and get it ready and motivated to change. But once readiness exists, further pressure is not needed. Indeed it can be counterproductive. At this point facilitation strategies are needed to help people in the organization change their attitudes and behaviors to alleviate the tensions created by the pressures. In other words, the optimum sequence is pressure strategies accompanied and mostly followed by facilitation strategies. In any change process this sequence may be repeated several times as the organization unfreezes due to pressures, changes, and refreezes due to facilitation, and once again requires pressure to unfreeze it for further change. Figure 7.1 presents this model of change showing a predominance of pressure strategies early in the change process when the organization is not yet unfrozen, and a predominance of facilitation strategies later in the process as the organization becomes unfrozen.

Our discussion of phasing pressure and facilitation strategies suggests that change in quality of work life will be a planned and rational process. Indeed the whole thrust of this chapter has implied this. Although it has been our intent to present the various strategies available in the context of a rational cost benefit analysis, we do not believe that most change unfolds in such a rational manner. Individuals and groups will adopt varying strategies as pressures and needs dictate. No one person or agency in a pluralistic society such as ours is powerful enough or knowledgeable enough to orchestrate change on a societal level. The government comes closest to having an overall societal concern, and might make optimum use of this rational analysis of alternative strategies for change. An understanding of all change strategies available and the effects of each might at least help in analyzing where the quality of work life change process is at any point in time, and what strategies might warrant additional resources or support to achieve further change.

This chapter has purposefully presented a whole range of strat-

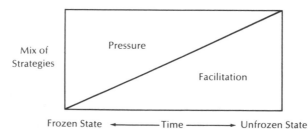

Figure 7.1   Phasing of Pressure and Facilitation Strategies

egies, from more conventional approaches such as organization development, community development, and government support of research and development, to more radical alternatives such as protests, union pressures, and government standards. This has not been done because we advocate any of these strategies, but because they are known social change strategies, they can be adapted to improving quality of work life, and they will probably be used at some point in the process of change.

We have tried to provide a basis for evaluating these strategies by outlining their consequences within the framework of strategic considerations discussed at the beginning of this chapter. There are no right or wrong consequences and therefore no right or wrong strategies. The consequence of each strategy must be evaluated by the change agent from the place in society he occupies, the attitudes and frustrations he has, and the values he holds.

Workers with high levels of frustration about their assembly line jobs may feel that organizing to protest, union agitation, or court action are justifiable and correct strategies to create the changes they desire. Social workers may want to raise community consciousness by organizing other health and welfare workers, because they see the effects of poor quality of work life on family life. The manager, on the other hand, may feel that these strategies are too radical, too destructive, and inappropriate for changing quality of work life. The government may have yet another view. Most likely it will be caught in the middle. The choice of strategies will depend on the point of view, the situation, and the place in society the change agent occupies.

EPILOGUE

In introducing his editorship of the case studies section of the *Journal of Applied Behavioral Science,* Warren Bennis wrote in 1968: "We call ourselves 'change agents,' but the real changes in our society have been wrought by the pill, the bomb, the automobile, industrialization, communication media, and other forces of modernization. The change agents of our society are the lawyers, the architects, the engineers, the politicians, and the assassins" (p. 228).

That statement is as true, and as unsettling, today as it was a decade ago. Behavioral science still has had no major impact on organized life in society, and the quality of life of the populace continues to be buffeted by forces over which policy-makers in government and industry appear to have little systematic control.

This book has been an attempt to lay the groundwork for increasing the effectiveness of behavioral science contributions to one particular set of challenges for change—namely, improving the quality of the work experience of people in organizations simultaneously with an increase in the productive effectiveness of organizations.

Part of the complexity of this particular change problem derives from the multiplicity of approaches available for addressing it. We have seen, for example, how the quality of work life and organizational productivity are affected by career paths, the design of work, reward systems, the design of human groups and systems, managerial practices, and several other attributes of organizations and their environments. We have tried to provide in the book some perspectives and tools that may facilitate the development of useful and usable strategies for change within each of these general areas. And, although the book provides neither final solutions nor specific recipes for change, one can distill from the various chapters a sense of what will be required if the behavioral sciences are to increase their potency as guides for individual and organizational development.

For one thing, new and innovative *ideas* about how organizations can be designed and managed must be put forth. There is reason for optimism here—most of the chapters of the book show that the level and quality of innovation in organizations appear to be on a marked upswing. In the past, for example, there were few "correct" ways to manage a compensation system in an organization. Now, as shown in Chapter 4, numerous innovative pay systems are being conceived and tried out, and the climate of the times is encouraging even more experimentation with ways of managing organizational rewards for high productivity and high employee satisfaction. Similar movement toward increased innovation and experimentation also is seen in the other areas reviewed in the book.

Second, well-articulated theories need to be developed for *understanding* the phenomena one wishes to change and improve. New ideas, by themselves, run the risk of leading managers and practitioners of change in several different directions simultaneously—with predictable and unfortunate consequences for the quality and the permanence of the changes made. Only when the innovative ideas are linked to some systematic theory is a coherent, powerful, and reasonably general strategy for carrying out and nurturing change likely to evolve.

Measurement tools for diagnosing work systems (and the people who populate them) prior to change, and for evaluating the impact of change on people and on the organization are a third requirement. As we have seen, many organizational innovations are conceived and implemented when someone in an organization develops a "good idea" that others can be persuaded to try out. Sometimes such ideas work, and sometimes they do not. But all too rarely does the change process include either diagnostic or evaluative measurements that can be used to develop a *cumulative* body of knowledge about when various kinds of changes are called for—and when they are not. Part of the reason for the paucity of systematic measurement and evaluation, to be sure, is poor understanding of the importance of this aspect of the change process. Another part of the reason, however, is the relative unavailability of appropriate and valid tools for carrying out such measurements and evaluations—a problem that is only gradually being remedied by behavioral scientists.

Finally, we must focus on acquiring knowledge of the *contingencies* that determine which quality of work life innovations are most appropriate for given circumstances, and which strategies for implementing those changes are most likely to be effective. As the chapters of this book make abundantly clear, there are many alternative approaches available for undertaking improvements in the quality of work life, none of which are universally effective. Moreover, there are many choices to be confronted in installing even those changes that seem most straightforward. The success of a change project often hinges on which of these choices are made under what specific circumstances. Additional knowledge about such contingencies is a prominent and a pressing research need, if we are to develop a behavioral science that is broadly useful in guiding the selection and installation of quality of work life improvements.

As pointed out several times in the earlier chapters, more progress has been made on these four items in some areas than in others. Our understanding of strategies for improving reward systems (Chapter 4) and for redesigning jobs (Chapter 3), for example, appears to be further along than is our knowledge of ways to enhance career development processes (Chapter 2) or ways to improve intra- and inter-group dynamics (Chapter 5). Approaches to change involving alteration of managerial practices are, in this context, somewhat unique as seen in Chapter 6. Enormous amounts of research on leadership and management have been carried out, but so far the direct usefulness of this knowledge in initiating and executing quality of work life improvements has been relatively limited.

What, then, are the research strategies that will be required for the development of behavioral science theory and techniques that are increasingly useful for improving the quality of work life and organizational productivity? It seems doubtful that either rigorous laboratory studies or one-shot case studies in organizations will figure prominently in such an undertaking. Laboratory studies are too often compromised by the need to control (in the interest of rigor) precisely those variables that turn out to affect behavior most strongly in real-world organizational settings. And case studies typically are tailored so specifically to the particular settings in which they are conducted that they cannot be used as building blocks in developing a *general* understanding of organizational change.

Even controlled experiments conducted in organizations, which bypass many of the problems inherent in laboratory experiments and one-shot case studies, are not without difficulties. It is a source of some problems that such experiments often are placed under a protective umbrella, to ensure that they can be conducted without meddling by management and without the constraints on change built into many union contracts. Although such protection often is necessary for the experiments to be carried out with any real chance of success, diffusion of the innovations throughout the sponsoring organization may be seriously compromised as a result. That is, even though real learnings about how (and how not) to proceed with quality of work changes may be obtained, the spread of such innovations may be impeded or halted because, under conditions of "business as usual," managers *do* meddle in planned change (especially when threatened by them) and union leadership *does* worry at the long-term consequences of such changes (especially if they appear likely to reduce the size or power of the bargaining unit).

So, although field experiments represent an excellent device for building the systematic body of knowledge that will be required for broad-scale application of behavioral science to improvements in the quality of work life, their limitations also make it clear that the behavioral sciences (and behavioral scientists) simply cannot do the job by themselves. Without the cooperation, understanding, and commitment of those responsible for organizational management and policy—managers, union leadership, government officials—real and system-wide change seems impossible.

How can such commitment be secured? Probably not by speeches, research articles, or books such as this one. Instead, it may be necessary to mount a coordinated, society-wide attack on issues of quality of work life and organizational productivity—an attack that centrally involves leaders of management, labor, and government as well as behavioral scientists. Because such an approach would require close collaboration among these parties, it could result in an increase in understanding, on *all* sides, of the contributions that can be made by others, and in better informed decisions about whether (and how) such collaboration might proceed in the future.

Moreover, a coordinated set of experiments on quality of work life innovations would make possible a comparison of various changes tried in different organizational settings and circumstances. This, in turn, would further the development of a cumulative body of knowledge about their effects, and about the contingencies that determine when they will and will not achieve their intended outcomes. Ultimately, such knowledge (coupled with the mutual understanding gained by those who participated in generating it) should make possible the design and installation of innovations that have a reasonable chance of persisting over time and diffusing throughout and across organizations.

The value of this general approach now is being tested in various experiments being carried out across the country (see Chapter 7), and further support for this type of activity may be forthcoming from federal and state legislation. It is clear, however, that a full test of the value of the approach will require an investment of societal resources many times greater than presently is the case, and will involve commitment and collaboration among segments of society that presently find themselves more often in a conflictful relationship than not.

Even if the resources for a large scale and coordinated attack on quality of work life issues should become available, there is no assurance that the outcomes of that venture would be commensurate with the resources expended. Although it is likely that significant learnings about organizations and about change would emerge from such an undertaking, it is much less clear that real improvements in the quality of work life would be realized. Can planned change, beginning deep within functioning organizations and working upward and outward, counter the powerful influences that operate from the top down, and from the outside in? Or is it true that even our best efforts in designing and carrying out planned change can never accomplish basic alterations in how organizations function? Perhaps, for fundamental change, the focus must be at the very roots of the economic system of society, or in the political system, or in the fast-flowing river of technological development that seems, at times, to defy control by any organized segment of society.

The answers to such questions cannot be known at present, because as yet we have not marshaled even modest resources to probe the limits of what planned behavioral science change can achieve in organizations. What does seem clear is that without further experimentation, on a broad scale and with cooperation among the many parties to the quality of work life phenomenon, we are unlikely to find out.

References

Adams, J. S. "Injustice in Social Exchange." In *Advances in Experimental Social Psychology*, Vol. 2, edited by L. Berkowitz, pp. 267–299. New York: Academic Press, 1965.

Adams, J. S., and Rosenbaum, W. B. "The Relationship of Worker Productivity to Cognitive Dissonance about Wage Inequities." *Journal of Applied Psychology* 46 (1962): 161–164.

Alderfer, C. P. "An Empirical Test of a New Theory of Human Needs." *Organizational Behavior and Human Performance* 4 (1969): 142–175 (a).

Alderfer, C. P. "Job Enlargement and the Organizational Context." *Personnel Psychology* 22 (1969): 418–426 (b).

Alderfer, C. P. "Effects of Individual, Group, and Intergroup Relations on Attitudes Toward a Management Development Program." *Journal of Applied Psychology* 55 (1971): 302–311.

Alderfer, C. P. "Improving Organizational Communication Through Long-Term Intergroup Intervention." New Haven: Yale University School of Organization and Management Technical Report, 1975.

Alderfer, C. P. "Change Processes in Organizations." In *Handbook of Industrial and Organizational Psychology*, edited by M. D. Dunnette. Chicago: Rand McNally, 1976.

Alfred, T. "Checkers or Choice in Manpower Management." *Harvard Business Review*, January-February 1967, pp. 157–169.

Alinsky, S. *Rules for Radicals.* New York: Vintage Books, 1972.

Anderson, J. W. "The Impact of Technology on Job Enrichment." *Personnel* 47 (1970): 29–37.

Argyle, M., Gardner, G., and Cioffi, F. "Supervisory Methods Related to Productivity, Absenteeism, and Labor Turnover." *Human Relations* 11 (1958): 33–40.

Argyris, C. *Organization of a Bank.* New Haven: Yale University Labor and Management Center, 1954.

Argyris, C. *Personality and Organization.* New York: Harper, 1957.

Argyris, C. *Understanding Organizational Behavior.* Homewood, Ill.: Dorsey, 1960.

Argyris, C. *Integrating the Individual and the Organization.* New York: Wiley, 1964.

Argyris, C. *On Organizations of the Future.* Beverly Hills, Calif.: Sage, 1973 (a).

Argyris, C. "Personality and Organization Theory Revisited." *Administrative Science Quarterly* 18 (1973): 141–167 (b).

"Arthur Friedman's Outrage: Employees Decide Their Own Pay." *The Washington Post*, February 23, 1975, pp. C1 and C8.

Bailyn, L. "Career and Family Orientation of Husbands and Wives in Relation to Marital Happiness." *Human Relations* 23 (1970): 97–113.

Bailyn, L. Family Constraints on Women's Work. *Annals of the New York Academy of Science* 208 (1973): 82–90.

Bailyn, L. "Accommodation as a Career Strategy: Implications for the Realm of Work." Cambridge, Mass.: Sloan School of Management Working Paper No. 728–74, 1974.

Bailyn, L., and Schein, E. H. "Work Involvement in Technically Based Careers: A Study of MIT Alumni at Mid-Career." Manuscript in preparation. Cambridge, Mass.: Sloan School of Management, 1975.

Bakan, P., Belton, J. A., and Toth, J. C. "Extraversion–Introversion and Decrement in an Auditory Vigilance Task." In *Vigilance: A Symposium*, edited by D. N. Buckner and J. J. McGrath. New York: McGraw-Hill, 1963.

Baldamus, W. *Efficiency and Work*. London: Tavistock, 1961.

Bandura, A. *Principles of Behavior Modification*. New York: Holt, Rinehart and Winston, 1969.

Barnard, C. *The Functions of the Executive*. Cambridge, Mass.: Harvard University Press, 1938.

Bass, B. *A Program for Executives*. Pittsburgh: Management Development Associates, 1966.

Bauer, R. S., and Fenn, D. H., Jr. *The Corporate Social Audit*. New York: Russell Sage Foundation, 1972.

Bavelas, A., and Strauss, G. "Group Dynamics and Intergroup Relations." In *Money and Motivation: An Analysis of Incentives in Industry*, edited by W. F. Whyte. New York: Harper & Row, 1955.

de Beauvoir, S. *The Second Sex*. New York: Random House, 1952.

Becker, H. S. "The Culture of a Deviant Group: The Dance Musician." *American Journal of Sociology* 57 (1951): 412–427.

Becker, H. S. "A School is a Lousy Place to Learn Anything In." In *Learning to Work*, edited by B. Greer. Beverly Hills, Calif.: Sage, 1972.

Becker, H. S., Greer, B., Hughes, E. C., and Strauss, A. *Boys in White: Student Culture in Medical School*. Chicago: University of Chicago Press, 1961.

Beer, M. "The Technology of Organizational Development." In *Handbook of Industrial and Organizational Psychology*, edited by M. D. Dunnette. Chicago: Rand McNally, 1976.

Beer, M. *Organization Development: A Systems Approach*. Santa Monica, Calif.: Goodyear, in press.

Beer, M., and Gery, G. "Pay Systems Preferences and Their Correlates." Paper presented at the American Psychological Association Convention, San Francisco, California, 1968.

Beer, M., and Huse, E. F. "A Systems Approach to Organization Development." *Journal of Applied Behavioral Science* 8 (1972): 79–101.

Behavioral Science: Concepts and Management Applications. Studies in Personnel Problems No. 216. New York: National Industrial Conference Board, 1969.

Belcher, D. *Compensation Administration*. Englewood Cliffs, N.J.: Prentice-Hall, 1974.

Bem, D. J. *Beliefs, Attitudes, and Human Affairs*. Monterey, Calif.: Brooks/Cole, 1970.

Bengston, V. L., Furlong, M. J., and Laufer, R. S. "Time, Aging, and the Continuity of Social Structure: Themes and Issues in Generational Analysis." *Journal of Social Issues* 30 (1974): 1–30.

Bennett, L. *Before the Mayflower*. Baltimore: Penguin, 1962.

Bennis, W. G. *Changing Organizations: Essays on the Development and Evolution of Human Organizations*. New York: McGraw-Hill, 1966.

Bennis, W. G. *Organization Development: Its Nature, Origins, and Prospects*. Reading, Mass.: Addison-Wesley, 1969.

Bennis, W. G., Schein, E. H., Steele, F. I., and Berlew, D. E. *Interpersonal Dynamics* rev. ed. Homewood, Ill.: Dorsey, 1968.

Berger, P. L., ed. *The Human Shape of Work*. New York: Macmillan, 1964.

Berkowitz, L. "Group Standards, Cohesiveness, and Productivity." *Human Relations* 7 (1954): 509–519.

Berlew, D. E., and Hall, D. T. "The Socialization of Managers: Effects of Expectations on Performance." *Administrative Science Quarterly* 11 (1966): 207–223.

Berlyne, D. E. "Arousal and Reinforcement." *Nebraska Symposium on Motivation* 15 (1967): 1–110.

Bernard, J. "The Housewife: Between Two Worlds." In *Varieties of Work Experience*, edited by P. L. Stewart and M. G. Cantor, pp. 49–66. New York: Halsted, 1974.

Best, F. "Flexible Work Scheduling: Beyond the Forty-Hour Impasse." In *The Future of Work*, edited by F. Best. Englewood Cliffs, N.J.: Prentice-Hall, 1973.

Bidwell, C. W. "Pre-adult Socialization." Paper read at the Social Science Research Council Conference on Socialization and Social Structure, May 1962.

Bion, W. R. *Experiences in Groups.* New York: Basic Books, 1961.

Bishop, R. C., and Hill, J. W. "Effects of Job Enlargement and Job Change on Continuous but Nonmanipulated Jobs as a Function of Workers' Status." *Journal of Applied Psychology* 55 (1971): 175–181.

Blake, R. R., and Mouton, J. S. *The Managerial Grid.* Houston: Gulf Publishing, 1964,

Blake, R. R., Mouton, J. S., and Sloma, R. L. "An Actual Case History of Resolving Intergroup Conflict in Union-Management Relations." In *Managing Intergroup Conflict in Industry,* edited by R. R. Blake, A. Shepard, and J. S. Mouton, pp. 155–195. Houston: Gulf Publishing, 1964.

Blake, R. R., Shepard, A., and Mouton, J. S., eds. *Managing Intergroup Conflict in Industry.* Houston: Gulf Publishing, 1964.

Blankenship, V., and Miles, R. "Organizational Structure and Management Decision Making." *Administrative Science Quarterly 13 (1968):* 106–120.

Blau, P. M. *The Dynamics of Industrial Bureaucracy.* Chicago: University of Chicago Press, 1955.

Blau, P. M. *Exchange and Power in Social Life.* New York: Wiley, 1964.

Blau, P. M., and Schoenherr, R. A. *The Structure of Organizations.* New York: Basic Books, 1971.

Blau, P. M., and Scott, W. R. *Formal Organization.* San Francisco: Chandler, 1962.

Blauner, R. *Alienation and Freedom.* Chicago: University of Chicago Press, 1964.

Blood, M. R., and Hulin, C. L. "Alienation, Environmental Characteristics, and Worker Responses." *Journal of Applied Psychology* 51 (1967): 284–290.

Bluestone, I. "Comments on Job Enrichment." *Organizational Dynamics,* Winter 1974, pp. 46–47.

Bowers, D. G., and Seashore, S. "Predicting Organizational Effectiveness with a Four-Factor Theory of Leadership." *Administrative Science Quarterly* 11 (1966): 238–263.

Bradford, D. L., Sargent, A. G., and Sprague, M. S. "Executive Man and Woman: The Issue of Sexuality." In *Bringing Women into Management,* edited by F. E. Gordon and M. H. Stober, pp. 39–58. New York: McGraw-Hill, 1975.

Bramwell, J. *Courage in Crisis.* New York: Bobbs-Merrill, 1972.

Bray, D. W., Campbell, R. J., and Grant, D. L. *Formative Years in Business.* New York: Wiley, 1974.

Bray, D. W., and Grant, D. L. "The Assessment Center in the Measurement of Potential Business Management." *Psychological Monographs* 80 (1966): entire issue.

Breer, P. E., and Locke, E. A. *Task Experience as a Source of Attitudes.* Homewood, Ill.: Dorsey, 1965.

Brief, A. P., and Aldag, R. J. "Employee Reactions to Job Characteristics: A Constructive Replication." *Journal of Applied Psychology* 60 (1975): 182–186.

Brim, O. G. "Socialization Through the Life Cycle." In *Socialization After Childhood,* edited by O. G. Brim and S. Wheeler. New York: Wiley, 1966.

Brooks, T. R. "Job Satisfaction: An Elusive Goal." *AFL-CIO American Federationist,* October 1972, pp. 1–8.

Brown, L. D. "Haves and Have-Nots in Dialogue: Third Party Interventions to Promote Intergroup Cooperation." Manuscript in preparation, 1975.

Brummet, R. L., Framholtz, E., and Pyle, W. *Human Resource Accounting: Development and Implementation in Industry.* Ann Arbor: Foundation for Research on Human Behavior, 1969.

Buchanan, P. C. "Crucial Issues in Organizational Development." In *Change in School Systems,* edited by G. Watson. Arlington: NTL Institute, 1967.

Bucklow, M. "A New Role for the Work Group. *Administrative Science Quarterly* 11 (1966): 59–78.

Burke, W. W. Managing Conflict Between Groups. In *Theory and Method in Organization Development: An Evolutionary Process,* edited by J. D. Adams, pp. 255–268. Arlington: NTL Institute, 1972.

Burling, T., Lentz, E., and Wilson, R. *The Give and Take in Hospitals.* New York: Putnam, 1956.

Burns, T., and Stalker, G. M. *The Management of Innovation.* London: Tavistock, 1961.

Buss, A. R. "Generational Analysis: Description, Explanation, and Theory." *Journal of Social Issues* 30 (1974): 55–71.

Calame, B. E. "Wary Labor Eyes Job Enrichment." *Wall Street Journal,* February 26, 1973, p. 12.

Cammann, C., and Lawler, E. E. "Employee Reactions to a Pay Incentive Plan." *Journal of Applied Psychology* 58 (1973): 163–172.

Campbell, J. P., Dunnette, M. D., Lawler, E. E., and Weick, K. E. *Managerial Behavior, Performance, and Effectiveness.* New York: McGraw-Hill, 1970.

Campbell, H. T., Otis, J. L., Liske, R. E., and Prien, E. P. "Assessments of Higher Level Personnel II: Validity of the Overall Assessment Process." *Personnel Psychology* 15 (1962): 63–74.

Caplow, T. *Principles of Organization.* New York: Harcourt, Brace and World, 1964.

Carroll, S. J., and Tosi, H. "Goal Characteristics and Personality Factors in a Management-by-Objectives Program." *Administrative Science Quarterly* 15 (1970): 295–305.

Cartwright, D., and Zander, A. *Group Dynamics.* 3rd ed. Evanston: Row-Peterson, 1968.

Chesler, P. "Patient and Patriarch: Women in the Psychotherapeutic Relationship." In *Woman in Sexist Society,* edited by V. Gornick and B. K. Moran, pp. 362–392. New York: Signet, 1972.

Chinoy, E. *Automobile Workers and the American Dream.* New York: Doubleday, 1955.

Cobbs, P. M. "Ethnotherapy in Groups." In *New Perspectives on Encounter Groups,* edited by L. N. Solomon and B. Berzon, pp. 383–403. San Francisco: Jossey-Bass, 1972.

Cofer, C., and Appley, M. *Motivation: Theory and Research.* New York: Wiley, 1964.

Coleman, J. S. "Conflicting Theories of Social Change." In *Processes and Phenomena of Social Change,* edited by G. Zaltman. New York: Wiley, 1973.

Conant, E. H., and Kilbridge, M. "An Interdisciplinary Analysis of Job Enlargement: Technology, Costs, and Behavioral Implications." *Industrial and Labor Relations Review* 18 (1965): 377–395.

Cook, F. J. "The Pusher Cop: The Institutionalization of Police Corruption." *New York Magazine,* August 16, 1971, pp. 32–37.

Coser, L. *The Functions of Social Conflict.* New York: Free Press, 1956.

Cottle, T. J. *A Family Album: Portraits of Intimacy and Kinship.* New York: Harper and Row, 1974.

Crozier, M. *The Bureaucratic Phenomenon.* Chicago: University of Chicago Press, 1964.

Dalton, M. *Men Who Manage.* New York: Wiley, 1959.

Davis, F. "The Cabdriver and His Fare: Facets of a Fleeting Relationship." *American Journal of Sociology* 65 (1959): 158–165.

Davis, L. E. "Toward a Theory of Job Design." *Journal of Industrial Engineering* 8 (1957): 19–23.

Davis, L. E. "The Design of Jobs." *Industrial Relations* 6 (1966): 21–45.

Davis, L. E. "Developments in Job Design." In *Personal Goals and Work Design,* edited by P. B. Warr. London: Wiley, 1975.

Davis, L. E., and Taylor, J. C. *Design of Jobs.* Middlesex, England: Penguin, 1972.

Davis, L. E., and Trist, E. L. "Improving the Quality of Work Life: Sociotechnical Case Studies." In *Work and the Quality of Life,* edited by J. O'Toole. Cambridge, Mass.: MIT Press, 1974.

Deep, S. D., Bass, B. M., and Vaughan, J. A. "Some Effects on Business Gaming of Previous Quasi-T Group Affiliations." *Journal of Applied Psychology* 51 (1967): 426–431.

DePasquale, J. A., and Lange, R. A. "Job Hopping and the MBA." *Harvard Business Review,* November-December 1971, pp. 4–8.

Deutsch, M. *The Resolution of Conflict.* New Haven: Yale University Press, 1973.

Dierkes, M., and Bauer, R. A., eds. *Corporate Social Accounting.* New York: Praeger, 1973.

Dowling, W. F., Jr. "Job Redesign on the Assembly Line." *Organizational Dynamics,* Winter 1973, pp. 51–67.

Downes, J. F. "Environment, Communications, and Status Change Aboard an American Aircraft Carrier." *Human Organization* 17 (1958): 14–19.

Dubin, R. "Industrial Workers' Worlds: A Study of the 'Central Life Interests' of Industrial Workers." *Social Problems* 3 (1956): 131–142.

Dubin, R. "Industrial Research and the Discipline of Sociology." *Proceedings of the Industrial Relations Research Association.* Madison, Wisc.: Industrial Relations Research Association, 1959.

Dubin, R. "Leadership in Union-Management Relations as an Intergroup System." In *Intergroup Relations and Leadership,* edited by M. Sherif, pp. 70–93. New York: Wiley, 1962.

Dubin, R. "Supervision and Productivity: Some Empirical Findings and Theoretical Considerations." In *Leadership and Productivity,* edited by R. Dubin et al. San Francisco: Chandler, 1965.

Dunnette, M. D. *Personnel Selection and Placement.* Belmont, Calif.: Wadsworth, 1966.

Dunnette, M.D., Campbell, J. P., and Hakel, M.D. "Factors Contributing to Job Satisfaction and Dissatisfaction in Six Occupational Groups." *Organizational Behavior and Human Performance* 2 (1967): 143–174.

Dyer, L., and Kochan, T. A. "Labor Unions and Organizational Change: A New Frontier for OD?" Manuscript, New York State School of Industrial and Labor Relations, Cornell University, 1974.

Emery, F. E., and Trist, E. L. "Socio-technical systems." In *Systems Thinking,* edited by F. E. Emery. Middlesex, England: Penguin, 1969.

Engelstad, P. H. "Socio-technical Approach to Problems of Process Control." In *Design of Jobs,* edited by L. E. Davis and J. C. Taylor. Middlesex, England: Penguin, 1972.

Erikson, E. H. *Childhood and Society.* New York: Norton, 1950.

Erikson, E. H. "Identity and the Life Cycle." *Psychological Issues* 1 (1959): 31–32.

Erikson, E. *Identity: Youth and Crisis.* New York: Norton, 1968.

Etzioni, A. *Complex Organizations.* Glencoe, Ill.: Free Press, 1961.

Ewing, D. W. "Who Wants Employee Rights?" *Harvard Business Review,* November–December 1971, pp. 22–28.

Factory. "What the Factory Worker Really Thinks about His Job Unemployment and Industry's Profit." *Factory Management and Maintenance* 105 (1947): 86–92.

Fein, M. "The Real Needs and Goals of Blue-Collar Workers." *The Conference Board Record,* February 1972, pp. 26–33.

Fein, M. "Job Enrichment: A Reevaluation." *Sloan Management Review* 15 (1974): 69–88.

Fein, M. "Motivation for Work." In *Handbook of Work, Organization and Society,* edited by R. Dubin. Chicago: Rand McNally, 1976.

Feurer, L. S. *The Conflict of Generations.* New York: Basic Books, 1969.

Filene, P. G. *Him, Her, Self.* New York: Harcourt, Brace, Jovanovich, 1974.

Fine, S. A. "Functional Job Analysis." *Journal of Personnel and Industrial Relations* 2 (1955): 1–16.

Finley, G. J. *Policies on Leaves for Political and Social Action.* New York: Conference Board, 1972.

Firestone, S. "On American Feminism." In *Woman in Sexist Society,* edited by V. Gornick and B. K. Moran, pp. 665–686. New York: Signet, 1972.

Fiss, B. *Flexitime in Federal Government.* Washington, D.C.: Government Printing Office, 1974.

Flamholtz, E. "Toward a Theory of Human Resource Value in Formal Organizations." *The Accounting Review* 47 (1972): 666-678.

Flamholtz, E. *Human Resource Accounting.* Encino, Calif.: Dickenson, 1974.

Fleishman, E. A. "A Leader Behavior Description for Industry." In *Leader Behavior: Its Description and Measurement,* edited by R. M. Stogdill and A. E. Coons. Columbus, Ohio: Ohio State University, Bureau of Business Research, 1957.

Fleishman, E. A., and Harris, E. F. "Patterns of Leadership Behavior Related to Employee Grievances and Turnover." *Personnel Psychology* 15 (1962): 43–56.

Fleishman, E. A., Harris, E. F., and Burtt, H. E. *Leadership and Supervision in Industry.* Columbus, Ohio: Ohio State University, Bureau of Educational Research, 1955.

Ford, R. N. *Motivation Through the Work Itself.* New York: American Management Association, 1969.

Ford, R. N. "A Prescription for Job Enrichment Success." In *New Perspectives in Job Enrichment,* edited by J. R. Maher. New York: Van Nostrand-Reinhold, 1971.

Ford, R. N. "Job Enrichment Lessons from AT&T." *Harvard Business Review,* January–February 1973, pp. 96–106.

Ford, G. A., and Lippitt, G. L. *A Life Planning Workbook.* Fairfax, Va.: NTL Learning Resources Workbook, 1972.

Foulkes, F. K. "Learning to Live with OSHA." *Harvard Business Review,* November–December 1973, pp. 57–67.

Frank, J. D. *Sanity and Survival: Psychological Aspects of War and Peace.* New York: Random House, 1967.

Frank, L. L., and Hackman, J. R. "A Failure of Job Enrichment: The Case of the Change That Wasn't." *Journal of Applied Behavioral Science,* in press.

Fraser, R. *Work.* Middlesex, England: Penguin, 1968.

Fraser, R., ed. *Work Volume 2: Twenty Personal Accounts.* Middlesex, England: Penguin, 1969.

French, J. R. P., Jr., Israel, J., and As, D. "An Experiment in a Norwegian Factory." *Human Relations* 13 (1960): 3–20.

French, J. R. P., Jr., Kay, E., and Meyer, H. H. "Participation and the Appraisal System." *Human Relations* 19 (1966): 3–29.

French, J. R. P., Jr., and Raven, B. "The Bases of Social Power." In *Studies in Social Power,* edited by D. Cartwright. Ann Arbor: University of Michigan, Institute for Social Research, 1959.

Freud, S. *New Introductory Lectures on Psychoanalysis.* New York: Norton, 1933.

Friedlander, F., and Brown, L. D. "Organization Development." *Annual Review of Psychology* 25 (1974): 313–341.

Frost, C., Wakeley, J., and Ruh, R. *The Scanlon Plan for Organization Development: Identity, Participation, and Equity.* East Lansing, Mich: Michigan State University Press, 1974.

Galbraith, J. *Designing Complex Organizations.* Reading, Mass.: Addison-Wesley, 1973.

Ganguli, H. *Structure and Process of Organization.* New York: Asia Publishing House, 1964.

General Electric Company *CDP 1: Orientation to Your Career Development Program.* Crotonville, N.Y.: General Electric Company, 1972.

Gillespie, J. *Free Expression in Industry.* London: Pilot Press, 1948.

Ginzberg, E. *Life Styles of Educated Women.* New York: Columbia University Press, 1966.

Ginzberg, E., Ginsburg, S. W., Axelrad, S., and Herma, J. L. *Occupational Choice: An Approach to a General Theory.* New York: Columbia University Press, 1951.

Glaser, B. G. *Organizational Scientists: Their Professional Career.* New York: Bobbs-Merrill, 1964.

Glaser, E. M. *Improving the Quality of Worklife . . . And in the Process, Improving Productivity.* Los Angeles: Human Interaction Research Institute, 1975.

Gluskines, U. M., and Kestelman, B. J. "Management and Labor Leaders' Perception of Worker Needs as Compared with Self-Reported Needs." *Personnel Psychology* 24 (1971): 239–246.

Goffman, E. *Asylums.* New York: Anchor Books, 1961 (a).

Goffman, E. *Encounters.* Indianapolis: Bobbs-Merrill, 1961 (b).

Goffman, E. *Interaction Ritual.* Chicago: Aldine, 1967.

Gold, L. "In the Basement—The Apartment Building Janitor." In *The Human Shape of Work: Studies in the Sociology of Occupations,* edited by P. L. Berger, pp. 1–49. New York: Macmillan, 1964.

Goldthorpe, J. H., Lockwood, D., Bechhofer, F., and Platt, J. *The Affluent Worker: Industrial Attitudes and Behavior.* London: Cambridge University Press, 1968.

Gomberg, W. "Job Satisfaction: Sorting Out the Nonsense." *AFL-CIO American Federationist,* June 1973.

Goode, W. J. *Family and Mobility: A Report to the Institute of Life Insurance,* 1964.

Goode, W. J. "The Theoretical Limits of Professionalization." In *The Semi-professions and Their Organization,* edited by A. Etzioni, pp. 226–314. New York: Free Press, 1969.

Gooding, J. "The Accelerated Generation Moves into Management." *Fortune* March 1971, p. 101.

Gooding, J. *The Job Revolution.* New York: Walker, 1972.

Gould, R. "Adult Life Stages: Growth Toward Self-Tolerance." *Psychology Today,* February 1975, pp. 74–78..

Gouldner, A. W. *Patterns of Industrial Bureaucracy.* New York: Free Press, 1954.

Gouldner, A. W. "Cosmopolitans and Locals: Towards an Analysis of Latent Social Roles—I, II." *Administrative Science Quarterly* 2 (1957–1958): 281–306; 444–480.

Graen, G. B. "Testing Traditional and Two-Factor Hypotheses Concerning Job Satisfaction." *Journal of Applied Psychology* 52 (1968): 366–371.

Graen, G. B., and Davis, R. V. "A Measure of Work Attitudes for High-School Youth." *Journal of Vocation Behavior* 1 (1971): 343–353.

Greer, B., ed. *Learning to Work.* Beverly Hills, Calif.: Sage, 1972.

Greiner, L. E. "Patterns of Organization Change." *Harvard Business Review,* May-June 1967, pp. 119–128.

Greiner, L. E., and Barnes, L. B. "Organization Change and Development." In *Organizational Change and Development,* edited by G. W. Dalton, P. R. Lawrence, and L. E. Greiner. Homewood, Ill.: Irwin-Dorsey, 1970.

Guest, R. H. Work Careers and Aspirations of Automobile Workers. In *Labor and Trade Unionism,* edited by W. Galenson and S. M. Lipset. New York: Wiley, 1960.

Gulland, E. "The Disenchanted Generation." *Business Today* 3 (1969): 47–49.

Gulowsen, J. "A Measure of Work Group Autonomy." In *Design of Jobs,* edited by L. E. Davis and J. C. Taylor. Middlesex, England: Penguin, 1972.

Gurin, G., Veroff, J., and Feld, S. *Americans View Their Mental Health.* New York: Basic Books, 1960.

Gutman, H. G. "Work, Culture, and Society in Industrializing America, 1815–1919." *American Historical Review* 78 (1973): 531–588.

Hackman, J. R. *Improving the Quality of Work Life: Work Design.* Washington, D.C.: Office of Research, ASPER, U.S. Dept. of Labor, 1975 (a).

Hackman, J. R. "On the Coming Demise of Job Enrichment." In *Man and Work in Society,* edited by E. L. Cass and F. G. Zimmer. New York: Van Nostrand-Reinhold, 1975 (b).

Hackman, J. R. "Group Influences on Individuals in Organizations." In *Handbook of Industrial and Organizational Psychology,* edited by M. D. Dunnette. Chicago: Rand McNally, 1976.

Hackman, J. R., and Lawler, E. E. "Employee Reactions to Job Characteristics." *Journal of Applied Psychology Monograph* 55 (1971): 259–286.

Hackman, J. R., and Morris, C. G. "Group Tasks, Group Interaction Process, and Group Performance Effectiveness: A Review and Proposed Integration." In *Advances in Experimental Social Psychology,* Vol. 8, edited by L. Berkowitz. New York: Academic Press, 1975.

Hackman, J. R., and Oldham, G. R. "Development of the Job Diagnostic Survey." *Journal of Applied Psychology* 60 (1975): 159–170.

Hackman, J. R., and Oldham, G. R. "Motivation Through the Design of Work: Test of a Theory." *Organizational Behavior and Human Performance,* in press.

Hackman, J. R., Oldham, G. R., Janson, R., and Purdy, K. "A New Strategy for Job Enrichment." *California Management Review,* Summer 1975, pp. 57–71.

Hall, D. T., "A Theoretical Model of Career Sub-identity Development in Organizational Settings. *Organizational Behavior and Human Performance* 6 (1971): 50–76.

Hall, J., and Williams, M. S. "A Comparison of Decision-Making Performances in Established and Ad Hoc Groups." *Journal of Personality and Social Psychology* 3 (1966): 214–222.

Harris, N. *The Police Academy: An Inside View.* New York: Wiley, 1973.

Hartman, H. "Codetermination in West Germany." *Industrial Relations* 9 (1970): 137–147.

Helfgott, R. *Group Wage Incentives: Experiences with the Scanlon Plan.* New York: Industrial Relations Counselors, Industrial Relations Memo No. 14, 1962.

Hellebrandt, E. T., and Stinson, J. E. "The Effects of T-Group Training on Business Game Results." *Journal of Psychology* 77 (1971): 271–272.

Heller, F. A. *Managerial Decision-Making.* London: Tavistock, 1971.

Heller, J. *Something Happened.* New York: Knopf, 1974.

Henry, J. *Culture Against Man.* New York: Random House, 1963.

Herald, K., and Dann, A. "Exploring Male/Female Issues in a Management Work Conference." Manuscript, 1975.

Herbst, P. G. *Autonomous Group Functioning.* London: Tavistock, 1962.

Herrick, N. W. "Who's Unhappy at Work and Why." *Manpower,* January 1972.

Herrick, N. W., and Quinn, R. P. "The Working Conditions Survey as a Source of Social Education." *Monthly Labor Review* April 1971, pp. 15–24.

Herzberg, F. *Work and the Nature of Man.* Cleveland: World, 1966.

Herzberg, F. "One More Time: How Do You Motivate Employees?" *Harvard Business Review,* January-February 1968, pp. 53–62.

Herzberg, F. "The Wise Old Turk." *Harvard Business Review,* September-October 1974, pp. 70–80.

Herzberg, F., Mausner, B., and Snyderman, B. *The Motivation to Work.* New York: Wiley, 1959.

Hinton, B. L. "An Empirical Investigation of the Herzberg Methodology and Two-Factor Theory." *Organizational Behavior and Human Performance,* 3 (1968): 286–309.

Holland, J. L. *The Psychology of Vocational Choice: A Theory of Personality Types and Environmental Models.* London: Ginn, 1966.

Homans, G. *The Human Group.* New York: Harcourt, Brace, 1950.

Homans, G. *Social Behavior: Its Elementary Forms.* New York: Harcourt, Brace & World, 1961.

Hornady, J. A., and Kuder, G. F. "A Study of Male Occupational Interest Scales Applied to Women." *Educational and Psychological Measurement* 21 (1961): 859–864.

Horner, J. *Studies in Industrial Democracy.* London: Gollanez, 1974.

Horney, K. *Feminine Psychology.* New York: Norton, 1967.

Horvath, L. *Career Development System in a Socialist Country–A Case Study of Hungary.* Round Table on Career Development in European Enterprises, International Labor Office, Budapest, Hungary, April 1975.

House, R. J. A Path-Goal Theory of Leader Effectiveness. *Administrative Science Quarterly* 16 (1971): 321–339.

House, R. J., and Wigdor, L. "Herzberg's Dual-Factor Theory of Job Satisfaction and Motivation: A Review of the Evidence and a Criticism." *Personnel Psychology* 20 (1967): 369–389.

Howell, W. "A New Look at Profit-Sharing, Pension, and Productivity Plans." *Business Management,* 1967, 26–42.

Huberman, J. "Discipline Without Punishment." *Harvard Business Review,* July 1964, pp. 62–68.

Hughes, E. C. *Men and Their Work.* Glenco, Ill.: Free Press, 1958.

Hughes, E. C. *The Sociological Eye.* Chicago: Aldine, 1971.

Hulin, C. L. Individual Differences and Job Enrichment. In *New Perspectives in Job Enrichment,* edited by J. R. Maher. New York: Van Nostrand-Reinhold, 1971.

Hulin, C. L., and Blood, M. R. "Job Enlargement, Individual Differences, and Worker Responses." *Psychological Bulletin* 69 (1968): 41–55.

Hulme, R., and Bevan, R. "The Blue-Collar Worker Goes on Salary." *Harvard Business Review,* March-April 1975, pp. 104–112.

Hundert, A. T. "Application of the Organization Development Process to Intergroup Conflict: A Case with Union and Management." Text of a presentation to the Division of Industrial and Organizational Psychology of the American Psychology Association, New Orleans, Louisiana, 1974.

Hunnius, G., Garson, G. D., and Case, J., eds. *Workers' Control: A Reader on Labor and Social Change.* New York: Random House, 1973.

Huse, E. F., and Beer, M. "Eclectic Approach to Organizational Development." *Harvard Business Review,* September-October 1971, pp. 103–112.

Indik, B. P., Georgopoulos, B. S., and Seashore, S. "Superior-Subordinate Relationships and Performance." *Personnel Psychology* 14 (1961): 347–374.

Jablonsky, S., and DeVries, R. "Operant Conditioning Principles Extrapolated to the Theory of Management." *Organizational Behavior and Human Performance* 7 (1972): 340–358.

Jaques, E. *Equitable Payment: A General Theory of Work Differential Payment and Industrial Progress.* New York: Wiley, 1961.

Jenkins, D. *Job Power.* New York: Doubleday, 1973.

Jenkins, G. D., Jr., Nadler, D. A., Lawler, E. E. III, and Cammann, C. "Standardized Observations: An Approach to Measuring the Nature of Jobs." *Journal of Applied Psychology* 60 (1975): 171–181.

Journal for Humanistic Management. Special Issue on Human Productivity and the Rearranged Work Week, 1 (1973): 8–54.

Kahn, R. L., Wolfe, D. M., Quinn, R. P., Snoek, J. D., and Rosenthal, R. A. *Organizational Stress.* New York: Wiley, 1964.

Kanter, R. M. "Women and the Structure of Organizations." Paper delivered at New Technology in Organization Development Conference, February 1974.

Kaplan, R. E. *Managing Interpersonal Relations in Task Groups: A Study of Two Contrasting Strategies.* Technical Report No. 2. New Haven: Department of Administrative Sciences, Yale University, 1973.

Katz, D., and Kahn, R. *The Social Psychology of Organizations.* New York: Wiley, 1966.

Katz, D., Macoby, N., and Morse, N. C. *Productivity, Supervision, and Morale in an Office Situation.* Ann Arbor: University of Michigan, Institute for Social Research, 1950.

Katzell, R. A., and Yankelovich, D. *Work, Productivity and Job Satisfaction.* New York: The Psychological Corporation, 1975.

Kelman, H. C. "Compliance, Identification, and Internalization: Three Processes of Attitude Change." *Conflict Resolution* 2 (1958): 51–60.

Kelman, H. C., and Warwick, D. P. "Bridging Micro and Macro Approaches to Social Change: A Social-Psychological Perspective." In *Processes and Phenomena of Social Change,* edited by G. Zaltman. New York: Wiley, 1973.

Kerner, O. et al. *Report on the National Advisory Commission on Civil Disorders.* New York: New York Times Company, 1968.

Kiesler, C. A., Collins, B. E., and Miller, N. *Attitude Change.* New York: Wiley, 1969.

Kilbridge, M. D. "Reduced Costs Through Job Enrichment: A Case." *The Journal of Business* 33 (1960): 357–362.

King, N. "A Clarification and Evaluation of the Two-Factor Theory of Job Satisfaction." *Psychological Bulletin* 74 (1970): 18–31.

Knapp, W. *Report to the Commission to Investigate Alleged Police Corruption (City of New York).* New York: Braziller, 1972.

Kochan, T. A., Lipsky, D. B., and Dyer, L. "Collective Bargaining and the Quality of Work: The Views of Local Union Activists." In *Proceedings of the Twenty-Seventh Annual Winter Meeting of the Industrial Relations Research Association,* San Francisco, December 28–29, 1974.

Kohlberg, L. "Development of Moral Character and Moral Ideology." In *Review of Child Research,* Vol. 1, edited by M. L. Hoffman and L. W. Hoffman, pp. 383–431. New York: Russell Sage Foundation, 1964.

Kohn, M. *Class and Conformity: A Study in Values.* Homewood, Ill.: Dorsey, 1969.

Kopelman, R., Dalton, G., and Thompson, P. "The Distinguishing Characteristics of High, Middle, and Low Performing Engineers: A Study of Four Age Groups." Manuscript, Graduate School of Business Administration, Harvard University, August 1971.

Korman, A. K. "'Consideration,' 'Initiating Structure,' and Organizational Criteria—A Review." *Personnel Psychology* 19 (1966): 349–361.

Kornhauser, A. *Mental Health of the Industrial Worker.* New York: Wiley, 1965.

Kotter, J. "The Psychological Contract." *California Management Review,* Spring 1973, pp. 91–99.

Krause, E. *The Sociology of Occupations.* Boston: Little, Brown, 1971.

Kraut, A. "A Hard Look at Management Assessment Centers and Their Future." *Personnel Journal* 51 (1972): 317–326.

Kroll, A. M., Dinklage, L. B., Lee, J., Morley, E. D., and Wilson, E. H. *Career Development: Growth and Crisis.* New York: Wiley, 1970.

Lammers, C. J. "Power and Participation in Decision-Making in Formal Organizations." *American Journal of Sociology* 73 (1967): 201–216.

Lancashire, R. D. "Occupational Choice Theory and Occupational Guidance Practice." In *Psychology at Work,* edited by P. Warr. Middlesex, England: Penguin, 1971.

Larson, K. *The Workers.* New York: Bantam, 1971.

Latham, G., Yukl, G., and Scott, R. *Motivating Tree Planters Through Schedules of Reinforcement.* Weyerhaeuser Company Technical Report, Tacoma, Washington, 1974.

Lawler, E. E. III. "Managers' Attitudes Toward How They Pay Is and Should Be Determined." *Journal of Applied Psychology* 50 (1966): 273–279.

Lawler, E. E. III. *Pay and Organizational Effectiveness: A Psychological View.* New York: McGraw-Hill, 1971.

Lawler, E. E. III. "Secrecy and the Need to Know." In *Managerial Motivation and Compensation,* edited by H. L. Tosi, R. J. House, and M. D. Dunnette, pp. 455–476. East Lansing: Michigan State University Press, 1972.

Lawler, E. E. III. *Motivation in Work Organizations.* Monterey, Calif.: Brooks/Cole, 1973 (a).

Lawler, E. E. III. "Quality of Working Life and Social Accounts." In *Corporate Social Accounting,* edited by M. Dierkes and R. A. Bauer, pp. 154–165. New York: Praeger, 1973 (b).

Lawler, E. E. III. "The Individualized Organization: Problems and Promise." *California Management Review,* Winter 1974, pp. 31–39.

Lawler, E. E. III, and Cammann, C. "What Makes a Work Group Successful?" In *The Failure of Success,* edited by A. J. Marrow. New York: Amacom, 1972.

Lawler, E. E. III, and Hackman, J. "The Impact of Employee Participation in the Development of Pay Incentive Plans: A Field Experiment." *Journal of Applied Psychology* 53 (1969): 467–471.

Lawler, E. E. III, Hackman, J. R., and Kaufman, S. "Effects of Job Redesign: A Field Experiment." *Journal of Applied Social Psychology* 3 (1973): 49–62.

Lawler, E. E. III, and Hall, D. T. "The Relationship of Job Characteristics to Job Involvement, Satisfaction and Intrinsic Motivation." *Journal of Applied Psychology* 54 (1970): 305–312.

Lawler, E. E. III, and Levin, E. "Union Officers' Perceptions of Members' Pay Preferences." *Industrial and Labor Relations Review* 21 (1968): 509–517.

Lawrence, P., and Lorsch, J. *Organization and Environment.* Boston: Division of Research, Graduate School of Business Administration, Harvard University, 1967.

Leavitt, H. J. "Applied Organizational Change in Industry: Structural, Technological and Humanistic Approaches." In *Handbook of Organizations,* edited by J. March. Chicago: Rand McNally, 1965.

Leavitt, H. J. *Managerial Psychology.* 3rd ed. Chicago: University of Chicago Press, 1972.

LeMasters, E. E. *Blue-Collar Aristocrats.* Madison: University of Wisconsin Press, 1975.

Lesieur, F. G., ed. *The Scanlon Plan.* Cambridge, Mass.: MIT Press, 1958.

Lesieur, F. G., and Puckett, E. "The Scanlon Plan Has Proved Itself." *Harvard Business Review,* September-October 1969, pp. 109–118.

Levine, R. A., and Campbell, D. T. *Ethnocentrism.* New York: Wiley, 1972.

Levinson, D. H., Darrow, C. M., Klein, E. B., Levinson, M. H., and McKee, B. "The Psycho-Social Development of Men in Early Adulthood and the Mid-Life Transition." In *Life History Research,* Vol. 3, edited by D. F. Ricks, A. Thomas, and M. Roof. Minneapolis: University of Minnesota Press, 1974.

Lewicki, R. J., and Alderfer, C. P. "The Tensions Between Research and Intervention in Intergroup Conflict." *Journal of Applied Behavioral Science* 9 (1973): 424–449.

Lewin, K. *Field Theory in Social Science.* New York: Harper and Row, 1951.

Likert, R. *New Patterns of Management.* New York: McGraw-Hill, 1961.

Likert, R. *The Human Organization: Its Management and Value.* New York: McGraw-Hill, 1967.

Lindholm, R. *Payment by Results*–Leading System in Production Development. Paper presented at EEPS-EAPM Conference, Amsterdam, 1974.

Linestad, H., and Norstedt, J. *Autonomous Groups and Payment by Results.* Stockholm: Swedish Employers' Confederation, 1972.

Locke, E. "What Is Job Satisfaction?" *Organizational Behavior and Human Performance* 4 (1969): 309–336.

Lopata, H. Z. *Occupation: Housewife.* New York: Oxford University Press, 1971.

Loring, R., and Wells, T. *Breakthrough: Women into Management.* New York: Van Nostrand-Reinhold, 1972.

Lorsch, J., and Morse, J. *Organizations and Their Members: A Contingency Approach.* New York: Harper and Row, 1974.

Lortie, D. C. *Schoolteacher.* Chicago: University of Chicago Press, 1975.

Lowin, A., Hrapchak, W. J., and Kavanagh, M. J. "Consideration and Initiating Structure: An Experimental Investigation of Leadership Traits." *Administrative Science Quarterly* 14 (1969): 238–253.

Lufton, M. "Decision-making in a Mental Hospital." *American Sociological Review* 24 (1959): 822–829.

Lynn, N. B., Vaden, A. G., and Vaden, R. E. "Challenges of Men in a Woman's World." *Public Personnel Management* 4 (1975): 4–17.

Maas, P. *Serpico.* New York: Viking, 1973.

Macedonia, R. M. "Expectation: Press and Survival." Ph.D. dissertation, New York University, 1969.

Macy, B., and Mirvis, P. "Measuring Quality of Work and Organizational Effectiveness in Behavioral Economic Terms." Paper presented at American Psychological Association Convention, New Orleans, Louisiana, September 1974.

Maier, N. R. F. *Psychology in Industry,* 2nd ed. Boston: Houghton Mifflin, 1955.

Maier, N. R. F., and Hoffman, L. R. "Acceptance and Quality of Solutions as Related to Leaders' Attitudes Toward Disagreement in Group Problem-Solving." *Journal of Applied Behavioral Science* 1 (1965): 373–386.

Mallino, D. L., and Werner, S. M., eds. *Occupational Safety and Health: A Policy Analysis.* Washington, D.C.: Government Research Corporation, 1973.

March, J. G., and Simon, H. A. *Organizations.* New York: Wiley, 1958.

Marris, P., and Rein, M., eds. *Dilemmas of Social Reform: Poverty and Community Action in the United States,* 2nd ed. Chicago: Aldine, 1973.

Marrow, A. J., Bowers, D. G., and Seashore, S. E. *Management by Participation.* New York: Harper and Row, 1967.

Mayer, M. *The Bankers.* New York: Weybright and Talley, 1974.

McClelland, D. C. *The Achieving Society.* Princeton: Van Nostrand, 1961.

McClelland, D. C., Atkinson, J. W., Clark, R. A., and Lowell, E. L. *The Achievement Motive.* New York: Appleton-Century-Crofts, 1953.

McConnell, J., and Parker T. "An Assessment Center Program for Multi-organizational Use." *Training and Development Journal* 26 (1972): 6–14.

McCormick, E. J., Jeanneret, P. R., and Mecham, R. C. "A Study of Job Characteristics and Job Dimensions as Based on the Position Analysis Questionnaire (PAQ)." *Journal of Applied Psychology Monograph* 56 (1972): 347–368.

McGrath, J. E. "Stress and Behavior in Organizations." In *Handbook of Industrial and Organizational Psychology,* edited by M. D. Dunnette, Chicago: Rand McNally, 1976.

McGregor, D. "Conditions of Effective Leadership in the Industrial Organization." *Journal of Consulting Psychology* 8 (1944): 55–63.

McGregor, D. *The Human Side of Enterprise.* New York: McGraw-Hill, 1960.

McKersie, R. "Wage Payment Method of the Future." *British Journal of Industrial Relations* 8 (1963): 191–212.

Meador, B., Solomon, E., and Bowen, M. "Encounter Groups for Women Only." In *New Perspectives on Encounter Groups,* edited by L. N. Solomon and B. Berzon, pp. 335–348. San Francisco: Jossey-Bass, 1972.

Meissner, M. *Technology and the Worker: Technical Demands and Social Processes in Industry.* San Francisco: Chandler, 1969.

Meyer, H. "The Pay-for-Performance Dilemma." *Organizational Dynamics,* Winter 1975, pp. 39–50.

Milkovich, G., and Anderson, P. "Management Compensation and Secrecy." *Personnel Psychology* 25 (1972): 293–302.

Miller, D. C., and Form, W. H. *Industrial Sociology.* New York: Harper and Row, 1964.

Miller, J. A. *Overcoming Some Organizational Obstacles to the Implementation of Individual Career Plans.* Round Table on Career Development in European Enterprises, International Labor Office, Budapest, Hungary, April 1975.

Mills, T. "Human Resources—Why the New Concern?" *Harvard Business Review,* March-April 1975, pp. 120–134.

Moore, B., and Goodman, P. *"Factors Affecting the Impact of a Company-Wide Incentive Program on Productivity."* Report submitted to the National Commission on Productivity, January 1973.

Morgan, W. R. "Campus Conflict as Formative Influence." In *Collective Violence,* edited by J. F. Short and M. E. Wolfgang, pp. 278–291. Chicago: Aldine-Atherton, 1972.

Morris, R., ed. *"Centrally-Planned Change: Prospects and Concepts."* New York: National Association of Social Workers, 1964.

Morse, N. *Satisfactions in White-Collar Jobs.* Ann Arbor: University of Michigan, Survey Research Center, 1953.

Myers, C. A. "Management and the Employee." In *Social Responsibility and the Business Predicament,* edited by J. W. McKie. Washington, D.C.: Brookings, 1974.

Nader, R., Petkas, P. J., and Blackwell, K., eds. *Whistle Blowing: The Report of the Conference on Professional Responsibility.* New York: Grossman, 1972.

Nealey, S. "Pay and Benefit Preferences." *Industrial Relations* 3 (1963): 17–28.

Neff, W. S. *Work and Human Behavior.* Chicago: Aldine, 1968.

Neilsen, E. H. "Understanding and Managing Intergroup Conflict." In *Managing Group and Intergroup Relations,* edited by J. W. Lorsch and P. R. Lawrence, pp. 329–343. Homewood, Ill.: Irwin-Dorsey, 1972.

Nord, W. "Beyond the Teaching Machine: The Neglected Area of Operant Conditioning in the Theory and Practice of Management." *Organizational Behavior and Human Performance,* 4 (1969): 375–401.

Novak, M. "How American Are You If Your Grandparents Came from Servia in 1888?" In *The Rediscovery of Ethnicity,* edited by S. Te Selle, pp. 1–20. New York: Harper and Row, 1975.

Oaklander, H., and Fleishman, E. A. "Patterns of Leadership Related to Organizational Stress in Hospital Settings." *Administrative Science Quarterly* 8 (1964): 520–532.

OSHA and the Unions: Bargaining on Job Safety and Health. Washington, D.C.: Bureau of National Affairs, 1973.

Oldham, G. R. "Some Determinants and Consequences of the Motivational Strategies Used by Supervisors." Ph.D. dissertation, Yale University, 1974.

Oldham, G., R. "Job Characteristics and Internal Motivation: The Moderating Effect of Interpersonal and Individual Variables." *Human Relations,* in press (a).

Oldham, G. R. "The Motivational Strategies Used by Supervisors: Relationships to Effectiveness Indicators." *Organizational Behavior and Human Performance,* in press (b).

Oldham, G. R., Hackman, J. R., and Pearce, J. L. *Conditions Under Which Employees Respond Positively to Enriched Work.* Technical Report No. 10. New Haven: Department of Administrative Sciences, Yale University, 1975.

Olsen, J. *The Girls in the Office.* New York: Simon and Schuster, 1972.

Opinion Research Corporation. *Wage Incentives.* Princeton: Opinion Research Corporation, 1946.

Patchen, M. *The Choice of Wage Comparisons.* Englewood Cliffs, N.J.: Prentice-Hall, 1961.

Patchen, M. "Supervisory Methods and Group Performance Norms." *Administrative Science Quarterly* 7 (1962): 275–294.

Patchen, M. *Participation, Achievement, and Involvement on the Job.* Englewood Cliffs, N.J.: Prentice-Hall, 1970.

Paul, W. J., Jr., Robertson, K. B., and Herzberg, F. "Job Enrichment Pays Off." *Harvard Business Review* March-April 1969, pp. 61–78.

Peabody, G. L. "Power, Alinsky, and Other Thoughts." In *Social Intervention: A Behavioral Science Approach,* edited by H. A. Horstein, B. B. Bunker, W. W. Burke, M. Gindes, and R. J. Lewicki, pp. 521–532. New York: Free Press, 1971.

Pedalino, E., and Gamboa, V. "Behavior Modification and Absenteeism: Intervention in One Industrial Setting." *Journal of Applied Psychology* 59 (1974): 694–698.

Pelz, D. C. "Leadership Within a Hierarchical Organization." *Journal of Social Issues* 7 (1951): 48–55.

Perrow, C. "A Framework for the Comparative Analysis of Organizations." *American Sociological Review* 32 (1967): 194–208.

Piaget, J. *The Moral Judgment of the Child.* New York: Collier, 1962.

Piaget, J. *The Child's Conception of Time.* Translated by A. J. Pomerans. London: Routledge and Kegan Paul, 1969 (first published in 1927).

A Plant-Wide Productivity Plan in Action: Three Years of Experience with the Scanlon Plan. Washington, D.C.: National Commission on Productivity and Work Quality, 1975.

Platt, A., and Pollack, R. "Channeling Lawyers: The Careers of Public Defenders." In *The Potential for Reform of Criminal Justice,* edited by H. Jacob. Beverly Hills, Calif.: Sage, 1974.

Pondy, L. R. "Budgeting and Intergroup Conflict in Organizations." In *Readings in Managerial Psychology,* edited by H. Leavitt. 2nd ed. Chicago: University of Chicago Press, 1973.

Porter, L. W., and Lawler, E. E. "Properties of Organization Structure in Relation to Job Attitudes and Job Behavior." *Psychological Bulletin* 64 (1965): 23–51.

Porter, L. W., and Lawler, E. E. *Managerial Attitudes and Performance.* Homewood, Ill.: Irwin-Dorsey, 1968.

Porter, L. W., Lawler, E. E., and Hackman, J. R. *Behavior in Organizations.* New York: McGraw-Hill, 1975.

Porter, L., and Steers, R. "Organizational, Work and Personal Factors in Employee Turnover and Absenteeism." *Psychological Bulletin* 80 (1973): 151–176.

Porter, L. W., Van Maanen, J., and Crampton, W. J. "Continuous Monitoring of Employee's Motivational Attitudes During the Initial Employment Period." Manuscript, University of California, Irvine, 1972.

Potratz, J. "Working on the Railroad: Job Satisfaction and Bid and Grievance Behavior." Master's thesis, Massachusetts Institute of Technology, June 1975.

Puckett, E. S. "Measuring Performance under the Scanlon Plan." In *The Scanlon Plan,* edited by F. G. Lesieur, pp. 65–79. Cambridge: MIT Press, 1958.

Purcell, T. V., and Cavanagh, G. F. *Blacks in the Industrial World.* New York: Free Press, 1972.

Quinn, R. P., Staines, G. L., and McCullough, M. R. *Job Satisfaction: Is There a Trend?* Washington, D.C.: U.S. Government Printing Office, Document 2900-00195, 1974.

Radano, G. *Walking the Beat.* New York: World, 1969.

Radano, G. *Stories Cops Only Tell to Each Other.* New York: Stein and Day, 1974.

Rapoport, R. N. "Some Notes on Paratechnical Factors in Cross-cultural Consultation." *Human Organization* 23 (1964): 8–9.

Reif, W. E., and Luthans, F. "Does Job Enrichment Really Pay Off?" *California Management Review,* Fall 1972, pp. 30–37.

Reiss, A. J. *The Police and the Public.* New Haven: Yale University Press, 1971.

Research Institute of America. *Sales Compensation Practices: An R.I.A. Survey.* File No. 32. New York: Research Institute of America, 1965.

Rhode, J. G., Lawler, E. E., and Sundam, G. L. "Human Resource Accounting: An Assessment." Industrial Relations, in press, 1976.

Rice, A. K. *Productivity and Social Organization: The Ahmedabad Experiment.* London: Tavistock, 1958.

Rice, A. K. *Learning for Leadership.* London: Tavistock, 1965.

Richardson, S. A. "Organization Contrasts on British and American Ships." *Administrative Science Quarterly* 1 (1956): 189–207.

Ritchie, J. B. "Supervision." In *Organizational Behavior: Research and Issues,* edited by G. Strauss, R. E. Miles, C. E. Snow, and A. S. Tannenbaum. Madison, Wisc.: Industrial Relations Research Association, 1974.

Ritchie, J. B., and Miles, R. E. "An Analysis of Quantity and Quality of Participation as Mediating Variables in the Decision-Making Process." *Personnel Psychology* 23 (1970): 347–359.

Robey, D. "Task Design, Work Values, and Worker Response: An Experimental Test." *Organizational Behavior and Human Performance* 12 (1974): 264–273.

Roe, A. "Early Determinants of Vocational Choice." *Journal of Counseling Psychology* 4 (1957): 212–217.

Roethlisberger, F. J., and Dickson, W. J. *Management and the Worker.* Cambridge, Mass.: Harvard University, 1939.

Rogers, E. M. "Effects of Incentives on the Diffusion of Innovations: The Case of Family Planning in Asia." In *Processes and Phenomena of Social Change,* edited by G. Zaltman. New York: Wiley, 1973.

Rose, A. "Strategies for Implementing Social Change." In *The Role of Government in Promoting Social Change,* edited by M. Silberman. Harriman, N.Y.: Proceedings of Arden House Conference, Columbia University School of Social Work, 1965.

Ross, A. M. "The Natural History of the Strike." In *Industrial Conflict,* edited by A. Kornhauser, R. Dubin, and A. M. Ross, pp. 23–36. New York: McGraw-Hill, 1954.

Roth, J. A. *Timetables: Structuring the Passage of Time in Hospital Treatment and Other Careers.* Indianapolis: Bobbs-Merrill, 1963.

Rowat, D. C. "The Spread of the Ombudsman Idea." In *Ombudsman for American Government?* Englewood Cliffs, N.J.: Prentice-Hall, 1968, pp. 7–36.

Roy, D. "Quota Restriction and Goldbricking in a Machine Shop." *American Journal of Sociology* 4 (1952): 426–442.

Roy, D. "Banana Time: Job Satisfaction and Informal Interaction." *Human Organization* 18 (1960): 158–169.

Rubenstein, J. *City Police.* New York: Farrar, Strauss and Giroux, 1973.

Rush, H. M. F. *Job Design for Motivation.* New York: The Conference Board, 1971.

Salaman, G. *Community and Occupation: An Exploration of Work/Leisure Relationships.* London: Cambridge University Press, 1974.

Salaman, G., and Thompson, K., eds. *People and Organizations.* London: Longman, 1973.

Sales, S. M. "Some Effects of Role Overload and Role Underload." *Organizational Behavior and Human Performance* 5 (1970): 592–608.

Salpukas, A. "Unions: A New Role?" In *The Worker and the Job: Coping with Change,* edited by J. M. Rosnow, pp. 99–117. Englewood Cliffs, N.J.: Prentice-Hall, 1974.

Salvo, V. J. "Familial and Occupational Roles in a Technical Society." In *The Engineer and the Social System,* edited by R. Perrucci and J. E. Gerstl. New York: Wiley, 1969.

Sayles, L. R. *Behavior of Industrial Work Groups.* New York: Wiley, 1958.

Sayles, L., and Strauss, G. *The Local Union: Its Place in the Industrial Plant.* New York: Harper and Brothers, 1953.

Scanlon, J. "Talk on Union Management Relations." *Proceedings of Conference on Productivity.* Madison: Industrial Relations Center, University of Wisconsin, 1949, pp. 10–18.

Schachter, S., Ellertson, N., McBride, D., and Gregory, D. "An Experimental Test of Cohesiveness and Productivity." *Human Relations* 4 (1951): 229–238.

Schachter, S., Willerman, B., Festinger, L., and Human, R. "Emotional Disruption and Industrial Productivity." *Journal of Applied Psychology* 45 (1961): 201–213.

Scheff, T. J. *Being Mentally Ill.* Chicago: Aldine, 1966.

Scheflen, K., Lawler, E. E., and Hackman, J. R. "Long-Term Impact of Employee Participation in the Development of Pay Incentive Plans: A Field Experiment Revisited." *Journal of Applied Psychology* 55 (1971): 182–186.

Schein, E. H. "Management Development as a Process of Influence." *Industrial Management Review* 2 (1961): 59–77.

Schein, E. H. "Problems of the First Year at Work: Report of the First Panel Re-union." Cambridge, Mass.: Massachusetts Institute of Technology, Contract NONR 1841 (83), Office of Naval Research, 1962.

Schein, E. H. "How to Break in the College Graduate." *Harvard Business Review,* November-December 1964, pp. 68–76.

Schein, E. H. "Organizational Socialization and the Profession of Management." Third Douglas McGregor Memorial Address, *Industrial Management Review* 9 (1968): 1–15.

Schein, E. H. "The Mechanisms of Change." In *The Planning of Change,* edited by W. G. Bennis, K. D. Benne, and R. Chin. 2nd ed. New York: Holt, Rinehart and Winston, 1969 (a).

Schein, E. H. *Process Consultation: Its Role in Organization Development.* Reading, Mass.: Addison-Wesley, 1969 (b).

Schein, E. H. *Organizational Psychology.* Englewood Cliffs, N.J.: Prentice-Hall, 1970.

Schein, E. H. "The Individual, the Organization, and the Career: A Conceptual Scheme." *Journal of Applied Behavioral Science* 7 (1971): 401–426.

Schein, E. H. "Personal Change Through Interpersonal Relationships." In *Interpersonal Dynamics,* edited by W. G. Bennis, D. E. Berlew, E. H. Schein, and F. I. Steel. 3rd ed. Homewood, Ill.: Dorsey, 1973.

Schein, E. H. "Career Anchors and Career Paths: A Panel Study of Management School Graduates." Cambridge, Mass.: Sloan School of Management Working Paper No. 707-74, May 1974.

Schein, E. H. "Career Anchors Hold Executives to Their Career Paths." *Personnel* 52 (1975): 11–24 (a).

Schein, E. H. *Career Development: Theoretical and Practical Issues for Organizations.* Round Table on Career Development in European Enterprises, International Labor Office, Budapest, Hungary, April 1975 (b).

Schein, E. H., and Bailyn, L. "Life/Career Considerations as Indicators of the Quality of Employment." Manuscript. Cambridge, Mass.: Sloan School of Management, 1974.

Schein, V. E. "Relationships Between Sex Role Stereotypes and Requisite Management Characteristics Among Female Managers." *Journal of Applied Psychology* 60 (1975): 340–344.

Schrank, R. "Work in America: What Do Workers Really Want?" *Industrial Relations* 13 (1974): 24–29.

Scott, R. *Muscle and Blood: The Massive, Hidden Agony of Industrial Slaughter in America.* New York: Dutton, 1974.

Scott, W. E. "Activation Theory and Task Design." *Organizational Behavior and Human Performance* 1 (1966): 3–30.

Scott, W. E. "The Behavioral Consequences of Repetitive Task Design: Research and Theory." In *Readings in Organizational Behavior and Human Performance,* edited by L. L. Cummings and W. E. Scott. Homewood, Ill.: Irwin-Dorsey, 1969.

Scott, W. E., and Rowland, K. M. "The Generality and Significance of Semantic Differential Scales as Measures of 'Morale.' " *Organizational Behavior and Human Performance* 5 (1970): 576–591.

Scott, W. G. *The Management of Conflict.* Homewood, Ill.: Irwin-Dorsey, 1965.

Seashore, S. E. *Group Cohesiveness in the Industrial Work Group.* Ann Arbor: Institute for Social Research, University of Michigan, 1954.

Seashore, S. E., and Bowers, G. D. *Changing the Structure and Functioning of an Organization: Report of a Field Experiment.* Monograph No. 23. Ann Arbor: University of Michigan, Survey Research Center, Institute for Social Research, 1963.

Seeman, M. "On the Meaning of Alienation." *American Sociological Review* 24 (1959): 783–791.

Seidenberg, R. *Corporate Wives—Corporate Casualties?* New York: Doubleday, 1975.

Seybolt, J. *Worker Participation and Power Evaluation.* Manuscript. Ithaca: New York State School of Industrial and Labor Relations, undated.

Sheehy, G. *Hustling.* New York: Dell, 1973.

Shepard, H. A., and Hawley, J. A. *Life Planning: Personal and Organizational.* Washington, D.C.: National Training and Development Service, 1974.

Shepard, J. M. "Functional Specialization, Alienation, and Job Satisfaction." *Industrial and Labor Relations Review* 23 (1970): 207–219.

Sheppard, H. L. and Herrick, N. *Where Have All the Robots Gone?* New York: Free Press, 1972.

Sheridan, J. "Should Your Production Workers Be Salaried?" *Industry Week* 184 (1975): 28–37.

Sherif, M., and Sherif, C. *Social Psychology.* New York: Harper and Row, 1969.

Sherman, L. W., ed. *Police Corruption: A Sociological Perspective.* New York: Anchor, 1974.

Shoestak, A. B. *Blue Collar Life.* New York: Random House, 1959.

Shultz, G. P. "Worker Participation on Production Problems." *Personnel* 28 (1951): 24–29.

Shultz, G. P. "Variations in the Environment and the Scanlon Plan." In *The Scanlon Plan,* edited by F. G. Lesieur, pp. 100–108. Cambridge, Mass.: MIT Press, 1958 (a).

Shultz, G. P. "Worker Participation on Production Problems: A Discussion of Experience with the Scanlon Plan." *Personnel* 28 (1958): 201–211 (b).

Sims, H. P., and Szilagyi, A. D. "Individual Moderators of Job Characteristic Relationships." Manuscript. Bloomington: Graduate School of Business, Indiana University, 1974.

Singerman, P. *Black Workers, White Workers, and Labor Unions.* Yale ISPS Working Paper W5-1. New Haven: Yale University, 1975.

Sirota, D., and Wolfson, A. D. "Job Enrichment: What Are the Obstacles? *Personnel,* May-June 1972, pp. 8–17 (a).

Sirota, D., and Wolfson, A. D. "Job Enrichment: Surmounting the Obstacles. *Personnel,* July-August 1972, 8–19 (b).

Skinner, B. *The Behavior of Organisms: An Experimental Analysis.* New York: Appleton-Century-Crofts, 1938.

Skinner, B. *Contingencies of Reinforcement: A Theoretical Analysis.* New York: Appleton-Century-Crofts, 1969.

Slater, P. *Microcosm.* New York: Wiley, 1966.

Slater, P. *The Pursuit of Loneliness: American Culture at the Breaking Point.* Boston: Beacon, 1970.

Smith, K. K. "Behavioral Consequences of Hierarchical Structures." Ph.D. dissertation, Yale University, 1974.

Smith, R. L. *The Tarnished Badge.* New York: Crowell, 1965.

Sofer, C. *Organizations in Theory and Practice.* New York: Basic Books, 1972.

Solomon, L. N., and Berzon, B. eds. *New Perspectives on Encounter Groups.* San Francisco: Jossey-Bass, 1972.

Sorokin, P., and Merton, R. K. "Social Time: A Methodology and Functional Analysis." *American Journal of Sociology* 42 (1937): 614–629.

Spiegel, A. H. II. "How Outsiders Overhauled a Public Agency." *Harvard Business Review,* January-February 1975, pp. 116–124.

Stanton, A. H., and Schwartz, M. S. *The Mental Hospital.* New York: Basic Books, 1954.

Steele, F. *The Open Organization.* Reading, Mass.: Addison-Wesley, 1975.

Steiner, I. D. "Perceived Freedom." In *Advances in Experimental Social Psychology,* edited by L. Berkowitz. Vol. 5. New York: Academic Press, 1970.

Stewart, P. L., and Cantor, M. G., eds. *Varieties of Work Experience.* New York: Wiley, 1974.

Stiles, L. J., and Robinson, B. "Change in Education." In *Processes and Phenomena of Social Change,* edited by G. Zaltman. New York: Wiley, 1973.

Stoddard, E. R. "The Informal Code of Police Deviancy: A Group Approach to Blue-Coat Crime." *Journal of Criminal Law, Criminology and Police Science* 59 (1968): 201–213.

Stone, E. F. "The Moderating Effect of Work-Related Values on the Job Scope-Job Satisfaction Relationship." *Organizational Behavior and Human Performance,* in press.

Storey, W. D. *Career Action Planning.* Crotonville, N.Y.: General Electric Company, 1973.

Stouffer, S. A., ed. *The American Soldier.* Vols. 1 and 2. Princeton, N.J.: Princeton University Press, 1949.

Strauss, A. *Mirrors and Masks: The Search for Identity.* Glencoe, Ill.: Free Press, 1959.

Strauss, G. "Group Dynamics and Intergroup Relations." In *Money and Motivation,* edited by W. F. Whyte. New York: Harper, 1955.

Strauss, G. "Tactics of Lateral Relationship: The Purchasing Agent." *Administrative Science Quarterly* 7 (1962): 161–187.

Strauss, G. "Some Notes on Power Equalization." In *The Social Science of Organization,* edited by H. J. Leavitt. Englewood Cliffs, N.J.: Prentice-Hall, 1963.

Strauss, G. "Workflow Frictions, Interfunctional Rivalry, and Professionalism: A Cast Study of Purchasing Agents." *Human Organization* 23 (1964): 137–149.

Strauss, G. "MBO: A Critical View." *Training and Development Journal* 26 (1972): 10–15.

Strauss, G. "Job Satisfaction, Motivation, and Job Redesign. In *Organizational Behavior: Research and Issues,* edited by G. Strauss, R. E. Miles, C. C. Snow, and A. S. Tannenbaum. Madison, Wisc.: Industrial Relations Research Association, 1974 (a).

Strauss, G. "Workers: Attitudes and Adjustments." In *The Worker and The Job: Coping with Change,* edited by J. M. Rosow. Englewood Cliffs, N.J.: Prentice-Hall, 1974 (b).

Strauss, G., and Rosenstein, E. "Worker Participation: A Critical Review." *Industrial Relations* 9 (1970): 197–214.

Strauss, G., and Sayles, L. R. "The Scanlon Plan: Some Organizational Problems." *Human Organization* 16 (1957): 15–22.

Strauss, G., and Sayles, L. R. *Personnel.* Englewood Cliffs, N.J.: Prentice-Hall, 1972.

Strong, E. K., Jr. *Vocational Interests of Men and Women.* Stanford, Calif.: Stanford University Press, 1943.

Sumner, W. G. *Folkways.* New York: Ginn, 1906.

Super, D. E. *The Psychology of Careers.* New York: Harper and Row, 1957.

Super, D. E., Starishevsky, R., Matlin, N., and Jordaan, J. P. *Career Development: Self-Concept Theory.* Princeton, N.J.: College Entrance Examination Board, 1963.

Susman, G. I. "The Impact of Automation on Work Group Autonomy and Task Specialization." *Human Relations* 23 (1970): 567–577.

Susman, G. I. "Job Enlargement: Effects of Culture on Worker Responses." *Industrial Relations* 12 (1973): 1–15.

Sutherland, H. *The Professional Thief.* Chicago: University of Chicago Press, 1937.

Tannenbaum, A. S. "Control in Organizations." *Administrative Science Quarterly* 7 (1962): 236–257.

Tannenbaum, A. S. *Control in Organizations.* New York: McGraw-Hill, 1968.

Tannenbaum, R., and Schmidt, W. "How to Choose a Leadership Pattern." *Harvard Business Review,* March-April 1958, pp. 95–101.

Tarnowieski, D. *The Changing Success Ethic.* New York: American Management Association, 1973.

Tausky, C. *Work Organizations: Major Theoretical Perspectives.* Itasca, Ill.: Peacock, 1970.

Taylor, F. W. *The Principles of Scientific Management.* New York: Harper, 1911.

Taylor, J. C. "Some Effects of Technology in Organizational Change." *Human Relations* 24 (1971): 105–123.

Terkel, S. *Division Street: America.* New York: Random House, 1968.

Terkel, S. *Working.* New York: Pantheon, 1974.

Thayer, R. E. "Measurement of Activation Through Self-Report." *Psychological Reports* 20 (1967): 663–678.

Thayer, R. E. "Activation States as Assessed by Verbal Report and Four Psychophysiological Variables." *Psychophysiology* 7 (1970): 86–94.

Thompson, C. "The Role of Women in this Culture." In *A Study of Interpersonal Relations,* edited by P. Mullahy, pp. 147–161. New York: Science House, 1949.

Thompson, V. *Modern Organization.* New York: Knopf, 1961.

Three Productive Years. The Three-Year Report of the Labor-Management Committee of the Jamestown Area. Jamestown, N.Y., 1975.

Tiedeman, D. V., and O'Hara, R. P. *Career Development: Choice and Adjustment.* Princeton, N.J.: College Entrance Examination Board, 1963.

Tosi, H., House, R., and Dunnette, M. eds. *Managerial Motivation and Compensation.* East Lansing: Michigan State University Business Studies, 1972.

Trist, E. L., Higgin, G. W., Murray, H., and Pollock, A. B. *Organizational Choice.* London: Tavistock, 1963.

Turner, A. N. "Foreman, Job, and Company." *Human Relations* 10 (1957): 99–112.

Turner, A. N., and Lawrence, P. R. *Industrial Jobs and the Worker.* Boston: Harvard Graduate School of Business Administration, 1965.

Tushman, M. *Organizational Change: An Exploratory Study and Case History.* Ithaca, N.Y.: New York State School of Industrial and Labor Relations, Cornell University, 1974.

University of Michigan, Survey Research Center. *Survey of Working Conditions.* Washington, D.C.: U.S. Department of Labor, Employment Standards Administration, 1971.

University of Michigan, Survey Research Center. *A Proposal to the Ford Foundation for the Further Support of a Quality of Work Program.* Ann Arbor: Survey Research Center, March 15, 1975.

Vaillant, G. E., and McArthur, C. "Natural History of Male Psychological Health." *Seminars in Psychiatry* 4 (1972): 417–429.

Van Den Berghe, P. *Intergroup Relations.* New York: Basic Books, 1972.

Van Gennep, A. *The Rites of Passage.* Translated by M. B. Vizedom and G. L. Caffee. Chicago: University of Chicago Press, 1960.

Van Maanen, J. "Observations on the Making of a Policeman." *Human Organizations* 32 (1973): 407–418.

Van Maanen, J. "Working the Street: A Developmental View of Police Behavior." In *The Potential for Reform of Criminal Justice,* edited by H. Jacob, pp. 83–130. Beverly Hills, Calif.: Sage, 1974.

Van Maanen, J. "Police Socialization." *Administrative Science Quarterly* 20 (1975): 207–228 (a).

Van Maanen, J. "Experiencing Organizations: Notes on the Structure and Meaning of Organizational Socialization." Cambridge, Mass.: Massachusetts Institute of Technology, March 1975 (b).

Van Maanen, J. "Breaking-in: Socialization to Work." In *Handbook of Work, Organization and Society,* edited by R. Dubin. Chicago: Rand McNally, 1976.

Van Maanen, J., Katz, R., and Gregg, R. *Job Satisfaction in the Public Sector.* Report prepared for the Economic Development Administration, November 1974.

Van Zelst, R. "Sociometrically Selected Work Teams Increase Production." *Personnel Psychology* 5 (1952): 175–185.

Vernon, H. M. *On the Extent and Effects of Variety in Repetitive Work.* Industrial Fatigue Research Board Report No. 26. London: H. M. Stationary Office, 1924.

Vicino, F. L., and Miller, J. A. *PROSPECTS: A Program in Self-Planning and Evaluation of Career and Training Needs.* Scottsville, N.Y.: Transnational Programs, 1971.

Vollmer, H. M., and Mills, D. J. eds. *Professionalization.* Englewood Cliffs, N.J.: Prentice-Hall, 1966.

Vroom, V. H. *Some Personality Determinants of the Effects of Participation.* Englewood Cliffs, N.J.: Prentice-Hall, 1960.

Vroom, V. *Work and Motivation.* New York: Wiley, 1964.

Vroom, V. H. "Industrial Social Psychology." In *Handbook of Social Psychology,* edited by G. Lindzey and E. Aronson. 2nd ed. Reading, Mass.: Addison-Wesley, 1969.

Vroom, V. H. "A New Look at Managerial Decision-Making. *Organizational Dynamics,* Spring 1973, pp. 66–80.

Vroom, V. H., and Deci, E. L. "The Stability of Post-Decisional Dissonance: A Follow-up Study on the Job Attitudes of Business School Graduates." *Organizational Behavior and Human Performance* 6 (1971): 34–49.

Vroom, V. H., and Yetton, P. *Leadership and Decision-Making.* Pittsburgh: University of Pittsburgh Press, 1973.

Wagner, A. B. "The Use of Process Analysis in Business Decision Games." *Journal of Applied Behavioral Science* 1 (1964): 387–408.

Waldorf, D. *Careers in Dope.* New York: Spectrum, 1973.

Walker, C. R., and Guest, R. H. *The Man on the Assembly Line.* Cambridge, Mass.: Harvard University Press, 1952.

Walker, C. R., Guest, R. H., and Turner, A. N. *The Foreman on the Assembly Line.* Cambridge, Mass.: Harvard University Press, 1956.

Walker, K. F. "Worker Participation in Management—Problems, Practice, and Prospects." International Institute for Labor Studies Bulletin No. 12, undated.

Walsh, J. L. "Police Career Styles and Counting Cops on the Beat. Sources of Police Incivility." Paper presented at the American Sociological Association Convention, San Francisco, Fall 1975.

Walters, R. W. "A Long-Term Look at the Shorter Work Week." *Personnel Administrator* July-August 1971.

Walters, R. W. and Associates. *Job Enrichment for Results.* Reading, Mass.: Addison-Wesley, 1975.

Walton, R. E. *"Two Strategies of Social Change and Their Dilemmas." Journal of Applied Behavioral Science* 1 (1965): 167–179.

Walton, R. E. *Interpersonal Peacemaking.* Reading, Mass.: Addison-Wesley, 1969.

Walton, R. E. "How to Counter Alienation in the Plant." *Harvard Business Review,* November-December 1972, pp. 70–81.

Walton, R. E. "Improving the Quality of Work Life." *Harvard Business Review,* May-June 1974, pp. 12ff (a).

Walton, R. E. "Innovative Restructuring of Work." In *The Worker and the Job: Coping with Change,* edited by J. M. Rosnow. Englewood Cliffs, N.J.: Prentice-Hall, 1974 (b).

Walton, R. E. "The Diffusion of New Work Structures: Explaining Why Success Didn't Take." *Organizational Dynamics,* Winter 1975, pp. 3–22 (a).

Walton, R. E. "From Hawthorne to Topeka and Kalmar." In *Man and Work in Society,* edited by E. L. Cass and F. G. Zimmer. New York: Van Nostrand-Reinhold, 1975 (b).

Walton, R. E., Dutton, J. M., and Fitch, H. G. "A Study in the Process, Structure, and Attitudes of Lateral Relationships." In *Operational Research and the Social Sciences,* edited by J. R. Lawrence, pp. 444–465. London: Tavistock, 1966.

Walton, R. E., and McKersie, R. B. *A Behavioral Theory of Labor Negotiations.* New York: McGraw-Hill, 1965.

Wambaugh, J. *The New Centurions.* Boston: Little, Brown, 1970.

Wambaugh, J. *The Blue Knight.* Boston: Little, Brown, 1972.

Wanous, J. P. "Individual Differences and Reactions to Job Characteristics." *Journal of Applied Psychology* 59 (1974): 616–622.

Warren, E. K., Ference, T., and Stoner, J. A. F. "Case of the Plateaued Performer." *Harvard Business Review,* January-February 1975, pp. 30–38.

Westley, W. *Violence and the Police.* Cambridge, Mass.: MIT Press, 1971.

Wheeler, S. "The Structure of Formally Organized Socialization Settings." In *Socialization after Childhood,* edited by O. G. Brim, Jr. and S. Wheeler. New York: Wiley, 1966.

Whitsett, D. A. "Where are Your Unenriched Jobs?" *Harvard Business Review,* January-February 1975, pp. 74–80.

Whitsett, D. A., and Winslow, E. K. "An Analysis of Studies Critical of the Motivator-Hygiene Theory." *Personnel Psychology* 20 (1967): 391–415.

Whittemore, L. H. *The Super Cops.* New York: Stein and Day, 1973.

Whyte, W. F. *Human Relations in the Restaurant Industry.* New York: McGraw-Hill, 1948.

Whyte, W. F., ed. *Money and Motivation: An Analysis of Incentives in Industry.* New York: Harper, 1955.

Whyte, W. F. *Men at Work.* Homewood: Dorsey, 1961.

Whyte, W. F., and Hamilton, E. I. *Action Research for Management.* Homewood, Ill.: Irwin-Dorsey, 1964.

Whyte, W. H. *The Organization Man.* New York: Simon and Schuster, 1956.

Wilensky, H. L. "Orderly Careers and Social Participation." *American Sociological Review* 26 (1961): 521–539.

Wilensky, H. L. "The Professionalization of Everyone?" *American Journal of Sociology* 70 (1964): 137–158.

Wispe, L. G., and Lloyd, K. E. "Some Situational and Psychological Determinants of the Desire for Structured Interpersonal Relations." *Journal of Abnormal and Social Psychology* 55 (1955): 57–60.

Wohlwill, J. F. "The Age Variable in Psychological Research." *Psychology Review* 77 (1970): 49–64.

Woodward, J. *Management and Technology.* London: H. M. Stationary Office, 1958.

Work in America. Cambridge, Mass.: MIT Press, 1973.

Worthy, J. C. "Organizational Structure and Employee Morale." *American Sociological Review* 15 (1950): 169–179.

Wyatt, S., and Langdon, J. N. *Fatigue and Boredom in Repetitive Work.* Industrial Health Research Council, Reprint No. 77. London: H. M. Stationary Office, 1933.

Yankelovich, D. *The Changing Values on Campus.* New York: Pocket, 1972.

Yoder, D. *Personnel Management and Industrial Relations.* Englewood Cliffs, N.J.: Prentice-Hall, 1956.

Yukl, G. "Toward a Behavioral Theory of Leadership." *Organizational Behavior and Human Performance* 6 (1971): 414–440.

Yukl, G., and Latham, G. "Consequences of Reinforcement Schedules and Incentive Magnitudes for Employee Performance: Problems Encountered in an Industrial Setting." *Journal of Applied Psychology* 60 (1975): 294–298.

Yukl, G., Wexley, K., and Seymour, J. "Effectiveness of Pay Incentives under Variable Ratio and Continuous Reinforcement Schedules." *Journal of Applied Psychology* 56 (1972): 19–23.

Zald, M. *Occupations and Organizations in American Society: The Organization Dominated Man.* Chicago: Markham, 1971.

Zaleznik, A., Christensen, C. R., Roethlisberger, F. J., and Homans, G. *The Motivation, Productivity, and Satisfaction of Workers.* Boston: Harvard University Press, 1958.

Zierden, W. E. "The Person, the Manager, the Job: Interactive Effects on Job-Related Satisfactions. Ph.D. dissertation, Yale University, 1975.

About the authors

J. Richard Hackman is Associate Professor of Administrative Sciences and of Psychology at Yale University. He earned his undergraduate degree in mathematics at MacMurray College in 1962, and his doctorate in social psychology at the University of Illinois in 1966. He has been at Yale since then. Professor Hackman conducts research on a variety of topics in organizational psychology, including the design of jobs, the task effectiveness of work groups, and the social influences on individual work behavior. He is on the editorial board of several professional journals, and has consulted with a number of organizations on quality of work life issues.

J. Lloyd Suttle is Associate Director of the Office of Institutional Research and a lecturer in the School of Organization and Management at Yale University. He earned both his undergraduate and doctorate degrees from the Department of Administrative Sciences at Yale. His primary research interests involve the determinants of individual motivation and behavior in organizational settings. Dr. Suttle is also concerned with the problems of evaluation in organizations as a critical step in an organizational change process, both in work and educational settings. He is currently in charge of the evaluation of a major change in the Yale College undergraduate curriculum—the conversion from two-term to year-round operation through the introduction of a summer term.

John Van Maanen is Associate Professor of Organizational Psychology at the Sloan School of Management, Massachusetts Institute of Technology. He received his bachelor's degree in political science from California State University at Long Beach in 1965, and his Ph.D. in organization theory from the University of California at Irvine in 1972. He has been at MIT since then. Professor Van Maanen's research interests include career socialization, organizational ethnography, and managerial processes in public sector organizations such as police departments, courts, and welfare agencies. He is the author of numerous articles and two books on these topics.

Edgar H. Schein is Professor of Organizational Psychology and Management at the Sloan School of Management, MIT, where he also heads the Organization Studies Group. He received his undergraduate training at the University of Chicago and Stanford University, and obtained his Ph.D. in 1953 from Harvard's Department of Social Relations in social psychology. After four years of research at the Walter Reed Army Institute of Research, he joined the MIT faculty. Professor Schein has done research on the interaction of the individual and the organization, socialization processes, career development throughout the life cycle, and how different kinds of managerial and organizational careers evolve. He has also written a book on consultation and on the use of group methods in organizational change (with Warren Bennis). He is a consultant on organization development, management development, and career development to a number of companies.

Edward E. Lawler, III is a Professor of Psychology and a Program Director in the Institute for Social Research at the University of Michigan. He also serves as Visiting Scientist at Battelle Memorial Institute in Seattle. Professor Lawler earned his undergraduate degree in psychology at Brown University in 1960 and his doctorate in organizational psychology at the University of California at Berkeley in 1964. He was at Yale from 1964 to 1972. Professor Lawler conducts research on a variety of topics in organizational psychology including the design of work, the relationship of extrinsic rewards to motivation, and labor-management cooperation to improve the quality of work life. He is on the editorial board of several professional journals and has consulted with a number of organizations on quality of work life issues. His most recent book is *Information and Control in Organizations*, which was published by Goodyear.

Clayton P. Alderfer is Associate Professor of Administrative Sciences and Director of Professional Studies in the School of Organization and Management at Yale University. He earned a B.S. with high honors from Yale in 1962 and a Ph.D. from the same institution in 1966. From 1966 to 1968 he taught in the Graduate School of Business and Public Administration at Cornell and then returned to Yale. Author of two books and more than twenty-five articles on the subjects of human needs, intergroup relations, organizational diagnosis, and organizational development, Alderfer has consulted with a variety of public and private organizations on the application of behavioral science to organizational problems.

George Strauss is a Professor of Business Administration at the University of California. He received his B.A. in economics from Swarthmore College in 1947 and Ph.D. in economics and social science from MIT in 1952. After serving on the faculties of Cornell University and the University of Buffalo, he came to Berkeley in 1960. Among his duties have been those of Associate Dean in the School of Business Administration, Associate Director of the Institute of Industrial Relations, and Managing Editor of the journal, *Industrial Relations*. He has done research work on participation and interaction patterns in a variety of areas, especially with industrial and construction trade unions. Other recent interests have included organization development, worker attitudes toward work, and the status of industrial relations as an academic discipline.

Michael Beer is a Lecturer on Business Administration at the Harvard Business School. He earned his undergraduate degree in psychology at Queens College in 1957. After completing a master's degree in industrial psychology at North Carolina State in 1958, he served as an officer in the U.S. Air Force and worked as a research psychologist on problems of training. Following four years in the Air Force, he attended Ohio State University where he obtained a doctorate in industrial psychology in 1964. Between 1964 and 1975 Dr. Beer worked at Corning Glass Works where he held the successive positions of Research Associate, Manager of Personnel Research, and Director of Organization Development. While at Corning he initiated a variety of organization change efforts aimed at improving organizational effectiveness and quality of work life. Dr. Beer has contributed to a number of professional journals and books and has been on the editorial board of two journals. He is currently completing a book on Organization Development, teaching in the Advanced Management Program at Harvard, and consulting on problems of organization change and development.

James W. Driscoll is an Assistant Professor of Industrial Relations in the Sloan School of Management at Massachusetts Institute of Technology. He earned both his undergraduate and master's degrees at Harvard, the former in government and the latter in business administration with a concentration in organizational behavior. His doctorate in organizational behavior is from Cornell University where he studied in the New

York State School of Industrial and Labor Relations. Professor Driscoll conducts research on various topics including collective bargaining, organizational decision making, and the management of human resources.

Name Index

Subject Index